ACCA

PAPER F6

TAXATION (UK)

FA 2014

STUDY TEXT

BPP Learning Media is an **ACCA Approved Learning Partner – content**. This means we work closely with ACCA to ensure this Study Text contains the information you need to pass your exam.

In this Study Text, which has been reviewed by the **ACCA examining team,** we:

- Highlight the **most important elements** in the syllabus and the **key skills** you need

- Signpost how each chapter links to the syllabus and the study guide

- Provide lots of **exam focus points** demonstrating what is expected of you in the exam

- Emphasise key points in regular **fast forward summaries**

- Test your knowledge in **quick quizzes**

- Examine your understanding in our **practice question bank**

- Reference all the important topics in our **full index**

BPP's **Practice & Revision Kit and i-Pass** products also support this paper.

FOR EXAMS FROM 1 APRIL 2015 TO 31 MARCH 2016

First edition 2007
Eighth edition October 2014

ISBN 9781 4727 2239 3
(Previous ISBN 9781 4727 5302 1)
eISBN 9781 4727 2564 6

British Library Cataloguing-in-Publication Data
A catalogue record for this book is available from
the British Library

Published by

BPP Learning Media Ltd
BPP House, Aldine Place
142–144 Uxbridge Road
London W12 8AA

www.bpp.com/learningmedia

Printed in the United Kingdom by

Polestar Wheatons
Hennock Road
Marsh Barton
Exeter
EX2 8RP

Your learning materials, published by BPP
Learning Media Ltd, are printed on paper
obtained from traceable sustainable sources.

We are grateful to the Association of Chartered Certified
Accountants for permission to reproduce past
examination questions. The suggested solutions in the
practice answer bank have been prepared by BPP
Learning Media Ltd, unless otherwise stated.

Contents

BPP
LEARNING MEDIA

A note about copyright

Helping you to pass

BPP Learning Media – ACCA Approved Learning Partner – content

As ACCA's **Approved Learning Partner – content**, BPP Learning Media gives you the **opportunity** to use study materials reviewed by the ACCA examination team. By incorporating the examination team's comments and suggestions regarding the depth and breadth of syllabus coverage, the BPP Learning Media Study Text provides excellent, **ACCA-approved** support for your studies.

The PER alert!

Before you can qualify as an ACCA member, you not only have to pass all your exams but also fulfil a three year **practical experience requirement** (PER). To help you to recognise areas of the syllabus that you might be able to apply in the workplace to achieve different performance objectives, we have introduced the 'PER alert' feature. You will find this feature throughout the Study Text to remind you that what you are **learning to pass** your ACCA exams is **equally useful to the fulfilment of the PER requirement**.

Your achievement of the PER should now be recorded in your online *My Experience* record.

Tackling studying

Studying can be a daunting prospect, particularly when you have lots of other commitments. The **different features** of the text, the **purposes** of which are explained fully on the **Chapter features** page, will help you whilst studying and improve your chances of **exam success**.

Developing exam awareness

Our Texts are completely **focused** on helping you pass your exam.

Our advice on **Studying F6** outlines the **content** of the paper and the **necessary skills** you are expected to be able to demonstrate and any **brought forward knowledge** you are expected to have.

Exam focus points are included within the chapters to highlight when and how specific topics were examined, or how they might be examined in the future.

Using the Syllabus and Study Guide

You can find the Syllabus and Study Guide on pages x – xxiii of this Study Text.

Testing what you can do

Testing yourself helps you develop the skills you need to pass the exam and also confirms that you can recall what you have learnt.

We include **Questions** – lots of them – both within chapters and in the **Practice Question Bank**, as well as **Quick Quizzes** at the end of each chapter to test your knowledge of the chapter content.

Chapter features

Each chapter contains a number of helpful features to guide you through each topic.

Topic list

Topic list	Syllabus reference

Tells you what you will be studying in this chapter and the relevant section numbers, together with ACCA syllabus references.

Introduction

Puts the chapter content in the context of the syllabus as a whole.

Study Guide

Links the chapter content with ACCA guidance.

Exam Guide

Highlights how examinable the chapter content is likely to be and the ways in which it could be examined.

Knowledge brought forward from earlier studies

What you are assumed to know from previous studies/exams.

FAST FORWARD

Summarises the content of main chapter headings, allowing you to preview and review each section easily.

Examples

Demonstrate how to apply key knowledge and techniques.

Key terms

Definitions of important concepts that can often earn you easy marks in exams.

Exam focus points

Tell you when and how specific topics were examined, or how they may be examined in the future.

Gives you a useful indication of syllabus areas that closely relate to performance objectives in your Practical Experience Requirement (PER).

 Question

Gives you essential practice of techniques covered in the chapter.

 Case Study

Real world examples of theories and techniques.

Chapter Roundup

A full list of the Fast Forwards included in the chapter, providing an easy source of review.

Quick Quiz

A quick test of your knowledge of the main topics in the chapter.

Practice Question Bank

Found at the back of the Study Text with more comprehensive chapter questions. Cross referenced for easy navigation.

Studying F6

As the name suggests, this paper examines the basic principles of taxation. This is a very important area for certified accountants as many areas of practice involve a consideration of taxation issues. It also provides a foundation for P6: Advanced Taxation which will be chosen by those who work in a tax environment.

The F6 exam requires candidates to show that they have a solid understanding of the UK tax system and the main taxes which are income tax, corporation tax, national insurance contributions, capital gains tax, inheritance tax and value added tax.

Members of the F6 examining team have written several technical articles including two on Inheritance Tax, two on chargeable gains, one on groups, two on VAT, one on benefits, one on motor cars, one on adjustment of profit and one on Finance Act 2014. All these articles are available on the ACCA website. Make sure you read them to gain further insight into what the F6 examining team is looking for.

1 What F6 is about

The UK tax system and its administration

The syllabus introduces the rationale behind – and the functions of – the tax system. This part of the syllabus also covers the **compliance obligations** of the taxpayer. This is likely to form an element in one or more questions in the exam. A knowledge of tax is incomplete without an understanding of how the tax is collected.

The taxes

The syllabus then covers the **main UK taxes** which apply to individuals and businesses.

The two major areas of the syllabus are first, income tax and second, corporation tax. These will be tested in Section A (multiple choice questions), in the two 15-mark questions in Section B, one of which will be focused on income tax and one of which will be focused on corporation tax, and possibly also in one or more of the four 10-mark questions in Section B. The other taxes are national insurance contributions, capital gains tax, inheritance tax and value added tax. These taxes will mainly be tested in Section A and in the four 10-mark questions in Section B.

You will be expected to have a detailed knowledge of these taxes, but **no previous knowledge is assumed**. You should **study the basics** carefully and **learn the pro forma computations**. It then becomes straightforward to complete these by slotting in figures from your detailed workings.

As well as being able to calculate tax liabilities, in Section B questions you may be required to explain the basis of the calculations and how a taxpayer can minimise or defer tax liabilities.

2 What skills are required?

- Be able to **integrate** knowledge and understanding from across the syllabus to enable you to complete detailed computations of tax liabilities.

- Be able to **explain** the underlying principles of taxation by providing a simple summary of the rules and how they apply to the particular situation.

- Be able to **apply** tax planning techniques by identifying available options and testing them to see which has the greater effect on tax liabilities.

3 How to improve your chances of passing

3.1 Study the whole syllabus

Study the **entire** syllabus – all the questions in the exam are **compulsory**. This gives the examiner the opportunity to test all major areas of the syllabus on every paper.

Section A consists of 15 multiple choice questions, each worth two marks. These will inevitably cover a wide range of the syllabus.

3.2 Lots of question practice

Practise as many questions as you can under **timed conditions** – this is the best way of developing good exam technique. Make use of the **Practice Question Bank** at the back of this Text. **BPP's Practice and Revision Kit** contains numerous exam standard questions as well as three mock exams for you to try.

Answer selectively – the examiner will expect you to consider carefully what is relevant and significant enough to include in your answer. Don't include unnecessary information.

Present your answers in a **professional** manner when answering **Section B** questions – use subheadings, leave spaces between paragraphs and make sure that your numerical workings are clearly set out. Even if you make a mistake in your calculations, you will still gain marks if you show that you understand the principles involved.

Answer all parts of the question – leaving out a five mark part may be the difference between a pass and a fail.

Syllabus

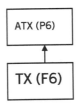

AIM

To develop knowledge and skills relating to the tax system as applicable to individuals, single companies, and groups of companies.

MAIN CAPABILITIES

On successful completion of this paper candidates should be able to:

A Explain the operation and scope of the tax system and the obligations of tax payer and/or their agents and the implications of non-compliance

B Explain and compute the income tax liabilities of individuals and the effect of national insurance contributions (NIC) on employees, employers and the self-employed

C Explain and compute the chargeable gains arising on individuals

D Explain and compute the inheritance tax liabilities of individuals

E Explain and compute the corporation tax liabilities of individual companies and groups of companies

F Explain and compute the effects of value added tax on incorporated and unincorporated businesses

RELATIONAL DIAGRAM OF MAIN CAPABILITIES

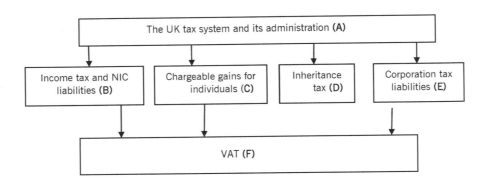

RATIONALE

The syllabus for Paper F6, *Taxation,* introduces candidates to the subject of taxation and provides the core knowledge of the underlying principles and major technical areas of taxation as they affect the activities of individuals and businesses.

Candidates are introduced to the rationale behind – and the functions of – the tax system. The syllabus then considers the separate taxes that an accountant would need to have a detailed knowledge of, such as income tax from self-employment, employment and investments, the corporation tax liability of individual companies and groups of companies, the national insurance contribution liabilities of both employed and self employed persons, the value added tax liability of businesses, the chargeable gains arising on disposals of investments by both individuals and companies, and the inheritance tax liabilities arising on chargeable lifetime transfers and on death.

Having covered the core areas of the basic taxes, candidates should be able to compute tax liabilities, explain the basis of their calculations, apply tax planning techniques for individuals and companies and identify the compliance issues for each major tax through a variety of business and personal scenarios and situations.

DETAILED SYLLABUS

A. The UK tax system and its administration

1. The overall function and purpose of taxation in a modern economy

2. Principal sources of revenue law and practice

3. The systems for self-assessment and the making of returns

4. The time limits for the submission of information, claims and payment of tax, including payments on account

5. The procedures relating to compliance checks, appeals and disputes

6. Penalties for non-compliance

B. Income tax and NIC liabilities

1. The scope of income tax

2. Income from employment

3. Income from self-employment

4. Property and investment income

5. The comprehensive computation of taxable income and income tax liability

6. National insurance contributions for employed and self-employed persons

7. The use of exemptions and reliefs in deferring and minimising income tax liabilities

C. Chargeable gains for individuals

1. The scope of the taxation of capital gains

2. The basic principles of computing gains and losses

3. Gains and losses on the disposal of movable and immovable property

4. Gains and losses on the disposal of shares and securities

5. The computation of capital gains tax

6. The use of exemptions and reliefs in deferring and minimising tax liabilities arising on the disposal of capital assets

D. Inheritance tax

1. The basic principles of computing transfers of value

2. The liabilities arising on chargeable lifetime transfers and on the death of an individual

3. The use of exemptions in deferring and minimising inheritance tax liabilities

4. Payment of inheritance tax

E.   Corporation tax liabilities

1.   The scope of corporation tax

2.   Taxable total profits

3.   Chargeable gains for companies

4.   The comprehensive computation of corporation tax liability

5.   The effect of a group corporate structure for corporation tax purposes

6.   The use of exemptions and reliefs in deferring and minimising corporation tax liabilities

F.   Value added tax

1.   The VAT registration requirements

2.   The computation of VAT liabilities

3.   The effect of special schemes

APPROACH TO EXAMINING THE SYLLABUS

The syllabus is assessed by a three-hour paper-based examination.

The paper will be predominantly computational and all questions are compulsory.

Section A of the exam comprises 15 multiple choice questions of 2 marks each.

Section B of the exam comprises four 10 mark questions and two 15 mark questions.

The two 15 mark questions will focus on income tax (syllabus area B) and corporation tax (syllabus area E).

The section A questions and the other questions in section B can cover any areas of the syllabus.

BPP
LEARNING MEDIA

Study Guide

A THE UK TAX SYSTEM AND ITS ADMINISTRATION

1. The overall function and purpose of taxation in a modern economy

a) Describe the purpose (economic, social etc) of taxation in a modern economy.[1]

b) Explain the difference between direct and indirect taxation.[2]

c) Identify the different types of capital and revenue tax.[1]

2. Principal sources of revenue law and practice

a) Describe the overall structure of the UK tax system.[1]

b) State the different sources of revenue law.[1]

c) Describe the organisation HM Revenue & Customs (HMRC) and its terms of reference.[1]

d) Explain the difference between tax avoidance and tax evasion, and the purposes of the General Anti-Abuse Rule (GAAR).[1]

e) Appreciate the interaction of the UK tax system with that of other tax jurisdictions.[2]

f) Appreciate the need for double taxation agreements.[2]

g) Explain the need for an ethical and professional approach.[2]

Excluded topics

- *Specific anti-avoidance legislation.*

3. The systems for self-assessment and the making of returns

a) Explain and apply the features of the self-assessment system as it applies to individuals.[2]

b) Explain and apply the features of the self-assessment system as it applies to companies, including the use of iXBRL.[2]

4. The time limits for the submission of information, claims and payment of tax, including payments on account

a) Recognise the time limits that apply to the filing of returns and the making of claims.[2]

b) Recognise the due dates for the payment of tax under the self-assessment system, and compute payments on account and balancing payments/repayments for individuals.[2]

c) Explain how large companies are required to account for corporation tax on a quarterly basis and compute the quarterly instalment payments.[2]

d) List the information and records that taxpayers need to retain for tax purposes.[1]

Excluded topics

- *The payment of CGT by annual instalments.*

5. The procedures relating to compliance checks, appeals and disputes

a) Explain the circumstances in which HM Revenue & Customs can make a compliance check into a self-assessment tax return.[2]

b) Explain the procedures for dealing with appeals and First and Upper Tier Tribunals.[2]

Excluded topics

- *Information powers.*

- *Pre-return compliance checks.*

- *Detailed procedures on the carrying out and completion of a compliance check.*

6. Penalties for non-compliance

a) Calculate late payment interest and state the penalties that can be charged.[2]

B INCOME TAX AND NIC LIABILITIES

1. The scope of income tax

a) Explain how the residence of an individual is determined.[1]

Excluded topics

- The split year treatment where a person comes to the UK or leaves the UK.

- Foreign income, non-residents and double taxation relief.

- Income from trusts and settlements.

2. Income from employment

a) Recognise the factors that determine whether an engagement is treated as employment or self-employment.[2]

b) Recognise the basis of assessment for employment income.[2]

c) Recognise the income assessable.[2]

d) Recognise the allowable deductions, including travelling expenses.[2]

e) Discuss the use of the statutory approved mileage allowances.[2]

f) Explain the PAYE system.[1]

g) Identify P11D employees.[1]

h) Explain and compute the amount of benefits assessable.[2]

i) Explain the purpose of a dispensation from HM Revenue & Customs.[2]

Excluded topics

- The calculation of a car benefit where emission figures are not available.

- The exemption for zero emission company motor cars.

- The exemption where an employer pays for medical treatment.

- Share and share option incentive schemes for employees.

- Payments on the termination of employment, and other lump sums received by employees.

- Real time reporting late filing penalties.

3. Income from self-employment

a) Recognise the basis of assessment for self-employment income.[2]

b) Describe and apply the badges of trade.[2]

c) Recognise the expenditure that is allowable in calculating the tax-adjusted trading profit.[2]

d) Explain and compute the assessable profits using the cash basis for small businesses.[2]

e) Recognise the relief which can be obtained for pre-trading expenditure.[2]

f) Compute the assessable profits on commencement and on cessation.[2]

g) Recognise the factors that will influence the choice of accounting date.[2]

h) Capital allowances
   i) Define plant and machinery for capital allowances purposes.[1]
   ii) Compute writing down allowances, first-year allowances and the annual investment allowance.[2]
   iii) Compute capital allowances for motor cars.[2]
   iv) Compute balancing allowances and balancing charges.[2]
   v) Recognise the treatment of short life assets.[2]
   vi) Recognise the treatment of assets included in the special rate pool.[2]

i) Relief for trading losses
   i) Understand how trading losses can be carried forward.[2]

ii) Understand how trading losses can be claimed against total income and chargeable gains, and the restriction that can apply.[2]

iii) Explain and compute the relief for trading losses in the early years of a trade.[1]

iv) Explain and compute terminal loss relief.[1]

v) Recognise the factors that will influence the choice of loss relief claim.[2]

j) Partnerships and limited liability partnerships

i) Explain and compute how a partnership is assessed to tax.[2]

ii) Explain and compute the assessable profits for each partner following a change in the profit sharing ratio.[2]

iii) Explain and compute the assessable profits for each partner following a change in the membership of the partnership.[2]

iv) Describe the alternative loss relief claims that are available to partners.[1]

Excluded topics

- *Change of accounting date.*

- *The 100% allowance for expenditure on renovating business premises in disadvantaged areas, flats above shops and water technologies.*

- *Capital allowances for industrial buildings, agricultural buildings, patents, scientific research and know how.*

- *CO^2 emission thresholds for capital allowances for motor cars prior to 6 April 2013.*

- *Apportionment in order to determine the amount of annual investment allowance where a period of account spans 6 April 2014.*

- *Enterprise zones.*

- *Investment income of a partnership.*

- *The allocation of notional profits and losses for a partnership.*

- *Farmers averaging of profits.*

- *The averaging of profits for authors and creative artists.*

- *Loss relief following the incorporation of a business.*

- *Loss relief for shares in unquoted trading companies.*

- *The loss relief restriction that applies to the partners of a limited liability partnership.*

4. Property and investment income

a) Compute property business profits.[2]

b) Explain the treatment of furnished holiday lettings.[1]

c) Understand rent-a-room relief.[1]

d) Compute the amount assessable when a premium is received for the grant of a short lease.[2]

e) Understand how relief for a property business loss is given.[2]

f) Compute the tax payable on savings and dividends income.[2]

g) Recognise the treatment of new individual savings accounts (NISAs) and other tax exempt investments.[1]

Excluded topics

- *The deduction for expenditure by landlords on energy-saving items.*

- *Premiums for granting subleases.*

- *The ISA investment rules and limits that applied prior to 1 July 2014.*

- *Junior ISAs.*

5. The comprehensive computation of taxable income and income tax liability

a) Prepare a basic income tax computation involving different types of income.[2]

b) Calculate the amount of personal allowance available generally, and for people born before 6 April 1948.[2]

c) Compute the amount of income tax payable.[2]

d) Understand the treatment of interest paid for a qualifying purpose.[2]

e) Understand the treatment of gift aid donations and charitable giving.[1]

f) Explain and compute the child benefit tax charge.[1]

g) Understand the treatment of property owned jointly by a married couple, or by a couple in a civil partnership.[1]

Excluded topics

- *The blind person's allowance and the married couple's allowance.*

- *Tax credits.*

- *Maintenance payments.*

- *The income of minor children.*

6. National insurance contributions for employed and self-employed persons

a) Explain and compute national insurance contributions payable:
i) Class 1 and 1A NIC.[2]
ii) Class 2 and 4 NIC. [2]

b) Understand the annual employment allowance.[2]

Excluded topics

- *The calculation of directors' national insurance on a month by month basis.*

- *Contracted out contributions.*

- *The offset of trading losses against non-trading income.*

7. The use of exemptions and reliefs in deferring and minimising income tax liabilities

a) Explain and compute the relief given for contributions to personal pension schemes, and to occupational pension schemes.[2]

b) Understand how a married couple or a couple in a civil partnership can minimise their tax liabilities.[2]

Excluded topics

- *The conditions that must be met in order for a pension scheme to obtain approval from HM Revenue & Customs.*

- *The enterprise investment scheme and the seed enterprise investment scheme.*

- *Venture capital trusts.*

- *Tax reduction scheme for gifts of pre-eminent objects.*

C   CHARGEABLE GAINS FOR INDIVIDUALS

1. The scope of the taxation of capital gains

a) Describe the scope of capital gains tax.[2]

b) Recognise those assets which are exempt.[1]

Excluded topics

- *Assets situated overseas and double taxation relief.*

- *Partnership capital gains.*

2. The basic principles of computing gains and losses

a) Compute and explain the treatment of capital gains.[2]

b) Compute and explain the treatment of capital losses [2]

c) Understand the treatment of transfers between a husband and wife or between a couple in a civil partnership.[2]

d) Understand the amount of allowable expenditure for a part disposal.[2]

© ACCA 2015 All rights reserved.

e) Recognise the treatment where an asset is damaged, lost or destroyed, and the implications of receiving insurance proceeds and reinvesting such proceeds.[2]

Excluded topics

- *Small part disposals of land, and small capital sums received where an asset is damaged.*

- *Losses in the year of death.*

- *Relief for losses incurred on loans made to traders.*

- *Negligible value claims.*

3. **Gains and losses on the disposal of movable and immovable property**

a) Identify when chattels and wasting assets are exempt.[1]

b) Compute the chargeable gain when a chattel or a wasting asset is disposed of.[2]

c) Calculate the chargeable gain when a principal private residence is disposed of.[2]

Excluded topics

- *The disposal of leases and the creation of sub-leases.*

4. **Gains and losses on the disposal of shares and securities**

a) Recognise the value of quoted shares where they are disposed of by way of a gift.[2]

b) Explain and apply the identification rules as they apply to individuals including the same day and 30 day matching rules.[2]

c) Explain and apply the pooling provisions.[2]

d) Explain and apply the treatment of bonus issues, rights issues, takeovers and reorganisations.[2]

e) Identify the exemption available for gilt-edged securities and qualifying corporate bonds.[1]

Excluded topics

- *The exemption for employee shareholders.*

- *The small part disposal rules applicable to rights issues, takeovers and reorganisations.*

- *Gilt-edged securities and qualifying corporate bonds other than the fact that they are exempt.*

5. **The computation of capital gains tax**

a) Compute the amount of capital gains tax payable.[2]

b) Explain and apply entrepreneurs' relief. [2]

Excluded topics

- *Entrepreneurs' relief for associated disposals.*

6. **The use of exemptions and reliefs in deferring and minimising tax liabilities arising on the disposal of capital assets**

a) Explain and apply capital gains tax reliefs:
(i) rollover relief.[2]
(ii) holdover relief for the gift of business assets.[2]

Excluded topics

- *Incorporation relief.*

- *Reinvestment relief.*

D INHERITANCE TAX

1. **The basic principles of computing transfers of value**

a) Identify the persons chargeable.[2]

b) Understand and apply the meaning of transfer of value, chargeable transfer and potentially exempt transfer.[2]

c) Demonstrate the diminution in value principle.[2]

d) Demonstrate the seven year accumulation principle taking into account changes in the level of the nil rate band.[2]

Excluded topics

- *Pre 18 March 1986 lifetime transfers.*

- *Transfers of value by close companies.*

- *Domicile, deemed domicile, and non-UK domiciled individuals.*

- *Trusts.*

- *Excluded property.*

- *Related property.*

- *The tax implications of the location of assets.*

- *Gifts with reservation of benefit.*

- *Associated operations.*

2. **The liabilities arising on chargeable lifetime transfers and on the death of an individual**

a) Understand the tax implications of lifetime transfers and compute the relevant liabilities.[2]

b) Understand and compute the tax liability on a death estate.[2]

c) Understand and apply the transfer of any unused nil rate band between spouses.[2]

Excluded topics

- *Specific rules for the valuation of assets (values will be provided).*

- *Business property relief.*

- *Agricultural relief.*

- *Relief for the fall in value of lifetime gifts.*

- *Quick succession relief.*

- *Double tax relief.*

- *Variation of wills and disclaimers of legacies.*

- *Grossing up on death.*

- *Post mortem reliefs.*

- *Double charges legislation.*

- *The reduced rate of inheritance tax payable on death when a proportion of a person's estate is bequeathed to charity.*

3. **The use of exemptions in deferring and minimising inheritance tax liabilities**

a) Understand and apply the following exemptions:
   i) small gifts exemption[2]
   ii) annual exemption[2]
   iii) normal expenditure out of income[2]
   iv) gifts in consideration of marriage[2]
   v) gifts between spouses.[2]

Excluded topics

- *Gifts to charities.*

- *Gifts to political parties.*

- *Gifts for national purposes.*

4. **Payment of inheritance tax**

a) Identify who is responsible for the payment of inheritance tax and the due date for payment of inheritance tax.[2]

Excluded topics

- *Administration of inheritance tax other than listed above.*

- *The instalment option for the payment of tax.*

- *Interest and penalties.*

E   CORPORATION TAX LIABILITIES

1.   The scope of corporation tax

a)   Define the terms 'period of account', 'accounting period', and 'financial year'.[1]

b)   Recognise when an accounting period starts and when an accounting period finishes.[1]

c)   Explain how the residence of a company is determined.[2]

Excluded topics

- *Investment companies.*

- *Close companies.*

- *Companies in receivership or liquidation.*

- *Reorganisations.*

- *The purchase by a company of its own shares.*

- *Personal service companies.*

2.   Taxable total profits

a)   Recognise the expenditure that is allowable in calculating the tax-adjusted trading profit.[2]

b)   Recognise the relief which can be obtained for pre-trading expenditure.[1]

c)   Compute capital allowances (as for income tax).[2]

d)   Compute property business profits and understand how relief for a property business loss is given.[2]

e)   Understand how trading losses can be carried forward.[2]

f)   Understand how trading losses can be claimed against income of the current or previous accounting periods.[2]

g)   Recognise the factors that will influence the choice of loss relief claim.[2]

h)   Recognise and apply the treatment of interest paid and received under the loan relationship rules.[1]

i)   Recognise and apply the treatment of qualifying charitable donations.[2]

j)   Compute taxable total profits.[2]

Excluded topics

- *Research and development expenditure.*

- *Non-trading deficits on loan relationships.*

- *Relief for intangible assets.*

- *Patent box.*

3   Chargeable gains for companies

a)   Compute and explain the treatment of chargeable gains.[2]

b)   Explain and compute the indexation allowance available.[2]

c)   Explain and compute the treatment of capital losses.[1]

d)   Understand the treatment of disposals of shares by companies and apply the identification rules including the same day and nine day matching rules.[2]

e)   Explain and apply the pooling provisions.[2]

f)   Explain and apply the treatment of bonus issues, rights issues, takeovers and reorganisations.[2]

g)   Explain and apply rollover relief.[2]

Excluded topics

- *A detailed question on the pooling provisions as they apply to limited companies.*

- *Substantial shareholdings.*

4. The comprehensive computation of corporation tax liability

a) Compute the corporation tax liability and apply marginal relief.[2]

b) Recognise the implications of receiving franked investment income.[2]

5. The effect of a group corporate structure for corporation tax purposes

a) Define an associated company and recognise the effect of having associated companies for corporation tax purposes.[2]

b) Define a 75% group, and recognise the reliefs that are available to members of such a group.[2]

c) Define a 75% chargeable gains group, and recognise the reliefs that are available to members of such a group.[2]

Excluded topics

- *Relief for trading losses incurred by an overseas subsidiary.*

- *Consortia.*

- *Pre-entry gains and losses.*

- *The anti-avoidance provisions where arrangements exist for a company to leave a group.*

- *The tax charge that applies where a company leaves a group within six years of receiving an asset by way of a no gain/no loss transfer.*

- *Overseas aspects of corporation tax.*

- *Transfer pricing*

6. The use of exemptions and reliefs in deferring and minimising corporation tax liabilities:

The use of such exemptions and reliefs is implicit within all of the above sections 1 to 5 of part E of the syllabus, concerning corporation tax.

F VALUE ADDED TAX

1. The VAT registration requirements

a) Recognise the circumstances in which a person must register or deregister for VAT (compulsory) and when a person may register or deregister for VAT (voluntary).[2]

b) Recognise the circumstances in which pre-registration input VAT can be recovered.[2]

c) Explain the conditions that must be met for two or more companies to be treated as a group for VAT purposes, and the consequences of being so treated.[1]

2. The computation of VAT liabilities

a) Understand how VAT is accounted for and administered.[2]

b) Recognise the tax point when goods or services are supplied.[2]

c) List the information that must be given on a VAT invoice.[1]

d) Explain and apply the principles regarding the valuation of supplies.[2]

e) Recognise the principal zero rated and exempt supplies [1]

f) Recognise the circumstances in which input VAT is non-deductible.[2]

g) Recognise the relief that is available for impairment losses on trade debts.[2]

h) Understand when the default surcharge, a penalty for an incorrect VAT return, and default interest will be applied.[1]

i) Understand the treatment of imports, exports and trade within the European Union.[2]

Excluded topics

- *VAT periods where there is a change of VAT rate.*

- *Partial exemption.*
- *In respect of property and land: leases, do-it-yourself builders, and a landlord's option to tax.*

- *Penalties apart from those listed in the study guide.*

3. **The effect of special schemes**

a) Understand the operation of, and when it will be advantageous to use, the VAT special schemes:
    i) cash accounting scheme.[2]
    ii) annual accounting scheme.[2]
    iii) flat rate scheme. [2]

Excluded topics

- *The second-hand goods scheme.*

- *The capital goods scheme.*

- *The special schemes for retailers.*

SUMMARY OF CHANGES TO F6 (UK)

ACCA periodically reviews it qualification syllabuses so that they fully meet the needs of stakeholders such as employers, students, regulatory and advisory bodies and learning providers.

Some of the syllabus areas have been reordered as shown in Table 1 below:

Table 1 – Reordering within F6 (UK)

Section and subject area	Syllabus content
Reordering of syllabus areas	The syllabus areas have been reordered so that syllabus area A covers the UK tax system and its administration, B covers income tax and NIC liabilities, C covers chargeable gains for individuals, D covers inheritance tax, E covers corporation tax (including chargeable gains) and F covers VAT.
Enlarged syllabus area A	Syllabus area H (the obligations of the taxpayer and/or their agents) has been combined with syllabus area A to create an enlarged syllabus area A (the UK tax system and its administration).
National insurance	National insurance has been moved and is now included in syllabus area B (Income tax and NIC liabilities)
E3 Chargeable gains for companies	Chargeable gains have been split between individuals (syllabus area C) and companies (syllabus area E3 Corporation tax)

The main areas that have been added to the syllabus are shown in Table 2 below:

Table 2 - Additions to F6 (UK)

Section and subject area	Syllabus content
A2c) Principal sources of revenue law and practice	New part (c) on the organisation HMRC and its terms of reference added
B2 Income from employment – *Excluded topics*	*The exemption where an employer pays for medical treatment.* *Real time reporting late filing penalties.*
B3 Income from self-employment – *Excluded topics*	*The loss relief restriction that applies to the partners of a limited liability partnership.*
B3i)v) Income from self-employment	New part v) on the factors that will influence the choice of loss relief claim added for clarity
B4 Property and investment income – *Excluded topics*	*The ISA investment rules and limits that applied prior to 1 July 2014.*
B6b) National insurance contributions for employed and self-employed persons	New part (b) on the annual employment allowance.
E5 The effect of a group corporate structure for corporation tax purposes – *Excluded topics*	*Relief for trading losses incurred by an overseas subsidiary*

The main areas that have been deleted from the syllabus are shown in Table 3 below:

Table 3 – Deletions from F6 (UK)

Section and subject area	Syllabus content
B3 Income from self employment	Part B3j) (v) on the loss relief restriction that applies to the partners of a limited liability partnership deleted.

The exam paper

Format of the paper

The syllabus is assessed by a **three-hour paper-based examination**.

The paper will be **predominantly computational** and **all questions are compulsory**.

Section A of the exam comprises **15 multiple choice questions** of **2 marks** each.

Section B of the exam comprises **four 10 mark questions** and **two 15 mark questions**.

The **two 15 mark questions** will focus on **income tax (syllabus area B)** and **corporation tax (syllabus area E)**.

The **section A questions** and the **other questions in section B** can cover **any areas of the syllabus**.

UK tax system

Introduction to
the UK tax system

1

Topic list	Syllabus reference
1 The overall function and purpose of taxation in a modern economy	A1(a)
2 Different types of taxes	A1(b), (c)
3 Principal sources of revenue law and practice	A2(a)-(c), (e), (f)
4 Tax avoidance and tax evasion	A2(d), (g)

Introduction

We start our study of tax with an introduction to the UK tax system.

First we consider briefly the purpose of raising taxes, focussing on economic, social and environmental factors. We next consider the specific UK taxes, both revenue and capital, and also direct and indirect.

We see how the collection of tax is administered in the UK, and where the UK tax system interacts with overseas tax jurisdictions.

Finally we highlight the difference between tax avoidance and tax evasion and explain the need for a professional and ethical approach in dealing with tax. In particular, we look at the situation where a client has failed to disclose information to the tax authorities.

When you have finished this chapter you should be able to discuss the broad features of the tax system. In the following chapters we will consider specific UK taxes, starting with income tax.

Study guide

		Intellectual level
A1	**The overall function and purpose of taxation in a modern economy**	
(a)	Describe the purpose (economic, social etc) of taxation in a modern economy.	1
(b)	Explain the difference between direct and indirect taxation.	2
(c)	Identify the different types of capital and revenue tax.	1
A2	**Principal sources of revenue law and practice**	
(a)	Describe the overall structure of the UK tax system.	1
(b)	State the different sources of revenue law.	1
(c)	Describe the organisation of HM Revenue and Customs (HMRC) and its terms of reference.	1
(d)	Explain the difference between tax avoidance and tax evasion, and the purposes of the General Anti-Abuse Rule (GAAR).	1
(e)	Appreciate the interaction of the UK tax system with that of other tax jurisdictions.	2
(f)	Appreciate the need for double taxation agreements.	2
(g)	Explain the need for an ethical and professional approach.	2

Exam guide

You are unlikely to be asked a whole Section B question on this part of the syllabus. You may, however, be asked to comment on one aspect, such as the difference between tax avoidance and tax evasion or how to act if a client has failed to disclose information to the tax authorities, as part of a question.

1 The overall function and purpose of taxation in a modern economy

FAST FORWARD

Economic, social and environmental factors may affect the government's tax policies.

1.1 Economic factors

In terms of economic analysis, government **taxation represents a withdrawal from the UK economy** while its expenditure acts as an injection into it. So the government's net position in terms of taxation and expenditure, together with its public sector borrowing policies, has an effect on the level of economic activity within the UK.

The government favours longer-term planning, and regularly sets out proposed plans for expenditure. These show the proportion of the economy's overall resources which will be allocated by the government and how much will be left for the private sector.

This can have an effect on demand for particular types of goods, eg health and education on the one hand, which are predominately the result of public spending, and consumer goods on the other, which results from private spending. Changing demand levels will have an impact on employment levels within the different sectors, as well as on the profitability of different private sector suppliers.

Within that overall proportion left in the private sector, **the government uses tax policies to encourage and discourage certain types of activity**.

It **encourages**:

(a) **Saving** on the part of the individual, by offering tax incentives such as tax-free New Individual Savings Accounts and tax relief on pension contributions

(b) **Donations to charities**, through the Gift Aid scheme

(c) **Entrepreneurs** who build their own business, through reliefs from capital gains tax

(d) **Investment in plant and machinery** through capital allowances

It **discourages**:

(a) **Smoking** and **alcoholic drinks**, through the duties placed on each type of product
(b) **Motoring**, through fuel duties

Governments can and do argue that these latter taxes and duties to some extent mirror the extra costs to the country as a whole of such behaviours, such as the cost of coping with smoking related illnesses. However, the Government needs to raise money for spending in areas where there are no consumers on whom the necessary taxes can be levied, such as defence, law and order, overseas aid and the cost of running the government and Parliament.

1.2 Social factors

Social justice lies at the heart of politics, since what some think of as just is regarded by others as completely unjust. Attitudes to the redistribution of wealth are a clear example.

In a free market some individuals generate greater amounts of income and capital than others and once wealth has been acquired, it tends to grow through the reinvestment of investment income received. This can lead to the rich getting richer and the poor poorer, with economic power becoming concentrated in relatively few hands.

Some electors make the value judgement that these trends should be countered by **taxation policies which redistribute income and wealth** away from the rich towards the poor. This is one of the key arguments in favour of some sort of capital gains tax and inheritance tax, taxes which, relative to the revenue raised, cost a great deal to collect.

Different taxes have different social effects:

(a) **Direct taxes** based on income and profits (income tax), gains (capital gains tax) or wealth (inheritance tax) **tax only those who have these resources**.

(b) **Indirect taxes** paid by the consumer (VAT) **discourage spending** and encourage saving. Lower or nil rates of tax can be levied on essentials, such as food.

(c) **Progressive taxes** such as income tax, where the proportion of the income or gains paid over in tax increases as income/gains rise, **target those who can afford to pay**. Personal allowances and the rates of taxation can be adjusted so as to ensure that those on very low incomes pay little or no tax.

(d) Taxes on capital or wealth ensure that that people cannot avoid taxation by having an income of zero and just living off the sale of capital assets.

Almost everyone would argue that taxation should be **equitable** or 'fair', but there are many different views as to what is equitable.

An **efficient tax** is one where the costs of collection are low relative to the tax paid over to the government. The government publishes figures for the administrative costs incurred by government departments in operating the taxation systems, but there are also compliance costs to be taken into account. Compliance costs are those incurred by the taxpayer, whether they be the individual preparing tax returns under the self assessment system or the employer operating the PAYE system to collect income tax or the business collecting value added tax. Some of the more equitable taxes may be less efficient to collect.

1.3 Environmental factors

The taxation system is moving slowly to accommodate the environmental concerns which have come to the fore over the last twenty years or so, especially the concerns about renewable and non-renewable sources of energy and global warming.

Examples of tax changes which have been introduced for environmental reasons are:

(a) The **climate change levy**, raised on businesses in proportion to their consumption of energy. Its claimed purpose is to encourage reduced consumption.

(b) The **landfill tax** levied on the operators of landfill sites on each tonne of rubbish/waste processed at the site. Its claimed purpose is to encourage recycling by taxing waste which has to be stored.

(c) The changes to rules on the **lease or purchase of cars**, and taxation of **cars and private fuel provided for employees** to be dependent on CO_2 emissions. Its claimed purpose is to encourage the manufacture and purchase of low CO_2 emission cars to reduce emissions into the atmosphere caused by driving.

Only the last of these will be directly felt by individuals, even if the other taxes are passed on by being factored into a business's overheads.

2 Different types of taxes

FAST FORWARD Central government raises revenue through a wide range of taxes. Tax law is made by statute.

2.1 Taxes in the UK

Central government raises revenue through a wide range of taxes. Tax law is made by **statute**.

The main taxes, their incidence and their sources, are set out in the table below.

Tax	Suffered by	Source
Income tax	**Individuals** **Partnerships**	Capital Allowances Act 2001 (CAA 2001); Income Tax (Earnings and Pensions) Act 2003 (ITEPA 2003); Income Tax (Trading and Other Income) Act 2005 (ITTOIA 2005); Income Tax Act 2007 (ITA 2007)
Corporation tax	**Companies**	CAA 2001 as above, Corporation Tax Act 2009 (CTA 2009), Corporation Tax Act 2010 (CTA 2010)
Capital gains tax	**Individuals** **Partnerships** **Companies** (which pay tax on capital gains in the form of corporation tax)	Taxation of Chargeable Gains Act 1992 (TCGA 1992)
Inheritance tax	**Individuals** **Trustees**	Inheritance Tax Act 1984 (IHTA 1984)
Value added tax	**Businesses**, both incorporated and unincorporated	Value Added Tax Act 1994 (VATA 1994)

You will also meet National Insurance. **National insurance is payable by employers, employees and the self employed.**

Further details of all these taxes are found later in this Text.

The other taxes referred to in the previous section, such as landfill tax, are not examinable at F6.

Finance Acts are passed each year, incorporating proposals set out in the **Budget**. They make changes which apply mainly to the tax year ahead. **This Study Text includes the provisions of the Finance Act 2014.** This is the **Finance Act examinable** in the sessions from **1 April 2015 to 31 March 2016**.

2.2 Revenue and capital taxes

Revenue taxes are those charged on income. In this Text this covers:

(a)   **Income tax**
(b)   **Corporation tax** (on income profits)
(c)   **National insurance**

Capital taxes are those charged on capital gains or on wealth. In this Text this covers:

(a)   **Capital gains tax**
(b)   **Corporation tax** (on capital gains)
(c)   **Inheritance tax**

2.3 Direct and indirect taxes

Direct taxes are those charged on **income, gains and wealth. Income tax, national insurance, corporation tax, capital gains tax** and **inheritance tax** are **direct taxes**. Direct taxes are collected directly from the taxpayer.

Indirect taxes are those **paid by the consumer to the supplier** who then passes the tax to the Government. **Value added tax** is an indirect tax.

3 Principal sources of revenue law and practice

FAST FORWARD

Tax is administered by HM Revenue and Customs (HMRC).

3.1 The overall structure of the UK tax system

3.1.1 Her Majesty's Treasury

Her Majesty's Treasury formally imposes and collects taxation. The management of the Treasury is the responsibility of the Chancellor of the Exchequer.

3.1.2 Her Majesty's Revenue and Customs (HMRC)

The administrative function for the collection of tax is undertaken by Her Majesty's Revenue and Customs (HMRC).

The HMRC staff are referred to in the tax legislation as **'Officers of Revenue and Customs'**. They are responsible for supervising the self-assessment system and raising queries about tax liabilities.

3.1.3 Crown Prosecution Service (CPS)

The **Crown Prosecution Service (CPS)** provides legal advice and institutes and conducts criminal prosecutions in England and Wales where there has been an investigation by HMRC.

3.1.4 Tax Tribunal

Tax appeals are heard by the **Tax Tribunal** which is made up of **two tiers**:

(a)   **First Tier Tribunal**
(b)   **Upper Tribunal**

The **First Tier Tribunal deals with most cases** other than complex cases. The **Upper Tribunal deals with complex cases** which either involve an important issue of tax law or a large financial sum. The Upper Tribunal **also hears appeals** against decisions of the First Tier Tribunal. We look at the appeals system in more detail later in this Text.

3.2 Different sources of revenue law

FAST FORWARD The sources of revenue law are Acts of Parliament, Statutory Instruments and case law.

As stated above, taxes are imposed by statute. This comprises not only **Acts of Parliament** but also regulations laid down by **Statutory Instruments**. Statute is interpreted and amplified by **case law**.

HMRC also issue:

(a) **Statements of practice**, setting out how they intend to apply the law

(b) **Extra-statutory concessions**, setting out circumstances in which they will not apply the strict letter of the law where it would be unfair. Following the case of *R v HM Commissioners of Inland Revenue ex p Wilkinson (2005)* which clarified the scope of HM Revenue and Custom's power to make extra-statutory concessions, a number of concessions have been withdrawn and instead their effect given statutory force by statutory instrument.

(c) A wide range of **explanatory leaflets**

(d) **Revenue and Customs Brief.** This is gives HMRC's view on specific points.

(e) The **Internal Guidance**, a series of manuals used by HMRC staff

(f) **Working Together**, for tax practitioners

A great deal of information and HMRC publications can be found on the HM Revenue and Customs Internet site (www.hmrc.gov.uk).

Although the HMRC publications do not generally have the force of law, some of the VAT notices do where power has been delegated under regulations. This applies, for example, to certain administrative aspects of the cash accounting scheme.

3.3 The interaction of the UK tax system with that of other tax jurisdictions

3.3.1 The European Union

FAST FORWARD UK membership of the European Union has a significant effect on UK taxes, in particular value added tax (VAT).

Membership of the European Union has a significant effect on UK taxes although there is not yet a general requirement imposed on the EU member states to move to a common system of taxation or to harmonise their individual tax systems. The states may, however, agree jointly to enact specific laws, known as '**Directives**', which provide for a common code of taxation within particular areas of their taxation systems.

The most important example to date is **Value Added Tax (VAT)**, where the UK is obliged to pass its laws in conformity with the rules laid down in the European legislation. The VAT Directives still allow for a certain amount of flexibility between member states, eg in setting rates of taxation. There are only limited examples of Directives in the area of Direct Taxes, generally concerned with cross-border dividend and interest payments and corporate reorganisations.

However, under the EU treaties, member states are also obliged to permit freedom of movement of workers, freedom of movement of capital and freedom to establish business operations within the EU. These treaty provisions have '**direct effect**', ie a taxpayer is entitled to claim that a UK tax provision is ineffective because it **breaches one or more of the freedoms** guaranteed under European Law.

The European Court of Justice has repeatedly held that taxation provisions which discriminate against non-residents (ie treat a non-resident less favourably than a resident in a similar situation) are contrary to European Law, unless there is a very strong public interest justification.

There are provisions regarding the **exchange of information** between European Union Revenue authorities.

3.3.2 Other countries

In general, the rules of tax jurisdictions of other countries do not have a direct interaction with UK tax. However, the UK has entered into **double tax agreement** with various countries, as discussed below.

3.4 Double taxation agreements

FAST FORWARD

Double taxation agreements are designed to protect against the risk of double taxation where the same income or gains are taxable in two countries.

Double Taxation agreements between two countries are primarily designed to protect against the risk of double taxation where the same income or gains are taxable in two countries.

For example an individual may have a **source of income which is taxed in the country in which the income arose** but **is also taxed in the individual's country of residence**. The agreement could provide that the **income is only to be taxed in one country** or that **credit is to be given for tax arising in one country against the tax charge in the other country**.

Double taxation agreements may also include **non-discrimination provisions** which prevent a foreign national from being treated more harshly than a national of a country.

Double taxation agreement also usually include rules for the **exchange of information** between the different Revenue authorities.

4 Tax avoidance and tax evasion

FAST FORWARD

Tax avoidance is the legal minimisation of tax liabilities; tax evasion is illegal.

4.1 Tax evasion

Tax evasion consists of seeking to pay too little tax by deliberately misleading HMRC by either:

(a) **Suppressing information to which they are entitled** (eg failing to notify HMRC that you are liable to tax, understating income or gains or omitting to disclose a relevant fact, eg that business expenditure had a dual motive), or

(b) **Providing them with deliberately false information** (eg deducting expenses which have not been incurred or claiming capital allowances on plant that has not been purchased)

Tax evasion is illegal. Minor cases of tax evasion have generally been settled out of court on the payment of penalties. However, there is now a **statutory offence of evading income tax**, which enables such matters as deliberate failure to operate PAYE to be dealt with in magistrates' courts.

Serious cases of tax evasion, particularly those involving fraud, will continue to be the subject of **criminal prosecutions** which may lead to **fines and/or imprisonment on conviction**.

4.2 Tax avoidance

Tax avoidance is more difficult to define.

In a very broad sense, it could include **any legal method of reducing your tax burden**, eg taking advantage of tax shelter opportunities explicitly offered by tax legislation such as NISAs. However, the term is more commonly used in a more narrow sense, to denote ingenious arrangements designed to produce unintended tax advantages for the taxpayer.

The effectiveness of tax avoidance schemes has often been examined in the courts. Traditionally the tax rules were applied to the legal form of transactions, although this principle was qualified in later cases. It was held that the Courts could disregard transactions which were preordained and solely designed to avoid tax.

Traditionally, the response of HMRC has been to seek to mend the **loopholes** in the law as they come to their attention. In general, there is a presumption that the effect of such changes should not be backdated.

There are **disclosure obligations** on promoters of certain tax **avoidance schemes**, and on taxpayers, to provide details to HMRC of any such schemes used by the taxpayer. This enables HMRC to introduce anti avoidance measures at the earliest opportunity.

4.3 The distinction between avoidance and evasion

The **distinction between tax evasion and tax avoidance should generally be clear cut**, since tax avoidance is an entirely legal activity and does not entail misleading HMRC. However, some tax avoidance arrangements may be subject to the General Anti-Abuse Rule discussed below.

Care should also be taken in giving advice in some circumstances. For example, a taxpayer who does not return income or gains because he wrongly believes that he has successfully avoided having to pay tax on them may, as a result, be accused of tax evasion.

4.4 General anti-abuse rule (GAAR)

FAST FORWARD

There is a general anti-abuse rule (GAAR) which enables HMRC to counteract tax advantages arising from abusive tax arrangements.

Tax avoidance is usually targeted with legislation which applies in specific circumstances. **The GAAR provides additional means for HMRC to 'counteract' tax advantages arising from abusive 'tax arrangements'**, ie arrangements that involve obtaining a **tax advantage** as (one of) their main purpose(s).

Arrangements are **abusive** if they **cannot be regarded as a reasonable course of action**, for example, where they **lead to unintended results involving one or more contrived or abnormal steps and exploit any shortcomings in the tax provisions**.

Examples of abusive arrangements include those that result in:

(a) Significantly less income, profits or gains
(b) Significantly greater deductions or losses, or
(c) A claim for the repayment or crediting of tax that has not been, and is unlikely to be, paid

A 'tax advantage' includes:

(a) Relief or increased relief from tax
(b) Repayment or increased repayment of tax
(c) Avoidance or reduction of a charge to tax
(d) Avoidance of a possible assessment to tax
(e) Deferral of a payment of tax or advancement of a repayment of tax
(f) Avoidance of an obligation to deduct or account for tax

HMRC may counteract tax advantages arising by, for example, increasing the taxpayer's tax liability. HMRC must follow certain procedural requirements and, if it makes any adjustments, these must be on a 'just and reasonable' basis.

4.5 The need for an ethical and professional approach

If a client makes a material error or omission in a tax return, or fails to file a tax return, and does not correct the error, omission or failure when advised, the accountant should cease to act for the client, inform HMRC of this cessation and make a money laundering report.

Under self assessment, all taxpayers (whether individuals or companies) are responsible for disclosing their taxable income and gains and the deductions and reliefs they are claiming against them.

Many taxpayers arrange for their accountants to prepare and submit their tax returns. **The taxpayer is still the person responsible for submitting the return and for paying whatever tax becomes due**: the accountant is only acting as the taxpayer's agent.

The practising accountant often acts for taxpayers in their dealings with HMRC and situations can arise where the accountant has concerns as to whether the taxpayer is being honest in providing information to the accountant for onward transmission.

How the accountant deals with such situations is a matter of **professional judgement**, but in deciding what to do, the accountant will be expected to uphold the standards of the Association of Chartered Certified Accountants. He must act **honestly** and **objectively**, with **due care and diligence**, and showing the highest standards of **integrity**.

If an accountant learns of a material error or omission in a client's tax return or of a **failure to file a required tax return**, the accountant has a responsibility to **advise the client of the error, omission or failure** and **recommend that disclosure be made to HMRC**.

If the client, after having had a reasonable time to reflect, does not correct the error, omission or failure or authorise the accountant to do so on the client's behalf, the accountant should **inform the client in writing that it is not possible for the accountant to act for that client**.

The accountant should also **notify HMRC that the accountant no longer acts for the client but should not provide details of the reason for ceasing to act**.

An accountant whose client refuses to make disclosure to HMRC, after having had notice of the error, omission or failure and a reasonable time to reflect, **must also report the client's refusal and the facts surrounding it to the Money Laundering Reporting Officer within the accountancy firm or to the appropriate authority (National Crime Agency) if the accountant is a sole practitioner.**

Accountants who suspect or are aware of tax evasion activities by a client may themselves commit an offence if they do not report their suspicions. The accountant must not disclose to the client, or any one else, that such a report has been made if the accountant knows or suspects that to do so would be likely to prejudice any investigation which might be conducted following the report as this might constitute the criminal offence of 'tipping-off'.

Exam focus point

You may be asked to explain how you, as a trainee Chartered Certified Accountant, should deal with a situation where a client is evading tax, for example by not disclosing income or gains to HMRC.

Chapter Roundup

- Economic, social and environmental factors may affect the government's tax policies.
- Central government raises revenue through a wide range of taxes. Tax law is made by statute.
- Tax is administered by HM Revenue and Customs (HMRC).
- The sources of revenue law are Acts of Parliament, Statutory Instruments and case law.
- UK membership of the European Union has a significant effect on UK taxes, in particular value added tax (VAT).
- Double taxation agreements are designed to protect against the risk of double taxation where the same income or gains are taxable in two countries.
- Tax avoidance is the legal minimisation of tax liabilities; tax evasion is illegal.
- There is a general anti-abuse rule (GAAR) which enables HMRC to counteract tax advantages arising from abusive tax arrangements.
- If a client makes a material error or omission in a tax return, or fails to file a tax return, and does not correct the error, omission or failure when advised, the accountant should cease to act for the client, inform HMRC of this cessation and make a money laundering report.

Quick Quiz

1 What is the difference between a direct and an indirect tax?

2 What is an Extra Statutory Concession?

3 How might a double taxation agreement benefit a UK taxpayer who has income arising in a country which has such an agreement with the UK?

4 Tax avoidance is legal. True/False?

5 When may HMRC use the general anti-abuse rule (GAAR)?

Answers to Quick Quiz

1   A direct tax is one charged on income or gains; an indirect tax is paid by a consumer to the supplier, who then passes it to HMRC.

2   An Extra Statutory Concession is a relaxation by HMRC of the strict rules where their imposition would be unfair.

3   The agreement could provided that the income is only to be taxed in one country or that credit is to be given for tax arising in one country against the tax charge in the other country.

4   True. Tax avoidance is legal; tax evasion is illegal.

5   The GAAR may be used by HMRC where a taxpayer has used abusive tax arrangements to obtain a tax advantage.

Now try the question below from the Practice Question Bank

Number	Type	Marks	Time
Q1	Section A	6	11 mins

Income tax and national insurance contributions

Computing taxable income

Topic list	Syllabus reference
1 Scope of income tax	B1(a)
2 Computing taxable income	B5(a)
3 Various types of income	B4(f), B5(a)
4 Tax exempt income	B4(g)
5 Deductible interest	B5(d)
6 Personal allowance	B5(b)

Introduction

In the previous chapter we considered the UK tax system generally. Now we look at income tax, which is the tax applied on the income individuals make from their jobs, their businesses and their savings and investments. We consider the scope of income tax and see how to collect together all of an individual's income in a personal tax computation, and we also see which income can be excluded as being exempt from tax.

Next we look at the circumstances in which interest paid can be deducted in the income tax computation.

Each individual is entitled to a personal allowance, and only if that is exceeded will any tax be due. Older taxpayers are entitled to a higher personal allowance.

In later chapters, we learn how to calculate income tax on taxable income and look at particular types of income in more detail.

Study guide

		Intellectual level
B1	**The scope of income tax**	
(a)	Explain how the residence of an individual is determined.	1
B4	**Property and investment income**	
(f)	Compute the tax payable on savings and dividends income.	2
(g)	Recognise the treatment of new individual savings accounts (NISAs) and other tax exempt investments.	1
B5	**The comprehensive computation of taxable income and income tax liability**	
(a)	Prepare a basic income tax computation involving different types of income.	2
(b)	Calculate the amount of personal allowance available generally, and for people born before 6 April 1948.	2
(d)	Explain the treatment of interest paid for a qualifying purpose.	2

Exam guide

Section A questions on the topics in this chapter may include identification of different types of income or calculation of the personal allowance for an individual who was born before 6 April 1948.

It is very likely that you will have to prepare a computation of taxable income in a Section B question, in a 15 mark question or a 10 mark question. You should familiarise yourself with the layout of the computation, and the three types of income: non-savings, savings and dividends. It is then a simple matter of slotting the final figures into the computation from supporting workings for the different types of income.

1 Scope of income tax

An individual who is UK resident is taxed on worldwide income.

1.1 Introduction

A taxpayer's **residence** has important consequences in establishing the **tax treatment of his UK and overseas income and capital gains**.

1.2 Residence

1.2.1 Statutory residence test

An individual will automatically not be UK resident if he meets any of the automatic overseas tests. An individual, who does not meet any of the automatic overseas tests, will automatically be UK resident if he meets any of the automatic UK tests. An individual who has not met any of the automatic overseas tests nor any of the automatic UK tests will be UK resident if he meets the sufficient ties test.

Statute sets out a test to determine whether or not an individual is UK resident in a tax year.

The **operation of the test** can be summarised as follows.

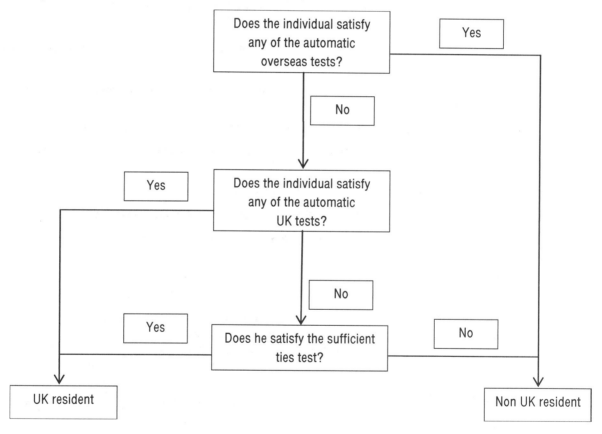

1.2.2 Automatic overseas tests

The **automatic overseas tests must be considered first.**

The **automatic overseas tests** treat an individual as **not resident in the UK in a tax year** if that individual:

(a) **Spends less than 16 days in the UK in that tax year** and **was resident in the UK for one or more of the three previous tax years** (typically someone who is leaving the UK); or

(b) **Spends less than 46 days in the UK in that tax year** and **was not resident in the UK for any of the previous three tax years** (typically someone who is arriving in the UK); or

(c) **Works full-time overseas in that tax year** and **does not spend more than 90 days in the UK during that tax year**

1.2.3 Automatic UK tests

If **none of the automatic overseas tests are met**, then the **automatic UK tests are considered**.

The **automatic UK tests treat an individual as UK resident in a tax year** if that individual:

(a) **Spends 183 days or more in the UK** during that tax year; or
(b) Has a **home in the UK** and **no home overseas**; or
(c) **Works full-time in the UK** during that tax year

1.2.4 Sufficient UK ties tests

If the **individual meets none of the automatic overseas tests and none of the automatic UK tests**, the **'sufficient ties' test** must be considered.

The **sufficient ties test** compares the **number of days spent in the UK** and the **number of connection factors or 'ties' to the UK**.

An **individual who was not UK resident in any of the previous three tax years** (typically someone who is arriving in the UK) must determine whether any of the following ties apply:

(a) **UK resident close family** (eg spouse/civil partner, child under the age of 18)

(b) **Available UK accommodation in which the individual spends at least one night during the tax year**

(c) **Substantive UK work** (employment or self-employment)

(d) **More than 90 days spent in the UK in either or both of the previous two tax years**

An **individual who was UK resident in any of the previous three tax years** (typically someone who is leaving the UK) must also determine whether any of the ties in (a) to (d) above apply plus whether an additional tie applies:

(e) **Present in the UK at midnight for the same or more days** in that tax year than in any other country

The following table shows **how an individual's UK residence status is found** by comparing **the number of days in the UK** during a tax year and the **number of UK ties**:

Days in UK	Previously resident	Not previously resident
Less than 16	Automatically not UK resident	Automatically not UK resident
Between 16 and 45	Resident if 4 UK ties (or more)	Automatically not UK resident
Between 46 and 90	Resident if 3 UK ties (or more)	Resident if 4 UK ties
Between 91 and 120	Resident if 2 UK ties (or more)	Resident if 3 UK ties (or more)
Between 121 and 182	Resident if 1 UK tie (or more)	Resident if 2 UK ties (or more)
183 or more	Automatically UK resident	Automatically UK resident

Exam focus point

This table will be given in the tax rates and allowances section of the examination paper.

1.2.5 Days spent in UK

Generally, **if a taxpayer is present in the UK at the end of a day (ie midnight)**, that **day counts as a day spent by the taxpayer in the UK**.

1.2.6 Examples

(a)   James spent 40 days in the UK during the tax year 2014/15. He had not previously been resident in the UK. James did not work during 2014/15.

James is arriving in the UK. He satisfies one of the automatic overseas tests since he spent less than 46 days in the UK in 2014/15 and was not resident in the UK for any of the previous three tax years. James is therefore not UK resident for the tax year 2014/15.

(b)   Caroline had not previously been resident in the UK before she arrived on 6 April 2014. She spent 60 days in the UK during the tax year 2014/15. She did not work during 2014/15. Her only home during 2014/15 is in the UK.

Caroline is arriving in the UK. She does not satisfy any of the automatic overseas tests since she spends 46 days or more in the UK and does not work overseas. She satisfies one of the automatic UK tests since her only home is in the UK. Caroline is therefore UK resident for the tax year 2014/15.

(c)   Miranda had always been resident in the UK before the tax year 2014/15 and has previously spent more than 90 days in the UK in every tax year. Miranda does not work during 2014/15. Miranda is married to Walter who is UK resident in 2014/15. They own a house in the UK which is available to them for the whole of 2014/15. On 6 April 2014, Miranda bought an overseas apartment where she spent 285 days during 2014/15. The remaining 80 days were spent in her UK house.

Miranda is leaving the UK. She does not satisfy any of the automatic overseas tests since she spends 16 days or more in the UK and does not work overseas. She does not satisfy any of the automatic UK tests since she spends less than 183 days in the UK, has an overseas home and does not work in the UK. The 'sufficient ties' test is therefore relevant. Miranda has three UK ties:

(i)   Close family resident in the UK (spouse)
(ii)   Available accommodation in the UK in which she spends at least one night in the tax year
(iii)   More than 90 days spent in the UK in both of the previous two tax years

Miranda spends between 46 and 90 days in the UK in 2014/15. These three ties are therefore sufficient to make her UK resident in 2014/15.

(d)   Norman has not been resident in, or visited, the UK in any tax year before 2014/15. On 6 April 2014, he bought a house in the UK and spent 160 days in the UK during the tax year 2014/15. Norman also has an overseas house in which he spent the remainder of the tax year 2014/15. Norman did not work in 2014/15 and his close family are not UK resident in 2014/15.

Norman is arriving in the UK. He does not satisfy any of the automatic overseas tests since he spends 46 days or more in the UK and does not work overseas. He does not satisfy any of the automatic UK tests as he spent less than 183 days in the UK, has an overseas home and does not work in the UK. The 'sufficient ties' test is therefore relevant. Norman spends between 121 and 182 days in the UK during 2014/15 and so he would need two UK ties to be UK resident for that tax year. Since Norman has only one tie with the UK in 2014/15 (available accommodation), he is therefore not UK resident for the tax year 2014/15.

1.3 Tax consequences

Generally, a **UK resident is liable to UK income tax on his UK and overseas income** whereas a **non-UK resident is liable to UK income tax only on income arising in the UK**. We deal with the capital gains tax consequences later in this Text.

The taxation of the overseas income of a UK resident and the taxation of non-UK residents is outside the scope of your syllabus.

2 Computing taxable income

FAST FORWARD

In a personal income tax computation, we bring together, for each tax year, income from all sources, splitting the sources into non-savings, savings and dividend income.

One of the competencies you require to fulfil performance objective 19 of the PER is the ability to evaluate and compute taxes payable. You can apply the knowledge you obtain from this section of the text to help to demonstrate this competence.

An individual's income from all sources is brought together (aggregated) in a personal tax computation for each tax year.

Key terms

The **tax year**, or **fiscal year**, or **year of assessment** runs from 6 April to 5 April. For example, the tax year 2014/15 runs from 6 April 2014 to 5 April 2015.

In the computation, three columns are needed to distinguish between non-savings income, savings income and dividend income. Here is an example. All items are explained later in this Text.

RICHARD: INCOME TAX COMPUTATION 2014/15

	Non-savings income £	Savings income £	Dividend income £	Total £
Income from employment	47,015			
Building society interest		1,000		
National Savings & Investments interest		400		
UK dividends			1,000	
Total income	47,015	1,400	1,000	
Less interest paid	(2,000)			
Net income	45,015	1,400	1,000	47,415
Less personal allowance	(10,000)			
Taxable income	35,015	1,400	1,000	37,415

	£	£
Income tax		
Non savings income		
£31,865 × 20%		6,373
£3,150 × 40%		1,260
		7,633
Savings income		
£1,400 × 40%		560
Dividend income		
£1,000 × 32.5%		325
Tax liability c/f		8,518

		£	£
Tax liability b/f			8,518
Less tax suffered			
Tax credit on dividend income		100	
PAYE tax on salary (say)		7,450	
Tax on building society interest		200	
			(7,750)
Tax payable			768

Key terms

> **Total income** is all income subject to income tax. Each of the amounts which make up total income is called a component. **Net income** is total income after deductible interest and trade losses. **Taxable income** is net income less the personal allowance or higher personal allowance.

Income tax is charged on **taxable income**. Non-savings income is dealt with first, then savings income and then dividend income. We look at how to compute the income tax liability in the next chapter.

2.1 The complete proforma for computing taxable

Here is a complete proforma computation of taxable income. It is probably too much for you to absorb at this stage, but refer back to it as you come to the chapters dealing with the types of income shown. You will also see how trading losses fit into the proforma later in this Text.

	Non-savings income £	Savings income £	Dividend income £	Total £
Trading income	X			
Employment income	X			
Property business income	X			
Bank/building society interest (gross)		X		
Other interest (gross)		X		
(as many lines as necessary)				
Dividends (gross)			X	
Total income	X	X	X	
Less interest paid	(X)	(X)	(X)	
Net income	X	X	X	X
Less personal allowance	(X)	(X)	(X)	
Taxable income	X	X	X	X

3 Various types of income

3.1 Classification of income

All income received must be **classified** according to the nature of the income. This is because different computational rules apply to different types of income. The main types of income are:

(a) **Income from employment and pensions**
(b) **Profits of trades, professions and vocations**
(c) **Income from property letting**
(d) **Savings and investment income, including interest and dividends**

The rules for computing employment income, profits from trades, professions and vocations and property letting income will be covered in later chapters. These types of income are **non-savings income**. Pension income is also non-savings income.

An individual may receive interest net of 20% tax suffered at source. The amount received must be grossed up by multiplying by 100/80 and must be included gross in the income tax computation. Dividends are received net of a 10% tax credit and must be grossed up by 100/90 for inclusion in the tax computation.

3.2 Savings income

3.2.1 What is savings income?

Savings income is interest. Interest is paid on bank and building society accounts, on Government securities, such as Treasury Stock, and on company debentures and loan stock.

Interest may be paid net of 20% tax or it may be paid gross.

3.2.2 Savings income received net of 20% tax

The following savings income is received net of 20% tax. **This is called income taxed at source.**

(a) Bank and building society interest paid to individuals
(b) Interest from company loan stock which is not listed on a recognised stock exchange

The reason this income is received net of 20% tax is that HMRC initially assumes that all taxpayers are only liable to income tax at the basic rate of 20%. The bank or building society deducts the basic rate tax at source and pays it to HMRC on behalf of the taxpayers. This eliminates the need for a large number of taxpayers to fill out a tax return. There may however be further tax to pay on the savings income, if, for example, the taxpayer is a higher or additional rate taxpayer and so a tax return will have to be completed.

The amount received is grossed up by multiplying by 100/80 and is included gross (reflecting the amount actually earned) in the income tax computation. The basic rate tax deducted at source is then deducted in computing tax payable and may be repaid. We will see how this works later in this Text.

Exam focus point

> In examinations you may be given either the net or the gross amount of such income: read the question carefully. If you are given the net amount (the amount received or credited), you should gross up the figure at the rate of 20%. For example, net building society interest of £160 is equivalent to gross income of £160 × 100/80 = £200 on which tax of £40 (20% of £200) has been suffered.

3.2.3 Savings income received gross

Some savings income is received gross, ie without tax having been deducted. Examples are:

(a) National Savings & Investments interest including interest from Direct Saver Accounts, Investment Accounts, Income Bonds
(b) Interest on government securities (these are also called 'gilts'). An example is 5% Treasury Stock 2025 – the government pays the investor 5% interest each year for each £1 of stock held, until it redeems the stock in 2025.
(c) Interest from company loan stock which is listed on a recognised stock exchange

3.3 Dividend income

Dividends on UK shares are received net of a 10% tax credit. This means a dividend of £90 has a £10 tax credit, giving gross income of £100 to include in the income tax computation. The tax credit can be deducted in computing tax payable **but it cannot be repaid**. We will see how this works later in this Text.

4 Tax exempt income

4.1 Types of tax exempt investments

One of the competencies you require to fulfil performance objective 20 of the PER is the ability to assist with tax planning. You can apply the knowledge you obtain from this section of the text to help to demonstrate this competence.

Income from certain investments is exempt from income tax. They are therefore useful for tax planning to minimise tax from investments.

Exam focus point

In the examination you may be given details of exempt income. You should state in your answer that the income is exempt to show that you have considered it and have not just overlooked it, otherwise the relevant marks will not be awarded.

4.2 New individual savings accounts

Key term

NISAs are tax efficient savings accounts. There are three types of NISA.

- Cash NISA (which only has a cash component)
- Stocks and shares NISA (which only has a stocks and shares component, although some cash may be held in a stocks and shares NISA if the provider allows this)
- Combined NISA (which has both a cash component and a stocks and shares component)

The annual subscription limit **for NISAs is £15,000 per tax year**. This can be invested in cash, stocks and shares, or any combination of the two.

Exam focus point

The NISA limit will be given to you in the Tax Rates and Allowances in the examination paper.

Dividend income and interest received from NISAs is exempt from income tax, whether it is paid out to the investor or retained and reinvested within the NISA. Similarly, **capital gains made within a NISA are exempt from capital gains tax.**

NISAs replaced Individual Savings Accounts (ISAs) from 1 July 2014. Existing ISAs were automatically converted to NISAs on that date.

Exam focus point

A question will not be set on the ISA investment rules and limits that applied prior 1 July 2014.

4.3 Savings certificates

Savings certificates are issued by National Savings and Investments (NS&I). They may be fixed rate certificates or index linked and are for fixed terms of between two and five years. On maturity the profit is tax exempt. This profit is often called interest.

4.4 Premium bonds

Prizes received from premium bonds are exempt from tax.

4.5 Child benefit

Child benefit is a benefit paid to people responsible for caring for at least one child. It is usually paid to the mother of the child.

Child benefit is usually exempt from income tax. However, an **income tax charge** applies if a taxpayer receives child benefit (or their partner receives child benefit) and has **adjusted net income over £50,000 in a tax year**. This charge is covered later in this Text.

5 Deductible interest

Deductible interest is deducted from total income to compute net income.

5.1 Interest payments

An individual who pays interest on a loan in a tax year is entitled to relief in that tax year if the loan is for one of the following purposes:

(a)   **Loan to buy plant or machinery for partnership use.** Interest is allowed for three years from the end of the tax year in which the loan was taken out. If the plant is used partly for private use, the allowable interest is apportioned.

(b)   **Loan to buy plant or machinery for employment use.** Interest is allowed for three years from the end of the tax year in which the loan was taken out. If the plant is used partly for private use, the allowable interest is apportioned.

(c)   **Loan to buy interest in employee-controlled company.** The company must be an unquoted trading company resident in the UK with at least 50% of the voting shares held by employees.

(d)   **Loan to invest in a partnership.** The investment may be a share in the partnership or a contribution to the partnership of capital or a loan to the partnership. The individual must be a partner (other than a limited partner) and relief ceases when he ceases to be a partner.

(e)   **Loan to invest in a co-operative.** The investment may be shares or a loan. The individual must spend the greater part of his time working for the co-operative.

Tax relief is given by deducting the interest from total income to calculate net income for the tax year in which the interest is paid. It is deducted from **non-savings income first, then from savings income and lastly from dividend income**.

5.2 Example

In 2014/15, Frederick has taxable trading income of £45,000, savings income of £1,320 (gross) and dividend income of £1,000 (gross).

Frederick pays interest of £1,370 in 2014/15 on a loan to invest in a partnership.

Frederick's net income for 2014/15 is:

	Non-savings income £	Savings income £	Dividend income £	Total £
Total income	45,000	1,320	1,000	
Less: interest paid	(1,370)			
Net income	43,630	1,320	1,000	45,950

6 Personal allowance

6.1 Standard personal allowance

All individuals are entitled to a personal allowance. It is deducted from net income, first against non savings income, then against savings income and lastly against dividend income. The personal allowance is reduced by £1 for every £2 that adjusted net income exceeds £100,000 and can be reduced to nil.

Once income from all sources has been aggregated and any deductible interest deducted, the remainder is the taxpayer's net income. An allowance, the **personal allowance,** is **deducted from net income**. Like deductible interest, it reduces non **savings income first, then savings income and lastly dividend income**.

All individuals **born after 5 April 1948** (including children) **are entitled to the standard personal allowance of £10,000.**

However, if the **individual's adjusted net income exceeds £100,000, the personal allowance is reduced by £1 for each £2 by which adjusted net income exceeds £100,000 until the personal allowance is nil (which is when adjusted net income is £120,000 or more).**

Key term

> **Adjusted net income** is net income less the gross amounts of personal pension contributions and gift aid donations.

We will look at personal pension contributions and gift aid donations later in this Text and revisit this topic again then. At the moment, we will look at the situation where net income and adjusted net income are the same amounts.

Question
                                                        Standard personal allowance

Clare was born in 1976. In 2014/15, she receives employment income of £95,000, bank interest of £6,400 and dividends of £6,750.

Calculate Clare's taxable income for 2014/15.

Answer

	Non-savings income £	Savings income £	Dividend income £	Total £
Employment income	95,000			
Bank interest £6,400 × 100/80		8,000		
Dividends £6,750 × 100/90			7,500	
Net income	95,000	8,000	7,500	110,500
Less: personal allowance (W)	(4,750)			
Taxable income	90,250	8,000	7,500	105,750

Working

Net income	110,500
Less income limit	(100,000)
Excess	10,500
Personal allowance	10,000
Less half excess £10,500 × ½	(5,250)
	4,750

Where an individual has an adjusted net income between £100,000 and £120,000, the rate of tax on the income between these two amounts will usually be 60%. This is calculated as 40% (the higher rate on income) plus 40% of half (ie 20%) of the excess adjusted net income over £100,000 used to restrict the personal allowance. The individual should consider **making personal pension contributions and/or gift aid donations to reduce adjusted net income to below £100,000.**

6.2 Higher personal allowance

FAST FORWARD

Taxpayers born between 6 April 1938 and 5 April 1948 are entitled to a higher personal allowance of £10,500 and taxpayers born before 6 April 1938 are entitled to a higher personal allowance of £10,660. The higher personal allowance is reduced by £1 for every £2 that adjusted net income exceeds £27,000 but is generally not reduced below the amount of the personal allowance for taxpayers born after 5 April 1948.

An individual born between 6 April 1938 and 5 April 1948 **is entitled to a higher personal allowance of £10,500** instead of the standard personal allowance of £10,000.

An individual born before 6 April 1938 **is entitled to a higher personal allowance of £10,660** instead of the standard personal allowance of £10,000.

If the individual's adjusted net income exceeds £27,000 the higher personal allowance is reduced by £1 for each £2 by which adjusted net income exceeds £27,000. The higher personal allowance **cannot usually be reduced below the amount of the standard personal allowance for taxpayers born after 5 April 1948 (£10,000).** However, **if the individual has adjusted net income in excess of £100,000, the personal allowance will be reduced** as described in Section 6.1 above.

Question	Higher personal allowance

Three taxpayers have the following net income for 2014/15.

A   £27,550
B   £36,900
C   £27,510

Calculate their taxable income assuming taxpayers A and B were born between 6 April 1938 and 5 April 1948 and taxpayer C was born before 6 April 1938.

Answer

	A	B	C
	£	£	£
Net income	27,550	36,900	27,510
Less higher personal allowance (W)	(10,225)	(10,000)	(10,405)
Taxable income	17,325	26,900	17,105
Working			
Net income	27,550	36,900	27,510
Less income limit	(27,000)	(27,000)	(27,000)
Excess	550	9,900	510
Higher personal allowance	10,500	10,500	10,660
Less half excess £550/9,900/510 × 1/2	(275)	(4,950)	(255)
	10,225	5,550	10,405
Minimum		10,000	

Chapter Roundup

- An individual who is UK resident is taxed on worldwide income.

- An individual will automatically not be UK resident if he meets any of the automatic overseas tests. An individual, who does not meet any of the automatic overseas tests, will automatically be UK resident if he meets any of the automatic UK tests. An individual who has not met any of the automatic overseas tests nor any of the automatic UK tests will be UK resident if he meets the sufficient ties test.

- In a personal income tax computation, we bring together, for each tax year, income from all sources, splitting the sources into non-savings, savings and dividend income.

- An individual may receive interest net of 20% tax suffered at source. The amount received must be grossed up by multiplying by 100/80 and must be included gross in the income tax computation. Dividends are received net of a 10% tax credit and must be grossed up by 100/90 for inclusion in the tax computation.

- Deductible interest is deducted from total income to compute net income.

- All individuals are entitled to a personal allowance. It is deducted from net income, first against non savings income, then against savings income and lastly against dividend income. The personal allowance is reduced by £1 for every £2 that adjusted net income exceeds £100,000 and can be reduced to nil.

- Taxpayers born between 6 April 1938 and 5 April 1948 are entitled to an higher personal allowance of £10,500 and taxpayers born before 6 April 1938 are entitled to a higher personal allowance of £10,660. The higher personal allowance is reduced by £1 for every £2 that adjusted net income exceeds £27,000 but is generally not reduced below the amount of the personal allowance for taxpayers born after 5 April 1948.

Quick Quiz

1   If an individual meets none of the automatic overseas tests and none of the automatic UK tests of residence in a tax year, what determines whether the individual is resident in the UK?

2   Give one type of savings income that is received by individuals net of 20% tax.

3   What is the amount of the tax credit received with a dividend? Can the tax credit be repaid?

4   What are the tax advantages of holding investments in a New Individual Savings Account (NISA)?

5   Who is entitled to a higher personal allowance?

Answers to Quick Quiz

1 The number of ties the individual has to the UK and the number of days spent in the UK that year. Whether the individual is leaving the UK or arriving in the UK also determines how many ties are to be satisfied for UK residence.

2 Bank (or building society) interest.

3 The tax credit received with a dividend is 10% of the grossed up dividend. The tax credit can be deducted in computing tax payable but it cannot be repaid.

4 Dividend income and interest received from NISAs are exempt from income tax. Capital gains made within a NISA are exempt from capital gains tax.

5 Individuals born before 6 April 1948.

Now try the questions below from the Practice Question Bank

Number	Type	Marks	Time
Q2	Section A	6	11 mins
Q3	Section B	11	20 mins
Q4	Section B	4	7 mins

Computing the income tax liability

Topic list	Syllabus reference
1 Computing income tax liability and income tax payable	B4(f), B5(c)
2 Gift aid	B5(e)
3 Child benefit income tax charge	B5(f)
4 Jointly held property	B5(g), B7(b)

Introduction

In the previous chapter we learned how to compute an individual's taxable income.

We now learn how to work out the income tax liability on taxable income and how much tax remains to be paid in cash.

We see how donations to charity under the gift aid scheme can save tax. We also look at the income tax charge in relation to child benefit.

Finally we consider how income from property held jointly by married couples or civil partners is allocated for tax purposes.

In the next chapter we look at employment income.

Study guide

		Intellectual level
B4	**Property and investment income**	
(f)	Compute the tax payable on savings and dividends income.	2
B5	**The comprehensive computation of taxable income and income tax liability**	
(c)	Compute the amount of income tax payable.	2
(e)	Understand the treatment of gift aid donations.	1
(f)	Explain and compute the child benefit tax charge.	1
(g)	Understand the treatment of property owned jointly by a married couple, or by a couple in a civil partnership.	1
B7	**The use of exemptions and reliefs in deferring and minimising income tax liabilities**	
(b)	Understand how a married couple or a couple in a civil partnership can minimise their tax liabilities.	2

Exam guide

Section A questions on the topics in this chapter could include a simple computation of income tax liability, for example for savings income within the starting rate band, and a computation of the child benefit income tax charge.

It is very likely that you will have to prepare a full computation of income tax liability (and possibly income tax payable) in a Section B question, either in a 15 mark question or a 10 mark question.

Gift aid donations are likely to feature regularly in both Sections A and B. You will come across the technique of increasing the basic rate and higher rate limits again when you deal with pensions later in this Text.

1 Computing income tax liability and income tax payable

FAST FORWARD

To work out the income tax liability on the taxable income, first compute the tax on non-savings income, then on savings income and, finally, on dividend income. To work out tax payable, deduct the tax credit on dividend income and any income tax suffered at source to arrive at tax payable. The tax credit on dividend income cannot be repaid if it exceeds the tax liability calculated so far. Other tax suffered at source can be repaid.

One of the competencies you require to fulfil performance objective 19 of the PER is the ability to evaluate and compute taxes payable. You can apply the knowledge you obtain from this section of the text to help to demonstrate this competence.

Key terms

The **income tax liability** is the amount of tax charged on the individual's taxable income. **Income tax payable** is the balance of the income tax liability still to be settled in cash.

1.1 The complete proforma for computing taxable income

Here is the complete proforma computation of taxable income which you met in Chapter 2. You will need to refer to this proforma when working through the questions and examples in this chapter as the first step in computing the income tax liability is to work out the amount of the individual's taxable income.

	Non-savings income £	Savings income £	Dividend income £	Total £
Trading income	X			
Employment income	X			
Property business income	X			
Bank/building society interest (gross)		X		
Other interest (gross)		X		
(as many lines as necessary)				
Dividends (gross)			X	
Total income	X	X	X	
Less interest paid	(X)	(X)	(X)	
Net income	X	X	X	X
Less personal allowance	(X)	(X)	(X)	
Taxable income	X	X	X	X

1.2 Tax rates

Income tax payable is computed on an individual's taxable income as computing using the proforma in the previous paragraph. The tax rates are applied to taxable income which is non-savings income first, then to savings income and finally to dividend income.

1.2.1 Savings income starting rate

There is a **tax rate of 10% for savings income up to £2,880 (the savings income starting rate limit)**. This rate is called the **savings income starting rate**.

The savings income starting rate only applies where the savings income falls wholly or partly below the starting rate limit. Remember that income tax is charged first on non-savings income. So, in most cases, an individual's non-savings income will exceed the savings income starting rate limit and the savings income starting rate will not be available on savings income.

1.2.2 Basic rate

The basic rate of tax is 20% for 2014/15 for both non-savings income and savings income. The basic rate of tax is 10% for 2014/15 for dividend income. The basic rate limit for 2014/15 is £31,865.

Question	Savings income starting rate and basic rate

Joe was born in 1958. In 2014/15, he earns a salary of £11,150 from a part-time job and receives bank interest of £4,000. Calculate Joe's tax liability for 2014/15.

Answer

	Non-savings income £	Savings income £	Total £
Employment income	11,150		
Bank interest £4,000 × 100/80		5,000	
Net income	11,150	5,000	16,150
Less: personal allowance	(10,000)		
Taxable income	1,150	5,000	6,150

	£
Income tax	
Non-savings income	
£1,150 × 20%	230
Savings income	
£(2,880 – 1,150) = 1,730 × 10%	173
£(5,000 – 1,730) = 3,270 × 20%	654
Tax liability	1,057

1.2.3 Higher rate

The higher rate of tax is 40% for 2014/15 for non-savings and savings income. The higher rate of tax is 32.5% for 2014/15 for dividend income. The higher rate limit for 2014/15 is £150,000.

Question	Basic rate and higher rate

Margery was born in 1978. In 2014/15, she has employment income of £37,315, receives building society interest of £1,200 and dividends of £9,000. Calculate Margery's tax liability for 2014/15.

Answer				

	Non-savings income £	Savings income £	Dividend income £	Total £
Employment income	37,315			
BSI £1,200 × 100/80		1,500		
Dividends £9,000 × 100/90			10,000	
Net income	37,315	1,500	10,000	48,815
Less: personal allowance	(10,000)			
Taxable income	27,315	1,500	10,000	38,815

Income tax	
	£
Non-savings income	
£27,315 × 20%	5,463
Savings income	
£1,500 × 20%	300
Dividend income	
£(31,865 – 27,315 – 1,500) = 3,050 × 10%	305
£(10,000 – 3,050) = 6,950 × 32.5%	2,259
Tax liability	8,327

1.2.4 Additional rate

The additional rate of tax is 45% for 2014/15 for non-savings and savings income.

The additional rate of tax is 37.5% for 2014/15 for dividend income.

The additional rate of tax applies to taxable income in excess of the higher rate limit which is £150,000 for 2014/15.

Question	Additional rate

Julian was born in 1980. In 2014/15, he has employment income of £148,000, receives bank interest of £5,000 and dividends of £18,000. Calculate Julian's tax liability for 2014/15.

BPP
LEARNING MEDIA

	Non-savings income £	Savings income £	Dividend income £	Total £
Employment income	148,000			
Bank interest £5,000 × 100/80		6,250		
Dividends £18,000 × 100/90			20,000	
Net income/taxable income (no PA available)	148,000	6,250	20,000	174,250

Income tax
Non-savings income

£31,865 × 20%	6,373
£(148,000 − 31,865) = 116,135 × 40%	46,454
Savings income	
£(150,000 − 148,000) = 2,000 × 40%	800
£(6,250 − 2,000) = 4,250 × 45%	1,912
Dividend income	
£20,000 × 37.5%	7,500
Tax liability	63,039

Julian is not entitled to the personal allowance as his net income exceeds £120,000.

1.3 Steps in computing the income tax liability

We now summarise the **steps required to compute the income tax liability**.

Step 1   **The first step in preparing a personal tax computation is to set up three columns**
One column for non-savings income, one for savings income and one for dividend income. Add up income from different sources. The sum of these is known as 'total income'. Deduct deductible interest and trade losses to compute 'net income'. Deduct the personal allowance or higher personal allowance to compute 'taxable income'.

Step 2   **Deal with non-savings income first**
Any non-savings income up to the basic rate limit of £31,865 is taxed at 20%. Non-savings income between the basic rate limit and the higher rate limit of £150,000 is taxed at 40%. The maximum non-savings income to which the higher rate applies is therefore £(150,000 − 31,865) = £118,135. Any further non-savings income is taxed at 45%.

Step 3   **Now deal with savings income**
If savings income is below the starting rate limit of £2,880, it is taxed at the savings income starting rate of 10% up to the starting rate limit. Savings income between the starting rate limit and the basic rate limit of £31,865 is taxed at 20%. Savings income between the basic rate limit and the higher rate limit of £150,000 is taxed at 40%, so again, the maximum savings income to which the higher rate applies is therefore £(150,000 − 31,865) = £118,135. Any further savings income is taxed at 45%. In most cases, non-savings income and savings income can be added together and tax calculated on the total, provided that the savings income starting rate does not apply.

Step 4   **Lastly, tax dividend income**
If dividend income is below the basic rate limit of £31,865, it is taxed at 10%. Dividend income between the basic rate limit and the higher rate limit of £150,000 (maximum £118,135) is taxed at 32.5%. Any further dividend income is taxed at 37.5%.

Step 5   Add the amounts of tax together. The resulting figure is the **income tax liability**.

1.4 Additional steps in computing income tax payable

The following **two additional steps** are needed to compute income tax payable when the income tax liability has been calculated.

Step 6   Next, **deduct the tax credit on dividends**. This tax credit cannot be repaid if it exceeds the tax liability calculated so far.

Step 7   Finally **deduct the tax deducted at source** from savings income such as bank interest and from employment income under the Pay As You Earn (PAYE) scheme (we look at this scheme in detail later in this text). These **amounts can be repaid to the extent that they exceed the income tax liability**.

1.5 Examples: personal tax computations

(a)   Kathy was born in 1980. In 2014/15 she has trading income of £17,560 and receives dividends of £4,500.

	Non-savings income £	Dividend income £	Total £
Trading income	17,560		
Dividends £4,500 × 100/90		5,000	
Net income	17,560	5,000	22,560
Less personal allowance	(10,000)		
Taxable income	7,560	5,000	12,560

	£
Income tax	
Non savings income	
£7,560 × 20%	1,512
Dividend income	
£5,000 × 10%	500
Tax liability	2,012
Less tax credit on dividend £5,000 × 10%	(500)
Tax payable	1,512

The dividend income falls below the basic rate limit so it is taxed at 10%.

(b)   Jules was born in 1954. In 2014/15, he has trading income of £34,815, property business income of £20,000, net building society interest of £3,000 and net dividends of £6,750. He is entitled to relief on interest paid of £2,000.

	Non-savings income £	Savings income £	Dividend income £	Total £
Trading income	34,815			
Property business income	20,000			
Building society interest £3,000 × 100/80		3,750		
Dividends £6,750 × 100/90			7,500	
Total income	54,815	3,750	7,500	66,065
Less interest paid	(2,000)			
Net income	52,815	3,750	7,500	64,065
Less personal allowance	(10,000)			
Taxable income	42,815	3,750	7,500	54,065

Income tax	£
Non savings income	
£31,865 × 20%	6,373
£(42,815 − 31,865) = 10,950 × 40%	4,380
Savings income	
£3,750 × 40%	1,500
Dividend income	
£7,500 × 32.5%	2,437
Tax liability	14,690
Less tax credit on dividend income £7,500 × 10%	(750)
Less tax deducted at source on building society interest £3,750 × 20%	(750)
Tax payable	13,190

Savings income and dividend income fall above the basic rate limit but below the higher rate limit so they are taxed at 40% and 32.5% respectively.

(c) Jim was born in 1966. He does not work. In 2014/15, he receives net bank interest of £38,732.

	Savings income £	Total £
Bank interest £38,732 × 100/80/Net income	48,415	48,415
Less personal allowance	(10,000)	
Taxable income	38,415	38,415

	£
Savings income	
£2,880 × 10%	288
£(31,865 − 2,880) = 28,985 × 20%	5,797
£(38,415 − 31,865) = 6,550 × 40%	2,620
Tax liability	8,705
Less tax deducted at source £50,415 × 20%	(10,083)
Tax repayable	(1,378)

The savings income starting rate applies to the first £2,880 of savings income. The income up to the basic rate limit is then £(31,865 − 2,880) = £28,985.

(d) Duncan was born in 1983. In 2014/15, he has a salary of £160,000 (PAYE deducted £45,000) and receives dividends of £45,000.

	Non-savings income £	Dividend income £	Total £
Employment income	160,000		
Dividends £45,000 × 100/90		50,000	
Net income/Taxable income (no PA available)	160,000	50,000	210,000

	£
Income tax	
Non savings income	
£31,865 × 20%	6,373
£(150,000 − 31,865) = 118,135 × 40%	47,254
£10,000 × 45%	4,500
Dividend income	
£50,000 × 37.5%	18,750
Tax liability	76,877
Less tax credit on dividend £50,000 × 10%	(5,000)
Less tax deducted under PAYE	(45,000)
Tax payable	26,877

Duncan is not entitled to the personal allowance as his net income exceeds £120,000.

(e) Moira was born in 1960. In 2014/15, she receives net dividends of £54,000. She has no other income.

	Dividend income £	Total £
Dividends £54,000 × 100/90/Total income	60,000	
Less personal allowance	(10,000)	
Taxable income	50,000	50,000

	£
Dividend income	
£31,865 × 10%	3,186
£(50,000 – 31,865) = 18,135 × 32.5%	5,894
Tax liability	9,080
Less tax deducted at source £50,000 × 10%	(5,000)
Tax payable	4,080

The tax credit on the dividend is restricted to that relating to taxable income.

2 Gift aid

 FAST FORWARD

> Increase the basic rate limit and the higher rate limit by the gross amount of any gift aid payment to give tax relief at the higher and additional rates.

2.1 Gift aid donations

Key term

> One-off and regular charitable gifts of money qualify for tax relief under the **gift aid scheme** provided the donor gives the charity a gift aid declaration.

Gift aid declarations can be made in writing, electronically through the internet or orally over the phone. A declaration can cover a one-off gift or any number of gifts made after a specified date (which may be in the past).

The gift must not be repayable and must not confer any more than a minimal benefit on the donor.

2.2 Tax relief for gift aid donations

A gift aid donation is treated as though it is paid net of basic rate tax (20%). This gives basic rate tax relief when the payment is made. For example, if you would like your charity to receive a donation of £1,000, you would only need to make a payment to them of £800. The charity reclaims the 20% tax relief that you have received, resulting in a gross gift of £1,000.

Additional tax relief for higher rate and additional rate taxpayers is given in the personal tax computation by increasing the donor's basic rate limit and higher rate limit by the gross amount of the gift. To arrive at the gross amount of the gift you must multiply the amount paid by 100/80. In the above example, the gross amount would be the amount paid of £800 × 100/80 = £1,000. The effect of increasing the basic rate limit is to increase the amount on which basic rate tax is payable. This is sometimes called 'extending the basic rate band'.

The effect of increasing the higher rate limit is simply to preserve the amount of taxable income on which higher rate tax is payable.

No additional relief is due for basic rate taxpayers. Increasing the basic rate limit is irrelevant as taxable income is below this limit.

Question

James was born in 1976. He earns a salary of £66,000 but has no other income. In 2014/15 he paid £8,000 (net) under the gift aid scheme. Compute James' income tax liability for 2014/15.

Answer

		Non-savings Income £
Employment income/Net income		66,000
Less: personal allowance		(10,000)
Taxable income		56,000

Income tax	£	£
Basic rate	41,865 (W) × 20%	8,373
Higher rate	14,135 × 40%	5,654
	56,000	14,027

Working
Basic rate limit £31,865 + (£8,000 × 100/80) = £41,865

Question

Matt was born in 1956. He has trading income of £182,000 in 2014/15. In January 2015, he made a gift aid donation of £12,000 (net). Compute Matt's income tax liability for 2014/15.

Answer

		Non-savings Income £
Taxable income (no personal allowance as income over £120,000)		182,000

Income tax	£	£
Basic rate	46,865 (W1) × 20%	9,373
Higher rate	118,135 (W2) × 40%	47,254
Additional rate	17,000 × 45%	7,650
	182,000	64,277

Workings

1   Basic rate limit £31,865 + (£12,000 × 100/80) = £46,865

2   Higher rate limit £150,000 + (£12,000 × 100/80) = £165,000. The higher rate band is therefore £(165,000 − 46,865) = £118,135 ie the same as the usual £(150,000 − 31,865).

2.3 Adjusted net income

Key term

> **Adjusted net income** is net income less the gross amounts of personal pension contributions and gift aid donations.

The restrictions on the personal allowance and higher personal allowance are calculated in relation to adjusted net income.

Question

Margaretta was born in 1966. She earns a salary of £110,000 in 2014/15. In January 2015, she made a gift aid donation of £5,000. Compute Margaretta's income tax liability for 2014/15.

Answer

		Non-savings income £
Employment income/Net income		110,000
Less: personal allowance (W1)		(8,125)
Taxable income		101,875

Income tax	£	£
Basic rate (W2)	38,115 × 20%	7,623
Higher rate	63,760 × 40%	25,504
	101,875	33,127

Workings

1   Personal allowance

	£
Net income	110,000
Less: gift aid donation £5,000 × 100/80	(6,250)
Adjusted net income	103,750
Less: income limit	(100,000)
Excess	3,750
Personal allowance	10,000
Less half excess £3,750 × ½	(1,875)
	8,125

2   Basic rate limit
    £31,865 + (£5,000 × 100/80)   £38,115

3 Child benefit income tax charge

FAST FORWARD

> There is an income tax charge to recover child benefit if the recipient or their partner has adjusted net income over £50,000 in a tax year.

An **income tax charge** applies if a taxpayer receives child benefit (or their partner receives child benefit) and the taxpayer has **adjusted net income over £50,000 in a tax year. Adjusted net income is defined in the same way as for the restriction of the personal allowance** described earlier in this chapter. The effect of the charge is to recover child benefit from taxpayers who have higher incomes.

A 'partner' is a **spouse**, a **civil partner,** or an **unmarried partner** where the couple are **living together as though they were married or were civil partners**. Civil partners are members of a same sex couple which has registered as a civil partnership under the Civil Partnerships Act 2004. Same sex couples can also marry in England, Wales and Scotland (but not Northern Ireland).

If the taxpayer has **adjusted net income over £60,000,** the charge is equal to the **full amount of child benefit received**.

If the taxpayer has **adjusted net income between £50,000 and £60,000**, the charge is **1% of the child benefit amount for each £100 of adjusted net income in excess of £50,000. The calculation**, at all stages, **is rounded down to the nearest whole number.**

If **both partners have adjusted net income in excess of £50,000**, the **partner with the higher adjusted net income** is liable for the charge.

The child benefit income tax charge is collected through the self-assessment system (dealt with later in this text). This includes the need for **taxpayers to submit tax returns,** which can be time consuming and costly. To avoid this, **taxpayers can opt not to receive child benefit at all** so that the income tax charge does not apply.

Question — Child benefit income tax charge (1)

Robert and Roslyn are not married but live together as though they were married. They have a five year old son.

Robert has net income of £52,000 in 2014/15. His adjusted net income is also £52,000 since he made no gift aid donations or personal pension contributions in 2014/15. Roslyn has no income. She receives child benefit of £1,066 in 2014/15.

Calculate Robert's child benefit income tax charge for 2014/15.

Answer

Robert will be liable to the child benefit income tax charge in 2014/15 since his partner receives child benefit during that year and he has adjusted net income over £50,000.

	£
Adjusted net income	52,000
Less: threshold	(50,000)
Excess	2,000
÷ £100	20
Child benefit income tax charge: 1% × £1,066 × 20	213

Question — Child benefit income tax charge (2)

Samantha is divorced and has two children aged ten and six. She has net income of £56,000 in 2014/15. Samantha made personal pension contributions of £4,500 (gross) during 2014/15. She receives child benefit of £1,771 in 2014/15.

Calculate Samantha's child benefit income tax charge for 2014/15.

	£
Net income	56,000
Less: personal pension contributions (gross)	(4,500)
Adjusted net income	51,500
Less: threshold	(50,000)
Excess	1,500
÷ £100	15
Child benefit income tax charge: 1% × £1,771 × 15	265

At all stages of the calculation, round down to the nearest whole number.

Tutorial note

If Samantha had made an extra gross personal pension contribution of £1,500 during 2014/15, her adjusted net income would not have exceeded £50,000 and she would not have been subject to the child benefit income tax charge.

4 Jointly held property

FAST FORWARD Income on property held jointly by married couples and members of a civil partnership is treated as if it were shared equally unless the couple make a joint declaration of the actual shares of ownership.

 One of the competencies you require to fulfil performance objective 20 of the PER is the ability to assist with tax planning. You can apply the knowledge you obtain from this section of the text to help to demonstrate this competence.

4.1 Allocation of joint income

If property is held jointly by a married couple or civil partners the income arising from that property is taxed as if it was shared equally between the members of the couple.

This 50:50 split of income from jointly held property applies even if the property is not owned in equal shares, **unless the members of the couple make a joint declaration to HMRC specifying the actual proportion to which each is entitled**.

4.2 Example: joint income

Janet owns 40% of a holiday cottage and John, her husband, owns the other 60%.

If no declaration is made each will be taxed on one half of the income arising when the property is let out.

If a declaration is made, Janet will be taxed on her 40% of the income and John will be taxed on his 60%.

4.3 Tax planning for married couples/civil partners

Where one member of a married couple/civil partnership is a basic rate taxpayer and the other a higher rate taxpayer, **income tax liabilities can be minimised by transferring income producing assets from the higher rate taxpayer to the other spouse or civil partner**.

If assets are owned jointly but in unequal proportions, then:

(a)   If the taxpayer who pays tax at a higher rate of tax than the other spouse/civil partner owns more than 50% of the asset, no declaration of beneficial interest should be made so that the income is shared equally, or

(b)   If the taxpayer who pays tax at a higher rate of tax than the other spouse/civil partner owns less than 50% of the asset, a declaration of beneficial interest should be made so that the other spouse or civil partner is taxed on their full amount of income at the lower tax rate.

Thus in the above example a declaration is beneficial, for example, if Janet is a higher rate taxpayer whilst John is a basic rate taxpayer or if Janet is an additional rate taxpayer and John is either a higher rate or basic rate taxpayer.

Chapter Roundup

- To work out the income tax liability on the taxable income, first compute the tax on non-savings income, then on savings income and, finally, on dividend income. To work out income tax payable, deduct the tax credit on dividend income and any income tax suffered at source to arrive at tax payable. The tax credit on dividend income cannot be repaid if it exceeds the tax liability calculated so far. Other tax suffered at source can be repaid.

- Increase the basic rate limit and the higher rate limit by the gross amount of any gift aid payment to give tax relief at the higher and additional rates.

- There is an income tax charge to recover child benefit if the recipient or their partner has adjusted net income over £50,000 in a tax year.

- Income on property held jointly by married couples and members of a civil partnership is treated as if it were shared equally unless the couple make a joint declaration of the actual shares of ownership.

Quick Quiz

1 Income tax on non-savings income is charged at _ % below the basic rate limit, at _% between the basic rate limit and the higher rate limit, and at _% above the higher rate limit. Fill in the blanks.

2 How is dividend income taxed?

3 If Dennis has taxable income of £32,565 and makes gift aid payments of £400, on how much of his income will he pay higher rate tax?

4 Mike and Matt are a married couple. Mike owns 25% of an investment property and Matt owns 75%. How will the income be taxed?

Answers to Quick Quiz

1   Income tax on non-savings income is charged at **20%** below the basic rate limit, at **40%** between the basic rate limit and the higher rate limit, and at **45%** above the higher rate limit.

2   Dividend income below the basic rate limit is taxed at 10%, at 32.5% between the basic rate limit and the higher rate limit, and at 37.5% above the higher rate limit.

3   The basic rate limit is increased by £400 × 100/80 = £500 to £32,365. Dennis will be liable to higher rate tax on £32,565 − £32,365 = £200.

4   Mike and Matt will each be taxed on 50% of the income from the investment property unless they make a joint declaration to specify the actual proportions in which case Mike will be taxed on 25% of the income and Matt on 75%.

Now try the questions below from the Practice Question Bank

Number	Type	Marks	Time
Q5	Section A	6	11 mins
Q6	Section B	15	27 mins
Q7	Section B	15	27 mins

3: Computing the income tax liability │ Part B Income tax and national insurance contributions

Employment income

Topic list	Syllabus reference
1 Employment and self employment	B2(a)
2 Basis of assessment for employment income	B2(b), B2(c)
3 Allowable deductions	B2(c), B2(d)
4 Statutory approved mileage allowances	B2(c), B2(e)
5 Charitable donations under the payroll deduction scheme	B5(e)

Introduction

In the previous chapters we saw how to construct the income tax computation. Now we start to look in greater detail at the different types of income that people may receive so that the income can be slotted into the computation.

Many people earn money by working. We look at the important distinction between employment and self employment, so that we can consider the way in which people are taxed on the wages or salaries from their jobs.

Sometimes the employee may incur expenses when carrying out his job. We look at the rules determining when these can be deducted from employment income for tax purposes. We also look at the rules covering mileage payments made by employers to employees who use their own cars for business journeys. Finally employees can make tax efficient contributions to charity under the payroll giving scheme.

In the next chapter we look at how benefits received as a result of employment are taxed and at how tax is deducted from employment income under the PAYE system.

Study guide

		Intellectual level
B2	**Income from employment**	
(a)	Recognise the factors that determine whether an engagement is treated as employment or self-employment.	2
(b)	Recognise the basis of assessment for employment income.	2
(c)	Recognise the income assessable.	2
(d)	Recognise the allowable deductions, including travelling expenses.	2
(e)	Discuss the use of the statutory approved mileage allowances.	2
B5	**The comprehensive computation of taxable income and income tax liability**	
(e)	Understand the treatment of charitable giving.	1

Exam guide

You are very likely to be asked a question concerning at least one aspect of employment taxation in your exam. This could range from identifying the date on which earnings are received in Section A to a discussion of the distinction between employment and self employment in Section B, either as part of a 15 mark question or a 10 mark question.

1 Employment and self employment

FAST FORWARD

Employment involves a contract of service whereas self employment involves a contract for services. The distinction between employment and self employment is decided by looking at all the facts of the engagement.

1.1 Employment income

Employment income includes income arising from an employment under a **contract of service**.

Some people, however, set themselves up in business and carry out work for customers under a **contract for services**.

Before we can calculate employment income, we must be sure that the individual is employed rather than self employed. This can only be decided by looking at all the facts of the engagement.

1.2 Employment and self employment

Exam focus point

Many of the tax rules have come about as a result of legal cases. In the exam you are not required to know the relevant cases. However we have included the case names in the Text for your information.

It can be difficult to distinguish between employment (receipts taxable as earnings) and self employment (receipts taxable as trading income). Employment involves a contract of service, whereas self employment involves a contract for services. Taxpayers tend to prefer self employment, because the rules on deductions for expenses are more generous.

Factors which may be of importance include:

- The degree of control exercised over the person doing the work (a high level of control indicates employment)

- Whether the worker must accept further work (if yes, indicates employment)

- Whether the person who has offered work must provide further work (if yes, indicates employment)

- Whether the worker provides his own equipment (if yes, indicates self-employment)

- Whether the worker is entitled to employment benefits such as sick pay, holiday pay and pension facilities (entitlement indicates employment)

- Whether the worker hires his own helpers (if yes, indicates self-employment)

- What degree of financial risk the worker takes (if high risk, indicates self-employment)

- What degree of responsibility for investment and management the worker has (if most of responsibility is the worker's, indicates self-employment)

- Whether the worker can profit from sound management (if can do so, indicates self-employment)

- Whether the worker can work when he chooses (if can do so, indicates self-employment)

- Whether the worker works for a number of different people or organisations (working for just one person or organisation indicates employment)

- The wording used in any agreement between the worker and the person for whom he performs work (but not conclusive about the actual legal relationship between them)

Relevant cases include:

(a) *Edwards v Clinch 1981*

A civil engineer acted occasionally as an inspector on temporary unplanned appointments.

Held: there was no ongoing office which could be vacated by one person and held by another so the fees received were from self employment not employment.

(b) *Hall v Lorimer 1994*

A vision mixer was engaged under a series of short-term contracts.

Held: the vision mixer was self employed, not because of any one detail of the case but because the overall picture was one of self-employment.

(c) *Carmichael and Anor v National Power plc 1999*

Individuals engaged as visitor guides on a casual 'as required' basis were not employees. An exchange of correspondence between the company and the individuals was not a contract of employment as there was no provision as to the frequency of work and there was flexibility to accept work or turn it down as it arose. Sickness, holiday and pension arrangements did not apply and neither did grievance and disciplinary procedures.

A worker's status also affects national insurance contributions (NIC). The self-employed generally pay less than employees. National insurance contributions are covered later in this Text.

2 Basis of assessment for employment income

FAST FORWARD

General earnings are taxed in the year of receipt. Money earnings are generally received on the earlier of the time payment is made and the time entitlement to payment arises.

2.1 Outline of the charge

Employment income includes income arising from an employment under a contract of service and the income of office holders, such as directors. The term 'employee' is used in this Text to mean anyone who receives employment income (ie both employees and directors).

General earnings are an employee's earnings (see key term below) plus the 'cash equivalent' of any taxable non-monetary benefits.

Key term

> **'Earnings'** means any salary, wage or fee, any gratuity or other profit or incidental benefit obtained by the employee if it is money or money's worth (something of direct monetary value or convertible into direct monetary value) or anything else which constitutes a reward of the employment.

Taxable earnings from an employment in a tax year are the general earnings received in that tax year.

2.2 When are earnings received?

2.2.1 General earnings consisting of money

General earnings consisting of money are treated as received at the earlier of:

- **The time when payment is made**
- **The time when a person becomes entitled to payment of the earnings**

If the employee is a **director** of a company, earnings from the company are received on the **earliest** of:

- The earlier of the two alternatives given in the general rule (above)
- The time when the amount is **credited in the company's accounting records**
- **The end of the company's period of account** (if the amount was determined by then)
- The **time the amount is determined** (if after the end of the company's period of account)

Question	Receipt of money earnings

Josephine and Vincent are employed by D plc. Josephine is a director of D plc. Vincent is not a director of D plc. D plc makes up its accounts to 31 March each year.

Bonuses were awarded by D plc as follows:

Josephine: £5,000. This amount was determined by the directors on 28 February 2015 and credited to Josephine's director's account on 10 March 2015, subject to a condition that she was could not draw down the bonus until 15 April 2015, on which date she became entitled to payment of the bonus. Josephine was actually paid the bonus on 28 April 2015.

Vincent: £3,000. Vincent became entitled to be paid this bonus on 31 March 2014, but agreed that payment should be delayed due to D plc's cash flow problems. He was actually paid the bonus on 30 April 2014.

Explain when each of the bonuses is received for the purposes of employment income and so determine the tax year in which it will be taxed.

Answer

Josephine

Josephine is a director and so her bonus is received for the purposes of employment income on the earliest of:

Time payment made: 28 April 2015
Time of entitlement: 15 April 2015
Credited in records   10 March 2015
End of period of account   31 March 2015 (amount determined before end of period)

The earliest of these dates is 10 March 2015 and so this is the date of receipt of the bonus. The tax year in which the bonus is taxed is therefore 2014/15.

Vincent

Vincent is not a director so his bonus is received for the purposes of employment income on the earlier of:

Time payment made: 30 April 2014
Time of entitlement: 31 March 2014

The earlier of these dates is 31 March 2014 and so this is the date of receipt of the bonus. The tax year in which the bonus is taxed is therefore 2013/14.

2.2.2 General earnings consisting taxable benefits

Taxable benefits (see next chapter) are generally treated as received when they are provided to the employee.

2.2.3 Pension income

The receipts basis does not apply to pension income. Pension income is taxed on the amount accruing in the tax year, whether or not it has actually been received in that year.

2.3 Net taxable earnings

Total taxable earnings less total allowable deductions (see below) **are net taxable earnings of a tax year.** Deductions cannot usually create a loss: they can only reduce the net taxable earnings to nil. If there is more than one employment in the tax year, separate calculations are required for each employment.

3 Allowable deductions

Deductions for expenses are extremely limited. Relief is available for the costs that an employee is obliged to incur in travelling in the performance of his duties or in travelling to the place he has to attend in performance of his duties. Relief is **not** available for normal commuting costs.

3.1 The general rules

Deductions for expenses are extremely limited and are notoriously hard to obtain. Although there are some specific deductions, which are covered below, the general rule is that relief is limited to:

- **Qualifying travel expenses**
- **Other expenses the employee is obliged to incur and pay as holder of the employment which are incurred wholly, exclusively and necessarily in the performance of the duties of the employment**

3.2 Travel expenses

3.2.1 Qualifying travel expenses

Tax relief is not available for an employee's normal commuting costs. This means relief is not available for any costs an employee incurs in getting from home to his normal place of work. However **employees are entitled to relief for travel expenses that they are obliged to incur and pay in travelling in the performance of their duties or travelling to or from a place which they have to attend in the performance of their duties (other than a permanent workplace).**

Question   Relief for travelling costs (1)

Judi is an accountant. She often travels to meetings at the firm's offices in Scotland returning to her office in Leeds after the meetings. What tax relief is available for Judi's travel costs?

Answer

Relief is available for the full cost of these journeys as the travel is undertaken in the performance of Judi's duties.

Question   Relief for travelling costs (2)

Zoe lives in Wycombe and normally works in Chiswick. Occasionally she visits a client in Wimbledon and travels direct from home. Distances are shown in the diagram below:

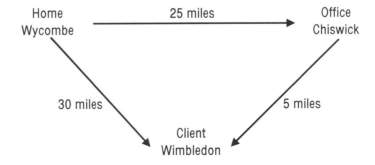

What tax relief is available for Zoe's travel costs?

Zoe is not entitled to tax relief for the costs incurred in travelling between Wycombe and Chiswick since these are normal commuting costs. However, relief is available for all costs (30 miles) that Zoe incurs when she travels from Wycombe to Wimbledon to visit her client.

To prevent manipulation of the basic rule normal commuting will not become a business journey just because the employee stops during the journey to perform a business task (eg to send an email). Nor will relief be available if the journey is essentially the same as the employee's normal journey to work.

Question   Relief for travelling costs (3)

Jeremy is based in an office in Birmingham City Centre. One day he is required to attend a 9.00 am meeting with a client whose premises are around the corner from his Birmingham office. Jeremy travels from home directly to the meeting. What tax relief is available for Jeremy's travel costs?

Answer

Since the journey is substantially the same as Jeremy's ordinary journey to work, tax relief is not available.

3.2.2 Site based employees

Site based employees (eg construction workers, management consultants etc) **who do not have a permanent workplace, are entitled to relief for the costs of all journeys made from home to wherever they are working.** This is because these employees do not have an ordinary commuting journey or any normal commuting costs.

3.2.3 Temporary workplace

If an employee is seconded to work at another location for some considerable time, then the question arises as to whether the journey from home to that workplace can become normal commuting. There is a 24 month rule.

Tax relief is available for travel, accommodation and subsistence expenses incurred by an employee who is working at a temporary workplace on a secondment expected to last up to 24 months. If a secondment is initially expected not to exceed 24 months, but it is extended, relief ceases to be due from the date the employee becomes aware of the change.

When looking at how long a secondment is expected to last, HMRC will consider not only the terms of the written contract but also any verbal agreement by the employer and other factors such as whether the employee buys a house etc.

Question   Relief for travelling costs (4)

Philip works for Vastbank at its Newcastle City Centre branch. Philip is sent to work full-time at another branch in Morpeth for 20 months at the end of which he will return to the Newcastle branch. Morpeth is about 20 miles north of Newcastle. What tax relief is available for Philip's travel costs?

Although Philip is spending all of his time at the Morpeth branch it will not be treated as his normal work place because his period of attendance will be less than 24 months. Thus Philip can claim relief in full for the costs of travel from his home to the Morpeth branch.

3.3 Other expenses

Relief is given for other expenses incurred **wholly, exclusively and necessarily in the performance of the duties** of the employment. The word 'exclusively' strictly implies that the expenditure must **give no private benefit at all**. If it does, none of it is deductible. In practice HMRC may ignore a small element of private benefit or make an apportionment between business and private use.

Whether an expense is 'necessary' is not determined by what the employer requires. The test is **whether the duties of the employment could not be performed without the outlay**.

The following cases illustrate how the requirements are interpreted. Remember you are not expected to know the case names, they are given for information only.

- *Sanderson v Durbridge 1955*

  The cost of evening meals taken when attending late meetings was not deductible because it was not incurred in the performance of the duties.

- *Blackwell v Mills 1945*

  As a condition of his employment, an employee was required to attend evening classes. The cost of his text books and travel was not deductible because it was not incurred in the performance of the duties.

- *Lupton v Potts 1969*

  Examination fees incurred by a solicitor's articled clerk were not deductible because they were incurred neither wholly nor exclusively in the performance of the duties, but in furthering the clerk's ambition to become a solicitor.

- *Brown v Bullock 1961*

  The expense of joining a club that was virtually a condition of an employment was not deductible because it would have been possible to carry on the employment without the club membership, so the expense was not necessary.

- *Elwood v Utitz 1965*

  A managing director's subscriptions to two residential London clubs were claimed by him as an expense on the grounds that they were cheaper than hotels.

  The expenditure was deductible as it was necessary in that it would be impossible for the employee to carry out his London duties without being provided with appropriate accommodation. The residential facilities (which were cheaper than hotel accommodation) were given to club members only.

- *Lucas v Cattell 1972*

  The cost of business telephone calls on a private telephone is deductible, but **no part of the line or telephone rental charges is deductible**.

- *Fitzpatrick v IRC 1994; Smith v Abbott 1994*

  Journalists could not claim a deduction for the cost of buying newspapers which they read to keep themselves informed, since they were merely preparing themselves to perform their duties.

The cost of clothes for work is not deductible, except for certain trades requiring protective clothing where there are annual deductions on a set scale.

An employee required to work at home may be able to claim a deduction for the additional costs of working from home, such as an appropriate proportion of expenditure on lighting and heating. Employers can pay up to £4 per week (or £18 per month for monthly paid employees) without the need for supporting evidence of the costs incurred by the employee. Payments above the £4 (or £18) limit require evidence of the employee's actual costs.

3.4 Other deductions

Some expenditure is specifically deductible in computing net taxable earnings:

(a) **Contributions to registered occupational pension schemes**

(b) **Subscriptions to professional bodies** on the list of bodies issued by the HMRC (which includes most UK professional bodies such as the ACCA), if relevant to the duties of the employment

(c) Payments for certain liabilities relating to the employment and for insurance against them (see below)

Employees may also claim capital allowances on plant and machinery (other than cars or other vehicles) necessarily provided for use in the performance of those duties. The computation of capital allowances is discussed later in this Text.

3.5 Liabilities and insurance

If a director or employee incurs a liability related to his employment or pays for insurance against such a liability, the cost is a deductible expense. If the employer pays such amounts, there is no taxable benefit.

A liability relating to employment is one which is imposed in respect of the employee's acts or omissions as employee. Thus, for example, liability for negligence would be covered. Related costs, for example the costs of legal proceedings, are included.

For insurance premiums to qualify, the insurance policy:

(a) Must cover only liabilities relating to employment, vicarious liability in respect of liabilities of another person's employment, related costs and payments to the employee's own employees in respect of their employment liabilities relating to employment and related costs

(b) Must not last for more than two years (although it may be renewed for up to two years at a time), and the insured person must not be required to renew it

4 Statutory approved mileage allowances

FAST FORWARD

> Employers may pay a mileage allowance to employees who use their own car on business journeys. Payments up to the statutory limits are tax free, any excess is taxable, and a deduction can be claimed if the payment is lower.

A single approved mileage allowance for business journeys in an employee's own vehicle applies to all cars and vans. There is no income tax on payments up to this allowance and employers do not have to report mileage allowances up to this amount. The allowance for 2014/15 is **45p per mile on the first 10,000 miles** in the tax year with **each additional mile over 10,000 miles at 25p per mile.**

The authorised mileage allowance for **employees using their own motor cycle is 24p per mile.** For **employees using their own pedal cycle it is 20p per mile.**

If employers pay less than the statutory approved mileage allowance, employees can claim tax relief up to that level.

The statutory approved mileage allowance does not prevent employers from paying higher rates, but any excess will be subject to income tax. There is a similar (but slightly different) system for NICs, covered later in this Text.

Employers can make income tax and NIC free payments of up to 5p per mile for each fellow employee making the same business trip who is carried as a passenger. If the employer does not pay the employee for carrying business passengers, the employee cannot claim any tax relief.

Question

Mileage allowance

Sophie uses her own car for business travel. During 2014/15, Sophie drove 15,400 miles in the performance of her duties. Sophie's employer paid her a mileage allowance. How is the mileage allowance treated for tax purposes assuming that the rate paid is:

(a)   40p a mile?
(b)   25p a mile?

Answer

(a)

	£
Mileage allowance received (15,400 × 40p)	6,160
Less: tax free [(10,000 × 45p) + (5,400 × 25p)]	(5,850)
Taxable benefit	310

£5,850 is tax free and the excess amount received of £310 is a taxable benefit.

(b)

	£
Mileage allowance received (15,400 × 25p)	3,850
Less: tax free amount [(10,000 × 45p) + (5,400 × 25p)]	(5,850)
Allowable deduction	(2,000)

There is no taxable benefit and Sophie can claim a deduction from her employment income of £2,000.

5 Charitable donations under the payroll deduction scheme

FAST FORWARD

Employees can make tax deductible donations to charity under the payroll deduction scheme. The amount paid is deducted from gross pay.

Employees can make charitable donations under the payroll deduction scheme by asking their employer to make deductions from their gross earnings. The deductions are then passed to a charitable agency which will either distribute the funds to the employees' chosen charities on receipt of their instructions, or provide the employee with vouchers that can be redeemed by the recipient charities.

The donation is an allowable deduction from the employee's earnings for tax purposes. Tax relief is given at source as the employer must deduct the donation from gross pay before calculating PAYE.

Exam focus point

Make sure you understand the difference between how tax relief is given for gift aid donations and how tax relief is given through the payroll deduction scheme.

Chapter Roundup

- Employment involves a contract of service whereas self employment involves a contract for services. The distinction between employment and self employment is decided by looking at all the facts of the engagement.

- General earnings are taxed in the year of receipt. Money earnings are generally received on the earlier of the time payment is made and the time entitlement to payment arises.

- Deductions for expenses are extremely limited. Relief is available for the costs that an employee is obliged to incur in travelling in the performance of his duties or in travelling to the place he has to attend in performance of his duties. Relief is **not** available for normal commuting costs.

- Employers may pay a mileage allowance to employees who use their own car on business journeys. Payments up to the statutory limits are tax free, any excess is taxable, and a deduction can be claimed if the payment is lower.

- Employees can make tax deductible donations to charity under the payroll deduction scheme. The amount paid is deducted from gross pay.

Quick Quiz

1   On what basis are earnings taxed?

2   In order for general expenses of employment to be deductible, they must be incurred _____, _____ and _____ in the performance of the duties of the employment. Fill in the blanks.

3   What relief can Karen claim if she is paid 40p for each mile that she drives her own car on company business and she drives 5,000 miles in 2014/15?

    A   £250
    B   £1,750
    C   £2,000
    D   £2,250

4   Could Karen claim any extra relief if she was accompanied by a work colleague for 1,000 of those miles?

1   Earnings are taxed on a receipts basis.

2   In order for general expenses of employment to be deductible, they must be incurred **wholly, exclusively** and **necessarily** in the performance of the duties of the employment.

3   A. Karen could claim relief of 5,000 × (45 − 40)p = £250. The 40p per mile received would not be taxable.

4   Karen could not claim any extra relief if she was accompanied by a work colleague for 1,000 of those miles. If her employer had made extra payments of up to 5p per mile for those journeys the extra payment would have been tax free.

Now try the questions below from the Practice Question Bank

Number	Type	Marks	Time
Q8	Section A	6	11 mins
Q9	Section B	10	18 mins

Taxable and exempt benefits. The PAYE system

Topic list	Syllabus reference
1 P11D employees	B2(g)
2 Benefits taxable on all employees	B2(h)
3 Benefits taxable on P11D employees	B2(h)
4 Exempt benefits	B2(h)
5 P11D dispensations	B2(i)
6 The PAYE system	B2(f)

Introduction

In the previous chapter we discussed when a worker was an employee and when he was self employed. We then considered the taxation of salaries and wages and the deduction of expenses and charitable donations.

In this chapter we look at benefits provided to employees. Benefits are an integral part of many remuneration packages, but the tax cost of receiving a benefit must not be overlooked. Special rules apply to fix the taxable value of certain benefits.

Finally we look at how tax is deducted from employment income under the PAYE system. Tax is deducted from cash payments, and benefits are dealt with through the PAYE code.

In the next chapter we look at how employees can save for their retirement through pension provision and the tax reliefs available.

Study guide

		Intellectual level
B2	**Income from employment**	
(f)	Explain the PAYE system.	1
(g)	Identify P11D employees.	1
(h)	Explain and compute the amount of benefits assessable.	2
(i)	Explain the purpose of a dispensation from HM Revenue & Customs.	2

Exam guide

Benefits are a very important part of employment income and you are likely to come across them in your exam in both Section A and Section B, in a 15 mark question or a 10 mark question. Most employees these days are P11D employees, but you may need to know which benefits apply to excluded employees. If you come across exempt benefits in a Section B question, note this in your answer to show that you have considered each item.

The PAYE system is a system of deduction of tax at source. You should be able to explain how it collects tax. The forms for the PAYE system are important as are the dates for submission.

1 P11D employees

FAST FORWARD

Most employees are taxed on benefits under the benefits code. 'Excluded employees' (lower paid/non-directors) are only subject to part of the provisions of the code.

1.1 Excluded employees

There is comprehensive legislation which covers the taxation of benefits.

The legislation generally applies to all employees. However, only certain parts of it apply to 'excluded employees'.

An excluded employee is an employee in lower paid employment who is either not a director of a company or is a director but has no material interest in the company ('material' means control of more than 5% of the ordinary share capital) and either:

(a) He is full time working director, or
(b) The company is non-profit-making or is established for charitable purposes only.

The term 'director' refers to any person who acts as a director or any person in accordance with whose instructions the directors are accustomed to act (other than a professional adviser).

1.2 Lower paid employment

A lower paid employment is one where earnings for the tax year are less than £8,500. To decide whether this applies, add together the total earnings and benefits that would be taxable if the employee were **not** an excluded employee.

A number of specific deductions must be taken into account to determine lower paid employment. These include contributions to registered pension schemes and payroll charitable deductions. However, general deductions from employment income (see earlier in this Text) are not taken into account.

Tim earns £6,500 per annum working full time as a sales representative at Chap Co Ltd. The company provides the following staff benefits to Tim:

Private health insurance	£300
Company car	£1,500
Expense allowance	£2,000

Tim used £1,900 of the expense allowance on business mileage petrol.

Is Tim an excluded employee?

Answer

No. Although Tim's taxable income is less than £8,500 this is only after his expense claim. The figure to consider and compare to £8,500 is the £10,300 as shown below.

		£
Salary		6,500
Benefits:	health insurance	300
	car	1,500
	expense allowance	2,000
Earnings to consider if Tim is an 'excluded employee'		10,300
Less claim for expenses paid out		(1,900)
Taxable income		8,400

1.3 P11D employees

Employees, including directors, who are not excluded employees may be referred to as 'P11D employees'; the P11D is the form that the employer completes for each such employee with details of expenses and benefits.

2 Benefits taxable on all employees

2.1 Introduction

All employees, including excluded employees, are taxable on the provision of:

- Vouchers
- Living accommodation

For excluded employees, other benefits are taxed on their 'second-hand value', which is usually nil. The special rules for P11D employees are covered in the next Section.

2.2 Vouchers

If any employee (including an excluded employee):

(a)   receives cash vouchers (vouchers exchangeable for cash)
(b)   uses a credit token (such as a credit card) to obtain money, goods or services, or
(c)   receives exchangeable vouchers (such as book tokens), also called non-cash vouchers

he is taxed on the **cost to the employer of providing the benefit**, less any amount made good.

2.3 Accommodation

FAST FORWARD

The benefit in respect of accommodation is its annual value. There is an additional benefit if the property cost over £75,000.

2.3.1 Annual value charge

The taxable value of accommodation provided to an employee (including an excluded employee) is the rent that would have been payable if the premises had been let at their annual value (sometimes called 'rateable value'). If the premises are rented rather than owned by the employer, then the taxable benefit is the higher of the rent actually paid and the annual value.

2.3.2 Additional benefit charge

If a property was bought by the employer for a cost of more than £75,000, an additional amount is chargeable as follows:

(Cost of providing the living accommodation – £75,000) × the official rate of interest at the start of the tax year. The official rate of interest at the start of the 2014/15 tax year is 3.25%.

Exam focus point

The 'official rate' of interest will be given to you in the exam.

Thus with an official rate of 3.25%, the total benefit for accommodation costing £95,000 and with an annual value of £2,000 would be £2,000 + £(95,000 – 75,000) × 3.25% = £2,650.

The 'cost of providing' the living accommodation is the total of the cost of purchase and the cost of any improvements made before the start of the tax year for which the benefit is being computed. It is therefore not possible to avoid the charge by buying an inexpensive property requiring substantial repairs and improving it.

Where the property was acquired more than six years before first being provided to the employee, the market value when first so provided plus the cost of subsequent improvements is used as the cost of providing the living accommodation. However, unless the actual cost plus improvements up to the start of the tax year in question exceeds £75,000, the additional charge cannot be imposed, however high the market value.

2.3.3 Job related accommodation

There is no taxable benefit in respect of job related accommodation. Accommodation is job related if:

(a)   Residence in the accommodation is necessary for **the proper performance of the employee's duties (as with a caretaker)**, or

(b)   The accommodation is provided **for the better performance of the employee's duties** and the employment is of a kind in which it is customary for accommodation to be provided (as with a policeman), or

(c)   The **accommodation is provided as part of arrangements in force because of a special threat to the employee's security**.

Directors can only claim exemptions (a) or (b) if:

(i)   They have no **material interest** ('material' means over 5%) in the company.
(ii)   Either they are **full time working directors** or the company is **non-profit making or is a charity**.

2.3.4 Contribution by employee

Any contribution paid by the employee is deducted from the annual value of the property and then from the additional benefit.

Question	Accommodation

Mr Quinton was provided with a company flat in Birmingham in January 2014. The rateable value of the flat is £1,200. The property cost his employer £125,000, but was valued at £150,000 in January 2014. Mr Quinton paid rent of £500 pa.

What is the taxable benefit for 2014/15 assuming:

(a) His employer purchased the property in 2012, or

(b) His employer purchased the property in 2006, or

(c) Mr Quinton was required to live in the flat as he was employed as the caretaker for the company premises (of which the flat was part).

Answer

(a)

	£
Annual value	1,200
Less: rent paid	(500)
	700
Additional amount £(125,000 − 75,000) × 3.25%	1,625
Taxable benefit	2,325

(b)

	£
Annual value	1,200
Less: rent paid	(500)
	700
Additional amount £(150,000 − 75,000) × 3.25%	2,437
Taxable benefit	3,137

As Mr Quinton first moved in more than six years after the company bought the flat, the value at the date he moved in is used.

(c) Job related accommodation: taxable benefit   £ nil

3 Benefits taxable on P11D employees

3.1 Introduction

Special rules apply to determine the taxable value of expenses and benefits paid to or provided for P11D employees.

3.2 Expenses

3.2.1 General business expenses

If business expenses on such items as travel or hotel stays are reimbursed by an employer, the reimbursed amount is a taxable benefit for P11D employees. To avoid being taxed on this amount, an employee must then make a claim to deduct it as an expense under the rules set out below.

A P11D dispensation may be obtained from HMRC to avoid the need to report expenses and claim a deduction (see later in this chapter).

BPP LEARNING MEDIA

Part B Income tax and national insurance contributions | **5: Taxable and exempt benefits. The PAYE system**   **63**

3.2.2 Private incidental expenses

When an individual has to spend one or more nights away from home, his employer may reimburse expenses on items incidental to his absence (for example laundry and private telephone calls). **Such incidental expenses are exempt** if:

(a) The expenses of travelling to each place where the individual stays overnight, throughout the trip, are incurred necessarily in the performance of the duties of the employment (or would have been, if there had been any expenses).

(b) The total (for the whole trip) of incidental expenses not deductible under the usual rules is **no more than £5 for each night spent wholly in the UK** and **£10 for each other night**. If this limit is exceeded, all of the expenses are taxable, not just the excess. The expenses include any VAT.

This incidental expenses exemption applies to expenses reimbursed, and to benefits obtained using credit tokens and non-cash vouchers.

3.2.3 Expenses related to living accommodation

In addition to the benefit of living accommodation itself, P11D **employees are taxed on related expenses paid by the employer**, such as:

(a) **Heating, lighting or cleaning the premises**
(b) **Repairing, maintaining or decorating the premises**
(c) **The provision of furniture (the annual value is 20% of the cost)**

If the accommodation is 'job related', however, the **taxable amount is restricted to a maximum of 10% of the employee's 'net earnings'.** For this purpose, net earnings comprises the total employment income, net of expenses and pension contributions, but excluding these related expenses.

Council tax and water or sewage charges paid by the employer are taxable in full as a benefit unless the accommodation is 'job-related'.

3.3 Cars

FAST FORWARD

> Employees who have a company car are taxed on a % of the car's list price which depends on the level of the car's CO_2 emissions. The same % multiplied by £21,700 determines the benefit where private fuel is also provided.

3.3.1 Cars provided for private use

A car provided by reason of the employment to a P11D employee or member of his family or household for private use gives rise to a taxable benefit. 'Private use' includes home to work travel.

A tax charge arises whether the car is provided by the employer or by some other person. The benefit is computed as shown below, even if the car is taken as an alternative to another benefit of a different value.

The starting point for calculating a car benefit is the list price of the car (plus accessories). **The percentage of the list price that is taxable depends on the car's CO_2 emissions.**

3.3.2 Taxable benefit

For cars that emit **CO_2 of 95 g/km (2014/15), the taxable benefit is 12% of the car's list price. This percentage increases by 1% for every 5g/km (rounded down to the nearest multiple of 5) by which CO_2 emissions exceed 95g/km up to a maximum of 35%.** Therefore the 12% rate also applies to cars with emissions between 96g/km and 99g/km as these are rounded down to 95g/km. Then, for cars with emissions between 100g/km and 104g/km, the relevant percentage will be 12 + ((100 – 95)/5) = 13% etc.

Exam focus point

> The CO_2 baseline figure of 95g/km will be given to you in the tax rates and allowances section of the exam paper.

For cars that emit CO_2 between 76g/km and 94g/km, the taxable benefit is 11% of the car's list price. For cars that emit 75g/km or less, the taxable benefit is 5% of the car's list price.

Exam focus point

The examiner has stated that zero emission company cars are not examinable.

Diesel cars have a supplement of 3% of the car's list price added to the taxable benefit. The maximum percentage, however, remains 35% of the list price.

3.3.3 List price

The price of the car is the sum of the following items:

(a) **The list price of the car** for a single retail sale at the time of first registration, including charges for delivery and standard accessories. The manufacturer's, importer's or distributor's list price must be used, even if the retailer offered a discount. A notional list price is estimated if no list price was published.

(b) **The price (including fitting) of all optional accessories provided when the car was first provided** to the employee, excluding mobile telephones and equipment needed by a disabled employee. The extra cost of adapting or manufacturing a car to run on road fuel gases is not included.

(c) **The price (including fitting) of all optional accessories fitted later** and costing at least £100 each, excluding mobile telephones and equipment needed by a disabled employee. Such accessories affect the taxable benefit from and including the tax year in which they are fitted. However, accessories which are merely replacing existing accessories and are not superior to the ones replaced are ignored. Replacement accessories which *are* superior are taken into account, but the cost of the old accessory is then deducted.

There is a special rule for **classic cars**. If the car is at least 15 years old (from the time of first registration) at the end of the tax year, and its market value at the end of the year (or, if earlier, when it ceased to be available to the employee) is over £15,000 and greater than the price found under the above rules, that market value is used instead of the price. The market value takes account of all accessories (except mobile telephones and equipment needed by a disabled employee).

Capital contributions made by the employee in that and previous tax years up to a maximum of £5,000 are deducted from the list price. Capital contributions are payments by the employee in respect of the price of the car or accessories for the same car. Contributions beyond the maximum are ignored.

Question

Car benefit (1)

Nigel Issan is provided with a diesel car which had a list price of £22,000 when it was first registered. The car has CO_2 emissions of 173g/km.

You are required to calculate Nigel's car benefit for 2014/15.

Answer

Car benefit £22,000 × 30% (12% + (170 − 95)/5 + 3%) = £6,600

Note that 173 is rounded down to 170 to be exactly divisible by 5.

BPP
LEARNING MEDIA

Part B Income tax and national insurance contributions | 5: Taxable and exempt benefits. The PAYE system | 65

Question

Car benefit (2)

Robyn is provided with a petrol car which had a list price of £18,000 when it was first registered. The car has CO_2 emissions of 90 g/km.

You are required to calculate Robyn's car benefit for 2014/15.

Answer

Car benefit £18,000 × 11% = £1,980

3.3.4 Reductions in the benefit

The benefit is reduced on a time basis where a car is first made available or ceases to be made available during the tax year or is incapable of being used for a continuous period of not less than 30 days (for example because it is being repaired).

The benefit is reduced by any payment the user must make for the private use of the car (as distinct from a capital contribution to the cost of the car). The benefit cannot become negative to create a deduction from the employee's income.

Question

Time apportioning benefits

Vicky Olvo starts her employment on 6 January 2015 and is immediately provided with a new petrol car with a list price of £25,000. The car was more expensive than her employer would have provided and she therefore made a capital contribution of £6,200. The employer was able to buy the car at a discount and paid only £23,000. Vicky contributed £100 a month for being able to use the car privately. CO_2 emissions are 238g/km.

You are required to calculate her car benefit for 2014/15.

Answer

	£
List price *	25,000
Less capital contribution (maximum)	(5,000)
	20,000

	£
£20,000 × 35%** × 3/12 ***	1,750
Less contribution to running costs (£100 × 3)	(300)
Car benefit	1,450

* The discounted price is not relevant
** 12% + (235 − 95) × 1/5 = 40% restricted to 35% max
*** Only available for three months in 2014/15

3.3.5 Pool cars

Pool cars are exempt. A car is a pool car if **all** the following conditions are satisfied:

(a) It is used by more than one employee and is not ordinarily used by any one of them to the exclusion of the others.

(b) Any private use is merely incidental to business use.

(c) It is not normally kept overnight at or near the residence of an employee.

3.3.6 Ancillary benefits

There are many ancillary benefits associated with the provision of cars, such as insurance, repairs, vehicle licences and a parking space at or near work. No extra taxable benefit arises as a result of these, with the exception of the cost of providing a driver.

3.4 Fuel for cars

3.4.1 Introduction

Where fuel is provided there is a further benefit in addition to the car benefit.

No taxable benefit arises where either

(a)   **All the fuel provided was made available only for business travel, or**

(b)   **The employee is required to make good, and has made good, the whole of the cost of any fuel provided for his private use.**

Unlike most benefits, a reimbursement of only part of the cost of the fuel available for private use does not reduce the benefit.

3.4.2 Taxable benefit

The taxable benefit is a percentage of a base figure. The base figure for 2014/15 is £21,700. The percentage is the same percentage as is used to calculate the car benefit (see above).

Exam focus point

> The fuel base figure will be given to you in the tax rates and allowances section of the exam paper.

3.4.3 Reductions in the benefit

The fuel benefit is reduced in the same way as the car benefit **if the car is not available for 30 days or more.**

The fuel benefit is also reduced if private fuel is not available for part of a tax year. However, if private fuel later becomes available in the same tax year, the reduction is not made. If, for example, fuel is provided from 6 April 2014 to 30 June 2014, then the fuel benefit for 2014/15 will be restricted to just three months. This is because the provision of fuel has permanently ceased. However, if fuel is provided from 6 April 2014 to 30 June 2014, and then again from 1 September 2014 to 5 April 2015, then the fuel benefit will not be reduced since the cessation was only temporary.

Question	Car and fuel benefit

An employee was provided with a new car costing £15,000 on 6 April 2014. The car emits 161g/km of CO_2. During 2014/15 the employer spent £900 on insurance, repairs and a vehicle licence. The firm paid for all petrol, costing £1,500, without reimbursement. The employee paid the firm £270 for the private use of the car. Calculate the taxable benefits for private use of the car and private fuel.

Answer

Round CO_2 emissions figure down to the nearest 5, ie 160g/km.

Amount by which CO_2 emissions exceed the baseline:

(160 − 95) = 65 g/km

Divide by 5 = 13

Taxable percentage = 12% + 13% = 25%

	£
Car benefit £15,000 × 25%	3,750
Less contribution towards use of car	(270)
	3,480
Fuel benefit £21,700 × 25%	5,425
Total benefits	8,905

If the contribution of £270 had been towards the petrol the benefit would have been £(3,750 + 5,425) = £9,175 since partial reimbursement of private use fuel does not reduce the fuel benefit.

Note there is no additional benefit for the insurance, repairs and licence costs. The car benefit is deemed to cover all these expenses incurred by the employer.

3.5 Vans and heavier commercial vehicles

If a van (of normal maximum laden weight up to 3,500 kg) **is made available for an employee's private use, there is an annual scale charge of £3,090.** The scale charge covers ancillary benefits such as insurance and servicing. The benefit is scaled down if the van is not available for the full year (as for cars) and is reduced by any payment made by the employee for private use.

There is, however, **no taxable benefit where an employee takes a van home** (ie uses the van for home to work travel) but is not allowed any other private use.

Where private fuel is provided, there is an additional charge of £581. If the van is unavailable for part of the year, or fuel for private use is only provided for part of the year, the benefit is scaled down.

If a commercial vehicle of normal maximum laden weight over 3,500 kg is made available for an employee's private use, but the employee's use of the vehicle is not wholly or mainly private, no taxable benefit arises except in respect of the provision of a driver.

3.6 Beneficial loans

FAST FORWARD

Cheap loans are charged to tax on the difference between the official rate of interest and any interest paid by the employee.

3.6.1 Taxable benefit

Employment related loans to P11D employees and their relatives give rise to a benefit equal to:

(a) **Any amounts written off** (unless the employee has died)

(b) The excess of the interest based on an official rate prescribed by the Treasury, over any interest actually charged ('taxable cheap loan'). Interest payable during the tax year but paid after the end of the tax year is taken into account.

The following loans are normally not treated as taxable cheap loans for calculation of the interest benefits (but are taxable for the purposes of the charge on loans written off).

(a) A loan on normal commercial terms made in the ordinary course of the employer's money-lending business.

(b) A loan made by an individual in the ordinary course of the lender's domestic, family or personal arrangements.

3.6.2 Calculating the interest benefit

There are two alternative methods of calculating the taxable benefit. The simpler **'average' method** automatically applies unless the taxpayer or HMRC elect for the alternative **'strict' method. The taxpayer should make the election for the 'strict' method** if this results in a **lower taxable benefit,** as this will give a **lower charge to income tax. HMRC normally only make the election** where it appears that the

'average' method is **being deliberately exploited.** In both methods, the benefit is the interest at the official rate minus the interest payable.

For the purposes of the F6 (UK) exam, the official rate of interest is assumed to be 3.25% throughout 2014/15.

The 'average' method averages the balances at the beginning and end of the tax year (or the dates on which the loan was made and/or repaid if it was not in existence throughout the tax year) and applies the official rate of interest to this average. If the loan was not in existence throughout the tax year only the number of complete tax months (from the 6th of the month) for which it existed are taken into account.

The 'strict' method is to compute interest at the official rate on the actual amount outstanding on a daily basis. However, for exam purposes, it is acceptable to work on a monthly basis.

Question   Loan benefit

At 6 April 2014 a taxable cheap loan of £40,000 was outstanding to an employee earning £50,000 a year, who repaid £15,000 on 6 December 2014. The remaining balance of £25,000 was outstanding at 5 April 2015. Interest paid during the year was £650. What was the benefit under both the 'average' and the 'strict' methods for 2014/15?

Answer

Average method

	£
$3.25\% \times \dfrac{40,000 + 25,000}{2}$	1,056
Less interest paid	(650)
Benefit	406

Strict method

	£
£40,000 × $\dfrac{8}{12}$ (6 April – 5 December) × 3.25%	867
£25,000 × $\dfrac{4}{12}$ (6 December – 5 April) × 3.25%	271
	1,138
Less interest paid	(650)
Benefit	488

HMRC could elect for the 'strict' method, although this is unlikely given the difference between the methods is relatively small and it does not appear that the 'average' method is being deliberately exploited.

Note. You must always show the workings for the average method. If it appears likely that the taxpayer should or HMRC might elect for the 'strict' method you will need to show those workings as well.

3.6.3 The de minimis test

The interest benefit is not taxable if the total of all non-qualifying loans to the employee did not exceed £10,000 at any time in the tax year.

A qualifying loan is one on which all or part of any interest paid would qualify for tax relief (see further below).

When the £10,000 threshold is exceeded, a benefit arises on interest on the whole loan, not just on the excess of the loan over £10,000.

3.6.4 Qualifying loans

If the whole of the interest payable on a qualifying loan is eligible for tax relief as deductible interest (as seen earlier in this Text), then no taxable benefit arises. If the interest is only partly eligible for tax relief, then the employee is treated as receiving earnings because the actual rate of interest is below the official rate. He is also treated as paying interest equal to those earnings. This **deemed interest paid may qualify as a business expense or as deductible interest in addition to any interest actually paid**.

Question	Beneficial loans

Anna, who is single, has an annual salary of £30,000, and two loans from her employer.

(a)   A season ticket loan of £8,300 at no interest

(b)   A loan, 90% of which was used to buy a partnership interest, of £54,000 at 0.75% interest

What is Anna's tax liability for 2014/15?

Answer	

	£
Salary	30,000
Season ticket loan (non-qualifying): not over £10,000	0
Loan to buy partnership interest (qualifying): £54,000 × (3.25 − 0.75 = 2.5%)	1,350
Earnings/Total income	31,350
Less deductible interest deemed paid (£54,000 × 3.25% × 90%)	(1,580)
Net income	29,770
Less personal allowance	(10,000)
Taxable income	19,770
Income tax	
Tax liability £19,770 × 20%	3,954

3.7 Private use of other assets

FAST FORWARD

> 20% of the value of assets made available for private use is taxable.

When assets are made available for private use to employees or members of their family or household, the taxable benefit is the higher of 20% of the market value when first provided as a benefit to any employee and the rent paid by the employer. The 20% charge is time-apportioned when the asset is provided for only part of the year. The charge after any time apportionment is reduced by any contribution made by the employee.

There is an additional taxable benefit of any other amounts that the employer pays during the tax year relating to the provision of the asset such as running costs.

Bicycles provided for journeys to work, as well as being available for private use, are exempt from the private use benefit rules.

If an asset made available is subsequently acquired by the employee, **the taxable benefit on the acquisition is the *greater* of:**

• The **current market value minus the price paid by the employee**

• The **market value when first provided minus any amounts already taxed (ignoring contributions by the employee) minus the price paid by the employee**

This rule prevents tax free benefits arising on rapidly depreciating items through the employee purchasing them at their low second-hand value.

There is an exception to this rule for bicycles which have previously been provided as exempt benefits (see above). The taxable benefit on acquisition is restricted to current market value, minus the price paid by the employee.

3.8 Example: assets made available for private use

A suit costing £400 is purchased by an employer for use by an employee on 6 April 2013. On 6 April 2014 the suit is purchased by the employee for £30, its market value then being £50.

The benefit in 2013/14 is £400 × 20% = £80.

The benefit in 2014/15 is £290, being the *greater* of:

		£
(a)	Market value at acquisition by employee	50
	Less price paid	(30)
		20
(b)	Original market value	400
	Less taxed in respect of use	(80)
		320
	Less price paid	(30)
		290

Question   Bicycles

Rupert is provided with a new bicycle by his employer on 6 April 2014. The bicycle is available for private use as well as commuting to work. It cost the employer £1,500 when new. On 6 October 2014 the employer transfers ownership of the bicycle to Rupert when it is worth £800. Rupert does not pay anything for the bicycle. What is the total taxable benefit on Rupert for 2014/15 in respect of the bicycle?

Answer

Use benefit	Exempt
Transfer benefit (use MV at acquisition by employee only)	
MV at transfer	£800

3.9 Scholarships

If scholarships are given to members of an employee's family, the **employee is taxable on the cost** unless the scholarship fund's or scheme's payments by reason of people's employments are not more than 25% of its total payments.

3.10 Childcare

FAST FORWARD Workplace childcare is an exempt benefit. Employer-supported childcare and childcare vouchers are exempt up to £55 per week. Maximum tax relief is limited to £11 per week (the equivalent of £55 × 20%).

The cost of running a **workplace nursery or playscheme is an exempt benefit (without limit)**.

Otherwise a certain amount of childcare is tax free if the employer contracts with an approved childcarer or provides childcare vouchers to pay an approved childcarer. The childcare must usually be available to all employees and the childcare must either be registered or approved home-childcare.

A **£55 per week limit applies to basic rate employees** who use employer-supported childcare schemes or receive childcare vouchers. The amount of tax relief for a basic rate taxpayer is therefore £55 × 20% = £11 per week.

Higher rate and additional rate employees have their tax relief restricted so that it is the equivalent of that received by a basic rate taxpayer. Higher and additional rate employees can therefore receive vouchers tax-free up to £28 per week and £25 per week respectively, each giving £11 of tax relief which is the same amount a basic rate taxpayer would receive.

Question
Childcare

Archie is employed by M plc and is paid a salary of £80,000 in 2014/15. He starts receiving childcare vouchers from M plc worth £50 per week for his daughter in June 2014 and receives them for 26 weeks during 2014/15. What is Archie's employment income for 2014/15?

Answer

	£
Salary (higher rate employee)	80,000
Childcare vouchers £(50 − 28) × 26 weeks	572
Employment income 2014/15	80,572

3.11 Other benefits

FAST FORWARD

There is a residual charge for other benefits, usually equal to the cost to the employer of the benefits.

We have seen above how certain specific benefits are taxed. **There is a sweeping up charge for all other benefits. Under this rule the taxable value of a benefit is the cost of the benefit less any part of that cost made good by the employee to the persons providing the benefit.**

The residual charge applies to any benefit provided for a P11D employee or a member of his family or household, by reason of the employment. There is an exception where the employer is an individual and the provision of the benefit is made in the normal course of the employer's domestic, family or personal relationships.

3.12 Example: other benefits

A private school offers free places to the children of its staff. The marginal cost to the school of providing the place is £2,000 pa, although the fees charged to other pupils is £5,000 pa.

The taxable value of the benefit to the staff is the actual cost of £2,000 per pupil, not the full £5,000 charged to other pupils.

4 Exempt benefits

FAST FORWARD

There are a number of exempt benefits including removal expenses, sporting facilities, and workplace parking.

Various benefits are exempt from tax. These include:

(a) **Entertainment provided to employees by genuine third parties** (eg seats at sporting/cultural events), even if it is provided by giving the employee a voucher

72   **5: Taxable and exempt benefits. The PAYE system** | Part B Income tax and national insurance contributions

(b) **Gifts of goods** (or vouchers exchangeable for goods) from third parties (ie not provided by the employer or a person connected to the employer) if the total cost (incl. VAT) of all gifts by the same donor to the same employee in the tax year is £250 or less. If the £250 limit is exceeded, the full amount is taxable, not just the excess.

(c) **Non-cash awards for long service** if the period of service was at least 20 years, no similar award was made to the employee in the past ten years and the cost is not more than £50 per year of service

(d) **Awards under staff suggestion schemes** if:

    (i)   There is a formal scheme, open to all employees on equal terms.

    (ii)   The suggestion is outside the scope of the employee's normal duties.

    (iii)   Either the award is not more than £25, or the award is only made after a decision is taken to implement the suggestion.

    (iv)   Awards over £25 reflect the financial importance of the suggestion to the business, and either do not exceed 50% of the expected net financial benefit during the first year of implementation or do not exceed 10% of the expected net financial benefit over a period of up to five years.

    (v)   Awards of over £25 are shared on a reasonable basis between two or more employees putting forward the same suggestion.

If an award exceeds £5,000, the excess is always taxable.

(e) **The first £8,000 of removal expenses** if:

    (i)   The employee does not already live within a reasonable daily travelling distance of his new place of employment, but will do so after moving.

    (ii)   The expenses are incurred or the benefits provided by the end of the tax year following the tax year of the start of employment at the new location.

(f) **Some childcare** (see earlier in this Chapter)

(g) **Sporting or recreational facilities available to employees generally and not to the general public**, unless they are provided on domestic premises, or they consist of an interest in or the use of any mechanically propelled vehicle or any overnight accommodation. Vouchers only exchangeable for such facilities are also exempt, but membership fees for sports clubs are taxable.

(h) **Assets or services used in performing the duties of employment** provided any private use of the item concerned is insignificant. This exempts, for example, the benefit arising on the private use of employer-provided tools.

(i) **Welfare counselling** and similar minor benefits if the benefit concerned is available to employees generally

(j) **Bicycles or cycling safety equipment** provided to enable employees to get to and from work or to travel between one workplace and another. The equipment must be available to the employer's employees generally. Also, it must be used mainly for the aforementioned journeys.

(k) **Workplace parking**

(l) **Up to £15,480 a year paid to an employee who is on a full-time course lasting at least a year**, with average full-time attendance of at least 20 weeks a year. If the £15,480 limit is exceeded, the whole amount is taxable.

(m) **Work related training** and related costs. This includes the costs of training material and assets either made during training or incorporated into something so made.

(n) **Air miles** or car fuel coupons obtained as a result of business expenditure but used for private purposes

(o) **The cost of work buses and minibuses or subsidies to public bus services**

A works bus must have a seating capacity of 12 or more and a works minibus a seating capacity of nine or more but not more than 12 and be available generally to employees of the employer concerned. The bus or minibus must mainly be used by employees for journeys to and from work and for journeys between workplaces.

(p) **Transport/overnight costs where public transport is disrupted by industrial action,** late night taxis and travel costs incurred where car sharing arrangements unavoidably breakdown

(q) The private use of one **mobile phone, which can be a smartphone.** Top up vouchers for exempt mobile phones are also tax free. If more than one mobile phone is provided to an employee for private use only the second or subsequent phone is a taxable benefit valued using the rules for assets made available to employees.

(r) **Employer provided uniforms** which employees must wear as part of their duties

(s) The cost of **staff parties** which are open to staff generally provided that the **cost per head per year (including VAT) is £150 or less.** The £150 limit may be split between several parties.

(t) **Private medical insurance premiums paid to cover treatment when the employee is outside the UK in the performance of his duties.** Other medical insurance premiums are taxable as is the cost of medical diagnosis and treatment except for routine check ups. Eye tests and glasses for employees using VDUs are exempt.

(u) **Cheap loans that do not exceed £10,000** at any time in the tax year (see above)

(v) **Job related accommodation** (see above)

(w) **Employer contributions towards additional household costs incurred by an employee who works wholly or partly at home.** Payments up to £4 a week (£18 per month for monthly paid employees) may be made without supporting evidence (see earlier in this Text).

(x) **Personal incidental expenses** (see earlier in this Text)

Exam focus point

> An exemption will be introduced in autumn 2014 for payments by an employer in respect of employees' medical treatment in certain circumstances. This exemption **will not be examined** in exams in the financial year 1 April 2015 to 31 March 2016.

Where a voucher is provided for a benefit which is exempt from income tax the provision of the voucher itself is also exempt.

5 P11D dispensations

As we have seen expense payments to P11D employees should be reported to HMRC. They form part of the employee's employment income and a claim must be made to deduct the expenses in computing net employment income.

To avoid this cumbersome procedure **the employer and HMRC can agree for a dispensation to apply to avoid the need to report expenses covered by the dispensation, and the employee then need not make a formal claim for a deduction**.

Dispensations can only apply to genuine business expenses. Some employers only reimburse business expenses, so that a dispensation may be agreed to cover all payments. Other employers may agree to cover a particular category of expenses, such as travel expenses.

A dispensation cannot be given for mileage allowances paid to employees using their own cars for business journeys as these payments are governed by a statutory exemption (see earlier in this Text).

6 The PAYE system

FAST FORWARD

> Most tax in respect of employment income is deducted under the PAYE system. The objective of the PAYE system is to collect the correct amount of tax over the year. An employee's PAYE code is designed to ensure that allowances etc are given evenly over the year.

6.1 Introduction

6.1.1 Cash payments

The objective of the PAYE system is to deduct the correct amount of income tax and national insurance contributions from employees over the year. Its scope is very wide. It applies to most cash payments, other than reimbursed business expenses, and to certain non cash payments.

In addition to wages and salaries, PAYE applies to round sum expense allowances and payments instead of benefits. It also applies to any readily convertible asset.

A readily convertible asset is any asset which can effectively be exchanged for cash. The amount subject to PAYE is the amount that would be taxed as employment income. This is usually the cost to the employer of providing the asset.

Tips paid direct to an employee are normally outside the PAYE system (although still assessable as employment income).

It is the employer's duty to deduct income tax and national insurance contributions from the pay of his employees, whether or not he has been directed to do so by HMRC. **If he fails to do this he** (or sometimes the employee) **must pay over the tax which he should have deducted and the employer may be subject to penalties.**

6.1.2 Benefits

PAYE is not normally operated on benefits; instead the employee's PAYE code is restricted (see below).

However, PAYE must be applied to remuneration in the form of a taxable non-cash voucher if at the time it is provided:

(a) The voucher is capable of being exchanged for readily convertible assets; or
(b) The voucher can itself be sold, realised or traded.

PAYE must normally be operated on cash vouchers and on each occasion when a director/employee uses a credit-token (eg a credit card) to obtain money or goods which are readily convertible assets. However, a cash voucher or credit token which is used to pay expenses is not subject to PAYE.

6.2 How PAYE works

Employers must report PAYE information to HMRC under the Real Time Information (RTI) system.

Under RTI, **an employer is required to submit information to HMRC electronically**. This can be done by:

(a) Using commercial payroll software

(b) Using HMRC's Basic PAYE Tools software (designed for use by an employer who has up to nine employees)

(c) Using a payroll provider (such as an accountant or payroll bureau) to do the reporting on behalf of the employer

The employer reports payroll information electronically to HMRC, on or before any day when the employer pays someone (ie in 'real time'). This report will normally be carried out by the payroll software (or the payroll provider) at the same time that the payments are calculated and is called **a Full Payment Submission (FPS)**. The FPS includes include details of:

(a) The amounts paid to employees
(b) Deductions made under PAYE such as income tax and national insurance contributions
(c) Details of employees who have started employment or left employment since the last FPS

The software works out the amount of PAYE tax to deduct on any particular pay day by using the employees' code numbers (see below). Tax is normally worked out on a cumulative basis. This means that with each payment of earnings the running total of tax paid is compared with tax due on total earnings to that date. The difference between the tax due and the tax paid is the tax to be deducted on that particular payday.

National insurance contributions are also calculated by the software in relation to the earnings period (see later in this Text).

6.3 Payment under the PAYE system

Under PAYE, income tax and national insurance is normally paid over to HMRC monthly, 17 days after the end of the tax month (if paid electronically) or 14 days after the end of the tax month (if paid by cheque). Large employers (with 250 or more employees) must make electronic payments. **A tax month runs from 6th of one calendar month to the 5th of the following calendar month.** For example, for the tax month from 6 June 2014 to 5 July 2014, payment must be made by 22 July 2014 (electronically) or 19 July 2014 (cheque).

If an employer's average monthly payments under the PAYE system are less than £1,500, the employer may choose to pay quarterly, within 17 or 14 days (depending on the method of payment) **of the end of each tax quarter**. Tax quarters end on 5 July, 5 October, 5 January and 5 April. Payments can continue to be made quarterly during a tax year even if the monthly average reaches or exceeds £1,500, but a new estimate must be made and a new decision taken to pay quarterly at the start of each tax year.

6.4 PAYE codes

An employee is normally entitled to various allowances. Under the PAYE system an amount reflecting the effect of a proportion of these allowances is set against his pay each pay day. To determine the amount to set against his pay the allowances are expressed in the form of a code.

An employee's code may be any one of the following:

L   Tax code for people born after 5 April 1948
P   Tax code for people born between 6 April 1938 and 5 April 1948
Y   Tax code for people before 6 April 1938

The codes BR, DO and OT are generally used where there is a second source of income and all allowances have been used in a tax code which is applied to the main source of income. The BR code means that basic rate tax will be deducted without any allowances.

Generally, a tax code number is arrived at by deleting the last digit in the sum representing the employee's tax free allowances. Every individual is entitled to a personal tax free allowance of £10,000. The code number for an individual who is entitled to this but no other allowance is 1000L.

The code number may also reflect other items. For example, **it will be restricted to reflect benefits, small amounts of untaxed income** and **unpaid tax on income from earlier years**. If an amount of tax is in point, it is necessary to gross up the tax in the code using the taxpayer's estimated marginal rate of income tax.

Question	PAYE codes

Adrian was born in 1975 (suffix letter L) and earns £15,000 each tax year. He has benefits of £560 and his unpaid tax for 2012/13 was £58. Adrian is entitled to a tax free personal allowance of £10,000 in 2014/15. Adrian is a basic rate taxpayer. What is Adrian's PAYE code for 2014/15?

	£
Personal allowance	10,000
Benefits	(560)
Unpaid tax £58 × 100/20	(290)
Available allowances	9,150

Adrian's PAYE code is 915L

Codes are determined and amended by HMRC. They are normally notified to the employer on a code list. The employer must act on the code until amended instructions are received from HMRC, even if the employee has appealed against the code.

When the payroll is run, an employee is generally given 1/52nd or 1/12th of his tax free allowances against each week's/month's pay. However because of the cumulative nature of PAYE, if an employee is first paid in, say, September, that month he will receive six months' allowances against his gross pay. In cases where the employee's previous PAYE history is not known, this could lead to under-deduction of tax. To avoid this, codes for the employees concerned have to be operated on a 'week 1/month1' basis, so that only 1/52nd or 1/12th of the employee's allowances are available each week/month.

6.5 PAYE forms

FAST FORWARD

Employers must complete forms P60, P9D, P11D and P45 as appropriate. Form P60 is a year end return. A P45 is needed when an employee leaves. Forms P9D and P11D record details of benefits.

At the end of each tax year, the employer must provide each employee with a form P60. This shows total taxable earnings for the year, tax deducted, code number, NI number and the employer's name and address. **The P60 must be provided by 31 May following the year of assessment.**

Following the end of each tax year, the employer must submit to HMRC by 6 July:

(a) **Forms P11D** (benefits etc for directors and employees paid £8,500+ pa)
(b) **Forms P11D(b)** (return of Class 1A NICs (see later in this Text))
(c) **Forms P9D** (benefits etc for other employees)

A copy of the form P11D (or P9D) must also be provided to the employee by 6 July. The details shown on the P11D include the full cash equivalent of all benefits, so that the employee may enter the details on his self-assessment tax return. Specific reference numbers for the entries on the P11D are given to assist with the preparation of the employee's self assessment tax return.

When an employee leaves, a form P45 (particulars of Employee Leaving) must be prepared. This form shows the employee's code and details of his income and tax paid to date and is handed to the employee. One of the parts is the employee's personal copy. If the employee takes up a new employment, he must hand another part of the form P45 to the new employer. The details on the form are used by the new employer to calculate income tax due under PAYE when the payroll is next run.

6.6 Interest and penalties

Daily interest is charged on late payments of income tax and NICs under PAYE by taking the number of days by which a payment is late and applying the relevant late payment interest rate. HMRC make the charge after the end of the tax year.

Late payment penalties may be charged on PAYE amounts that are not paid in full and on time. For 2014/15 there will be no penalty if there is only a small underpayment, and penalties will be charged on a risk-assessed basis rather than automatically. Employers are not charged a penalty for the first late PAYE payment in a tax year, unless that payment is over six months late. The amounts of the penalties on

subsequent late payments in the tax year depends on how much is late each time and the number of times payments are late in a tax year. The maximum penalty is 4% of the amount that is late in the relevant tax month and applies to the 11th (or more) late payment that tax year. **Where a penalty has been imposed and the tax remains unpaid at six months, the further penalty is 5% of tax unpaid**, with a further 5% if tax remains unpaid at 12 months, even if there is only one late payment in the year.

There are also penalties for making late returns under RTI.

Exam focus point

Late filing penalties **will not be examined** in F6 (UK) exams from 1 April 2015 to 31 March 2016.

Penalties for inaccurate returns are subject to the common penalty regime for errors (see later in this Text).

6.7 PAYE settlement agreements

PAYE settlement agreements (PSAs) are arrangements under which employers can make single payments to settle their employees' income tax liabilities on expense payments and benefits which are minor, irregular or where it would be impractical to operate PAYE.

Chapter Roundup

- Most employees are taxed on benefits under the benefits code. 'Excluded employees' (lower paid/non-directors) are only subject to part of the provisions of the code.

- The benefit in respect of accommodation is its annual value. There is an additional benefit if the property cost over £75,000.

- Employees who have a company car are taxed on a % of the car's list price which depends on the level of the car's CO_2 emissions. The same % multiplied by £21,700 determines the benefit where private fuel is also provided.

- Cheap loans are charged to tax on the difference between the official rate of interest and any interest paid by the employee.

- 20% of the value of assets made available for private use is taxable.

- Workplace childcare is an exempt benefit. Employer-supported childcare and childcare vouchers are exempt up to £55 per week. Maximum tax relief is limited to £11 per week (the equivalent of £55 × 20%).

- There is a residual charge for other benefits, usually equal to the cost to the employer of the benefits.

- There are a number of exempt benefits including removal expenses, sporting facilities, and workplace parking.

- Most tax in respect of employment income is deducted under the PAYE system. The objective of the PAYE system is to collect the correct amount of tax over the year. An employee's PAYE code is designed to ensure that allowances etc are given evenly over the year.

- Employers must complete forms P60, P9D, P11D and P45 as appropriate. Form P60 is a year end return. A P45 is needed when an employee leaves. Forms P9D and P11D record details of benefits.

Quick Quiz

1   What accommodation does not give rise to a taxable benefit?

2   Mike is provided with a petrol-engined car by his employer throughout 2014/15. The car has a list price of £15,000 (although the employer actually paid £13,500 for it) and has CO_2 emissions of 125g/km. Mike's taxable car benefit is:

    A   £2,430
    B   £2,700
    C   £4,050
    D   £4,500

3   When may an employee who is provided with fuel by his employer avoid a fuel benefit?

4   To what extent are qualifying removal expenses paid for by an employer taxable?

5   Give an example of a PAYE code.

1   Job related accommodation

2   B. Amount by which CO_2 emissions exceed the baseline is $(125 - 95)$ $= 30 \div 5 = 6 + 12\%$
                                                                                $= 18\% \times £15,000$
                                                                                $= £2,700$

3   There is no fuel benefit if:

     (a)   All the fuel provided was made available only for business travel, or
     (b)   The full cost of any fuel provided for private use was completely reimbursed by the employee.

4   The first £8,000 of qualifying removal expenses are exempt. Any excess is taxable.

5   1000L.

Now try the questions below from the Practice Question Bank

Number	Type	Marks	Time
Q10	Section A	6	11 mins
Q11	Section B	10	18 mins
Q12	Section B	5	9 mins

Pensions

Topic list	Syllabus reference
1 Types of pension scheme and membership	B7(a)
2 Contributing to a pension scheme	B7(a)
3 Receiving benefits from pension arrangements	B7(a)

Introduction

In the previous two chapters we have discussed the taxation of employment income. Many employers offer their employees the option of joining an occupational pension scheme, and they may choose instead, or in addition, to take out a personal pension scheme run by a financial institution such as a bank or building society.

Self-employed or non-working individuals can only make provision for a pension using a personal pension scheme.

Whichever type of scheme is chosen the amount of tax relief available is the same. However, the method for giving the relief can be different: contributions to occupational schemes are usually deducted from gross pay before PAYE is calculated whilst contributions to personal pensions are paid net of basic rate tax and further tax relief is given through the personal tax computation. We cover both methods of giving tax relief in detail in this Chapter.

Study guide

		Intellectual level
B7	**The use of exemptions and reliefs in deferring and minimising income tax liabilities**	
(a)	Explain and compute the relief given for contributions to personal pension schemes and to occupational pension schemes.	2

Exam guide

Pension contributions can be paid by all individuals and you may come across them as part of an income tax question in Section B. In Section B you may also be required to discuss the types of pension schemes available and the limits on the tax relief due, or you may have to deal with them in an income tax computation. Pensions may be tested in a 15 mark question or a 10 mark question. Section A questions might test a specific aspect of pensions such as the amount of the annual allowance.

You must be sure that you know how to deal with the two ways of giving relief – contributions to occupational schemes are deducted from earnings whilst contributions to personal pensions are paid net of basic rate tax and further tax relief is given by increasing the basic rate and higher rate limits.

1 Types of pension scheme and membership

FAST FORWARD

An employee may be a member of his employer's occupational pension scheme. Any individual whether a member of an occupational pension scheme or not, can take out a 'personal pension' plan with a financial institution such as an insurance company, bank or building society.

1.1 Introduction

An individual is encouraged by the Government to make financial provision to cover his needs when he reaches a certain age. There are state pension arrangements which provide some financial support, but the Government are keen for individuals to make their own pension provision to supplement their state pensions.

Therefore tax relief is given for private pension provision. This includes both relief for contributions paid into pension schemes during an individual's working life and an exemption from tax on income and gains arising in the pension fund itself.

1.2 Pension arrangements

An individual may make pension provision in a number of ways.

1.2.1 Occupational pension scheme

Key term

Employers may set up an **occupational pension scheme**. Such schemes may either require contributions from employees or be non-contributory. The employer may use the services of an insurance company (an insured scheme) or may set up a totally self administered pension fund.

There are two kinds of occupational pension scheme – earnings-related (**defined benefits arrangements**) and investment-related (**money purchase arrangements**). In a **defined benefits arrangements** the pension is generally based on employees' earnings either at retirement (a **final salary** scheme) or throughout their employment (a **career average** scheme) and linked to the number of years they have worked for the employer.

A **money purchase pension** – also known as a **defined contribution scheme** – does not provide any guarantee regarding the level of pension which will be available. The individual invests in the pension scheme and the amount invested is used to build up a pension.

1.2.2 Personal pensions

Key term

> **Personal pensions** are money purchase schemes, which are provided by banks, insurance companies and other financial institutions.

Stakeholder pensions are a particular type of personal pension scheme. They must satisfy certain rules, such as a maximum level of charges, ease of transfer and so on.

Any individual (whether employed or not) may join a personal pension scheme.

1.2.3 More than one pension arrangement

An individual may make a number of different pension arrangements depending on his circumstances. For example, he may be a member of an occupational pension scheme and also make pension arrangements independently with a financial provider. If the individual has more than one pension arrangement, the rules we will be looking at in detail later apply to all the pension arrangements he makes. For example, **there is a limit on the amount of contributions that the individual can make in a tax year. This limit applies to all the pension arrangements that he makes, not** *each* **of them.**

The rules below apply to registered pension schemes, ie those registered with HMRC.

2 Contributing to a pension scheme

FAST FORWARD

> Anyone can contribute to a personal pension scheme, even if they are not earning, subject to the contributions threshold of £3,600 (gross).

2.1 Contributions by a scheme member

Any individual **under the age of 75 can make tax relievable pension contributions** in a tax year.

The maximum amount of contributions attracting tax relief made by an individual in a tax year is the higher of:

(a)   **The individual's relevant UK earnings chargeable to income tax in the year**
(b)   **The basic amount (set at £3,600 for 2014/15)**

These figures are gross contributions (see further below) and apply whether the individual pays into an occupational scheme, a personal pension scheme or both.

Relevant UK earnings are broadly employment income, trading income and income from furnished holiday lettings (see later in this Text).

If the individual does not have any UK earnings in a tax year, the maximum pension contribution he can obtain tax relief on is £3,600.

Where an individual contributes to more than one pension scheme, the aggregate of his contributions will be used to give the total amount of tax relief.

2.2 Methods of giving tax relief

Contributions to personal pension plans are paid net of basic rate tax. Higher/additional rate relief is given through the personal tax computation. Contributions to occupational pension schemes are usually paid under the net pay scheme.

2.2.1 Pension tax relief given at source

This method will be used where an individual makes a contribution to a pension scheme run by a personal pension provider such as an insurance company.

Relief is given at source by the contributions being deemed to be made net of basic rate tax. This applies whether the individual is an employee, self-employed or not employed at all and whether or not he has taxable income. HMRC then pay an amount of basic rate tax to the pension provider.

Further tax relief is given if the individual is a higher rate or additional rate taxpayer. The relief is given by increasing the basic rate limit and the higher rate limit for the year by the gross amount of contributions for which the taxpayer is entitled to relief. You will recognise this method as the same way in which relief is given for gift aid donations.

Exam focus point

Make sure your workings show clearly how you have increased the basic rate and higher rate limits. Note the difference between this method and that used for net pay arrangements (see below).

Question

Pension tax relief given at source

Joe has earnings of £60,000 in 2014/15. He pays a personal pension contribution of £7,200 (net). He has no other taxable income.

Show Joe's tax liability for 2014/15.

Answer

	Non savings Income £
Earnings/Net income	60,000
Less PA	(10,000)
Taxable income	50,000

Tax

	£
£40,865 (W) × 20%	8,173
£9,135 × 40%	3,654
50,000	11,827

Basic rate limit £31,865 + (£7,200 × 100/80) = £40,865

Remember that **gross personal pension contributions** are also used to compute **adjusted net income** and that **restrictions on the personal allowance and higher personal allowance** are calculated in relation to adjusted net income.

2.2.2 Net pay arrangements

An occupational scheme will normally operate **net pay arrangements**.

In this case, the employer will deduct gross pension contributions from the individual's earnings before operating PAYE. The individual therefore obtains tax relief at his marginal rate of tax automatically.

Question	Net pay arrangements

Maxine has taxable earnings of £60,000 in 2014/15. Her employer deducts a pension contribution of £9,000 from these earnings before operating PAYE. She has no other taxable income.

Show Maxine's tax liability for 2014/15.

Answer

	Non-savings Income £
Earnings/Total income	60,000
Less pension contribution	(9,000)
Net income	51,000
Less PA	(10,000)
Taxable income	41,000

Tax

	£
£31,865 × 20%	6,373
£9,135 × 40%	3,654
41,000	10,027

This is the same result as Joe in the previous example. Joe had received basic rate tax relief of £(9,000 – 7,200) = £1,800 at source, so his overall tax position was £(11,827 – 1,800) = £10,027.

2.3 Contributions not attracting tax relief

An individual can also make contributions to his pension arrangements which **do not attract tax relief, for example out of capital.** The member must notify the scheme administrator if he makes contributions in excess of the higher of his UK relevant earnings and the basic amount.

Such contributions do not count towards the annual allowance limit (discussed below) but will affect the value of the pension fund for the lifetime allowance.

2.4 Employer pension contributions

Where the individual is an employee, his **employer may make contributions to his pension scheme** as part of his employment benefits package. Such contributions are **exempt benefits** for the employee.

There is **no limit** on the amount of the contributions that may be made by an employer but **they always count towards the annual allowance** and will also affect the value of the pension fund for the lifetime allowance (see further below).

All contributions made by an employer are made gross and the employer will usually obtain tax relief for the contribution by deducting it as an expense in calculating trading profits for the period of account in which the payment is made.

2.5 Annual allowance

There is an overriding limit on the amount that can be paid into an individual's pension scheme for each tax year. This is called the annual allowance. Unused annual allowance can be carried forward for up to three years.

2.5.1 Introduction

The annual allowance effectively restricts the amount of tax relievable contributions that can be paid into an individual's pension scheme each year. The annual allowance for 2014/15 is £40,000. The amount of the annual allowance for 2011/12, 2012/13 and 2013/14 was £50,000.

Exam focus point

These amounts will be shown in the tax rates and allowances in the exam.

2.5.2 Carry forward of unused annual allowance

Where **an individual is a member of a registered pension scheme** but **does not make contributions of at least the annual allowance in a tax year**, the individual can **carry forward the unused amount of the annual allowance for up to three years**. In any year for which the individual is not a member of a pension scheme, the annual allowance does not apply and so there can be no carry forward.

The annual allowance in the current tax year is treated as being used first, then any unused annual allowance is brought forward from earlier years, using the earliest tax year first. For tax years before 2011/12, a notional £50,000 annual allowance applies to calculate the unused annual allowance in those years.

Question
Carry forward of annual allowance

Ted is a sole trader. His gross contributions to his personal pension scheme have been as follows:

2010/11	£21,000
2011/12	£26,000
2012/13	£46,000
2013/14	£35,000

In 2014/15 Ted has a good trading year and wishes to make a large pension contribution.

(a) What is the maximum gross tax relievable pension contribution Ted can make in 2014/15, taking into account any brought forward annual allowance?

(b) If Ted makes a gross personal pension contribution of £43,000 in 2014/15, what are the unused annual allowances he can carry forward to 2015/16?

Answer

(a)

	£
Annual allowance 2014/15	40,000
Annual allowance unused in 2011/12 £(50,000 – 26,000)	24,000
Annual allowance unused in 2012/13 £(50,000 – 46,000)	4,000
Annual allowance unused in 2013/14 £(50,000 – 35,000)	15,000
Maximum gross pension contribution in 2014/15	83,000

Note

The unused allowance from 2010/11 cannot be used in 2014/15 as this is more than three years after 2010/11.

(b)

	£
Annual allowance 2014/15 used in 2014/15	40,000
Annual allowance unused in 2011/12 used in 2014/15	3,000
Contribution in 2014/15	43,000

The remaining £(24,000 – 3,000) = £21,000 of the 2011/12 annual allowance cannot be carried forward to 2015/16 since this is more than three years after 2011/12. The unused annual allowances are therefore £4,000 from 2012/13 and £15,000 from 2013/14 and these are carried forward to 2015/16.

2.5.3 Contributions in excess of annual allowance

FAST FORWARD

An annual allowance charge arises if tax-relievable contributions exceed the available annual allowance.

If tax-relievable pension contributions exceed the annual allowance, there is a charge to income tax based on the individual's taxable income. This will occur if the taxpayer has relevant earnings in excess of the available annual allowance and makes a contribution in excess of the available annual allowance (including any brought forward annual allowance). **The taxpayer is primarily liable for the tax on the excess contribution.**

The annual allowance charge is calculated by taxing the excess contribution as an extra amount of income received by the taxpayer. The calculation therefore claws back the tax relief given on the pension contribution.

Question   Annual allowance charge

Jaida had employment income of £240,000 in 2014/15. She made a gross personal pension contribution of £70,000 in 2014/15. She does not have any unused annual allowance brought forward. What is Jaida's income tax liability for 2014/15?

Answer

	Non-savings Income £
Taxable income (no personal allowance available)	240,000
Tax	
£101,865 (W1) × 20%	20,373
£118,135 × 40%	47,254
£220,000 (W2)	
£20,000 × 45%	9,000
£240,000	
£30,000 (W3) × 45%	13,500
Tax liability	90,127

Workings

1   Basic rate limit £31,865 + £70,000 = £101,865
2   Higher rate limit £150,000 + £70,000 = £220,000
3   Excess pension contribution £(70,000 – 40,000) = £30,000

3 Receiving benefits from pension arrangements

3.1 Pension benefits

After reaching the minimum pension age of 55, an individual may 'vest' the benefits, ie set aside all or part of the pension fund to provide pension benefits. Normally an individual may take one quarter of his pension fund as a tax free lump sum, and the balance of the fund is usually used to purchase a pension (annual income) often referred to as an annuity. An individual under the age of 75 can usually both make tax-relieved contributions and receive pension benefits.

3.2 The lifetime allowance

FAST FORWARD

> An individual is not allowed to build up an indefinitely large pension fund. There is a maximum value for a pension fund called the lifetime allowance.

The amount of the **lifetime allowance for 2014/15 is £1,250,000**.

If the pension fund exceeds the lifetime allowance at the time the benefit starts to be taken ('vested') this will give rise to an income tax charge on the excess value of the fund. The rate of the charge is 55% if the excess value is taken as a lump sum, or 25% if the funds are left in the scheme to provide a pension.

Chapter Roundup

- An employee may be a member of his employer's occupational pension scheme. Any individual whether a member of an occupational pension scheme or not, can take out a 'personal pension' plan with a financial institution such as an insurance company, bank or building society.

- Anyone can contribute to a personal pension scheme, even if they are not earning, subject to the contributions threshold of £3,600 (gross).

- Contributions to personal pension plans are paid net of basic rate tax. Higher/additional rate relief is given through the personal tax computation. Contributions to occupational pension schemes are usually paid under the net pay scheme.

- There is an overriding limit on the amount that can be paid into an individual's pension scheme for each tax year. This is called the annual allowance. Unused annual allowance can be carried forward for up to three years.

- An annual allowance charge arises if tax-relievable contributions exceed the available annual allowance.

- An individual is not allowed to build up an indefinitely large pension fund. There is a maximum value for a pension fund called the lifetime allowance.

Quick Quiz

1   Martha has UK earnings of £3,000 in 2014/15. What is the maximum actual amount of pension contribution she can pay in 2014/15 to a personal pension?

    A   £2,400
    B   £2,880
    C   £3,000
    D   £3,600

2   Fern joined a registered pension scheme in 2012/13 and made a gross contribution of £24,000. She had not been a member of registered pension scheme before this time. She did not make any contribution in 2013/14. What is the maximum gross pension contribution Fern can make in 2014/15 without incurring an annual allowance charge, taking into account any brought forward annual allowance?

3   What are the consequences of the total of employee and employer pension contributions exceeding the annual allowance?

4   What are the consequences of exceeding the lifetime allowance?

1   B. The maximum gross contribution that Martha can pay is the higher of her relevant earnings (£3,000) and the basic amount (£3,600). She will actually pay £3,600 × 80% = £2,880 to the pension provider.

2   Fern will not be able to use any unused personal allowance from 2011/12 as she was not a member of a registered pension scheme in this year. She has £(50,000 − 24,000) = £26,000 unused from 2012/13 and £50,000 from 2013/14. Her total maximum contribution in 2014/15 without incurring an annual allowance charge is therefore £(26,000 + 50,000 + 40,000) = £116,000.

3   The excess is subject to the annual allowance charge primarily chargeable on the employee.

4   If the lifetime allowance is exceeded the excess is charged at 55% (if taken as a lump sum) or 25% (if taken as a pension).

Now try the questions below from the Practice Question Bank

Number	Type	Marks	Time
Q13	Section A	6	11 mins
Q14	Section B	6	11 mins

Property income

Topic list	Syllabus reference
1 Property business income	B4(a)
2 Furnished holiday lettings	B4(b)
3 Rent a room relief	B4(c)
4 Premiums on leases	B4(d)
5 Property business losses	B4(e)

Introduction

We have finished looking at an individual's employment income and can turn our attention to other income to be slotted into the tax computation.

We are now going to look at the computation and taxation of the profits of a property letting business. First we see how to work out the profit (you may like to return to this section once you have studied Chapters 8 and 9).

Next we look at the special conditions which must be satisfied if a letting is to be treated as a furnished holiday let and at the extra tax reliefs available if it is.

We then consider the special relief available to taxpayers who let out rooms in their own homes, rent a room relief.

Finally we see how part of a premium for granting a short lease is taxed as income, and briefly consider how to deal with property business losses.

In the following chapters we shall turn our attention to the profits of an actual trade, profession or vocation.

Study guide

		Intellectual level
B4	**Property and investment income**	
(a)	Compute property business profits.	2
(b)	Explain the treatment of furnished holiday lettings.	1
(c)	Understand rent-a-room relief.	1
(d)	Compute the amount assessable when a premium is received for the grant of a short lease.	2
(e)	Understand how relief for a property business loss is given.	2

Exam guide

You are likely to be required to compute property income as part of 10 or 15 mark question in Section B. You may find it in the context of income tax or corporation tax – the basic computational rules are the same (apart from interest paid which is not included as an expense when computing property income for corporation tax purposes). Specific aspects of property income such as lease premiums may be tested in a Section A question. Rent a room relief is an important relief for individuals (it does not apply to companies), and the special rules for furnished holiday lettings will only be examined in an income tax context. Remember that property income is non-savings income even though a property portfolio is usually regarded as an investment.

1 Property business income

FAST FORWARD   Property business profits are calculated on an accruals basis.

1.1 Profits of a property business

Income from land and buildings in the UK is taxed as non-savings income.

The profits of the UK property business are computed for tax years. Each tax year's profit is taxed in that year.

1.2 Computation of profits

A taxpayer with UK rental income is treated as running a business, his 'UK property business'. All the rents and expenses for all properties are pooled, to give a single profit or loss. Profits and losses are computed in the same way as trading profits are computed for tax purposes, on an **accruals basis**.

Expenses will often include rent payable where a landlord is himself renting the land which he in turn lets to others. For individuals, interest on loans to buy or improve properties is treated as an expense (on an accruals basis).

Relief is available for irrecoverable rent as an impairment loss.

1.3 Capital allowances

FAST FORWARD   If a residential property is let furnished a wear and tear allowance may be claimed in respect of the furniture. Capital allowances are not available.

Capital allowances are given on plant and machinery used in the UK property business in the same way as they are given for a trading business with an accounting date of 5 April (we will study capital allowances in

greater detail later in this Text). However, **capital allowances are not normally available on plant or machinery used in a dwelling but someone who lets a furnished property used as a dwelling (residential property) can instead claim the wear and tear allowance**.

If the wear and tear allowance is claimed, the actual cost of furniture is ignored, but an annual allowance is given of **10% of rents**. The rents are first reduced by amounts which are paid by the landlord but are normally a tenant's burden. These amounts include any **water rates** and **council tax** paid by the landlord.

Question
Property business income

Over the last few years Peter has purchased several residential properties in Manchester as 'buy to let' investments.

5 Whitby Ave is let out furnished at £500 per month. A tenant moved in on 1 March 2014 but left unexpectedly on 1 May 2015 having paid rent only up to 31 December 2014. The tenant left no forwarding address.

17 Bolton Rd has been let furnished to the same tenant for a number of years at £800 per month.

A recent purchase, 27 Turner Close, has been let unfurnished since 1 August 2014 at £750 per month. Before then, it had been empty whilst Peter redecorated it after its purchase in March 2014.

Pete's expenses during 2014/15 are:

	No 5 £	No 17 £	No 27 £
Insurance	250	250	200
Letting agency fees	–	–	100
Repairs	300	40	–
Redecoration	–	–	500

No 27 was in a fit state to let when Peter bought it but he wanted to redecorate the property as he felt this would allow him to achieve a better rental income. Water rates and council tax are paid by the tenants.

Calculate Peter's property business income for 2014/15.

Answer

	No 5 £	No 17 £	No 27 £
Accrued income			
12 × £500	6,000		
12 × £800		9,600	
8 × £750			6,000
Less:			
Insurance	(250)	(250)	(200)
Letting agency fees			(100)
Repairs	(300)	(40)	
Redecoration (N)			(500)
Impairment loss (irrecoverable rent) 3 × £500	(1,500)		
Wear and Tear Allowance			
£(6,000 – 1,500) × 10%	(450)		
£9,600 × 10%		(960)	
Property business income	3,500	8,350	5,200

Taxable property income for 2014/15	£17,050

Note: The redecoration of No.27 is an allowable expense. This is an example of the application of the case of *Odeon Associated Theatres Ltd v Jones 1971* (covered in more detail later in this Text) which showed that the cost of initial repairs to remedy normal wear and tear of a recently acquired asset was an allowable expense. This contrasts with the case of *Law Shipping v. CIR 1921* where the cost of initial

repairs to improve an asset recently acquired to make it fit to earn profits was disallowable capital expenditure. The key point in relation to No. 27 is that it was in a fit state to let when acquired.

2 Furnished holiday lettings

FAST FORWARD

Special rules apply to income from furnished holiday lettings. Whilst the income is taxed as normal as property business income, the letting is treated as if it were a trade. Capital allowances are available on the furniture and the income is relevant earnings for pension purposes. However, only carry forward trade loss relief is available.

2.1 Introduction

There are special rules for furnished holiday lettings (FHLs). The letting is treated as if it were a trade. This means that, although the income is taxed as income from a property business, the provisions which apply to actual trades also apply to furnished holiday lettings.

(a) **Capital allowances are available on furniture instead of the 10% wear and tear allowance.**

(b) The income qualifies as **relevant earnings for pension relief** (see earlier in this Text).

(c) **Capital gains tax rollover relief, entrepreneurs' relief and relief for gifts of business assets are available** (see later in this Text).

However, losses from FHLs are not treated as trade losses for relief against general income, early years loss relief and terminal loss relief. If a loss arises on a FHL, the only trade loss relief available is carry forward loss relief by deduction from the first available future profits of the same FHL business. Trading loss reliefs are dealt with later in this Text.

2.2 Conditions

Exam focus point

A FHL must be situated in the UK or in another state within the European Economic Area. However, only FHL situated within the UK are within the F6 syllabus.

The letting must be of furnished accommodation made on a **commercial basis with a view to the realisation of profit**. The property must also satisfy the following three conditions.

(a) **The availability condition** – the accommodation is available for commercial let as holiday accommodation to the public generally, for **at least 210 days during the year**.

(b) **The letting condition** – the accommodation is commercially let as holiday accommodation to members of the public for **at least 105 days during the year**.

   If the **landlord has more than one FHL**, at least one of which satisfies the 105 day rule ('qualifying holiday accommodation') and at least one of which does not, ('the underused accommodation'), he may elect to **average the occupation of the qualifying holiday accommodation and any or all of the underused accommodation**. If the average of occupation is at least 105 days, the under-used accommodation will be treated as qualifying holiday accommodation.

Exam focus point

It is possible to make an election so that a rental property continues to qualify as a furnished holiday letting for up to two years after the 105 day test ceases to be met. This election is not examinable.

(c) **The pattern of occupation condition** – **not more than 155 days in the year** fall during periods of longer term occupation. Longer term occupation is defined as a **continuous period of more than 31 days during which the accommodation is in the same occupation** unless there are abnormal circumstances.

If someone has furnished holiday lettings and other lettings, **draw up two income statements as if they had two separate property businesses**. This is so that the profits and losses can be identified for the special rules which apply to FHLs.

3 Rent a room relief

FAST FORWARD

> Rents received from letting a room in the taxpayer's home may be tax free under the rent a room scheme.

3.1 The exemption

If an individual lets a room or rooms, furnished, in his main residence as living accommodation, then a special exemption may apply under the rent a room scheme.

The limit on the exemption is gross rents (before any expenses or capital allowances) of £4,250 a year. This limit is halved if any other person (eg spouse/civil partner) also received income from renting accommodation in the property.

If gross rents are not more than the limit, the rents are wholly exempt from income tax and expenses are ignored. However, the taxpayer may claim to ignore the exemption, for example to generate a loss by taking into account both rent and expenses.

Exam focus point

> If you are asked to calculate property income in an exam don't overlook rent a room relief, but be sure to state whether the relief applies.

3.2 Alternative basis

If gross rents exceed the limit, the taxpayer will be taxed in the ordinary way, ignoring the rent a room scheme, unless he elects for the 'alternative basis'. If he so elects, he will be taxable on gross receipts less £4,250 (or £2,125 if the limit is halved), with no deductions for expenses.

3.3 Election

An election to ignore the exemption (if gross profits are below £4,250), or an election for the alternative basis (if gross profits exceed £4,250) must be made by the 31 January which is 22 months from the end of the tax year concerned. An election to ignore the exemption applies only for the tax year for which it is made, but an election for the alternative basis remains in force until it is withdrawn or until a year in which gross rents do not exceed the limit.

Question   Rent a room relief

Sylvia owns a house near the sea in Norfolk. She has a spare bedroom and during 2014/15 this was let to a chef working at a nearby restaurant for £85 per week which includes the cost of heating and electricity.

Sylvia estimates that her lodger costs her an extra £50 on gas, £25 on electricity, and £50 on buildings insurance each year. The wear and tear allowance applicable under the normal method would be £435. What is Sylvia's property income for 2014/15?

Answer

Sylvia's gross rents are above the rent a room limit. Therefore she has the following choices:

(1)   Under the normal method (no election needed), she can be taxed on her actual profit:

	£
Rental income £85 × 52	4,420
Less expenses (50 + 25 + 50 + 435)	(560)
	3,860

(2)   Under the 'alternative basis' (elect for rent a room relief):

Total rental income of £4,420 exceeds £4,250 limit, so taxable income is £170 (ie 4,420 – 4,250) if rent a room relief claimed.

Sylvia should claim rent a room relief and so be taxed on the 'alternative basis'.

4 Premiums on leases

FAST FORWARD A premium received on the grant of a lease may be partly taxable as property income.

When a premium or similar consideration **is received on the grant** (that is, by a landlord to a tenant) **of a short lease (50 years or less), part of the premium is treated as property income received in the year of grant.**

The premium taxed as property income is the whole premium, less 2% of the premium for each complete year of the lease, except the first year.

This rule does not apply on the **assignment** of a lease (one tenant selling his entire interest in the property to another).

4.1 Example: income element of premium

Janet granted a lease to Jack on 1 March 2015 for a period of 40 years. Jack paid a premium of £16,000. How much of the premium received by Janet is taxed as property income?

	£
Premium received	16,000
Less 2% × (40 –1) × £16,000	(12,480)
Taxable as property income	3,520

Note that if Janet **owned a 40 year lease and assigned it to Jack**, no part of the amount received would be taxed as property income.

4.2 Premiums paid by traders

FAST FORWARD If the premium is paid by a trader, a deduction can be made in computing taxable trading profits.

Where a trader pays a premium for a lease he may deduct an amount when computing his taxable trading profits in each year of the lease. The amount deductible is the figure taxed as property income on the landlord divided by the number of years of the lease.

You may want to look at this point again once you have studied trade profits later in this Text.

4.3 Example: deduction for premium paid by trader

On 1 July 2014 Bryony, a trader, pays Scott, the landlord, a premium of £30,000 for a ten year lease on a shop. Bryony makes up accounts to 31 December each year.

Scott is taxable on property income in 2014/15 of £30,000 – (£30,000 × (10 – 1) × 2%) = £24,600.

Bryony can therefore deduct £24,600/10 = £2,460 in each of the ten years of the lease. She starts with the accounts year in which the lease starts (year ended 31 December 2014) and apportions the relief to the nearest month. Her deduction for 2014/15 is therefore:

1 July 2014 to 31 December 2014: 6/12 × £2,460   £1,230

5 Property business losses

A loss on a property letting business is carried forward to set against future property business profits.

A loss from a UK property business is carried forward to set against the **first future profits from the UK property business**. It may be carried forward until the UK property business ends, but it must be used as soon as possible.

As explained above, however, FHL losses are dealt with under special rules so that **losses from a FHL business must be kept separate and can only be used against profits of the same FHL business**.

Chapter Roundup

- Property business profits are calculated on an accruals basis.

- If residential property is let furnished a wear and tear allowance may be claimed in respect of the furniture. Capital allowances are not available.

- Special rules apply to income from furnished holiday lettings. Whilst the income is taxed as normal as property business income, the letting is treated as if it were a trade. Capital allowances are available on the furniture and the income is relevant earnings for pension purposes. However, only carry forward trade loss relief is available.

- Rents received from letting a room in the taxpayer's home may be tax free under the rent a room scheme.

- A premium received on the grant of a lease may be partly taxable as property income.

- If the premium is paid by a trader, a deduction can be made in computing taxable trading profits.

- A loss on a property letting business is carried forward to set against future property business profits.

Quick Quiz

1   How is capital expenditure relieved for furnished lettings?

2   In order for property to be a furnished holiday letting it must be:

    (a)   Available for letting for at least _____ days during the year

    (b)   Actually let for at least _____ days during the year

    (c)   Not let as longer term accommodation for more than _____ days in the year (longer term occupation is a continuous period of more than _____ days in the same occupation)

    Fill in the blanks.

3   How much income per annum is tax free under the rent a room scheme?

    A   £2,125
    B   £4,250
    C   £4,500
    D   £8,105

BPP
LEARNING MEDIA

Answers to Quick Quiz

1   Except for furnished holiday lettings where capital allowances are available for the cost of furniture, capital expenditure on furnishings is relieved through the wear and tear allowance. The allowance is equal to 10% of rents less council tax and water rates (if paid by the landlord).

2   In order for property to be a furnished holiday letting it must be:

    (a)   Available for letting for at least **210** days during the year

    (b)   Actually let for at least **105** days during the year

    (c)   Not let as longer term accommodation for more than **155** days in the year (longer term occupation is a continuous period of more than **31** days in the same occupation)

3   B. £4,250

Number	Type	Marks	Time
Q15	Section A	6	11 mins
Q16	Section B	10	18 mins

Now try the questions below from the Practice Question Bank

Computing trading income

Topic list	Syllabus reference
1 The badges of trade	B3(b)
2 The adjustment of profits	B3(c)
3 Cash basis of accounting for small businesses	B3(d)
4 Pre-trading expenditure	B3(e)

Introduction

The final figure to slot into the income tax computation is income from self employment (trading income).

We are therefore going to look at the computation of profits of unincorporated businesses. We work out a business's profit as if it were a separate entity (the separate entity concept familiar to you from basic bookkeeping) but, as an unincorporated business has no legal existence apart from its trader, we cannot tax it separately. We have to feed its profit into the owner's personal tax computation.

Later chapters will consider capital allowances, which are allowed as an expense in the computation of profits, the taxation of business profits, and how trading losses can be relieved. We will then extend our study to partnerships, ie to groups of two or more individuals trading together.

Study guide

		Intellectual level
B3	**Income from self-employment**	
(b)	Describe and apply the badges of trade.	2
(c)	Recognise the expenditure that is allowable in calculating the tax-adjusted trading profit.	2
(d)	Explain and compute the assessable profits using the cash basis for small businesses.	2
(e)	Recognise the relief that can be obtained for pre-trading expenditure.	2

Exam guide

Section A questions on computing taxable trading income may test two or three particular adjustments such as the restriction for motor cars with high CO_2 emissions.

You are likely to have to compute trading profits in a Section B question. The computation may be for an individual, a partnership or a company. In each case the same principles are applied. You must however watch out for the adjustments which only apply to individuals, such as private use expenses. You may also be asked to explain the badges of trade in a Section B question. These topics may be tested as part of a 15 mark or a 10 mark question.

1 The badges of trade

FAST FORWARD

The badges of trade are used to decide whether or not a trade exists. If one does exist, the accounts profits need to be adjusted in order to establish the taxable profits.

Key term

A trade is defined in Income Tax Act 2007 only as 'any venture in the nature of trade'. Further guidance about the scope of this definition is found in a number of cases which have been decided by the Courts. This guidance is summarised in a collection of principles known as the **'badges of trade'**. These are set out below. They apply to both corporate and unincorporated businesses.

Exam focus point

You are not expected to know case names – we have included these below for your information only.

1.1 The subject matter

Whether a person is trading or not may sometimes be decided by examining the subject matter of the transaction. Some assets are commonly held as investments for their intrinsic value: an individual buying some shares or a painting may do so in order to enjoy the income from the shares or to enjoy the work of art. A subsequent disposal may produce a gain of a capital nature rather than a trading profit. But **where the subject matter of a transaction is such as would not be held as an investment** (for example 34,000,000 yards of aircraft linen (*Martin v Lowry 1927*) or 1,000,000 rolls of toilet paper (*Rutledge v CIR 1929*)), **it is presumed that any profit on resale is a trading profit.**

1.2 The frequency of transactions

Transactions which may, in isolation, be of a capital nature will be interpreted as **trading transactions where their frequency indicates the carrying on of a trade.** It was decided that whereas normally the purchase of a mill-owning company and the subsequent stripping of its assets might be a capital transaction, where the taxpayer was embarking on the same exercise for the fourth time he must be carrying on a trade (*Pickford v Quirke 1927*).

1.3 Existence of similar trading transactions or interests

If there is an **existing trade**, then a **similarity to the transaction which is being considered** may point to that transaction having a trading character. For example, a builder who builds and sells a number of houses may be held to be trading even if he retains one or more houses for longer than usual and claims that they were held as an investment (*Harvey v Caulcott 1952*).

1.4 The length of ownership

The courts may infer a venture in the nature of trade where **items purchased are sold soon afterwards**.

1.5 The organisation of the activity as a trade

The courts may infer that a trade is being carried on if the transactions are **carried out in the same manner as someone who is unquestionably trading**. For example, an individual who bought a consignment of whiskey and then sold it through an agent, in the same way as others who were carrying on a trade, was also held to be trading (*CIR v Fraser 1942*). On the other hand, if an **asset has to be sold in order to raise funds in an emergency, this is less likely to be treated as trading**.

1.6 Supplementary work and marketing

When work is done to make an asset more marketable, or **marketing steps are taken to find purchasers**, the Courts will be more ready to ascribe a trading motive. When a group of accountants bought, blended and recasked a quantity of brandy, they were held to be taxable on a trading profit when the brandy was later sold (*Cape Brandy Syndicate v CIR 1921*).

1.7 A profit motive

The absence of a profit motive will not necessarily preclude a tax charge as trading income, but its presence is a strong indication that a person is trading. The purchase and resale of £20,000 worth of silver bullion by the comedian Norman Wisdom, as a hedge against devaluation, was held to be a trading transaction (*Wisdom v Chamberlain 1969*).

1.8 The way in which the asset sold was acquired

If goods are acquired deliberately, trading may be indicated. If goods are acquired unintentionally, for example by gift or inheritance, their later sale is unlikely to be trading.

1.9 Method of finance

If the **purchaser has to borrow money to buy an asset such that he has to sell that asset quickly to repay the loan**, it may be inferred that trading was taking place. This was a factor in the *Wisdom v Chamberlain* case as Mr Wisdom financed his purchases by loans at a high rate of interest. It was clear that he had to sell the silver bullion quickly in order to repay the loan and prevent the interest charges becoming too onerous. On the other hand, taking out a long term loan to buy an asset (such as a mortgage on a house) would not usually indicate that trading is being carried on.

1.10 The taxpayer's intentions

Where a transaction is clearly trading on objective criteria, **the taxpayer's intentions are irrelevant**. If, however, a transaction has (objectively) a dual purpose, the taxpayer's intentions may be taken into account. An example of a transaction with a dual purpose is the acquisition of a site partly as premises from which to conduct another trade, and partly with a view to the possible development and resale of the site.

This test is not one of the traditional badges of trade, but it may be just as important.

2 The adjustment of profits

The net profit in the statement of profit or loss must be adjusted to find the taxable trading profit.

2.1 Illustrative adjustment

Exam focus point

The rules relating to profits from trades apply equally to profits from all professions and vocations.

Although the **net profit** shown in the statement of profit or loss is the starting point in computing the taxable trade profits, many adjustments may be required to calculate the taxable amount.

Exam focus point

Only international accounting standard terminology is used when presenting accounting information contained within an examination question. This applies for companies, sole traders and partnerships.

Here is an illustrative adjustment of a statement of profit or loss:

	£	£
Net profit		140,000
Add: expenditure charged in the accounts which is not deductible from trading profits	50,000	
income taxable as trading profits which has not been included in the accounts	30,000	
		80,000
		220,000
Less: profits included in the accounts but which are not taxable as trading profits	40,000	
expenditure which is deductible from trading profits but has not been charged in the accounts (eg capital allowances)	20,000	
		(60,000)
Adjusted taxable trading profit		160,000

You may refer to deductible and non-deductible expenditure as allowable and disallowable expenditure respectively. The two sets of terms are interchangeable.

Exam focus point

An examination question requiring adjustment to profit will direct you to start the adjustment with the net profit of £XXXX and to deal with all the items listed, indicating with a zero (0) any items which do not require adjustment. Marks will not be given for relevant items unless this approach is used. Therefore students who attempt to rewrite the statement of profit or loss will be penalised.

2.2 Accounting policies

The fundamental concept is that the profits of the business must be calculated in accordance with generally accepted accounting principles. These profits are subject to any adjustment specifically required for income tax purposes.

2.3 Deductible and non-deductible expenditure

Disallowable (ie non-deductible) expenditure must be added back to the net profit in the computation of the taxable trading profit. Any item not deducted wholly and exclusively for trade purposes is disallowable expenditure. Certain other items, such as depreciation, are specifically disallowable.

2.3.1 Introduction

Certain expenses are specifically disallowed by the legislation. These are covered below. If however a deduction is specifically permitted this overrides the disallowance.

2.3.2 Payments contrary to public policy and illegal payments

Fines and penalties are not deductible. However, **HMRC usually allow employees' parking fines incurred in parking their employer's cars while on their employer's business. Fines relating to traders, however, are never allowed.**

A payment is not deductible if making it constitutes an offence by the payer. This covers protection money paid to terrorists, and also bribes. Statute also prevents any deduction for payments made in response to blackmail or extortion.

2.3.3 Capital expenditure

Capital expenditure is not deductible. This means that depreciation is non-deductible.

Profits and losses on the sale of non-current assets must be deducted or added back respectively. Chargeable gains or allowable losses may be dealt with under capital gains tax (see later in this Text).

The most contentious items of expenditure will often be repairs (revenue expenditure) **and improvements** (capital expenditure).

- **The cost of restoration of an asset by, for instance, replacing a subsidiary part of the asset is revenue expenditure.** Expenditure on a new factory chimney replacement was allowable since the chimney was a subsidiary part of the factory (*Samuel Jones & Co (Devondale) Ltd v CIR 1951*). However, in another case a football club demolished a spectators' stand and replaced it with a modern equivalent. This was held not to be repair, since repair is the restoration by renewal or replacement of subsidiary parts of a larger entity, and the stand formed a distinct and *separate* part of the club (*Brown v Burnley Football and Athletic Co Ltd 1980*).

- **The cost of initial repairs to improve an asset recently acquired to make it fit to earn profits is disallowable capital expenditure.** In *Law Shipping Co Ltd v CIR 1923* the taxpayer failed to obtain relief for expenditure on making a newly bought ship seaworthy prior to using it.

- **The cost of initial repairs to remedy normal wear and tear of recently acquired assets is allowable revenue expenditure.** *Odeon Associated Theatres Ltd v Jones 1971* can be contrasted with the *Law Shipping* judgement. Odeon were allowed to charge expenditure incurred on improving the state of recently acquired cinemas.

Capital allowances may, however, be available as a deduction for capital expenditure from trading profits (see later in this Text).

Two exceptions to the 'capital' rule are worth noting.

(a) **The costs of registering patents and trade marks are deductible.**

(b) **Incidental costs of obtaining loan finance**, or of attempting to obtain or redeeming it, are deductible, other than a discount on issue or a premium on redemption (which are really alternatives to paying interest).

2.3.4 Expenditure not wholly and exclusively for the purposes of the trade

Expenditure is not deductible if it is not for trade purposes (the remoteness test), or if it reflects more than one purpose (the duality test). The private proportion of payments for motoring expenses, rent, heat and light and telephone expenses of a trader is non-deductible. If an exact apportionment is possible, relief is given on the business element. Where the payments are to or on behalf of employees, the full amounts are deductible but the employees are taxed under the benefits code (see earlier in this Text).

The **remoteness test** is illustrated by the following cases.

- *Strong & Co of Romsey Ltd v Woodifield 1906*
  A customer injured by a falling chimney when sleeping in an inn owned by a brewery claimed compensation from the company. The compensation was not deductible: 'the loss sustained by the appellant was not really incidental to their trade as innkeepers and fell upon them in their character not of innkeepers but of householders'.

- *Bamford v ATA Advertising Ltd 1972*
  A director misappropriated £15,000. The loss was not allowable: 'the loss is not, as in the case of a dishonest shop assistant, an incident of the company's trading activities. It arises altogether outside such activities'.

- Expenditure which is wholly and exclusively to benefit the trades of several companies (for example in a group) but is not wholly and exclusively to benefit the trade of one specific company is not deductible *(Vodafone Cellular Ltd and others v Shaw 1995)*.

- *McKnight (HMIT) v Sheppard (1999)* concerned expenses incurred by a stockbroker in defending allegations of infringements of Stock Exchange regulations. It was found that the expenditure was incurred to prevent the destruction of the taxpayer's business and that as the expenditure was incurred for business purposes it was deductible. It was also found that although the expenditure had the effect of preserving the taxpayer's reputation, that was not its purpose, so there was no duality of purpose.

The **duality test** is illustrated by the following cases.

- *Caillebotte v Quinn 1975*
  A self-employed carpenter spent an average of 40p per day when obliged to buy lunch away from home but just 10p when he lunched at home. He claimed the excess 30p. It was decided that the payment had a dual purpose and was not deductible: a taxpayer 'must eat to live not eat to work'.

- *Mallalieu v Drummond 1983*
  Expenditure by a lady barrister on black clothing to be worn in court (and on its cleaning and repair) was not deductible. The expenditure was for the dual purpose of enabling the barrister to be warmly and properly clad as well as meeting her professional requirements.

- *McLaren v Mumford 1996*
  A publican traded from a public house which had residential accommodation above it. He was obliged to live at the public house but he also had another house which he visited regularly. It was held that the private element of the expenditure incurred at the public house on electricity, rent, gas, etc was not incurred for the purpose of earning profits, but for serving the non-business purpose of satisfying the publican's ordinary human needs. The expenditure, therefore had a dual purpose and was disallowed.

However, the cost of overnight accommodation when on a business trip may be deductible and reasonable expenditure on an evening meal and breakfast in conjunction with such accommodation is then also deductible.

2.3.5 Impairment losses (bad debts)

Only impairment losses where the liability was incurred wholly and exclusively for the purposes of the trade are deductible for taxation purposes. For example, **loans to employees written off are not deductible** unless the business is that of making loans, or it can be shown that the writing-off of the loan was earnings paid out for the benefit of the trade.

Under generally accepted accounting principles, a review of all trade receivables should be carried out to assess their fair value at the balance sheet date and any impairment losses written off. **The tax treatment follows the accounting treatment so no adjustment is required for tax purposes.** General provisions (ie those calculated as a percentage of total trade receivables, without reference to specific receivables) will now rarely be seen. In the event that they do arise, increases or decreases in a general provision are not allowable /taxable and an adjustment will need to be made.

Where a tax deduction has been taken for an impairment loss, but the relevant debt is later recovered, the recovery is taxable so no adjustment is required to the amount of the recovery shown in the statement of profit or loss.

2.3.6 Unpaid remuneration and employee benefit contributions

If earnings for employees are charged in the accounts but are not paid within nine months of the end of the period of account, the cost is only deductible for the period of account in which the earnings are paid. When a tax computation is made within the nine month period, it is initially assumed that unpaid earnings will not be paid within that period. The computation is adjusted if they are so paid.

Earnings are treated as paid at the same time as they are treated as received for employment income purposes.

Similar rules apply to employee benefit contributions.

2.3.7 Entertaining and gifts

The general rule is that expenditure on entertaining and gifts is non-deductible. This applies to amounts reimbursed to employees for specific entertaining expenses and gifts, and to round sum allowances which are exclusively for meeting such expenses. There is no distinction between UK and overseas customer entertaining for income tax and corporation tax purposes (you will find out later in this Text that a different rule applies for value added tax).

There are specific exceptions to the general rule:

- **Entertaining for and gifts to employees are normally deductible** although where gifts are made, or the entertainment is excessive, a charge to tax may arise on the employee under the benefits legislation.

- Gifts to customers not costing more than £50 per donee per year are allowed if they carry a conspicuous advertisement for the business and are not food, drink, tobacco or vouchers exchangeable for goods.

- **Gifts to charities may also be allowed** although many will fall foul of the 'wholly and exclusively' rule above (see further later in this Chapter). If a gift aid declaration is made by an individual in respect of a gift, tax relief will be given under the gift aid scheme, not as a trading expense. If a qualifying charitable donation is made by a company, it will be given tax relief by deduction from total profits (we deal with companies later in this Text).

2.3.8 Lease charges for cars with CO_2 emissions exceeding 130g/km

There is a restriction on the leasing costs of a car with CO_2 emissions exceeding 130 g/km. 15% of the leasing costs will be disallowed in the adjustment of profits calculation.

Question

Restriction for car leasing costs

Mandy is a sole trader. In May 2014 she leased a car for use in her business. The leasing costs for 2014/15 were £4,000. The car had CO_2 emissions of 141g/km.

What is the amount of the leasing costs that will be disallowed in the adjustment of profits calculation?

Answer

Since the car has CO_2 emissions exceeding 130 g/km, 15% of the leasing costs will be disallowed ie £4,000 × 15% = £600. This disallowed amount will be added back to the net profit assuming the full leasing cost of £4,000 has originally been deducted in calculating the net profit. If the leasing cost has not been deducted in calculating the net profit, then the allowable 85% of the leasing cost can be deducted.

2.3.9 Patent royalties and copyright royalties

Patent royalties and copyright royalties paid in connection with an individual's trade are deductible as trading expenses.

2.3.10 National insurance contributions

No deduction is allowed for any national insurance contributions **except for employer's contributions**. For your exam, these are Class 1 secondary contributions and Class 1A contributions (see later in this Text).

2.3.11 Penalties and interest on tax

Penalties and interest on late paid tax are not allowed as a trading expense. For the purpose of your exam, tax includes income tax, capital gains tax, corporation tax (for companies), and VAT.

2.3.12 Appropriations

Salary or interest on capital paid to a trader are not deductible. A salary paid to a member of the trader's family is allowed as long as it is not excessive in respect of the work performed by that family member.

The private proportion of payments for motoring expenses, rent, heat and light and telephone expenses of a trader is not deductible. Where the payments are to or on behalf of employees, the full amounts are deductible but are taxed on the employees as benefits for income tax.

Payments of the trader's income tax and national insurance contributions are not deductible.

Question

Adjusted taxable trade profits

Here is the statement of profit or loss of John Dodd, a trader.

Statement of profit or loss for year ended 31 May 2014

	£	£
Gross profit		79,500
Other income		
Bank interest received		500
Expenses		
Wages and salaries (N1)	47,000	
Rent and rates	12,000	
Depreciation	1,500	
Motor expenses – cars owned by business (N2)	5,000	
Motor expenses – cost of leased car CO_2 emissions 150g/km (N4)	500	
Entertainment expenses – customers	750	
Office expenses	1,350	
		(68,100)
Finance costs		
Interest payable on overdraft		(1,500)
Net profit		10,400

Notes

1   Salaries include £10,000 paid to John Dodd's wife, Julie, who works part time in the business. If John had employed another person to do this work, John would have had to pay at least this amount.

2   Motor expenses on cars owned by the business are £3,000 for John Dodd's car used 20% privately and £2,000 for his part-time salesman's car used 40% privately.

3   Capital allowances are £860.

4   The lease of the car started on 1 May 2014. No private use on the leased car.

Compute the adjusted taxable trade profit for the year ended 31 May 2014. You should start with the net profit figure of £10,400 and indicate by the use of zero (0) any items which do not require adjustment.

Answer

Adjusted taxable trading profit for year 31 May 2014

		£	£
Net profit			10,400
Add:	wages and salaries	0	
	rents and rates	0	
	depreciation	1,500	
	trader private motor expenses (£3,000 × 20%)	600	
	salesman's car	0	
	leased car cost disallowed (£500 × 15%)	75	
	entertainment expenses customers	750	
	office expenses	0	
	interest payable on overdraft	0	
			2,925
			13,325
Deduct:	bank interest received	(500)	
	capital allowances	(860)	
			(1,360)
Profit adjusted for tax purposes			11,965

Note. The employee's private motor expenses are allowable for the trader but the provision of the car will be taxed on the employee as an income tax benefit. The salary paid to John Dodd's wife is allowed as it is reasonable remuneration for the work actually done.

2.3.13 Subscriptions and donations

The general 'wholly and exclusively' rule determines the deductibility of expenses. Subscriptions and donations are not deductible unless the expenditure is for the benefit of the trade. The following are the main types of subscriptions and donations you may meet and their correct treatments.

- Trade subscriptions (such as to a professional or trade association) are generally deductible.

- Charitable donations are generally deductible only if they are small and to local charities.

- Political subscriptions and donations are generally not deductible.

- When a business makes a gift of equipment manufactured, sold or used in the course of its trade to an educational establishment or for a charitable purpose, nothing need be brought into account as a trading receipt.

2.3.14 Legal and professional charges

Legal and professional charges relating to capital or non-trading items are not deductible. These include charges incurred in acquiring new capital assets or legal rights, issuing shares, drawing up partnership agreements and litigating disputes over the terms of a partnership agreement.

Professional charges are deductible if they relate directly to trading. Deductible items include:

*   Legal and professional charges incurred defending the taxpayer's title to non-current assets
*   Charges connected with an action for breach of contract
*   Expenses of the **renewal** (not the original grant) of a lease for less than 50 years
*   Charges for trade debt collection
*   Normal charges for preparing accounts/assisting with the self assessment of tax liabilities

Accountancy expenses arising out of an enquiry into the accounts information in a particular year's return are not allowed where the enquiry reveals discrepancies and additional liabilities for the year of enquiry, or any earlier year, which arise as a result of negligent or fraudulent conduct.

Where, however, the enquiry results in no addition to profits, or an adjustment to the profits for the year of enquiry only and that assessment does not arise as a result of negligent or fraudulent conduct, the additional accountancy expenses are allowable.

2.3.15 Interest

Interest paid by an individual on borrowings for trade purposes is deductible as a trading expense on an accruals basis, so no adjustment to the accounts figure is needed.

Individuals cannot deduct interest on overdue tax.

2.3.16 Miscellaneous deductions

Here is a list of various other items that you may meet.

Item	Treatment	Comment
Educational courses for staff	Allow	
Educational courses for trader	Allow	If to update existing knowledge or skills, not if to acquire new knowledge or skills
Removal expenses (to new business premises)	Allow	Only if not an expansionary move
Travelling expenses to the trader's place of business	Disallow	*Ricketts v Colquhoun 1925*: unless an itinerant trader (*Horton v Young 1971*)
Counselling services for employees leaving employment	Allow	If qualify for exemption from employment income charge on employees
Pension contributions (to schemes for employees and company directors)	Allow	If paid, not if only provided for; special contributions may be spread over the year of payment and future years
Premiums for insurance: • against an employee's death or illness • to cover locum costs or fixed overheads whilst the policyholder is ill	Allow	Receipts are taxable
Damages paid	Allow	If not too remote from trade: *Strong and Co v Woodifield 1906*
Improving an individual's personal security	Allow	Provision of a car, ship or dwelling is excluded

2.4 Income taxable as trading income but excluded from the accounts

The usual example is when a trader takes goods for his own use. In such circumstances the selling price of the goods if sold in the open market is added to the accounting profit. If the trader pays anything for the goods, this is left out of the account. In other words, the trader is treated for tax purposes as having made a sale to himself.

This rule does not apply to supplies of services, which are treated as sold for the amount (if any) actually paid (but the cost of services to the trader or his household is not deductible).

2.5 Accounting profits not taxable as trading income

FAST FORWARD

Receipts not taxable as trading profit must be deducted from the net profit. For example, rental income and interest received are not taxable as trading profit. The rental income is taxed instead as property business income, whilst the interest is taxed as savings income.

There are three types of receipts which may be found in the accounting profits but which must be excluded from the taxable trading profit computation. These are:

(a) **Capital receipts**
(b) **Income taxed in another way** (at source or as another type of income)
(c) **Income specifically exempt from tax**

However, compensation received in one lump sum for the loss of income is likely to be treated as income (*Donald Fisher (Ealing) Ltd v Spencer 1989*).

Income taxed as another type of income, for example rental income, is excluded from the computation of taxable trading profits but it is brought back into the income tax computation further down as property business income. Similarly capital receipts are excluded from the computation of taxable trading profits but they may be included in the computation of chargeable gains (see later in this Text).

2.6 Deductible expenditure not charged in the accounts

FAST FORWARD

Amounts not charged in the accounts that are deductible from trading profits must be deducted when computing the taxable trading income. An example is capital allowances.

Capital allowances (see the next Chapter) are an example of deductible expenditure not charged in the accounts.

A second example is **an annual sum which can be deducted by a trader that has paid a lease premium to a landlord who is taxable on the premium as property business income** (see earlier in this Text). Normally, the amortisation of the lease will have been deducted in the accounts and must be added back as an appropriation of profit.

Question		Adjustment of profits

Here is the statement of profit or loss of Steven Pring, a trader.

	£	£
Gross profit		90,000
Other income		
Bank interest received		860
c/f		90,860

	£	£
c/f		90,860
Expenses		
Wages and salaries	59,000	
Rent and rates	8,000	
Depreciation	1,500	
Impairment losses (trade)	150	
Entertainment expenses for customers	750	
Patent royalties paid	3,200	
Legal expenses on acquisition of new factory	250	
		(72,850)
Finance costs		
Bank interest paid		(300)
Net profit		17,710

Salaries include £15,000 paid to Steven Pring's wife, Melanie, who works full time in the business.

Compute the adjusted taxable trade profit. You should start with the net profit figure of £17,710 and indicate by the use of zero (0) any items which do not require adjustment.

Answer

	£	£
Net profit		17,710
Add: wages and salaries (Melanie's salary not excessive for full time work)	0	
rent and rates	0	
depreciation	1,500	
impairment losses (trade)	0	
entertainment expenses for customers	750	
patent royalties	0	
legal expenses (capital)	250	
bank interest paid	0	
		2,500
		20,210
Less bank interest received		(860)
Profit adjusted for tax purposes		19,350

3 Cash basis of accounting for small businesses

3.1 Introduction

FAST FORWARD

An election can be made for an unincorporated business to calculate trading profits on the cash basis (instead of in accordance with generally accepted accounting principles) in certain circumstances.

Usually, **businesses prepare accounts using generally accepted accounting principles for tax purposes.** In particular, this means that **income and expenses are dealt with on an accruals basis**. This is referred to as **'accruals accounting'** in this section.

Certain small unincorporated businesses may elect to use cash accounting (known as 'the cash basis') rather than accruals accounting for the purposes of calculating their taxable trading income.

Exam focus point

The detailed cash basis rules are quite complex. These **more complex aspects are not examinable at Paper F6 (UK)**. In any examination question involving an unincorporated business, **it should be assumed that the cash basis is not relevant unless it is specifically mentioned**.

3.2 Which businesses can use the cash basis?

The cash basis can only be used by **unincorporated businesses** (sole traders and partnerships) **whose receipts for the tax year do not exceed the value added tax (VAT) registration threshold** (currently £81,000 – this figure is given in the Tax rates and Allowances available in the exam).

An election must be made for the cash basis to apply. The election is generally effective for the tax year for which it is made and all subsequent tax years.

However **a business must cease to use the cash basis** if:

(a)   (i)   **Receipts in the previous tax year exceeded twice the VAT registration threshold for that year** (the threshold in 2013/14 was £79,000), and

       (ii)   **Receipts for the current year exceed the VAT registration for that year**; or

(b)   Its **'commercial circumstances' change** such that the **cash basis is no longer appropriate** and **an election is made to use accruals accounting.**

3.3 Calculation of taxable profits under the cash basis

3.3.1 Introduction

The taxable trading profits under the cash basis are calculated as:

(a)   **Cash receipts**; less
(b)   **Deductible business expenses actually paid in the period.**

3.3.2 Cash receipts

Cash receipts include all amounts received relating to the business including cash and card receipts. They include **amounts received from the sale of plant and machinery, other than on the sale of motor cars.** We look at the definition of plant and machinery when we look at capital allowances later in this Text.

Receipts from the sale of motor cars and capital assets which are not classed as plant and machinery (eg land) are not taxable receipts.

3.3.3 Deductible business expenses

Under the cash basis, business expenses are deductible when they are paid.

Business expenses for the cash basis of accounting include capital expenditure on plant and machinery (except motor cars). Other capital expenses are not business expenses eg purchase of land, motor cars, and legal fees on such purchases.

The majority of the specific tax rules covered earlier in this chapter concerning the deductibility of business expenses also apply when the cash basis is used. It should be remembered, in particular, that only business expenses are tax deductible so that any private element must be disallowed. **Fixed rate expenses** for private use of motor cars and business premises used for private purposes may be used instead (see further below).

3.3.4 Fixed rate expenses

FAST FORWARD

> Fixed rate expenses can be used in relation to expenditure on motor cars and business premises partly used as the trader's home.

Exam focus point

> Although the **use of fixed rate expenses is optional**, in **any examination question involving the cash basis**, it should be assumed that, where relevant, **expenses are claimed on this basis.**
>
> The option of claiming expenses on a fixed rate basis is also available to unincorporated businesses generally, but it will **only be examined in F6 (UK) within the context of the cash basis.**

Where a business elects to use the cash basis, for Paper F6 (UK) purposes, it will be assumed to use **fixed rate expenses** rather than make deductions on the usual basis of actual expenditure incurred.

For Paper F6 (UK) purposes, fixed rate expenses relate to:

(a) **Expenditure on motor cars**
(b) **Business premises partly used as the trader's home**

These are dealt with in detail in the following two subsections.

3.3.5 Fixed rate mileage expense

The **fixed rate mileage (FRM) expense** can be claimed in respect of **motor cars** which are **owned or leased by the business** and which are **used for business purposes by the sole trader/partner or an employee of the business.**

The **FRM expense is calculated as the business mileage times the appropriate rate per mile.** The appropriate mileage rates for motor cars are **45p per mile for the first 10,000 miles**, then **25p per mile thereafter**.

Exam focus point

These rates are the **same as the authorised mileage rates for employment income** given in the Tax rates and Allowances available in the exam.

3.3.6 Business premises used partly as trader's home

A **fixed rate monthly adjustment can be made where a sole trader/partner uses part of the business premises as his home eg where a sole trader runs a small hotel or guesthouse and also lives in it.** The adjustment is deducted from the actual allowable business premises costs to reflect the private portion of household costs, including food, and utilities (eg heat and light). It does not include mortgage interest, rent, council tax or rates: apportionment of these expenses must be made based on the extent of the private occupation of the premises.

The deductible fixed rate amount depends on **how many people use the business premises each month as a private home**:

Number relevant occupants	Non-business use amount
1	£350
2	£500
3 or more	£650

Exam focus point

These rates will be **given in the examination question**, if relevant.

Be careful when using these amounts – they are **not the deductible expense itself but the disallowable amount**.

3.4 Example

Larry started trading as an interior designer on 6 April 2014. The following information is relevant for the year to 5 April 2015.

Revenue was £65,000 of which £8,000 was owed as receivables at 5 April 2015.

A motor car was acquired on 6 April 2014 for £15,000. Larry drove 10,000 miles in the car during the year to 5 April 2015 of which 3,000 miles were for private journeys. The car qualifies for a capital allowance of £1,890, after taking account of private use. The motoring costs were £2,000. The fixed rate mileage expense for motoring is 45p per mile for the first 10,000 miles, then 25p per mile after that.

Machinery was acquired on 1 May 2014 for £4,000. The machinery qualifies for a capital allowance of £4,000.

Other allowable expenses were £12,000 of which £1,000 was owed as payables at 5 April 2015.

If Larry uses the accruals accounting basis and does not use fixed rate expenses, his trading profit will be calculated as follows:

	£	£
Revenue (accruals)		65,000
Less: capital allowance on motor car	1,890	
business motoring expenses £2,000 × 7,000/10,000	1,400	
capital allowance on machinery	4,000	
other allowable expenses (accruals)	12,000	
		(19,290)
Taxable trading profit		45,710

If Larry uses the cash basis of accounting and fixed rate expenses, his trading profit will be calculated as follows:

	£	£
Revenue (cash received £65,000 – £8,000)		57,000
Less: FRM on car 7,000 × 45p	3,150	
cost of machinery	4,000	
other allowable expenses (cash paid £12,000 – £1,000)	11,000	
		(18,150)
Taxable trading profit		38,850

3.5 Basis of assessment

A trader using the cash basis can, like any other trader, prepare his accounts to any date in the year. The basis of assessment rules which determine in which tax year the profits of an accounting period are taxed apply in the same way for accruals accounting and cash basis traders (see later in this Text).

3.6 Losses

A net cash deficit (ie a loss) can normally only be relieved against future cash surpluses (ie future trading profits). Cash basis traders cannot offset a loss against other income or gains. Trading losses for the accruals accounting traders are dealt with in detail later in this Text.

4 Pre-trading expenditure

FAST FORWARD

Pre-trading expenditure incurred within the seven years prior to the commencement of trade is allowable if it would have been allowable had the trade already started.

Expenditure incurred before the commencement of trade is deductible, if it is incurred within seven years of the start of trade and it is of a type that would have been deductible had the trade already started. **It is treated as a trading expense incurred on the first day of trading.**

Chapter Roundup

- The badges of trade are used to decide whether or not a trade exists. If one does exist, the accounts profits need to be adjusted in order to establish the taxable profits.

- The net profit in the statement of profit or loss must be adjusted to find the taxable trading profit.

- Disallowable (ie non-deductible) expenditure must be added back to the net profit in the computation of the taxable trading profit. Any item not deducted wholly and exclusively for trade purposes is disallowable expenditure. Certain other items, such as depreciation, are specifically disallowable.

- Receipts not taxable as trading profit must be deducted from the net profit. For example, rental income and interest received are not taxable as trading profit. The rental income is taxed instead as property business income, whilst the interest is taxed as savings income.

- Amounts not charged in the accounts that are deductible from trading profits must be deducted when computing the taxable trading income. An example is capital allowances.

- An election can be made for an unincorporated business to calculate trading profits on the cash basis (instead of in accordance with generally accepted accounting principles) in certain circumstances.

- Fixed rate expenses can be used in relation to expenditure on motor cars and business premises partly used as the trader's home.

- Pre-trading expenditure incurred within the seven years prior to the commencement of trade is allowable if it would have been allowable had the trade already started.

1   List the traditional badges of trade.

2   What are the remoteness test and the duality test?

3   No adjustment for taxation is required to the accounts for deduction of a trader's salary. True/False?

4   Sid is a sole trader. Included in his most recent statement of profit or loss are the following deductions:

£3,000 legal fees for acquiring a new 15-year lease of his business premises.

£180 car parking fines incurred by Sid whilst on business trips.

£40 interest for late payment of Sid's previous year's income tax.

How much must be added back to the net profit figure when calculating the tax adjusted profit figure?

A   £3,180
B   £3,220
C   £220
D   £3,040

5   Which ONE of the following items of expenditure will Leila, a fashion designer, be allowed to deduct in calculating her tax adjusted trading profit?

A   The cost of building a new wall in front of her retail shop

B   The cost of installing air conditioning in her workshop

C   The cost of initial repairs to a recently acquired second-hand office building which was not usable until the repairs were carried out

D   The cost of redecorating her retail shop

6   Which ONE of the following is an allowable trading expense for a sole trader?

A   Gift of fleece jackets to customers with trade logo costing £60 each
B   A subscription to a political party
C   Legal fees in respect of employment contracts
D   A Gift Aid donation

7   Which businesses can use the cash basis of accounting?

8   Pre-trading expenditure is deductible if it is incurred within ____ years of the start of trade and is of a type that would have been deductible if the trade had already started. Fill in the blank.

1   The subject matter
    The frequency of transactions
    Existence of similar trading transactions or interests
    The length of ownership
    The organisation of the activity as a trade
    Supplementary work and marketing
    Method of finance
    A profit motive
    The way in which the goods were acquired

2   Expenditure is not deductible if it is not for trade purposes (the remoteness test) or if it reflects more than one purpose (the duality test).

3   False. The trader's salary must be added back as it is an appropriation of profit.

4   B   All three items are disallowed and must be added back.

5   D   The cost of redecoration is an allowable expense in calculating trading profit. The other expenditure is capital expenditure and so is not allowable.

6   C   Legal fees on employment contracts are an allowable income expense.

7   Unincorporated businesses (sole traders and partnerships) whose receipts for the tax year do not exceed the value added tax (VAT) registration threshold can elect to use the cash basis of accounting.

8   Pre-trading expenditure is deductible if it is incurred within **seven** years of the start of the trade and is of a type that would have been deductible if the trade had already started.

Now try the question below from the Practice Question Bank

Number	Type	Marks	Time
Q17	Section A	6	11 mins
Q18	Section B	15	27 mins
Q19	Section B	6	11 mins

Capital allowances

Topic list	Syllabus reference
1 Capital allowances in general	B3(h)
2 Plant and machinery – qualifying expenditure	B3(h)(i)
3 The main pool	B3(h)(ii), (iii), (iv)
4 Special rate pool	B3(h)(ii), (iii), (vi)
5 Private use assets	B3(h)(ii), (iv)
6 Motor cars	B3(h)(iii)
7 Short life assets	B3(h)(v)

Introduction

We saw in the last chapter that depreciation cannot be deducted in computing taxable trade profits and that capital allowances may be given instead. In this chapter, we look at the rules for calculating capital allowances, starting with plant and machinery.

Our study of plant and machinery falls into three parts. First, we look at what qualifies for allowances: many business assets obtain no allowances at all.

Secondly, we see how to compute the allowances on the main pool and the special rate pool.

Lastly, we look at the special rules for assets with private use, motor cars and assets with short lives.

You may wish to return to this chapter while you are studying Chapter 20 on companies.

Study guide

		Intellectual level
B3	**Income from self-employment**	
(h)	Capital allowances	
(i)	Define plant and machinery for capital allowances purposes.	1
(ii)	Compute writing down allowances, first year allowances and the annual investment allowance.	2
(iii)	Compute capital allowances for motor cars.	2
(iv)	Compute balancing allowances and balancing charges.	2
(v)	Recognise the treatment of short life assets.	2
(vi)	Recognise the treatment of assets included in the special rate pool.	2

Exam guide

Section A questions on capital allowances may focus on one particular type of asset such as a motor car.

In Section B, you may have to answer a whole question on capital allowances or a capital allowances computation may be included as a working in a computation of taxable trading profits. This may be as part of a 15 mark question or a 10 mark question.

The computations may be for either income tax or corporation tax purposes; the principles are basically the same. Look out for private use assets; only restrict the capital allowances if there is private use by **traders**, never restrict capital allowances for private use by **employees**. This means that when you calculate capital allowances for a company there will never be any private use adjustments. Also watch out for the length of the period of account; you may need to scale WDAs and the AIA up (income tax only) or down (income tax or corporation tax).

1 Capital allowances in general

Capital allowances are available to give tax relief for certain capital expenditure.

Capital expenditure is not deducted in computing taxable trade profits when using the accruals method of accounting, but it *may* attract capital allowances. Capital allowances are treated as a trading expense and are deducted in arriving at taxable trade profits. Balancing charges, effectively negative allowances, are added in arriving at those profits.

Capital expenditure on plant and machinery qualifies for capital allowances. Both unincorporated businesses (sole traders and partnerships) and companies are entitled to capital allowances. For completeness, in this Chapter we will look at the rules for companies alongside those for unincorporated businesses. We will look at companies in more detail later in this Text.

For the purposes of the F6 (UK) exam, if an unincorporated business uses the cash basis of accounting (as seen in the previous chapter), **capital allowances are not available.**

For unincorporated businesses, capital allowances are calculated for periods of account. These are simply the periods for which the trader chooses to make up accounts. For companies, capital allowances are calculated for accounting periods (see later in this Text).

For capital allowances purposes, expenditure is generally deemed to be incurred when the obligation to pay becomes unconditional. This will often be the date of delivery, even if payment is actually required later than this date. For example, the sales contract may require payment to be made within four weeks of delivery but the obligation to pay still becomes unconditional on the delivery date. However, amounts due

more than four months after the obligation becomes unconditional are deemed to be incurred when they fall due.

2 Plant and machinery – qualifying expenditure

FAST FORWARD

> There are various statutory rules on what does or does not qualify as plant.

2.1 Definition of plant and machinery

Capital expenditure on plant and machinery qualifies for capital allowances if the plant or machinery is used for a qualifying activity, such as a trade. 'Plant' is not fully defined by the legislation, although some specific exclusions and inclusions are given. The word 'machinery' may be taken to have its normal everyday meaning.

2.2 The statutory exclusions

2.2.1 Buildings

Expenditure on a building and on any asset which is incorporated in a building or is of a kind normally incorporated into buildings does not usually qualify as expenditure on plant. (There are exceptions to this (see Section 2.2.3 below) and also certain 'integral features' (see later in this chapter) are specifically treated as plant).

In addition to complete buildings, **the following assets count as 'buildings', and are therefore not plant (except if they qualify as 'integral features').**

- Walls, floors, ceilings, doors, gates, shutters, windows and stairs
- Mains services, and systems, of water, electricity and gas
- Waste disposal, sewerage and drainage systems
- Shafts or other structures for lifts etc

2.2.2 Structures

Expenditure on structures and on works involving the alteration of land **does not qualify as expenditure on plant**, but see below for exceptions.

A 'structure' is a fixed structure of any kind, other than a building. An example is a bridge.

2.2.3 Exceptions

Over the years a large body of case law has been built up under which plant and machinery allowances have been given on certain types of expenditure which might be thought to be expenditure on a building or structure. Statute therefore gives a list of various assets which *may* still be plant. These include:

- Any machinery not within any other item in this list
- Gas and sewerage systems:
    - Provided mainly to meet the particular requirements of the trade, or
    - Provided mainly to serve particular machinery or plant used for the purposes of the trade
- Manufacturing or processing equipment, storage equipment, including cold rooms, display equipment, and counters, checkouts and similar equipment
- Cookers, washing machines, refrigeration or cooling equipment, sanitary ware and furniture and furnishings
- Hoists
- Sound insulation provided mainly to meet the particular requirements of the trade
- Refrigeration or cooling equipment
- Computer, telecommunication and surveillance systems

- Sprinkler equipment, fire alarm and burglar alarm systems
- Partition walls, where movable and intended to be moved
- Decorative assets provided for the enjoyment of the public in the hotel, restaurant or similar trades; advertising hoardings
- Movable buildings intended to be moved in the course of the trade
- Expenditure on altering land for the purpose only of installing machinery or plant

Items falling within the above list of exclusions will only qualify as plant if they fall within the meaning of plant as established by case law. This is discussed below.

2.2.4 Land

Land or an interest in land does not qualify as plant and machinery. For this purpose 'land' excludes buildings, structures and assets which are installed or fixed to land in such a way as to become part of the land for general legal purposes.

2.2.5 Integral features

The following **integral features of a building or structure** qualify for capital allowances as plant (in the special rate pool, see later in this chapter):

- Electrical systems (including lighting systems)
- Cold water system
- Space or water heating system, a powered system of ventilation, air cooling or air purification, and any floor or ceiling comprised in such a system
- Lift, an escalator or a moving walkway
- External solar shading

When a building is sold, the vendor and purchaser can make a joint election to determine how the sale proceeds are apportioned between the building and its integral features.

2.2.6 Computer software

Capital expenditure on computer software (both programs and data) **normally qualifies as expenditure on plant and machinery.**

2.3 Case law

FAST FORWARD
There are also cases on the definition of plant. To help you to absorb them, try to see the function/setting theme running through them.

Exam focus point

In this chapter we mention the names of cases where it was decided what was or wasn't 'plant'. You are **not** expected to know the names of cases for your examination. We have included them for your information only.

The original case law **definition of plant** (applied in this case to a horse) is '**whatever apparatus is used by a businessman for carrying on his business: not his stock in trade which he buys or makes for sale; but all goods and chattels, fixed or movable, live or dead, which he keeps for permanent employment in the business**' (*Yarmouth v France 1887*).

Subsequent cases have refined the original definition and have largely been concerned with the **distinction between plant actively used in the business (qualifying) and the setting in which the business is carried on (non-qualifying). This is the 'functional' test.** Some of the decisions have now been enacted as part of statute law, but they are still relevant as examples of the principles involved.

A barrister succeeded in his claim for his law library: 'Plant includes a man's tools of his trade. It extends to what he uses day by day in the course of his profession. It is not confined to physical things like the dentist's chair or the architect's table' (*Munby v Furlong 1977*).

Office partitioning was allowed. Because it was movable, it was not regarded as part of the setting in which the business was carried on (*Jarrold v John Good and Sons Ltd 1963*) (actual item now covered by statute).

At a motorway service station, false ceilings contained conduits, ducts and lighting apparatus. **They did not qualify because they did not perform a function in the business. They were merely part of the setting in which the business was conducted** (*Hampton v Fortes Autogrill Ltd 1979*).

Similarly, it has been held that when an attractive floor is provided in a restaurant, the fact that the floor performs the function of making the restaurant attractive to customers is not enough to make it plant. It functions as premises, and the cost therefore does not qualify for capital allowances (*Wimpy International Ltd v Warland 1988*).

Conversely, light fittings, decor and murals can be plant. A company carried on business as hoteliers and operators of licensed premises. The function of the items was the creation of an atmosphere conducive to the comfort and well being of its customers (*CIR v Scottish and Newcastle Breweries Ltd 1982*) (decorative assets used in hotels etc, now covered by statute).

General lighting in a department store was held not to be plant, as it was merely setting. Special display lighting, however, could be plant (*Cole Brothers Ltd v Phillips 1982*). Note that changes in legislation mean that it is now possible to claim allowances on lighting as an integral feature (see earlier in this chapter), but the case is still a useful example of the distinction between setting and function.

3 The main pool

FAST FORWARD

> With capital allowances computations, the main thing is to get the layout right. Having done that, you will find that the figures tend to drop into place.

3.1 Main pool expenditure

Most expenditure on plant and machinery, including expenditure on cars with CO$_2$ emissions of 130g/km or less, is put into a pool of expenditure (the main pool) on which capital allowances may be claimed. An addition increases the pool whilst a disposal decreases it.

Exceptionally the following items are not put into the main pool:

(a)   Assets dealt with in the special rate pool
(b)   Assets with private use by the trader
(c)   Short life assets where an election has been made

These exceptions are dealt with later in this chapter.

Expenditure on plant and machinery by a person about to begin a trade is treated as incurred on the first day of trading. Assets previously owned by a trader and then brought into the trade (at the start of trading or later) are treated as bought for their market values at the times when they are brought in.

3.2 Annual investment allowance

FAST FORWARD

> Businesses are entitled to an annual investment allowance (AIA) of £500,000 for a 12 month period of account.

Businesses can claim an **annual investment allowance (AIA) on the first £500,000 spent each year on plant or machinery**, including assets in the main pool, but not including motor cars. Expenditure on motorcycles does qualify for the AIA.

Where the period of account is more or less than a year, the maximum allowance is proportionately increased or reduced.

After claiming the AIA, the balance of expenditure on main pool assets is transferred to the main pool immediately and is eligible for writing down allowances in the same period.

3.3 First year allowance for low emission cars

FAST FORWARD

A first year allowance (FYA) at the rate of 100% is available on new low emission cars. The FYA is not pro-rated in short or long periods of account.

Key term

A **low emission car** is one which has CO_2 emissions of 95g/km or less.

A **100% first year allowance (FYA) is available for expenditure incurred on new** (ie unused and not second hand) **low emission motor cars.**

If the FYA is not claimed in full (for example if the trader does not want to create a loss – see later in this Study Text), the balance of expenditure is transferred to the main pool after any writing down allowance has been calculated on the main pool.

The FYA is not adjusted pro-rata in a short or long period of account, unlike the AIA and writing down allowances.

3.4 Writing down allowances

FAST FORWARD

Expenditure on plant and machinery in the main pool qualifies for a WDA at 18% every 12 months.

Key term

A **writing down allowance (WDA)** is given on main pool expenditure **at the rate of 18% a year** (on a reducing balance basis). The WDA is calculated on the tax written down value (TWDV) of pooled plant, after adding the current period's additions and taking out the current period's disposals.

When plant is sold, proceeds, limited to a maximum of the original cost, are taken out of the pool. Provided that the trade is still being carried on, the pool balance remaining is written down in the future by WDAs, even if there are no assets left.

3.5 Example

Elizabeth has tax written down value on her main pool of plant and machinery of £16,000 on 6 April 2014. In the year to 5 April 2015 she bought a car with CO_2 emissions of 110g/km for £8,000 (no non-business use) and she disposed of plant, which originally cost £4,000, for £6,000.

Calculate the maximum capital allowances claim for the year.

	Main pool £	Allowances £
TWDV b/f	16,000	
Addition (not qualifying for AIA)	8,000	
Less disposal (limited to cost)	(4,000)	
	20,000	
WDA @ 18%	(3,600)	3,600
TWDV c/f	16,400	
Maximum capital allowances claim		3,600

Julia is a sole trader making up accounts to 5 April each year. At 5 April 2014, the tax written down value on her main pool is £12,500.

In the year to 5 April 2015, Julia bought the following assets:

1 June 2014	Machinery	£490,000
12 November 2014	Van	£17,500
10 February 2015	Car for salesman (CO_2 emissions 120g/km)	£9,000

She disposed of plant on 15 December 2014 for £12,000 (original cost £16,000).

Calculate the maximum capital allowances claim that Julia can make for the year ended 5 April 2015.

Answer

	AIA £	Main pool £	Allowances £
y/e 5 April 2015			
TWDV b/f		12,500	
Additions qualifying for AIA			
1.6.14 Machinery	490,000		
12.11.14 Van	17,500		
	507,500		
AIA	(500,000)		500,000
	7,500		
Transfer balance to pool	(7,500)	7,500	
Additions not qualifying for AIA			
10.2.15 Car		9,000	
Disposal			
15.12.14 Plant		(12,000)	
		17,000	
WDA @ 18%		(3,060)	3,060
TWDV c/f		13,940	
Maximum capital allowances			503,060

3.6 Short and long periods of account

WDAs are 18% × number of months/12:

(a) For unincorporated businesses where the period of account is longer or shorter than 12 months. For individuals, capital allowances computations are computed for periods of account not tax years.

(b) For companies where the accounting period is shorter than 12 months (a company's accounting period for tax purposes is never longer than 12 months), or where the trade concerned started in the accounting period and was therefore carried on for fewer than 12 months. For companies, capital allowances computations are computed for accounting periods, (we will be studying companies in detail later in this Text).

Question

Venus is a sole trader and has made up accounts to 30 April each year. At 30 April 2014, the tax written down value of her main pool was £66,667. She decides to make up her next set of accounts to 31 December 2014.

In the period to 31 December 2014, the following acquisitions were made:

1 May 2014	Plant	£346,666
10 July 2014	Car (CO_2 emissions 110 g/km)	£9,000
3 August 2014	Car (CO_2 emissions 85 g/km) – new	£11,000

Venus disposed of plant on 1 November 2014 for £20,000 (original cost £28,000).

Calculate the maximum capital allowances that Venus can claim for the period ending 31 December 2014.

Answer

	AIA £	FYA £	Main pool £	Allowances £
p/e 31 December 2014				
TWDV b/f			66,667	
Additions qualifying for AIA				
1.5.14 Plant	346,666			
AIA £500,000 × 8/12	(333,333)			333,333
	13,333			
Transfer balance to pool	(13,333)		13,333	
Additions qualifying for FYA				
3.8.14 Car (new – low emission)		11,000		
Less: 100% FYA		(11,000)		11,000
Additions not qualifying for AIA or FYA				
10.7.14 Car			9,000	
Disposals				
1.11.14 Plant			(20,000)	
			69,000	
WDA @ 18% × 8/12			(8,280)	8,280
TWDVs c/f			60,720	
Maximum allowances claim				352,613

Note that the annual investment allowance and the writing down allowance are reduced for the short period of account, but the first year allowance is given in full.

Question

Oscar started trading on 1 July 2014 and made up his first set of accounts to 31 December 2015. He bought the following assets:

10 July 2014	Plant	£325,000
1 October 2014	Car for business use only (CO_2 emissions 120g/km)	£11,000
12 February 2015	Plant	£490,000

Calculate the maximum capital allowances claim that Oscar can make for the period ended 31 December 2015. Assume that the rates of capital allowances in 2014/15 also apply in 2015/16.

	AIA £	Main pool £	Allowances £
p/e 31 December 2015			
Additions qualifying for AIA			
10.7.14 Plant	325,000		
12.2.15 Plant	490,000		
	815,000		
AIA £500,000 × 18/12	(750,000)		750,000
	65,000		
Transfer balance to main pool	(65,000)	65,000	
Additions not qualifying for AIA			
1.10.14 Car		11,000	
		76,000	
WDA @ 18% × 18/12		(20,520)	20,520
TWDV c/f		55,480	
Maximum capital allowances			770,520

Note that the annual investment allowance and the writing down allowance are increased for the long period of account.

3.7 Small balance on main pool

A writing down allowance equal to unrelieved expenditure in the main pool can be claimed where this is **£1,000 or less**. If the maximum WDA is claimed, the main pool will then have a nil balance carried forward.

Question — **Small balance on main pool**

Alan has traded for many years, making up accounts to 5 April each year. At 5 April 2014, the tax written down value of his main pool was £15,000. On 1 October 2014, he sold some plant and machinery for £14,200 (original cost £16,000).

Calculate the maximum capital allowances claim that Alan can make for the period ending 5 April 2015.

Answer

	Main pool £	Allowances £
y/e 5 April 2015		
TWDV b/f	15,000	
Disposal	(14,200)	
	800	
WDA (small pool)	(800)	800
TWDV c/f	nil	
Maximum capital allowances		800

Note the tax planning opportunities available. If plant is bought just before an accounting date, allowances become available as soon as possible. Alternatively, it may be desirable to claim less than the maximum allowances to even out annual taxable profits and avoid a higher rate of tax in later years. However, in the exam you should always claim the maximum available capital allowances unless you are told otherwise.

3.8 Balancing charges and allowances

Balancing charges occur when the disposal value deducted exceeds the balance remaining in the pool. The charge equals the excess and is effectively a negative capital allowance, increasing profits. Most commonly this happens when the trade ceases and the remaining assets are sold. It may also occur, however, whilst the trade is still in progress.

Balancing allowances on the main and special pools of expenditure arise only when the trade ceases. The balancing allowance is equal to the remaining unrelieved expenditure after deducting the disposal value of all the assets. Balancing allowances may also arise on single pool items (see later in this Chapter) whenever those items are disposed of.

3.9 Interaction with value added tax (VAT)

We deal with VAT in Chapters 26 and 27. You may want to make a note to re-read this section when you study VAT.

Qualifying expenditure includes irrecoverable value added tax (VAT). The VAT may be irrecoverable because the trader is not VAT registered, or because it is type of expenditure on which the VAT is not recoverable (eg the acquisition of a car not used wholly for business purposes).

If the trader is VAT registered and can reclaim VAT on a purchase, only the expenditure net of VAT will be qualifying expenditure. Similarly, on a disposal of an asset on which capital allowances have been claimed, if VAT is charged by the trader on the disposal, **only the disposal proceeds net of VAT will be deducted**.

Not all capital allowances questions will require you to consider VAT. Take care, if the question mentions VAT inclusive or exclusive amounts or states that the trader is VAT-registered, that you make the appropriate VAT adjustments when performing capital allowances calculations.

3.10 Example

Frank is registered for VAT. He had the following transactions in capital assets during the year ended 5 April 2015:
Purchases:

12 May 2014	Plant for £42,000 (including VAT of £7,000)
4 October 2014	A car with CO_2 emissions of 115 g/km for £15,000 (including VAT of £2,500), 20% private use by one of Frank's employees.

Disposal:

30 September 2014	Machinery, which had originally cost £24,000 (including VAT of £4,000), was sold for £21,000 (including VAT of £3,500)

The tax written down value of Frank's main pool on 6 April 2014 was £70,000.

The maximum capital allowances that Frank can claim for the year ended 5 April 2015 are:

	AIA £	Main pool £	Allowances £
y/e 5 April 2015			
TWDV b/f		70,000	
Addition qualifying for AIA			
12.5.14 Plant			
£(42,000 – 7,000)	35,000		
AIA	(35,000)		35,000
Addition not qualifying for AIA			
4.10.14 Car (N)		15,000	
Disposal			
30.9.14 Machinery			
£(21,000 – 3,500)		(17,500)	
		67,500	
WDA @ 18%		(12,150)	12,150
TWDV c/f		55,350	
Maximum capital allowances			47,150

Note: The VAT on the car is irrecoverable because an employee uses it partly for private purposes (see Chapter 26). Whilst private use by the employee does not restrict the rate of capital allowances (as private use by Frank would), for VAT purposes *any* private use prevents the recovery of VAT.

3.11 Cessation of trade

For plant and machinery, **when a business ceases to trade, no AIAs, FYAs or WDAs are given in the final period of account** (unincorporated businesses) or accounting period (companies – see later in this Text). Each asset is deemed to be disposed of on the date the trade ceased (usually at the then market value). Additions (if any) in the relevant period are brought in and then the disposal proceeds (limited to cost) are deducted from the balance of qualifying expenditure. If the proceeds exceed the balance then a balancing charge arises. If the balance of qualifying expenditure exceeds the proceeds then a balancing allowance is given.

4 Special rate pool

FAST FORWARD

The special rate pool contains expenditure on thermal insulation, long life assets, features integral to a building and cars with CO_2 emissions over 130g/km. The AIA can be used against such expenditure except cars. The WDA is 8%.

4.1 Operation of the special rate pool

Expenditure on thermal insulation, long life assets, features integral to a building (see earlier in this chapter), **solar panels, and cars with CO_2 emissions over 130g/km is not dealt with in the main pool but in a special rate pool.**

The annual investment allowance can apply to expenditure on such assets except on cars. The taxpayer can decide how to allocate the AIA. It will be more tax efficient to set the allowance against special rate pool expenditure in priority to main pool expenditure where there is expenditure on assets in both pools in the period. Expenditure in excess of the AIA is added to the special rate pool and will be eligible for writing down allowance in the same period in which the expenditure is incurred.

The writing down allowance for the special rate pool is 8% for a 12 month period. As with the writing down allowance on the main pool, this is adjusted for short and long periods of account.

Where the **tax written down balance of the special rate pool is £1,000 or less**, a writing down allowance can be claimed of up to £1,000. This is in addition to any similar claim in relation to the main pool.

4.2 Long life assets

Key term

> **Long life assets** are assets with an expected working life of 25 years or more.

The **long life asset rules only apply to businesses whose total expenditure on assets with an expected working life of 25 years or more in a chargeable period is more than £100,000**. If the expenditure exceeds £100,000, the whole of the expenditure enters the special rate pool, not just the excess over £100,000. If the expenditure is £100,000 or less, the long life asset rules do not apply and the expenditure will be added to the main pool in the normal way. For this purpose all expenditure incurred under a contract is treated as incurred in the first chargeable period to which that contract relates.

The £100,000 limit is reduced or increased proportionately in the case of a chargeable period of less or more than 12 months.

The following are **not** treated as long life assets:

(a)   **Plant and machinery in dwelling houses, retail shops, showrooms, hotels and offices**
(b)   **Cars**

4.3 Example

Lucy has been trading for many years, making up accounts to 5 April each year. The tax written down value of her main pool at 5 April 2014 was £110,000. In the year to 5 April 2015, Lucy had the following expenditure:

10 June 2014	General plant costing £45,000
12 December 2014	Lighting system in shop £245,000
15 January 2015	Car for business use only (CO_2 emissions 155 g/km) £25,000
26 January 2015	Delivery van £15,000
4 March 2015	Lifts £257,500

The maximum capital allowances claim that Lucy can make for the year to 5 April 2015 is:

		AIA £	Main pool £	Special rate pool £	Allowances £
y/e 5 April 2015					
TWDV b/f			110,000		
Additions for AIA (best use)					
12.12.14	Lighting	245,000			
4.3.15	Lifts	257,500			
		502,500			
AIA		(500,000)			500,000
		2,500			
Transfer balance to special rate pool		(2,500)		2,500	
Additions not given AIA					
10.6.14	Plant		45,000		
26.1.15	Van		15,000		
Additions not qualifying for AIA					
15.1.15	Car			25,000	
			170,000	27,500	
WDA @ 18%			(30,600)		30,600
WDA @ 8%				(2,200)	2,200
TWDVs c/f			139,400	25,300	
Allowances					532,800

5 Private use assets

An asset which is used privately by a trader is dealt with in a single asset pool and the capital allowances are restricted.

An asset which is used partly for private purposes by a sole trader or a partner is put into its own pool (single asset pool).

Capital allowances are calculated on the full cost. However, only the business use proportion of the allowances is allowed as a deduction from trading profits. This restriction applies to the AIA, FYAs, WDAs, balancing allowances and balancing charges.

An asset with some private use by an employee (not the owner of the business) suffers no such restriction. The employee may be taxed under the benefits code (see earlier in this Text) so the business receives capital allowances on the full cost of the asset.

Exam focus point

Capital allowances on assets with some private use is a common exam topic. Check carefully whether the private use is by the owner of the business or by an employee.

Question
Capital allowances on private use asset

Jacinth has been in business as a sole trader for many years, making up accounts to 31 March.
On 1 November 2014 she bought computer equipment for £2,700 which she uses 75% in her business and 25% privately. She has already used the AIA against other expenditure in the year to 31 March 2015.

Calculate the maximum capital allowance that Jacinth can claim in respect to the computer equipment in the year to 31 March 2015.

Answer

	Computer equipment £	Allowances @ 75% £
y/e 31 March 2015		
Acquisition	2,700	
WDA @ 18%	(486)	365
TWDV c/f	2,214	
Maximum capital allowance on computer equipment		365

6 Motor cars

Motor cars are generally dealt with in the main pool or the special rate pool (cars emitting over 130g/km), unless there is private use by the trader in which case the car is held in a single asset pool.

As we have already seen, motor cars are categorised in accordance with their CO_2 emissions:

(a)   **Cars emitting over 130g/km**: expenditure is added to the special rate pool

(b)   **Cars emitting between 96 and 130 g/km**: expenditure is added to the main pool

(c)   **Cars emitting 95 g/km or less**: expenditure on new cars eligible for 100% first year allowance, if allowance not claimed in full, excess added to main pool; expenditure on second hand cars is added to main pool

Cars with an element of private use are kept separate from the main and special pools and are dealt with in single asset pools. Such cars are entitled to a WDA of 18% (car with CO_2 emissions between 96 and 130 g/km) or 8% (car with CO_2 emissions over 130 g/km).

Quodos started to trade on 1 July 2014, making up accounts to 31 December 2014 and each 31 December thereafter. On 1 August 2014 he bought a car for £17,000 with CO_2 emissions of 110 g/km. The private use proportion is 10%. The car was sold in July 2017 for £4,000. Quodos has no other assets which qualify for capital allowances.

Calculate the capital allowances, assuming:

(a)   The car was used by an employee, or
(b)   The car was used by Quodos

and that the capital allowances rates in 2014/15 apply throughout.

Answer

(a)

	Main pool £	Allowances £
1.7.14 – 31.12.14		
Purchase price	17,000	
WDA 18% × 6/12 × £17,000	(1,530)	1,530
	15,470	
1.1.15 – 31.12.15		
WDA 18% × £15,470	(2,785)	2,785
	12,685	
1.1.16 – 31.12.16		
WDA 18% × £12,685	(2,283)	2,283
	10,402	
1.1.17 – 31.12.17		
Proceeds	(4,000)	
	6,402	
WDA 18% × £6,402	(1,152)	1,152
TWDV c/f	5,250	

The private use of the car by the employee has no effect on the capital allowances due to Quodos. The car will be placed in the main pool. No balancing allowance is available on the main pool until trade ceases even though the car has been sold.

(b)

	Car £	Allowances 90% £
1.7.14 – 31.12.14		
Purchase price	17,000	
WDA 18% × 6/12 x £17,000	(1,530)	1,377
	15,470	
1.1.15 – 31.12.15		
WDA 18% × £15,470	(2,785)	2,507
	12,685	
1.1.16 – 31.12.16		
WDA 18% × £12,685	(2,283)	2,055
	10,402	
1.1.17 – 31.12.17		
Proceeds	(4,000)	
Balancing allowance	6,402	5,762

The car is placed in a single asset pool because of the private use by the trader, Quodos. Only 90% of the WDAs and balancing allowance are available as a result of this private use.

7 Short life assets

FAST FORWARD

Short life asset elections can bring forward the allowances due on an asset.

A trader can elect that specific items of plant, which are expected to have a short working life, be kept separately from the main pool.

Key term

> Any asset subject to this election is known as a **'short life asset'**, and the election is known as a 'de-pooling election'.

The election is irrevocable. For an unincorporated business, the time limit for electing is the 31 January which is 22 months after the end of the tax year in which the period of account of the expenditure ends. (For a company, it is two years after the end of the accounting period of the expenditure.) **Short life asset treatment cannot be claimed for any motor cars, or plant used partly for non-trade purposes.**

The short life asset is kept in a single asset pool. Provided that the short life asset is disposed of **within eight years of the end of the accounting period** in which it was bought, a balancing charge or allowance arises on its disposal.

If the asset is not disposed of within this time period, its tax written down value is added to the main pool at the beginning of the next period of account (accounting period for companies). This will be after allowances have been claimed nine times on the asset; once in the period of acquisition and then each year for the following eight years.

The election should therefore be made for assets likely to be sold for less than their tax written down values within eight years. It should not usually be made for assets likely to be sold within eight years for more than their tax written down values. There is no requirement to show from the outset that the asset will actually have a 'short life', so it is a matter of judgment whether the election should be made.

The annual investment allowance can be set against short life assets. The taxpayer can decide how to allocate the AIA. It will be more tax efficient to set the allowance against main pool expenditure in priority to short life asset expenditure.

Question — Short life assets

Caithlin bought a machine for business use on 1 May 2014 for £9,000 and elected for de-pooling. She did not claim the AIA in respect of this asset. Her accounting year end is 30 April.

Calculate the capital allowances due if:

(a)   The asset is scrapped for £300 in August 2022
(b)   The asset is scrapped for £200 in August 2023

and assuming that the capital allowances rates in 2014/15 apply throughout.

		£
(a)	*Year to 30.4.15*	
	Cost	9,000
	WDA 18%	(1,620)
		7,380
	Year to 30.4.16	
	WDA 18%	(1,328)
		6,052
	Year to 30.4.17	
	WDA 18%	(1,089)
		4,963
	Year to 30.4.18	
	WDA 18%	(893)
		4,070
	Year to 30.4.19	
	WDA 18%	(733)
		3,337
	Year to 30.4.20	
	WDA 18%	(601)
		2,736
	Year to 30.4.21	
	WDA 18%	(492)
		2,244
	Year to 30.4.22	
	WDA 18%	(404)
		1,840
	Year to 30.4.23	
	Disposal proceeds	(300)
	Balancing allowance	1,540

(b) If the asset is still in use at 30 April 2022, WDAs up to 30.4.22 will be as above. In the year to 30.4.23, a WDA can be claimed of 18% × £1,840 = £331. The tax written down value of £1,840 − £331 = £1,509 will be added to the main pool at the beginning of the next period of account. The disposal proceeds of £200 will be deducted from the main pool in that period's capital allowances computation. No balancing allowance will arise and the main pool will continue.

Chapter Roundup

- Capital allowances are available to give tax relief for certain capital expenditure.

- There are various statutory rules on what does or does not qualify as plant.

- There are also cases on the definition of plant. To help you to absorb them, try to see the function/setting theme running through them.

- With capital allowances computations, the main thing is to get the layout right. Having done that, you will find that the figures tend to drop into place.

- Businesses are entitled to an annual investment allowance (AIA) of £500,000 for a 12 month period of account.

- A first year allowance (FYA) at the rate of 100% is available on new low emission cars. The FYA is not pro-rated in short or long periods of account.

- Expenditure on plant and machinery in the main pool qualifies for a WDA at 18% every 12 months.

- The special rate pool contains expenditure on thermal insulation, long life assets, features integral to a building and cars with CO_2 emissions over 130g/km. The AIA can be used against such expenditure except cars. The WDA is 8%.

- An asset which is used privately by a trader is dealt with in a single asset pool and the capital allowances are restricted.

- Motor cars are generally dealt with in the main pool or the special rate pool (cars emitting over 130g/km), unless there is private use by the trader in which case the car is held in a single asset pool.

- Short life asset elections can bring forward the allowances due on an asset.

Quick Quiz

1   Writing down allowances are pro-rated in a six month period of account. True/False?

2   Lucas makes up accounts for a 15 month period to 30 June 2015. What Annual Investment Allowance is he entitled to?

    A   £125,000
    B   £375,000
    C   £500,000
    D   £625,000

3   Is a first year allowance on a low emission car pro-rated in a six month period of account?

4   When may balancing allowances arise?

5   An asset must be disposed of within ____ years of the end of the accounting period (or period of account) in which it was acquired in order for it to be advantageous to treat it as a short life asset. Fill in the blank.

6   Paula makes up accounts to 5 April each year. She buys a car in August 2014 costing £20,000 for use in her business. Her private use of the car is 30%. The CO_2 emissions of the car are 150g/km.

    What WDA is available on the car for the year ended 5 April 2015?

    A   £1,120
    B   £1,600
    C   £2,520
    D   £3,600

1 True. In a six month period, writing down allowance are pro-rated by multiplying by 6/12.

2 D. £500,000 × 15/12 = £625,000.

3 No. A first year allowance is given in full in a short period of account.

4 Balancing allowances may arise in respect of main or special rate pool expenditure only when the trade ceases. Balancing allowances may arise on single pool assets whenever those assets are disposed of.

5 An asset must be disposed of within **8** years of the end of the accounting period (or period of account) in which it was acquired in order for it to be advantageous to treat it as a short life asset.

6 A. £20,000 × 8% (CO_2 emissions of the car exceed 130g/km) = £1,600. WDA is £1,600 × 70% = £1,120.

Now try the questions below from the Practice Question Bank

Number	Type	Marks	Time
Q20	Section A	6	11 mins
Q21	Section B	15	27 mins
Q22	Section B	8	14 mins

Assessable trading income

Topic list	Syllabus reference
1 Recognise the basis of assessment	B3(a)
2 Commencement and cessation	B3(f)
3 The choice of an accounting date	B3(g)

Introduction

In the previous two chapters we have seen how to calculate the taxable trading profits after capital allowances. We are now going to look at how these are taxed in the owner's hands.

Businesses do not normally prepare accounts for tax years so we look at the basis of assessment which is the method by which the taxable trading profits of periods of account are allocated to tax years. As well as the normal rules for a continuing business we need special rules for the opening years of a trade, and again in the closing years.

A business may choose its accounting date and this may have an effect on when the tax is payable on profits.

In the next chapter we will look at the tax reliefs available should the business make a loss.

Study guide

		Intellectual level
B3	**Income from self-employment**	
(a)	Recognise the basis of assessment for self-employment income.	2
(f)	Compute the assessable profits on commencement and on cessation.	2
(g)	Recognise the factors that will influence the choice of accounting date.	2

Exam guide

You are likely to have to deal with a tax computation for an unincorporated business in either Section A or Section B. It may be a simple computation for a continuing business, or you may have to deal with a business in its opening or closing years, including computing taxable trading profits and allocating them to tax years. You must be totally familiar with the rules and be able to apply them in the exam. These topics may be tested in a 15 mark question or a 10 mark question in Section B. A specific point, such as computing an amount of overlap profits, may be tested in Section A.

1 Recognise the basis of assessment

FAST FORWARD

Basis periods are used to link periods of account to tax years. Broadly, the profits of a 12 month period of account ending in a tax year are taxed in that year (current year basis).

1.1 Basis periods and tax years

A tax year runs from 6 April to 5 April, but most businesses do not have periods of account ending on 5 April. **Thus there must be a link between a period of account of a business and a tax year**. The procedure is to **find a period to act as the basis period for a tax year. The profits for a basis period are taxed in the corresponding tax year.** If a basis period is not identical to a period of account, the profits of periods of account are time-apportioned as required on the assumption that profits accrue evenly over a period of account. We will apportion to the nearest month for exam purposes.

The same rules apply to link periods of account to tax years regardless of whether the normal accruals method of accounting or the cash basis is used.

The general rule is that **the basis period is the year of account ending in the tax year**. This is known as the **current year basis of assessment**. For example, if a trader prepares accounts to 31 December each year, the profits of the year to 31 December 2014 will be taxed in the tax year 2014/15.

This general rule does not apply in the opening or closing years of a business. This is because in the first few years the business has not normally established a pattern of annual accounts, and very few businesses cease trading on the annual accounting date.

Apart from the first tax year of trade and the last tax year of trade, HMRC will expect to see 12 months of profits showing in the income tax computation each year. As the periods of account may not be 12 months long in the opening and closing years, the current year basis may be impossible to apply, therefore special rules need to be applied to establish which 12 months should be allocated to which tax year.

2 Commencement and cessation

FAST FORWARD

In the first tax year of trade actual profits of the tax year are taxed. In the second tax year, the basis period is either the first 12 months, the 12 months to the accounting date ending in year two or the actual profits from April to April. Profits of the 12 months to the accounting date are taxed in year three.

2.1 The first tax year

The first tax year is the year during which the trade commences. For example, if a trade commences on 1 June 2014 the first tax year is 2014/15.

The **basis period for the first tax year runs from the date the trade starts to the next 5 April** (or to the date of cessation if the trade does not last until the end of the tax year).

So continuing the above example a trader commencing in business on 1 June 2014 will be taxed on profits arising from 1 June 2014 to 5 April 2015 in 2014/15, the first tax year.

2.2 The second tax year

(a) **If the accounting date falling in the second tax year is at least 12 months after the start of trading, the basis period is the 12 months to that accounting date.**

(b) **If the accounting date falling in the second tax year is less than 12 months after the start of trading, the basis period is the first 12 months of trading.**

(c) **If there is no accounting date falling in the second tax year, because the first period of account is a very long one which does not end until a date in the third tax year, the basis period for the second tax year is the year itself (from 6 April to 5 April).**

The following flowchart may help you determine the basis period for the second tax year.

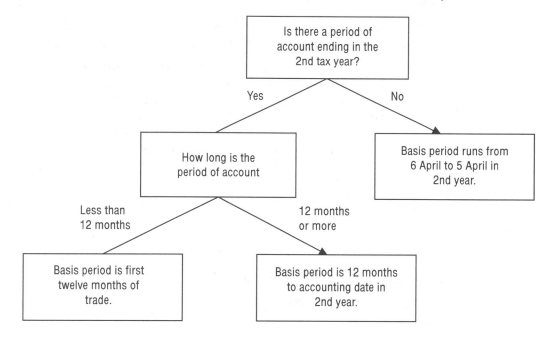

2.3 Example: period of 12 months or more ending in second year

John starts to trade on 1 January 2015 making up accounts to 31 December 2015.

1st tax year: 2014/15 – tax profits 1 January 2015 to 5 April 2015, ie 3/12 × year ended 31 December 2015

2nd tax year: 2015/16

- Is there a period of account ending in 2015/16?

  Yes – year ended 31 December 2015 ends in 2015/16

- How long is the period of account?

  12 months or more, ie 12 months (exactly) to 31 December 2015.

- So in 2015/16 tax profits of 12 months to 31 December 2015.

2.4 Example: short period ending in second year

Janet starts to trade on 1 January 2015 making up accounts as follows:

- Six months to 30 June 2015
- 12 months to 30 June 2016

1st tax year: 2014/15 – tax profits 1 January 2015 to 5 April 2015, ie 3/6 × 6 months ended 30 June 2015

2nd tax year: 2015/16

- Is there a period of account ending in 2015/16?

  Yes – period ended 30 June 2015 ends in 2015/16

- How long is the period of account?

  Less than 12 months

- So in 2015/16 tax profits of first 12 months of trade ie 1 January 2015 to 31 December 2015, ie 6 month period ended 30 June 2015 profits plus 6/12 of year ended 30 June 2016 profits

- You may notice that profits between 1 January 2015 to 5 April 2015 have been taxed in both 2014/15 and 2015/16 because the basis periods for these tax years overlap. These profits are therefore called 'overlap profits'. Relief for overlap profits is usually given when the trade ceases. The treatment of overlap profits is dealt with in more detail in Section 2.11

2.5 Example: no period ending in second year

Jodie starts to trade on 1 March 2015 making up a 14 month set of accounts to 30 April 2016.

1st tax year: 2014/15 – tax profits 1 March 2015 to 5 April 2015, ie 1/14 × 14 months ended 30 April 2016

2nd tax year: 2015/16

- Is there a period of account ending in 2015/16?

  No – period ended 30 April 2016 ends in 2016/17

- So in 2015/16 tax profits of 6 April 2015 to 5 April 2016, ie 12/14 × 14 months ended 30 April 2016

2.6 The third tax year

(a) **If there is an accounting date falling in the second tax year, the basis period for the third tax year is the 12 month period of account ending in the third tax year (current year basis).**

(b) If there is no accounting date falling in the second tax year, the basis period for the third tax year is the 12 months to the accounting date falling in the third tax year.

2.7 Example: accounting date in second year

Wilma starts to trade on 1 October 2014. She made taxable profits of £9,000 for the first nine months to 30 June 2015 and £30,000 for the year to 30 June 2016.

The taxable profits for the first three tax years are as follows:

Year	Basis period	Working	Taxable profits £
2014/15	1.10.14 – 5.4.15	£9,000 × 6/9	6,000
2015/16	1.10.14 – 30.9.15	£9,000 + £30,000 × 3/12	16,500
2016/17	1.7.15 – 30.6.16		30,000
	(period of account ending in 3rd year)		

2.8 Example: no accounting date in the second year

Thelma starts to trade on 1 March 2015. Her first accounts, covering the 16 months to 30 June 2016 show a profit of £36,000. The taxable profits for the first three tax years are as follows.

Year	Basis period	Working	Taxable profits £
2014/15	1.3.15 – 5.4.15	£36,000 × 1/16	2,250
2015/16	6.4.15 – 5.4.16	£36,000 × 12/16	27,000
2016/17	1.7.15 – 30.6.16	£36,000 × 12/16	27,000
	(12 months to the accounting date in 3rd year)		

2.9 Later tax years

For later tax years, except the year in which the trade ceases, the normal current year basis of assessment applies, ie the basis period is the 12 month period of account ending in the tax year (see above).

Question · Basis periods

Peter commenced trading on 1 September 2010 preparing accounts to 30 April each year with the following results.

Period	Profit £
1.9.10 – 30.4.11	8,000
1.5.11 – 30.4.12	15,000
1.5.12 – 30.4.13	9,000
1.5.13 – 30.4.14	10,500

Show the profits to be taxed in each year from 2010/11 to 2014/15.

Answer

Year	Basis period	Working	Taxable Profits £
2010/11	1.9.10 – 5.4.11	£8,000 × 7/8	7,000
2011/12	1.9.10 – 31.8.11	£8,000 + (£15,000 × 4/12)	13,000
2012/13	1.5.11 – 30.4.12		15,000
2013/14	1.5.12 – 30.4.13		9,000
2014/15	1.5.13 – 30.4.14		10,500

2.10 The final year

FAST FORWARD On a cessation the basis period runs from the end of the basis period for the previous tax year.

(a) If a trade starts and ceases in the same tax year, the basis period for that year is the whole lifespan of the trade.

(b) If the final year is the second year, the basis period runs from 6 April at the start of the second year to the date of cessation. This rule overrides the rules that normally apply for the second year.

(c) If the final year is the third year or a later year, **the basis period runs from the end of the basis period for the previous year to the date of cessation**. This rule overrides the rules that normally apply in the third and later years.

Question
Ceasing to trade

Harriet, who has been trading since 2000, ceases her trade on 31 March 2015.

Her results for recent years were:

Year ended 31 December	£
2012	10,000
2013	14,000
2014	21,000
Period ended 31 March 2015	4,000

Show the taxable trade profits for the last three tax years of trading.

Answer

Trade ceases in 2014/15.

Year	Basis period	Working	Assessment £
2012/13	Y/e 31.12.12		10,000
2013/14	Y/e 31.12.13		14,000
2014/15	1.1.14 – 31.3.15	Y/e 31.12.14 plus p/e 31.3.15	25,000

2.11 Overlap profits

Key term

Profits which have been taxed more than once are called **overlap profits**.

When a business starts, some profits may be taxed twice because the basis period for the second year includes some or all of the period of trading in the first year or because the basis period for the third year overlaps with that for the second year, or both.

Overlap profits are relieved when the trade ceases by being deducted from the final year's taxable profits. Any deduction of overlap profits may create or increase a loss. The usual loss reliefs (covered later in this Text) are then available.

Exam focus point

A business with a 31 March year end will have no overlap profits as its accounting year coincides with the tax year. A business with a 31 December year end, for example, will have three months of overlap profit as its accounting year ends three months before the end of the tax year. Use this rule of thumb to check your calculation of overlap profits.

2.12 Examples: overlap profits

(a) John starts to trade on 1 January 2015 making up accounts to 31 December 2015. Show the overlap period.

Tax year	Basis period
2014/15	1.1.15 – 5.4.15
2015/16	1.1.15 – 31.12.15
2016/17	1.1.16 – 31.12.16

Overlap period: 1.1.15 – 5.4.15 (three months)

(b) Janet starts to trade on 1 January 2015 making up accounts as follows:

6m to 30 June 2015
12m to 30 June 2016

Show the overlap period.

Tax year	Basis period
2014/15	1.1.15 – 5.4.15
2015/16	1.1.15 – 31.12.15
2016/17	1.7.15 – 30.6.16

Overlap period: 1.1.15 – 5.4.15 plus 1.7.15 – 31.12.15 (nine months)

(c) Jodie starts to trade on 1 March 2015 making up a 14 month set of accounts to 30 April 2016. Show the overlap period.

Tax year	Basis period
2014/15	1.3.15 – 5.4.15
2015/16	6.4.15 – 5.4.16
2016/17	1.5.15 – 30.4.16

Overlap period: 1.5.15 – 5.4.16 (11 months)

Question	Ceasing to trade and overlap profits

Jenny trades from 1 July 2009 to 31 December 2014, with the following results.

Period	Profit £
1.7.09 – 31.8.10	7,000
1.9.10 – 31.8.11	12,000
1.9.11 – 31.8.12	15,000
1.9.12 – 31.8.13	21,000
1.9.13 – 31.8.14	18,000
1.9.14 – 31.12.14	5,600
	78,600

Calculate the taxable trade profits to be taxed from 2009/10 to 2014/15, the overlap profits and state when these overlap profits can be relieved.

Answer

The profits to be taxed in each tax year from 2009/10 to 2014/15 and the total of these taxable profits are calculated as follows.

Year	Basis period	Working	Taxable profit £
2009/10	1.7.09 – 5.4.10	£7,000 × 9/14	4,500
2010/11	1.9.09 – 31.8.10	£7,000 × 12/14	6,000
2011/12	1.9.10 – 31.8.11		12,000
2012/13	1.9.11 – 31.8.12		15,000
2013/14	1.9.12 – 31.8.13		21,000
2014/15	1.9.13 – 31.12.14	£(18,000 + 5,600 – 3,500)	20,100
			78,600

The overlap profits are those in the period 1 September 2009 to 5 April 2010, a period of seven months. They are £7,000 × 7/14 = £3,500. Overlap profits are deducted from the final year's taxable profit when the business ceases.

Exam focus point

Over the life of the business, the total taxable profits equal the total actual profits.

3 The choice of an accounting date

FAST FORWARD

The choice of an accounting date may affect when tax is payable on trading profits. It may also create overlap profits and help or hinder tax planning.

A new trader should consider which accounting date would be best. There are **a number of factors to consider** from the point of view of taxation.

- **If profits are expected to rise, a date early in the tax year** (such as 30 April) will delay the time when rising accounts profits feed through into rising taxable profits, whereas a date late in the tax year (such as 31 March) will accelerate the taxation of rising profits. This is because with an accounting date of 30 April, the taxable profits for each tax year are mainly the profits earned in the previous tax year. With an accounting date of 31 March the taxable profits are almost entirely profits earned in the current year.

- If the accounting date in the second tax year is less than 12 months after the start of trading, the taxable profits for that year will be the profits earned in the first 12 months. If the accounting date is at least 12 months from the start of trading, they will be the profits earned in the 12 months to that date. **Different profits may thus be taxed twice**, and if profits are fluctuating this can make a considerable difference to the taxable profits in the first few years.

- **The choice of an accounting date affects the profits shown in each set of accounts**, and this may affect the taxable profits.

- **An accounting date of 30 April gives the maximum interval between earning profits and paying the related tax liability.** For example if a trader makes up accounts to 30 April 2015, this falls into the tax year 2015/16 with payments on account being due on 31 January 2016 and 31 July 2016, and a balancing payment due on 31 January 2017 (details of payment of income tax are dealt with later in this Text). If the trader makes up accounts to 31 March 2015, this falls in the tax year 2014/15 and the payments will be due one year earlier (ie on 31 January 2015, 31 July 2015 and 31 January 2016).

- **Knowing profits well in advance of the end of the tax year makes tax planning much easier.** For example, if a trader wants to make personal pension contributions and makes up accounts to 30 April 2015 (2015/16), he can make contributions up to 5 April 2016 based on those relevant earnings. If he makes up accounts to 31 March 2015, he will probably not know the amount of his relevant earnings until after the end of the tax year 2014/15, too late to adjust his pension contributions for 2014/15.

- **However, a 31 March or 5 April accounting date means that the application of the basis period rules is more straightforward and there will be no overlap profits.** This may be appropriate for small traders.

- **With an accounting date of 30 April, the assessment for the year of cessation could be based on up to 23 months of profits.** For example, if a trader who has made up accounts to 30 April ceases trading on 31 March 2015 (2014/15), the basis period for 2014/15 will run from 1 May 2013 to 31 March 2015. This could lead to larger than normal trading profits being assessable in the year of cessation. However, this could be avoided by carrying on the trade for another month so that a cessation arises on 30 April 2015 so that the profits from 1 May 2013 to 30 April 2014 are taxable in 2014/15 and those from 1 May 2014 to 30 April 2015 are taxable in 2015/16. Each case must be looked at in relation to all relevant factors, such as other income which the taxpayer may have and loss relief – there is no one rule which applies in all cases.

Question

The choice of an accounting date

Christine starts to trade on 1 December 2012. Her monthly profits are £1,000 for the first seven months, and £2,000 thereafter. Show the taxable profits for the first three tax years with each of the following accounting dates (in all cases starting with a period of account of less than 12 months).

(a)   31 March
(b)   30 April
(c)   31 December

Answer

(a)   *31 March*

Period of account	Working	Profits £
1.12.12 – 31.3.13	£1,000 × 4	4,000
1.4.13 – 31.3.14	£1,000 × 3 + £2,000 × 9	21,000
1.4.14 – 31.3.15	£2,000 × 12	24,000

Year	Basis period	Taxable profits £
2012/13	1.12.12 – 5.4.13	4,000
2013/14	1.4.13 – 31.3.14	21,000
2014/15	1.4.14 – 31.3.15	24,000

(b)   *30 April*

Period of account	Working	Profits £
1.12.12 – 30.4.13	£1,000 × 5	5,000
1.5.13 – 30.4.14	£1,000 × 2 + £2,000 ×10	22,000

Year	Basis period	Working	Taxable profits £
2012/13	1.12.12 – 5.4.13	£5,000 × 4/5	4,000
2013/14	1.12.12 – 30.11.13	£5,000 + £22,000 × 7/12	17,833
2014/15	1.5.13 – 30.4.14		22,000

(c) *31 December*

Period of account	Working	Profits
		£
1.12.12 – 31.12.12	£1,000 × 1	1,000
1.1.13 – 31.12.13	£1,000 × 6 + £2,000 × 6	18,000
1.1.14 – 31.12.14	£2,000 × 12	24,000

Year	Basis period	Working	Taxable profits
			£
2012/13	1.12.12 – 5.4.13	£1,000 + £18,000 × 3/12	5,500
2013/14	1.1.13 – 31.12.13		18,000
2014/15	1.1.14 – 31.12.14		24,000

Chapter Roundup

- Basis periods are used to link periods of account to tax years. Broadly, the profits of a 12 month period of account ending in a tax year are taxed in that year (current year basis).

- In the first tax year of trade actual profits of the tax year are taxed. In the second tax year, the basis period is either the first 12 months, the 12 months to the accounting date ending in year two or the actual profits from April to April. Profits of the 12 months to the accounting date are taxed in year three.

- On a cessation the basis period runs from the end of the basis period for the previous tax year.

- The choice of an accounting date may affect when tax is payable on trading profits. It may also create overlap profits and help or hinder tax planning.

Quick Quiz

1   What is the normal basis of assessment?

2   Isabella started trading on 1 September 2014. She made up her first set of accounts to 31 December 2015. The basis period for the year of commencement is:

    A   1 September 2014 to 31 December 2014
    B   1 September 2014 to 5 April 2015
    C   1 September 2014 to 31 August 2015
    D   1 September 2014 to 31 December 2015

3   Ernie started trading on 1 January 2014. He decided to make up accounts to 31 October each year. His taxable trading profits is as follows:

p/e 31.10.14	£3,000
y/e 31.10.15	£23,760

What are Ernie's overlap profits?

    A   £900
    B   £2,880
    C   £3,960
    D   £4,860

4   Gita ceased trading on 31 March 2015. Her taxable trading profits were:

y/e 31.12.14	£5,600
p/e 31.3.15	£4,500

Gita had £2,300 of unused overlap profits.

What is her taxable trading profit for 2014/15?

    A   £10,100
    B   £7,800
    C   £6,400
    D   £2,200

5   How are overlap profits relieved?

Answers to Quick Quiz

1   The normal basis of assessment is that the profits for a tax year are those of the 12 month accounting period ending in the tax year.

2   B. 1 September 2014 to 5 April 2015 ie the actual tax year.

3   D £4,860

First tax year (2013/14)
Actual basis
Basis period 1.1.14 to 5.4.14

Second tax year (2014/15)
Period of account in 2nd year less than 12 months
Basis period 1.1.14 to 31.12.14

Third tax year (2015/16)
Current year basis
Basis period 1.11.14 to 31.10.15

Overlap profits
Period of overlap 1.1.14 to 5.4.14 and 1.11.14 to 31.12.14

Overlap profits

	£
3/10 × £3,000	900
2/12 × £23,760	3,960
	4,860

4   B £7,800

Last tax year (2014/15) Basis period 1.1.14 to 31.3.15

	£
y/e 31.12.14	5,600
p/e 31.3.15	4,500
	10,100
Less: overlap profits	(2,300)
	7,800

5   On the cessation of a business by deduction from the final year's taxable profits.

Now try the questions below from the Practice Question Bank

Number	Type	Marks	Time
Q23	Section A	6	11 mins
Q24	Section B	15	27 mins
Q25	Section B	15	27 mins

11

Trading losses

Topic list	Syllabus reference
1 Losses	B3(i)
2 Carry forward trade loss relief	B3(i)(i)
3 Trade loss relief against general income	B3(i)(ii), (i)(v)
4 Losses in the early years of a trade	B3(i)(iii)
5 Terminal trade loss relief	B3(i)(iv)

Introduction

We have seen how to calculate taxable trading profits and how to allocate them to tax years so that they can be slotted into the income tax computation.

Traders sometimes make losses rather than profits. In this chapter we consider the reliefs available for losses. A loss does not in itself lead to getting tax back from HMRC. Relief is obtained by setting a loss against trading profits, against general income or against capital gains (which are covered later in this Text), so that tax need not be paid on them. There are restrictions on how much loss relief can be claimed in a tax year.

An important consideration is the choice between different reliefs. The aim is to use a loss to save as much tax as possible, as quickly as possible.

In the next chapter we will see how the rules on trading profits and losses for sole traders are extended to those trading in partnership.

Study guide

		Intellectual level
B3	**Income from self-employment**	
(i)	Relief for trading losses	
(i)(i)	Understand how trading losses can be carried forward.	2
(i)(ii)	Understand how trading losses can be claimed against total income and chargeable gains, and the restriction that can apply.	2
(i)(iii)	Explain and compute the relief for trading losses in the early years of a trade.	1
(i)(iv)	Explain and compute terminal loss relief.	1
(i)(v)	Recognise the factors that will influence the choice of loss relief claim.	2

Exam guide

Section A questions on loss relief may deal with a specific aspect such as the cap on loss relief against general income.

Section B could have a detailed computational question involving the carry back and carry forward of losses for a sole trader. Ensure you know the rules for ongoing trades and the additional relief in the early years of trading. On cessation, terminal loss relief may be used. Once you have established the reliefs available look to see which is most beneficial.

1 Losses

FAST FORWARD

> Trading losses may be relieved against future profits of the same trade, against general income and against capital gains.

1.1 Introduction

When computing taxable trade profits, profits may turn out to be negative, meaning a loss has been made in the basis period. **A loss is computed in exactly the same way as a profit**, making the same adjustments to the accounts profit or loss.

If there is a loss in a basis period, the taxable trade profits for the tax year based on that basis period are nil.

This chapter considers how losses are calculated and how a loss-suffering taxpayer can use a loss to reduce his tax liability.

The rules in this chapter apply only to individuals, trading alone or in partnership. They do not apply to a business using the cash basis. Loss reliefs for companies are completely different and are covered later in this Text.

1.2 The computation of the loss

The trade loss for a tax year is the trade loss in the basis period for that tax year.

1.3 Example: computation of trade loss

Here is an example of a trader with a 31 December year end who has been trading for many years.

Period of account		Loss
		£
Y/e 31.12.14		9,000
Y/e 31.12.15		24,000

Tax year	Basis period	Trade loss for the tax year
		£
2014/15	Y/e 31.12.14	9,000
2015/16	Y/e 31.12.15	24,000

1.4 How loss relief is given

Loss relief is given by deducting the loss from total income to calculate net income. Carry forward loss relief and terminal loss relief can only be set against the trading profits of the same trade. Other loss reliefs may be set against general income (ie any component of total income).

2 Carry forward trade loss relief

Trading losses may be relieved against future profits of the same trade. The relief is against the first available profits of the same trade.

2.1 The relief

A trade loss not relieved in any other way will be **carried forward to set against the first available trade profits of the same trade** in the calculation of net trading income. Losses may be carried forward for any number of years unless they have been entirely used up.

Carry forward trade loss relief is the only trade loss relief which applies to furnished holiday lettings (see earlier in this Text).

2.2 Example: carrying forward losses

Brian has the following results.

Year ending	£
31 December 2012	(6,000)
31 December 2013	5,000
31 December 2014	11,000

Brian's net trading income, assuming that he claims carry forward loss relief only are:

	2012/13		2013/14		2014/15
	£		£		£
Trade profits	0		5,000		11,000
Less carry forward loss relief	(0)	(i)	(5,000)	(ii)	(1,000)
Net trading income	0		0		10,000

Loss memorandum		£
Trading loss, y/e 31.12.12		6,000
Less: claim in y/e 31.12.13 (13/14)	(i)	(5,000)
claim in y/e 31.12.14 (balance of loss) (14/15)	(ii)	(1,000)
		0

3 Trade loss relief against general income

A trading loss may be set against general income in the year of the loss and/or the preceding year. Personal allowances may be lost as a result of a claim. Once a claim has been made in any year, the remaining loss can be set against net chargeable gains.

3.1 The relief

Instead of carrying a trade loss forward against future trade profits, a claim may be made to relieve it against general income.

3.2 Relieving the loss

Relief is against the income of the tax year in which the loss arose. In addition or instead, relief may be claimed against the income of the preceding year.

If there are losses in two successive years, and relief is claimed against the first year's income both for the first year's loss and for the second year's loss, relief is given for the first year's loss before the second year's loss.

A claim for a loss must be made by the 31 January which is 22 months after the end of the tax year of the loss: thus by 31 January 2017 for a loss in 2014/15.

The taxpayer cannot choose the amount of loss to relieve: thus the loss may have to be set against income part of which would have been covered by the personal allowance. However, the taxpayer can choose whether to claim full relief in the current year and then relief in the preceding year for any remaining loss, or the other way round.

Question	Loss relief against general income

Janet has a loss in her period of account ending 31 December 2014 of £27,000. Her other income is £20,000 part time employment income a year, and she wishes to claim loss relief against general income for the year of loss and then for the preceding year. Her trading income in the previous year was £nil. Show her taxable income for each year, and comment on the effectiveness of the loss relief. Assume that tax rates and allowances for 2014/15 have always applied.

Answer

The loss-making period ends in 2014/15, so the year of the loss is 2014/15.

	2013/14 £	2014/15 £
Total income	20,000	20,000
Less loss relief against general income	(7,000)	(20,000)
Net income	13,000	0
Less personal allowance	(10,000)	(10,000)
Taxable income	3,000	0

In 2014/15, £10,000 of the loss has been wasted because that amount of income would have been covered by the personal allowance. If Janet just claims loss relief against general income, there is nothing she can do about this waste of loss relief.

3.3 Capital allowances

The trader may adjust the size of the loss relief claim by not claiming all the capital allowances he is entitled to: a reduced claim will increase the balance carried forward to the next year's capital allowances

computation. This may be a useful **tax planning point to preserve the personal allowance or where the effective rate of relief for capital allowances in future periods will be greater than the rate of tax relief for the loss relief**.

Question | Capital allowances and loss relief

Mario is a sole trader making up accounts to 31 December each year. In the year to 31 December 2014, he makes a trading loss, before taking capital allowances into account, of £7,500. Mario has a tax written down value on his main pool at 1 January 2014 of £12,000. He does not make any additions or disposals in the year to 31 December 2014 and does not intend to make any additions or disposals in the year to 31 December 2015.

Mario has gross savings income of £19,000 in 2014/15 and wishes to use trade loss relief against general income in 2014/15 only (ie without any carry back to 2013/14). He expects to make a trading profit of £30,000 in the year to 31 December 2015.

What advice would you give Mario?

Answer

Mario should make a reduced capital allowance claim so that the loss relief claim will preserve his personal allowance in 2014/15.

The maximum capital allowances claim that Mario could make in 2014/15 is £12,000 × 18% = £2,160. He should only claim £(19,000 – 7,500 – 10,000) = £1,500. The tax written down value of the pool at 1 January 2015 will then be £(12,000 – 1,500) = £10,500 on which Mario can claim the maximum allowance at 18% for relief in 2015/16.

3.4 Trading losses relieved against capital gains

Where relief is claimed against general income of a given year, the taxpayer may include **a further claim to set the loss against his chargeable gains for the year** less any allowable capital losses for the same year or for previous years. This amount of net gains is computed ignoring the annual exempt amount (see later in this Text).

The trading loss is first set against general income of the year of the claim, and only any excess loss is set against capital gains. The taxpayer cannot specify the amount to be set against capital gains, so the annual exempt amount may be wasted. We include an example here for completeness. You will study chargeable gains later in this Text and we suggest that you come back to this example at that point.

Question | Loss relief against income and gains

Sibyl had the following results for 2014/15.

	£
Loss available for relief against general income	27,000
Income	19,500
Capital gains less current year capital losses	15,000
Annual exempt amount for capital gains tax purposes	11,000
Capital losses brought forward	9,000

Show how the loss would be relieved against income and gains.

Answer

	£
Income	19,500
Less loss relief against general income	(19,500)
Net income	0
Capital gains	15,000
Less loss relief: lower of £(27,000 – 19,500) = £7,500 (note 1) and	
£(15,000 – 9,000) = £6,000 (note 2)	(6,000)
	9,000
Less annual exempt amount (restricted)	(9,000)
	0

Notes:

1   This equals the loss left after the loss relief claim against general income
2   This equals the gains left after losses b/fwd but ignoring the annual exempt amount.

A trading loss of £(7,500 – 6,000) = £1,500 is carried forward. Sibyl's personal allowance and £(11,000 – 9,000) = £2,000 of her capital gains tax annual exempt amount are wasted. Her capital losses brought forward of £9,000 are carried forward to 2015/16. Although we deducted this £9,000 in working out how much trading loss we were allowed to use in the claim, we do not actually need to use any of the £9,000 as the remaining gain is covered by the annual exempt amount.

3.5 Restrictions on trade loss relief against general income

3.5.1 Commercial basis

FAST FORWARD
> Loss relief cannot be claimed against general income unless the loss-making business is conducted on a commercial basis.

Relief cannot be claimed against general income unless the loss-making business is conducted on a commercial basis with a view to the realisation of profits throughout the basis period for the tax year.

3.5.2 Relief cap

FAST FORWARD
> An individual taxpayer can only deduct the greater of £50,000 and 25% of adjusted total income when making a claim for loss relief against general income.

There is a **restriction on certain deductions which may be made by an individual from total income for a tax year**. For F6 (UK) purposes, the restricted deduction concerns **trade loss relief against general income, whether claimed for the tax year of the loss or the previous year**.

The total deductions in a tax year cannot exceed the greater of:

(a)   **£50,000**; and
(b)   **25% of the taxpayer's adjusted total income for the tax year.**

Key term

> For F6 (UK) purposes, **adjusted total income** is total income less the gross amounts of personal pension contributions.

If a claim is made for relief against general income in the previous year, there is no restriction on the amount of loss that can be used against trading income (of the same trade). The restriction only applies to the other income in that year. Any restricted loss can still be carried forward against future profits from the same trade.

The limits apply in each year for which relief is claimed. If a current year and a prior year claim are made, the relief in the current year is restricted to the greater of £50,000 and 25% of the adjusted total income in the current year. The relief in the prior year is restricted to the greater of £50,000 and 25% of the adjusted total income in the prior year.

Question

Grace has been trading for many years, preparing accounts to 5 April each year. Her recent results have been as follows:

	Profit/(loss) £
Year to 5 April 2014	20,000
Year to 5 April 2015	(210,000)

Grace also owns a number of investment properties and her property business income is £130,000 in 2013/14 and £220,000 in 2014/15.

Show Grace's taxable income for the tax years 2013/14 and 2014/15 assuming that she claims relief for her trading loss against general income in both of those years.

Answer

	2013/14 £	2014/15 £
Trading income	20,000	0
Property business income	130,000	220,000
Total income	150,000	220,000
Less loss relief against general income	(70,000)	(55,000)
Net income	80,000	165,000
Less personal allowance	(10,000)	(0)
Taxable income	70,000	165,000

Loss relief for 2014/15 is capped at £(220,000 × 25%) = £55,000 since this is greater than £50,000. The personal allowance is not available as adjusted net income exceeds £120,000.

In 2013/14, the loss relief claim is not capped against the trading profit of £20,000. Relief against other income is capped at £50,000 since this is greater than £(150,000 × 25%) = £37,500. The total loss relief claim is therefore £(20,000 + 50,000) = £70,000. The balance of the loss is £(210,000 – 55,000 – 70,000) = £85,000 is carried forward against future profits of the same trade.

Note that the restriction on loss relief means that the loss has been relieved at the additional rate in 2014/15 and at the higher rate in 2013/14. The personal allowance has also been restored for 2013/14.

3.6 The choice between loss reliefs

FAST FORWARD

It is important for a trader to choose the right loss relief, so as to save tax at the highest possible rate and so as to obtain relief reasonably quickly.

When a trader has a choice between loss reliefs, he should aim to obtain relief both quickly and at the highest possible tax rate. However, do consider that losses relieved against income which would otherwise be covered by the personal allowance are wasted. Consideration also needs to be given to any restriction on loss relief.

Another consideration is that a trading loss cannot be set against the capital gains of a year unless relief is first claimed against general income of the same year. It may be worth making the claim against income and wasting the personal allowance in order to avoid a CGT liability.

Question

Felicity's trading results are as follows.

Year ended 30 September	Trading profit/(loss) £
2012	3,900
2013	(21,000)
2014	14,000

Her other income (all non-savings income) is as follows.

	£
2012/13	5,800
2013/14	32,500
2014/15	17,000

Show the most efficient use of Felicity's trading loss. Assume that the personal allowance has been £10,000 throughout.

Answer

Relief could be claimed against general income for 2012/13 and/or 2013/14, with any unused loss being carried forward. Relief in 2012/13 would be against general income of £(3,900 + 5,800) = £9,700, all of which would be covered by the personal allowance anyway, so this claim should not be made.

A claim against general income should be made for 2013/14 as this saves tax quicker than a carry forward claim in 2014/15.

The final results will be as follows:

	2012/13 £	2013/14 £	2014/15 £
Trading income	3,900	0	14,000
Less carry forward loss relief	(0)	(0)	(0)
	3,900	0	14,000
Other income	5,800	32,500	17,000
	9,700	32,500	31,000
Less loss relief against general income	(0)	(21,000)	(0)
Net income	9,700	11,500	31,000
Less personal allowance	(10,000)	(10,000)	(10,000)
Taxable income	0	1,500	21,000

Exam focus point

Before recommending loss relief against general income consider whether it will result in the waste of the personal allowance. Such waste is to be avoided if at all possible.

4 Losses in the early years of a trade

4.1 The computation of the loss

Under the rules determining the basis period for the first three tax years of trading, there may be periods where the basis periods overlap. If profits arise in these periods, they are taxed twice but are relieved later, usually on cessation. However, a loss in an overlap period can only be relieved once. It must not be double counted.

If basis periods overlap, **a loss in the overlap period is treated as a loss for the earlier tax year only**.

4.2 Example: losses in early years

Here is an example of a trader who starts to trade on 1 July 2014 and makes losses in opening periods.

Period of account			Loss
			£
P/e 31.12.14			9,000
Y/e 31.12.15			24,000

Tax year	Basis period	Working	Trade loss for the tax year
			£
2014/15	1.7.14 – 5.4.15	£9,000 + (£24,000 × 3/12)	15,000
2015/16	1.1.15 – 31.12.15	£24,000 less loss already used in 2014/15 (£24,000 × 3/12 = 6,000)	18,000

4.3 Example: losses and profits in early years

The rule against using losses twice also applies when losses are netted off against profits in the same basis period. Here is an example, with a commencement on 1 July 2014.

Period of account			(Loss)/profit
			£
1.7.14 – 30.4.15			(10,000)
1.5.15 – 30.4.16			24,000

Tax year	Basis period	Working	Trade (Loss)/Profit
			£
2014/15	1.7.14 – 5.4.15	£(10,000) × 9/10	(9,000)
2015/16	1.7.14 – 30.6.15	£24,000 × 2/12 + £(10,000) × 1/10	3,000

4.4 Early trade losses relief

FAST FORWARD

In opening years, a special relief involving the carry back of losses against general income is available. Losses arising in the first four tax years of a trade may be set against general income in the three years preceding the loss making year, taking the earliest year first.

Early trade losses relief is available for **trading losses incurred in the first four tax years of a trade**.

Relief is obtained by **setting the allowable loss against general income in the three years preceding the year of loss**, applying the loss to the earliest year first. Thus a loss arising in 2014/15 may be set off against income in 2011/12, 2012/13 and 2013/14 in that order.

A claim for early trade losses relief applies to all three years automatically, provided that the loss is large enough. The taxpayer cannot choose to relieve the loss against just one or two of the years, or to relieve only part of the loss. However, the taxpayer could reduce the size of the loss by not claiming the full capital allowances available to him. This will result in higher capital allowances in future years.

Claims for the relief must be made by the 31 January which is 22 months after the end of the tax year in which the loss is incurred.

Early trade losses relief is an alternative to using trade loss relief against general income or using carry forward loss relief. The advantage of early trade losses relief is that it enables losses to be carried back for three years and so gives relief earlier than the other loss reliefs. Whether that is advantageous or not depends on the particular circumstances of the trader, for example whether the trader has any other income and whether there are different rates of tax in the tax years which might be affected by a particular loss relief claim.

Mr A is employed as a dustman until 1 January 2013. On that date he starts up his own business as a scrap metal merchant, making up his accounts to 30 June each year. His earnings as a dustman are:

	£
2009/10	5,000
2010/11	6,000
2011/12	7,000
2012/13 (nine months)	6,000

His trading results as a scrap metal merchant are:

	Profit/ (Loss) £
Six months to 30 June 2013	(3,000)
Year to 30 June 2014	(1,500)
Year to 30 June 2015	(1,200)

Assuming that loss relief is claimed as early as possible, show the net income for each of the years 2009/10 to 2015/16 inclusive.

Answer

Since reliefs are to be claimed as early as possible, early trade loss relief is applied. The losses available for relief are as follows.

	£	£	Years against which relief is available
2012/13 (basis period 1.1.13 – 5.4.13)			
Three months to 5.4.13 £(3,000) × 3/6		(1,500)	2009/10 to 2011/12
2013/14 (basis period 1.1.13 – 31.12.13)			
Three months to 30.6.13			
(omit 1.1.13 – 5.4.13 : overlap) £(3,000) ×3/6	(1,500)		
Six months to 31.12.13 £(1,500) × 6/12	(750)		
		(2,250)	2010/11 to 2012/13
2014/15 (basis period 1.7.13 – 30.6.14)			
Six months to 30.6.14			
(omit 1.7.13 – 31.12.13: overlap) £(1,500) × 6/12		(750)	2011/12 to 2013/14
2015/16 (basis period 1.7.14 – 30.6.15)			
12 months to 30.6.15		(1,200)	2012/13 to 2014/15

The net income is as follows.

	£	£
2009/10		
Original	5,000	
Less 2012/13 loss	(1,500)	
		3,500
2010/11		
Original	6,000	
Less 2013/14 loss	(2,250)	
		3,750
2011/12		
Original	7,000	
Less 2014/15 loss	(750)	
		6,250
2012/13		
Original	6,000	
Less 2015/16 loss	(1,200)	
		4,800

The taxable trade profits for 2012/13 to 2015/16 are zero because there were losses in the basis periods.

5 Terminal trade loss relief

FAST FORWARD

On the cessation of trade, a loss arising in the last 12 months of trading may be set against trade profits of the tax year of cessation and the previous three years, taking the latest year first.

5.1 The relief

Trade loss relief against general income will often be insufficient on its own to deal with a loss incurred in the last months of trading. For this reason there is a special relief, **terminal trade loss relief, which allows a loss on cessation to be carried back for relief against taxable trading profits in previous years**.

5.2 Computing the terminal loss

A terminal loss is **the loss of the last 12 months of trading**.

It is built up as follows.

		£
(a)	The actual trade loss for the tax year of cessation (calculated from 6 April to the date of cessation)	X
(b)	The actual trade loss for the period from 12 months before cessation until the end of the penultimate tax year	X
	Total terminal trade loss	X

If the result of either (a) or (b) is a profit rather than a loss, it is treated as zero.

Any unrelieved overlap profits are included within (a) above.

If any loss cannot be included in the terminal loss (eg because it is matched with a profit) it can be relieved instead against general income.

5.3 Relieving the terminal loss

The loss is relieved against trade profits only.

Relief is given in the tax year of cessation and the three preceding years, later years first.

Question   Terminal loss relief

Set out below are the results of a business up to its cessation on 30 September 2014.

	Profit/(loss) £
Year to 31 December 2011	2,000
Year to 31 December 2012	400
Year to 31 December 2013	300
Nine months to 30 September 2014	(1,950)

Unrelieved overlap profits were £450.

Show the available terminal loss relief, and suggest an alternative claim if the trader had had other non-savings income of £13,000 in each of 2013/14 and 2014/15. Assume that 2014/15 tax rates and allowances apply to all years.

Answer

The terminal loss comes in the last 12 months, the period 1 October 2013 to 30 September 2014. This period is split as follows.

2013/14   Six months to 5 April 2014
2014/15   Six months to 30 September 2014

The terminal loss is made up as follows.

Unrelieved trading losses		£	£
2014/15			
6 months to 30.9.14	£(1,950) × 6/9		(1,300)
Overlap relief	£(450)		(450)
2013/14			
3 months to 31.12.13	£300 × 3/12	75	
3 months to 5.4.14	£(1,950) × 3/9	(650)	
			(575)
			(2,325)

Taxable trade profits will be as follows.

Year	Basis period	Profits £	Terminal loss relief £	Final taxable Profits £
2011/12	Y/e 31.12.11	2,000	1,625	375
2012/13	Y/e 31.12.12	400	400	0
2013/14	Y/e 31.12.13	300	300	0
2014/15	1.1.14 – 30.9.14	0	0	0
			2,325	

If the trader had had £13,000 of other income in 2013/14 and 2014/15 we could consider loss relief claims against general income for these two years, using the loss of £(1,950 + 450) = £2,400 for 2013/14.

The final results would be as follows. (We could alternatively claim loss relief in 2014/15, but a claim in either year would save income tax at the same (basic) rate, so the preference is to save tax earlier rather than later.)

	2011/12	2012/13	2013/14	2014/15
	£	£	£	£
Trade profits	2,000	400	300	0
Other income	0	0	13,000	13,000
	2,000	400	13,300	13,000
Less loss relief against general income	0	0	(2,400)	0
Net income	2,000	400	10,900	13,000

Another option would be to make a claim for terminal loss relief (as above) and a claim against general income for the balance of the loss not relieved as a terminal loss £(2,400 – 2,325) = £75 in either 2013/14 or 2014/15.

However, as there is only taxable income (after the personal allowance) in 2013/14 and 2014/15 the terminal loss relief claim in fact saves no tax in earlier years, and the full claim against general income is more tax efficient.

Chapter Roundup

- Trading losses may be relieved against future profits of the same trade, against general income and against capital gains.

- Trading losses may be relieved against future profits of the same trade. The relief is against the first available profits of the same trade.

- A trading loss may be set against general income in the year of the loss and/or the preceding year. Personal allowances may be lost as a result of the claim. Once a claim has been made in any year, the remaining loss can be set against net chargeable gains.

- Loss relief cannot be claimed against general income unless the loss-making business is conducted on a commercial basis.

- An individual taxpayer can only deduct the greater of £50,000 and 25% of adjusted total income when making a claim for loss relief against general income.

- It is important for a trader to choose the right loss relief, so as to save tax at the highest possible rate and so as to obtain relief reasonably quickly.

- In opening years, a special relief involving the carry back of losses against general income is available. Losses arising in the first four tax years of a trade may be set against general income in the three years preceding the loss making year, taking the earliest year first.

- On the cessation of trade, a loss arising in the last 12 months of trading may be set against trade profits of the tax year of cessation and the previous three years, taking the latest year first.

Quick Quiz

1   Against what income can trade losses carried forward be set off?

   A   General income
   B   Non-savings income
   C   Any trading income
   D   Trading income from the same trade

2   When a loss is to be relieved against general income, how are losses linked to particular tax years?

3   Against which years' general income may a loss be relieved, for a continuing business which has traded for many years?

4   Maggie has been trading as a decorator for many years. In 2013/14, she made a trading profit of £10,000. She has savings income of £16,000 each year. She makes no capital gains.

   Maggie makes a loss of £(48,000) in 2014/15 and expects to make either a loss or smaller profits in the foreseeable future. How can Maggie obtain loss relief?

5   Marie has total income of £230,000 in 2014/15, consisting of employment income. She has also carried on a sole trade for many years, preparing accounts to 31 December. For the year to 31 December 2014, the sole trade business made a loss of £80,000. What is the maximum amount of the loss that Marie can relieve in 2014/15 under loss relief against general income?

6   Joe starts trading on 6 April 2014, having previously been employed for many years. He makes a loss in his first year of trading. Against income of which years can he set the loss under early trade loss relief?

7   Terminal loss relief can be given in the year of _____ and then in the _____ preceding years, _____ years first. Fill in the blanks.

Answers to Quick Quiz

1 D. Against trading income from the same trade.

2 The loss for a tax year is the loss in the basis period for that tax year. However, if basis periods overlap, a loss in the overlap period is a loss of the earlier tax year only.

3 The year in which the loss arose and/or the preceding year.

4 Maggie can make a claim to set the loss against general income of £16,000 in 2014/15. She can also claim loss relief against general income of £(10,000 + 16,000) = £26,000 in 2013/14. The remaining £(48,000 − 16,000 − 26,000) = £6,000 will be carried forward and set against the first available trading profits of her decorating trade.

5 Greater of £50,000 and (25% × £230,000) = £57,500.

6 Loss incurred 2014/15: set against general income of 2011/12, 2012/13 and 2013/14 in that order.

7 Terminal loss relief can be given in the year of **cessation** and then in the **three** preceding years, **later** years first.

Now try the question below from the Practice Question Bank

Number	Type	Marks	Time
Q26	Section A	6	11 mins
Q27	Section B	10	18 mins
Q28	Section B	5	9 mins

12

Partnerships and limited liability partnerships

Topic list	Syllabus reference
1 Assessment of partnerships to tax	B3(j)(i)
2 Change in profit sharing ratios	B3(j)(ii)
3 Change in membership of partnership	B3(j)(iii)
4 Loss reliefs for partners	B3(j)(iv)

Introduction

We have covered sole traders, learning how to calculate taxable trading profits after capital allowances and allocate them to tax years and how to deal with losses.

We now see how the income tax rules for traders are adapted to deal with business partnerships. On the one hand, a partnership is a single trading entity, making profits as a whole. On the other hand, each partner has a personal tax computation, so the profits must be apportioned to the partners. The general approach is to work out the profits of the partnership, then tax each partner as if he were a sole trader running a business equal to his slice of the partnership (for example 25% of the partnership).

This chapter concludes our study of the income tax computation. In the next chapter we will turn our attention to national insurance.

Study guide

		Intellectual level
B3	Income from self-employment	
(j)	Partnerships and limited liability partnerships	
(j)(i)	Explain and compute how a partnership is assessed to tax.	2
(j)(ii)	Explain and compute the assessable profits for each partner following a change in the profit sharing ratio.	2
(j)(iii)	Explain and compute the assessable profits for each partner following a change in the membership of the partnership.	2
(j)(iv)	Describe the alternative loss relief claims that are available to partners.	1

Exam guide

Section A questions on partnerships may involve allocation of profits to partners, possibly involving salaries and/or interest on capital.

A Section B question, which may be for 15 marks or 10 marks, may involve changes in partnerships such as a partner joining or leaving. As long as you remember to allocate the profits between the partners according to their profit sharing arrangements for the period of account, you should be able to cope with any aspect of partnership tax. Remember that each partner is taxed as a sole trader, and you should apply the opening and closing year rules and loss reliefs as appropriate to that partner.

1 Assessment of partnerships to tax

FAST FORWARD

A partnership is simply treated as a source of profits and losses for trades being carried on by the individual partners.

1.1 Introduction

A partnership is **a group of individuals who are trading together**. They will agree amongst themselves how the business should be run and how profits and losses should be shared. Most partnerships have **unlimited liability** for the partners for the debts of the partnership. A **partnership** is **not treated as a separate entity from the partners for tax purposes** (in contrast to a company).

It is possible to set up a **limited liability partnership** (LLP) where the liability of the partners for debts of the partnership is limited. A LLP is a legal person in its own right (similar to a company). However, LLPs and their partners are generally taxed on the same basis as unlimited partnerships, as described in the rest of this chapter.

1.2 Computing partnership profits

A business partnership is **treated like a sole trader for the purposes of computing its profits.** Partners' salaries and interest on capital are not deductible expenses and must be added back in computing profits, because they are a form of drawings.

Where the partners own assets (such as their cars) individually, capital allowances must be calculated in respect of such assets (not forgetting any adjustment for private use). **The capital allowances must go into the partnership's tax computation as they must be claimed by the partnership, not by the individual partner.**

Question

Gustav and Melanie have been in partnership for many years, preparing accounts to 31 March each year. They share profits in the ratio 3:2. In the year to 31 March 2015, the partnership's trading profit is £60,000. The partnership does not own any assets which qualify for capital allowances but Gustav owns a car (which he acquired for £22,000 in May 2014) which he uses 75% for the business of the partnership. The car has CO_2 emissions of 150 g/km.

Show the trade profits allocated to each partner for the period of account to 31 March 2015, assuming that the partnership makes the maximum capital allowances claim.

Answer

	Total £	Gustav £	Melanie £
Partnership profit	60,000		
Less: capital allowance on car £22,000 × 8% × 75%	(1,320)		
Trade profits allocated to partners (3:2)	58,680	35,208	23,472

1.3 Allocating partnership profits between partners

FAST FORWARD

Divide profits or losses between the partners according to the profit sharing arrangements in the period of account concerned. If any of the partners are entitled to a salary or interest on capital, apportion this first, not forgetting to pro-rate in periods of less than 12 months.

Once the partnership's profits for a period of account have been computed, they are shared between the partners according to the profit sharing arrangements for that period of account.

Question

Steve and Tanya have been in partnership for many years, preparing accounts to 31 October each year. For the year ended 31 October 2014, taxable trading profits were £70,000. Steve is allocated an annual salary of £12,000 and Tanya's salary is £28,000. The profit sharing ratio is 2:1.

Show the trade profits allocated to each partner for the period of account ended 31 October 2014.

Answer

Allocate the profits for the period of account ended 31 October 2014.

	Total £	Steve £	Tanya £
Profit	70,000		
Salaries	40,000	12,000	28,000
Balance (2:1)	30,000	20,000	10,000
Trade profits allocated to partners	70,000	32,000	38,000

BPP LEARNING MEDIA

1.4 The tax positions of individual partners

Each partner is taxed like a sole trader who runs a business which:

- Starts when he joins the partnership
- Finishes when he leaves the partnership
- Has the same periods of account as the partnership (except that a partner who joins or leaves during a period will have a period which starts and/or ends part way through the partnership's period)
- Makes profits or losses equal to the partner's share of the partnership's profits or losses

Exam focus point

Partners are effectively taxed in the same way as sole traders with just one difference. Before you tax the partner you need to take each set of accounts (as adjusted for tax purposes) and divide the trade profit (or loss) between each partner.

Then carry on as normal for a sole trader – each partner is treated in the same way as a sole trader in respect of his trade profits for each period of account.

Question

Taxing partnership profits

Ursula and Victor have been in partnership for many years, preparing accounts to 30 April each year. For the year ended 30 April 2014, taxable trading profits were £45,000. Victor is allocated an annual salary of £5,000 and the remaining profits are then shared between Ursula and Victor in the ratio 3:1. Neither Ursula nor Victor have any other sources of income. They were both born in 1970.

Compute the taxable income for Ursula and Victor for the tax year 2014/15.

Answer

First, allocate the profits for the period of account ended 30 April 2014.

	Total £	Ursula £	Victor £
Profit	45,000		
Salary to Victor	5,000	0	5,000
Balance (3:1)	40,000	30,000	10,000
Trade profits allocated to partners	45,000	30,000	15,000

Then compute the taxable income for the tax year 2014/15. The current year basis of assessment applies so the partnership income is the share of profits for each partner for the period of account ended 30 April 2014. It is important to note that Victor's 'salary' is not taxable as employment income but is part of his trading income.

	Ursula £	Victor £
Trading income	30,000	15,000
Less: personal allowance	(10,000)	(10,000)
Taxable income	20,000	5,000

2 Change in profit sharing ratios

If the **profit sharing arrangements change part way through the period of account**, the **profits, salaries and interest** for the period of account must be **pro-rated** accordingly.

Sue and Tim have been in partnership for many years, preparing accounts to 31 December each year. For the year ended 31 December 2014, taxable trading profits were £50,000. Sue is allocated an annual salary of £10,000 and Tim's salary is £15,000.

The profit sharing ratio was 1:1 until 31 August 2014 when it changed to 1:2 with no provision for salaries.

Show the trade profits allocated to each partner for the period of account ended 31 December 2014.

Answer

Allocate the profits for the period of account ended 31 December 2014.

	Total £	Sue £	Tim £
Profit	50,000		
1 January – 31 August (8 months)	33,333		
Salaries (8/12 × £10,000/£15,000)	16,667	6,667	10,000
Balance (1:1)	16,666	8,333	8,333
	33,333		
1 September – 31 December (four months)	16,667		
Salaries	Nil	–	–
Balance (1:2)	16,667	5,556	11,111
	16,667		
Trade profits allocated to partners	50,000	20,556	29,444

Note. Since the profit sharing arrangements changed part way through the period of account, the profits and salaries for the period of account must be pro-rated accordingly.

3 Change in membership of partnership

FAST FORWARD   Commencement and cessation rules apply to partners individually when they join or leave.

When a trade continues but partners join or leave (including cases when a sole trader takes in partners or a partnership breaks up leaving only one partner as a sole trader), **the special rules for basis periods in opening and closing years do not apply to the people who were carrying on the trade both before and after the change. They carry on using the period of account ending in each tax year as the basis period for the tax year (ie the current year basis). The commencement rules only affect joiners, and the cessation rules only affect leavers.**

Daniel and Ashley have been in partnership for many years preparing accounts to 31 December each year and sharing profits in the ratio 2:1.

On 1 June 2014, Kate joined the partnership. From that date, profits were shared Daniel 50% and Ashley and Kate 25% each.

The partnership profits for the year ended 31 December 2014 were £72,000 and for the year ended 31 December 2015 were £90,000.

Compute the partnership profits taxable on Daniel, Ashley and Kate for 2014/15 and 2015/16 and the overlap profits for Kate on commencement.

Answer

Allocation of partnership profits

	Total £	Daniel £	Ashley £	Kate £
y/e 31.12.14				
1.1.14 – 31.5.14				
Profits (5/12) 2:1	30,000	20,000	10,000	n/a
1.6.14 – 31.2.14				
Profits (7/12) 50:25:25	42,000	21,000	10,500	10,500
Profit allocation	72,000	41,000	20,500	10,500
y/e 31.12.15				
Profits 50:25:25	90,000	45,000	22,500	22,500

Taxable partnership profits for 2014/15 and 2015/16

	Daniel £	Ashley £	Kate £
2014/15			
CYB y/e 31.12.14	41,000	20,500	
First year – actual basis			
1.6.14 – 31.12.14			10,500
1.1.15 – 5.4.15			
3/12 × £22,500			5,625
			16,125
2015/16			
CYB y/e 31.12.15	45,000	22,500	
Second year – 12 months to 31.12.15			22,500

Overlap profits

Kate has overlap profits for the period 1.1.15 to 5.4.15 of £5,625.

Question

Partner leaving partnership

Maxwell, Laura and Wesley traded in partnership for many years, preparing accounts to 30 September.

Each partner was entitled to 5% interest per annum on capital introduced into the partnership. Each partner had introduced £60,000 of capital on the commencement of the partnership. From that date, profits were shared in the ratio 50% to Maxwell, 30% to Laura and 20% to Wesley.

On 1 May 2014, Wesley left the partnership. From that date profits were shared equally between the two remaining partners and no interest was paid on capital. The partnership taxable trading income for the year to 30 September 2014 was £120,000. Wesley had overlap profits on commencement of £5,000.

Compute the partnership profits taxable on Maxwell, Laura and Wesley for 2014/15.

Answer

Allocation of partnership profits

	Total £	Maxwell £	Laura £	Wesley £
1.10.13 – 30.4.14				
Interest 7/12 × £60,000 × 5% each	5,250	1,750	1,750	1,750
Profits (7/12) 50:30:20	64,750	32,375	19,425	12,950
	70,000	34,125	21,175	14,700
1.5.14 – 30.9.14				
Profits (5/12) 1:1	50,000	25,000	25,000	n/a
Profits allocated for year	120,000	59,125	46,175	14,700

Taxable partnership profits for 2014/15

	Maxwell £	Laura £	Wesley £
2014/15			
CYB y/e 30.9.14	59,125	46,175	
Final year			
1.10.13 – 30.4.14			14,700
Less: overlap relief			(5,000)
			9,700

When no-one carries on the trade both before and after the change, as when a partnership transfers its trade to a completely new owner or set of owners, the **cessation rules apply to the old owners** and the **commencement rules apply to the new owners.**

4 Loss reliefs for partners

FAST FORWARD Partners are individually entitled to loss relief in the same way as sole traders.

4.1 Entitlement to loss relief

Partners are entitled to the same loss reliefs as sole traders. The reliefs are:

(a) **Carry forward against future trading profits.**

(b) **Set off against general income of the same and/or preceding year.** This claim can be extended to set off against capital gains. The restriction on loss relief (see earlier in this Text) applies.

(c) **For a new partner, losses in the first four tax years of trade can be set off against general income of the three preceding years.** This is so even if the actual trade commenced many years before the partner joined.

(d) **For a ceasing partner, terminal loss relief is available** when he is treated as ceasing to trade. This is so even if the partnership continues to trade after he leaves.

Different partners may claim loss reliefs in different ways.

Question — Partnership losses

Mary and Natalie have been trading for many years sharing profits equally. On 1 January 2015 Mary retired and Oliver joined the partnership. Natalie and Oliver share profits in the ratio of 2:1. Although the partnership had previously been profitable it made a loss of £24,000 for the year to 31 March 2015. The partnership is expected to be profitable in the future.

Calculate the loss accruing to each partner for 2014/15 and explain what reliefs are available.

Answer

We must first share the loss for the period of account between the partners.

	Total £	Mary £	Natalie £	Oliver £
y/e 31.3.15				
1.4.14 – 31.12.14				
Total £24,000 × 9/12	(18,000)	(9,000)	(9,000)	
1.1.15 – 31.3.15				
Total £24,000 × 3/12	(6,000)		(4,000)	(2,000)
Total for y/e 31.03.15	(24,000)	(9,000)	(13,000)	(2,000)

BPP LEARNING MEDIA

Part B Income tax and national insurance contributions | **12: Partnerships and limited liability partnerships** | **171**

Mary

For 2014/15, Mary has a loss of £9,000. She may claim relief against general income of 2014/15 and/or 2013/14 and may extend the claim to capital gains.

Mary has ceased trading and may instead claim terminal loss relief. The terminal loss will be £9,000 (a profit arose in the period 1.1.14 – 31.3.14 which would be treated as zero) and this may be set against her taxable trade profits for 2014/15 (£nil), 2013/14, 2012/13 and 2011/12.

Natalie

For 2014/15, Natalie has a loss of £13,000. She may claim relief against general income of 2014/15 and/or 2013/14 and may extend the claim to capital gains. Any loss remaining unrelieved may be carried forward against future income from the same trade.

Oliver

Oliver's loss for 2014/15 is £2,000. He may claim relief for the loss against general income (and gains) of 2014/15 and/or 2013/14. As he has just started to trade he may claim relief for the loss against general income of 2011/12, 2012/13 and 2013/14. Any loss remaining unrelieved may be carried forward against future income from the same trade.

Chapter Roundup

- A partnership is simply treated as a source of profits and losses for trades being carried on by the individual partners.

- Divide profits or losses between the partners according to the profit sharing arrangements in the period of account concerned. If any of the partners are entitled to a salary or interest on capital, apportion this first, not forgetting to pro-rate in periods of less than 12 months.

- Commencement and cessation rules apply to partners individually when they join or leave.

- Partners are individually entitled to loss relief in the same way as sole traders.

Quick Quiz

1   How are partnership trading profits divided between the individual partners?

2   Janet and John are partners sharing profits 60:40. For the years ended 30 June 2014 and 2015 the partnership made profits of £100,000 and £150,000 respectively. John's taxable trading profits in 2014/15 are:

    A   £30,000
    B   £40,000
    C   £50,000
    D   £60,000

3   Yolanda and Yan are in partnership sharing profits 80:20. For the year ended 31 December 2014 the business makes a loss of £40,000. Yan decides to use his share of the loss against general income.

Yolanda must also use her share of the loss against general income. True/False?

4   Pete and Doug have been partners for many years, sharing profits equally. On 1 January 2014 Dave joins the partnership and it is agreed to share profits 40:40:20. For the year ended 30 June 2014 profits are £100,000.

Doug's share of these profits is:

    A   £42,500
    B   £45,000
    C   £47,500
    D   £50,000

5   What loss reliefs are partners entitled to?

BPP
LEARNING MEDIA

Part B Income tax and national insurance contributions | **12: Partnerships and limited liability partnerships**   **173**

Answers to Quick Quiz

1   Profits are divided in accordance with the profit sharing arrangements that existed during the period of account in which the profits arose.

2   B. £40,000.

    2014/15: y/e 30 June 2014

    £100,000 × 40% = £40,000.

3   False. Yolanda has a choice of loss reliefs:

    Loss relief against general income or carry forward loss relief.

    Her loss relief claim is unaffected by Yan's.

4   B. £45,000

	Pete £	Doug £	Dave £
Y/e 30 June 2014			
1.7.13 – 31.12.13			
6m × £100,000			
£50,000 50:50	25,000	25,000	
1.1.14 – 30.6.14			
6m × £100,000			
£50,000 40:40:20	20,000	20,000	10,000
	45,000	45,000	10,000

5   Partners are entitled to the same loss reliefs as sole traders. These are loss relief against general income, early years trade loss relief, carry forward loss relief and terminal loss relief.

Now try the questions below from the Practice Question Bank

Number	Type	Marks	Time
Q29	Section A	6	11 mins
Q30	Section B	9	16 mins
Q31	Section B	6	11 mins

National insurance contributions

Topic list	Syllabus reference
1 Scope of national insurance contributions (NICs)	B6
2 Class 1 and Class 1A NICs for employed persons	B6(a)(i), (b)
3 Class 2 and Class 4 NICs for self-employed persons	B6(a)(ii)

Introduction

In the previous chapters we have covered income tax for employees and for the self-employed.

We look at the national insurance contributions payable under Classes 1 and 1A in respect of employment and under Classes 2 and 4 in respect of self-employment.

In the next chapter we will turn our attention to the taxation of chargeable gains.

Study guide

		Intellectual level
B6	**National insurance contributions for employed and self-employed persons**	
(a)	Explain and compute national insurance contributions payable	
(i)	Class 1 and Class 1A NIC.	2
(ii)	Class 2 and Class 4 NIC.	2
(b)	Understand the annual employment allowance.	2

Exam guide

National insurance contributions may be tested in Section A or as part of a 15 mark or 10 mark question in Section B. You must be absolutely clear who is liable for which class of contributions; only employers, for example, pay Class 1A.

1 Scope of national insurance contributions (NICs)

Four classes of national insurance contribution (NIC) exist, as set out below.

(a) **Class 1**. This is divided into:

    (i) **Primary**, paid by employees

    (ii) **Secondary**, **Class 1A** and **Class 1B** paid by employers

(b) **Class 2**. Paid by the self-employed

(c) **Class 3**. Voluntary contributions (paid to maintain rights to certain state benefits)

(d) **Class 4**. Paid by the self-employed

Exam focus point

Class 1B and Class 3 contributions are outside the scope of your syllabus.

The National Insurance Contributions Office (NICO), which is part of HM Revenue and Customs, examines employers' records and procedures to ensure that the correct amounts of NICs are collected.

2 Class 1 and Class 1A NICs for employed persons

2.1 Class 1 NICs

FAST FORWARD

Class 1 NICs are payable by employees and employers on earnings.

Both **employees** and **employers pay NICs** related to the employee's earnings. NICs are not deductible from an employee's gross salary for income tax purposes. However, employers' contributions are deductible trade expenses.

2.1.1 Earnings

'Earnings' broadly comprise gross pay, excluding benefits which cannot be turned into cash by surrender (eg holidays). Earnings also include payments for use of the employee's own car on business over the approved amount of 45p per mile (irrespective of total mileage). Therefore, where an employer reimburses an employee using his own car for business mileage, the earnings element is the excess of the mileage rate paid over 45 per mile. This applies even where business mileage exceeds 10,000 in a tax year.

Certain payments are exempt. In general the income tax and NIC exemptions mirror one another. For example, payment of personal incidental expenses covered by the £5/£10 a night income tax de minimis exemption are excluded from NIC earnings. Relocation expenses of a type exempt from income tax are also excluded from NIC earnings but without the income tax £8,000 upper limit (although expenses exceeding £8,000 are subject to Class 1A NICs as described below).

An expense with a business purpose is not treated as earnings. For example, if an employee is reimbursed for business travel or for staying in a hotel on the employer's business this is not normally 'earnings'. Again the NIC rules for travel expenses follow the income tax rules.

One commonly met expenses payment is telephone calls. If an employee is reimbursed for his own telephone charges the reimbursed cost of private calls (and all reimbursed rental) is earnings.

In general, non cash vouchers are subject to Class 1 NICs. However, the following are exempt.

- Childcare vouchers up to the amount exempt from income tax (see earlier in this Text)
- Any other voucher which is exempt from income tax

An employer's contribution to an employee's occupational or private registered pension scheme is excluded from the definition of 'earnings'.

2.1.2 Rates of Class 1 NICs

The rates of contribution for 2014/15, and the income bands to which they apply, are set out in the Rates and Allowance Tables in this Text.

Employees pay main primary contributions of 12% of earnings between the primary earnings threshold of £7,956 and the upper earnings limit (UEL) of £41,865 or the equivalent monthly or weekly limit (see below). They also pay additional primary contributions of 2% on earnings above the upper earnings limit.

Employers pay secondary contributions of 13.8% on earnings above the secondary earnings threshold of £7,956 or the equivalent monthly or weekly limit. There is no upper limit.

If an individual has more than one job then NIC is calculated on the earnings from each job separately and independently. However there is an overall annual maximum amount of Class 1 NIC any individual will be due to pay. If the total NIC paid from those different jobs exceeds the maximum that individual can claim a refund of the excess.

2.1.3 Earnings period

NICs are calculated in relation to an earnings period. This is the period to which earnings paid to an employee are deemed to relate. Where earnings are paid at regular intervals, the earnings period will generally be equated with the payment interval, for example a week or a month. An earnings period cannot usually be less than seven days long.

Exam focus point

In the exam NICs will generally be calculated on an annual basis.

Question	Class 1 contributions

Sally works for Red plc. She is paid £4,000 per month.

Show Sally's primary contributions and the secondary contributions paid by Red plc for 2014/15.

Answer

Primary earnings threshold £7,956
Secondary earnings threshold £7,956
Upper earnings limit £41,865
Annual salary £4,000 × 12 = £48,000

Sally
Primary contributions
£(41,865 − 7,956) = £33,909 × 12% (main)
£(48,000 − 41,865) = £6,135 × 2% (additional)
Total primary contributions

	£
	4,069
	123
	4,192

Red plc
Secondary contributions
£(48,000 − 7,956) = £40,044 × 13.8%

	£
	5,526

Special rules apply to company directors, regardless of whether they are paid at regular intervals or not. Where a person is a director at the beginning of the tax year, his earnings period is the tax year, even if he ceases to be director during the year. **The annual limits as shown in the Tax Tables apply.**

Question

Bill and Ben work for Weed Ltd. Bill is a monthly paid employee. Ben who is a director of Weed Ltd, is also paid monthly. Each is paid an annual salary of £40,800 in 2014/15 and each also received a bonus of £3,000 in December 2014.

Show the primary and secondary contributions for both Bill and Ben, using a monthly earnings period for Bill.

Answer

Bill
Primary and secondary earnings thresholds £7,956/12 = £663
Upper earnings limit £41,865/12 = £3,489
Regular monthly earnings £40,800/12 = £3,400

Primary contributions

	£
11 months	
£(3,400 − 663) = £2,737 × 12% × 11 (main only)	3,613
1 month (December)	
£(3,489 − 663) = £2,826 × 12% (main)	339
£(3,400 + 3,000 − 3,489) = £2,911 × 2% (additional)	58
Total primary contributions	4,010

Secondary contributions

	£
11 months	
£(3,400 − 663) = £2,737 × 13.8% × 11	4,155
1 month (December)	
£(3,400 + 3,000 − 663) = £5,737 × 13.8%	792
Total secondary contributions	4,947

Ben
Total earnings £(40,800 + 3,000) = £43,800

Primary contributions

	£
Total earnings exceed UEL	
£(41,865 − 7,956) = £33,909 × 12% (main)	4,069
£(43,800 − 41,865) = £1,935 × 2% (additional)	39
Total primary	4,108

Secondary contributions

£(43,800 − 7,956) = £35,844 × 13.8%	4,946

Because Ben is a director an annual earnings period applies. The effect of this is that increased primary contributions are due.

2.1.4 Employment allowance

The employment allowance enables an employer to reduce its total Class 1 secondary contributions by up to £2,000 per tax year.

An employer can make a claim to **reduce its total Class 1 secondary contributions** by an **employment allowance equal to those contributions**, subject to a **maximum allowance of £2,000 per tax year.**

Some employers are **excluded employers** for the purposes of the employment allowance. These include those who employ **employees for personal, household or domestic work**, **public authorities** and employers who **carry out functions either wholly or mainly of a public nature** such as provision of National Heath Service services.

Question
Employment allowance

Blue plc is a trading company which has two employees, one who earns £20,000 per year and the other who earns £15,000 per year. Each employee is paid in equal monthly amounts and so an annual computation of Class 1 computation can be made.

Calculate the Class 1 secondary contributions payable by Blue plc for 2014/15.

Answer

	£
Employee 1: £(20,000 − 7,956) = 12,044 × 13.8%	1,662
Employee 2: £(15,000 − 7,956) = 7,044 × 13.8%	972
	2,634
Less: employment allowance (maximum)	(2,000)
Secondary contributions 2014/15	634

2.2 Class 1A NICs

Class 1A NICs are payable by employers on benefits provided for employees.

Employers must pay Class 1A NIC at 13.8% in respect of most taxable benefits. Taxable benefits are calculated in accordance with income tax rules. There is no Class 1A in respect of any benefits already treated as earnings for Class 1 purposes (eg non cash vouchers). Tax exempt benefits are not liable to Class 1A NIC.

No contributions are levied when an employee is earning less than £8,500 a year.

 **Question**   Class 1A NIC

James has the following benefits for income tax purposes

	£
Company car	5,200
Living accommodation	10,000
Medical insurance	800

Calculate the Class 1A NICs that the employer will have to pay.

Answer

Total benefits are £16,000 (£10,000 + £5,200 + £800)

Class 1A NICs:

13.8% × £16,000 = £2,208

2.3 Miscellaneous points

Class 1 contributions are collected under the PAYE system described earlier in this Text.

Class 1A contributions are collected annually in arrears. If the payment is made electronically, payment must reach HMRC's bank account no later than 22 July following the end of the tax year. Payment by cheque must reach HMRC no later than 19 July following the end of the tax year.

It is important to note that Class 1 and 1A contributions broadly apply to amounts which are taxable as employment income. They do not apply to dividends paid to directors and employees who are also shareholders in the company. This means that it may be more tax-efficient for an employee/shareholder to receive payment from a company in the form of dividends. We look at this situation when we consider the company's liability to corporation tax later in this Text.

3 Class 2 and Class 4 NICs for self-employed persons

FAST FORWARD
> The self-employed pay Class 2 and Class 4 NICs. Class 2 NICs are paid at a flat weekly rate. Class 4 NICs are based on the level of the individual's profits.

3.1 Class 2 contributions

The self-employed (sole traders and partners) pay NICs in two ways.

Class 2 contributions are payable at a flat rate. It is possible, however, to be excepted from payment of Class 2 contributions (or to obtain a repayment of contributions already paid) if **annual accounts profits are less than the small earnings exception limit which is £5,885 (2014/15). The Class 2 rate for 2014/15 is £2.75 a week.**

HMRC recommend that Class 2 contributions be paid monthly or six monthly by direct debit. Alternatively payments can be made in response to notices issued by HMRC twice yearly. Whichever method is used, payment for the first six months of Class 2 NICs for the tax year must be received by HMRC no later than 31 January in the tax year, and payment for the remaining six months must be received by HMRC no later than 31 July following the end of the tax year. Payment by direct debit will guarantee that these deadlines are met.

If the individual is also employed, unpaid Class 2 contributions can be collected by HMRC through the individual's PAYE tax code.

Self-employed people must register with HMRC for Class 2 contributions as soon as they start self employment. People who fail to register by 31 January following the end of the tax year in which the business starts may incur a late notification penalty (see later in this Text).

3.2 Class 4 contributions

Additionally, **the self-employed pay Class 4 NICs,** based on the level of the individual's taxable business profits.

Main rate Class 4 NICs are calculated by applying a fixed percentage (9% for 2014/15) to the individual's profits between the lower profits limit (£7,956 for 2014/15) and the upper profits limit (£41,865 for 2014/15). Additional rate contributions are 2% (for 2014/15) on profits above that limit.

3.3 Example: Class 4 contributions

If a sole trader had profits of £16,811 for 2014/15 his Class 4 NIC liability would be as follows.

	£
Profits	16,811
Less lower profits limit	(7,956)
	8,855

Class 4 NICs = 9% × £8,855 = £797 (main only)

3.4 Example: additional Class 4 contributions

If an individual's profits are £47,000, additional Class 4 NICs are due on the excess over the upper profits limit. Thus the amount payable in 2014/15 is as follows.

	£
Profits (upper limit)	41,865
Less lower limit	(7,956)
	33,909
Main rate Class 4 NICs 9% × £33,909	3,052
Additional rate Class 4 NICs £(47,000 − 41,865) = £5,135 × 2%	103
	3,155

For Class 4 NIC purposes, profits are the trade profits taxable for income tax purposes, less trading losses.

There is no deduction for personal pension premiums.

Class 4 NICs are collected by HMRC. They are paid at the same time as the associated income tax liability. Interest is charged on overdue contributions. The administration of tax is covered later in this Text.

Chapter Roundup

- Class 1 NICs are payable by employees and employers on earnings.

- The employment allowance enables an employer to reduce its total Class 1 secondary contributions by up to £2,000 per tax year.

- Class 1A NICs are payable by employers on benefits provided for employees.

- The self-employed pay Class 2 and Class 4 NICs. Class 2 NICs are paid at a flat weekly rate. Class 4 NICs are based on the level of the individual's profits.

Quick Quiz

1   What national insurance contributions are payable by employers and employees?
2   On what are Class 1A NICs based?
3   Class 2 NICs are paid by an employer. True/False?
4   How are Class 4 NICs calculated?

1   Employees – Class 1 primary contributions

    Employers – Class 1 secondary contributions
                Class 1A contributions

2   Class 1A NICs are based on taxable benefits paid to P11D employees.

3   False. Class 2 contributions are paid by the self-employed.

4   The main rate is a fixed percentage (9% in 2014/15) of an individual's tax profits between an upper profits limit and lower profits limit. The additional rate (2%) applies above the upper profits limit.

Now try the questions below from the Practice Question Bank

Number	Type	Marks	Time
Q32	Section A	6	11 mins
Q33	Section B	9	16 mins
Q34	Section B	15	27 mins

BPP
LEARNING MEDIA

Chargeable gains for individuals

Computing chargeable gains

Topic list	Syllabus reference
1 Chargeable persons, disposals and assets	C1(a), (b)
2 Computing a gain or loss	C2(a), (b)
3 The annual exempt amount	C5(a)
4 Capital losses	C2(b)
5 CGT payable by individuals	C5(a)
6 Transfers between spouses/civil partners	C2(c)
7 Part disposals	C2(d)
8 The damage, loss or destruction of an asset	C2(e)

Introduction

Now that we have completed our study of the income tax and national insurance liabilities we turn our attention to the capital gains tax computation. We deal with individuals in this chapter. Chargeable gains for companies are dealt with later in this Study Text.

We look at the circumstances in which a chargeable gain or allowable loss may arise. Then we look at the detailed calculation of the gain or loss on a disposal of an asset.

We then consider the annual exempt amount and look at the relief for capital losses, including the interaction between capital losses brought forward and the annual exempt amount. This enables us to compute CGT payable by individuals.

Following on from this, we start to identify the different types of disposals you may be presented with in the exam. We look first at part disposals. If only part of an asset has been disposed of we need to know how to allocate the cost between the part disposed of and the part retained.

Finally, for this chapter we consider the damage or destruction of an asset and the receipt of compensation or insurance proceeds, and look at the reliefs available where the proceeds are applied in restoring or replacing the asset.

In the following chapters we look at further rules, including those for disposals of shares, and various CGT reliefs that may be available.

Study guide

			Intellectual level
C1	**The scope of the taxation of capital gains**		
(a)	Describe the scope of capital gains tax.		2
(b)	Recognise those assets which are exempt.		1
C2	**The basic principles of computing gains and losses**		
(a)	Compute and explain the treatment of capital gains.		2
(b)	Compute and explain the treatment of capital losses.		2
(c)	Understand the treatment of transfers between a husband and wife or between a couple in a civil partnership.		2
(d)	Understand the amount of allowable expenditure for a part disposal.		2
(e)	Recognise the treatment where an asset is damaged, lost or destroyed, and the implications of receiving insurance proceeds and reinvesting such proceeds.		2
C5	**The computation of capital gains tax**		
(a)	Compute the amount of capital gains tax payable.		2

Exam guide

Section A questions on the topics in this chapter may include dealing with losses or computing the amount of capital gains tax payable.

You are almost certain to have to prepare a detailed capital gains computation, whether for an individual or company in Section B. Learn the basic layout, so that slotting in the figures becomes automatic. Then in the exam you will be able to turn your attention to the particular points raised in the question. The A/(A+B) formula for part disposals must be learnt.

1 Chargeable persons, disposals and assets

FAST FORWARD

A gain is chargeable if there is a chargeable disposal of a chargeable asset by a chargeable person.

Key term

For a chargeable gain to arise there must be:

- A **chargeable person**; and
- A **chargeable disposal**; and
- A **chargeable asset**

otherwise no charge to tax occurs.

1.1 Chargeable persons

FAST FORWARD

Capital gains are chargeable on individuals and companies.

The following are chargeable persons.

- **Individuals**
- **Companies**

UK resident individuals are chargeable persons in relation to the disposal of assets situated anywhere in the world. Residence is defined for CGT in the same way as for income tax (see Section 1.2 in Chapter 2).

We will look at the taxation of chargeable gains on companies later in this Text. Note that individuals pay capital gains tax (CGT) on capital gains, whilst companies bring chargeable gains into their corporation tax computation and pay corporation tax on them.

1.2 Chargeable disposals

The following are chargeable disposals.

- **Sales of assets or parts of assets**
- **Gifts of assets or parts of assets**
- **The loss or destruction of assets**

A chargeable disposal occurs on the date of the contract (where there is one, whether written or oral), or the date of a conditional contract becoming unconditional. This may differ from the date of transfer of the asset. However, when a capital sum is received for example on the loss or destruction of an asset, the disposal takes place on the day the sum is received.

Where a disposal involves an acquisition by someone else, the date of acquisition for that person is the same as the date of disposal.

Transfers of assets on death are exempt disposals.

1.3 Chargeable assets

All forms of property, wherever in the world they are situated, are chargeable assets unless they are specifically designated as exempt (see further below).

1.4 Exempt assets

The following are exempt assets.

- **Motor vehicles** suitable for private use
- **National Savings and Investments certificates** and **premium bonds**
- **Gilt-edged securities (treasury stock)**
- **Qualifying corporate bonds (QCBs)**
- **Certain chattels**
- **Investments held in new individual savings accounts (NISAs)**
- Foreign currency bank accounts held by individuals
- Decorations for bravery where awarded, not purchased
- Damages for personal or professional injury
- Debts (except debts on a security)

If an asset is an exempt asset any gain is not chargeable and any loss is not allowable.

2 Computing a gain or loss

FAST FORWARD

A gain or loss is computed by taking the proceeds and deducting the cost. Incidental costs of acquisition and disposal are deducted together with any enhancement expenditure reflected in the state and nature of the asset at the date of disposal.

2.1 Basic calculation

A gain (or an allowable loss) is generally calculated as follows.

	£
Disposal consideration	45,000
Less incidental costs of disposal	(400)
Net proceeds	44,600
Less allowable costs	(21,000)
Gain	23,600

Usually the disposal consideration is the proceeds of sale of the asset, but a disposal is deemed to take place at market value:

- **Where the disposal is not a bargain at arm's length**
- **Where the disposal is made for a consideration which cannot be valued**
- **Where the disposal is by way of a gift**

Special valuation rules apply for shares (see later in this Text).

Incidental costs of disposal may include:

- Valuation fees
- Estate agency fees
- Advertising costs
- Legal costs

Allowable costs include:

- The original cost of acquisition
- Incidental costs of acquisition
- Capital expenditure incurred in enhancing the asset

Enhancement expenditure is capital expenditure which enhances the value of the asset and is reflected in the state or nature of the asset at the time of disposal, or expenditure incurred in establishing, preserving or defending title to, or a right over, the asset. Excluded from this category are:

- Costs of repairs and maintenance
- Costs of insurance
- Any expenditure deductible from trading profits
- Any expenditure met by public funds (for example council grants)

Question | Calculating the gain

Joanne bought a piece of land as an investment for £20,000. The legal costs of purchase were £250. Joanne spent £2,000 on installing drainage pipes on the land which enhanced its value.

Joanne sold the land on 12 December 2014 for £35,000. She incurred estate agency fees of £700 and legal costs of £500 on the sale.

Calculate Joanne's gain on sale.

	£
Proceeds of sale	35,000
Less costs of disposal £(700 + 500)	(1,200)
	33,800
Less costs of acquisition £(20,000 + 250)	(20,250)
costs of enhancement	(2,000)
Gain	11,550

3 The annual exempt amount

An individual is entitled to an annual exempt amount for each tax year.

There is an annual exempt amount for each tax year. For each individual for 2014/15 it is £11,000.

The annual exempt amount is deducted from the **chargeable gains** for the year after the deductions of losses and other reliefs. The resulting amount is the individual's **taxable gains**.

An individual who has gains taxable at more than one rate of tax may deduct the annual exempt amount for that year in the way that produces the lowest possible tax charge.

4 Capital losses

Losses are set off against gains of the same year and any excess carried forward. Brought forward losses are only set off to reduce net gains down to the amount of the annual exempt amount.

4.1 Allowable losses of the same year

Allowable capital losses arising in a tax year are deducted from gains arising in the same tax year.

An individual who has gains taxable at more than one rate of tax may deduct any allowable losses in the way that produces the lowest possible tax charge.

Any loss which cannot be set off is carried forward to set against future gains. Losses must be used as soon as possible (but see below).

4.2 Allowable losses brought forward

Allowable losses brought forward are only set off to reduce net current year gains to the annual exempt amount. No set-off is made if net chargeable gains for the current year do not exceed the annual exempt amount.

Net current year gains are current year gains less current year allowable losses. Note that if a claim is made to set trading losses against capital gains in any tax year (as we saw earlier in this Text), they will be set off before capital losses brought forward. Unlike capital losses brought forward, trading losses cannot be restricted to preserve the annual exempt amount.

4.3 Example: the use of losses

(a) George has gains for 2014/15 of £13,000 and allowable losses of £6,000. As the losses are *current year losses* they must be fully relieved against the £13,000 of gains to produce net gains of £7,000 despite the fact that net gains are below the annual exempt amount.

(b) Bob has gains of £14,900 for 2014/15 and allowable losses brought forward of £6,000. Bob restricts his loss relief to £3,900 so as to leave net gains of £(14,900 – 3,900) = £11,000, which will be exactly covered by his annual exempt amount for 2014/15. The remaining £2,100 of losses will be carried forward to 2015/16.

(c) Tom has gains of £10,500 for 2014/15 and losses brought forward from 2013/14 of £4,000. He will not use any of his brought forward losses in 2014/15 and instead will carry forward all of his losses to 2015/16. His gains of £10,500 are covered by his annual exempt amount for 2014/15.

5 CGT payable by individuals

Capital gains tax is usually payable at the rate of 18% or 28% depending on the individual's taxable income.

One of the competencies you require to fulfil performance objective 19 of the PER is the ability to evaluate and compute taxes payable. You can apply the knowledge you obtain from this section of the text to help to demonstrate this competence.

Taxable gains are usually chargeable to capital gains tax at the rate of 18% or 28% depending on the individual's taxable income.

To work out which rate applies, follow these rules:

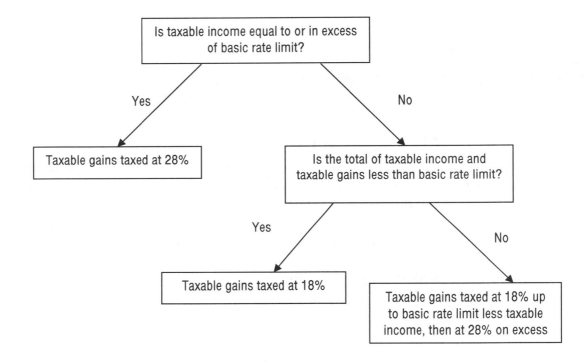

Remember that the basic rate band limit will usually be £31,865 for 2014/15 but the limit will be increased by the gross amount of gift aid donations and personal pension contributions.

Question

Mo has taxable income of £22,495 in 2014/15. He made personal pension contributions of £242 (net) per month during 2014/15. In December 2014, he makes a chargeable gain of £28,900. The gain does not qualify for entrepreneurs' relief (see below).

Calculate the CGT payable by Mo for 2014/15.

Answer

	£
Chargeable gain	28,900
Less: annual exempt amount	(11,000)
Taxable gain	17,900
Basic rate limit	31,865
Add: personal pension contributions £(242 × 12) = £2,904 × 100/80	3,630
Increased basic rate limit	35,495
CGT	
£(35,495 – 22,495) = £13,000 @ 18%	2,340
£(17,900 – 13,000) = £4,900 @ 28%	1,372
Total CGT payable	3,712

There is also a special 10% rate of tax for gains on which the taxpayer claims entrepreneurs' relief. We will look at this situation later in this Text when we deal with entrepreneurs' relief.

6 Transfers between spouses/civil partners

FAST FORWARD

Disposals between spouses or members of a civil partnership are made on a no gain no loss basis and do not give rise to a chargeable gain or allowable loss.

Spouses/civil partners are taxed as two separate people. Each has an annual exempt amount, and losses of one spouse/civil partner cannot be set against gains of the other.

Disposals between spouses/civil partners living together give rise to no gain no loss, whatever actual price (if any) was charged by the transferor. **This means that there is no chargeable gain or allowable loss, and the transferee takes over the transferor's cost.** This is not the same as the disposal being exempt from CGT.

Since transfers between spouses/civil partners are on a no gain no loss basis, it may be beneficial to transfer the whole or part of an asset to the spouse/civil partner with an unused annual exempt amount or with taxable income below the basic rate limit.

Question

Inter spouse transfer

Harry is a higher rate taxpayer who always makes gains of at least £20,000 each year on disposals of investments. His wife, Margaret, has taxable income of £1,995 each year and has no chargeable assets.

Harry bought a plot of land for £150,000 in 2010. He gave it to Margaret when it was worth £180,000 on 10 May 2013. Margaret sold it on 27 August 2014 for £190,000. The land does not qualify for entrepreneurs' relief.

Calculate any chargeable gains arising to Harry and Margaret and show the tax saving arising from the transfer between Harry and Margaret, followed by the disposal by Margaret, instead of a disposal in August 2014 by Harry.

The disposal from Harry to Margaret in May 2013 is a no gain no loss disposal. Harry has no chargeable gain, and the cost for Margaret is Harry's original cost.

The gain on the sale by Margaret in August 2014 is:

	£
Proceeds of sale	190,000
Less cost	(150,000)
Gain	40,000

If Harry had made the disposal in August 2014, the whole of the gain would have been taxed at 28%.

Margaret's gain will be reduced by her annual exempt amount, saving tax at 28% on that amount compared with the situation where Harry makes the disposal.

Margaret also has £(31,865 − 1,995) = £29,870 of her basic rate band remaining. She will be taxable at 18% on the gain within the basic rate band, instead of 28% if Harry makes the disposal.

The tax saving is therefore:

	£
Tax saved on annual exempt amount £11,000 @ 28%	3,080
Tax saved at basic rate £(40,000 − 11,000) = £29,000 @ (28 − 18)%	2,900
Tax saving on disposal by Margaret instead of Harry	5,980

7 Part disposals

FAST FORWARD

On a part disposal, the cost must be apportioned between the part disposed of and the part retained.

The disposal of part of a chargeable asset is a chargeable event. The chargeable gain (or allowable loss) is computed by deducting a fraction of the original cost of the whole asset from the disposal value. The balance of the cost is carried forward until the eventual disposal of the remaining part of the asset.

Exam formula

The fraction is:

$$\text{Cost} \times \frac{A}{A+B} = \frac{\text{value of the part disposed of}}{\text{value of the part disposed of} + \text{market value of the remainder}}$$

In this fraction, A is the proceeds *before* deducting incidental costs of disposal.

The part disposal fraction should not be applied indiscriminately. Any expenditure incurred wholly in respect of a particular part of an asset should be treated as an allowable deduction in full for that part and not apportioned. An example of this is incidental selling expenses, which are wholly attributable to the part disposed of.

Question

Part disposal

Mr Heal owns a four hectare plot of land which originally cost him £150,000. He sold one hectare in July 2014 for £60,000. The incidental costs of sales were £3,000. The market value of the three hectares remaining is estimated to be £180,000. What is the gain on the sale of the one hectare?

Answer

The amount of the cost attributable to the part sold is

$$\frac{60,000}{60,000+180,000} \times £150,000 = £37,500$$

	£
Proceeds	60,000
Less: disposal cost	(3,000)
Net proceed of sale	57,000
Less cost (see above)	(37,500)
Gain	19,500

8 The damage, loss or destruction of an asset

 FAST FORWARD

The gain which would otherwise arise on the receipt of insurance proceeds may, subject to certain conditions, be deferred.

8.1 Destruction or loss of an asset

If an asset is destroyed any compensation or insurance monies received will normally be brought into an ordinary CGT disposal computation as proceeds.

If all the proceeds are applied for the replacement of the asset within 12 months, any gain can be deducted from the cost of the replacement asset. The replacement asset can be any type of asset as long as it falls within the charge to CGT.

If only part of the proceeds are used, the gain immediately chargeable can be limited to the amount not used. The rest of the gain is then deducted from the cost of the replacement.

Question

Asset destroyed

Fiona bought an asset for £25,000. It was destroyed in July 2014. Insurance proceeds were £34,000, and Fiona spent £30,500 on a replacement asset in January 2015. Compute the gain immediately chargeable and the base cost of the new asset.

Answer

	£
Proceeds	34,000
Less cost	(25,000)
Gain	9,000
Gain immediately chargeable £(34,000 – 30,500)	(3,500)
Deduction from base cost	5,500

The base cost of the new asset is £(30,500 – 5,500) = £25,000.

8.2 Damage to an asset

If an asset is damaged then the receipt of any compensation or insurance monies received will normally be treated as a part disposal.

If all the proceeds are applied in restoring the asset the taxpayer can elect to disregard the part disposal. The proceeds will instead be deducted from the cost of the asset.

Question   Asset damaged

Frank bought an investment property for £100,000 in May 2014. It was damaged two and a half months later. Insurance proceeds of £20,000 were received in November 2014, and Frank spent a total of £25,000 on restoring the property. Prior to restoration the property was worth £120,000. Compute the chargeable gain immediately chargeable, if any, and the base cost of the restored property assuming Frank elects for there to be no part disposal.

How would your answer differ if no election were made?

Answer

As the proceeds have been applied in restoring the property Frank has elected to disregard the part disposal.

The base cost of the restored property is £(100,000 − 20,000 + 25,000) = £105,000.

If no election were made, the receipt of the proceeds would be a part disposal in November 2014:

	£
Proceeds	20,000
Less cost £100,000 × 20,000/(20,000 + 120,000)	(14,286)
Gain	5,714

The base cost of the restored asset is £(100,000 − 14,286 + 25,000) = £110,714.

Assuming this is Frank's only disposal in the tax year, the gain is covered by the annual exempt amount. It may therefore be preferable not to make the election.

Chapter Roundup

- A gain is chargeable if there is a chargeable disposal of a chargeable asset by a chargeable person.

- Capital gains are chargeable on individuals and companies.

- A gain or loss is computed by taking the proceeds and deducting the cost. Incidental costs of acquisition and disposal are deducted together with any enhancement expenditure reflected in the state and nature of the asset at the date of disposal.

- An individual is entitled to an annual exempt amount for each tax year.

- Losses are set off against gains of the same year and any excess carried forward. Brought forward losses are only set off to reduce net gains down to the amount of the annual exempt amount.

- Capital gains tax is usually payable at the rate of 18% or 28% depending on the individual's taxable income.

- Disposals between spouses or members of a civil partnership are made on a no gain no loss basis and do not give rise to a chargeable gain or allowable loss.

- On a part disposal, the cost must be apportioned between the part disposed of and the part retained.

- The gain which would otherwise arise on the receipt of insurance proceeds may, subject to certain conditions, be deferred.

Quick Quiz

1   Give some examples of chargeable disposals.

2   On what assets does a UK resident pay CGT?

3   What is enhancement expenditure?

4   To what extent must allowable losses be set against chargeable gains?

5   At what rate or rates do individuals pay CGT on gains which do not qualify for entrepreneurs' relief?

6   Ten acres of land are sold for £15,000 out of 25 acres. Original cost for the 25 acres was £9,000. Costs of sale are £2,000. Rest of land valued at £30,000. What is the total amount deductible from proceeds?

    A   £2,000
    B   £2,872
    C   £5,000
    D   £5,600

7   Emma drops and destroys a vase. She receives compensation for £2,000 from her insurance company. How can she avoid a charge to CGT arising?

1   The following are chargeable disposals

  - Sales of assets or parts of assets
  - Gifts of assets or parts of assets
  - Receipts of capital sums following the loss or destruction of an asset

2   All assets, whether situated in the UK or abroad, unless specifically exempt.

3   Enhancement expenditure is capital expenditure enhancing the value of the asset and reflected in the state/nature of the asset at disposal, or expenditure incurred in establishing, preserving or defending title to asset.

4   Current year losses must be set off against gains in full, even if this reduces net gains below the annual exempt amount. Losses brought forward are set off to bring down gains to the level of the annual exempt amount.

5   Individuals pay CGT at the rate of 18% or 28% depending on their taxable income.

6   C. $\dfrac{15,000}{15,000 + 30,000} \times £9,000 = £3,000 + £2,000$ (costs of disposal) $= £5,000$

7   Emma can avoid a charge to CGT on receipt of the compensation by investing at least £2,000 in a replacement asset within 12 months.

Now try the question below from the Practice Question Bank

Number	Type	Marks	Time
Q35	Section A	6	11 mins
Q36	Section B	10	18 mins

Chattels and the principal private residence exemption

15

Topic list	Syllabus reference
1 Chattels	C3(a), (b)
2 Wasting assets	C3(a), (b)
3 Private residences	C3(c)

Introduction

In the previous chapter we have considered the basic rules for the capital gains computation and the calculation of CGT payable by an individual, together with the rules for part disposals and assets damaged or destroyed.

We now turn our attention to specific assets, starting with chattels. Where there is a disposal of low value assets, the chattels rules may apply to restrict the gain or allowable loss. The gain may even be exempt in certain circumstances. We look at the detailed rules.

The highest value item that an individual is likely to sell is his home. We look at the rules to see when the gain may be wholly or partly exempt.

In the next chapter we will consider the reliefs specifically available on business assets, and later we will turn our attention to the special rules for shares.

Study guide

		Intellectual level
C3	**Gains and losses on the disposal of movable and immovable property**	
(a)	Identify when chattels and wasting assets are exempt.	1
(b)	Compute the chargeable gain when a chattel or a wasting asset is disposed of.	2
(c)	Calculate the chargeable gain when a principal private residence is disposed of.	2

Exam guide

You are quite likely to come across a question on either chattels or the reliefs available on the disposal of a principal private residence.

With chattels always look for the exemption for wasting chattels, a restriction of the gain if proceeds exceed £6,000, or a restriction of loss relief if proceeds are less than £6,000. The rules for chattels apply to companies as well as individuals, but watch out for assets on which capital allowances have been given.

On the disposal of a principal private residence if there has been any non-occupation or business use make a schedule of the relevant dates before you start to calculate the gain in case it turns out to be wholly exempt.

1 Chattels

1.1 What is a chattel?

Key terms

> A **chattel** is tangible moveable property.
>
> A **wasting asset** is an asset with an estimated remaining useful life of 50 years or less.

Plant and machinery, whose predictable useful life is always deemed to be less than 50 years, is an example of a wasting chattel (unless it is immoveable, in which case it will be wasting but not a chattel). Machinery includes, in addition to its ordinary meaning, motor vehicles (unless exempt as cars), railway and traction engines, engine-powered boats and clocks.

1.2 Wasting chattels

FAST FORWARD

> Gains on most wasting chattels are exempt and losses are not allowable.

Wasting chattels are exempt (so that there are no chargeable gains and no allowable losses).

There is one exception to this: assets used for the purpose of a trade, profession or vocation in respect of which capital allowances have been or could have been claimed. This means that items of plant and machinery used in a trade are not exempt merely on the ground that they are wasting (see below). However, cars are always exempt.

1.3 Gains on non-wasting chattels

FAST FORWARD

> When a non-wasting chattel is sold for less than £6,000, any gain is exempt. There is marginal relief for gains where sale proceeds exceed £6,000.

If a chattel is not exempt under the wasting chattels rule, any gain arising on its disposal will still be exempt if the asset is sold for gross proceeds of £6,000 or less, even if capital allowances were claimed on it.

If sale proceeds exceed £6,000, any gain is limited to a maximum of 5/3 × (gross proceeds − £6,000).

Question

Chattels: gains

Adam purchased a Chippendale chair for £1,800. On 10 October 2014 he sold the chair at auction for £6,300 (which was net of the auctioneer's 10% commission). What is the gain?

Answer

	£
Proceeds (£6,300 × 100/90)	7,000
Less incidental costs of sale	(700)
Net proceeds	6,300
Less cost	(1,800)
Gain	4,500

The maximum gain is 5/3 × £(7,000 − 6,000) = £1,667.

The chargeable gain is the lower of £4,500 and £1,667, so it is £1,667.

1.4 Losses on non-wasting chattels

FAST FORWARD

> A loss on the sale of a non-wasting chattel is restricted where proceeds are less than £6,000.

Where a chattel which is not exempt under the wasting chattels rule is sold for less than £6,000 and a loss arises, the allowable loss is restricted by assuming that the chattel was sold for gross proceeds of £6,000. This rule cannot turn a loss into a gain, only reduce the loss, perhaps to zero.

Question

Chattels: losses

Eve purchased a rare first edition for £8,000 which she sold in October 2014 at auction for £2,700 (which was net of 10% commission). Compute the gain or loss.

Answer

	£
Proceeds (assumed)	6,000
Less incidental costs of disposal (£2,700 × 10/90)	(300)
	5,700
Less cost	(8,000)
Allowable loss	(2,300)

1.5 Chattels and capital allowances

FAST FORWARD The CGT rules are modified for assets eligible for capital allowances.

The wasting chattels exemption does not apply to chattels on which capital allowances have been claimed or could have been claimed. The chattels rules based on £6,000 do apply.

Where a chattel on which capital allowances have been obtained is sold at a loss, the allowable cost for chargeable gains purposes is reduced by the lower of the loss and the net amount of allowances given (taking into account any balancing allowances or charges). **The result is no gain and no loss.** This is because relief for the loss has already been given through the capital allowances computation.

If the chattel is sold at a gain the cost is not adjusted for capital allowances. This is because the capital allowances will have been repaid through the balancing charge.

2 Wasting assets

FAST FORWARD When a wasting asset is disposed of its cost must be depreciated over its estimated useful life.

2.1 Introduction

A wasting asset is one which has an estimated remaining useful life of 50 years or less and whose original value will depreciate over time. Examples of such assets are copyrights and registered designs.

2.2 The computation

The normal capital gains computation is amended to reflect the anticipated depreciation over the life of the asset.

The cost is written down on a straight line basis, and it is this depreciated cost which is deducted in the computation.

Thus if a taxpayer acquires a wasting asset with a remaining life of 40 years and disposes of it after 15 years, so that 25 years of useful life remain, only 25/40 of the cost is deducted in the computation.

Any enhancement expenditure must be separately depreciated.

2.3 Example: wasting asset

Harry bought a copyright on 1 July 2010 for £20,000. The copyright is due to expire in July 2030. He sold it on 1 July 2014 for £22,000.

Harry's gain is:

	£
Proceeds of sale	22,000
Less depreciated cost £20,000 × 16/20	(16,000)
Gain	6,000

2.4 Capital allowances

If capital allowances have been given on a wasting asset its cost is not depreciated over time.

3 Private residences

FAST FORWARD
There is an exemption for gains on principal private residences, but the exemption may be restricted because of periods of non-occupation or because of business use.

3.1 General principles

A gain arising on the sale of an individual's only or main private residence (sometimes called **his principal private residence or PPR**) **is exempt from CGT.** The exemption covers total grounds, including the house, of up to half a hectare. The total grounds can exceed half a hectare if the house is large enough to warrant it, but if not, the gain on the excess grounds is taxable.

For the exemption to be available the taxpayer must have occupied the property as a residence rather than just as temporary accommodation.

3.2 Occupation

The gain is wholly exempt where the owner has occupied the whole of the residence throughout his period of ownership. Where occupation has been for only part of the period, the proportion of the gain exempted is

$$\text{Total gain} \times \frac{\text{Period of occupation}}{\text{Total period of ownership}}$$

The **last 18 months of ownership are always** treated as **a period of occupation**, if at some time the residence has been the taxpayer's main residence, even if within those last 18 months the taxpayer also has another house which is his actual principal private residence.

Where a loss arises and all, or a proportion of, any gain would have been exempt, all or the same proportion of the loss is not allowable.

3.3 Deemed occupation

The **period of occupation is also deemed to include certain periods of absence, provided the individual had no other exempt residence at the time and the period of absence was at some time both preceded and followed by a period of actual occupation.** The last 18 months rule (see above) takes precedence over this rule.

These periods of **deemed occupation** are:

(a)   **Any period** (or periods taken together) of absence, **for any reason, up to three years**, and

(b)   **Any periods** during which the owner was **required by his employment** (ie employed taxpayer) **to live abroad**, and

(c)   **Any period** (or periods taken together) **up to four years** during which the owner was **required to live elsewhere due to his work** (ie both employed and self employed taxpayer) so that he could not occupy his private residence.

It does not matter if the residence is let during the absence.

Exempt periods of absence must normally be preceded and followed by periods of actual occupation. This rule is relaxed where an individual who has been required to work abroad or elsewhere (ie (b) and (c) above) is unable to resume residence in his home because the terms of his employment require him to work elsewhere.

Mr A purchased a house on 1 April 1989 for £88,200. He lived in the house until 31 December 1990. He then worked abroad for two years before returning to the UK to live in the house again on 1 January 1993. He stayed in the house until 30 June 2009 before retiring and moving out to live with friends in Spain until the house was sold on 31 December 2014 for £150,000.

Calculate the gain arising.

Answer

	£
Proceeds	150,000
Less cost	(88,200)
Gain before PPR exemption	61,800
Less PPR exemption (working)	
$\dfrac{261}{309} \times £61,800$	(52,200)
Gain	9,600

Working

Exempt and chargeable periods

Period		Total months	Exempt months	Chargeable Months
(i)	April 1989 – December 1990 (occupied)	21	21	0
(ii)	January 1991 – December 1992 (working abroad)	24	24	0
(iii)	January 1993 – June 2009 (occupied)	198	198	0
(iv)	July 2009 – June 2013 (see below)	48	0	48
(v)	July 2013 – December 2014 (last 18 months)	18	18	0
		309	261	48

No part of the period from July 2009 to June 2013 can be covered by the exemption for three years of absence for any reason because it is not followed at any time by actual occupation.

Exam focus point

> To help you to answer questions such as that above it is useful to draw up a table showing the period of ownership, exempt months (actual/deemed occupation) and chargeable months (non-occupation) similar to that in the working.

3.4 Business use

Where part of a residence is used exclusively for business purposes throughout the entire period of ownership, the gain attributable to use of that part is taxable. The 'last 18 months always exempt' rule does not apply to that part.

Question

Business use of PPR

Mr Smail purchased a property for £35,000 on 31 May 2008 and began operating a dental practice from that date in one quarter of the house. He closed the dental practice on 31 December 2014, selling the house on that date for £130,000.

Compute the gain arising.

Answer

	£
Proceeds	130,000
Less: cost	(35,000)
Gain before PPR exemption	95,000
Less PPR exemption 0.75 × £95,000	(71,250)
Gain	23,750

Exemption is lost on one quarter throughout the period of ownership (including the last 18 months) because of the use of that fraction for business purposes.

If part of a residence was used for business purposes for only part of the period of ownership, the gain is apportioned between chargeable and exempt parts. If the business part was *at some time* used as part of the residence, the gain apportioned to that part *will* qualify for the last 18 months exemption.

3.5 Letting relief

The principal private residence exemption is extended to any gain accruing while the property is let, up to a certain limit. The two main circumstances in which the letting exemption applies are:

(a)   When the owner is absent and lets the property, where the absence is not a deemed period of occupation.

(b)   When the owner lets part of the property while still occupying the rest of it. The absence from the let part cannot be a deemed period of occupation, because the owner has another residence (the rest of the property). However, the let part will qualify for the last 18 months exemption **if** the let part has *at some time* been part of the only or main residence.

In both cases the letting must be for residential use. **The extra exemption is restricted to the lowest of:**

(a)   The amount of the total **gain** which is already **exempt under the PPR provisions**
(b)   The gain accruing during the letting period (the **letting part of the gain**)
(c)   **£40,000** (maximum)

Letting relief cannot convert a gain into an allowable loss.

If a lodger lives as a member of the owner's family, sharing their living accommodation and eating with them, the **whole** property is regarded as the owner's main residence.

Question   Letting relief (1)

Mr Ovett purchased a house in Truro on 5 October 2000 and sold it on 5 April 2015 making a gain of £290,000.

On 5 July 2003 he had been sent to work in Edinburgh, and he did not return to his own house until 6 January 2013. The property was let out during his absence, and he lived in a flat provided for him by his employer. What is the gain arising?

Answer

	£
Gain before PPR exemption	290,000
Less PPR exemption (working)	
£290,000 × 144/174	(240,000)
	50,000

Less letting exemption: Lowest of:

(a)   gain exempt under PPR rules: £240,000

(b)   gain attributable to letting: $£290,000 \times \dfrac{30}{174} = £50,000$

(c) £40,000 (maximum)	(40,000)
Gain	10,000

Working

Period	Notes	Total ownership months	Exempt months	Chargeable Months
5.10.00 – 4.7.03	Actual occupation	33	33	0
5.7.03 – 4.7.07	Four years absence working in the UK	48	48	0
5.7.07 – 4.7.10	Three year of absence for any reason	36	36	0
5.7.10 – 5.1.13	Absent – let	30	0	30
6.1.13 – 5.4.15	Occupied (includes last 18 months)	27	27	0
		174	144	30

 ## Question

Letting relief (2)

Miss Coe purchased a house on 31 March 2000 for £90,000. She sold it on 31 August 2014 for £340,000. In 2005 the house was redecorated and Miss Coe began to live on the top floor renting out the balance of the house (constituting 60% of the total house) to tenants between 1 July 2005 and 1 January 2014. On 2 January 2014 Miss Coe put the whole house on the market but continued to live only on the top floor until the house was sold. What is the gain arising?

Answer

	£
Proceeds	340,000
Less: cost	(90,000)
Gain before PPR exemption	250,000
Less PPR exemption (working)	
$£250,000 \times \dfrac{117.8}{173}$	(170,231)
	79,769

Less letting exemption: Lowest of:

(a)   gain exempt under PPR rules: £170,231

(b)   gain attributable to letting: $£250,000 \times \dfrac{55.2}{173} = £79,769$

(c) £40,000 (maximum)	(40,000)
Gain	39,769

Working

Period	Notes	Total ownership months	Exempt months	Chargeable months
1.4.00 – 30.06.05	100% of house occupied	63	63	0
1.7.05 – 28.2.13	40% of house occupied	92	36.8	
	60% of house let			55.2
1.3.13 – 31.8.14	Last 18 months treated as 100% of house occupied	18	18	0
		173	117.8	55.2

Note. The gain on the 40% of the house always occupied by Miss Coe is fully covered by PPR relief. The other 60% of the house has not always been occupied by Miss Coe and thus any gain on this part of the house is taxable where it relates to periods of time when Miss Coe was not actually (or deemed to be) living in it.

Even if Miss Coe reoccupied all floors prior to the sale, she cannot claim exemption for part of the period of letting under the 'three year absence for any reason' rule since during this time she has a main residence which qualifies for relief (ie the rest of the house). However, she can claim exemption for the whole of the house for the last 18 months since the let part was part of her only residence prior to the letting.

Chapter Roundup

- Gains on most wasting chattels are exempt and losses are not allowable.
- When a non-wasting chattel is sold for less than £6,000, any gain is exempt. There is marginal relief for gains where sale proceeds exceed £6,000.
- A loss on the sale of a non-wasting chattel is restricted where proceeds are less than £6,000.
- The CGT rules are modified for assets eligible for capital allowances.
- When a wasting asset is disposed of its cost must be depreciated over its estimated useful life.
- There is an exemption for gains on principal private residences, but the exemption may be restricted because of periods of non-occupation or because of business use.

Quick Quiz

1 How are gains on non-wasting chattels sold for more than £6,000 restricted?
2 How are losses on non-wasting chattels sold for less than £6,000 restricted?
3 For what periods may an individual be deemed to occupy his principal private residence?
4 The maximum letting exemption is

    A   £30,000
    B   £40,000
    C   £60,000
    D   £80,000

1   Gain restricted to 5/3 × (gross proceeds − £6,000)

2   Allowable loss restricted by deeming proceeds to be £6,000

3   Periods of deemed occupation are:

- Last 18 months of ownership

- Any period of absence up to three years

- Any period during which the owner was required by his employment to work abroad

- Any period up to four years during which the owner was required to live elsewhere due to his work (employed or self employed) or that he could not occupy his private residence

4   B. £40,000

> Now try the question below from the Practice Question Bank

Number	Type	Marks	Time
Q37	Section A	6	11 mins
Q38	Section B	10	18 mins

16

Business reliefs

Topic list	Syllabus reference
1 Entrepreneurs' relief	C5(b)
2 The replacement of business assets (rollover relief)	C6(a)(i)
3 Gift relief (holdover relief)	C6(a)(ii)

Introduction

Having discussed the general rules for capital gains we now turn our attention to specific reliefs for businesses.

Entrepreneurs' relief is a very important relief. It applies on the sale of a business and certain trading company shares. It reduces the rate of tax payable from 18% or 28% to 10% on all or part of the chargeable gains arising on such disposals.

Another important relief is rollover relief, which enables a gain on the disposal of a business asset to be rolled over if a new asset is purchased for business use. This enables the payment of tax to be deferred until the business has actually retained the proceeds of sale uninvested so that it can meet the liability. This is the only relief that is available to both individuals and companies.

Finally, we consider the relief for gifts of business assets. This relief allows an entrepreneur to give away his business during his lifetime and pass any gains to the donee.

In the next chapter we will cover the computation of capital gains on the disposal of shares.

Study guide

		Intellectual level
C5	**The computation of capital gains tax**	
(b)	Explain and apply entrepreneurs' relief.	2
C6	**The use of exemptions and reliefs in deferring and minimising tax liabilities arising on the disposal of capital assets**	
(a)	Explain and apply capital gains tax reliefs:	
(i)	Rollover relief.	2
(ii)	Holdover relief for the gift of business assets.	2

Exam guide

Business reliefs are an important part of the F6 exam and may be tested in both Section A and Section B. Rollover relief may be met in either an unincorporated business or a company context, and as it is an extremely important relief for all businesses it is likely to be examined. If you are required to compute a gain on a business asset look out for the purchase of a new asset, but carefully check the date and cost of the acquisition. Do not be caught out by the purchase of an investment property. The relief for gifts of assets is only available to individuals, and effectively passes the gain to the donee. Entrepreneurs' relief is only available to individuals but is a particularly valuable relief as it reduces the rate of capital gains tax to 10%.

One of the competencies you require to fulfil objective 20 of the PER is the ability to assist with tax planning. You can apply the knowledge you obtain from this chapter of the text to help to demonstrate this competence.

1 Entrepreneurs' relief

FAST FORWARD

Entrepreneurs' relief applies on the disposal of a business and certain trading company shares. Gains on assets qualifying for the relief are taxed at 10%.

1.1 Conditions for entrepreneurs' relief

Entrepreneurs' relief is available where there is a **material disposal of business assets**.

A **material disposal** of **business assets** is:

- A disposal of the **whole or part of a business** which has been **owned by the individual** throughout the period of **one year** ending with the date of the disposal

- A disposal of **one or more assets in use for the purposes of a business at** the time at which the business **ceases to be carried on** provided that:

  - The business was owned by the individual throughout **the period of one year** ending with the date on which the business ceases to be carried on; **and**

  - The date of cessation is within **three years** ending with the date of the disposal

- A disposal of **shares or securities of a company where** the company is the individual's **personal company**; the company is either a **trading company** or the **holding company of a trading group**; the individual is an **officer or employee** of the company (or a group company) and these conditions are met either:

  - Throughout the period of **one year** ending with the date of the disposal; **or**

      –   Throughout the period of **one year** ending with the date on which the company (or group) **ceases to be a trading company (or trading group)** and that date is within the period of **three years** ending with the date of the disposal

For the first category to apply, there has be a **disposal of the whole or part of the business as a going concern**, not just a disposal of individual assets. A business includes one carried on as a partnership of which the individual is a partner. The business must be a **trade, profession or vocation** conducted on a **commercial basis with a view to the realisation of profits**. Note that gains on all business assets on such a disposal are eligible for entrepreneurs' relief, provided the business has been owned for more than a year. This is the case regardless of how long the assets themselves have been owned.

In relation to the third category, a **personal company** in relation to an individual is one where:

* The individual holds **at least 5% of the ordinary share capital;** and

* The individual can exercise **at least 5% of the voting rights in the company** by virtue of that holding of shares

For both the first and second category, relief is only available on **relevant business assets**. These are assets **used for the purposes of the business** and **cannot include shares and securities** or **assets held as investments**.

1.2 The operation of the relief

Where there is a material disposal of business assets which results in both gains and losses, losses are netted off against gains to give a single chargeable gain on the disposal of the business assets.

The rate of tax on this chargeable gain is 10%.

An individual may use losses on assets not qualifying for entrepreneurs' relief and the annual exempt amount in the most beneficial way. This means that these amounts should **first be set against gains which do not qualify for entrepreneurs' relief** in order to save tax at either 18% or 28% rather than at 10%.

The chargeable gain qualifying for entrepreneurs' relief is treated as the lowest part of the amount on which an individual is chargeable to capital gains tax. This means chargeable gains qualifying for entrepreneurs' relief will use up any unused basic rate band before those gains that do not qualify for the relief. Although this does not affect the tax on the gain qualifying for entrepreneurs' relief (which is always at 10%), it may have an effect on the rate of tax on other taxable gains.

1.3 Example

Simon sells his business, all the assets of which qualify for entrepreneurs' relief, in September 2014. The chargeable gain arising is £10,000.

Simon also made a chargeable gain of £24,900 in December 2014 on an asset which did not qualify for entrepreneurs' relief.

Simon has taxable income of £14,865 in 2014/15.

The CGT payable for 2014/15 is calculated as follows:

	Gains £	CGT £
Gain qualifying for entrepreneurs' relief		
Taxable gain	10,000	
CGT @ 10%		1,000
Gain not qualifying for entrepreneurs' relief		
Gain	24,900	
Less: annual exempt amount (best use)	(11,000)	
Taxable gain	13,900	
CGT on £(31,865 – 14,865 – 10,000)		
= 7,000 @ 18%		1,260
CGT on £(13,900 – 7,000) = 6,900 @ 28%		1,932
CGT 2014/15		4,192

Note that the £10,000 gain qualifying for entrepreneurs' relief is deducted from the basic rate limit for the purposes of computing the rate of tax on the gain not qualifying for entrepreneurs' relief.

1.4 Lifetime limit

There is a limit of £10 million of gains on which entrepreneurs' relief can be claimed. **This is a lifetime amount applicable to disposals made on or after 6 April 2008.**

Question	Limit on entrepreneurs' relief

Maureen sells a shareholding in January 2015 realising a gain of £9,300,000. The conditions for entrepreneurs' relief are satisfied for this disposal and Maureen makes a claim for the relief to apply. Maureen had already made a claim for entrepreneurs' relief in 2013/14 in respect of gains totalling £900,000. Maureen also makes an allowable loss of £(20,000) in 2014/15 on an asset not qualifying for entrepreneurs' relief. Her taxable income for 2014/15 is £200,000.

Calculate the CGT payable by Maureen for 2014/15.

Answer

	Gains £	CGT £
Gain qualifying for entrepreneurs' relief		
£(10,000,000 – 900,000)	9,100,000	
CGT @ 10% on £9,100,000		910,000
Gain not qualifying for entrepreneurs' relief		
£(9,300,000 – 9,100,000)	200,000	
Less: allowable loss (best use)	(20,000)	
Net gain	180,000	
Less: annual exempt amount (best use)	(11,000)	
Taxable gain	169,000	
CGT @ 28% on £169,000		47,320
Total CGT due		957,320

Exam focus point

The entrepreneurs' relief lifetime limit of £10,000,000 and rate of tax of 10% will be given in the tax rates and allowances section of the examination paper.

1.5 Claim

An individual must claim entrepreneurs' relief: it is not automatic. The claim deadline is the first anniversary of 31 January following the end of the tax year of disposal. For a 2014/15 disposal, the taxpayer must claim by 31 January 2017.

FAST FORWARD

2 The replacement of business assets (rollover relief)

Rollover relief is available to all businesses that reinvest in qualifying assets in the period commencing one year before and ending 36 months after the disposal concerned.

2.1 Conditions

A gain may be 'rolled over' (deferred) where the proceeds received on the disposal of a business asset are spent on a replacement business asset. This is **rollover relief**. A claim cannot specify that only part of a gain is to be rolled over.

All the following conditions must be met.

(a) **The old asset sold and the new asset bought are both used only in the trade** or trades carried on **by the person claiming rollover relief.** Where part of a building is in non-trade use for all or a substantial part of the period of ownership, the building (and the land on which it stands) is treated as two separate assets, the trade part (qualifying) and the non-trade part (non-qualifying). This split cannot be made for other assets.

(b) **The old asset and the new asset both fall within one** (but not necessarily the same one) **of the following classes.**

   (i) Land and buildings (including parts of buildings) occupied as well as used only for the purpose of the trade

   (ii) Fixed (that is, immovable) plant and machinery

   (iii) Goodwill

(c) **Reinvestment of the proceeds received on the disposal of the old asset** takes place in a period beginning one year before and ending three years after the date of the disposal.

(d) **The new asset is brought into use in the trade on its acquisition** (not necessarily immediately, but not after any significant and unnecessary delay).

The new asset can be used in a different trade from the old asset.

A claim for the relief must be made by the later of four years of the end of the tax year in which the disposal of the old asset takes place and four years of the end of the tax year in which the new assets is acquired.

2.2 Operation of relief

FAST FORWARD

A rolled over gain is deducted from the base cost of the replacement asset acquired.

Deferral is obtained by deducting the chargeable gain from the cost of the new asset. For full relief, the whole of the proceeds must be reinvested. Where only part is reinvested, a gain equal to the amount not reinvested or the full gain, if lower, will be chargeable to tax immediately.

The new asset will have a base cost for chargeable gains purposes of its purchase price less the gain rolled over.

Question

A freehold factory was purchased by Zoë for business use in August 2005. It was sold in December 2014 for £70,000, giving rise to a gain of £17,950. A replacement factory was purchased in June 2015 for £60,000. Compute the base cost of the replacement factory, taking into account any possible rollover of the gain from the disposal in December 2014.

Answer

	£
Gain	17,950
Less: rollover relief (balancing figure)	(7,950)
Chargeable gain: amount not reinvested £(70,000 – 60,000)	10,000
Cost of new factory	60,000
Less rolled over gain	(7,950)
Base cost of new factory	52,050

2.3 Non-business use

Where the old asset has not been used in the trade for a fraction of its period of ownership, the amount of the gain that can be rolled over is reduced by the same fraction. When considering proceeds not reinvested the restriction on rollover relief is based on the proportion of proceeds relating to the part of the asset used in the trade or the proportion relating to the period of trade use.

Exam focus point

> Look out for both the old and the new asset having some non-business use. You must compare the proceeds of the business use proportion with the amount reinvested in the business use portion of the new asset.

Question

John bought a factory for £150,000 on 11 January 2010, for use in his business. From 11 January 2011, he let the factory out for a period of two years. He then used the factory for his own business again, until he sold it on 10 July 2014 for £225,000. On 13 January 2015, he purchased another factory for use in his business. This second factory cost £100,000.

Calculate the chargeable gain on the sale of the first factory and the base cost of the second factory.

Answer

Gain on first factory

	Non business £	Business £
Proceeds of sale (24:30) (W1)	100,000	125,000
Less: cost (24:30)	(66,667)	(83,333)
Gain	33,333	41,667
Less: rollover relief		(16,667)
Chargeable gain (W2)	33,333	25,000

Base cost of second factory

	£
Cost	100,000
Less gain rolled over	(16,667)
Base cost c/f	83,333

Workings

1   *Use of factory*

Total ownership period:

11.1.10 – 10.07.14 = 54 months

Attributable to non business use:

11.1.11 – 10.1.13 = 24 months

Attributable to business use (balance: 54m – 24m) = 30 months

2   *Proceeds not reinvested*

	£
Proceeds of business element	125,000
Less: cost of new factory	(100,000)
Not reinvested	25,000

2.4 Depreciating assets

FAST FORWARD

When the replacement asset is a depreciating asset, the gain on the old asset is 'frozen' rather than rolled over.

Where the replacement asset is a depreciating asset, the gain is not rolled over by reducing the cost of the replacement asset. Rather it is deferred until it crystallises on the earliest of:

(a)   The disposal of the replacement asset

(b)   The date the replacement asset ceases to be used in the trade (but the gain does not crystallise on the taxpayer's death)

(c)   Ten years after the acquisition of the replacement asset (maximum)

Key term

An asset is a **depreciating asset** if it is, or within the next ten years will become, a wasting asset. Thus, any asset with an expected life of 60 years or less is covered by this definition. Plant and machinery is always treated as depreciating.

Question   **Gain deferred into depreciating asset**

Norma bought a freehold shop for use in her business in June 2013 for £125,000. She sold it for £140,000 on 1 August 2014. On 10 July 2014, Norma bought some fixed plant and machinery to use in her business, costing £150,000. She then sells the plant and machinery for £167,000 on 19 November 2016. Show Norma's gains in relation to these transactions.

2014/15 – Gain deferred

	£
Proceeds of shop	140,000
Less cost	(125,000)
Gain	15,000

This gain is deferred in relation to the purchase of the plant and machinery as all the proceeds have been reinvested.

2016/17 – Sale of plant and machinery

	£
Proceeds	167,000
Less cost	(150,000)
Gain	17,000

Total gain chargeable on sale in 2016/17 (gain on plant and machinery plus deferred gain) £(15,000 + 17,000) = £32,000

Where a gain on disposal is deferred against a replacement depreciating asset it is possible to transfer the deferred gain to a non-depreciating asset provided the non-depreciating asset is bought before the deferred gain has crystallised.

3 Gift relief (holdover relief)

FAST FORWARD Gift relief can be claimed on gifts of business assets.

3.1 The relief

If an individual gives away a qualifying asset, the transferor and the transferee can jointly claim within four years of the end of the tax year of the transfer, that the transferor's gain be reduced to nil. The transferee is then deemed to acquire the asset for market value at the date of transfer less the transferor's deferred gain.

If a disposal involves actual consideration rather than being an outright gift, but is still not a bargain made at arm's length (so that the proceeds are deemed to be the market value of the asset), this is known as a sale at undervalue. **Any excess of actual consideration over actual cost is chargeable immediately and only the balance of the gain is deferred.** The amount chargeable immediately is limited to the full gain.

Exam focus point

The asset need only be a business asset in the hands of the donor. It is immaterial if the donee does not use it for business purposes.

3.2 Qualifying assets

Gift relief can be claimed on gifts or sales at undervalue on transfers of **business assets.** The definition of a business asset for gift relief is **not** the same as for entrepreneurs' relief.

Business assets are:

(a)   Assets used in a trade, profession or vocation carried on:

   (i)   By the donor

   (ii)   By the donor's personal company (ie one where the individual holds at least 5% of the voting rights)

If the asset was used for the purposes of the trade, profession or vocation for only part of its period of ownership, the gain to be held over is the gain otherwise eligible × period of such use/total period of ownership.

If the asset was a building or structure only partly used for trade, professional or vocational purposes, only the **part of the gain attributable to the part so used is eligible for gift relief**.

(b) **Shares and securities in trading companies**

    (i)   The shares or securities are **not listed on a recognised stock exchange** (but they may be on the AIM); or

    (ii)   If the donor is an individual, the company concerned is his **personal company** (defined as above)

If the company has chargeable non-business assets at the time of the gift, and point (2) above applied at any time in the last 12 months, **the gain to be held over is:**

Exam formula

$$\text{Gain} \times \frac{\text{the market value of the chargeable business assets (CBA)}}{\text{the market value of the chargeable assets (CA)}}$$

Question
Gift relief

On 6 May 2014 Angelo sold to his son Michael a freehold shop valued at £200,000 for £50,000, and claimed gift relief. Angelo had originally purchased the shop from which he had run his business for £30,000. Michael continued to run a business from the shop premises but decided to sell the shop in March 2015 for £195,000. Compute any chargeable gains arising.

Answer

(a) *Angelo's gain*

	£
Proceeds (market value)	200,000
Less cost	(30,000)
Gain	170,000
Less gain deferred (balance)	(150,000)
Chargeable gain £(50,000 – 30,000)(actual proceeds less actual cost)	20,000

(b) *Michael's gain*

	£
Proceeds	195,000
Less cost £(200,000 – 150,000) (MV less deferred gain)	(50,000)
Gain	145,000

Question
Gift of shares – CBA/CA restriction

Morris gifts shares in his personal company to his son Minor realising a gain of £100,000. The market values of the assets owned by the company at the date of the gift are:

	£
Freehold factory and offices	150,000
Leasehold warehouse	80,000
Investments	120,000
Current assets	200,000

Show the gain qualifying for hold-over relief and the chargeable gain.

Gain qualifying for hold-over relief:

$$£100,000 \times \frac{\text{Chargeable business assets (CBA)}}{\text{Chargeable assets (CA)}} = £100,000 \times \frac{150+80}{150+80+120}$$

$$= £100,000 \times \frac{230}{350}$$

$$= \underline{\underline{£65,714}}$$

The gain which is not held-over (ie chargeable in current year) is £100,000 − £65,714 = $\underline{\underline{£34,286}}$

Chapter Roundup

- Entrepreneurs' relief applies on the disposal of a business and certain trading company shares. Gains on assets qualifying for the relief are taxed at 10%.

- Rollover relief is available to all businesses that reinvest in qualifying assets in the period commencing one year before and ending 36 months after the disposal concerned.

- A rolled over gain is deducted from the base cost of the replacement asset acquired.

- When the replacement asset is a depreciating asset, the gain on the old asset is 'frozen' rather than rolled over.

- Gift relief can be claimed on gifts of business assets.

Quick Quiz

1 Patrick has been running a trading business for five years. In 2014/15 he sold the business to Andrew realising gains of £75,000. Patrick has already used his annual exempt amount for 2014/15 against other gains. He had not made any previous claim for entrepreneurs' relief. What is Patrick's CGT liability?

2 Alice sells a factory for £500,000 realising a gain of £100,000. She acquires a factory two months later for £480,000. How much rollover relief is available?

    A   £20,000

    B   £60,000

    C   £80,000

    D   £100,000

3 What deferral relief is available when a business asset is replaced with a depreciating business asset?

4 Which disposals of shares qualify for gift relief?

1   CGT @ 10% on £75,000   £7,500

2   C. Amount not reinvested £(500,000 – 480,000) = £20,000. Rollover relief £(100,000 – 20,000) = £80,000.

3   The gain is frozen on the acquisition of a depreciating asset until the earliest of: disposal of that asset; the date the asset is no longer used in the trade; ten years after the acquisition of replacement asset.

4   Shares which qualify for gift relief are those in trading companies

     • Which are not listed on a recognised stock exchange, or
     • Which are in the individual's personal company ie the individual holds at least 5% of the voting rights

Now try the questions below from the Practice Question Bank

Number	Type	Marks	Time
Q39	Section A	6	11 mins
Q40	Section B	8	14 mins
Q41	Section B	7	13 mins
Q42	Section B	10	18 mins

17

Shares and securities

Topic list	Syllabus reference
1 Valuing quoted shares	C4(a)
2 The matching rules for individuals	C4(b)
3 The share pool	C4(c)
4 Bonus and rights issues	C4(d)
5 Reorganisations and takeovers	C4(d)
6 Gilts and qualifying corporate bonds	C4(e)

Introduction

We have now covered most aspects of the capital gains computation apart from shares and securities.

Shares and securities need special rules because an individual may hold several shares or securities in the same company, bought at different times for different prices but otherwise identical. We need to identify the shares which are disposed to compute the gain or loss.

We also discuss bonus and rights issues, takeovers and reorganisations.

In the next chapter we will conclude our study of personal taxation by considering administration.

Study guide

		Intellectual level
C4	**Gains and losses on the disposal of shares and securities**	
(a)	Recognise the value of quoted shares where they are disposed of by way of a gift.	2
(b)	Explain and apply the identification rules as they apply to individuals including the same day and 30 day matching rules.	2
(c)	Explain and apply the pooling provisions.	2
(d)	Explain and apply the treatment of bonus issues, rights issues, takeovers and reorganisations.	2
(e)	Identify the exemption available for gilt-edged securities and qualifying corporate bonds.	1

Exam guide

Shares and securities are likely to form at least part of a question on capital gains in Section B. You must learn the identification rules as they are crucial in calculating the gain correctly. The identification rules for companies are covered later in this Text. Takeovers and reorganisations are important; remember to apportion the cost across the new holding.

1 Valuing quoted shares

FAST FORWARD

Quoted shares are valued at the lower of the 'quarter-up' value and the average of the highest and lowest marked bargains.

Where quoted shares are disposed of by way of a gift, the market value of these shares is needed as 'proceeds' in order to calculate the chargeable gain or allowable loss.

Quoted shares and securities are valued using prices in The Stock Exchange Daily Official List, taking the lower of:

- The 'quarter-up' value: lower quoted price + $\frac{1}{4}$ × (higher quoted price − lower quoted price)
- The average of the highest and lowest marked bargains (ignoring bargains marked at special prices)

Question
CGT value of shares

Shares in A plc are quoted at 100–110p. The highest and lowest marked bargains were 99p and 110p. What would be the market value for CGT purposes?

Answer

The value will be the lower of:

(a) $100 + \frac{1}{4} \times (110 - 100) = 102.5$

(b) $\frac{110 + 99}{2} = 104.5$

The market value for CGT purposes will therefore be 102.5p per share.

2 The matching rules for individuals

FAST FORWARD

> There are special rules for matching shares sold with shares purchased. Disposals are matched first with shares acquired on the same day, then within the following 30 days and finally with the share pool.

Quoted and unquoted shares and securities present special problems when attempting to compute gains or losses on disposal. For instance, suppose that an individual buys some quoted shares in X plc as follows.

Date	Number of shares	Cost £
5 May 2001	220	150
17 August 2014	100	375

On 15 August 2014, he sells 120 of the shares for £1,450. To determine the chargeable gain, we need to be able to work out which shares out of the two original holdings were actually sold.

We therefore need **matching rules**. These **allow us to decide which shares have been sold and so work out what the allowable cost on disposal should be**.

At any one time, we will only be concerned with shares or securities of the same class in the same company. If an individual owns both ordinary shares and preference shares in X plc, we will deal with the two classes of share entirely separately, because they are distinguishable.

Below 'shares' refers to both shares and securities.

For individuals, share disposals are matched with acquisitions in the following order.

(a)   **Same day acquisitions**

(b)   **Acquisitions within the following 30 days** (known as the 'bed and breakfast rule') if more than one acquisition, use a 'first in, first out' (FIFO) basis

(c)   **Any shares in the share pool (see below)**

The 'bed and breakfast' rule stops shares being sold to crystallise a capital gain or loss, usually to use the annual exempt amount, and then being repurchased a day or so later. Without the rule a gain or loss would arise on the sale, since it would be 'matched' to the original acquisition.

Exam focus point

> Learn the 'matching rules' because a crucial first step to getting a shares question right is to correctly match the shares sold to the original shares purchased.

3 The share pool

3.1 Composition of pool

We treat any shares acquired (other than those acquired on the same day or within the next 30 days) as a 'pool' which grows as new shares are acquired and shrinks as they are sold.

In making computations which use the share pool, we must keep track of:

(a)   The **number** of shares
(b)   The **cost** of the shares

3.2 Disposals from the share pool

In the case of a disposal the cost attributable to the shares disposed of are deducted from the amounts within the share pool. The proportion of the cost to take out of the pool should be computed using the A/(A + B) fraction that is used for any other part disposal. However, we are not usually given the value of the remaining shares (B in the fraction). We just use numbers of shares.

Question

In August 2006 Oliver acquired 4,000 shares in Twist plc at a cost of £10,000. Oliver sold 3,000 shares on 10 July 2014 for £17,000. Compute the gain and the value of the share pool following the disposal.

Answer

The gain is computed as follows:

	£
Proceeds	17,000
Less cost (working)	(7,500)
Gain	9,500

Working – share pool

	No of shares	Cost £
Acquisition – August 2006	4,000	10,000
Disposal – July 2014	(3,000)	
Cost $\dfrac{3,000}{4,000} \times £10,000$		(7,500)
	1,000	2,500

Question

Anita acquired shares in Kent Ltd as follows:

1 July 1996	1,000 shares for £2,000
11 April 2001	2,500 shares for £7,500
17 July 2014	400 shares for £1,680
10 August 2014	500 shares for £2,000

Anita sold 4,000 shares for £16,400 on 17 July 2014.

Calculate Anita's net gain on sale.

Answer

First match the disposal with the acquisition on the same day:

	£
Proceeds $\dfrac{400}{4,000} \times £16,400$	1,640
Less: cost	(1,680)
Loss	(40)

Next match the disposal with the acquisition in the next thirty days:

	£
Proceeds $\dfrac{500}{4,000} \times £16,400$	2,050
Less: cost	(2,000)
Gain	50

Finally, match the disposal with the shares in the share pool:

		£
Proceeds $\frac{3,100}{4,000} \times £16,400$		12,710
Less: cost (working)		(8,414)
Gain		4,296
Net gain £(50 + 4,296 − 40)		4,306

Working

	No. of shares	Cost
		£
1.7.96 Acquisition	1,000	2,000
11.4.01 Acquisition	2,500	7,500
	3,500	9,500
17.7.14 Disposal	(3,100)	(8,414)
c/f	400	1,086

4 Bonus and rights issues

 FAST FORWARD

Bonus shares are shares acquired at no cost. Rights issue shares are acquired for payment.

4.1 Bonus issues

Bonus shares are shares issued by a company in proportion to each shareholder's existing holding. For example, a shareholder may have 1,000 shares. If the company makes a 2 shares for each 1 share held bonus issue (called a '2 for 1 bonus issue'), the shareholder will receive 2 bonus shares for each 1 share held. So the shareholder will end up with 1,000 original shares and 2,000 bonus shares making 3,000 shares in total.

When a company issues bonus shares all that happens is that the size of the original holding is increased. Since bonus shares are issued at no cost there is no need to adjust the original cost.

4.2 Rights issues

In a rights issue the company offers shareholders rights issue shares in proportion to their existing shareholdings.

The difference between a bonus issue and a rights issue is that in a rights issue the new shares are paid for by the shareholder and this results in an adjustment to the original cost.

Question

Rights issue

Simon had the following transactions in S Ltd.

1.10.97	Bought 10,000 shares for £15,000
1.2.10	Took up rights issue 1 for 2 at £2.75 per share
14.10.14	Sold 2,000 shares for £6,000

Compute the gain arising in October 2014.

Answer

Share pool

	Number	Cost £
1.10.97 Acquisition	10,000	15,000
1.2.10 Rights issue (1 for 2)	5,000	13,750
	15,000	28,750
14.10.14 Sale	(2,000)	(3,833)
c/f	13,000	24,917

Gain

	£
Proceeds	6,000
Less cost	(3,833)
Gain	2,167

5 Reorganisations and takeovers

FAST FORWARD The costs of the original holding are allocated to the new holdings pro rata to their values on a takeover or reorganisation.

5.1 Reorganisations

A reorganisation takes place where new shares or a mixture of new shares and debentures are issued in exchange for the original shareholdings. The new shares take the place of the old shares. The problem is how to apportion the original cost between the different types of capital issued on the reorganisation.

If the new shares and securities are quoted, then the cost is apportioned by reference to the market values of the new types of capital on the first day of quotation after the reorganisation.

Question
Reorganisations

An original quoted shareholding of 3,000 shares is held in a share pool with a cost of £13,250.

In 2014 there is a reorganisation whereby each ordinary share is exchanged for two 'A' ordinary shares (quoted at £2 each) and one preference share (quoted at £1 each). Show how the original cost will be apportioned.

Answer

Share pool

	New holding	MV £	Cost £
Ords 2 new shares	6,000	12,000	10,600 (W)
Prefs 1 new shares	3,000	3,000	2,650 (W)
Total		15,000	13,250

Working

$^{12}/_{15} \times £13,250$ = cost of ordinary shares
$^{3}/_{15} \times £13,250$ = cost of preference shares

5.2 Takeovers

A chargeable gain does not arise on a 'paper for paper' takeover. **The cost of the original holding is passed on to the new holding** which takes the place of the original holding. **If part of the takeover consideration is cash then a gain must be computed**: the normal part disposal rules will apply.

The takeover rules apply where the company issuing the new shares ends up with **more than 25%** of the ordinary share capital of the old company or the majority of the voting power in the old company, or the company issuing the new shares makes a general offer to shareholders in the other company which is initially made subject to a condition which, if satisfied, would give the first company control of the second company.

The exchange must take place for bona fide commercial reasons and does not have as its main purpose, or one of its main purposes, the avoidance of CGT or corporation tax.

Question	Takeover

Mr Le Bon held 20,000 £1 shares in Duran plc out of a total number of issued shares of one million. They were bought in 2002 for £2 each. In 2014 the board of Duran plc agreed to a takeover bid by Spandau plc under which shareholders in Duran plc received three ordinary Spandau plc shares plus one preference share for every four shares held in Duran plc. Immediately following the takeover, the ordinary shares in Spandau plc were quoted at £5 each and the preferences shares at 90p. Show the base costs of the ordinary shares and the preference shares.

Answer

The total value due to Mr Le Bon on the takeover is as follows.

		£
Ordinary	20,000 × 3/4 × £5	75,000
Preference	20,000 × 1/4 × 90p	4,500
		79,500

The base costs are therefore:

	£
Ordinary shares: 75,000/79,500 × 20,000 × £2	37,736
Preference shares: 4,500/79,500 × 20,000 × £2	2,264
	40,000

6 Gilts and qualifying corporate bonds

FAST FORWARD

> Gilts and qualifying corporate bonds held by individuals are exempt from CGT. You should never waste time computing gains and losses on them.

Key term

> **Gilts are UK Government securities issued by HM Treasury** as shown on the Treasury list. You may assume that the list includes all issues of Treasury Loan, Treasury Stock, Exchequer Loan, Exchequer Stock and War Loan.

Disposals of gilt edged securities (gilts) and qualifying corporate bonds by individuals are exempt from CGT.

A **qualifying corporate bond (QCB)** is a security (whether or not secured on assets) which:

(a) Represents a **'normal commercial loan'**. This excludes any bonds which are convertible into shares (although bonds convertible into other bonds which would be QCBs are not excluded), or which carry the right to excessive interest or interest which depends on the results of the issuer's business.

(b) Is **expressed in sterling** and for which no provision is made for conversion into or redemption in another currency

(c) Was **acquired** by the person now disposing of it **after 13 March 1984**

(d) Does not have a redemption value which depends on a published index of share prices on a stock exchange

Chapter Roundup

- Quoted shares are valued at the lower of the 'quarter-up' value and the average of the highest and lowest marked bargains.

- There are special rules for matching shares sold with shares purchased. Disposals are matched first with acquisitions on the same day, then within the following 30 days and finally with the share pool.

- Bonus shares are shares acquired at no cost. Rights issue shares are acquired for payment.

- The costs of the original holding are allocated to the new holdings pro rata to their values on a takeover or reorganisation.

- Gilts and qualifying corporate bonds held by individuals are exempt from CGT. You should never waste time computing gains and losses on them.

Quick Quiz

1   In what order are acquisitions of shares matched with disposals for individuals?

2   In July 2006 an individual acquired 1,000 shares. He acquired 1,000 more shares on each of 15 January 2008 and 15 January 2015 in X plc. He sells 2,500 shares on 10 January 2015. How are the shares matched on sale?

3   Sharon acquired 10,000 shares in Z plc in 2007. She takes up a 1 for 2 rights offer in May 2014. How many shares does Sharon have in her share pool after the rights offer?

4   What is a qualifying corporate bond?

1   The matching of shares sold is in the following order.

   (a)   Same day acquisitions
   (b)   Acquisitions within the following 30 days
   (c)   Shares in the share pool

2   January 2015 1,000 shares (following 30 days)
     Share pool 1,500 shares

3   10,000 + 5,000 = 15,000 shares

4   A qualifying corporate bond is a security which:

   •   Represents a normal commercial loan
   •   Is expressed in sterling
   •   Was acquired after 13 March 1984
   •   Is not redeemable in relation to share prices on a stock exchange

Now try the question below from the Practice Question Bank

Number	Typo	Marks	Time
Q43	Section A	6	11 mins
Q44	Section B	10	18 mins

Tax administration for individuals

Self assessment and payment of tax by individuals

Topic list	Syllabus reference
1 The self assessment system	A3(a)
2 Tax returns and keeping records	A4(a), (d)
3 Self assessment and claims	A4(a)
4 Payment of income tax and capital gains tax	A4(b)
5 HMRC powers	A5(a)
6 Interest and penalties	A6(a)
7 Disputes and appeals	A5(b)

Introduction

In the earlier chapters we have learned how to calculate an individual's liability to income tax, capital gains tax and national insurance.

In this chapter we see how individuals (including partners) must 'self assess' their liability to income tax, capital gains tax and Class 4 NICs.

We also look at how HMRC enforces compliance with tax law, including compliance checks and imposing penalties and interest.

In the remaining chapters we will consider the other taxes within the syllabus: inheritance tax, corporation tax and VAT.

Study guide

		Intellectual level
A3	**The systems for self-assessment and the making of returns**	
(a)	Explain and apply the features of the self assessment system as it applies to individuals.	2
A4	**The time limits for the submission of information, claims and payment of tax, including payments on account**	
(a)	Recognise the time limits that apply to the filing of returns and the making of claims.	2
(b)	Recognise the due dates for the payment of tax under the self-assessment system and compute payments on account and balancing payments/repayments for individuals.	2
(d)	List the information and records that taxpayers need to retain for tax purposes.	1
A5	**The procedures relating to compliance checks, appeals and disputes**	
(a)	Explain the circumstances in which HM Revenue & Customs can make a compliance check into a self assessment tax return.	2
(b)	Explain the procedures for dealing with appeals and First and Upper Tier Tribunals.	2
A6	**Penalties for non-compliance**	
(a)	Calculate late payment interest and state the penalties that can be charged.	2

Exam guide

Section A questions on the topics in this chapter might relate to the dates for filing returns or the amount of interest or penalties.

In Section B you might be asked to explain an aspect of the self assessment system, such as the filing of a return, the payment of tax or compliance checks by HMRC. Your knowledge should include the penalties used to enforce the self assessment system.

1 The self assessment system

One of the competencies you require to fulfil performance objective 19 of the PER is the ability to evaluate and compute taxes payable. You can apply the knowledge you obtain from this section of the text to help to demonstrate this competence.

1.1 Introduction

The self assessment system relies upon the taxpayer completing and filing a tax return and paying the tax due. The system is enforced by a system of penalties for failure to comply within the set time limits, and by interest for late payment of tax.

Many taxpayers have very simple affairs: receiving a salary under deduction of tax through PAYE, with a small amount of investment income which can be dealt with through the PAYE code. These individuals will not normally have to complete a tax return. Self-employed taxpayers, company directors and individuals with complicated affairs will have to complete a tax return.

Individuals within the self assessment system are required to complete and file a return every year unless HMRC recognise that their affairs have become sufficiently straightforward for no return to be required.

Conversely, individuals whose affairs become more complicated so that they are likely to owe tax must notify HMRC that they should be brought within the self assessment system.

1.2 Notification of liability to income tax and CGT

FAST FORWARD Individuals who do not receive a tax return must notify their chargeability to income tax or CGT.

Individuals who are chargeable to income tax or CGT for any tax year and who have not received a notice to file a return are required to give notice of chargeability to an Officer of the Revenue and Customs within six months from the end of the year ie by 5 October 2015 for 2014/15.

A person who has no chargeable gains and who is not liable to higher rate tax does not have to give notice of chargeability if all his income:

(a)   Is taken into account under PAYE
(b)   Is from a source of income not subject to tax under a self assessment
(c)   Has had (or is treated as having had) income tax deducted at source, or
(d)   Is UK dividends

A penalty may be imposed for late notification (see later in this chapter).

2 Tax returns and keeping records

FAST FORWARD Tax returns must usually be filed by 31 October (paper) or 31 January (electronic) following the end of the tax year.

2.1 Tax returns

The tax return comprises a basic six-page return form, **together with supplementary pages for particular sources of income.** Taxpayers are sent a return and a number of supplementary pages depending on their known sources of income, together with a Tax Return Guide and various notes relating to the supplementary pages. Taxpayers with new sources of income may have to ask for further supplementary pages. Taxpayers with simple tax returns may be asked to complete a short four-page tax return. If a return for the previous year was filed electronically the taxpayer may be sent a notice to file a return, rather than the official HMRC form.

The taxpayer must sign a declaration that the information given on the tax return and any supplementary pages is **correct and complete to the best of the taxpayer's knowledge and belief** and a statement that the **taxpayer understands** that he may have to **pay financial penalties and face prosecution if he gives false information.**

Partnerships must file a separate return which includes a Partnership Statement showing the firm's profits, losses, proceeds from the sale of assets, tax suffered, tax credits, and the division of all these amounts between partners. Each partner must then include his share of partnership profits on his personal tax return.

A partnership return must include a declaration of the name and tax reference of each partner, as well as the usual declaration that the return is correct and complete to the best of the signatory's knowledge. There is a warning on the form that if false information is given or any of the partnership's income or gains is concealed, the partners may be liable to financial penalties and/or HMRC may prosecute them.

2.2 Time limit for submission of tax returns

The **latest filing date** for a personal tax return for a tax year (Year 1) is:

- **31 October** in the next tax year (Year 2), for a **non-electronic return** (eg a paper return)
- **31 January** in Year 2, for an **electronic return** (eg made via the internet)

There are **two exceptions to this general rule**.

The **first exception applies if the notice to file a tax return is issued by HMRC to the taxpayer after 31 July in Year 2, but on or before 31 October in Year 2**. In this case, the **latest filing date is:**

- the end of three months following the notice, for a non-electronic return.
- 31 January in Year 2, for an electronic return.

The second exception applies **if the notice to file the tax return is issued to the taxpayer after 31 October in Year 2**. In this case, **the latest filing date is the end of three months following the notice**.

Question	Submission of tax returns

Advise each of the following clients of the latest filing date for her personal tax return for 2014/15 if the return is:

(a) Non-electronic
(b) Electronic

Norma	Notice to file tax return issued by HMRC on 6 April 2015
Melanie	Notice to file tax return issued by HMRC on 10 August 2015
Olga	Notice to file tax return issued by HMRC on 12 December 2015

Answer

	Non-electronic	Electronic
Norma	31 October 2015	31 January 2016
Melanie	9 November 2015	31 January 2016
Olga	11 March 2016	11 March 2016

A partnership return may be filed as a non-electronic return or an electronic return. **The general rule and the exceptions to the general rule for personal returns apply also to partnership returns.**

2.3 Keeping records

All taxpayers must retain all records required to enable them to make and deliver a correct tax return.

Records must be retained until the later of:

(a) (i) Five **years after the 31 January following the tax year where the taxpayer is in business** (as a sole trader or partner or letting property). Note that this applies to all of the records, not only the business records, or

   (ii) One **year after the 31 January following the tax year otherwise**, or

(b) Provided notice to deliver a return is given before the date in (a):

   (i) **The time after which a compliance check enquiry by HMRC into the return can no longer be commenced, or**

   (ii) **The date any such compliance check enquiry has been completed.**

HMRC can specify a shorter time limit for keeping records where the records are bulky and the information they contain can be provided in another way.

Where a person receives a notice to deliver a tax return after the normal record keeping period has expired, he must keep all records in his possession at that time until no compliance issues can be raised in respect of the return or until such a compliance check enquiry has been completed.

Taxpayers can keep 'information', rather than 'records', but must show that they have prepared a complete and correct tax return. The information must also be able to be provided in a legible form on request. Records can be kept in electronic format.

HMRC can inspect 'in-year' records, ie *before* a return is submitted, if they believe it is reasonably required to check a tax position.

3 Self assessment and claims

FAST FORWARD

If a paper return is filed the taxpayer can ask HMRC to compute the tax due. Electronic returns have tax calculated automatically.

3.1 Self assessment

Key term

A **self assessment** is a calculation of the amount of taxable income and gains after deducting reliefs and allowances, a calculation of income tax and CGT payable after taking into account tax deducted at source and tax credits on dividends.

If the taxpayer is filing a **paper return (other than a Short Tax Return), he may make the tax calculation on his return or ask HMRC to do so on his behalf.**

If the taxpayer wishes HMRC to make the calculation for Year 1, a paper return must be filed:

- **On or before 31 October in Year 2, or**

- **If the notice to file the tax return is issued after 31 August in Year 2, within two months of the notice**

If the taxpayer is filing an **electronic return, the calculation of tax liability is made automatically when the return is made online.**

3.2 Amending the self assessment

The taxpayer may amend his return (including the tax calculation) for Year 1 within twelve months after the filing date. For this purpose the filing date means:

- **31 January of Year 2; or**

- **Where the notice to file a return was issued after 31 October in Year 2, the last day of the three month period starting with the issue**

A return may be amended by the taxpayer at a time when a compliance check enquiry is in progress into the return. The amendment does not restrict the scope of a compliance check enquiry into the return but may be taken into account in that enquiry. If the amendment made during a compliance check enquiry to the amount of tax payable, the amendment does not take effect while the enquiry is in progress.

A return may be amended by HMRC to correct any obvious error or omission in the return (such as errors of principle and arithmetical mistakes) or anything else that an officer has reason to believe is incorrect in the light of information available. The correction must be usually be made within nine months after the day on which the return was actually filed. The taxpayer can object to the correction but must do so within 30 days of receiving notice of it.

3.3 Claims

All claims and elections which can be made in a tax return must be made in this manner if a return has been issued. A claim for any relief, allowance or repayment of tax must be quantified at the time it is made. **In general, the time limit for making a claim is four years from the end of tax year.** Where different time limits apply, these have been mentioned throughout this Text.

3.4 Recovery of overpaid tax

If a taxpayer discovers that he has overpaid tax, for example because he has made an error in his tax return, he can make a claim to have the overpaid tax repaid to him. The claim must be made within four years of the end of the tax year to which the overpayment relates.

4 Payment of income tax and capital gains tax

FAST FORWARD Two payments on account and a final balancing payment of income tax and Class 4 NICs are due. All capital gains tax is due on 31 January following the end of the tax year.

4.1 Payments on account and final payment

4.1.1 Introduction

The self assessment system may result in the taxpayer making three payments of income tax and Class 4 NICs.

Date	Payment
31 January in the tax year	1st payment on account
31 July after the tax year	2nd payment on account
31 January after the tax year	Final payment to settle the remaining liability

HMRC issue payslips/demand notes in a credit card type 'Statement of Account' format, but there is no statutory obligation for it to do so and **the onus is on the taxpayer to pay the correct amount of tax on the due date**.

4.1.2 Payments on account

Key term

Payments on account are usually required where the income tax and Class 4 NICs due in the previous year exceeded the amount of income tax deducted at source; this excess is known as **'the relevant amount'**. Income tax deducted at source includes tax deducted at source on interest, PAYE deductions and tax credits on dividends.

The payments on account are each equal to 50% of the relevant amount for the previous year.

Exam focus point

Payments on account of CGT are never required.

Question | Payments on account

Sue is a self employed writer who paid tax for 2013/14 as follows:

		£
Total amount of income tax charged		9,200
This included:	Tax deducted on savings income	3,200
She also paid:	Class 4 NIC	1,900
	Capital gains tax	4,800

How much are the payments on account for 2014/15 and by what dates are they due?

Answer

	£
Income tax:	
Total income tax charged for 2013/14	9,200
Less tax deducted for 2013/14	(3,200)
	6,000
Class 4 NIC	1,900
'Relevant amount'	7,900
Payments on account for 2014/15:	
31 January 2015 £7,900 × 50%	3,950
31 July 2015 £7,900 × 50%	3,950

There is no requirement to make payments on account of capital gains tax.

Payments on account are not required if the relevant amount falls below a de minimis limit of £1,000. Also, payments on account are not required from taxpayers who paid 80% or more of their tax liability for the previous year through PAYE or other deduction at source arrangements.

4.1.3 Reducing payments on account

Payments on account are normally fixed by reference to the previous year's tax liability but if a taxpayer expects his liability to be lower than this **he may claim to reduce his payments on account to:**

(a) **A stated amount, or**
(b) **Nil**

The claim must state the reason why he believes his tax liability will be lower, or nil.

If the taxpayer's eventual liability is higher than he estimated he will have reduced the payments on account too far. Although the payments on account will not be adjusted, the taxpayer will suffer an interest charge on late payment.

A penalty of the difference between the reduced payment on account and the correct payment on account may be levied if the reduction was claimed fraudulently or negligently.

4.1.4 Balancing payment

The balance of any income tax and Class 4 NICs together with all CGT due for a year, is normally payable on or before the 31 January following the year.

Question

Payment of tax

Giles made payments on account for 2014/15 of £6,500 each on 31 January 2015 and 31 July 2015, based on his 2013/14 liability. He then calculates his total income tax and Class 4 NIC liability for 2014/15 at £18,000 of which £2,750 was deducted at source. In addition he calculated that his CGT liability for disposals in 2014/15 is £5,120.

What is the final payment due for 2014/15?

Answer

Income tax and Class 4 NIC: £18,000 − £2,750 − £6,500 − £6,500 = £2,250. CGT = £5,120

Final payment due on 31 January 2016 for 2014/15: £2,250 + £5,120 = £7,370

In one case the due date for the final payment is later than 31 January following the end of the year. **If a taxpayer has notified chargeability by 5 October but the notice to file a tax return is not issued before 31 October, then the due date for the payment is three months after the issue of the notice.**

Tax charged in an amended self assessment is usually payable on the later of:

(a) The normal due date, generally 31 January following the end of the tax year
(b) The day following 30 days after the making of the revised self assessment

5 HMRC powers

5.1 Compliance check enquiries

FAST FORWARD

A compliance check enquiry into a return, claim or election can be started by an officer of HMRC within a limited period.

5.1.1 Starting compliance check enquiry

HM Revenue and Customs has powers to make compliance check enquiries into returns, claims or elections which have already been submitted.

Some returns, claims or elections are **selected for a compliance check enquiry at random**, others for a **particular reason**, for example, if HM Revenue and Customs believes that there has been an **underpayment of tax** due to the taxpayer's failure to comply with tax legislation.

An officer of HM Revenue and Customs has a limited period within which to commence a compliance check enquiry on a return or amendment. The officer must give written notice of his intention by:

(a) **The first anniversary of the actual filing date, if the return was delivered on or before the due filing date,** or

(b) **The quarter day following the first anniversary of the actual filing date, if the return is filed after the due filing date. The quarter days are 31 January, 30 April, 31 July and 31 October.**

If the taxpayer amends the return after the due filing date, the compliance check enquiry 'window' extends to the quarter day following the first anniversary of the date the amendment was filed. Where the compliance check enquiry was not started within the limit which would have applied had no amendment been filed, the enquiry is restricted to matters contained in the amendment.

The officer does not have to have, or give, any reason for starting a compliance check enquiry. In particular, the taxpayer will not be advised whether he has been selected at random for an audit. Compliance check enquiries may be full enquires, or may be limited to 'aspect' enquiries.

5.1.2 During the compliance check enquiry

In the course of the compliance check enquiry **the officer may require the taxpayer to produce documents, accounts or any other information required. The taxpayer can appeal to the Tax Tribunal against such a requirement.**

5.1.3 Completion of a compliance check enquiry

An officer must issue a notice that the compliance check enquiry is complete.

The officer cannot then make a further compliance check enquiry into that return. HMRC may, in limited circumstances, raise a discovery assessment if they believe that there has been a loss of tax.

5.2 Determinations

If notice has been served on a taxpayer to submit a return but the return is not submitted by the due filing date, an officer of HMRC may make a determination of the amounts liable to income tax and CGT and of the tax due. Such a determination must be made to the best of the officer's information and belief, and is then treated as if it were a self assessment. This enables the officer to seek payment of tax, including payments on account for the following year and to charge interest.

A determination must be made within four years following the end of the relevant tax year.

5.3 Discovery assessments

If an officer of HMRC discovers that profits have been omitted from assessment, that any assessment has become insufficient, or that any relief given is, or has become excessive, an assessment may be raised to recover the tax lost.

If the tax lost results from an error in the taxpayer's return but the return was made in accordance with prevailing practice at the time, no discovery assessment may be made.

A discovery assessment may only be raised where a return has been made if:

(a)   There has been **careless or deliberate understatement** by the taxpayer or his agent, or

(b)   At the time that compliance check enquiries on the return were completed, or could no longer be made, the officer **did not have information** to make him aware of the loss of tax.

Information is treated as available to an officer if it is contained in the taxpayer's return or claim for the year or either of the two preceding years, or it has been provided as a result of a compliance check enquiry covering those years, or it has been specifically provided.

The time limit for raising a discovery assessment is four years from the end of the tax year but this is extended to six years if there has been careless understatement and 20 years if there has been deliberate understatement. The taxpayer may appeal against a discovery assessment within 30 days of issue.

5.4 Dishonest conduct of tax agents

FAST FORWARD

> HMRC can investigate dishonest conduct by a tax agent and issue a civil penalty of up to £50,000 where there has been dishonest conduct.

HMRC can investigate whether there has been dishonest conduct by a tax agent (ie an individual who, in the course of business, assists clients with their tax affairs). Dishonest conduct occurs when a tax agent does something dishonest with a view to bringing about a loss of tax.

HMRC can issue a civil penalty of up to £50,000 where there has been **dishonest conduct and the tax agent fails to supply the information or documents that HMRC has requested.**

6 Interest and penalties

6.1 Interest on late paid tax

FAST FORWARD

> Interest is chargeable by HMRC on late payment of tax.

Interest is chargeable on late payment of both payments on account and balancing payments. Late payment interest is charged from the due date for payment until the day before the date on which payment is made.

Exam focus point

You will be given the rate of interest to use in the exam.

Interest is charged from 31 January following the tax year (or the normal due date for the balancing payment, in the rare event that this is later), even if this is before the due date for payment on:

(a)   Tax payable following an amendment to a self assessment
(b)   Tax payable in a discovery assessment
(c)   Tax postponed under an appeal, which becomes payable

Since a determination (see above) is treated as if it were a self assessment, interest runs from 31 January following the tax year.

If a taxpayer claims to reduce his payments on account and there is still a final payment to be made, interest is normally charged on the payments on account as if each of those payments had been the lower of:

(a)   The reduced amount, plus 50% of the final income tax liability
(b)   The amount which would have been payable had no claim for reduction been made

Question
Interest

Herbert's payments on account for 2014/15 based on his income tax liability for 2013/14 were £4,500 each. However when he submitted his 2013/14 income tax return in January 2015 he made a claim to reduce the payments on account for 2014/15 to £3,500 each. The first payment on account was made on 29 January 2015 and the second on 12 August 2015.

Herbert filed his 2014/15 tax return in December 2015. The return showed that his tax liabilities for 2014/15 (before deducting payments on account) were income tax and Class 4 NIC: £10,000, capital gains tax: £2,500. Herbert paid the balance of tax due of £5,500 on 19 February 2016.

For what periods and in respect of what amounts will Herbert be charged interest?

Answer

Herbert made an excessive claim to reduce his payments on account, and will therefore be charged interest on the reduction. The payments on account should have been £4,500 each based on the original 2013/14 liability (not £5,000 each based on the 2014/15 liability). Interest will be charged as follows:

(a)   First payment on account

    (i)   On £3,500 – nil – paid on time
    (ii)   On £1,000 from due date of 31 January 2015 to day before payment date, 18 February 2016 (384 days)

(b)   Second payment on account

    (i)   On £3,500 from due date of 31 July 2015 to day before payment date, 11 August 2015 (12 days)
    (ii)   On £1,000 from due date of 31 July 2015 to day before payment date, 18 February 2016 (203 days)

(c)   Balancing payment and capital gains tax

    (i)   On £3,500 from due date of 31 January 2016 to day before payment date, 18 February 2016 (19 days)

Where interest has been charged on late payments on account but the final balancing settlement for the year produces a repayment, all or part of the original interest is repaid.

6.2 Repayment of tax and repayment supplement

FAST FORWARD Interest (repayment supplement) is payable by HMRC on overpayment of tax.

Tax is repaid when claimed unless a greater payment of tax is due in the following 30 days, in which case it is set-off against that payment.

Interest is paid on overpayments of:

(a) **Payments on account**

(b) **Final payments** of income tax and Class 4 NICs and CGT, including tax deducted at source or tax credits on dividends

(c) **Penalties**

Repayment supplement runs from the original date of payment (even if this was prior to the due date), until the day before the date the repayment is made. Income tax deducted at source and tax credits are treated as if they were paid on the 31 January following the tax year concerned.

Repayment supplement is tax free.

6.3 Penalties for errors

FAST FORWARD There is a common penalty regime for errors in tax returns, including income tax, NICs, corporation tax and VAT. Penalties range from 30% to 100% of the Potential Lost Revenue. Penalties may be reduced.

A common penalty regime for errors in tax returns for income tax, national insurance contributions, corporation tax and value added tax.

A penalty may be imposed where **a taxpayer makes an inaccurate return** if he has:

- Been **careless** because he has not taken reasonable care in making the return or discovers the error later but does not take reasonable steps to inform HMRC; or

- Made a **deliberate error** but **does not make arrangements to conceal it**; or

- Made a **deliberate error** and **has attempted to conceal it** eg by submitting false evidence in support of an inaccurate figure

Note that **an error which is made where the taxpayer has taken reasonable care** in making the return and which he **does not discover later, does not result in a penalty**.

In order for a penalty to be charged, the **inaccurate return must result in**:

- **An understatement of the taxpayer's tax liability**; or
- **A false or increased loss for the taxpayer**; or
- **A false or increased repayment of tax to the taxpayer**

If a return contains more than one error, a penalty can be charged for each error.

The rules also extend to **errors in claims for allowances and reliefs** and in **accounts submitted in relation to a tax liability**.

Penalties for error also apply where **HMRC has issued an assessment estimating a person's liability** where:

- **A return has been issued to that person and has not been returned**, or
- The taxpayer was **required to deliver a return to HMRC but has not delivered it**

The taxpayer will be charged a penalty where

- The **assessment understates the taxpayer's liability** to income tax, capital gains tax, corporation tax or VAT, and

- **The taxpayer fails to take reasonable steps within 30 days of the date of the assessment** to tell HMRC that there is an under-assessment

The amount of **the penalty for error is based on the Potential Lost Revenue (PLR)** to HMRC as a result of the error. For example, if there is an understatement of tax, this understatement will be the PLR.

The maximum amount of the penalty for error depends on the type of error:

Type of error	Maximum penalty payable
Careless	30% of PLR
Deliberate not concealed	70% of PLR
Deliberate and concealed	100% of PLR

Question

Penalty for error

Alex is a sole trader. He files his tax return for 2014/15 on 10 January 2016. The return shows his trading income to be £60,000. In fact, due to carelessness, his trading income should have been stated to be £68,000. State the maximum penalty that could be charged by HMRC on Alex for his error.

Answer

The Potential Lost Revenue as a result of Alex's error is:

£(68,000 – 60,000) = £8,000 × [40% (income tax) + 2% (NICs)]   £3,360

Alex's error is careless so the maximum penalty for error is:

£3,360 × 30%   £1,008

A **penalty for error may be reduced if the taxpayer tells HMRC about the error** – this is called a **disclosure.** The reduction depends on the **circumstances of** the disclosure and the **help that the taxpayer gives to HMRC in relation to the disclosure.**

An **unprompted disclosure is one made at a time when the taxpayer has no reason to believe HMRC has discovered, or is about to discover, the error.** Otherwise, the disclosure will be a **prompted disclosure.** The **minimum penalties** that can be imposed are as follows:

Type of error	Unprompted	Prompted
Careless	0% of PLR	15% of PLR
Deliberate not concealed	20% of PLR	35% of PLR
Deliberate and concealed	30% of PLR	50% of PLR

Question

Reduction of penalty

Sue is a sole trader. She files her tax return for 2013/14 on 31 January 2015. The return shows a loss for the year of £(80,000). In fact, Sue has deliberately increased this loss by £(12,000) and has submitted false figures in support of her claim. HMRC initiate a review into Sue's return and in reply Sue then makes a disclosure of the error. Sue is a higher rate taxpayer due to her substantial investment income and she has made a claim to set the loss against general income in 2014/15.

State the maximum and minimum penalties that could be charged by HMRC on Sue for her error.

The potential lost revenue as a result of Sue's error is:

£12,000 × 40%   £4,800

Sue's error is deliberate and concealed so the maximum penalty for error is:

£4,800 × 100%   £4,800

Sue has made a prompted disclosure so the minimum penalty for error is:

£4,800 × 50%   £2,400

The help that the taxpayer gives to HMRC relates to when, how and to what extent the taxpayer:

- **Tells HMRC about the error,** making full disclosure and explaining how the error was made
- **Gives reasonable help** to HMRC to enable it **to quantify the error**
- **Allows access to business and other records** and other relevant documents

A taxpayer can appeal to the First Tier Tax Tribunal against:

- The **penalty being charged**
- The **amount of the penalty**

6.4 Penalties for late notification of chargeability

FAST FORWARD A common penalty regime also applies to late notification of chargeability.

A common penalty regime also applies to certain taxes for failures to notify chargeability to, or liability to register for, tax that result in a loss of tax. The taxes affected include income tax, NICs, PAYE, CGT, corporation tax and VAT. Penalties are behaviour related, increasing for more serious failures, and are based on the 'potential lost revenue'.

The minimum and maximum penalties as percentages of PLR are as follows:

Behaviour	Maximum penalty	Minimum penalty with unprompted disclosure		Minimum penalty with prompted disclosure	
Deliberate and concealed	100%	30%		50%	
Deliberate but not concealed	70%	20%		35%	
		≥12m	<12m	≥12m	<12m
Careless	30%	10%	0%	20%	10%

Note that there is no zero penalty for reasonable care (as there is for penalties for errors on returns – see above), although the penalty may be reduced to 0% if the failure is rectified within 12 months through unprompted disclosure. The penalties may also be reduced at HMRC's discretion in 'special circumstances'. However, inability to pay the penalty is not a 'special circumstance'.

The same penalties apply for failure to notify HMRC of a new taxable activity.

Where the taxpayer's failure is not classed as deliberate, there is no penalty if he can show he has a 'reasonable excuse'. Reasonable excuse does not include having insufficient money to pay the penalty. Taxpayers have a right of appeal against penalty decisions to the First Tier Tribunal.

6.5 Penalties for late filing of tax return

FAST FORWARD A penalty can be charged for late filing of a tax return based on how late the return is and how much tax is payable.

An individual is liable to a penalty where a tax return is filed after the due filing date. The penalty date is the date on which the return will be overdue (ie the date after the due filing date).

The initial penalty for late filing of the return is £100.

If the failure continues after the end of the period of three months starting with the penalty date, HMRC may give the individual notice specifying that a daily penalty of £10 is payable for a maximum of 90 days. The daily penalty runs from a date specified in the notice which may be earlier than the date of the notice but cannot be earlier than the end of the three month period.

If the failure continues after the end of the period of six months starting with the penalty date, a further penalty is payable. This penalty is the greater of:

- **5% of the tax liability** which would have been shown in the return
- **£300**

If the failure continues after the end of the period of 12 months starting with the penalty date, a further penalty is payable. This penalty is determined in accordance with the taxpayer's conduct in withholding information which would enable or assist HMRC in assessing the taxpayer's liability to tax. The penalty is computed as follows:

Type of conduct	Penalty
Deliberate and concealed	Greater of: • 100% of tax liability which would have been shown on return • £300
Deliberate not concealed	Greater of: • 70% of tax liability which would have been shown on return • £300
Any other case (eg careless)	Greater of: • 5% of tax liability which would have been shown on return • £300

6.6 Penalty for late payment of tax

FAST FORWARD A penalty is chargeable where tax is paid after the due date based on the amount of unpaid tax. Up to 15% of that amount is payable where the tax is more than 12 months late.

A penalty is chargeable where tax is paid after the penalty date. The penalty date is 30 days after the due date for the tax. Therefore no penalty arises if the tax is paid within 30 days of the due date.

The penalty chargeable is:

Date of payment	Penalty
Not more than five months after the penalty date	5% of tax which is unpaid at the penalty date.
More than five months after the penalty date but not more than 11 months after the penalty date	5% of tax which is unpaid at the end of the five month period. This is in addition to the 5% penalty above.
More than 11 months after the penalty date	5% of tax which is unpaid at the end of the 11 month period. This is in addition to the two 5% penalties above.

Penalties for late payment of tax apply to:

(a) **Balancing payments of income tax and Class 4 NICs and any CGT under self assessment or a determination**

(b) Tax due on the amendment of a self assessment

(c) Tax due on a discovery assessment

Penalties for late payment do not apply to late payments on account.

6.7 Penalty for failure to keep records

The maximum penalty for each failure to keep and retain records is £3,000 per tax year/accounting period. This penalty can be reduced by HMRC.

7 Disputes and appeals

FAST FORWARD

Disputes between taxpayers and HMRC can be dealt with by an HMRC internal review or by a Tribunal hearing.

7.1 Internal reviews

For direct taxes, appeals must first be made to HMRC, which will assign a 'caseworker'.

For indirect taxes, appeals must be sent directly to the Tax Tribunal, although the taxpayer can continue to correspond with his caseworker where, for example, there is new information.

At this stage the taxpayer may be offered, or may ask for, an **'internal review'**, which will be made by an objective HMRC review officer not previously connected with the case. This is a less costly and more effective way to resolve disputes informally, without the need for a Tribunal hearing. An appeal to the Tax Tribunal cannot be made until any review has ended.

The taxpayer must either accept the review offer, or notify an appeal to the Tax Tribunal within 30 days of being offered the review, otherwise the appeal will be treated as settled.

HMRC must usually carry out the review within 45 days, or any longer time as agreed with the taxpayer. The review officer may decide to uphold, vary or withdraw decisions.

After the review conclusion is notified, **the taxpayer has 30 days to appeal to the Tax Tribunal**.

7.2 Tribunal hearings

If there is no internal review, or the taxpayer is unhappy with the result of an internal review, the case may be heard by the Tax Tribunal. The person wishing to make an appeal (the appellant) must send a notice of appeal to the Tax Tribunal. The Tax Tribunal must then give notice of the appeal to the respondent (normally HMRC).

The Tax Tribunal is made up of two 'tiers':

(a)   A First Tier Tribunal
(b)   An Upper Tribunal

The case will be allocated to one of four case **'tracks':**

(a)   **Complex cases,** which the Tribunal considers will require lengthy or complex evidence or a lengthy hearing, or involve a complex or important principle or issue, or involves a large amount of money. Such cases will usually be heard by the Upper Tribunal

(b)   **Standard cases, heard by the First Tier Tribunal,** which have detailed case management and are subject to a more formal procedure than basic cases

(c)   **Basic cases, also heard by the First Tier Tribunal,** which will usually be disposed of after a hearing, with minimal exchange of documents before the hearing

(d)   **Paper cases, dealt with by the First Tier Tribunal,** which applies to straightforward matters such as fixed filing penalties and will usually be dealt with in writing, without a hearing

A decision of the First Tier Tribunal may be appealed to the Upper Tribunal.

Decisions of the Upper Tribunal are binding on the Tribunals and any affected public authorities. A decision of the Upper Tribunal may be appealed to the Court of Appeal.

Chapter Roundup

- Individuals who do not receive a tax return must notify their chargeability to income tax or CGT.

- Tax returns must usually be filed by 31 October (paper) or 31 January (electronic) following the end of the tax year.

- If a paper return is filed the taxpayer can ask HMRC to compute the tax due. Electronic returns have tax calculated automatically.

- Two payments on account and a final balancing payment of income tax and Class 4 NICs are due. All capital gains tax is due on 31 January following the end of the tax year.

- A compliance check enquiry into a return, claim or election can be started by an officer of HMRC within a limited period.

- HMRC can investigate dishonest conduct by a tax agent and issue a civil penalty of up to £50,000 where there has been dishonest conduct.

- Interest is chargeable by HMRC on late payment of tax.

- Interest (repayment supplement) is payable by HMRC on overpayment of tax.

- There is a common penalty regime for errors in tax returns, including income tax, NICs, corporation tax and VAT. Penalties range from 30% to 100% of the Potential Lost Revenue. Penalties may be reduced.

- A common penalty regime also applies to late notification of chargeability.

- A penalty can be charged for late filing of a tax return based on how late the return is and how much tax is payable.

- A penalty is chargeable where tax is paid after the due date based on the amount of unpaid tax. Up to 15% of that amount is payable where the tax is more than 12 months late.

- Disputes between taxpayers and HMRC can be dealt with by an HMRC internal review or by a Tribunal hearing.

Quick Quiz

1   A taxpayer who has not received a tax return must give notice of his chargeability to capital gains tax due in 2014/15 by_____. Fill in the blank.

2   By when must a taxpayer normally file a paper tax return for 2014/15?

    A   31 October 2015
    B   31 December 2015
    C   31 January 2016
    D   5 April 2016

3   What are the normal payment dates for income tax?

4   What penalty is due in respect of income tax payments on account that are paid two months after the due date?

5   What is the maximum penalty for failure to keep records?

6   Which body hears tax appeals?

Answers to Quick Quiz

1   A taxpayer who has not received a tax return must give notice to his chargeability to capital gains tax due in 2014/15 by **5 October 2015**.

2   A. 31 October 2015

3   Two payments on account of income tax are due on 31 January in the tax year and on 31 July following. A final balancing payment is due on 31 January following the tax year.

4   None. The penalty for late paid tax does not apply to late payment of payments on account.

5   £3,000

6   The Tax Tribunal which consists of the First Tier Tribunal and the Upper Tribunal.

Now try the questions below from the Practice Question Bank

Number	Type	Marks	Time
Q45	Section A	6	11 mins
Q46	Section B	10	18 mins

Inheritance tax

19

Inheritance tax: scope and transfers of value

Topic list	Syllabus reference
1 Chargeable persons	D1(a)
2 Transfers of value	D1(b), (c)
3 Calculation of tax on lifetime transfers	D1(d), D2(a)
4 Calculation of tax on death estate	D1(d), D2(b)
5 Transfer of unused nil rate band	D2(c)
6 Exemptions	D3(a)
7 Basic inheritance tax planning	D1, D2, D3
8 Payment of inheritance tax	D4(a)

Introduction

In this chapter we introduce inheritance tax (IHT). IHT is primarily a tax on wealth left on death. It also applies to gifts within seven years of death and to certain lifetime transfers of wealth.

The tax is different from income tax and CGT, where the basic question is: how much has the taxpayer made? With IHT, the basic question is, how much has been given away? We tax the amount which the taxpayer has transferred - the amount by which he is worse off. If the taxpayer pays IHT on a lifetime gift, he is worse off by the amount of the gift plus the tax due, and we have to take that into account. Some transfers are, however, exempt from IHT.

We will see that the first £325,000 of transfers is taxed at 0% (the 'nil rate band'), and is therefore effectively tax-free. To stop people from avoiding IHT by, for example, giving away £1,625,000 in five lots of £325,000, we need to look back seven years every time a transfer is made to decide how much of the nil rate band is available to set against the current transfer.

Next, we will see how to bring together all of a deceased person's assets at death, and compute the tax on the estate. Finally, we look at the administration and payment of IHT.

In the next chapter we will start our study of corporation tax.

Study guide

		Intellectual level
D1	**The basic principles of computing transfers of value**	
(a)	Identify the persons chargeable.	2
(b)	Understand and apply the meaning of transfer of value, chargeable transfer and potentially exempt transfer.	2
(c)	Demonstrate the diminution in value principle.	2
(d)	Demonstrate the seven year accumulation principle taking into account changes in the level of the nil rate band.	2
D2	**The liabilities arising on chargeable lifetime transfers and on the death of an individual**	
(a)	Understand the tax implications of lifetime transfers and compute the relevant liabilities.	2
(b)	Understand and compute the tax liability on a death estate.	2
(c)	Understand and apply the transfer of any unused nil rate band between spouses.	2
D3	**The use of exemptions in deferring and minimising inheritance tax liabilities**	
(a)	Understand and apply the following exemptions:	
(i)	Small gifts exemption.	2
(ii)	Annual exemption.	2
(iii)	Normal expenditure out of income.	2
(iv)	Gifts in consideration of marriage.	2
(v)	Gifts between spouses.	2
D4	**Payment of inheritance tax**	
(a)	Identify who is responsible for the payment of inheritance tax and the due date for payment of inheritance tax.	2

Exam guide

Inheritance tax (IHT) may be the subject of a 10 mark question in Section B and you may also find specific aspects being tested in Section A such as tax on a single transfer of value. You will need to know when IHT is charged: transfers of value (basically gifts) and chargeable persons. The concepts of potentially exempt transfers (PETs), chargeable lifetime transfers (CLTs) and the seven year accumulation principle are all fundamental to an understanding of IHT. Once you have worked out the amount of a transfer of value, you need to be able to work out the IHT liability on it. This could be payable during the donor's lifetime and/or on death for a lifetime transfer and on death for a death estate. There are a number of exemptions which may be used to reduce IHT liability such as gifts between spouses/civil partners. Finally, you need to have an understanding of how IHT is paid and who pays it.

1 Chargeable persons

FAST FORWARD

IHT is a tax on gifts made by individuals to other individuals or trustees.

Inheritance tax is a tax on gifts or '**transfers of value**' made by **chargeable persons**. This generally involves a transaction as a result of which wealth is transferred by one individual to another, either directly or via a trust.

Individuals are chargeable persons for inheritance tax.

Spouses and civil partners are taxed separately under inheritance tax although there is an exemption for transfers between the couple (dealt with later in this chapter).

The general principle is that all transfers of value of assets made by individuals, whether during lifetime or on death, are within the charge to IHT.

2 Transfers of value

FAST FORWARD

IHT applies to lifetime transfers of value and transfers of value made on death.

2.1 Introduction

There are **two main chargeable occasions** for inheritance tax:

(a)   Transfers of value made in the lifetime of the donor (**lifetime transfers**)

(b)   Transfers of value made on death, for example when property is left in a Will (**death estate**)

An example of a transfer of value is a **gift by an individual** to **another individual.**

Another example of a transfers of value is a **gift by an individual** to **trustees. A trust is a legal structure where one person (the settlor) gives property to one or more people (the trustees) to be held for the benefit of one or more people (the beneficiaries).**

2.2 Transfers of value

2.2.1 What is a transfer of value?

IHT cannot arise unless there is a transfer of value.

A transfer of value is any gratuitous disposition (eg a gift) made by a person which results in his being worse off, that is, he suffers a diminution (ie reduction) in the value of his estate. An individual's estate is basically all the assets which he owns.

Exam focus point

> The examiner has stated that, as far as Paper F6 is concerned, the terms 'transfer' and 'gift' can be taken to mean the same thing and that a transfer of value will always be a gift of assets.

2.2.2 Gratuitous intent

Transfers where there is no gratuitous intent are not chargeable to IHT. An example would be selling a painting for £1,000 at auction which later turns out to be worth £100,000 or other poor business deals.

2.2.3 Diminution in value

In many cases the diminution in value of the donor's estate will be the same as the increase in the value of the donee's estate, for example if there is a cash gift or the gift of a house. However, sometimes the two will not be the same. Typically this is the situation where unquoted shares are gifted.

The measure of the transfer for inheritance tax purposes is always the loss to the donor (the diminution in value of his estate), not the amount gained by the donee.

2.2.4 Example

Audrey holds 5,100 of the shares in an unquoted company which has an issued share capital of 10,000 shares. Currently Audrey's majority holding is valued at £15 per share.

Audrey wishes to give 200 shares to her son, Brian. However, the shares are worth only £2.50 each to Brian, since Brian will have only a small minority holding in the company. After the gift Audrey will hold 4,900 shares and these will be worth £10 each. The value per share to Audrey will fall from £15 to £10 per share since she will lose control of the company.

The diminution in value of Audrey 's estate is £27,500, as follows.

	£
Before the gift: 5,100 shares × £15	76,500
After the gift: 4,900 shares × £10	(49,000)
Diminution in value	27,500

Brian has only been given shares with a market value of 200 × £2.50 = £500. Remember, a gift is also a deemed disposal at market value for CGT purposes and it is this value that will be used in any CGT computation. IHT, however, uses the principle of diminution in value which can, as in this case, give a much greater value than the market value of the asset transferred.

2.3 Chargeable transfers and potentially exempt transfers

Inheritance tax is chargeable on a **chargeable transfer**. This is any transfer of value which is not an exempt transfer (see later in this Text).

Key terms

> A **potentially exempt transfer (PET)** is a **lifetime transfer** (other than an exempt transfer) **made by an individual to another individual**. Any other lifetime transfer by an individual (eg a gift to trustees) which is not an exempt transfer is a **chargeable lifetime transfer (CLT).**

A **potentially exempt transfer (PET)** is exempt from IHT when made and will remain exempt if the donor survives for at least seven years from making the gift. If the donor dies within seven years of making the PET, the transfer will become chargeable to IHT.

A **chargeable lifetime transfer (CLT)** is immediately chargeable to IHT when made.

On death, an individual is treated as if he had made a transfer of value of the property comprised in his estate immediately before death. This is a **chargeable transfer** to the extent that it is not covered by an exemption.

3 Calculation of tax on lifetime transfers

> One of the competencies you require to fulfil performance objective 19 of the PER is the ability to evaluate and compute taxes payable. You can apply the knowledge you obtain from this section of the text to help to demonstrate this competence.

FAST FORWARD

> The tax on a chargeable transfer is calculated with reference to chargeable transfers in the previous seven years.

There are two aspects of the calculation of tax on lifetime transfers:

(a) Lifetime tax on CLTs
(b) Additional death tax on CLTs and death tax on PETs, in both cases where the donor dies within seven years of making the transfer

Exam focus point

> You should always calculate the lifetime tax on any CLTs first, then move on to calculate the death tax on all CLTs and PETs made within seven years of death.

3.1 Lifetime tax

> IHT is charged on what a donor loses. If the donor pays the IHT on a lifetime gift he loses both the asset given away and the money with which he paid the tax due on it. Grossing up is required.

3.1.1 Donee pays tax

Lifetime inheritance tax on lifetime transfers is chargeable at two rates of tax: a 0% rate (the 'nil rate') and 20%. The nil rate is chargeable where accumulated transfers do not exceed the nil rate band limit. The excess is chargeable at 20%.

When a CLT is made and the donee (ie the trustees) pays the lifetime tax, follow these steps to work out the lifetime IHT on it:

Step 1   Look back seven years from the date of the transfer to see if any other CLTs have been made. If so, these transfers use up the nil rate band available for the current transfer. This is called **seven year accumulation**. Work out the value of any nil rate band still available.

Step 2   Compute the gross value of the CLT. You may be given this in the question or you may have to work out the diminution of value or deduct exemptions (such as the annual exemption described later in this Chapter).

Step 3   Any part of the CLT covered by the nil rate band is taxed at 0%. Any part of the CLT not covered by the nil rate band is charged at 20%.

Exam focus point

> The nil band and the lifetime rate will be given in the rates and allowances section of the exam paper. Where nil rate bands are required for previous years, these will be given in the question.

Question
Donee pays the lifetime tax

Eric makes a gift of £330,000 to a trust on 10 July 2014. There are no exemptions available (we will deal with exemptions later in this Text). The trustees agree to pay the tax due.

Calculate the lifetime tax payable by the trustees if Eric has made:

(a)   A lifetime chargeable transfer of value of £100,000 in August 2006
(b)   A lifetime chargeable transfer of value of £100,000 in August 2007
(c)   A lifetime chargeable transfer of value of £350,000 in August 2007

Answer

(a)   **Step 1**   No lifetime transfers in seven years before 10 July 2014 (transfers after 10 July 2007). Nil rate band of £325,000 available.

      Step 2   Value of CLT is £330,000.

      Step 3

	IHT
	£
£325,000 × 0%	0
£5,000 × 20%	1,000
£330,000	1,000

(b)   **Step 1**   Lifetime transfer of value of £100,000 in seven years before 10 July 2014 (transfers after 10 July 2007). Nil rate band of £(325,000 – 100,000) = £225,000 available.

      Step 2   Value of CLT is £330,000.

Step 3

	IHT £
£225,000 × 0%	0
£105,000 × 20%	21,000
£330,000	21,000

(c) **Step 1** Lifetime transfer of value of £350,000 in seven years before 10 July 2014 (transfers after 10 July 2007). No nil rate band available as all covered by previous transfer.

Step 2 Value of CLT is £330,000.

Step 3

	IHT £
£330,000 @ 20%	66,000

3.1.2 Donor pays tax

Where IHT is payable on a CLT, the **primary liability to pay tax is on the donor,** although the donor may agree with the donee (as in the above example) that the donee is to pay the tax instead.

If the donor pays the lifetime IHT due on a CLT, the total reduction in value of his estate is the transfer of value plus the IHT due on it. The transfer is therefore a net transfer and must be grossed up in order to find the gross value of the transfer. **We do this by working out the tax as follows.**

Formula to learn

$$\text{Chargeable amount (ie not covered by nil band)} \times \frac{20 \,(\text{rate of tax})}{80 \,(100 \,\text{minus the rate of tax})}$$

When a CLT is made and the donor pays the lifetime tax, follow these steps to work out the lifetime IHT on it:

Step 1 Look back seven years from the date of the transfer to see if any other CLTs have been made. If so, these transfers use up the nil rate band available for the current transfer. Work out the value of any nil rate band still available.

Step 2 Compute the net value of the CLT. You may be given this in the question or may have to work out the diminution of value or deduct exemptions (such as the annual exemption discussed later in this Chapter).

Step 3 Any part of the CLT covered by the nil rate band is taxed at 0%. Any part of the CLT not covered by the nil rate band is taxed at 20/80.

Step 4 Work out the gross transfer by adding the net transfer and the tax together. You can check your figure by working out the tax on the gross transfer.

Question	Donor pays the lifetime tax

James makes a gift of £330,000 to a trust on 10 July 2014. No exemptions are available. James will pay the tax due.

Calculate the lifetime tax payable, if James has made:

(a) A lifetime chargeable transfer of value of £100,000 in August 2006
(b) A lifetime chargeable transfer of value of £100,000 in August 2007
(c) A lifetime chargeable transfer of value of £350,000 in August 2007

(a) **Step 1**   No lifetime transfers in seven years before 10 July 2014 (transfers after 10 July 2007). Nil rate band of £325,000 available.

Step 2   Net value of CLT is £330,000.

Step 3

	IHT £
£325,000 × 0%	0
£5,000 × 20/80	1,250
£330,000	1,250

Step 4   Gross transfer is £(330,000 + 1,250) = £331,250.

Check: Tax on the gross transfer would be:

	IHT £
£325,000 × 0%	0
£6,250 × 20%	1,250
£331,250	1,250

(b) **Step 1**   Lifetime transfer of value of £100,000 in seven years before 10 July 2014 (transfers after 10 July 2007). Nil rate band of £(325,000 – 100,000) = £225,000 available.

Step 2   Net value of CLT is £330,000.

Step 3

	IHT £
£225,000 × 0%	0
£105,000 × 20/80	26,250
£330,000	26,250

Step 4   Gross transfer is £(330,000 + 26,250) = £356,250.

Check: Tax on the gross transfer would be:

	IHT £
£225,000 × 0%	0
£131,250 × 20%	26,250
£356,250	26,250

(c) **Step 1**   Lifetime transfer of value of £350,000 in seven years before 10 July 2014 (transfers after 10 July 2007). No nil rate band available as all covered by previous transfer.

Step 2   Net value of CLT is £330,000.

Step 3

	IHT £
£330,000 × 20/80	82,500

Step 4   Gross transfer is £(330,000 + 82,500) = £412,500.

Check: Tax on the gross transfer would be:

	IHT £
£412,500 × 20%	82,500

3.2 Death tax on chargeable lifetime transfers

FAST FORWARD

Death tax is chargeable on chargeable lifetime transfers if the donor dies within seven years of making the transfer. Taper relief reduces the death tax if the donor survives between three and seven years.

Death inheritance tax on lifetime transfers is chargeable if the donor dies within seven years of making the lifetime transfer. It is chargeable at two rates: 0% and 40%. The nil rate is chargeable where accumulated transfers do not exceed the nil rate band limit at the date of death. The excess is chargeable at 40%.

The longer the donor survives after making a gift, the lower the death tax. This is because taper relief applies to lower the amount of death tax payable as follows:

Years before death	% reduction
Over three but less than four years	20
Over four but less than five years	40
Over five but less than six years	60
Over six but less than seven years	80

Exam focus point

The taper relief table will be given in the tax rates and allowances section of the examination paper.

Death tax on a lifetime transfer is **always** payable by the donee, so grossing up is not relevant.

Follow these steps to work out the death tax on a CLT:

Step 1   Look back seven years from the **date of the transfer** to see if any other chargeable transfers were made. If so, these transfers use up the nil rate band available for the current transfer. Work out the value of any nil rate band remaining.

Step 2   Compute the value of the CLT. This is the gross value of the transfer that you worked out for computing lifetime tax.

Step 3   Any part of the CLT covered by the nil rate band is taxed at 0%. Any part of the CLT not covered by the nil rate band is charged at 40%.

Step 4   Reduce the death tax by taper relief (if applicable).

Step 5   Deduct any lifetime tax paid. The death tax may be reduced to nil, but there is **no repayment of lifetime tax**.

Exam focus point

The nil band and the death rate will be given in the rates and allowances section of the exam paper. Where nil rate bands are required for previous years, these will be given in the question.

 Question   Lifetime tax and death tax on CLTs

Trevor makes a gross chargeable transfer of value of £207,000 in December 2002. He then makes a gift to a trust of shares worth £200,000 on 15 November 2008. The trustees pay the lifetime tax due. There are no exemptions available. The nil rate band in 2008/09 was £312,000.

Trevor dies in February 2015. The shares held by the trustees were then worth £500,000.

Compute:

(a)   The lifetime tax payable by the trustees on the lifetime transfer in November 2008
(b)   The death tax (if any) payable on the lifetime transfer in November 2008

(a)   Lifetime tax

Step 1   Lifetime transfer of value of £207,000 in seven years before 15 November 2008 (transfers after 15 November 2001). Nil rate band of £(312,000 – 207,000) = £105,000 available.

Step 2   Value of CLT is £200,000.

Step 3

	IHT £
£105,000 × 0%	0
£ 95,000 × 20%	19,000
£200,000	19,000

(b)   Death tax

Step 1   Lifetime transfer of value of £207,000 in seven years before 15 November 2008 (transfers after 15 November 2001). Nil rate band of £(325,000 – 207,000) = £118,000 available.

Step 2   Value of CLT is £200,000. Note that the value of the transfer does not change even though the shares are worth £500,000 at the date of the donor's death.

Step 3

	IHT £
£118,000 × 0%	0
£ 82,000 × 40%	32,800
£200,000	32,800

Step 4   Transfer over six but less than seven years before death

	£
Death tax	32,800
Less: taper relief @ 80%	(26,240)
Death tax left in charge	6,560

Step 5   Tax due £(6,560 – 19,000) (no repayment of lifetime tax)   0

3.3 Death tax on potentially exempt transfers

FAST FORWARD

Death tax is chargeable on potentially exempt transfers if the donor dies within seven years of making the transfer. Taper relief reduces the death tax if the donor survives between three and seven years. Grossing up is never required on PET because the death tax is payable by the donee.

If the donor dies within seven years of making a PET it will become chargeable to death tax in the same way as a CLT. There will be no lifetime tax paid, so Step 5 above will not apply.

We will now work through an example where there is both a PET and a CLT.

Exam focus point

Calculate lifetime tax on CLTs first. Then move on to death tax, working through all CLTs and PETs in chronological order. Remember: on death, PETs become chargeable so must be taken into account when calculating the death tax on later CLTs.

Louise gave £340,000 to her son on 1 February 2011. There were no exemptions available. This was the first transfer that Louise had made.

On 10 October 2014, Louise gave £370,000 to a trust. The trustees paid the lifetime IHT due. There were no exemptions available.

On 11 January 2015, Louise died.

Compute:

(a)   The lifetime tax payable by the trustees on the lifetime transfer made in 2014
(b)   The death tax payable on the lifetime transfer made in 2011
(c)   The death tax payable on the lifetime transfer made in 2014

Answer

(a)   Lifetime tax – 2014 CLT

Step 1   There are no chargeable lifetime transfers in the seven years before 10 October 2014 because the 2011 transfer is a PET and therefore exempt during Louise's lifetime. Nil rate band of £325,000 available.

Step 2   Value of CLT £370,000

Step 3

	IHT £
£325,000 × 0%	0
£ 45,000 × 20%	9,000
£370,000	9,000

(b)   Death tax – 2011 PET becomes chargeable

Step 1   No lifetime transfers of value in seven years before 1 February 2011 (transfers after 1 February 2004). Nil rate band (at date of death) of £325,000 available.

Step 2   Value of PET £340,000

Step 3

	IHT £
£325,000 × 0%	0
£ 15,000 × 40%	6,000
£340,000	6,000

Step 4   Transfer over three but less than four years before death

	£
Death tax	6,000
Less: taper relief @ 20%	(1,200)
Death tax due	4,800

(c)   Death tax – 2014 CLT additional tax

Step 1   Lifetime transfer of value of £340,000 in seven years before 10 October 2014 (transfers after 10 October 2007). Note that as the PET becomes chargeable on death, its value is now included in calculating the death tax on the CLT. No nil rate band available.

Step 2   Value of CLT is £370,000 as before

Step 3

		IHT £
	£370,000 @ 40%	148,000
Step 4	Transfer within three years before death so no taper relief.	
Step 5	Tax due £(148,000 – 9,000)	139,000

3.4 Advantages of making lifetime transfers

One of the competencies you require to fulfil performance objective 20 of the PER is the ability to assist with tax planning. You can apply the knowledge you obtain from this section of the text to help to demonstrate this competence.

There are a number of inheritance tax advantages of making lifetime transfers:

(a) **If the donor makes a potentially exempt transfer and survives seven years, he has reduced his estate for IHT but the transfer is exempt.** No inheritance tax is payable on the transfer and it does not form part of the seven year cumulation for later transfers.

(b) **If the donor makes a chargeable lifetime transfer and survives seven years, he has reduced his estate for IHT and the only inheritance tax payable is that on the lifetime transfer at lifetime rates.** However, note that the chargeable lifetime transfer remains in cumulation and affects the calculation of tax on transfers made in the seven years after it.

(c) If the donor does not survive seven years, IHT is payable on lifetime transfers at death rates at the date of death but **taper relief reduces the death tax if the donor survives between three and seven years**.

(d) **The values of lifetime transfers cannot exceed the transfer of value when made.** Therefore, **it is good tax planning to give away assets which are likely to increase in value such as land and shares.**

However, there is one situation where **it may not be advantageous for the donor to make a lifetime transfer** in terms of overall tax liability. This is where a **gift of an asset would result in a large chargeable gain (either immediately chargeable or deferred under gift relief)**. In this case, it may be better for the donor to retain the asset until death as there is a tax-free uplift in value on death for capital gains tax purposes so that the donee will receive the asset at market value at the date of the donor's death. This is particularly relevant if the donor is unlikely to survive three years from the date of a lifetime gift and so death rates without the benefit of taper relief would apply to a lifetime transfer.

4 Calculation of tax on death estate

One of the competencies you require to fulfil performance objective 19 of the PER is the ability to evaluate and compute taxes payable. You can apply the knowledge you obtain from this section of the text to help to demonstrate this competence.

FAST FORWARD

When someone dies, we must bring together all their assets to find the value of their death estate and then charge inheritance tax on it to the extent that it is not exempt, taking account of transfers made in the seven years before death.

4.1 Death estate

4.1.1 What is in the death estate?

An individual's death estate consists of all the property he owned immediately before death (such as land and buildings, shares and other investments, cars and cash) **less debts and funeral expenses.**

The death estate also includes anything received as a result of death, for example the proceeds of a life assurance policy which pays out on the individual's death. The value of the policy immediately before the death is not relevant.

Exam focus point

> The specific rules for valuation of assets are not in the syllabus. Values will be provided in the question where relevant.

4.1.2 Debts and funeral expenses

The rules on debts are as follows.

(a) **Debts incurred by the deceased can be deducted** if they can be **legally enforced** as they are either **imposed by law** or they are a debt for which the deceased received **consideration**. Specific examples of the application of these rules include:

    (i) **Taxes** – deductible as imposed by law.

    (ii) **Electricity and gas bills** – deductible as incurred for consideration.

    (iii) **Gambling debts** – deductible if relates to legal gambling (eg in a licenced casino or betting shop), not deductible if relates to illegal gambling as not legally enforceable.

    (iv) **Promise to pay an amount to a relative** – not deductible as no consideration received.

    (v) **Oral agreement for sale of interest in land** – not deductible as not legally enforceable since contracts for such sales must be evidenced in writing.

(b) **Debts incurred by the deceased but payable after the death may be deductible under the above rules,** but the amount should be discounted because of the future date of payment.

(c) **Rent and similar amounts which accrue day by day should be accrued up to the date of death.**

(d) **If a debt is charged on a specific property it is deductible primarily from that property.** For example, a mortgage secured on a house is deductible from the value of that house.

This does not include endowment mortgages as these are repaid upon death by the life assurance element of the mortgage.

Repayment mortgages and interest-only mortgages are deductible (although there may be separate life assurance policies which become payable at death and which will effectively cancel out the mortgage).

Reasonable funeral expenses may also be deducted:

(a) What is reasonable depends on the deceased's condition in life.

(b) Reasonable costs of mourning for the family are allowed.

(c) **The cost of a tombstone is deductible.**

Zack died on 19 June 2014.

Zack's assets at the date of his death consisted of the following.
   10,000 shares in A plc valued at £8,525
   Cash in bank £9,280
   Freehold property valued at £150,000 subject to a repayment mortgage of £45,000

Zack's debts due at the date of his death were as follows:

   Electricity £150
   Council tax £300

Zack had also told his daughter on 10 June 2014 that he would pay £1,000 towards the cost of her summer holiday and that he would pay her this amount on 1 July 2014.

Zack's executors paid reasonable funeral expenses of £2,000 (including the cost of a tombstone) on 1 September 2014.

Calculate Zack's death estate for IHT purposes.

Answer

		£
A plc shares		8,525
Cash in bank		9,280
Freehold property	150,000	
Less: repayment mortgage	(45,000)	
		105,000
Gross estate		122,805
Less: debts and funeral expenses		
electricity (incurred for consideration)	150	
council tax (imposed by law)	300	
amount towards holiday for daughter (gratuitous promise)	0	
funeral expenses	2,000	
		(2,450)
Death estate		120,355

4.2 Computing death tax on the death estate

Inheritance tax on the death estate is chargeable at two rates: 0% and 40%. The nil rate is chargeable where accumulated transfers do not exceed the nil rate band limit. The excess is chargeable at 40%.

In order to calculate the tax on the death estate, use the following steps:

Step 1   Look back seven years from the date of death to see if any CLTs or PETs which have become chargeable have been made. If so, these transfers use up the nil rate band available for the death estate. Work out the value of any nil rate band still available.

Step 2   Compute the value of the death estate.

Step 3   Any part of the death estate covered by the nil rate band is taxed at 0%. Any part of the death estate not covered by the nil rate band is charged at 40%.

Question

Tax on death estate

Laura dies on 1 August 2014, leaving a death estate valued at £400,000. No exemptions were available. Laura had made a gift of £165,000 to her sister on 11 September 2013. No exemptions were available.

Compute the tax payable on Laura's death estate.

Death tax

Note. There is no death tax on the September 2013 PET which becomes chargeable as a result of Laura's death, as it is within the nil rate band at her death. However, it will use up part of the nil rate band, as shown below.

Step 1 Lifetime transfer of value of £165,000 in seven years before 1 August 2014 (transfers after 1 August 2007). Nil rate band of £(325,000 − 165,000) = £160,000 available.

Step 2 Value of death estate is £400,000.

Step 3

	IHT £
£160,000 × 0%	0
£240,000 × 40%	96,000
£400,000	96,000

5 Transfer of unused nil rate band

FAST FORWARD

If one spouse or civil partner does not use up the whole nil rate band on death, the excess may be transferred to the surviving spouse/civil partner.

5.1 How the transfer of unused nil rate band works

If:

- **An individual ("A") dies;** and
- **A had a spouse or civil partner ("B") who died before A;** and
- **A and B were married or in a civil partnership immediately before B's death;** and
- **B had unused nil rate band (wholly or in part) on death**

then **a claim may be made to increase the nil rate band maximum at the date of A's death by B's unused nil-rate band in order to calculate the IHT on A's death.**

The revised nil rate band will apply to the calculation of additional death tax on CLTs made by A, PETs made by A and death tax on A's death estate.

5.2 Example

Robert and Claudia were married for many years until the death of Robert on 10 April 2014. In his will, Robert left his death estate valued at £100,000 to his sister. He had made no lifetime transfers.

Claudia died on 12 January 2015 leaving a death estate worth £850,000 to her brother. Claudia had made a chargeable lifetime transfer of £50,000 in 2011.

The inheritance tax payable on the death of Claudia, assuming that a claim is made to transfer Robert's unused nil rate band, is calculated as follows:

Step 1 (a) Lifetime transfer of value of £50,000 in seven years before 12 January 2015 (transfers after 12 January 2008).

(b) Nil rate band at Claudia's death is £325,000. Nil rate band is increased by claim to transfer Robert's unused nil rate band at death £(325,000 − 100,000) = £225,000. The maximum nil rate band at Claudia's death is therefore £(325,000 + 225,000) = £550,000 and the available nil rate band for working out the tax on her estate is £(550,000 − 50,000) = £500,000.

Step 2   Value of Claudia's death estate is £850,000.

Step 3

	IHT
	£
£500,000 x 0%	0
£350,000 x 40%	140,000
£850,000	140,000

5.3 Changes in nil rate band between deaths of spouses/civil partners

If the nil rate band increases between the death of B and the death of A, the amount of B's unused nil rate band must be scaled up so that it represents the same proportion of the nil rate band at A's death as it did at B's death.

For example, if the nil rate band at B's death was £300,000 and B had an unused nil rate band of £90,000, the unused proportion in percentage terms is therefore 90,000/300,000 × 100 = 30%. If A dies when the nil rate band has increased to £325,000, B's unused nil rate band is £325,000 × 30% = £97,500 and this amount is transferred to increase the nil rate band maximum available on A's death.

The increase in the nil rate band maximum cannot exceed the nil rate band maximum at the date of A's death eg if the nil rate band is £325,000, the increase cannot exceed £325,000, giving a total of £650,000.

Question	Transfer of nil rate band

Jenna and Rebecca were civil partners until the death of Jenna on 19 August 2007.

Jenna made no lifetime transfers. Her death estate was £240,000 and she left it to her mother. The nil rate band at Jenna's death was £300,000.

Rebecca died on 24 February 2015. Her death estate was £550,000 and she left her entire estate to her brother. She had made no lifetime transfers.

Calculate the inheritance tax payable on the death of Rebecca, assuming that any beneficial claims are made.

Answer

Step 1   (a)   No lifetime transfers of value in seven years before 24 February 2015.

(b)   Nil rate band at Rebecca's death is £325,000. Nil rate band is increased by claim to transfer Jenna's unused nil rate band at death. Unused proportion was £(300,000 – 240,000) = 60,000/300,000 × 100 = 20%. The adjusted unused proportion is therefore £325,000 × 20% = £65,000. The maximum nil rate band at Rebecca's death is therefore £(325,000 + 65,000) = £390,000 and this is also the available nil rate band for her estate.

Step 2   Value of Rebecca's death estate is £550,000.

Step 3

	IHT
	£
£390,000 × 0%	0
£160,000 × 40%	64,000
£550,000	64,000

BPP
LEARNING MEDIA

5.4 Claim to transfer unused nil rate band

The claim to transfer the unused nil rate band is usually made by the personal representatives of A. The time limit for the claim is two years from the end of the month of A's death (or the period of three months after the personal representatives start to act, if later) or such longer period as an officer of HMRC may allow in a particular case.

If the personal representatives do not make a claim, a claim can be made by any other person liable to tax chargeable on A's death within such later period as an officer of HMRC may allow in a particular case.

6 Exemptions

Exemptions may apply to make transfers or parts of transfers non chargeable. Some exemptions only apply on lifetime transfers (annual, normal expenditure out of income, marriage/civil partnership), but the spouse/civil partner exemption applies on both life and death transfers.

One of the competencies you require to fulfil performance objective 20 of the PER is the ability to assist with tax planning. You can apply the knowledge you obtain from this section of the text to help to demonstrate this competence.

6.1 Introduction

There are various exemptions available to eliminate or reduce the chargeable amount of a lifetime transfer or property passing on an individual's death.

The lifetime exemptions apply to PETs as well as to CLTs. Only the balance of such gifts after the lifetime exemptions have been taken into account is then potentially exempt.

6.2 Exemptions applying to lifetime transfers only

6.2.1 The small gifts exemptions

Outright gifts to individuals totalling £250 or less per donee in any one tax year are exempt. If gifts total more than £250 the whole amount is chargeable. A donor can give up to £250 each year to each of as many donees as he wishes. The small gifts exemption cannot apply to gifts into trusts.

6.2.2 The annual exemption (AE)

The first £3,000 of value transferred in a tax year is exempt from IHT. The annual exemption is used only after all other exemptions (such as for transfers to spouses/civil partners (see below)). If several gifts are made in a year, the £3,000 exemption is applied to earlier gifts before later gifts. The annual exemption is used up by PETs as well as CLTs, even though the PETs might never become chargeable.

Exam focus point

Where CLTs and PETS made in the same year the CLTs should be made first to use any available annual exemptions. If used up against the PETs the exemption(s) will be wasted if the PET never becomes chargeable.

Any unused portion of the annual exemption is carried forward for one year only. Only use it the following year *after* that year's own annual exemption has been used.

Question

Annual exemptions

Frank has no unused annual exemption brought forward at 6 April 2013.

On 1 August 2013 he makes a transfer of £600 to his son Peter.
On 1 September 2013 he makes a transfer of £2,000 to his nephew Quentin.
On 1 July 2014 he makes a transfer of £3,300 to a trust for his grandchildren.
On 1 June 2015 he makes a transfer of £5,000 to his friend Rowan.

Show the application of the annual exemptions.

Answer

2013/14	£
1.8.13 Gift to Peter	600
Less AE 2013/14	(600)
	0

	£
1.9.13 Gift to Quentin	2,000
Less AE 2013/14	(2,000)
	0

The unused annual exemption carried forward is £3,000 − £600 − £2,000 = £400.

2014/15	£	£
1.7.14 Gift to trust		3,300
Less: AE 2014/15	3,000	
AE 2013/14 b/f	300	
		(3,300)
		0

The unused annual exemption carried forward is zero because the 2014/15 exemption must be used before the 2013/14 exemption brought forward. The balance of £100 of the 2013/14 exemption is lost, because it cannot be carried forward for more than one year.

2015/16	£
1.6.15 Gift to Rowan	5,000
Less AE 2015/16	(3,000)
	2,000

6.2.3 Normal expenditure out of income

Inheritance tax is a tax on transfers of capital, not income. A transfer of value is exempt if:

(a) It is made as part of the normal expenditure of the donor
(b) Taking one year with another, it was made out of income
(c) It leaves the donor with sufficient income to maintain his usual standard of living

As well as covering such things as regular presents **this exemption can cover regular payments out of income such as a grandchild's school fees or the payment of life assurance premiums on a policy for someone else.**

6.2.4 Gifts in consideration of marriage/civil partnership

Gifts in consideration of marriage/civil partnership are exempt up to:

(a) **£5,000 if from a parent of a party to the marriage/civil partnership**
(b) **£2,500 if from a remoter ancestor or from one of the parties to the marriage/civil partnership**
(c) **£1,000 if from any other person**

Part E Inheritance tax | **19: Inheritance tax: scope and transfers of value**   271

The limits apply to gifts from any one donor for any one marriage/civil partnership. The exemption is available only if the marriage/civil partnership actually takes place.

6.3 Exemption applying to both lifetime transfers and transfers on death

6.3.1 Transfers between spouses/civil partners

Any transfers of value between spouses/civil partners are exempt. The exemption covers lifetime gifts between them and property passing under a will or on intestacy.

Question	Exemptions

Dale made a gift of £153,000 to her son on 17 October 2010 on the son's marriage. Dale gave £100,000 to her spouse on 1 January 2014. Dale gave £70,000 to her daughter on 11 May 2014. The only other gifts Dale made were birthday and Christmas presents of £100 each to her grandchildren.

Show what exemptions are available in respect of these transfers.

Answer

17 October 2010

	£
Gift to Dale's son	153,000
Less: ME	(5,000)
AE 2010/11	(3,000)
AE 2009/10 b/f	(3,000)
PET	142,000

1 January 2014

	£
Gift to Dale's spouse	100,000
Less spouse exemption	(100,000)
	0

11 May 2014

	£
Gift to Dale's daughter	70,000
Less: AE 2014/15	(3,000)
AE 2013/14 b/f	(3,000)
PET	64,000

The gifts to the grandchildren are covered by the small gifts exemption.

7 Basic inheritance tax planning

FAST FORWARD

> Basic planning may reduce or eliminate inheritance tax payable. Where appropriate, donors should use exemptions, make gifts early in life, make use of the nil rate band in relation to gifts to trusts, and consider making gifts to grandchildren, rather than children.

7.1 Use exemptions

Donors should ensure that **use is made of exemptions in relation to lifetime gifts**, in particular the **annual exemption**, the **marriage/civil partnership exemption**, the **normal expenditure out of income exemption** and the **spouse/civil partner exemption**.

When considering how to pass on assets in the **death estate**, the **spouse/civil partner exemption may be used to ensure that no inheritance tax is payable when the first spouse/civil partner dies**. Remember

that an election can be made to ensure that unused nil rate band of the first spouse/civil partner is available to be used against the estate of the surviving spouse/civil partner.

7.2 Make gifts early in life

The earlier that a gift is made in lifetime which is, or may become, a chargeable transfer, the more likely it is that the donor will survive seven years from making it.

If a **gift is made shortly before death**, there will be **little or no inheritance benefit** as the gift will be chargeable on the death of the donor. In addition, if the **gift is of a chargeable asset for capital gains tax** (eg shares, land) there will be a **chargeable disposal at market value which may result in a chargeable gain**, whereas **transfers of chargeable assets on death are exempt disposals**.

7.3 Make use of the nil rate band

Gifts to trusts are chargeable transfers. If the gift is **within the nil rate band**, however, there will be **no inheritance tax payable when the gift is made**.

Transfers are only cumulated for seven years and therefore, after that time has elapsed, a **further gift within the nil rate band can be made to a trust**, again without incurring any immediate payment of inheritance tax.

7.4 Skip a generation

Donors may consider giving assets to their children, either during lifetime or on death. Such assets may then be passed by those children to their own children, the grandchildren of the donor.

If the **donor's children already have sufficient assets for their financial needs, it may be beneficial to skip a generation** so that **gifts are made to grandchildren, rather than children**. This **avoids a further charge to inheritance tax on the death of the children** so that gifts will then only be taxed once before being inherited by the grandchildren, rather than twice.

8 Payment of inheritance tax

8.1 Liability for IHT

FAST FORWARD

The liability to pay IHT depends on the type of transfer and whether it was made in lifetime or on death.

The donor is primarily liable for the tax due on chargeable lifetime transfers. However the donee (ie the trustees) may agree to pay the tax out of the trust assets.

On death, liability for payment is as follows.

(a)   **Tax on the death estate is paid by the deceased's personal representatives (PRs)** out of estate assets.

(b)   **Tax on a PET that has become chargeable is paid by donee.**

(c)   **Additional liabilities on a CLT is paid by the donee.**

8.2 Due dates

(a)   **For chargeable lifetime transfers the due date is the later of:**
    (i)   **30 April just after the end of the tax year of the transfer**
    (ii)   **Six months after the end of the month of the transfer**

(b)   **Tax arising on the death estate: the due date is six months from the end of the month of death.** However, if the personal representatives **submit an account of the death estate** within the six month period, they must **pay the IHT due on the death estate on the submission of the account**.

(c)   **Tax arising on death in respect of PETs and CLTs: the due date for additional tax is six months from the end of the month of death.**

Lisa gave some shares to a trust on 10 July 2010. She gave a house to her daughter on 12 December 2012. Lisa died on 17 May 2014 leaving her death estate to her son.

For each of these transfers of value, state who is liable to pay any inheritance tax due and the due date for payment.

Answer

10 July 2010

Chargeable lifetime transfer. Lifetime tax payable by Lisa (unless trustees agree to pay tax), due later of 30 April 2011 and 31 January 2011 ie 30 April 2011. Death tax payable by trustees, due 30 November 2014.

12 December 2012

Potentially exempt transfer – no lifetime tax. Death tax payable by daughter, due 30 November 2014.

17 May 2014

Death tax payable by personal representatives out of death estate, due on earlier of submission of account and 30 November 2014.

Chapter Roundup

- IHT is a tax on gifts made by individuals to other individuals or trustees.

- IHT applies to lifetime transfers of value and transfers of value made on death.

- The tax on a chargeable transfer is calculated with reference to chargeable transfers in the previous seven years.

- IHT is charged on what a donor loses. If the donor pays the IHT on a lifetime gift he loses both the asset given away and the money with which he paid the tax due on it. Grossing up is required.

- Death tax is chargeable on chargeable lifetime transfers if the donor dies within seven years of making the transfer. Taper relief reduces the death tax if the donor survives between three and seven years.

- Death tax is chargeable on potentially exempt transfers if the donor dies within seven years of making the transfer. Taper relief reduces the death tax if the donor survives between three and seven years. Grossing up is never required on a PET because the death tax is payable by the donee.

- When someone dies, we must bring together all their assets to find the value of their death estate and then charge inheritance tax on it to the extent that it is not exempt, taking account of transfers made in the seven years before death.

- If one spouse or civil partner does not use up the whole nil rate band on death, the excess may be transferred to the surviving spouse/civil partner.

- Exemptions may apply to make transfers or parts of transfers non chargeable. Some exemptions only apply on lifetime transfers (annual, normal expenditure out of income, marriage/civil partnership), but the spouse/civil partner exemption applies on both life and death transfers.

- Basic planning may reduce or eliminate inheritance tax payable. Where appropriate, donors should use exemptions, make gifts early in life, make use of the nil rate band in relation to gifts to trusts, and consider making gifts to grandchildren, rather than children.

- The liability to pay IHT depends on the type of transfer and whether it was made in lifetime or on death.

Quick Quiz

1   What is a transfer of value?

2   What type of transfer by an individual is a potentially exempt transfers?

3   Why must some lifetime transfers be grossed up?

4   What is taper relief?

5   Greg dies leaving the following debts:

   (a)   Grocery bill
   (b)   HM Revenue and Customs – income tax to death
   (c)   Mortgage on house
   (d)   Illegal gambling debt

   Which are deductible against his death estate and why?

6   Mark and Hilary had been married for many years. Mark died on 11 May 2014 leaving his estate to Hilary. He had made a chargeable lifetime transfer of £160,000 in July 2011. If Hilary dies in February 2015, what is the maximum nil rate band on her death?

7   To what extent may unused annual exemption be carried forward?

8   Don gives some money to his daughter on her marriage. What marriage exemption is applicable?

9   When is lifetime inheritance tax on a chargeable lifetime transfer due for payment?

Answers to Quick Quiz

1   A transfer of value is any gratuitous disposition by a person resulting in a diminution of the value of his estate.

2   A potentially exempt transfer is a lifetime transfer made by an individual to another individual.

3   Where the donor pays the lifetime tax due it must be grossed up to calculate the total reduction in value of the estate.

4   Taper relief reduces death tax where a transfer is made between three and seven years before death.

5   (a)   Grocery bill – deductible as incurred for consideration
    (b)   Income tax to death – deductible as imposed by law
    (c)   Mortgage – deductible, will be set against value of house primarily
    (d)   Illegal gambling debt – not deductible as not legally enforceable

6   Hilary's nil rate band is £325,000. Mark's unused nil rate band is £(325,000 – 160,000) = £165,000. The nil rate band maximum on Hilary's death is therefore £490,000.

7   An unused annual exemption can be carried forward one tax year.

8   The marriage exemption for a gift to the donor's child is £5,000.

9   The due date for lifetime tax on a chargeable lifetime transfer is the later of:

    (a)   30 April just after the end of the tax year of the transfer
    (b)   Six months after the end of the month of transfer

Now try the questions below from the Practice Question Bank

Number	Type	Marks	Time
Q47	Section A	6	11 mins
Q48	Section B	10	18 mins
Q49	Section B	10	18 mins

Corporation tax

Computing taxable total profits

20

Topic list	Syllabus reference
1 The scope of corporation tax	E1(a)-(c)
2 Taxable total profits	E2(j)
3 Trading income	E2(a)-(c)
4 Property business income	E2(d)
5 Loan relationships (interest income)	E2(h)
6 Miscellaneous income	E2(j)
7 Qualifying charitable donations	E2(i)
8 Long periods of account	E2(j)

Introduction

Now that we have completed our study of personal tax we turn our attention to corporation tax, ie the tax that a company must pay on its profits.

First we consider the scope of corporation tax and we see that a company must pay tax for an 'accounting period' which may be different from its period of account.

We then learn how to calculate taxable total profits. This involves first calculating total profits by adding together income from different sources, such as trading income, interest and property income, and capital gains, and then deducting trading and property losses and qualifying charitable donations. You have learnt the general rules for calculating income in your earlier studies, but here we see where there are special rules for companies.

In the next chapter you will learn how to compute the corporation tax liability on taxable total profits.

Study guide

		Intellectual level
E1	**The scope of corporation tax**	
(a)	Define the terms 'period of account', 'accounting period', and 'financial year'.	1
(b)	Recognise when an accounting period starts and when an accounting period finishes.	1
(c)	Explain how the residence of a company is determined.	2
E2	**Taxable total profits**	
(a)	Recognise the expenditure that is allowable in calculating the tax-adjusted trading profit.	2
(b)	Recognise the relief which can be obtained for pre-trading expenditure.	1
(c)	Compute capital allowances (as for income tax).	2
(d)	Compute property business profits and understand how relief for a property business loss is given.	2
(h)	Recognise and apply the treatment of interest paid and received under the loan relationship rules.	1
(i)	Recognise and apply the treatment of qualifying charitable donations.	2
(j)	Compute taxable total profits.	2

Exam guide

One of the 15 mark questions in Section B will focus on corporation tax. Corporation tax may also be tested in 10 mark questions in Section B. You should also expect to see one or more questions on corporation tax in Section A. When dealing with a corporation tax question in Section B you must first be able to identify the accounting period(s) involved; watch out for long periods of account. You must also be able to calculate taxable total profits; learn the standard layout so that you can easily slot in figures from your workings.

1 The scope of corporation tax

FAST FORWARD

Companies pay corporation tax on their taxable total profits.

1.1 Companies

Companies must pay corporation tax on their **taxable total profits** for each **accounting period**. We look at the meaning of these terms below.

Key term

A **company** is any corporate body (limited or unlimited) or unincorporated association, eg sports club.

1.2 Accounting periods

FAST FORWARD

An accounting period cannot exceed 12 months in length so a long period of account must be split into two accounting periods. The first accounting period of a long period of account is always 12 months in length.

Corporation tax is chargeable in respect of accounting periods. It is important to understand the difference between an accounting period and a period of account.

Key term

> A **period of account** is any period for which a company prepares accounts; usually this will be 12 months in length but it may be longer or shorter than this.

Key term

> An **accounting period** is the period for which corporation tax is charged and cannot exceed 12 months. Special rules determine when an accounting period starts and ends.

An accounting period starts on the earliest of:

- When a company starts to trade
- When the company otherwise becomes liable to corporation tax (eg it opens a bank account which pays interest)
- Immediately after the previous accounting period finishes

An accounting period finishes on the earliest of:

- 12 months after its start
- The end of the company's period of account
- The company starting or ceasing to trade
- The company entering/ceasing to be in administration
- The commencement of the company's winding up
- The company's ceasing to be resident in the UK
- The company's ceasing to be liable to corporation tax

If a company has a period of account exceeding 12 months (a long period of account), it is split into two accounting periods: the first 12 months and the remainder.

Question	Accounting periods

For each of the following companies, identify the accounting period(s).

(a) J Ltd, which has been trading for many years, prepares accounts for the twelve months to 30 September 2014.

(b) K plc is incorporated on 1 April 2014. On 1 June 2014, K plc starts to trade and makes up its first set of accounts to 31 August 2014.

(c) L Ltd, which has been trading for many years preparing accounts to 31 December each year, prepares accounts for the eleven months to 30 November 2014.

(d) M Plc, which has been trading for many years preparing accounts to 31 July each year, prepares accounts for the sixteen months to 30 November 2014.

(a) 1 October 2013 (immediately after previous accounting period finishes) to 30 September 2014 (12 months after start of accounting period and also the end of period of account).

(b) 1 June 2014 (company starts to trade) to 31 August 2014 (end of period of account).

(c) 1 January 2014 (immediately after previous accounting period finishes) to 30 November 2014 (end of period of account).

(d) First accounting period: 1 August 2013 (immediately after previous accounting period finishes) to 31 July 2014 (12 months after start).

Second accounting period: 1 August 2014 (immediately after previous accounting period finishes) to 30 November 2014 (end of period of account).

1.3 Financial year

FAST FORWARD

Tax rates are set for financial years.

The rates of corporation tax are fixed for financial years.

Key term

A **financial year** runs from 1 April to the following 31 March and is identified by the calendar year in which it begins. For example, the year ended 31 March 2015 is the Financial year 2014 (FY 2014). This should not be confused with a tax year, which runs from 6 April to the following 5 April.

1.4 Residence of companies

FAST FORWARD

A company is UK resident if it is incorporated in the UK or if it is incorporated overseas and its central management and control are exercised in the UK.

A company incorporated in the UK is resident in the UK. A company incorporated abroad is resident in the UK if its central management and control are exercised here. Central management and control are usually treated as exercised where the board of directors meet.

Question   Residence of a company

Supraville SARL is a company incorporated in France. It has its head office in London where the board of directors meet monthly. It trades throughout the European Union.

Is Supraville SARL resident in the UK?

Answer

Yes, Supraville SARL is resident in the UK.

The central management and control of Supraville SARL is in London (ie the UK) where the board of directors meet.

2 Taxable total profits

Taxable total profits comprises the company's income and chargeable gains (total profits) less some losses and qualifying charitable donations. It does not include dividends received from other companies.

One of the competencies you require to fulfil performance objective 19 of the PER is the ability to evaluate and compute taxes payable. You can apply the knowledge you obtain from this section of the text to help to demonstrate this competence.

2.1 Proforma computation

Income includes trading income, property income, income from non-trading loan relationships (interest) and miscellaneous income.

A company may have both income and gains. As a general rule income arises from receipts which are expected to recur regularly (such as the profits from a trade) whereas chargeable gains arise on the sale of capital assets which have been owned for several years (such as the sale of a factory used in the trade).

A company may receive income from various sources. All income received must be classified according to the nature of the income as different computational rules apply to different types of income. The main types of income for a company are:

- Profits of a trade
- Profits of a property business
- Interest income from non-trading loan relationships
- Miscellaneous income

The computation of chargeable gains for a company is dealt with later in this Text. At the moment, you will be given a figure for chargeable gains in order to compute taxable total profits. We also deal with losses in detail later in this Text so, at the moment, you just need to know that some losses are given tax relief by being deducted from total profits.

A company's taxable total profits are arrived at by aggregating its various sources of income and its chargeable gains and then deducting losses and qualifying charitable donations. Here is a pro forma computation.

	£
Trading profits	X
Property business income	X
Interest income from non-trading loan relationships	X
Miscellaneous income	X
Chargeable gains	X
Total profits	X
Less losses deductible from total profits	(X)
Less qualifying charitable donations	(X)
Taxable total profits for an accounting period	X

Exam focus point

It would be of great help in the exam if you could learn the above proforma. When answering a corporation tax question you could immediately reproduce the proforma and insert the appropriate numbers as you are given the information in the question.

Dividends received from other companies (UK resident and non-UK resident), for the purposes of the F6 exam, are usually exempt and so not included in taxable trading profits.

3 Trading income

3.1 Adjustment of profits

FAST FORWARD The adjustment of profits computation for companies broadly follows that for computing business profits subject to income tax. There are, however, some minor differences.

The trading income of companies is derived from the profit before taxation figure in the statement of profit or loss, just as for individuals, adjusted as follows.

	£	£
Profit before taxation		X
Add expenditure not allowed for taxation purposes		X
		X
Less: income not taxable as trading income	X	
expenditure not charged in the accounts but allowable for the purposes of taxation	X	
capital allowances	X	
		(X)
Profit adjusted for tax purposes		X

Exam focus point

> An examination question requiring adjustment to profit will direct you to start the adjustment with the profit before taxation of £XXXX and deal with all the items listed indicating with a zero (0) any items which do not require adjustment. Marks will not be given for relevant items unless this approach is used. Therefore students who attempt to rewrite the statement of profit or loss will be penalised.

The adjustment of profits computation for companies broadly follows that for computing business profits subject to income tax. There are, however, some minor differences. There is no disallowance for 'private use' for companies; instead the director or employee will be taxed on the benefit received.

Qualifying charitable donations are added back in the calculation of adjusted profit. They are treated instead as a deduction from total profits.

Investment income including rents is deducted from profit before taxation in arriving at trading income but brought in again further down in the computation (see below).

Exam focus point

> When adjusting profits as supplied in a statement of profit or loss confusion can arise as regards whether figures are net or gross. Properly drawn up company accounts should normally include all income gross. However, some examination questions include items 'net'. Read the question carefully.

3.2 Pre-trading expenditure

Pre-trading expenditure incurred by the company within the 7 years before trade commences is treated as an allowable expense incurred on the first day of trading provided it would have been allowable had the company been trading when the expense was actually incurred.

3.3 Capital allowances

The calculation of capital allowances follows income tax principles.

For companies, however, there is never any reduction of allowances to take account of any private use of an asset. The director or employee suffers a taxable benefit instead. As shown above capital allowances must be deducted in arriving at taxable trading income.

A company's accounting period can never exceed 12 months. If the period of account is longer than 12 months it is **divided into two**; one for the first 12 months and one for the balance. **The capital allowances computation must be carried out for each period separately**.

The calculation of trading income should be undertaken as a first step to the calculation of taxable total profits. However, it is important to realise that these are two distinct aspects when calculating a company's liability to corporation tax and you should not attempt to present them in one calculation.

4 Property business income

Rental income is deducted in arriving at trading income but brought in again further down in the computation as property business income.

The calculation of property business income follows income tax principles. The income tax rules for property businesses were set out earlier in this Text. In summary all UK rental activities are treated as a single source of income calculated in the same way as trading income.

However interest paid by a company on a loan to buy or improve property is not a property business expense. The loan relationship rules apply instead (see below).

5 Loan relationships (interest income)

5.1 General principle

If a company borrows or lends money, including issuing or investing in debentures or buying gilts, it has a loan relationship. This can be a creditor relationship (where the company lends or invests money) or a debtor relationship (where the company borrows money or issues securities). Loan interest paid or received is dealt with on a receivable (accruals) basis.

5.2 Treatment of trading loan relationships

If the company is a party to a loan relationship for trade purposes, any debits – ie interest paid or other debt costs – charged through its accounts are allowed as a trading expense and are therefore deductible in computing trading income. An example of a trading loan relationship is a loan to buy plant and machinery to use in the trade.

Similarly if any credits – ie interest income or other debt returns – arise on a trading loan these are treated as a trading receipt and are taxable as trading income. This is not likely to arise unless the trade is one of money lending.

5.3 Treatment of non-trading loan relationships

If a loan relationship is not one to which the company is a party for trade purposes any debits or credits must be pooled. A net credit on the pool is chargeable as interest income. Examples of non trading loan relationships would be cash on deposit at the bank (creditor relationship), or a loan to purchase a property that is rented out (debtor relationship).

Interest charged on underpaid tax is allowable and interest received on overpaid tax is assessable under the rules for non-trading loan relationships.

You will not be expected to deal with net deficits (ie losses) on non-trading loan relationships in your exam.

5.4 Accounting methods

Debits and credits must be brought into account using the UK generally accepted accounting practice (GAAP) or using the International Accounting Standards (IAS). This will usually be the accruals basis.

5.5 Incidental costs of loan finance

Under the loan relationship rules expenses ('debits') are allowed if incurred directly:

(a)   To bring a loan relationship into existence
(b)   Entering into or giving effect to any related transactions
(c)   Making payment under a loan relationship or related transactions or
(d)   Taking steps to ensure the receipt of payments under the loan relationship or related transaction.

A related transaction means 'any disposal or acquisition (in whole or in part) of rights or liabilities under the relationship, including any arising from a security issue in relation to the money debt in question'.

The above categories of incidental costs are also allowable even if the company does not enter into the loan relationship (ie abortive costs). Costs directly incurred in varying the terms of a loan relationship are also allowed.

5.6 Other matters

It is not only the interest costs of borrowing that are allowable or taxable. The capital costs are treated similarly. Thus if a company issues a loan at a discount and repays it eventually at par, the capital cost is usually allowed on Redemption (if the accruals basis is adopted).

6 Miscellaneous income

Patent royalties received which do not relate to the trade are taxed as miscellaneous income. Patent royalties which relate to the trade are included in trading income normally on an accruals basis.

7 Qualifying charitable donations

FAST FORWARD

> Qualifying charitable donations are deducted from total profits when computing taxable total profits.

Qualifying charitable donations are deductible from total profits when computing taxable total profits.

Almost all donations of money to charity by a company can be qualifying charitable donations whether they are single donations or regular donations. There is no need for a claim to be made in order for a payment to be treated as a qualifying charitable donation (compare with gift aid donations where a declaration is required).

Donations to local charities which are incurred wholly and exclusively for the purposes of a trade are deducted in the calculation of the tax adjusted trading profits.

Marlborough Ltd is a UK resident trading company. The company's statement of profit or loss for the year ended 31 March 2015 is as follows:

	£	£
Gross profit		700,000
Other income		
Loan stock interest (note 1)		14,500
Rental income (note 2)		18,000
Expenses		
Salaries	76,000	
Depreciation	37,900	
Loss on sale of non-current asset	1,400	
Impairment losses (all trade)	2,800	
Professional fees (note 3)	12,900	
Repairs and renewals (note 4)	17,100	
Other expenses (note 5)	25,600	
		(173,700)
Finance costs		
Loan interest (note 6)		(12,000)
Profit before taxation		546,800

Notes

(1)   *Loan stock interest*

The loan stock interest is in respect of loan stock held by Marlborough Ltd as an investment. The amount of £14,500 is the amount received and accrued to 31 March 2015.

(2)   *Rental income*

The rental income is in respect of a warehouse which is held as an investment and is let out to an unconnected company. The rental received of £18,000 is also the amount accrued to 31 March 2015.

(3)   *Professional fees*

Professional fees are as follows:

	£
Accountancy and audit fees	4,600
Debt collection of trade debts	5,000
Legal fees in connection with renewing a 25 year lease	1,300
Legal fees in connection with director's motoring offences	2,000
	12,900

(4)   *Repairs and renewals*

Repairs and renewals include:

	£
Extension to factory	7,988
Repainting exterior of company's offices	6,000

(5)   *Other expenses*

Other expenses include:

	£
100 pens with an advertisement for company, given to customers	2,100
Qualifying charitable donation	5,000

(6) *Loan interest*

The loan interest relates to the warehouse let out (see note (2)). The amount shown is the amount paid and accrued to 31 March 2015.

(7) *Plant and machinery*

On 1 April 2014 the tax written down value of the main pool was £22,500. The following transactions took place during the year ended 31 March 2015:

		Cost/(Proceeds) £
10 June 2014	Purchased general plant	20,200
25 January 2015	Sold a van (original cost £17,000)	(11,500)
15 March 2015	Purchased a motor car CO_2 emissions 128g/km	10,600

The motor car purchased on 15 March 2015 is used by the company's sales manager: 30% of the mileage is for private journeys.

(a) What are Marlborough Ltd's trading profits for the year ended 31 March 2015? Start with the profit before taxation figure of £546,800 and list all of the items in the statement of profit or loss indicating by the use of a zero (0) any items that do not require adjustment.

(b) What are Marlborough Ltd's taxable total profits for the year ended 31 March 2015?

Answer

(a) **Marlborough Ltd – trading profits for y/e 31 March 2015**

	£	£
Profit before taxation		546,800
Add:		
Salaries (trade)	0	
Depreciation (capital)	37,900	
Loss on sale of non-current asset (capital loss)	1,400	
Impairment losses (trade)	0	
Accountancy and audit fees	0	
Debt collection (trade)	0	
Legal fees – renewal of short lease	0	
Legal fees – motoring offences (not trade)	2,000	
Repairs and renewals: extension (capital)	7,988	
Repairs and renewals: repainting (revenue)	0	
Other expenses: pens (>£50, advertisement)	0	
Other expenses: qualifying charitable donation	5,000	
Loan interest (non-trading loan relationship)	12,000	
		66,288
Deduct:		
Loan stock interest (non-trading loan relationship)	14,500	
Rental income (property business income)	18,000	
Capital allowances (W)	24,088	
		(56,588)
Profit adjusted for tax purposes		556,500

Working

Capital allowances on plant and machinery

	AIA £	Main pool £	Allowances £
TWDV b/f		22,500	
Additions qualifying for AIA			
10.6.14 General plant	20,200		
AIA	(20,200)		20,200
Additions not qualifying for AIA			
15.3.15 Car		10,600	
Disposal			
25.1.15 Van		(11,500)	
		21,600	
WDA @ 18%		(3,888)	3,888
TWDVs c/f		17,712	
Allowances			24,088

Note. The private use of the car by the employee is not relevant for capital allowance purposes. No adjustment is ever made to a company's capital allowances to reflect the private use of an asset.

(b) **Marlborough Ltd – taxable total profits for y/e 31 March 2015**

	£	£
Trading profit (part (a))		556,500
Non-trading loan relationship credit (loan stock)	14,500	
Less non-trading loan relationship debit (warehouse loan)	(12,000)	
		2,500
Property business income		18,000
Total profits		577,000
Less qualifying charitable donation		(5,000)
Taxable total profits		572,000

8 Long periods of account

FAST FORWARD

Long periods of account are split into two accounting periods: the first 12 months and the remainder.

As we saw earlier in this chapter, if a company has a long period of account exceeding 12 months, it is split into two accounting periods: the first 12 months and the remainder.

Where the period of account differs from the corporation tax accounting periods, profits are **allocated to the relevant periods** as follows:

- **Trading income** before capital allowances and **property income** are apportioned on a **time basis**.
- **Capital allowances** and balancing charges are **calculated for each accounting period**.
- **Other income is allocated to the period to which it relates** (eg interest accrued). Miscellaneous income, however, is apportioned on a time basis.
- **Chargeable gains and losses** are allocated to the **period in which they are realised**.
- **Qualifying charitable donations** are deducted in the accounting **period in which they are paid**.

Xenon Ltd makes up an 18 month set of accounts to 30 September 2015 with the following results.

	£
Trading income (no capital allowances claimed)	180,000
Interest income	
18 months @ £500 accruing per month	9,000
Capital gain (1 August 2015 disposal)	250,000
Less: qualifying charitable donation (paid 31 March 2015)	(50,000)
	389,000

What are the taxable total profits for each of the accounting periods based on the above accounts?

Answer

The 18 month period of account is divided into:

Year ending 31 March 2015
6 months to 30 September 2015

Results are allocated:

	Y/e 31.3.15 £	6m to 30.9.15 £
Trading income 12:6	120,000	60,000
Interest income		
12 × £500	6,000	
6 × £500		3,000
Capital gain (1.8.15)		250,000
Total profits	126,000	313,000
Less: qualifying charitable donation (31.3.15)	(50,000)	
Taxable total profits	76,000	313,000

Chapter Roundup

- Companies pay corporation tax on their taxable total profits.

- An accounting period cannot exceed 12 months in length so a long period of account must be split into two accounting periods. The first accounting period of a long period of account is always 12 months in length.

- Tax rates are set for financial years.

- A company is UK resident if it is incorporated in the UK or if it is incorporated overseas and its central management and control are exercised in the UK.

- Taxable total profits comprises the company's income and chargeable gains (total profits) less some losses and qualifying charitable donations. It does not include dividends received from other companies.

- Income includes trading income, property income, income from non-trading loan relationships (interest) and miscellaneous income.

- The adjustment of profits computation for companies broadly follows that for computing business profits subject to income tax. There are, however, some minor differences.

- Qualifying charitable donations are deducted from total profits when computing taxable total profits.

- Long periods of account are split into two accounting periods: the first 12 months and the remainder.

Quick Quiz

1   When does an accounting period end?

2   What is the difference between a period of account and an accounting period?

3   Zed Ltd has been trading for many years, preparing accounts to 31 October. It decides to prepare accounts for the fifteen month period ending 31 January 2015. What are Zed Ltd's accounting period(s) for the long period of account?

    A   1 November 2013 to 31 January 2015
    B   1 November 2013 to 31 October 2014 and 1 November 2014 to 31 January 2015
    C   1 November 2013 to 31 January 2014 and 1 February 2014 to 31 January 2015
    D   1 November 2013 to 31 March 2014 and 1 April 2014 to 31 January 2015

4   Should interest paid on a trading loan be adjusted in the trading income computation?

5   How is trading income (before capital allowances) of a long period of account divided between accounting periods?

    A   On a receipts basis
    B   On an accruals basis
    C   On a time basis
    D   On any basis the company chooses

1. An accounting period ends on the earliest of:

    (a) 12 months after its start
    (b) The end of the company's period of account
    (c) The commencement of the company's winding up
    (d) The company ceasing to be resident in the UK
    (e) The company ceasing to be liable to corporation tax

2. A period of account is the period for which a company prepares accounts. An accounting period is the period for which corporation tax is charged. If a company prepares annual accounts the two will coincide.

3. B. 1 November 2013 to 31 October 2014 and 1 November 2014 to 31 January 2015. The first accounting period of a long period of account is always 12 months in length.

4. Interest paid on a trading loan should not be adjusted in the trading income computation as it is an allowable expense, computed on the accruals basis.

5. C. Trading income (before capital allowances) is apportioned on a time basis.

Now try the question below from the Practice Question Bank

Number	Type	Marks	Time
Q50	Section A	6	11 mins
Q51	Section B	15	27 mins

Computing the corporation tax liability

Topic list	Syllabus reference
1 Charge to corporation tax	E4(a), (b)
2 Associated companies	E4(a), E5(a)
3 Choice of business medium	E4(a)

Introduction

In the previous chapter you learnt how to identify a company's accounting period and how to compute the taxable total profits for that accounting period.

In this chapter you will learn how to compute the corporation tax liability on those profits. We will also investigate choice of business medium by comparing the tax effects of trading as a sole trader and through a company.

In the next chapter we will deal with chargeable gains for companies.

Study guide

		Intellectual level
E4	**The comprehensive computation of corporation tax liability**	
(a)	Compute the corporation tax liability and apply marginal relief.	2
(b)	Recognise the implications of receiving franked investment income.	2
E5	**The effect of a group corporate structure for corporation tax purposes**	
(a)	Define an associated company and recognise the effect of having associated companies for corporation tax purposes.	2

Exam guide

There will be a 15 mark question in Section B of your exam on corporation tax. Computing the corporation tax is usually an integral part of this question, and you must be sure that you understand the rules for marginal relief. Corporation tax may also be tested in 10 mark questions in Section B. You may also find a question in Section A dealing with a particular aspect of the corporation tax liability such as marginal relief.

Note in particular the consequences of short accounting periods and of having associated companies. It will be crucial for you to know the marginal rate of corporation tax for a company when you are dealing with loss relief and group relief later in your studies. You may also be asked to compare the tax implications of operating a business as a sole trader or through a company.

1 Charge to corporation tax

> One of the competencies you require to fulfil performance objective 19 of the PER is the ability to evaluate and compute taxes payable. You can apply the knowledge you obtain from this section of the text to help to demonstrate this competence.

1.1 Augmented profits

FAST FORWARD

> A company pays corporation tax on its taxable total profits, but the rate of tax depends on augmented profits. Augmented profits are taxable total profits plus franked investment income (FII).

Although we tax taxable total profits, another figure needs to be calculated, called augmented profits, to determine the rate of corporation tax to apply to taxable total profits.

Augmented profits means taxable total profits plus the grossed-up amount of dividends received from other companies. The exception to this rule is any dividends received from an associated company (see later in this chapter): **these dividends** (sometimes called 'group dividends') **are completely ignored for corporation tax purposes.**

The grossed-up amount of dividends is the dividend received multiplied by 100/90. You may see the grossed up amount of dividend received referred to as **franked investment income (FII)**.

1.2 The main rate

FAST FORWARD

> Companies may be taxed at the main rate, the small profits rate or obtain marginal relief, depending on their augmented profits.

The rates of corporation tax are fixed for financial years. **The main rate of corporation tax is 21% for FY 2014 and was 23% for FY 2013 and 24% for FY 2012. The main rate applies to taxable total profits of companies with augmented profits of £1,500,000 or more (for all relevant FYs). The £1,500,000 limit is called the 'upper limit'.** This limit is in the rates and allowances section of the exam paper.

Question
The main rate

A Ltd had the following results for the year ended 31 March 2015.

	£
Trading profits	1,142,000
Dividend received 1 May 2014 from non-associated company	340,200

Compute the corporation tax payable.

Answer

	£
Trading profits/Taxable total profits	1,142,000
Dividend plus tax credit £340,200 × 100/90	378,000
Augmented profits (above upper limit)	1,520,000
Corporation tax payable	
£1,142,000 × 21%	£239,820

Exam focus point

Be careful to charge corporation tax on taxable total profits, not on augmented profits.

1.3 The small profits rate

The small profits rate of corporation tax is 20% for FY 2014, FY 2013 and FY 2012. The small profits rate applies to the taxable total profits of UK resident companies whose augmented profits are not more than £300,000 (for all relevant FYs). The £300,000 limit is called the 'lower limit'. This limit is in the rates and allowances section of the exam paper.

Question
The small profits rate

B Ltd had the following results for the year ended 31 March 2015.

	£
Trading profits	42,000
Dividend received 1 May 2014 from non-associated company	9,000

Compute the corporation tax payable.

Answer

	£
Trading profits/Taxable total profits	42,000
Dividend plus tax credit £9,000 × 100/90	10,000
Augmented profits (less than lower limit)	52,000
Corporation tax payable	
£42,000 × 20%	£8,400

1.4 Marginal relief

Marginal relief applies where the augmented profits of an accounting period of a UK resident company are above the lower limit but less than the upper limit.

We first calculate the corporation tax at the main rate and then deduct:

Standard fraction × (U – A) × N/A

where U = upper limit (£1,500,000 for all relevant FYs)
A = augmented profits
N = taxable total profits

The standard fraction is 1/400 for FY 2014. It was 3/400 for FY 2013 and was 1/100 for FY 2012.

This information is given in the rates and allowances section of the exam paper.

Question	Marginal relief

Lenox Ltd has the following results for the year ended 31 March 2015.

	£
Taxable total profits	296,000
Dividend received 1 December 2014 from non-associated company	12,600

Calculate the corporation tax liability.

Answer	

	£
Taxable total profits	296,000
Dividend plus tax credit £12,600 × 100/90	14,000
Augmented profits	310,000

Augmented profits are above £300,000 but below £1,500,000, so marginal relief applies.

	£
Corporation tax on taxable total profits £296,000 × 21%	62,160
Less marginal relief	
£(1,500,000 – 310,000) × 296,000/310,000 × 1/400	(2,841)
	59,319

FAST FORWARD

The marginal rate of corporation tax between the small profits limits is 21.25% for FY 2014. The marginal rate of tax is an effective rate; it is never actually used in working out corporation tax.

In exam questions you often need to be aware that there is a **marginal rate of 21.25%** which applies to any taxable total profits that lie in between the small profits limits. This is calculated as follows:

	£				£
Upper limit	1,500,000	@	21%		315,000
Lower limit	(300,000)	@	20%		(60,000)
Difference	1,200,000				255,000

$$\frac{255,000}{1,200,000} = 21.25\%$$

Effectively the band of profits (here £1,200,000) falling between the upper and lower limits are taxed at a rate of 21.25%.

The marginal rate in FY 2013 was 23.75% and in FY 2012 was 25%.

1.5 Example: effective marginal rate of tax

A Ltd has taxable total profits of £350,000 for the year ended 31 March 2015. Its corporation tax liability is

	£
£350,000 × 21%	73,500
Less marginal relief	
£(1,500,000 − 350,000) × $\frac{1}{400}$	(2,875)
	70,625

This is the same as calculating tax at 20% × £300,000 + 21.25% × £50,000 = £60,000 + £10,625 = £70,625.

Consequently tax is charged at an effective rate of 21.25% on taxable total profits that exceed the small profits lower limit.

Note that although there is an effective corporation tax charge of 21.25%, this rate of tax is never used in actually calculating corporation tax. The rate is just an effective marginal rate that you must be aware of. It will be particularly important when considering loss relief and group relief (see later in this Text).

1.6 Accounting period in more than one financial year

An accounting period **may fall within more than one financial year. If the rates and limits for corporation tax are the same in both financial years, tax can be computed for the accounting period as if it fell within one financial year.**

However, **if the rates and/or limits for corporation tax are different in the financial years, taxable total profits are time apportioned between the financial years**. Strictly, augmented profits should also be time apportioned between the financial years in order to determine the rate of tax, but in practice this is not necessary since the upper and lower limits are the same for all financial years that you will deal with in your exam.

1.7 Example: accounting period in more than one financial year

Wentworth Ltd makes up its accounts to 31 December each year. For the year to 31 December 2014, it has taxable total profits of £1,480,000. It receives a dividend of £54,000 on 1 December 2014 from a non-associated company.

The corporation tax payable by Wentworth Ltd is calculated as follows.

	£
Taxable total profits	1,480,000
Dividend plus tax credit £54,000 × 100/90	60,000
Augmented profits	1,540,000
Main rate applies for both FY 2013 and FY2014	

	£
FY 2013 (1.1.14 to 31.3.14 – 3 months)	
£1,480,000 × 3/12 = 370,000 × 23%	85,100
FY 2014 (1.4.14 to 31.12.14 – 9 months)	
£1,480,000 × 9/12 = 1,110,000 × 21%	233,100
Corporation tax liability for year to 31 December 2014	318,200

Question

Elliot Ltd has the following results for the year to 30 September 2014.

	£
Taxable total profits	360,000
Dividend received 15 July 2014 from non-associated company	8,100

Calculate the corporation tax payable by Elliot Ltd.

Answer

	£
Taxable total profits	360,000
Add: FII £8,100 × 100/90	9,000
Augmented profits	369,000

Marginal relief applies for both FY 2013 and FY2014

	£
FY 2013 (1.10.13 to 31.3.14 – 6 months)	
£360,000 × 6/12 = 180,000 × 23%	41,400
Less: marginal relief £(1,500,000 – 369,000) × $\dfrac{360,000}{369,000}$ × 3/400 × 6/12	(4,138)
FY 2014 (1.4.14 to 30.9.14 – 6 months)	
£360,000 × 6/12 = 180,000 × 21%	37,800
Less: marginal relief £(1,500,000 – 369,000) × $\dfrac{360,000}{369,000}$ × 1/400 × 6/12	(1,379)
Corporation tax liability for year to 30 September 2014	73,683

1.8 Short accounting periods

The upper and lower limits which are used to be determine tax rates are pro-rated on a time basis if an accounting period lasts for less than 12 months.

Question

Ink Ltd prepared accounts for the six months to 31 March 2015. Taxable total profits for the period were £200,000. No dividends were received. Calculate the corporation tax payable for the period.

Answer

Upper limit £1,500,000 × 6/12 = £750,000
Lower limit £300,000 × 6/12 = £150,000

As augmented profits fall between the limits, marginal relief applies.

	£
Corporation tax (FY 14)	
£200,000 × 21%	42,000
Less marginal relief	
1/400 × (£750,000 – £200,000)	(1,375)
Corporation tax	40,625

1.9 Long periods of account

Remember that an accounting period cannot be more than 12 months long. If the period of account exceeds 12 months it must be split into two accounting periods, the first of 12 months and the second of the balance.

Exam focus point

If you have to deal with a long period of account remember to pro-rate the upper and lower limits on a time basis for the second (short) accounting period.

Question	Long period of account

Xenon Ltd (in the previous chapter) made up an 18 month set of accounts to 30 September 2015.

The 18 month period of account is divided into:

Year ending 31 March 2015
6 months to 30 September 2015

Results were allocated:

	Y/e 31.3.15 £	6m to 30.9.15 £
Trading profits 12:6	120,000	60,000
Property income	6,000	3,000
Capital gain (1.8.15)		250,000
Less: qualifying charitable donation (31.3.15)	(50,000)	
Taxable total profits	76,000	313,000

Assuming Xenon Ltd received FII of £27,000 on 31 August 2015, calculate the corporation tax payable for each accounting period. Assume that the corporation tax rates in FY15 are the same as in FY14.

Answer

	Y/e 31.3.15 £	6m to 30.9.15 £
Taxable total profits	76,000	313,000
FII	0	27,000
Augmented profits	76,000	340,000
Small profits lower limit	300,000	150,000
Small profits upper limit	1,500,000	750,000
	Small company	Marginal Relief
Corporation tax payable		
£76,000 × 20%	15,200	
£313,000 × 21% (assumed)		65,730
Less marginal relief £(750,000 − 340,000) × 313,000/340,000 × 1/400		(944)
		64,786
Total corporation tax payable £(15,200 + 64,786)		79,986

BPP
LEARNING MEDIA

2 Associated companies

> The upper and lower limits which are used to determine tax rates are divided by the total number of associated companies. Broadly, associated companies are trading companies resident anywhere in the world which are under common control.

2.1 What is an associated company?

Key term

> The expression **'associated companies'** in tax has no connection with financial accounting. For tax purposes a company is associated with another company if either controls the other or if both are under the control of the same person or persons (individuals, partnerships or companies). Whether such a company is UK resident or not is irrelevant. Control is given by holding over 50% of the share capital or the voting power or being entitled to over 50% of the distributable income or of the net assets in a winding up.

2.2 Effects of associated companies

If a company has one or more 'associated companies', then the profit limits are divided by the number of associated companies + 1 (for the company itself).

Companies which have only been associated for part of an accounting period are deemed to have been associated for the whole period for the purpose of determining the profit limits.

2.3 Exception

An associated company is ignored for these purposes if it has not carried on any trade or business at any time in the accounting period (or the part of the period during which it was associated) ie it is 'dormant'.

Question
Associated companies

For the year to 31 March 2015, Y Ltd had taxable total profits of £200,000. Y Ltd has three wholly owned subsidiary companies, V Ltd, X Ltd and Z Ltd. Y Ltd received a dividend of £9,000 from V Ltd on 1 December 2014. X Ltd did not carry on any trade or business during the year to 31 March 2015. Z Ltd is not resident in the UK. Compute the corporation tax payable by Y Ltd.

Answer

(a) Reduction in the lower limit

V Ltd and Z Ltd (residence not relevant) are associated companies for Y Ltd. X Ltd is not an associated company because it is dormant.

Divide by number of associated companies 2 + 1 = 3

£300,000 ÷ 3 = £100,000

(b) Reduction in the upper limit

£1,500,000 ÷ 3 = £500,000

(c) Augmented profits = £200,000

The dividend received from V Ltd is group income and is therefore not FII. Y Ltd's taxable total profits of £200,000 are therefore also its augmented profits.

As augmented profits fall between the lower and upper limits, the main rate less marginal relief applies.

(d)   Corporation tax for Y Ltd

	£
£200,000 × 21%	42,000
Less marginal relief £(500,000 − 200,000) × 1/400	(750)
Corporation tax	41,250

2.4 Associated companies and short accounting periods

If a company has associated companies and also a short accounting period, first reduce the upper and lower limits for the associated companies and then prorate them for the short accounting period.

2.5 Example: small profits limits

Alpha plc, a company with one subsidiary in which it owns 70% of the shares, prepares accounts for the 9 months to 31 December 2014.

The limits will be multiplied by ½ as there is one associated company, and then by 9/12 as the accounting period is only 9 months long.

The lower limit will be £300,000 × ½ × 9/12 = £112,500

The upper limit will be £1,500,000 × ½ × 9/12 = £562,500

3 Choice of business medium

FAST FORWARD

> An individual can choose between trading as a sole trader or trading through a company. Trading through a company may reduce the overall tax and national insurance liability.

3.1 Trading as a sole trader or through a company

An individual starting in business must decided whether to trade as a sole trader or as a company. If a company is used, the individual can be both a director and a shareholder of the company.

A sole trader pays **income tax on trading income** and also **Class 2 and Class 4 national insurance contributions**.

A company pays corporation tax on its taxable total profits. Any director's salary and its associated Class 1 secondary national insurance contributions are deducted in computing those profits. The employment allowance may cover the Class 1 secondary national insurance contributions, for example if the director is the only employee. An amount equal to the **remaining profits after corporation tax** can then be **paid out to shareholders as a dividend** with a 10% tax credit. The **individual as a director pays income tax on employment income** and **Class 1 primary contributions** on cash earnings. The **individual as shareholder pays income tax on dividend income** using the 10% tax credit to cover the basic rate liability on this income. There are **no national insurance contributions on dividends**.

3.2 Example: sole trader or company?

Sharif was born in 1975. He is starting a new business and expects to make profits of £36,000 before tax and national insurance.

Sharif wants to know how much net income he would receive from the business if he trades as a sole trader or, alternatively, through a company of which he would be the sole shareholder, director and employee, with the company paying him a salary of £12,000 and then an amount equal to the company's remaining profits (after corporation tax) as a dividend.

As a sole trader

	£
Profits	36,000
Less personal allowance	(10,000)
Taxable income	26,000
Income tax on £26,000 at 20%	5,200
National Insurance Classes 2 (52 × £2.75) and 4 (£(36,000 – 7,956) × 9%)	2,667
	7,867
Net income £(36,000 – 7,867)	28,133

Through a company

	£	£
Profits		36,000
Less: director's salary		(12,000)
Less: employer's secondary Class 1 contributions (12,000 – 7,956) × 13.8%	558	
Less: employment allowance (sole employee)	(558)	(0)
Taxable profits		24,000
Less: corporation tax 20% × £24,000		(4,800)
Net profits		19,200

A dividend of £19,200 can be paid to Sharif.

	Non-savings income £	Dividend income £	Total £
Earnings	12,000		
Dividend £19,200 × 100/90		21,333	
Net income	12,000	21,333	33,333
Less personal allowance	(10,000)		
Taxable income	2,000	21,333	23,333

	£
Non-savings income	
£2,000 × 20%	400
Dividend income	
£21,333 × 10%	2,133
	2,533
Less dividend credit £21,333 × 10%	(2,133)
Income tax payable	400

		£
Net income		
Salary		12,000
Dividend		19,200
	£	31,200
Less: income tax	400	
employee's primary Class 1 contributions		
£(12,000 – 7,956) × 12%	485	
		(885)
Net income		30,315

If Sharif trades through a company, he will receive £(30,315 – 28,133) = £2,182 more net income from the business than if he trades as a sole trader.

Chapter Roundup

- A company pays corporation tax on its taxable total profits, but the rate of tax depends on augmented profits. Augmented profits are taxable total profits plus franked investment income (FII).

- Companies may be taxed at the main rate, the small profits rate or obtain marginal relief, depending on their augmented profits.

- The marginal rate of corporation tax between the small profits limits is 21.25% for FY 2014. The marginal tax rate is an effective rate; it is never actually used in working out corporation tax.

- The upper and lower limits which are used to be determine tax rates are pro-rated on a time basis if an accounting period lasts for less than 12 months.

- The upper and lower limits which are used to determine tax rates are divided by the total number of associated companies. Broadly, associated companies are trading companies resident anywhere in the world which are under common control.

- An individual can choose between trading as a sole trader or trading through a company. Trading through a company may reduce the overall tax and national insurance liability.

Quick Quiz

1   Individual companies are entitled to the small profits rate of corporation tax if they have augmented profits for a 12 month period of up to £_____. Fill in the blank.

2   What is the marginal relief formula?

3   T plc had taxable total profits for the year to 31 December 2014 of £1,800,000. It did not receive any dividends.

     What is the amount of corporation tax payable by T plc for the year ended 31 December 2014?

     A   £378,000
     B   £382,500
     C   £387,000
     D   £414,000

4   M plc has the following relationships with other companies during the year to 31 March 2015:

     N plc – M plc owns 20% of the ordinary shares

     O Inc (not resident in the UK) – M plc owns 60% of the ordinary shares

     P Ltd – M plc owns 90% of the ordinary shares, which it acquired on 1 February 2015

     Q Ltd (has not carried on any trade or business since it was incorporated) – M plc owns 100% of the ordinary shares

     Which of these four companies are associated with M plc for the year to 31 March 2015?

5   What effect do associated companies have on the corporation tax computation?

Answers to Quick Quiz

1   Individual companies are entitled to the small profits rate of corporation tax if they have augmented profits for a 12 month period of up to **£300,000**.

2   Standard fraction × (U – A) × N/A

where:

U = upper limit
A = augmented profits
N = taxable total profits

3   C.

	£
FY 2013	
£1,800,000 × 23% × 3/12	103,500
FY 2014	
£1,800,000 × 21% × 9/12	283,500
Corporation tax	387,000

4   O Inc and P Ltd.

N plc is not controlled by M plc and so is not an associated company. O Inc's non-UK resident status is not relevant. P Ltd was associated with M plc from 1 February 2015 but is deemed to be associated for the whole of the year to 31 March 2015. Q Ltd is dormant and so is excluded from being an associated company.

5   If a company has associated companies the lower and upper limits are divided by the number of associated companies + 1.

Now try the questions below from the Practice Question Bank

Number	Type	Marks	Time
Q52	Section A	6	11 mins
Q53	Section B	10	18 mins
Q54	Section B	10	18 mins

Chargeable gains for companies

Topic list	Syllabus reference
1 Corporation tax on chargeable gains	E3(a)
2 Indexation allowance	E3(b)
3 Disposal of shares by companies	E3(d)–(f)
4 Relief for replacement of business assets (rollover relief)	E3(g)

Introduction

We studied chargeable gains for individuals earlier in this Text. In this chapter, we will consider the treatment of chargeable gains for companies.

Companies pay corporation tax on their chargeable gains, rather than capital gains tax. The computation of gains for companies is slightly more complicated than for individuals because companies are entitled to indexation allowance.

We also consider the matching rules for companies which dispose of shares in other companies. Again, these rules are slightly more complicated than for individuals.

Finally, we look at how the relief for replacement of business assets applies to companies.

In the next chapters we will deal with losses, groups and overseas matters.

Study guide

		Intellectual level
E3	**Chargeable gains for companies**	
(a)	Compute and explain the treatment of chargeable gains.	2
(b)	Explain and compute the indexation allowance available.	2
(d)	Understand the treatment of disposals of shares by companies and the identification rules including the same day and nine day matching rules.	2
(e)	Explain and apply the pooling provisions.	2
(f)	Explain and apply the treatment of bonus issues, rights issues, takeovers and reorganisations.	2
(g)	Explain and apply rollover relief.	2

Exam guide

There will be a 15 mark question on corporation tax in Section B. This may include the gains of a company so it is important that you can deal with the aspects covered in this chapter. Corporation tax may also be tested in 10 mark questions in Section B. A Section A question may test a specific point such as computation of the indexation allowance.

1 Corporation tax on chargeable gains

FAST FORWARD

Chargeable gains for companies are computed in broadly the same way as for individuals, but indexation allowance applies and there is no annual exempt amount.

Companies do not pay capital gains tax. Instead their chargeable gains are included in the calculation of taxable total profits.

A company's capital gains or allowable losses are computed in a similar way to individuals but with a few major differences:

- There is relief for inflation called the indexation allowance
- **No annual exempt amount** is available
- Different matching rules for shares apply if the shareholder is a company

2 Indexation allowance

FAST FORWARD

The indexation allowance gives relief for the inflation element of a gain.

The purpose of having an indexation allowance is to remove the inflation element of a gain from taxation.

Companies are entitled to indexation allowance from the date of acquisition until the date of disposal of an asset. It is based on the movement in the Retail Price Index (RPI) between those two dates.

For example, if J Ltd bought a painting on 2 January 2002 and sold it on 19 November 2014 the indexation allowance is available from January 2002 until November 2014.

Exam formula

The indexation factor is:

$$\frac{\text{RPI for month of disposal} - \text{RPI for month of acquisition}}{\text{RPI for month of acquisition}}$$

The calculation is expressed as a decimal and is rounded to three decimal places.

Indexation allowance is available on the allowable cost of the asset from the date of acquisition (including incidental costs of acquisition). It is also available on enhancement expenditure from the month in which such expenditure becomes due and payable. Indexation allowance is not available on the costs of disposal.

Question — The indexation allowance

An asset is acquired by a company on 15 February 2003 (RPI = 179.3) at a cost of £5,000. Enhancement expenditure of £2,000 is incurred on 10 April 2004 (RPI = 185.7). The asset is sold for £15,500 on 20 December 2014 (assumed RPI =260.2). Incidental costs of sale are £500. Calculate the chargeable gain arising.

Answer

The indexation allowance is available until December 2014 and is computed as follows.

	£
$\dfrac{260.2 - 179.3}{179.3} = 0.451 \times £5,000$	2,255
$\dfrac{260.2 - 185.7}{185.7} = 0.401 \times £2,000$	802
	3,057

The computation of the chargeable gain is as follows.

	£
Proceeds	15,500
Less incidental costs of sale	(500)
Net proceeds	15,000
Less allowable costs £(5,000 + 2,000)	(7,000)
Unindexed gain	8,000
Less indexation allowance (see above)	(3,057)
Indexed gain	4,943

Indexation allowance cannot create or increase an allowable loss. If there is a gain before the indexation allowance, the allowance can reduce that gain to zero but no further. If there is a loss before the indexation allowance, there is no indexation allowance.

If the indexation allowance calculation gives a negative figure, treat the indexation as nil: do not add to the unindexed gain.

3 Disposal of shares by companies

FAST FORWARD
There are special rules for matching shares sold by a company with shares purchased. Disposals are matched with acquisitions on the same day, the previous nine days and the FA 1985 share pool.

3.1 The matching rules

We have discussed the share matching rules for individuals earlier in this Text. We also need special rules for companies.

For companies the matching of shares sold is in the following order.

(a)   Shares acquired on the same day

(b)   Shares acquired in the **previous nine days**, if more than one acquisition on a "first in, first out" (FIFO) basis

(c)   Shares from the **FA 1985 pool**

The composition of the FA 1985 pool in relation to companies which are shareholders is explained below.

3.2 Example: share matching rules for companies

Nor Ltd acquired the following shares in Last plc:

Date of acquisition	No of shares
9.11.02	15,000
15.12.04	15,000
11.7.14	5,000
15.7.14	5,000

Nor Ltd disposed of 20,000 of the shares on 15 July 2014.

We match the shares as follows:

(a)   Acquisition on same day: 5,000 shares acquired 15 July 2014

(b)   Acquisitions in previous 9 days: 5,000 shares acquired 11 July 2014

(c)   FA 1985 share pool: 10,000 shares out of 30,000 shares in FA 1985 share pool (9.11.02 and 15.12.04)

3.3 The FA 1985 share pool

The FA 1985 pool comprises the following shares of the same class in the same company.

- **Shares held by a company on 1 April 1985 and acquired by that company on or after 1 April 1982**

- **Shares acquired by that company on or after 1 April 1985**

We must keep track of:

(a)   The **number** of shares

(b)   The **cost** of the shares ignoring indexation

(c)   The **indexed cost** of the shares

The first step in constructing the FA 1985 share pool is to calculate the value of the pool at 1 April 1985 by indexing the cost of each acquisition before that date up to April 1985.

3.4 Example: the FA 1985 pool

Oliver Ltd bought 1,000 shares in Judith plc for £2,750 in August 1984 and another 1,000 for £3,250 in December 1984. RPIs are August 1984 = 89.9, December 1984 = 90.9 and April 1985 = 94.8. The FA 1985 pool at 1 April 1985 is as follows.

	No of shares	Cost £	Indexed Cost £
August 1984 (a)	1,000	2,750	2,750
December 1984 (b)	1,000	3,250	3,250
	2,000	6,000	6,000

Indexation allowance

$\dfrac{94.8 - 89.9}{89.9} = 0.055 \times £2,750$ 151

$\dfrac{94.8 - 90.9}{90.9} = 0.043 \times £3,250$ 140

Indexed cost of the pool at 1 April 1985   6,291

Disposals and acquisitions of shares which affect the indexed value of the FA 1985 pool are termed **'operative events'. Prior to reflecting each such operative event within the FA 1985 share pool, a further indexation allowance (an 'indexed rise') must be computed up to the date of the operative event concerned from the date of the last such operative event** (or from the later of the first acquisition and April 1985 if the operative event in question is the first one).

Indexation calculations within the FA 1985 pool (after its April 1985 value has been calculated) **are not rounded to three decimal places**. This is because rounding errors would accumulate and have a serious effect after several operative events.

If there are several operative events between 1 April 1985 and the date of a disposal, the indexation procedure described above will have to be performed several times over.

Question
Value of FA 1985 pool

Following on from the above example, assume that Oliver Ltd acquired 2,000 more shares on 10 July 1986 at a cost of £4,000. Recalculate the value of the FA 1985 pool on 10 July 1986 following the acquisition. RPI July 1986 = 97.5.

Answer

	No of shares	Cost £	Indexed cost £
Value at 1.4.85 b/f	2,000	6,000	6,291
Indexed rise $\dfrac{97.5 - 94.8}{94.8} \times £6,291$			179
	2,000	6,000	6,470
Acquisition	2,000	4,000	4,000
Value at 10.7.86	4,000	10,000	10,470

In the case of a disposal, following the calculation of the indexed rise to the date of disposal, the cost and the indexed cost attributable to the shares disposed of are deducted from the amounts within the FA 1985 pool. The proportions of the cost and indexed cost to take out of the pool should be computed by using the proportion of cost that the shares disposed of bear to the total number of shares held.

The indexation allowance is the indexed cost taken out of the pool minus the cost taken out. As usual, the indexation allowance cannot create or increase a loss.

Continuing the above exercise, suppose that Oliver Ltd sold 3,000 shares on 10 July 2014 for £23,500. Compute the gain, and the value of the FA 1985 pool following the disposal. Assume RPI July 2014 = 256.4.

Answer

	No of shares	Cost £	Indexed cost £
Value at 10.7.86	4,000	10,000	10,470
Indexed rise			
$\dfrac{256.4 - 97.5}{97.5} \times £10,470$	___	___	17,063
	4,000	10,000	27,533
Disposal	(3,000)		
Cost and indexed cost $\dfrac{3,000}{4,000} \times £10,000$ and £27,533	___	(7,500)	(20,650)
Value at 10.7.14	1,000	2,500	6,883

The gain is computed as follows:

	£
Proceeds	23,500
Less: cost	(7,500)
Unindexed gain	16,000
Less: indexation allowance £(20,650 – 7,500)	(13,150)
Indexed gain	2,850

3.5 Bonus and rights issues

When **bonus issue shares are issued**, all that happens is that **the size of the original holding is increased**. Since **bonus issue shares are issued at no cost** there is **no need to adjust the original cost** and there is **no operative event for the FA 1985 pool** (so no indexation allowance needs to be calculated).

When **rights issue shares are issued**, the **size of the original holding is increased** in the same way as for a bonus issue. So if the original shareholding was part of the FA 1985 pool, the rights issue shares are added to that pool. This might be important for the matching rules if a shareholding containing the rights issue shares is sold shortly after the rights issue.

However, in the case of a rights issue, the **new shares are paid for and this results in an adjustment to the original cost**. For the purpose of **calculating the indexation allowance, expenditure on a rights issue is taken as being incurred on the date of the issue** and not the date of the original holding.

3.6 Example: bonus and rights issue

S Ltd bought 10,000 shares in T plc in May 2000 (RPI = 170.7) at a cost of £45,000.

There was a 2 for 1 bonus issue in October 2002.

There was a 1 for 3 rights issue in June 2006 (RPI = 198.5) at a cost of £4 per share. S Ltd took up all of its rights entitlement.

S Ltd sold 20,000 shares in T plc for £120,000 in January 2015 (assumed RPI = 259.4).

FA 1985 share pool

		No. of shares	Cost £	Indexed cost £
5.00	Acquisition	10,000	45,000	45,000
10.02	Bonus 2:1	20,000		
		30,000		
6.06	Indexed rise			
	$\dfrac{198.5-170.7}{170.7} \times £45,000$		.	7,329
	Rights 1:3	10,000	40,000	40,000
		40,000	85,000	92,329
1.15	Index rise			
	$\dfrac{259.4-198.5}{198.5} \times £92,329$			28,327
				120,656
	Disposal	(20,000)	(42,500)	(60,328)
c/f		20,000	42,500	60,328

The gain is:

	£
Proceeds	120,000
Less: cost	(42,500)
Unindexed gain	77,500
Less: indexation allowance £(60,328 – 42,500)	(17,828)
Indexed gain	59,672

3.7 Reorganisations and takeovers

The rules on reorganisation and takeovers apply in a similar way for company shareholders as they do for individuals.

In the case of a **reorganisation, the new shares or securities take the place of the original shares. The original cost and the indexed cost of the original shares is apportioned between the different types of capital issued on the reorganisation.**

Where there is a takeover of shares which qualifies for the 'paper for paper' treatment, the cost and indexed cost of the original holding is passed onto the new holding which take the place of the original holding.

Question   Takeover

J Ltd acquired 20,000 shares in G Ltd in August 1990 (RPI = 128.1) at a cost of £40,000. It acquired a further 5,000 shares in December 2006 (RPI = 202.7) at a cost of £30,000.

In September 2014, G Ltd was taken over by K plc and J Ltd received one ordinary share and two preference shares in K plc for each one share held in G Ltd. Immediately following the takeover, the ordinary shares in K plc were worth £4 per share and the preference shares in K plc were worth £1 per share.

(a)   Show the cost and indexed cost of the ordinary shares and the preference shares in K plc.

(b)   Calculate the gain arising if J Ltd sells 10,000 of its ordinary shares in K plc for £42,000 in February 2015 (assumed RPI = 261.1).

(a)   *G Ltd FA 1985 share pool*

		No. of shares	Cost £	Indexed cost £
8.90	Acquisition	20,000	40,000	40,000
12.06	Indexed rise			
	$\dfrac{202.7 - 128.1}{128.1} \times £40,000$			23,294
	Acquisition	5,000	30,000	30,000
		25,000	70,000	93,294

Note that the takeover is not an operative event because the pool of cost is not increased or decreased and so it is not necessary to calculate an indexed rise to the date of the takeover.

Apportionment of cost/indexed cost to K plc shares

	No. of shares	MV £	Cost £	Indexed cost £
Ords × 1	25,000	100,000	46,667	62,196
Prefs × 2	50,000	50,000	23,333	31,098
Totals		150,000	70,000	93,294

(b)   *K plc ordinary shares FA 1985 share pool*

		No. of shares	Cost £	Indexed cost £
12.06	Acquisition (deemed)	25,000	46,667	62,196
2.15	Indexed rise			
	$\dfrac{261.1 - 202.7}{202.7} \times £62,196$			17,919
				80,115
	Disposal	(10,000)	(18,667)	(32,046)
		15,000	28,000	48,069

Note that the indexation allowance on the ordinary shares is calculated from the December 2006, not from the date of the takeover.

The gain is:

	£
Proceeds	42,000
Less: cost	(18,667)
Unindexed gain	23,333
Less: indexation allowance £(32,046 – 18,667)	(13,379)
Indexed gain	9,954

4 Relief for replacement of business assets (rollover relief)

FAST FORWARD

Rollover relief for replacement of business assets is available to companies to defer gains arising on the disposal of business assets.

4.1 Conditions for relief

As for individuals, **a gain may be deferred by a company where the proceeds on the disposal of a business asset are spent on a replacement business asset under rollover relief**.

The conditions for the relief to apply to company disposals are:

(a)   The old assets sold and the new asset bought are both used only in the trade of the company (apportionment into business and non-business parts available for buildings).

(b)   The old asset and the new asset both fall within one (but not necessarily the same one) of the following classes.

   (i)   **Land and buildings** (including parts of buildings) occupied as well as used only for the purposes of the trade
   (ii)   Fixed plant and machinery

(c)   Reinvestment of the proceeds received on the disposal of the old asset takes place in a period beginning one year before and ending three years after the date of the disposal.

(d)   The new asset is brought into use in the trade on its acquisition.

Note that goodwill is not a qualifying asset for the purposes of corporation tax.

A claim for the relief must be made by the later of four years of the end of the accounting period in which the disposal of the old asset takes place and four years of the end of the accounting period in which the new assets is acquired.

4.2 Operation of relief

Deferral is obtained by deducting the indexed gain from the cost of the new asset. For full relief, the whole of the proceeds must be reinvested. If only part is reinvested, a gain equal to the amount not invested, or the full gain, if lower, will be chargeable to tax immediately.

The new asset will have a base cost for chargeable gains purposes of its purchase price less the gain rollover over.

Question	Rollover relief

D Ltd acquired a factory in April 2000 (RPI = 170.1) at a cost of £120,000. It used the factory in its trade throughout the period of its ownership.

In August 2014 (assumed RPI = 257.8), D Ltd sold the factory for £220,000. In November 2014, it acquired another factory at a cost of £190,000.

Calculate the gain chargeable on the sale of the first factory and the base cost of the second factory.

Chargeable gain on sale of first factory

	£
Proceeds	220,000
Less: cost	(120,000)
Unindexed gain	100,000
$\dfrac{257.8 - 170.1}{170.1} = 0.516 \times £120,000$	(61,920)
Indexed gain	38,080
Less: rollover relief (balancing figure)	(8,080)
Chargeable gain: amount not reinvested £(220,000 – 190,000)	30,000

Base cost of second factory

	£
Cost of second factory	190,000
Less: rolled over gain	(8,080)
Base cost	181,920

4.3 Depreciating assets

The relief for investment into depreciating assets works in the same way for companies as it does for individuals.

The indexed gain is calculated on the old asset and is deferred until the gain crystallises on the earliest of:

(a) The disposal of the replacement asset
(b) The date the replacement asset ceases to be used in the trade
(c) Ten years after the acquisition of the replacement asset

Chapter Roundup

- Chargeable gains for companies are computed in broadly the same way as for individuals, but indexation allowance applies and there is no annual exempt amount.

- The indexation allowance gives relief for the inflation element of a gain.

- There are special rules for matching shares sold by a company with shares purchased. Disposals are matched with acquisitions on the same day, the previous nine days and the FA 1985 share pool.

- Rollover relief for replacement of business assets is available to companies to defer gains arising on the disposal of business assets.

Quick Quiz

1   A company is entitled to an annual exempt amount against its chargeable gains. True/False?

2   Indexation allowance runs from the date of _____ to date of _____. Fill in the blanks.

3   What are the share matching rules for company shareholders?

4   H Ltd sells a warehouse for £400,000. The warehouse cost £220,000 and the indexation allowance available is £40,000. The company acquires another warehouse ten months later for £375,000. What is the amount of rollover relief?

1   False. A company is not entitled to an annual exempt amount against its chargeable gains.

2   Indexation allowance runs from the date of **acquisition** to date of **disposal**.

3   The matching rules for shares disposed of by a company shareholder are:

   (a)   Shares acquired on the same day
   (b)   Shares acquired in the previous nine days
   (c)   Shares from the FA 1985 pool

4   The gain on the sale of first warehouse is:

	£
Proceeds	400,000
Less: cost	(220,000)
Unindexed gain	180,000
Less: indexation allowance	(40,000)
Indexed gain	140,000
Less: rollover relief (balancing figure)	(115,000)
Chargeable gain: amount not reinvested £(400,000 – 375,000)	25,000

Now try the questions below from the Practice Question Bank

Number	Type	Marks	Time
Q55	Section A	6	11 mins
Q56	Section B	10	18 mins
Q57	Section B	10	18 mins

Losses

23

Introduction

In the previous three chapters we have seen how a company calculates its taxable total profits and the corporation tax payable.

We now look at how a company may obtain relief for losses. An important factor in deciding what relief to claim is the marginal rate of tax, which may be 20%, 21% or 21.25% as seen earlier.

In the next chapter we will look at groups, and in particular how losses can be relieved by group relief.

Study guide

		Intellectual level
E2	**Taxable total profits**	
(d)	Understand how relief for a property business loss is given.	2
(e)	Understand how trading losses can be carried forward.	2
(f)	Understand how trading losses can be claimed against income of the current or previous accounting periods.	2
(g)	Recognise the factors that will influence the choice of loss relief claim.	2
E3	**Chargeable gains for companies**	
(c)	Explain and compute the treatment of capital losses.	1

Exam guide

Losses could form part of a 15 mark question or a 10 mark question in Section B. They may also be included in Section A questions, for example dealing with carry forward loss relief. Dealing with losses involves a methodical approach: first establish what loss is available for relief, second identify the different reliefs available, and third evaluate the options. Do check the question for specific instructions; you may be told that loss relief should be taken as early as possible.

1 Trading losses – overview

FAST FORWARD

Trading losses may be relieved by deduction from current total profits, from total profits of earlier periods or from future trading income.

In summary, the following reliefs are available for trading losses incurred by a company.

(a)   Claim to deduct the loss from current total profits
(b)   Claim to deduct the loss from earlier total profits
(c)   Make no claim and automatically carry forward the loss to be deducted from future trading profits of the same trade

These **reliefs may be used in combination**. The options open to the company are:

(a)   Do nothing, so that the loss is automatically carried forward against future trading profits

(b)   Claim to deduct the loss from current total profits, then automatically carry forward any remaining unrelieved loss to be deducted future trading profits

(c)   Claim to deduct the loss from current total profits, then claim to carry any unused loss back and deduct from earlier total profits, and then automatically carry any remaining unrelieved loss forward to be deducted from future trading profits.

The reliefs are explained in further detail below.

Remember that total profits is income and gains before the deduction of qualifying charitable donations. This may lead to qualifying charitable donations becoming unrelieved.

2 Carry forward trade loss relief

FAST FORWARD

Trading losses carried forward can only be deducted from future trading profits arising from the same trade.

A company must deduct a trading loss which is carried forward against trading profits from the same trade in future accounting periods (unless it has been otherwise relieved by making a claim to deduct it from total profits). **Relief is against the first available profits.**

Question

A Ltd has the following results for the three years to 31 March 2015.

	Year ended		
	31.3.13	31.3.14	31.3.15
	£	£	£
Trading profit/(loss)	(8,550)	3,000	6,000
Property income	0	1,000	1,000
Qualifying charitable donation	300	1,400	1,700

Calculate the taxable total profits for all three years showing any losses available to carry forward at 1 April 2015 and the amounts of any qualifying charitable donations which become unrelieved.

Answer

	Year ended		
	31.3.13	31.3.14	31.3.15
	£	£	£
Trading profits	0	3,000	6,000
Less: carry forward loss relief		(3,000)	(5,550)
	0	0	450
Property income	0	1,000	1,000
Total profits	0	1,000	1,450
Less: Qualifying charitable donation	0	(1,000)	(1,450)
Taxable total profits	0	0	0
Unrelieved qualifying charitable donation	300	400	250

Note that the trading loss carried forward is deducted from the trading profit in future years. It cannot be deducted from the property income.

Loss memorandum

	£
Loss for y/e 31.3.13	8,550
Less used y/e 31.3.14	(3,000)
Loss carried forward at 1.4.14	5,550
Less used y/e 31.3.15	(5,550)
Loss carried forward at 1.4.15	0

3 Trade loss relief against total profits

FAST FORWARD

Loss relief by deduction from total profits is given before qualifying charitable donations and so qualifying charitable donations may become unrelieved.

3.1 Current year relief

A company may claim to deduct a trading loss incurred in an accounting period from total profits. This may make qualifying charitable donations unrelieved because such donations are deducted from total profits after this loss relief to compute taxable total profits.

3.2 Carry back relief

Loss relief by deduction from total profits may be given by deduction from current period profits and from the previous 12 months.

Such a loss may then be carried back and deducted from total profits of an accounting period falling wholly or partly within the 12 months of the start of the period in which the loss was incurred. Again, this may cause qualifying charitable donations to be unrelieved.

A claim for current period loss relief can be made without a claim for carry back relief. However, if a loss is to be carried back, a claim for current period relief must have been made first.

Any possible loss relief claim for the period of the loss must be made before any excess loss can be carried back to a previous period.

Any carry back is to more recent periods before earlier periods. Relief for earlier losses is given before relief for later losses.

Any loss remaining unrelieved after any loss relief claims against total profits is automatically carried forward to be deducted from future profits of the same trade.

Question	Loss relief against total profits

Helix Ltd has the following results.

	y/e 30.11.13	y/e 30.11.14 £
Trading profit/(loss)	22,500	(19,500)
Bank interest received	500	500
Chargeable gains	0	4,000
Qualifying charitable donation	250	250

Calculate the taxable total profits for both years affected assuming that loss relief by deduction from total profits is claimed. Show the amount of any qualifying charitable donations which become unrelieved.

Answer

	y/e 30.11.13 £	y/e 30.11.14 £
Trading profit	22,500	0
Investment income	500	500
Chargeable gains	0	4,000
Total profits	23,000	4,500
Less current period loss relief	0	(4,500)
	23,000	0
Less carry back loss relief	(15,000)	(0)
	8,000	0
Less qualifying charitable donation	(250)	0
Taxable total profits	7,750	0
Unrelieved qualifying charitable donation		250

Loss memorandum

Loss incurred in y/e 30.11.14		19,500
Less used:	y/e 30.11.14	(4,500)
	y/e 30.11.13	(15,000)
Loss available to carry forward		0

If a period falls partly outside the prior 12 months, loss relief is limited to the proportion of the period's profits (before qualifying charitable donations) equal to the proportion of the period which falls within the 12 months.

Question

Short accounting period and loss relief

Tallis Ltd had the following results for the three accounting periods to 31 December 2014.

	y/e 30.9.13	3 months to 31.12.13	y/e 31.12.14
	£	£	£
Trading profit (loss)	20,000	12,000	(39,000)
Building society interest received	1,000	400	1,800
Qualifying charitable donations	600	500	0

Calculate the taxable total profits for all years and show any qualifying charitable donations which become unrelieved. Assume loss relief is claimed by deduction from total profits where possible.

Answer

	y/e 30.9.13	3 months to 31.12.13	y/e 31.12.14
	£	£	£
Trading profit	20,000	12,000	0
Interest income	1,000	400	1,800
Total profits	21,000	12,400	1,800
Less current period loss relief			(1,800)
	21,000	12,400	0
Less carry back loss relief	(15,750)	(12,400)	
	5,250	0	0
Less qualifying charitable donations	(600)		0
Taxable total profits	4,650	0	0
Unrelieved qualifying charitable donations	0	500	0

Loss memorandum

	£
Loss incurred in y/e 31.12.14	39,000
Less used y/e 31.12.14	(1,800)
Less used p/e 31.12.13	(12,400)
Less used y/e 30.9.13 £21,000 × 9/12 (max)	(15,750)
C/f	9,050

Notes

1. The loss can be carried back to set against total profits of the previous 12 months. This means total profits in the y/e 30.9.13 must be time apportioned by multiplying by 9/12.

2. Losses remaining after the loss relief claims against total profits are carried forward to set against future trading profits.

3.3 Claims

A claim for relief by deduction from current or earlier period total profits must be made within two years of the end of the accounting period in which the loss arose. Any claim must be for the *whole* loss (to the extent that profits are available to relieve it). The loss can however be reduced by not claiming full capital allowances, so that higher capital allowances are given (on higher tax written down values) in future years (see later in this chapter).

3.4 Interaction with losses brought forward

A trading loss carried back is relieved after any trading losses brought forward have been offset.

Question	Losses carried forward and back

Chile Ltd has the following results.

	Year ended		
	30.11.13	*30.11.14*	*30.11.15*
	£	£	£
Trading profit/(loss)	21,000	(20,000)	40,000
Bank interest received	1,000	1,500	500
Chargeable gains	0	2,000	0
Qualifying charitable donations	500	500	500

Chile Ltd had a trading loss of £16,000 carried forward at 1 December 2012.

Compute the taxable trading profits for all the years affected assuming that loss relief by deduction from total profits is claimed. Show the amount of any qualifying charitable donations which become unrelieved.

Answer	

The loss of the year to 30 November 2014 is relieved by deduction from current year total profits and from total profits of the previous twelve months. The trading loss brought forward at 1 December 2012 is relieved in the year ended 30 November 2013 before the loss brought back.

	Year ended		
	30.11.13	*30.11.14*	*30.11.15*
	£	£	£
Trading profit	21,000	0	40,000
Less carry forward loss relief	(16,000)	0	(10,500)
	5,000	0	29,500
Interest income	1,000	1,500	500
Chargeable gains	0	2,000	0
Total profits	6,000	3,500	30,000
Less current period loss relief	0	(3,500)	0
	6,000	0	30,000
Less carry back loss relief	(6,000)	0	0
	0	0	30,000
Less qualifying charitable donation	0	0	(500)
Taxable total profits	0	0	29,500
Unrelieved qualifying charitable donations	500	500	

	£
Loss memorandum (1)	
Loss brought forward at 1 December 2012	16,000
Less used y/e 30.11.13	(16,000)
	0

Loss memorandum (2)

	£
Loss incurred in y/e 30.11.14	20,000
Less used: y/e 30.11.14	(3,500)
y/e 30.11.13	(6,000)
	10,500
Less used: y/e 30.11.15	(10,500)
C/f	0

3.5 Terminal trade loss relief

FAST FORWARD

Trading losses in the last 12 months of trading can be carried back and deducted from total profits of the previous three years.

For trading losses incurred in the 12 months up to the cessation of trade the carry back period is extended from 12 months to three years, later years first.

Question
Terminal losses

Brazil Ltd had the following results for the accounting periods up to the cessation of trade on 30 September 2014.

	y/e 30.9.11 £	y/e 30.9.12 £	y/e 30.9.13 £	y/e 30.9.14 £
Trading profits	60,000	40,000	15,000	(180,000)
Gains	0	10,000	0	6,000
Property income	12,000	12,000	12,000	12,000

You are required to show how the losses are relieved assuming the maximum use is made of loss relief by deduction from total profits.

Answer

	y/e 30.9.11 £	y/e 30.9.12 £	y/e 30.9.13 £	y/e 30.9.14 £
Trading profits	60,000	40,000	15,000	0
Property income	12,000	12,000	12,000	12,000
Gains	0	10,000	0	6,000
Total profits	72,000	62,000	27,000	18,000
Less current period loss relief				(18,000)
				0
Less carry back loss relief	(72,000)	(62,000)	(27,000)	
Taxable total profits	0	0	0	0

Loss memorandum

Loss in y/e 30.9.14	180,000
Less used y/e 30.9.14	(18,000)
Loss of y/e 30.9.14 available for 3 year carry back	162,000
Less used y/e 30.9.13	(27,000)
	135,000
Less used y/e 30.9.12	(62,000)
	73,000
Less used y/e 30.9.11	(72,000)
Loss remaining unrelieved	1,000

4 Choosing loss reliefs and other planning points

 FAST FORWARD

When selecting a loss relief, first consider the rate at which relief is obtained and, secondly, the timing of the relief.

⚠️ **PER alert**

One of the competencies you require to fulfil performance objective 20 of the PER is the ability to assist with tax planning. You can apply the knowledge you obtain from this section of the text to help to demonstrate this competence.

4.1 Making the choice

Several alternative loss reliefs may be available. In making a choice consider:

- **The rate at which relief will be obtained:**

    - 21% at the main rate for FY 2014 (23% for FY 2013)
    - 20% at the small profits rate for FY 2014 (20% for FY 2013)
    - 21.25% if the marginal relief applies for FY 2014 (23.75% for FY 2013)

    We previously outlined how the 21.25% marginal rate is calculated. Remember it is just a marginal rate of tax; it is never actually used in computing a company's corporation tax.

- **How quickly relief will be obtained**: loss relief against total profits is quicker than carry forward loss relief.

- **The extent to which relief for qualifying charitable donations might be lost.**

For the purposes of the F6 exam, when choosing between loss relief claims **always** consider the rate of tax 'saved' by the loss first.

If in the current period the loss 'saves' 20% tax but if carried forward saves 21% tax then a carry forward is the better choice (even though the timing of loss relief is later).

If the tax saved now is 21% and in the future is the same (21%) **then** consider timing (in this example a current claim is better timing wise).

So, first – rate of tax saved, second – timing.

M Ltd has had the following results.

	Year ended 31 March			
	2013	2014	2015	2016
	£	£	£	£
Trading profit/(loss)	2,000	(1,000,000)	200,000	138,000
Chargeable gains	35,000	750,000	0	0
Qualifying charitable donations	30,000	20,000	20,000	20,000

Recommend appropriate loss relief claims, and compute the corporation tax for all years based on your recommendations. Assume that future years' profits will be similar to those of the year ended 31 March 2016 and the small profits rate of corporation tax in FY15 and later years will be the same as in FY14.

Answer

A loss relief against total profits claim for the year ended 31 March 2014 will save tax partly in the marginal relief band and partly at the small profits rate. It will waste the qualifying charitable donation.

Taxable total profits in the previous year are £7,000 (£35,000 + £2,000 – £30,000) and fall in the small profits band. Carry back would waste qualifying charitable donations of £30,000 and would use £37,000 of loss to save tax on £7,000.

If no current period loss relief claim is made, £200,000 of the loss will be carried forward and will save tax at the small profits rate in the year ended 31 March 2015, with £20,000 of qualifying charitable donations being wasted. The remaining £800,000 of the loss, would be carried forward to the year ended 31 March 2016 and later years, to save tax at the small profits rate which is assumed to be 20%.

To conclude, a loss relief claim by deduction from total profits should be made for the year of the loss but not in the previous year. £20,000 of qualifying charitable donations would be wasted in the current year, but much of the loss would save tax at the marginal rate and relief would be obtained quickly. Carrying the loss back would mean that £30,000 of qualifying charitable donations would become unrelieved. Therefore it would be more advantageous to carry the loss forward to where it will also save tax at the assumed small profits rate of 20%.

The final computations are as follows.

	Year ended 31 March			
	2013	2014	2015	2016
	£	£	£	£
Trading income	2,000	0	200,000	138,000
Less carry forward loss relief	0	0	(200,000)	(50,000)
	2,000	0	0	88,000
Chargeable gains	35,000	750,000	0	0
Total profits	37,000	750,000	0	88,000
Less current period loss relief	0	(750,000)	0	0
	37,000	0	0	88,000
Less qualifying charitable donations	(30,000)	0	0	(20,000)
Taxable total profits	7,000	0	0	68,000

	Year ended 31 March			
	2013	2014	2015	2016
	£	£	£	£
CT at 20%	1,400	0	0	13,600
Unrelieved qualifying charitable donations	0	20,000	20,000	0

4.2 Other tax planning points

A company with losses should consider claiming less than the maximum amount of capital allowances available. This will result in a higher tax written down value to carry forward and therefore higher capital allowances in future years.

Reducing capital allowances in the current period reduces the loss available for relief against total profits. As this relief, if claimed, must be claimed for all of a loss available, a reduced capital allowance claim could be advantageous where all of a loss would be relieved at a lower tax rate in the current (or previous) period than the effective rate of relief for capital allowances in future periods.

5 Other losses

5.1 Capital losses

FAST FORWARD Capital losses can only be set against capital gains in the current or future accounting periods.

Capital losses can only be set against capital gains in the same or future accounting periods, never against income. Capital losses must be set against the first available gains and cannot be carried back.

5.2 Property business losses

FAST FORWARD Property business losses are set off first against total profits in the current period and then carried forward against future total profits.

Property business losses are first deducted from the company's total profits of the current accounting period. Any excess is then:

(a)   **Carried forward to the next accounting period** and treated as a loss made by the company in that period, or

(b)   Available for surrender as **group relief** (see later in this Text)

Chapter Roundup

- Trading losses may be relieved by deduction from current total profits, from total profits of earlier periods or from future trading income.

- Trading losses carried forward can only be deducted from future trading profits arising from the same trade.

- Loss relief by deduction from total profits is given before qualifying charitable donations and so qualifying charitable donations may become unrelieved.

- Loss relief by deduction from total profits may be given by deduction from current period profits and from profits of the previous 12 months.

- A claim for current period loss relief can be made without a claim for carry back relief. However, if a loss is to be carried back, a claim for current period relief must have been made first.

- Trading losses in the last 12 months of trading can be carried back and deducted from total profits of the previous three years.

- When selecting a loss relief, first consider the rate at which relief is obtained and, secondly, the timing of the relief.

- Capital losses can only be set against capital gains in the current or future accounting periods.

- Property business losses are set off first against total profits in the current period and then carried forward against future total profits.

Quick Quiz

1   Against what profits may trading losses carried forward be set?

    A   Against all trading profits
    B   Against total profits
    C   Against profits from the same trade
    D   Against trading profits and gains

2   To what extent may losses be carried back?

3   Why might a company make a reduced capital allowances claim?

1   C. Against profits from the same trade.

2   A loss may be carried back and set against total profits of the previous 12 months. The loss carried back is the trading loss left unrelieved after a claim to deduct the loss from total profits of the loss making accounting period has been made. A loss arising on the final 12 months of trading can be carried back and deducted from profits arising in the previous 36 months.

3   Reducing capital allowances in the current accounting period reduces the loss available for relief by deduction from total profits. Such a loss relief claim means that all of the available loss is utilised, possibly without making qualifying charitable donations unrelieved. Reducing capital allowances reduces the size of the available loss which could mean that tax is saved at a higher rate if increased capital allowances are available in future years.

Now try the question below from the Practice Question Bank

Number	Type	Marks	Time
Q58	Section A	6	11 mins
Q59	Section B	10	18 mins

Groups

Topic list	Syllabus reference
1 Types of group	E5(a)-(c)
2 Group relief	E5(b), E6
3 Chargeable gains group	E5(c), E6

Introduction

In the previous chapters in this section we have covered corporation tax on single companies, including the reliefs for losses.

In this chapter we consider the extent to which tax law recognises group relationships between companies. Companies in a group are still separate entities with their own tax liabilities, but tax law recognises the close relationship between group companies. They can, if they meet certain conditions, share their losses and also pass assets between each other without chargeable gains.

In the next chapter we consider administrative aspects of corporation tax.

Study guide

		Intellectual level
E5	**The effect of a group corporate structure for corporation tax purposes**	
(a)	Define an associated company and recognise the effect having associated companies for corporation tax purposes.	2
(b)	Define a 75% group, and recognise the reliefs that are available to members of such a group.	2
(c)	Define a 75% chargeable gains group, and recognise the reliefs that are available to members of such a group.	2
E6	**The use of exemptions and reliefs in deferring and minimising corporation tax liabilities**	

Exam guide

Section A questions on groups could included the identification of members of a 75% group relief group or a 75% chargeable gains group.

Groups may also feature in your examination as part of the 15 mark corporation tax question in Section B or in a 10 mark question in that Section. Your first step in dealing with any group question must be to establish the relationship between the companies and identify what group or groups exist. You may find it helpful to draw a diagram. You must be aware that 75% group relief groups and 75% chargeable gains groups do not always coincide. The next steps will be to identify the amounts eligible for relief and to work out your strategy for maximising tax relief. Look out for companies receiving marginal relief first; they will have the highest marginal tax rate of 21.25%.

1 Types of group

A group exists for taxation purposes where one company is a subsidiary of another. The percentage shareholding involved determines the taxation consequences of the fact that there is a group.

The three examinable types of relationship for tax purposes are:

- **Associated companies** (see earlier in this text)
- **75% subsidiaries**
- **Groups for chargeable gains purposes** (chargeable gains groups)

2 Group relief

FAST FORWARD

Within a 75% group, current period trading losses, excess property business losses and excess qualifying charitable donations can be surrendered between UK companies. Profits and losses of corresponding accounting periods must be matched up. Group relief is available where the existence of a group is established through companies resident anywhere in the world.

2.1 Group relief provisions

The group relief provisions enable companies within a 75% group to transfer trading losses to other companies within the group, in order to set these against taxable total profits and reduce the group's overall corporation tax liability.

2.2 Definition of a 75% group

For one company to be a **75% subsidiary** of another, the holding company must have:

- At least 75% of the ordinary share capital of the subsidiary
- A right to at least 75% of the distributable income of the subsidiary
- A right to at least 75% of the net assets of the subsidiary were it to be wound up

Two companies are members of a 75% group where one is a 75% subsidiary of the other, or both are 75% subsidiaries of a third company.

Two companies are in a 75% group only if there is a 75% effective interest. Thus an 80% subsidiary (T) of an 80% subsidiary (S) is not in a 75% group with the holding company (H), because the effective interest is only 80% × 80% = 64%. However, S and T are in a 75% group and can claim group relief from each other. S *cannot* claim group relief from T and pass it on to H; it can only claim group relief for its own use.

A 75% group may include non-UK resident companies. **However, losses may generally only be surrendered between UK resident companies.**

Relief for trading losses incurred by an overseas subsidiary is not examinable in your paper.

Illustration of a 75% group:

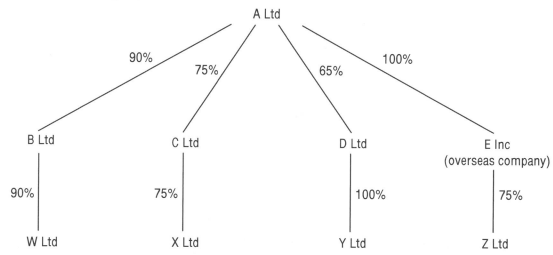

The companies in the 75% group are:

A Ltd
B Ltd
W Ltd (81% effective holding by A)
C Ltd
E Inc
Z Ltd (75% effective holding by A)

In addition C Ltd and X Ltd and also D Ltd and Y Ltd form their own separate mini-75% groups.

Note that a 75% group may also be called a 'group relief' group.

2.3 The relief

FAST FORWARD

A surrendering company can surrender any amount of its trading loss but a claimant company can only claim an amount up to its available taxable total profits. The best option is normally to surrender losses to set against taxable total profits of the company suffering the highest marginal rate of tax.

2.3.1 Transfer of loss

A company which has made a loss (the surrendering company) may transfer its loss to another member of the 75% group (the claimant company).

2.3.2 The claimant company

A **claimant company** is assumed to use its own current year losses or losses brought forward in working out the taxable total profits against which it may claim group relief, even if it does not in fact claim relief for current losses against total profits.

Furthermore, **group relief is against taxable total profits after all other reliefs for the current period (for example qualifying charitable donations) or brought forward from earlier periods.**

Group relief is given before relief for any amounts carried back from later periods.

2.3.3 The surrendering company

A surrendering company may group relieve a trading loss before setting it against its own total profits for the period of the loss, and may specify any amount to be surrendered.

This is **important** for **tax planning as it enables the surrendering company to leave taxable total profits in its own computation to be charged to corporation tax at the small profits rate**, while surrendering its losses to other companies to cover profits which would otherwise fall into the marginal relief band or be taxed at the main rate. Remember that taxable total profits in the marginal relief band are taxed at the marginal rate of 21.25%.

Question	Group relief of losses

In a group relief group of four companies, the results for the year ended 31 March 2015 are as follows.

	Profit/(loss) £
A Ltd	52,000
B Ltd	212,500
C Ltd	1,000,000
D Ltd	(400,000)

How should the loss be allocated to save as much tax as possible? How much tax is saved?

Answer

The upper and lower limits are £1,500,000/4 = £375,000 and £300,000/4 = £75,000 respectively.

	A Ltd £	B Ltd £	C Ltd £
Taxable total profits before group relief	52,000	212,500	1,000,000
Less group relief (note)	0	(137,500)	(262,500)
Taxable total profits after group relief	52,000	75,000	737,500
Tax saved			
£137,500 × 21.25%		29,219	
£262,500 × 21%			55,125
Total £(29,219 + 55,125) =	£84,344		

Note. We wish to save the most tax possible for the group.

Since A Ltd has taxable total profits below than the lower limit, any loss given to it will save tax at the small profits rate of 20%.

B Ltd has taxable total profits between the lower limit and the upper limit. Therefore, any loss given to B saves the effective marginal rate of 21.25% until the profits fall to £75,000 (the lower limit). After this only 20% is saved.

C Ltd pays tax at the main rate of 21% until profits fall to £375,000 (the upper limit).

So to conclude it is best to give B Ltd £137,500 of loss and save 21.25% tax on the profits between the lower limit and the upper limit. The balance of the loss is then given to C Ltd to save 21% tax.

2.4 Losses eligible for relief

A company may surrender to other group companies trading losses, excess property income losses and excess qualifying charitable donations. Qualifying charitable donations and property income losses can only be group relieved to the extent that they exceed total profits before taking account of any losses of the current period or brought forward or back from other accounting periods. Excess qualifying charitable donations must be surrendered before excess property income losses.

Only current period losses are available for group relief.

2.5 Corresponding accounting periods

Surrendered losses must be set against taxable total profits of a corresponding accounting period. If the accounting periods of a surrendering company and a claimant company are not the same this means that both the profits and losses must be apportioned so that only the results of the period of overlap may be set off. Apportionment is on a time basis. However, in the period when a company joins or leaves a group, an alternative method may be used if the result given by time-apportionment would be unjust or unreasonable.

Question — Corresponding accounting periods

	£
S Ltd incurs a trading loss for the year to 30 September 2014	(150,000)
H Ltd makes taxable total profits:	
for the year to 31 December 2013	200,000
for the year to 31 December 2014	100,000

What group relief can H Ltd claim from S Ltd?

Answer

H Ltd can claim group relief as follows.

	£
The lower of:	
For the year ended 31 December 2013 taxable total profits of the corresponding accounting period	50,000
(1.10.13 – 31.12.13) are £200,000 × 3/12	
Losses of the corresponding accounting period are £150,000 × 3/12	37,500

A claim for £37,500 of group relief may be made against H Ltd's taxable total profits for the year ended 31 December 2013.

	£
The lower of:	
For the year ended 31 December 2014 taxable total profits of the corresponding accounting period (1.1.14 – 30.9.14) are £100,000 × 9/12	75,000
Losses of the corresponding accounting period are £150,000 × 9/12	112,500

A claim for £75,000 of group relief may be made against H Ltd's taxable total profits for the year ended 31 December 2014.

If a claimant company claims relief for losses surrendered by more than one company, the total relief that may be claimed for a period that overlaps is limited to the proportion of the claimant's taxable total profits attributable to that period. Similarly, if a company surrenders losses to more than one claimant, the total losses that may be surrendered in a period that overlaps is limited to the proportion of the surrendering company's losses attributable to that period.

2.6 Claims

A claim for group relief is normally made on the claimant company's tax return. It is ineffective unless a notice of consent is also given by the surrendering company.

Groupwide claims/surrenders can be made as one person can act for two or more companies at once.

Any payment by the claimant company for group relief, up to the amount of the loss surrendered, is ignored for all corporation tax purposes.

2.7 Tax planning for group relief

One of the competencies you require to fulfil performance objective 20 of the PER is the ability to assist with tax planning. You can apply the knowledge you obtain from this section of the text to help to demonstrate this competence.

This section outlines some tax planning points to bear in mind when dealing with a group.

Group relief should first be given in this order:

1st   To companies in the marginal relief band paying **21.25%** tax (FY 2014) (but only **sufficient loss to bring augmented profits down to the lower limit**)

2nd   To companies paying the main rate of tax at **21%** (FY 2014)

3rd   To companies paying the small profits rate at **20%** (FY 2014)

Similarly, a company should make a claim to use a loss itself rather than surrender the loss to other group companies if the claim against its own total profits would lead to a tax saving at a higher rate.

Companies with profits may benefit by reducing their claims for capital allowances in a particular year. This may leave sufficient profits to take advantage of group relief which may only be available for the current year. The amount on which writing-down allowances can be claimed in later years is increased accordingly.

3 Chargeable gains group

FAST FORWARD

A chargeable gains group consists of the top company plus companies in which the top company has a 50% effective interest, provided there is a 75% holding at each level. Within a chargeable gains group, assets are transferred at no gain and no loss.

3.1 Definition

Companies are in a chargeable gains group if:

(a)   At each level, there is a 75% holding
(b)   The top company has an effective interest of over 50% in the group companies

If A holds 75% of B, B holds 75% of C and C holds 75% of D, then A, B and C are in such a group, but D is outside the group because A's interest in D is only 75% × 75% × 75% = 42.1875%. Furthermore, D is not in a group with C, because the group must include the top company (A).

The definition of a chargeable gains group is wider than that of a 75% group as only a effective 50% interest is needed compared to a 75% interest. However a company can only be in one chargeable gains group although it may be a member of more than one 75% group.

Illustration of a chargeable gains group:

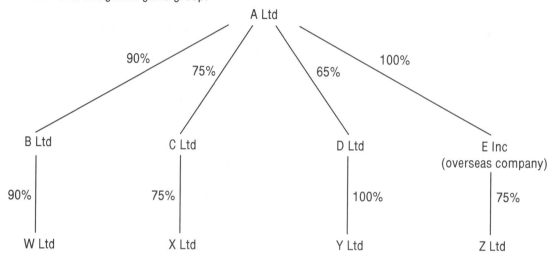

The companies in a group for chargeable gains purposes are:

A Ltd
B Ltd
W Ltd
C Ltd
X Ltd (75% subsidiary of 75% subsidiary, effective interest over 50%)
E Inc
Z Ltd

There is a separate chargeable gains group of D Ltd and Y Ltd.

3.2 Intra-group transfers

Companies in a chargeable gains group make intra-group transfers of chargeable assets without a chargeable gain or an allowable loss arising. No election is needed, as this relief is compulsory. The assets are deemed to be transferred at such a price as will give the transferor no gain and no loss (ie cost plus indexation allowance up to the date of transfer)

3.3 Matching group gains and losses

FAST FORWARD

Gains and losses can be matched within a group. This can be done by electing that all or part of any gain or loss is treated as transferred between group companies.

One of the competencies you require to fulfil performance objective 20 of the PER is the ability to assist with tax planning. You can apply the knowledge you obtain from this section of the text to help to demonstrate this competence.

Two members of a chargeable gains group can elect to transfer a chargeable gain or allowable loss, or any part of a gain or loss, between them. This election must be made within two years of the end of the accounting period in which the gain or loss accrues in the company which is making the transfer.

Only current year losses can be transferred, not brought forward losses.

From a tax planning point of view, elections(s) should be made to match gains and losses and ensure that net taxable gains arise in the company subject to the lowest rate of corporation tax.

Question
Matching gains and losses

D plc group has had the following results for the year ended 31 March 2015.

	D plc £	A Ltd £	B Ltd £	C Ltd £
Trading profit	400,000	46,000	20,000	220,000
Interest income	10,000	11,000	12,000	14,000
Chargeable gains/ (allowable losses)	18,000	(5,000)	6,000	(2,000)

Reliefs are always claimed as early as possible.

Required

Compute the taxable total profits for all companies and show all amounts to be carried forward at 31 March 2015.

Answer

Year ended 31.3.15

	D plc £	A Ltd £	B Ltd £	C Ltd £
Trading profit	400,000	46,000	20,000	220,000
Interest income	10,000	11,000	12,000	14,000
Income	410,000	57,000	32,000	234,000

There are 4 companies in the group.

Upper limit   1,500,000/4 = £375,000
Lower limit   300,000/4 = £75,000

D plc is paying tax at the main rate of 21%.

A Ltd and B Ltd are paying tax at the small profits rate of 20%.

C Ltd is paying tax at a marginal rate of 21.25%.

Since the election can be used to transfer all or part of any of the gains, the simplest way to achieve the optimum result is to identify where the resultant net gains should be taxed:

A Ltd up to the lower limit capacity = £75,000 – £57,000 = £18,000 of gains

B Ltd up to the lower limit capacity = £75,000 – £32,000 = £43,000 of gains

One way of achieving this would be to:

(a)   Elect that D plc's gain is transferred to A Ltd offsetting A Ltd's loss, and

(b)   Elect that C plc's loss is transferred to B Ltd offsetting B Ltd's gain

The total profits are:

	D plc £	A Ltd £	B Ltd £	C Ltd £
Income	410,000	57,000	32,000	234,000
Chargeable gains				
(18,000 – 5,000)/(6,000 – 2,000)		13,000	4,000	
Taxable total profits	410,000	70,000	36,000	234,000

Note that there are other alternatives: all the gains and losses could have been transferred to A Ltd, so that the total net gains of £17,000 resulted in A Ltd having taxable total profits of £74,000.

3.4 Rollover relief

FAST FORWARD Rollover relief is available in a chargeable gains group.

If a member of a chargeable gains group disposes of an asset eligible for chargeable gains rollover relief it may treat all of the group companies as a single unit for the purpose of claiming such relief. Acquisitions by other group members within the qualifying period of one year before the disposal to three years afterwards may therefore **be matched with the disposal**. However, both the disposing company and the acquiring company must make the claim. If an asset is transferred at no gain and no loss between group members, that transfer does not count as the acquisition of an asset for rollover or holdover relief purpose.

Exam focus point

Try to remember the following summary – it will be of great help in the exam.

Parent Co **controls** over 50% of subsidiary

- Associated companies for upper and lower limits

Parent Co **owns** 75% or more of subsidiary (directly and effectively)

- Surrender trading losses, excess property business losses, excess qualifying charitable donations to companies with some taxable total profits for same time period

Parent Co **owns** 75% or more of subsidiary and subsidiary owns 75% or more of its subsidiaries

- Transfer assets between companies automatically at no gain/no loss
- Chargeable gains and losses can be matched between group member companies
- All companies treated as one for rollover relief purposes

Chapter Roundup

- Within a 75% group, current period trading losses, excess property business losses and excess qualifying charitable donations can be surrendered between UK companies. Profits and losses of corresponding accounting periods must be matched up. Group relief is available where the existence of a group is established through companies resident anywhere in the world.

- A surrendering company can surrender any amount of its trading loss but a claimant company can only claim an amount up to its available taxable total profits. The best option is normally to surrender losses to set against taxable total profits of the company suffering the highest marginal rate of tax.

- A chargeable gains group consists of the top company plus companies in which the top company has a 50% effective interest, provided there is a 75% holding at each level. Within a chargeable gains group, assets are transferred at no gain and no loss.

- Gains and losses can be matched within a group. This can be done by electing that all or part of any gain or loss is treated as transferred between group companies.

- Rollover relief is available in a chargeable gains group.

Quick Quiz

1   List the types of losses which may be group relieved.
2   When may assets be transferred intra-group at no gain and no loss?
3   How can chargeable gains and losses within a group be matched with each other?

Answers to Quick Quiz

1   Trading losses, excess property business losses and excess qualifying charitable donations.

2   No gain no loss asset transfers are mandatory between companies in a chargeable gains group.

3   Two members of a gains group can elect that all or part of a gain or loss is transferred between them within two years of the end of the accounting period in which the gain or loss accrued. This election allows the group to match its gains and losses in one company.

Now try the questions below from the Practice Question Bank

Number	Type	Marks	Time
Q60	Section A	6	11 mins
Q61	Section B	10	18 mins
Q62	Section B	15	27 mins

Self assessment and payment of tax by companies

Topic list	Syllabus reference
1 Corporation tax self assessment	A3(b)
2 Returns, records and claims	A4(a), (d)
3 Compliance checks, appeals and disputes	A5(a), (b)
4 Payment of corporation tax and interest	A4(b), (c), A6(a)
5 Penalties	A6(a)

Introduction

We now complete our corporation tax studies by looking at the self assessment system for corporation tax, under which companies must file returns and pay the tax due.

In the following chapters we will turn our attention to VAT, which applies to both incorporated and unincorporated businesses.

Study guide

		Intellectual level
A3	**The systems for self assessment and the making of returns**	
(b)	Explain and apply the features of the self assessment system as it applies to companies, including the use of iXBRL.	2
A4	**The time limits for the submission of information, claims and payment of tax, including payments on account**	
(a)	Recognise the time limits that apply to the filing of returns and the making of claims.	2
(b)	Recognise the due dates for the payment of tax under the self-assessment system.	2
(c)	Explain how large companies are required to account for corporation tax on a quarterly basis and compute the quarterly instalment payments.	2
(d)	List the information and records that taxpayers need to retain for tax purposes.	1
A5	**The procedures relating to compliance checks, appeals and disputes**	
(a)	Explain the circumstances in which HM Revenue & Customs can make a compliance check into a self assessment tax return.	2
(b)	Explain the procedures for dealing with appeals and First and Upper Tier Tribunals.	2
A6	**Penalties for non-compliance**	
(a)	Calculate late payment interest and state the penalties that can be charged.	2

Exam guide

Section A questions on corporation tax administration could include the identification of filing dates and the calculation of interest on late paid tax or penalties.

In Section B you might be asked to explain an aspect of the tax administration system such as the appeals process.

1 Corporation tax self assessment

FAST FORWARD

A company that does not receive a notice requiring a return to be filed must, if it is chargeable to tax, notify HMRC within 12 months of the end of the accounting period.

1.1 Introduction

One of the competencies you require to fulfil performance objective 19 of the PER is the ability to evaluate and compute taxes payable. You can apply the knowledge you obtain from this section of the text to help to demonstrate this competence.

The self assessment system relies upon the company completing and filing a tax return and paying the tax due. The system is enforced by a system of penalties for failure to comply within the set time limits, and by interest for late payment of tax.

Dormant companies and companies which have not yet started to trade may not be required to complete tax returns. Such companies have a duty to notify HMRC when they should be brought within the self assessment system.

1.2 Notification of first accounting period

A company must notify HMRC of the beginning of its first accounting period (ie usually when it starts to trade) and the beginning of any subsequent period that does not immediately follow the end of a previous accounting period. The notice must be in the prescribed form and submitted within three months of the relevant date.

1.3 Notification of chargeability

A company that does not receive a notice requiring a return to be filed must, if it is chargeable to tax, **notify HMRC within twelve months of the end of the accounting period.**

2 Returns, records and claims

FAST FORWARD   A company must, in general, file a tax return within 12 months of the end of an accounting period.

2.1 Returns

A company's tax return must be filed electronically and must include a self assessment of any tax payable. Limited companies are also required to file electronically a copy of their accounts. The filing of accounts must be done in inLine eXtensible Business Reporting Language (iXBRL).

iXBRL is a standard for reporting business information in an electronic form which uses tags that can be read by computers. HMRC supplies software which can be used by small companies with simple accounts. This software automatically produces accounts and tax computations in the correct format. Other companies can use:

(a)   Other software that automatically produces iXBRL accounts and computations
(b)   A tagging service which will apply the appropriate tags to accounts and computations
(c)   Software that enables the appropriate tags to be added to accounts and computations

The tags used are contained in dictionaries known as taxonomies, with different taxonomies for different purposes. The tagging of tax computations is based on the corporation tax computational taxonomy, which includes over 1,200 relevant tags.

An obligation to file a return arises only when the company receives a notice requiring a return. A return is required for each accounting period ending during or at the end of the period specified in the notice requiring a return. A company also has to file a return for certain other periods which are not accounting periods (eg for a period when the company is dormant).

A notice to file a return may also require other information, accounts and reports. For a UK resident company the requirement to deliver accounts normally extends only to the accounts required under the Companies Act.

A return is due on or before the filing date. This is normally the later of:

(a)   **12 months after the end of the period to which the return relates**
(b)   **Three months from the date on which the notice requiring the return was made**

The relevant period of account is that in which the accounting period to which the return relates ends.

2.2 Amending a return

A company may amend a return within twelve months of the filing date.

HMRC may amend a return to correct obvious errors, or anything else that an officer has reason to believe is incorrect in the light of information available, within nine months of the day the return was filed, or if the correction is to an amended return, within nine months of the filing of an amendment. The company may amend its return so as to reject the correction. If the time limit for amendments has expired, the company may reject the correction by giving notice within three months.

2.3 Records

Companies must keep records until the latest of:

(a) **Six years from the end of the accounting period**
(b) **The date any compliance check enquiries are completed**
(c) **The date after which a compliance check enquiry may not be commenced**

All business records and accounts, including contracts and receipts, must be kept or information showing that the company has prepared a complete and correct tax return.

If a return is demanded more than six years after the end of the accounting period, any records or information which the company still has must be kept until the later of the end of a compliance check enquiry and the expiry of the right to start one.

2.4 Claims

Wherever possible claims must be made on a tax return or on an amendment to it and must be quantified at the time the return is made.

If a company believes that it has paid excessive tax, for example as a result of an error in its tax return, a claim may be made within four years from the end of the accounting period. An appeal against a decision on such a claim must be made within 30 days. A claim may not be made if the return was made in accordance with a generally accepted practice which prevailed at the time.

Other claims must be made by four years after the end of the accounting period, unless a different time limit is specified.

If HMRC amend a self assessment or issue a discovery assessment then the company has a further period to make, vary or withdraw a claim (unless the claim is irrevocable) even if this is outside the normal time limit. The period is one year from the end of the accounting period in which the amendment or assessment was made, or one year from the end of the accounting period in which the compliance check enquiry was complete if the amendment is the result of a compliance check enquiry. The relief is limited where there has been fraudulent or negligent conduct by the company or its agent.

3 Compliance checks, appeals and disputes

FAST FORWARD

HMRC can carry out compliance check enquiries on returns.

3.1 Compliance check enquiries

HM Revenue and Customs may decide to conduct a compliance check enquiry on a return, claim or election that has been submitted by a company, in the same way as for individuals.

The officer of HM Revenue and Customs must give written notice of his intention to conduct a compliance check enquiry. The notice must be given by:

(a) **The first anniversary of the due filing date** (most group companies) or **the actual filing date** (other companies), **if the return was delivered on or before the due filing date,** or

(b)   **The quarter day following the first anniversary of the actual filing date, if the return is filed after the due filing date. The quarter days are 31 January, 30 April, 31 July and 31 October.**

If the company amends the return after the due filing date, the compliance check enquiry 'window' extends to the quarter day following the first anniversary of the date the amendment was filed. Where the compliance check enquiry was not started within the limit which would have applied had no amendment been filed, the enquiry is restricted to matters contained in the amendment.

3.2 Appeals and disputes

The procedure for HMRC internal reviews and appeals relating to individuals, discussed earlier in this Text, also applies to companies.

4 Payment of corporation tax and interest

FAST FORWARD

In general, corporation tax is due nine months and one day after the end of an accounting period but large companies must pay their corporation tax in four quarterly instalments.

4.1 Payment dates – companies not paying tax at main rate

Corporation tax is due for payment by companies which do not pay tax at the main rate, **nine months and one day after the end of the accounting period**. For example, if a company has an accounting period ending on 31 December 2014, the corporation tax for the period is payable on 1 October 2015.

4.2 Payment dates –companies paying tax at main rate ('large' companies)

Large companies must pay their corporation tax in instalments. Broadly, a large company is any company that pays corporation tax at the main rate.

Instalments are due on the 14th day of the month, starting in the seventh month of the accounting period. Provided that the accounting period is twelve months long subsequent instalments are due in the tenth month during the accounting period and in the first and fourth months after the end of the accounting period. If an accounting period is less than twelve months long subsequent instalments are due at three monthly intervals but with the final payment being due in the fourth month of the next accounting period.

4.3 Example: quarterly instalments

X Ltd is a large company with a 31 December accounting year end. Instalments of corporation tax will be due to be paid by X Ltd on:

- 14 July and 14 October in the accounting period
- 14 January and 14 April after the accounting period ends

Thus for the year ended 31 December 2014 instalment payments are due on 14 July 2014, 14 October 2014, 14 January 2015 and 14 April 2015.

4.4 Calculating the instalments

Instalments are based on the estimated corporation tax liability for the current period (not the previous period). **A company is required to estimate its corporation tax liability before the end of the accounting period, and must revise its estimate each quarter.** It is extremely important for companies to forecast their tax liabilities accurately. Large companies whose directors are poor at estimating may find their companies incurring significant interest charges.

The amount of each instalment is computed by:

(a) **Working out 3 × CT/n** where CT is the amount of the estimated corporation tax liability payable in instalments for the period and n is the number of months in the period

(b) **Allocating the smaller of that amount and the total estimated corporation tax liability to the first instalment**

(c) **Repeating the process for later instalments until the amount allocated is equal to the corporation tax liability**

If the company has an accounting period of 12 months, there will be four instalments and each instalment will be 25% of the estimated amount due. The position is slightly more complicated if the company has an accounting period of less than 12 months, as is shown in the following question.

| Question | Short accounting period |

A large company has a corporation tax liability of £880,000 for the eight month period to 30 September 2014. Accounts had previously always been prepared to 31 January. Show when the corporation tax liability is due for payment.

Answer

£880,000 must be paid in instalments.

The amount of each instalment is $3 \times \dfrac{£880,000}{8} = £330,000$

The due dates are:

	£
14 August 2014	330,000
14 November 2014	330,000
14 January 2015	220,000 (balance)

Companies can have instalments repaid if they later conclude the instalments ought not to have been paid.

4.5 Exceptions

A company is not required to pay instalments in the first year that it is 'large', unless its augmented profits exceed £10 million. The £10 million limit is reduced proportionally if there are associated companies. For this purpose only, a company will be regarded as an associated company where it was an associated company on the last day of the previous accounting period. (This differs from the normal approach in corporation tax where being an associated company for any part of the accounting period affects the thresholds of both companies for the whole of the accounting period).

Any company whose liability does not exceed £10,000 need not pay by instalments.

4.6 Interest on late or overpaid tax

Interest runs from the due date on over/underpaid instalments. The position is looked at cumulatively after the due date for each instalment. HMRC calculate the interest position after the company submits its corporation tax return.

Companies which do not pay by instalments are charged interest if they pay their corporation tax after the due date, and will receive interest if they overpay their tax or pay it early.

Interest paid/received on late payments or over payments of corporation tax is dealt with as investment income as interest paid/received on a non-trading loan relationship. For the purpose of F6 (UK) exams for the financial year 1 April 2015 to 31 March 2016, the assumed rate of interest on underpaid tax is 3.0% and the assumed rate of interest on overpaid tax is 0.5%.

5 Penalties

Penalties may be levied for failure to notify the first accounting period, failure to notify chargeability, the late filing of returns, failure to keep records, and errors in returns.

5.1 Notification of first accounting period

Failure to notify, and provide information about, the first accounting period can mean a penalty of £300 plus £60 per day the information is outstanding, and a penalty of up to £3,000 for fraudulently or negligently giving incorrect information.

5.2 Notification of chargeability

The common penalty regime for late notification of chargeability discussed earlier in this Text in relation to individuals also applies to companies.

5.3 Late filing penalties

There is a £100 penalty for a failure to submit a return on time, rising to £200 if the delay exceeds three months. These penalties become £500 and £1,000 respectively when a return was late (or never submitted) for each of the preceding two accounting periods.

An additional tax geared penalty is applied if a return is more than six months late. The penalty is 10% of the tax unpaid six months after the return was due if the total delay is up to 12 months, and 20% of that tax if the return is over 12 months late.

There is a tax geared penalty for a fraudulent or negligent return and for failing to correct an innocent error without unreasonable delay. The maximum penalty is equal to the tax that would have been lost had the return been accepted as correct. HMRC can mitigate this penalty. If a company is liable to more than one tax geared penalty, the total penalty is limited to the maximum single penalty that could be charged.

5.4 Failure to keep records

Failure to keep records can lead to a **penalty of up to £3,000** for each accounting period affected.

5.5 Errors in returns

The common penalty regime for making errors in tax returns discussed earlier in this Text applies for corporation tax.

Chapter Roundup

- A company that does not receive a notice requiring a return to be filed must, if it is chargeable to tax, notify HMRC within 12 months of the end of the accounting period.

- A company must, in general, file a tax return within 12 months of the end of an accounting period.

- HMRC can carry out compliance check enquiries on returns.

- In general, corporation tax is due nine months and one day after the end of an accounting period, but large companies must pay their corporation tax in four quarterly instalments.

- Penalties may be levied for failure to notify the first accounting period, failure to notify chargeability, the late filing of returns, failure to keep records, and errors in returns.

Quick Quiz

1   When must HMRC give notice to a non-group company that it is going to start a compliance check enquiry if the return was filed on or before the due filing date?

2   Companies that pay corporation tax at the _____ rate must pay quarterly instalments of their corporation tax liability. Fill in the blank.

3   State the due dates for the payment of quarterly instalments of corporation tax for a 12 month accounting period.

4   What is the maximum penalty if a company fails to keep records?

   A   £1,000
   B   £2,000
   C   £3,000
   D   £4,000

Answers to Quick Quiz

1   Notice must be given by after the first anniversary of the actual filing date.

2   Companies that pay corporation tax at the **main** rate.

3   14th day of:

   (a)   7th month in AP
   (b)   10th month in AP
   (c)   1st month after AP ends
   (d)   4th month after AP ends

4   C. £3,000 for each accounting period affected.

Now try the questions below from the Practice Question Bank

Number	Type	Marks	Time
Q63	Section A	6	11 mins
Q64	Section B	5	9 mins
Q65	Section B	10	18 mins

P
A
R
T

G

Value added tax

An introduction to VAT

Topic list	Syllabus reference
1 The scope of VAT	F2
2 Zero-rated and exempt supplies	F2(e)
3 Registration	F1(a), (c)
4 Deregistration	F1(a)
5 Pre-registration input tax	F1(b)
6 Accounting for and administering VAT	F2(a)
7 The tax point	F2(b)
8 The valuation of supplies	F2(d)
9 The deduction of input tax	F2(f)
10 Relief for impairment losses	F2(g)

Introduction

The final topic in our studies is value added tax (VAT). We cover VAT in this and the next chapter.

VAT is a tax on turnover rather than on profits. As the name suggests, it is charged on the value added. The VAT is collected bit by bit along the chain of manufacturer, wholesaler, retailer, until it finally hits the consumer who does not add value, but uses up the goods.

In this chapter we look at the scope of VAT and then consider when a business must, or may, be registered for VAT. We also look at administration and accounting. VAT is a tax with simple computations but many detailed rules to ensure its enforcement. You may find it easier to absorb the detail if you ask yourself, in relation to each rule, exactly how it helps to enforce the tax.

Finally, we look at the rules regarding the deduction of input tax and relief for impairment losses on trade debts.

In the following chapter we will conclude our study of VAT and the F6 syllabus.

Study guide

		Intellectual level
F1	**The VAT registration requirements**	
(a)	Recognise the circumstances in which a person must register or deregister for VAT (compulsory) and when a person may register or deregister for VAT (voluntary).	2
(b)	Recognise the circumstances in which pre-registration input VAT can be recovered.	2
(c)	Explain the conditions that must be met for two or more companies to be treated as a group for VAT purposes, and the consequences of being so treated.	1
F2	**The computation of VAT liabilities**	
(a)	Explain how VAT is accounted for and administered.	2
(b)	Recognise the tax point when goods or services are supplied.	2
(d)	Explain and apply the principles regarding the valuation of supplies.	2
(e)	Recognise the principal zero rated and exempt supplies.	2
(f)	Recognise the circumstances in which input VAT is non-deductible.	2
(g)	Recognise the relief that is available for impairment losses on trade debts.	2

Exam guide

Section A questions on basic value added tax (VAT) topics could include identification of the date for registration and dealing with impairment losses.

In Section B, registration requirements may be examined in more detail; make sure that you know the difference between the historical test and the future test, and the dates by which HMRC must be notified and registration takes effect. Do not overlook pre-registration input VAT. You may be required to calculate the VAT due for a return period; watch out for non deductible input tax and check the dates if there are impairment losses.

1 The scope of VAT

FAST FORWARD

> VAT is charged on turnover at each stage in a production process, but in such a way that the burden is borne by the final consumer.

1.1 The nature of VAT

VAT is a tax on turnover, not on profits. The basic principle is that the VAT should be borne by the final consumer. Registered traders may deduct the tax which they suffer on supplies to them (input tax) from the tax which they charge to their customers (output tax) at the time this is paid to HMRC. Thus, at each stage of the manufacturing or service process, the net VAT paid is on the value added at that stage.

1.2 Example: the VAT charge

A forester sells wood to a furniture maker for £100 plus VAT. The furniture maker uses this wood to make a table and sells the table to a shop for £150 plus VAT. The shop then sells the table to the final consumer for £300 plus VAT of 20%. VAT will be accounted for to HMRC as follows.

	Cost £	Input tax 20% £	Net sale price £	Output tax 20% £	Payable to HMRC £
Forester	0	0	100	20.00	20.00
Furniture maker	100	20.00	150	30.00	10.00
Shop	150	30.00	300	60.00	30.00
					60.00

Because the traders involved account to HMRC for VAT charged less VAT suffered, their profits for income tax or corporation tax purposes are based on sales and purchases net of VAT.

1.3 Taxable supplies

FAST FORWARD

VAT is chargeable on taxable supplies made by a taxable person in the course or furtherance of any business carried on by him. Supplies may be of goods or services.

Key term

A **taxable supply** is a supply of goods or services made in the UK, other than an exempt supply.

PER alert

One of the competencies you require to fulfil performance objective 19 of the PER is the ability to evaluate and compute taxes payable. You can apply the knowledge you obtain from this section of the text to help to demonstrate this competence.

A taxable supply is either standard-rated or zero-rated. The standard rate is 20%.

Certain supplies, which fall within the classification of standard rate supplies, are charged at a reduced rate of 5%. An example is the supply of domestic fuel.

Zero-rated supplies are taxable at 0%. A taxable supplier whose outputs are zero-rated but whose inputs are standard-rated will obtain repayments of the VAT paid on purchases.

An exempt supply is not chargeable to VAT. A person making exempt supplies is unable to recover VAT on inputs. The exempt supplier thus has to shoulder the burden of VAT. Of course, he may increase his prices to pass on the charge, but he cannot issue a VAT invoice which would enable a taxable customer to obtain a credit for VAT, since no VAT is chargeable on his supplies.

1.4 Example: standard-rated, zero-rated and exempt supplies

Here are figures for three traders, the first with standard-rated outputs, the second with zero-rated outputs and the third with exempt outputs. All their inputs are standard-rated. The standard rate is 20%.

	Standard-rated £	Zero-rated £	Exempt £
Inputs	20,000	20,000	20,000
VAT	4,000	4,000	4,000
	24,000	24,000	24,000
Outputs	30,000	30,000	30,000
VAT	6,000	0	0
	36,000	30,000	30,000
Pay/(reclaim)	2,000	(4,000)	0
Net profit	10,000	10,000	6,000

VAT legislation lists zero-rated, reduced rate and exempt supplies. There is no list of standard-rated supplies. Therefore any supplies that do not appear on the zero-rated, reduced rate or exempt lists will be assumed to be standard-rated by default.

We look at the main categories of zero-rated and exempt supplies later in this chapter.

1.5 Supplies of goods

Goods are supplied if exclusive ownership of the goods passes to another person.

The following are treated as supplies of goods.

- The supply of any form of power, heat, refrigeration or ventilation, or of water

- The grant, assignment or surrender of a major interest (the freehold or a lease for over 21 years) in land

- Taking goods permanently out of the business for the non-business use of a taxable person or for other private purposes including the supply of goods by an employer to an employee for his private use

- Transfers under an agreement contemplating a transfer of ownership, such as a hire purchase agreement

Gifts of goods are normally treated as sales at cost (so VAT is due). **However, business gifts are not supplies of goods if**:

(a)   **The total cost of gifts made to the same person does not exceed £50 in any 12 month period**. If the £50 limit is exceeded, output tax will be due in full on the total of gifts made. Once the limit has been exceeded a new £50 limit and new 12 month period begins.

(b)   **The gift is a sample** (unlimited number of samples allowed).

1.6 Supplies of services

Apart from a few specific exceptions, **any supply which is not a supply of goods and which is done for a consideration is a supply of services**. A consideration is any form of payment in money or in kind, including anything which is itself a supply.

A supply of services also takes place if:

- Goods are lent to someone for use outside the business
- Goods are hired to someone
- Services bought for business purposes are used for private purposes

The European Court of Justice has ruled that restaurants supply services rather than goods.

1.7 Taxable persons

The term 'person' includes individuals, partnerships (which are treated as single entities, ignoring the individual partners) and **companies. If a person is in business making taxable supplies, then the value of these supplies is called the taxable turnover. If a person's taxable turnover exceeds certain limits then he is a taxable person and should be registered for VAT** (see later in this Text).

2 Zero-rated and exempt supplies

FAST FORWARD

Some supplies are taxable (either standard-rated, reduced-rate or zero-rated). Others are exempt.

2.1 Types of supply

We have seen that a trader may make standard rated, reduced-rate, zero-rated or exempt supplies.

If a trader makes a supply we need to categorise that supply for VAT as follows:

Step 1   Consider the zero-rated list to see if it is zero-rated. If not:

Step 2   Consider the exempt list to see if it is exempt. If not:

Step 3   Consider the reduced rate list to see if the reduced rate of VAT applies. If not:

Step 4   The supply is standard rated.

Exam focus point

In the exam you will not be expected to categorise all the zero-rated and exempt supplies. The main supplies in each group are highlighted below.

2.2 Zero-rated supplies

The following are items on the **zero-rated list**.

(a)   Human and animal food
(b)   Sewerage services and water
(c)   Printed matter used for reading (eg books, newspapers)
(d)   Construction work on new homes or the sale of the freehold of new homes by builders
(e)   Transport of goods and passengers
(f)   Drugs and medicines on prescription or provided in private hospitals
(g)   Clothing and footwear for young children and certain protective clothing eg motor cyclists' crash helmets

2.3 Exempt supplies

The following are items on the **exempt** list.

(a)   Financial services
(b)   Insurance
(c)   Public postal services provided by the Royal Mail under its duty to provide a universal postal service (eg first and second class letters)
(d)   Betting and gaming
(e)   Certain education and vocational training
(f)   Health services
(g)   Burial and cremation services
(h)   Sale of freeholds of buildings (other than commercial buildings less than 3 years old) and leaseholds of land and buildings.

2.4 Exceptions to the general rule

The zero-rated, exempt and reduced rate lists outline general categories of goods or services which are either zero-rated or exempt or charged at a rate of 5%. However, the VAT legislation then goes into great detail to outline exceptions to the general rule.

For example the zero-rated list states human food is zero-rated. However, the legislation then states that food supplied in the course of catering (eg restaurant meals, hot takeaways) is not zero-rated. Luxury items of food (eg crisps, peanuts, chocolate covered biscuits) are also not zero-rated.

In the exempt list we are told that financial services are exempt. However the legislation then goes on to state that credit management and processing services are not exempt. Investment advice is also not exempt.

Land and buildings is a complex topic. Broadly, sales of new homes are zero-rated, sales of new commercial buildings are standard rated and most other transactions are exempt.

Thus great care must be taken when categorising goods or services as zero-rated, exempt or standard-rated. It is not as straightforward as it may first appear.

3 Registration

FAST FORWARD

A trader becomes liable to register for VAT if the value of taxable supplies in any past period up to 12 months exceeds £81,000 or if there are reasonable grounds for believing that the value of the taxable supplies will exceed £81,000 in the next 30 days alone. A trader may also register voluntarily.

3.1 Compulsory registration

3.1.1 Historical test

At the end of every month a trader must calculate his cumulative turnover of taxable supplies for the previous 12 months to date. Taxable supplies are the total of standard rated supplies and zero rated supplies, but not exempt supplies. **The trader becomes liable to register for VAT if the value of his cumulative taxable supplies** (excluding VAT) **exceeds £81,000**. The person is required to notify HMRC within 30 days of the end of the month in which the £81,000 limit is exceeded. HMRC will then register the person with effect from the end of the month following the month in which the £81,000 was exceeded, or from an earlier date if they and the trader agree. For example, if a trader exceeds the limit on 30 April 2014, HMRC will register the trader for VAT from midnight on 31 May 2014 so the trader is effectively registered for VAT, and must charge VAT to customers, from 1 June 2014 onwards.

Registration under this rule is not required if HMRC are satisfied that the value of the trader's taxable supplies (excluding VAT) in the year then starting will not exceed £79,000.

Question   VAT registration

Fred started to trade cutlery on 1 January 2014. Sales (excluding VAT) were £7,500 a month for the first nine months and £7,900 a month thereafter. From what date should Fred be registered for VAT?

Answer

	£
Sales to 31 October 2014	75,400
Sales to 30 November 2014	83,300 (exceeds £81,000)

Fred must notify his liability to register by 30 December 2014 (not 31 December) and will be registered and charge VAT from 1 January 2015.

3.1.2 Future test

A person is also liable to register **at any time** (not necessarily at the end of the month) if there are reasonable grounds for believing that his taxable supplies (excluding VAT) in the following 30 days will exceed £81,000. Only taxable turnover of that 30 day period is considered **not** cumulative turnover. HMRC must be notified by the end of the 30 day period and registration will be with effect from the beginning of that period.

Question
Future test

Constant Ltd started to trade on 1 February 2014 with sales of goods as follows

	VAT status	£ per month
Goods A	standard-rated	7,000
Goods B	zero-rated	3,000

On 1 June 2014 Constant Ltd signed a contract to provide £40,000 of Goods A and £35,000 of Goods B to Unicorn plc by 25 June 2014. This is in addition to normal sales.

From which date should Constant Ltd be registered for VAT?

Answer

Goods A and B are taxable supplies.

Cumulative turnover at end of May 2014 is £40,000.

Cumulative turnover at end of June 2014 is £125,000.

But on 1 June 2014 the company signed a contract and hence 'knew' that within the next 30 days it would supply £85,000 of taxable supplies – this meets the future test conditions. Therefore the company needs to notify HMRC of their need to register within 30 days of 1 June 2014, ie by 30 June 2014.

HMRC will then register the company from 1 June 2014.

The historic test is met at the end of June 2014 (this would require notification by 30 July 2014 and registration from 1 August 2014).

However when a trader satisfies both tests HMRC will use the test that gives the earlier registration date.

In this case the future test gives the earliest date, 1 June 2014.

3.1.3 Other registration issues

When determining the value of a person's taxable supplies for the purposes of registration, supplies of goods and services that are *capital assets* of the business are to be disregarded, except for non zero-rated taxable supplies of interests in land.

When a person is liable to register in respect of a past period, it is his responsibility to pay VAT. If he is unable to collect it from those to whom he made taxable supplies, the VAT burden will fall on him. A person must start keeping VAT records and charging VAT to customers as soon as he is required to be registered. However, VAT should not be shown separately on any invoices until the registration number is known. The invoice should show the VAT inclusive price and customers should be informed that VAT invoices will be forwarded once the registration number is known. Formal VAT invoices should then be sent to such customers within 30 days of receiving the registration number.

Notification of liability to register must be made on form VAT 1. This can be downloaded from the HMRC website, can be requested by telephone, or an application to register can be made online through the website. Simply writing to, or telephoning, a local VAT office is not enough. On registration the VAT office will send the trader a certificate of registration. This shows the VAT registration number, the date of registration, the end of the first VAT period and the length of the VAT periods. We will look at VAT periods later in this chapter.

If a trader makes a supply before becoming liable to register, but gets paid after registration, VAT is not due on that supply.

3.2 Voluntary registration

A person may decide to become registered even though his taxable turnover falls below the registration limit. Unless a person is registered he cannot recover the input tax he pays on purchases.

Voluntary registration is advantageous where a person wishes to recover input tax on purchases. However, charging VAT may make the supply less competitive if customers are not VAT registered and the trader may have to absorb the VAT output tax thus reducing his profit.

Therefore, consideration needs to be given to the situation of the customer. For example, consider a trader who has one input during the period which cost £1,000 plus £200 VAT at 20%; he works on the input which becomes his sole output for the year and he decides to make a profit of £1,000.

(a)   If he is not registered he will charge £2,200 and his customer will obtain no relief for any VAT.

(b)   If he is registered he will charge £2,000 plus VAT of £400. His customer will have input tax of £400 which he will be able to recover if he, too, is registered.

If the customer is a non-taxable person he will prefer (a) as the cost to him is £2,200. If he is taxable he will prefer (b) as the net cost is £2,000. Thus, a decision whether or not to register voluntarily may depend upon the status of customers.

The decision to register may also depend on the image of the business the trader wishes to project (registration may give the impression of a substantial business). The **administrative burden of registration** should also be considered.

3.3 Group registration

FAST FORWARD

Two or more companies under common control can register as a group for VAT purposes. A single VAT return and payment are then made by a representative member for a VAT period but all members of the group are jointly and severally liable for VAT due. There is no need to account for VAT on supplies between group members.

Two or more companies under common control may apply for group registration.

The **effects and advantages of group registration** are as follows.

*   Each VAT group must appoint a representative member which must **account for the group's output tax and input tax, completing one VAT return and paying VAT on behalf of the group. Thus this simplifies VAT accounting, saving administrative costs,** and allows payments and repayments of VAT to be netted off. However, **all members of the group are jointly and severally liable for any VAT due from the representative member.**

*   **Any supply of goods or services by a member of the group to another member of the group is, in general, disregarded for VAT purposes,** reducing the VAT accounting required.

*   Any other supply of goods or services by or to a group member is in general treated as a supply by or to the representative member.

*   Any VAT payable on the import of goods by a group member is payable by the representative member.

Two or more companies are eligible to be treated as members of a group provided each of them is either established in the UK or has a fixed establishment in the UK, and:

*   **One of them controls each of the others, or**
*   **One person** (which could be an individual or a holding company) **controls all of them**, or
*   **Two or more persons carrying on a business in partnership control all of them**

An application to create, terminate, add to or remove a company from a VAT group may be made at any time.

It is not necessary for each company, which meets the requirements, to join a particular VAT group. It may be beneficial, for example, in the case of a company making largely zero-rated supplies (and so receiving VAT repayments) to remain outside the group and benefit from cash flow repayments from completing monthly VAT returns (see later in this Text).

4 Deregistration

FAST FORWARD

A trader may deregister voluntarily if he expects the value of his taxable supplies in the following one year period will not exceed £79,000. Alternatively, a trader who no longer makes taxable supplies may be compulsorily deregistered.

4.1 Voluntary deregistration

A person is eligible for voluntary deregistration if HMRC are satisfied that the value of his taxable supplies (net of VAT and excluding supplies of capital assets) in the following one year period will not exceed £79,000. However, voluntary deregistration will not be allowed if the reason for the expected fall in value of taxable supplies is the cessation of taxable supplies or the suspension of taxable supplies for a period of 30 days or more in that following year.

HMRC will cancel a person's registration from the date the request is made or from an agreed later date.

4.2 Compulsory deregistration

A trader may be compulsorily deregistered if HMRC are satisfied that he is no longer making nor intending to make taxable supplies. Failure to notify a requirement to deregister within 30 days may lead to a penalty. Compulsory deregistration may also lead to HMRC reclaiming input tax which has been wrongly recovered by the trader since the date on which he should have deregistered.

4.3 The consequences of deregistration

FAST FORWARD

VAT is chargeable on all goods and services on hand at the date of deregistration.

On deregistration, VAT is chargeable on all stocks and capital assets in a business on which input tax was claimed, since the registered trader is in effect making a taxable supply to himself as a newly unregistered trader. If the VAT chargeable does not exceed £1,000, it need not be paid.

4.4 Transfer of a going concern

FAST FORWARD

The transfer of a business as a going concern is outside the scope of VAT.

There is no VAT charge if a business (or a separately viable part of it) is sold as a going concern to another taxable person (or a person who immediately becomes a taxable person as a result of the transfer). Such a sale is outside the scope of VAT.

If a transfer of a going concern (TOGC) is from a VAT registered trader to a new owner who is not VAT registered, then it is possible to apply to transfer the registration number of the previous owner to the new owner. This would also transfer to the new owner the responsibility for the past VAT history of the old business. So, if the previous owner had committed any VAT misdemeanours the liability for those would transfer to the new owner of the business. As a result of this it may not be wise to apply to transfer the VAT registration number between old and new owners unless of course, it is a situation where there is a very close connection between the two.

If the VAT registration number is not transferred then the new owners do not have any responsibility for the VAT affairs of the previous owner of the business. This is probably a safer way to structure the transfer of a business.

5 Pre-registration input tax

5.1 Introduction

VAT incurred before registration can be treated as input tax and recovered from HMRC subject to certain conditions.

5.2 Pre-registration goods

If the claim is for input tax suffered on goods purchased prior to registration then the following conditions must be satisfied.

(a)   The **goods were acquired for the purpose of the business** which either was carried on or was to be carried on by him at the time of supply.

(b)   The **goods have not been supplied onwards or consumed before the date of registration** (although they may have been used to make other goods which are still held).

(c)   The **VAT must have been incurred in the four years prior to the date of registration**.

5.3 Pre-registration services

If the claim is for input tax suffered on the supply of services prior to registration then the following conditions must be satisfied.

(a)   The **services were supplied for the purposes of a business** which either was carried on or was to be carried on by him at the time of supply.

(b)   **The services were supplied within the six months prior to the date of registration.**

Input tax attributable to supplies made before registration is not deductible even if the input tax concerned is treated as having been incurred after registration.

6 Accounting for and administering VAT

6.1 Administration

FAST FORWARD

> VAT is administered by HMRC. Appeals are heard by the Tax Tribunal.

6.1.1 Introduction

The administration of VAT is dealt with by HM Revenue and Customs (HMRC).

Local offices are responsible for the local administration of VAT and for providing advice to registered persons whose principal place of business is in their area. They are controlled by regional collectors.

From time to time a registered person will be visited by HMRC staff from a local office to ensure that the law is understood and is being applied properly. If a trader disagrees with any decision as to the application of VAT given by HMRC he can ask his local office to reconsider the decision. It is not necessary to appeal formally while a case is being reviewed in this way. Where an appeal can be settled by agreement, a written settlement has the same force as a decision by the Revenue and Customs Prosecution Office.

6.1.2 Assessments

HMRC may issue assessments of VAT due to the best of their judgement if they believe that a trader has failed to make returns or if they believe those returns to be incorrect or incomplete. The time limit for making assessments is normally four years after the end of a VAT period, but this is extended to 20 years in the case of fraud, dishonest conduct, certain registration irregularities and the unauthorised issue of VAT invoices.

HMRC sometimes write to traders, setting out their calculations, before issuing assessments. The traders can then query the calculations.

6.1.3 Appeals

A trader may appeal to the Tax Tribunal in the same way as an appeal may be made for income tax and corporation tax (see earlier in this Text). VAT returns and payments shown thereon must have been made before an appeal can be heard.

6.2 VAT periods

FAST FORWARD

> VAT is accounted for on regular returns – most are submitted electronically. Extensive records must be kept.

The VAT period (also known as the tax period) is the period covered by a VAT return. It is usually three calendar months. The return shows the total input and output tax for the tax period.

HMRC allocate VAT periods according to the class of trade carried on (ending in June, September, December and March; July, October, January and April; or August, November, February and May), to spread the flow of VAT returns evenly over the year. When applying for registration a trader can ask for VAT periods which fit in with his own accounting year. It is also possible to have VAT periods to cover accounting systems not based on calendar months.

A registered person whose input tax will regularly exceed his output tax can elect for a one month VAT period, but will have to balance the inconvenience of making 12 returns a year against the advantage of obtaining more rapid repayments of VAT.

Certain small businesses may submit an annual VAT return (see later in this Text).

6.3 Electronic filing

Nearly all VAT registered businesses must file their VAT returns online and make payments electronically.

The time limit for submission and payment is one month plus seven days after the end of the VAT period. For example, a business which has a VAT quarter ending 31 March 2015 must file its VAT return and pay the VAT due by 7 May 2015.

6.4 Substantial traders

If a trader does not make monthly returns, and the total VAT liability over 12 months to the end of a VAT period exceeds £2,300,000, he must make payments on account of each quarter's VAT liability during the quarter.

The amount of each payment on account is 1/24th of the total VAT liability for the previous VAT year.

Payments are due one month before the end of the quarter, at the end of the month which is the final month of the quarter, and one month after the end of the quarter. Payments must be made electronically. There is no additional seven days, after the end of the month, for payment.

If the trader's annual liability falls below £1,800,000, the trader can apply to stop making payments on account.

6.5 Refunds of VAT

There is a four year time limit on the right to reclaim overpaid VAT. This time limit does not apply to input tax which a business could not have reclaimed earlier because the supplier only recently invoiced the VAT, even though it related to a purchase made some time ago. Nor does it apply to overpaid VAT penalties.

If a taxpayer has overpaid VAT and has recovered excessive input tax by reason of the same mistake, HMRC can set off any tax, penalty, interest or surcharge due to them against any repayment due to the taxpayer and repay only the net amount. In such cases the normal four year time limit for recovering VAT, penalties, interest, etc by assessment does not apply.

HMRC can refuse to make any repayment which would unjustly enrich the claimant. They can also refuse a repayment of VAT where all or part of the tax has, for practical purposes, been borne by a person other than the taxpayer (eg by a customer of the taxpayer) except to the extent that the taxpayer can show loss or damage to any of his businesses as a result of mistaken assumptions about VAT.

7 The tax point

FAST FORWARD

> The tax point is the deemed date of supply. The basic tax point is the date on which goods are removed or made available to the customer, or the date on which services are completed. If a VAT invoice is issued or payment is received before the basic tax point, the earlier of these dates becomes the actual tax point. If the earlier date rule does not apply, and the VAT invoice is issued within 14 days of the basic tax point, the invoice date becomes the actual tax point.

7.1 The basic tax point

The tax point of each supply is the deemed date of supply. The basic tax point is the date on which the goods are removed or made available to the customer, or the date on which services are completed.

The tax point determines the VAT period in which output tax must be accounted for and credit for input tax will be allowed. The tax point also determines which rate applies if the rate of VAT or a VAT category changes (for example when a supply ceases to be zero-rated and becomes standard-rated).

7.2 The actual tax point

If a VAT invoice is issued or payment is received before the basic tax point, the earlier of these dates automatically becomes the tax point. If the earlier date rule does not apply and if the VAT invoice is issued within 14 days after the basic tax point, the invoice date becomes the tax point (although the trader can elect to use the basic tax point for all his supplies if he wishes). This 14 day period may be extended to accommodate, for example, monthly invoicing; the tax point is then the VAT invoice date or the end of the month, whichever is applied consistently.

Question	Tax point

Julia sells a sculpture to the value of £1,000 net of VAT. She receives a payment on account of £250 plus VAT on 25 April 2014. The sculpture is delivered on 28 May 2014. Julia's VAT return period is to 30 April 2014. She issues an invoice on 4 June 2014.

Outline the tax point(s) and amount(s) due.

A separate tax point arises in respect of the £250 deposit and the £750 balance payable.

Julia should account for VAT as follows.

(a) Deposit

25 April 2014: tax at 20% × £250 = £50. This is accounted for in her VAT return to 30 April 2014. The charge arises on 25 April 2014 because payment is received before the basic tax point (which is 28 May 2014 – date of delivery).

(b) Balance

4 June 2014: tax at 20% × £750 = £150. This is accounted for on the VAT return to 31 July 2014. The charge arises on 4 June because the invoice was issued within 14 days of the basic tax point of 28 May 2014 (delivery date).

7.3 Miscellaneous points

Goods supplied on sale or return are treated as supplied on the earlier of adoption by the customer or 12 months after despatch.

Continuous supplies of services paid for periodically normally have tax points on the earlier of the receipt of each payment and the issue of each VAT invoice, unless one invoice covering several payments is issued in advance for up to a year. The tax point is then the earlier of each due date or date of actual payment. However, for connected businesses the tax point will be created periodically, in most cases based on 12 month periods.

8 The valuation of supplies

FAST FORWARD

In order to ascertain the amount of VAT on a supply, the supply must be valued. If a discount is offered for prompt payment, VAT is chargeable on the net amount even if the discount is not taken up.

8.1 Value of supply

The value of a supply is the VAT-exclusive price on which VAT is charged. The consideration for a supply is the amount paid in money or money's worth.

Thus with a standard rate of 20%:

Value + VAT = consideration
£100 + £20.00 = £120.00

The VAT proportion of the consideration is known as the 'VAT fraction'. It is:

$$\frac{\text{rate of tax}}{100 + \text{rate of tax}} = \frac{20}{100 + 20} = \frac{1}{6}$$

Provided the consideration for a bargain made at arm's length is paid in money, the value for VAT purposes is the VAT exclusive price charged by the trader. If it is paid in something other than money, as in a barter of some goods or services for others, it must be valued and VAT will be due on the value.

If the price of goods is effectively reduced with money off coupons, the value of the supply is the amount actually received by the taxpayer.

8.2 Discounts

Where a discount is offered for prompt payment, VAT is chargeable on the net amount, regardless of whether the discount is taken up.

Melissa sells furniture. She makes a standard-rated supply to a customer, Chris, on 10 March 2015 for £5,000 plus VAT. Chris is entitled to a 10% discount if he pays within 21 days. However, payment is actually made 28 days later. What is the VAT chargeable by Melissa?

Answer

	£
Full amount	5,000
Less: discount 10% × £5,000	(500)
Discounted amount	4,500
VAT @ 20% on £4,500	£900

VAT is chargeable on the *discounted amount* regardless of whether or not the discount is taken up. Therefore the customer will actually pay £5,900 (full amount plus the discounted VAT).

Exam focus point

This treatment of prompt payment discounts is being phased out so that output VAT will instead by charged on the actual amount received if a prompt payment discount is not taken. However, there will be no change as regards the majority of supplies until 1 April 2015, so the **current rules will continue to be examined** in F6 (UK) exams from 1 April 2015 to 31 March 2016.

8.3 Miscellaneous

For goods supplied under a hire purchase agreement VAT is chargeable on the cash selling price at the start of the contract.

When goods are permanently taken from a business for non-business purposes VAT must be accounted for on their market value. Where business goods are put to a private or non-business use, the value of the resulting supply of services is the cost to the taxable person of providing the services. If services bought for business purposes are used for non-business purposes (without charge), then VAT must be accounted for on their cost, but the VAT to be accounted for is not allowed to exceed the input tax deductible on the purchase of the services.

9 The deduction of input tax

9.1 Input tax recovery

FAST FORWARD

Not all input VAT is deductible, eg VAT on most motor cars.

For input tax to be deductible, the payer must be a taxable person, with the supply being to him in the course of his business. In addition a VAT invoice must be held (except for payments of up to £25 including VAT which are for telephone calls, or car park fees, or which are made through cash operated machines).

Input tax recovery can be denied to any business that does not hold a valid VAT invoice and cannot provide alternative evidence to prove the supply took place.

9.2 Capital items

The distinction between capital and revenue which is important in other areas of tax **does not apply to VAT**. Thus a manufacturer buying plant subject to VAT will be able to obtain a credit for all the VAT immediately. The plant must of course be used to make taxable supplies, and if it is only partly so used only part of the VAT can be reclaimed. Conversely, if plant is sold second-hand then VAT should be charged on the sale and is output tax in the normal way.

9.3 Non-deductible input tax

Exam focus point

In the F6 (UK) exam students are not required to know actual cases where VAT decisions were made. They are included below for your information only.

The following input tax is not deductible even for a taxable person with taxable outputs.

(a) **VAT on motor cars not used wholly for business purposes**. VAT on cars is never reclaimable unless the car is acquired new for resale or is acquired for use in or leasing to a taxi business, a self-drive car hire business or a driving school (see further below).

(b) **VAT on business entertaining** where the cost of the entertaining is not a tax deductible trading expense, unless the entertainment is of overseas customers in which case the input tax is deductible.

If the items bought are used partly for non-deductible entertaining and partly for other purposes, an apportionment of the expenses is required. In *Ernst & Young v CCE* the Tribunal held that staff entertaining was wholly for business purposes and a full input tax recovery was allowed. HMRC accept this decision in respect of staff entertainment but maintain that following the case *KPMG v CCE* input tax on entertaining guests at a staff party is non-deductible.

(c) **VAT on expenses incurred on domestic accommodation for directors.**

(d) **VAT on non-business items passed through the business accounts.** However, when goods are bought partly for business use, the purchaser may:

(i)   Deduct all the input tax, and account for output tax in respect of the private use, or
(ii) Deduct only the business proportion of the input tax

Where services are bought partly for business use, only method (ii) may be used. If services are initially bought for business use but the use then changes, a fair proportion of the input tax (relating to the private use) is reclaimed by HMRC by making the trader account for output tax.

(e) **VAT which does not relate to the** making of supplies by the buyer in the course of a **business**.

9.4 Irrecoverable VAT

Where all (as with many cars) or some (as for partial business use) of the input tax on a purchase is not deductible, the **non-deductible VAT is included in the cost for income tax, corporation tax, capital allowance or capital gains purposes. Deductible VAT is omitted from costs, so that only net amounts are included in accounts. Similarly, sales** (and proceeds in chargeable gains computations) **are shown net of VAT**, because the VAT is paid over to HMRC.

9.5 Motoring expenses

9.5.1 Cars

The VAT incurred on the purchase of a car not used wholly for business purposes is not recoverable (except as mentioned above). If accessories are fitted after the original purchase and a separate invoice is raised then the VAT on the accessories can be treated as input tax so long as the accessories are for business use. **If VAT is not recoverable on a car because it is not used wholly for business purposes, then VAT is not charged if the car is subsequently sold.**

If a car is used wholly for business purposes (including leasing, so long as the charges are at the open market rate), the input tax is recoverable but the buyer must account for VAT when he sells the car.

If a car is leased, the lessor recovered the input tax when the car was purchased and the lessee makes some private use of the car (for example private use by employees), the lessee can only recover 50% of the input tax on the lease charges. A hiring of five days or less is assumed to be for wholly business use.

If a car is used for business purposes then any VAT charged on repair and maintenance costs can be treated as input tax. No apportionment has to be made for private use.

9.5.2 Fuel

If fuel is supplied for private purposes all input VAT incurred on the fuel is allowed and the business will normally account for output VAT using a set of scale charges.

If a business pays for fuel which is only used for business purposes, it can claim all the input tax paid on that fuel. However, many businesses will pay for fuel which is used for private motoring by employees.

If a business does provide fuel to an employee for private and business use but the employee reimburses the business the full cost of the private fuel, there is an actual taxable supply by the business valued at the amount received from that employee. The business can claim its input tax on all fuel, but then must account for output tax on the amount paid by the employee. HM Revenue and Customs will accept that the full cost of all private fuel has been reimbursed where a log is kept recording private miles and the employee pays a fuel-only mileage rate that covers the average fuel cost (on its website, HM Revenue and Customs publish a set of such rates for different sizes of engine).

If a business provides fuel to its employees for private use without charge or at a charge below the full cost, there is a deemed taxable supply. The business then has the following options for how to account for VAT on fuel:

(a) **Not to claim any input tax in respect of fuel** purchased by the business. **No output tax is charged**. In effect, the fuel is not brought into the VAT system at all.

(b) **Claim input VAT only on the fuel purchased for business journeys**. This requires the business to keep detailed mileage records of business and private use. **No output tax is charged in respect of private use.** In effect, the private fuel is not brought into the VAT system.

(c) **Claim input tax on all fuel purchased and charge output tax based either on the full cost of the private fuel supplied** (again, this requires detailed mileage records to be kept) **or the fuel scale charge which reflects the deemed output in respect of private use. The fuel scale charge is based on the CO_2 emissions of the car.**

Exam focus point

In the F6 (UK) exam, questions on the treatment of private use fuel will normally involve the use of the fuel scale charge.

The above rules apply **even where employees pay for the fuel themselves and the business reimburses them**: as long as the business obtains VAT invoices for the fuel, it can treat the fuel as its own purchase/input.

Question   Fuel scale charge

Iain is an employee of ABC Ltd. He has the use of a car with CO_2 emissions of 176 g/km for one month and a car with CO_2 emissions of 208 g/km for two months during the quarter ended 31 August 2014.

ABC Ltd pays all the petrol costs in respect of both cars without requiring Iain to make any reimbursement in respect of private fuel. Total petrol costs for the quarter amount to £300 (including VAT). ABC Ltd wishes to use the fuel scale charge as detailed records of private mileage have not been kept.

What is the VAT effect of the above on ABC Ltd?

VAT scale rates (VAT inclusive) for three month periods

CO_2 emissions	£
175	391
205	485

Answer

Value added tax for the quarter:

	£
Car 1	
£391 × 1/3 =	130
Car 2	
£485 × 2/3 =	323
	453
Output tax:	
1/6 × £453	£76
Input tax	
1/6 × £300	£50

10 Relief for impairment losses

FAST FORWARD

Relief for VAT on impairment losses is available if the debt is over six months old (measured from when the payment is due) and has been written off in the trader's accounts.

Where a supplier of goods or services has accounted for VAT on the supply and the customer does not pay, the supplier may claim a refund of VAT on the amount unpaid. **Relief is available for VAT for impairment losses (bad debts) on trade debts if the debt is over six months old (measured from when payment is due) and has been written off in the creditor's accounts.** Where payments on account have been received, they are attributed to debts in chronological order. If the debtor later pays all or part of the amount owed, a corresponding part of the VAT repaid must be paid back to HMRC.

Impairment loss relief claims must be made within four years of the time the impairment loss became eligible for relief (in other words, within four years and six months from when the payment was due). The creditor must have a copy of the VAT invoice, and records to show that the VAT in question has been accounted for and that the debt has been written off. The VAT is reclaimed on the creditor's VAT return as an amount of input tax.

A business which has claimed input tax on a supply, but which has not paid the supplier of the goods or services within six months of date of supply (or the date on which the payment is due, if later), must repay the input tax, irrespective of whether the supplier has made a claim for bad debt relief. The input tax will be repaid by making an adjustment to the input tax on the VAT return for the accounting period in which the end of the six months falls.

Exam focus point

Watch out for the six month rule when claiming relief for impairment losses.

Elixir Ltd has VAT accounting periods ending on 31 March, 30 June, 30 September and 31 December. The company sold standard rated goods to Ben on 1 July 2014. The VAT inclusive amount on the invoice was £2,000 and payment was due by 15 July 2014. Ben paid Elixir Ltd £500 as part payment on 1 October 2014 but then became untraceable and Elixir Ltd has written off the remaining debt.

State how much impairment loss relief can be claimed by Elixir Ltd and the earliest VAT return on which the claim can be made.

Answer

The amount of the loss is £(2,000 – 500) = £1,500.

The VAT on the loss is £1,500 × 1/6 = £250, so this amount can be claimed as impairment loss relief.

Payment was due on 15 July 2014 and so the six month period ended on 15 January 2015. The earliest VAT return on which an impairment loss relief claim is that for the quarter ending 31 March 2015.

Chapter Roundup

- VAT is charged on turnover at each stage in a production process, but in such a way that the burden is borne by the final consumer.

- VAT is chargeable on taxable supplies made by a taxable person in the course or furtherance of any business carried on by him. Supplies may be of goods or services.

- Some supplies are taxable (either standard-rated, reduced-rate or zero-rated). Others are exempt.

- A trader becomes liable to register for VAT if the value of taxable supplies in any period up to 12 months exceeds £81,000 or if there are reasonable grounds for believing that the value of the taxable supplies will exceed £81,000 in the next 30 days alone. A trader may also register voluntarily.

- Two or more companies under common control can register as a group for VAT purposes. A single VAT return and payment are then made by a representative member for a VAT period but all members of the group are jointly and severally liable for VAT due. There is no need to account for VAT on supplies between group members.

- A trader may deregister voluntarily if he expects the value of his taxable supplies in the following one year period will not exceed £79,000. Alternatively, a trader who no longer makes taxable supplies may be compulsorily deregistered.

- VAT is chargeable on all goods and services on hand at the date of deregistration.

- The transfer of a business as a going concern is outside the scope of VAT.

- VAT is administered by HMRC. Appeals are heard by the Tax Tribunal.

- VAT is accounted for on regular returns – most are submitted electronically. Extensive records must be kept.

- The tax point is the deemed date of supply. The basic tax point is the date on which goods are removed or made available to the customer, or the date on which services are completed. If a VAT invoice is issued or payment is received before the basic tax point, the earlier of these dates becomes the actual tax point. If the earlier date rule does not apply, and the VAT invoice is issued within 14 days of the basic tax point, the invoice date becomes the actual tax point.

- In order to ascertain the amount of VAT on a supply, the supply must be valued. If a discount is offered for prompt payment, VAT is chargeable on the net amount even if the discount is not taken up.

- Not all input VAT is deductible, eg VAT on most motor cars.

- If fuel is supplied for private purposes all input VAT incurred on the fuel is allowed and the business will normally account for output VAT using a set of scale charges.

- Relief for VAT on impairment losses is available if the debt is over six months old (measured from when the payment is due) and has been written off in the trader's accounts.

Quick Quiz

1 On what transactions will VAT be charged?

2 What is a taxable person?

3 What are the two advantages of group registration?

4 When may a person choose to be deregistered?

5 What is the time limit in respect of claiming pre-registration input tax on goods?

6 On what amount is VAT charged if a discount is offered for prompt payment?

7 What input tax is never deductible?

8 What relief is available for impairment losses?

1   VAT is charged on taxable supplies of goods and services made in the UK by a taxable person in the course or furtherance of any business carried on by him.

2   Any 'person' whose taxable turnover exceeds the registration limit. The term 'person' includes individuals, partnerships and companies.

3   The two advantages of group registration are:

- Saving on administrative costs: only one VAT return needs to be completed for the group
- No VAT on supplies between group members

4   A person is eligible for voluntary deregistration if HMRC are satisfied that the value of his taxable supplies in the following year will not exceed £79,000.

5   The VAT must have been incurred in the four years prior to the effective date of registration.

6   VAT is chargeable on the net price, regardless of whether the discount is taken up.

7   VAT on:

- Motor cars
- UK business entertaining
- Expenses incurred on domestic accommodation for directors
- Non-business items passed through the accounts
- Items which do not relate to making business supplies

8   Where a supplier has accounted for VAT on a supply and the customer fails to pay, then the supplier may claim a refund of the VAT accounted for to HMRC but never actually collected from the customer.

Now try the questions below from the Practice Question Bank

Number	Type	Marks	Time
Q66	Section A	6	11 mins
Q67	Section B	10	18 mins
Q68	Section B	10	18 mins
Q69	Section B	10	18 mins

Further aspects of VAT

Topic list	Syllabus reference
1 VAT invoices and records	F2(c)
2 Penalties	F2(h)
3 Imports, exports, acquisitions and despatches	F2(i)
4 Special schemes	F3(a)(i)–(iii)

Introduction

In the previous chapter we looked at the scope of VAT and when businesses must, or may, register for VAT.

In this chapter we consider the contents of a valid VAT invoice and the main penalties used to enforce the VAT system.

VAT needs to be applied to imports, so that people do not have a tax incentive to buy abroad, and VAT is taken off many exports in order to encourage sales abroad. We see how this is achieved for transactions both within and outside the European Union.

Finally we look at the three special schemes which are intended to reduce the administrative burden for small businesses.

This chapter concludes our study of UK taxation and the F6 syllabus.

Study guide

		Intellectual level
F2	**The computation of VAT liabilities**	
(c)	List the information that must be given on a VAT invoice.	1
(h)	Understand when the default surcharge, a penalty for an incorrect VAT return, and default interest will be applied.	1
(i)	Understand the treatment of imports, exports and trade within the European Union.	2
F3	**The effect of special schemes**	
(a)	Understand the operation of, and when it will be advantageous to use, the VAT special schemes:	
(i)	Cash accounting scheme.	2
(ii)	Annual accounting scheme.	2
(iii)	Flat rate scheme.	2

Exam guide

The topics in this chapter could be examined in Section A or Section B. Penalties are an important topic as they are used to enforce the VAT system, but the special schemes are designed to make life simpler for small businesses. You may be asked to advise on the VAT treatment of imports and exports outside the European Union (EU) and on trade within the EU. The flat rate scheme may also lead to a small extra profit for the business, depending on the flat rate percentage and the level of inputs.

1 VAT invoices and records

1.1 VAT invoices

FAST FORWARD

> A taxable person making a taxable supply to another registered person must supply a VAT invoice within 30 days.

A taxable person making a taxable supply to another VAT registered trader must supply a VAT invoice within 30 days of the time of supply, and must keep a copy. There is no requirement supply a VAT invoice if the supply is exempt or if the supply is to a non-VAT registered customer.

The invoice must show:

(a)   The supplier's name, address and registration number

(b)   The date of issue, the tax point and an invoice number

(c)   The name and address of the customer

(d)   A description of the goods or services supplied, giving for each description the quantity, the unit price, the rate of VAT and the VAT exclusive amount

(e)   The rate of any cash discount

(f)   The total invoice price excluding VAT (with separate totals for zero-rated and exempt supplies)

(g)   Each VAT rate applicable and the total amount of VAT

If an invoice is issued, and a change in price then alters the VAT due, a credit note or debit note to adjust the VAT must be issued.

Credit notes must give the reason for the credit (such as 'returned goods'), and the number and date of the original VAT invoice. If a credit note makes no VAT adjustment, it should state this.

A less detailed VAT invoice may be issued by a taxable person where the invoice is for a total including VAT of up to £250. Such an invoice must show:

(a)   The supplier's name, address and registration number
(b)   The date of the supply
(c)   A description of the goods or services supplied
(d)   The rate of VAT chargeable
(e)   The total amount chargeable including VAT

Zero-rated and exempt supplies must not be included in less detailed invoices.

VAT invoices are not required for payments of up to £25 including VAT which are for telephone calls, or car park fees, or made through cash operated machines. In such cases, input tax can be claimed without a VAT invoice.

1.2 Records

FAST FORWARD

> Every VAT registered trader must keep records for six years.

Every VAT registered trader must keep records for six years, although HMRC may sometimes grant permission for their earlier destruction. They may be kept on paper, on microfilm or microfiche or on computer. However, there must be adequate facilities for HMRC to inspect records.

All records must be kept up to date and in a way which allows:

- The calculation of VAT due
- Officers of HMRC to check the figures on VAT returns

The following records are needed.

- Copies of VAT invoices, credit notes and debit notes issued

- A summary of supplies made

- VAT invoices, credit notes and debit notes received

- A summary of supplies received

- A VAT account

- Order and delivery notes, correspondence, appointment books, job books, purchases and sales books, cash books, account books, records of takings (such as till rolls), bank paying-in slips, bank statements and annual accounts

- Records of zero-rated and exempt supplies, gifts or loans of goods, taxable self-supplies and any goods taken for non-business use

2 Penalties

2.1 The default surcharge

FAST FORWARD

> A default occurs when a trader either submits his VAT return late, or submits the return on time but pays the VAT late. A default surcharge is applied if there is a default on payment during a default surcharge period.

A default occurs when a trader either submits his VAT return late, or submits the return on time but pays the VAT late. If a trader defaults, HMRC will serve a surcharge liability notice on the trader. The notice specifies a surcharge period running from the date of the notice to the anniversary of the end of the period for which the trader is in default.

If a further default occurs in respect of a return period ending during the specified surcharge period, the original surcharge period will be extended to the anniversary of the end of the period to which the new default relates. In addition, if the default involves the late payment of VAT (as opposed to simply a late return) **a surcharge is levied.**

The surcharge depends on the number of defaults involving late payment of VAT which have occurred in respect of periods ending in the surcharge period, as follows.

Default involving late payment of VAT in the surcharge period	Surcharge as a percentage of the VAT outstanding at the due date
First	2%
Second	5%
Third	10%
Fourth or more	15%

Surcharges at the 2% and 5% rates are not normally demanded unless the amount due would be at least £400 but for surcharges calculated using the 10% or 15% rates there is a minimum amount of £30 payable.

A trader must submit one year's returns on time and pay the VAT shown on them on time in order to break out of the surcharge liability period and the escalation of surcharge percentages.

Question

Peter Popper has an annual turnover of around £300,000. His VAT return for the quarter to 31.12.12 is late. He then submits returns for the quarters to 30.9.13 and 31.3.14 late as well as making late payment of the tax due of £12,000 and £500 respectively.

Peter's VAT return to 31.3.15 is also late and the VAT due of £1,100 is also paid late. All other VAT returns and VAT payments are made on time. Outline Peter Popper's exposure to default surcharge.

Answer

A surcharge liability notice will be issued after the late filing on the 31.12.12 return outlining a surcharge period extending to 31.12.13.

The late 30.9.13 return is in the surcharge period so the period is extended to 30.9.14. The late VAT payment triggers a 2% penalty. 2% × £12,000 = £240. Since £240 is less than the £400 de minimis limit it is not collected by HMRC.

The late 31.3.14 return is in the surcharge period so the period is now extended to 31.3.15. The late payment triggers a 5% penalty. 5% × £500 = £25. Since £25 is less than the £400 de minimis limit it is not collected by HMRC.

The late 31.03.15 return is in the surcharge period. The period is extended to 31.03.16. The late payment triggers a 10% penalty 10% × £1,100 = £110. This is collected by HMRC since the £400 de minimis does not apply to penalties calculated at the 10% (and 15%) rate.

Peter will have to submit all four quarterly VAT returns to 31.3.16 on time and pay the VAT on time to 'escape' the default surcharge regime.

A default will be ignored for all default surcharge purposes if the trader can show that the return or payment was sent at such a time, and in such a manner, that it was reasonable to expect that HMRC would receive it by the due date. Posting the return and payment first class the day before the due date is generally accepted as meeting this requirement. A default will also be ignored if the trader can demonstrate a reasonable excuse for the late submission or payment.

376   **27: Further aspects of VAT** | Part G Value added tax

The application of the default surcharge regime to small businesses is modified. **A small business is one with a turnover below £150,000.** When a small business is late submitting a VAT return or paying VAT it will receive a letter from HMRC offering help. No penalty will be charged. If a further default occurs within 12 months a surcharge liability notice will be issued.

2.2 Penalties for errors

There is a common penalty regime for errors in tax returns, including VAT. Errors in a VAT return up to certain amounts may be corrected in the next return.

2.2.1 Common penalty regime

The common penalty regime for making errors in tax returns discussed earlier in this Text applies for value added tax.

2.2.2 Errors corrected in next return

Errors on a VAT return not exceeding the greater of:

- **£10,000** (net under-declaration minus over-declaration)
- **1% x net VAT turnover for return period** (maximum £50,000)

may be **corrected on the next return.**

Other errors should be notified to HMRC in writing eg by letter.

In both cases, a penalty for the error may be imposed. Correction of an error on a later return is not, of itself, an unprompted disclosure of the error and fuller disclosure is required for the penalty to be reduced.

Default interest (see below) on the unpaid VAT as a result of the error is only charged where the limit is exceeded for the error to be corrected on the next VAT return.

2.3 Interest on unpaid VAT (default interest)

Default interest is charged on unpaid VAT if HMRC raise an assessment of VAT or the trader makes a voluntary payment before the assessment is raised. It runs from the date the VAT should have been paid to the actual date of payment but cannot run for more than three years before the assessment or voluntary payment.

Interest (not deductible in computing taxable profits) **is charged on VAT which is the subject of an assessment** (where returns were not made or were incorrect), **or which could have been the subject of an assessment but was paid before the assessment was raised. It runs from the reckonable date until the date of payment.** This interest is sometimes called 'default interest'.

The reckonable date is when the VAT should have been paid (usually one month and seven days from the end of the return period), or in the case of VAT repayments, seven days from the issue of the repayment order. However, where VAT is charged by an assessment, interest does not run from more than three years before the date of the assessment; where the VAT was paid before an assessment was raised, interest does not run for more than three years before the date of payment.

In practice, interest is only charged when there would otherwise be a loss to the Exchequer. It is not, for example, charged when a company failed to charge VAT but if it had done so another company would have been able to recover the VAT.

3 Imports, exports, acquisitions and despatches

3.1 Introduction

The terms **import and export** refer to purchases and sales of goods with countries **outside the European Union (EU)**.

The terms **acquisition and despatch** refer to purchases and sales of goods with countries **in the EU**.

3.2 Trade in goods outside the European Union

FAST FORWARD

Imports of goods from outside the EU are subject to VAT and exports of goods to outside the EU are zero-rated.

3.2.1 Imports

Goods imported into the UK from outside the EU are effectively treated in the same way as goods that are purchased within the UK. This is because imports are chargeable to VAT if the same goods supplied in the home market by a registered trader would be chargeable to VAT. The rate of VAT is the same as that which would have applied if the supply had been made in the home market.

An importer of goods from outside the EU must calculate VAT on the value of the goods imported and account for it at the point of entry into the UK. He can then deduct the VAT payable as input tax on his next VAT return. HMRC issue monthly certificates to importers showing the VAT paid on imports. VAT is chargeable on the onward sale of the goods in the UK in the normal way.

If security (such as a bank guarantee) can be provided, the deferred payment system can be used whereby VAT is automatically charged to the importer's bank account each month rather than payment being made for each import when the goods arrive in the UK. Approved importers are able to provide reduced (and in some cases zero) security in respect of the deferred payment scheme. Such importers need to seek the approval of HMRC.

3.2.2 Exports

There is a general zero-rating where a UK VAT registered trader exports goods outside of the EU.

It is not sufficient merely to export goods. The zero-rating only applies if HMRC 'are satisfied' that the supplier has exported the goods. Evidence of the export must therefore be retained by the trader and must take the form specified by HMRC.

3.3 Trade in goods within the European Union

FAST FORWARD

Sales of goods to registered traders in other EU states are zero-rated. Taxable acquisitions of goods to the UK from other EU states are subject to VAT in the UK as both output tax and input tax.

3.3.1 Sales (despatches)

Where goods are sold by a UK registered trader to a customer in another EU member state, the supply is usually zero-rated if the supply is made to a VAT registered trader.

3.3.2 Purchases (acquisitions)

Goods acquired in the UK by a VAT registered trader from another EU member state are liable to UK VAT. Consequently, output tax has to be accounted for by that UK trader on the relevant VAT return. **The 'tax point' for such acquisitions is the earlier of:**

- **The fifteenth day of the month following the month of acquisition**
- **The date of issue of an invoice**

The transaction is entered on the UK trader's VAT return as an output and an input so the effect is usually neutral. Thus the UK trader is effectively in the same overall position as he would have been if he had acquired the goods from another UK VAT registered trader.

Although the end result is the same as with an import from outside the EU, the difference with an EU acquisition is that there is no need to actually pay the VAT subsequent to its recovery as input VAT.

3.4 Supplies of services

FAST FORWARD

Services supplied to a business customer are generally treated as being supplied in the country where that customer is situated. Therefore, if the customer is a UK VAT registered trader, output VAT is payable by that trader on the supply. Supplies of services by a UK VAT registered trader to business customers outside the UK are generally outside the scope of UK VAT.

3.4.1 Place of supply of services

Services supplied to a business customer are generally treated as being supplied in the country where that customer is situated. A 'business customer' is anyone carrying on a business anywhere in the world, not just VAT registered traders and not just customers in the EU.

3.4.2 Supplies of services to a UK business customer

Where a UK business customer receives services from outside the UK, the place of supply will be the UK. Therefore, if the business customer is a VAT registered trader, output tax has to be accounted for by that UK trader on the relevant VAT return.

The tax point for a supply of such services is the earlier of:

- The time the service is completed
- The time the service is paid for.

The transaction is entered on the UK trader's VAT return as an output and an input so the effect is usually neutral. Thus the UK trader effectively in the same overall position as if the services have been supplied by another UK VAT registered trader.

3.4.3 Supplies of services by a UK trader

Supplies of services by a UK VAT registered trader to business customers outside the UK are generally outside the scope of UK VAT. This is because the place of supply is not in the UK.

Exam focus point

The rules on international services are complex. For F6 (UK) purposes, you only need to know the rules in outline as explained in this section.

4 Special schemes

FAST FORWARD

Special schemes include the cash accounting scheme, the annual accounting scheme and the optional flat rate scheme. These schemes can make VAT accounting easier and ease cash flow for certain types of trader.

One of the competencies you require to fulfil performance objective 19 of the PER is the ability to evaluate and compute taxes payable. You can apply the knowledge you obtain from this section of the text to help to demonstrate this competence.

4.1 The cash accounting scheme

The cash accounting scheme enables businesses to account for VAT on the basis of cash paid and received. That is, the date of payment or receipt determines the return in which the transaction is dealt with. This means that the cash accounting scheme gives automatic impairment loss relief (bad debt relief) because VAT is not due on a supply until payment has been received.

The scheme can only be used by a trader whose taxable turnover (exclusive of VAT) for the 12 months starting on their application to join the scheme is not expected to exceed £1,350,000. A trader can join the scheme only if all returns and VAT payments are up to date (or arrangements have been made to pay outstanding VAT by instalments).

If the value of taxable supplies exceeds £1,600,000 in the 12 months to the end of a VAT period a trader must leave the cash accounting scheme immediately.

Businesses which leave the scheme (either voluntarily or because they have breached the £1,600,000 limit) can account for any outstanding VAT due under the scheme on a cash basis for a further six months.

4.2 The annual accounting scheme

The annual accounting scheme is only available to traders who regularly pay VAT to HMRC, not to traders who normally receive repayments. It is available for traders **whose taxable turnover (exclusive of VAT) for the 12 months starting on their application to join the scheme is not expected to exceed £1,350,000**.

Under the annual accounting scheme traders file annual VAT returns but throughout the year they must make payments on account of their VAT liability by direct debit. The year for which each return is made may end at the end of any calendar month. Unless HMRC agree otherwise, the trader must pay 90% of the previous year's net VAT liability during the year by means of nine monthly payments commencing at the end of the fourth month of the year. The balance of the year's VAT is then paid with the annual return. There is an option for businesses to pay three larger interim instalments.

Late payment of instalments is not a default for the purposes of the default surcharge.

An annual VAT return must be submitted to HMRC along with any balancing payment due within two months of the end of the year.

It is not possible to use the annual accounting scheme if input tax exceeded output tax in the year prior to application. In addition, all VAT payments must be up to date.

If the expected value of a trader's taxable supplies exceeds £1,600,000, notice must be given to HMRC within 30 days and he may then be required to leave the scheme. If the £1,600,000 limit is in fact exceeded, the trader must leave the scheme.

If a trader fails to make the regular payments required by the scheme or the final payment for a year, or has not paid all VAT shown on returns made before joining the scheme, he may be expelled from the scheme. HMRC can also prevent a trader using the scheme 'if they consider it necessary to do so for the protection of the revenue'.

Advantages of annual accounting:

- Only one VAT return each year so fewer occasions to trigger a default surcharge
- Ability to manage cash flow more accurately
- Avoids need for quarterly calculations for input tax recovery

Disadvantages of annual accounting:

- Need to monitor future taxable supplies to ensure turnover limit not exceeded

- Timing of payments have less correlation to turnover (and hence cash received) by business

- Payments based on previous year's turnover may not reflect current year turnover which may be a problem if the scale of activities has reduced.

4.3 Flat rate scheme

The optional flat rate scheme enables businesses to calculate VAT due simply by applying a flat rate percentage to their turnover.

Under the scheme, businesses calculate VAT by applying a fixed percentage to their **tax inclusive turnover**, ie the total turnover, **including all reduced rate, zero-rated and exempt income.** However, the businesses **cannot reclaim any input tax suffered.**

The percentage depends upon the trade sector into which a business falls. It ranges from 4% for retailing food, confectionery or newspapers to 14.5% for accountancy and bookkeeping services.

A 1% reduction off the flat rate % can be made by businesses in their first year of VAT registration.

Exam focus point

The flat rate percentage will be given to you in your examination.

Businesses using the scheme must issue VAT invoices to their VAT registered customers but they do not have to record all the details of the invoices issued or purchase invoices received to calculate the VAT due. Invoices issued will show VAT at the normal rate rather than the flat rate.

To join the flat rate scheme businesses must have a VAT exclusive annual taxable turnover of up to £150,000.

A business must leave the flat rate scheme if the total value of its VAT inclusive supplies in the year (excluding sales of capital assets) is more than £230,000.

4.4 Example: flat rate scheme

An accountant undertakes work for individuals and for business clients. In a VAT year, the business client work amounts to £35,000 and the accountant will issue VAT invoices totalling £42,000 (£35,000 plus VAT at 20%). Turnover from work for individuals totals £18,000, including VAT. Total gross sales are therefore £60,000. The flat rate percentage for an accountancy businesses is 14.5%.

VAT due to HMRC will be 14.5% × £60,000 (VAT inclusive amount) = £8,700

Under the normal VAT rules the output tax due would be:

	£
£35,000 × 20%	7,000
£18,000 × 1/6	3,000
	10,000

Whether the accountant is better off under the scheme depends on the amount of input tax incurred as this would be offset, under normal rules, from output tax due.

Chapter Roundup

- A taxable person making a taxable supply to another registered person must supply a VAT invoice within 30 days.

- Every VAT registered trader must keep records for six years.

- A default occurs when a trader either submits his VAT return late, or submits the return on time but pays the VAT late. A default surcharge is applied if there is a default on payment during a default surcharge period.

- There is a common penalty regime for errors in tax returns, including VAT. Errors in a VAT return up to certain amounts may be corrected in the next return.

- Default interest is charged on unpaid VAT if HMRC raise an assessment of VAT or the trader makes a voluntary payment before the assessment is raised. It runs from the date the VAT should have been paid to the actual date of payment but cannot run for more than three years before the assessment or voluntary payment.

- Imports of goods from outside the EU are subject to VAT and exports of goods to outside the EU are zero-rated.

- Sales of goods to registered traders in other EU states are zero-rated. Taxable acquisitions of goods to the UK from other EU states are subject to VAT in the UK as both output tax and input tax.

- Services supplied to a business customer are generally treated as being supplied in the country where that customer is situated. Therefore, if the customer is a UK VAT registered trader, output VAT is payable by that trader on the supply. Supplies of services by a UK VAT registered trader to business customers outside the UK are generally outside the scope of UK VAT.

- Special schemes include the cash accounting scheme, the annual accounting scheme and the optional flat rate scheme. These schemes can make VAT accounting easier and ease cash flow for certain types of trader.

Quick Quiz

1   How long must a VAT trader keep records?

2   What is a default?

3   Dylan makes an error in his VAT for the quarter ending 31 March 2015 which results in a net under-declaration of £5,000. His net VAT turnover for the period is £150,000. How can Dylan correct the error?

4   Are goods despatched to the EU standard-rated or zero-rated?

5   Mr Higgins is registered for VAT in the UK. Mr Higgins is supplied with services by a French business on 1 September 2014. The value of the supply is £50,000. What are the VAT consequences of the supply?

6   How does the cash accounting scheme operate?

7   The turnover limits for the annual accounting scheme are not exceeding £_____m to join the scheme and once turnover exceeds £_____m the trade must leave the scheme. Fill in the blanks.

8   What is the optional flat rate scheme?

Answers to Quick Quiz

1   A VAT trader must keep records for six years.

2   A default occurs when a trader either submits his VAT return late or submits the return on time but pays the VAT late.

3   Dylan can correct the error in his VAT return for the quarter ending 30 June 2015. This is because the error is less than £10,000 and also less than 1% of his net VAT turnover for the return period.

4   In general, despatches to the EU are zero-rated.

5   Mr Higgins will have to account for output tax of £50,000 × 20% = £10,000 on the supply and also £10,000 of input tax. The supply is therefore tax neutral for him.

6   The cash accounting scheme operates by a trader accounting for VAT on the basis of cash paid and received (rather than invoices). The date of payment or receipt determines the return in which the transaction is dealt with. The scheme gives automatic impairment loss relief because VAT on a supply is not due until payment is received.

7   The turnover limits for the annual accounting scheme are not exceeding **£1.35m** to join the scheme and once turnover exceeds **£1.6m** the trade must leave the scheme.

8   The optional flat rate scheme enables businesses to calculate VAT simply by applying a percentage to their tax-inclusive turnover. Under the scheme, businesses calculate VAT due by applying a flat rate percentage to their tax inclusive turnover, ie the total turnover generated, including all reduced-rate, zero-rated and exempt income. The percentage depends upon the trade sector in which a business falls.

Now try the questions below from the Practice Question Bank

Number	Type	Marks	Time
Q70	Section A	6	11 mins
Q71	Section B	10	18 mins
Q72	Section B	10	18 mins
Q73	Section B	5	9 mins

Practice question and answer bank

1 Introduction to the UK tax system

1.1 Which of the following are functions of HM Revenue and Customs (HMRC) in the UK tax system?

(1) Formally imposes taxation
(2) Produces a wide range of explanatory notes
(3) Provides advice on minimising tax liability
(4) Has the administrative function for collection of tax.

A 1 and 2
B 2 and 3
C 1 and 4
D 2 and 4

(2 marks)

1.2 Which of the following are NOT revenue taxes?

(1) Income tax
(2) Capital gains tax
(3) National insurance
(4) Inheritance tax

A 1 and 2
B 2 and 4
C 3 and 4
D 2 and 3

(2 marks)

1.3 You work for a firm of accountants. A few weeks ago, you prepared a tax return for Serena. Serena has now told you that she forgot to include some bank interest in the return but that she does not intend to tell HM Revenue and Customs (HMRC) of the omission.

Which of the following actions should you take?

(1) Inform Serena in writing that it is not possible for your firm to act for her.

(2) Inform HMRC that your firm is no longer acting for Serena.

(3) Inform HMRC about the details of Serena's omission.

(4) Report to your firm's Money Laundering Reporting Officer Serena's refusal to disclose the omission to HMRC and the facts surrounding it.

A 1, 2 and 3
B 2, 3 and 4
C 1, 2 and 4
D 1, 3 and 4

(2 marks)

(Total = 6 marks)

2 Computing taxable income

11 mins

2.1   In 2014/15, Elaine received the following income.

£10,800 dividends from Z plc
£400 interest from Principality Building Society
£1,000 interest from 8¾% Treasury Stock 2017

What is Elaine's total income for the tax year 2014/15?

A   £13,444
B   £13,750
C   £15,000
D   £13,500   **(2 marks)**

2.2   Which of the following types of income are exempt from income tax?

(1)   Dividends from a company
(2)   Interest received from a New Individual Savings Account
(3)   £50 Premium Bond prize
(4)   Interest on NS&I Savings Certificates
(5)   Interest on government securities

A   1, 2 and 4
B   2, 3 and 5
C   2, 3 and 4
D   1, 4 and 5   **(2 marks)**

2.3   In 2014/15, Robert, born in 1945, had property business income of £105,000. This was his only
income in 2014/15.

What is the personal allowance available to Robert for the tax year 2014/15?

A   £2,500
B   £10,000
C   £7,500
D   £10,500   **(2 marks)**

                                                                                    (Total = 6 marks)

3 Julia, Sandeep, Harriet and Romelu

20 mins

(a)   Julia had always been UK-resident prior to the tax year 2014/15. She left the UK on 6 April 2014 to
live overseas. Julia returned to the UK for 14 days in October 2014.

Required

Explain why Julia is non-UK resident in the tax year 2014/15.   **(1 mark)**

(b)   Sandeep had not previously been UK-resident prior to the tax year 2014/15. He arrived in the UK on
6 April 2014 and remained in the UK for 190 days. Sandeep does not work during 2014/15.

Required

Explain why Sandeep is UK resident in the tax year 2014/15.   **(2 marks)**

(c)   Harriet had always been UK-resident prior to the tax year 2014/15, but she has not spent more than 90 days in the UK in the two previous tax years. Harriet is self-employed and does substantive (but not full-time) work in the UK during 2014/15. She has no close family. Harriet owns a house in the UK. On 6 April 2014, she started to rent an overseas apartment in which she lived for 255 days. She then returned to the UK where she lived in her house for the remainder of the tax year 2014/15.

Required

Explain why Harriet is UK resident in the tax year 2014/15.   **(4 marks)**

(d)   Romelu had not previously been UK-resident prior to the tax year 2014/15 and has never spent more than 60 days in the UK in previous tax years. His wife is UK resident. Romelu arrived in the UK on 6 April 2014 and remained in the UK for 92 days during which time he lived in a rented flat. He also has a home outside the UK where he spent the rest of 2014/15. Romelu does not work during 2014/15.

Required

Explain why Romelu is non-UK resident in the tax year 2014/15.   **(4 marks)**

(Total = 11 marks)

4 Luke   7 mins

Luke was born in 1935. In 2014/15, he has pension income of £22,900 and receives bank interest of £4,000.

Required

Calculate Luke's taxable income for 2014/15, clearly showing the amount of non-savings income and the amount of savings income.   **(4 marks)**

5 Computing the income tax liability   11 mins

5.1   Peter has taxable income for the tax year 2014/15 as follows:

Non-savings income	£2,000
Savings income	£3,290

What is Peter's income tax liability for the tax year 2014/15?

A   £970
B   £770
C   £529
D   £1,058   **(2 marks)**

5.2   Rhoda has taxable income of £175,000 in 2014/15 which is all employment income. PAYE of £40,000 was deducted.

What is Rhoda's income tax payable for the tax year 2014/15?

A   £64,877
B   £20,377
C   £24,877
D   £23,627   **(2 marks)**

5.3 John is a widower and has two children aged fourteen and twelve. He receives child benefit of £1,771 in 2014/15. John has net income of £53,400 in 2014/15 and he made a gift aid donation of £300 (gross) in January 2015.

What is John's child benefit income tax charge for the tax year 2014/15?

A £531
B £549
C £602
D £1,771

(2 marks)

(Total = 6 marks)

6 John and Helen

27 mins

John and Helen, who were both born in 1975, are a married couple. They have a twelve year old son, Marcus. John and Helen received the following income in 2014/15.

	John £	Helen £
Salary (gross)	64,955	22,190
PAYE tax deducted	15,200	2,200
Dividends (amount received)	1,090	2,538
Bank deposit interest (amount received)	600	76
Building society interest (amount received)	592	420

Required

(a) Compute the tax payable by John and by Helen for 2014/15. **(13 marks)**

(b) Explain the tax implications if Helen had received child benefit of £1,066 during 2014/15.

(2 marks)

(Total = 15 marks)

7 Michael and Josie

27 mins

Michael (born in 1968) and Josie (born in 1966) are a married couple. They received the following income in 2014/15.

	Michael £	Josie £
Salary (gross)	163,540	100,000
PAYE tax deducted	59,650	33,000
Dividends (amount received)	10,900	2,538
Bank deposit interest (amount received)	6,000	760
Building society interest (amount received)	5,920	4,200

Josie made a gift aid donation of £1,600 in December 2014.

Required

Compute the tax payable or repayable by or to Michael and Josie for 2014/15. **(15 marks)**

8 Employment income

11 mins

8.1 Jacob works part time for Z Ltd at a salary of £8,000 a year. He is not a director of Z Ltd. On 30 November 2014, Jacob received a bonus of £1,800 in respect of Z Ltd's trading results for the year ended 31 October 2014. He expects to receive a bonus of £2,400 in November 2015 in respect of Z Ltd's results for the year ended 31 October 2015.

What is Jacob's employment income for the tax year 2014/15?

    A   £8,000
    B   £9,800
    C   £10,050
    D   £10,400   **(2 marks)**

8.2 You are a tax advisor for the following clients.

    (1)   Ben, who is a computer systems advisor. He works in the Bristol office one day a week and spends the rest of his time visiting clients in London and Manchester.

    (2)   Colin, who is a computer technician. He works two days a week at the Bristol workshop depot and three days a week at the Swindon workshop.

    (3)   Diane, who works for an accountancy firm. She is based in the Birmingham office but has been seconded to the Bristol office for 12 months.

    (4)   Erica, who works permanently in the same Birmingham office as Diane. She occasionally travels from home to visit a client in Bristol.

Which of your clients can claim tax relief for travelling expenses between home and Bristol?

    A   1 and 2
    B   2 and 3
    C   3 and 4
    D   1 and 4   **(2 marks)**

8.3 Sarah is employed by Y plc. She uses her own car for business purposes and is reimbursed 35p per mile by Y plc. In 2014/15, Sarah travelled 15,000 miles on business.

What is the employment income consequence of the reimbursement for business mileage?

    A   £5,250 taxable benefit
    B   £(500) allowable expense
    C   £(1,500) allowable expense
    D   £(5,750) allowable expense   **(2 marks)**

(Total = 6 marks)

9 Danni

18 mins

Danni joined a UK company, Clifton plc, as purchasing director on 1 July 2014, based at their Nottingham office.

Until 31 December 2014, Danni's monthly salary as a director was £6,000. From 1 January 2015, her salary increased by 2.5%.

Clifton plc awarded Danni a bonus of £10,000 in relation to a special purchasing project during Clifton plc's period of account ended 31 March 2015. This bonus was determined by the board of directors on 15 March 2015, credited in the company's accounts on 10 April 2015, which was also the date when Danni became entitled to payment of the bonus. The bonus was paid to Danni on 31 May 2015.

From 1 July 2014, Danni traveled to Clifton plc's office in Nottingham from home using the Nottingham Tram Network. Danni bought a monthly tram season ticket at a cost of £45 per month for each of the months from July 2014 to December 2014.

From 1 January 2015, Danni was seconded to Clifton plc's office in Manchester for a period of six months. Danni bought a monthly rail season ticket at a cost of £543 per month for each month of her secondment.

Danni also used her own car for journeys to meet clients in Leicester, which is 24 miles from Nottingham. She made five return journeys between 1 July 2014 and 5 April 2015. Clifton plc paid Danni 30p per mile for these journeys.

Danni is a member of the Chartered Institute of Purchasing and Supply (MCIP) and paid her annual membership fee of £159 on 31 December 2014. Danni is also a member of her local tennis club at which she sometimes meets potential suppliers for Clifton plc. The membership fee is £180 per month.

Clifton plc has a payroll giving scheme. Danni donated £50 per month through the scheme from 31 December 2014.

Required

Calculate Danni's employment income for 2014/15, giving a brief explanation for your treatment of each item. **(10 marks)**

10 Taxable and exempt benefits. The PAYE system

11 mins

10.1 Lenny is employed by B plc at a salary of £42,000 each tax year. He is provided with a car available for private use throughout 2014/15. The car has CO_2 emissions of 133 g/km and a list price of £20,000. B plc paid £18,000 for the car as a result of a dealer discount. The car has a diesel engine. No private fuel is provided.

What is Lenny's taxable car benefit for the tax year 2014/15?

A £3,800
B £4,400
C £3,960
D £3,420 **(2 marks)**

10.2 Bernie is employed by N Ltd. N Ltd provided Bernie with the use of free accommodation (not job related) from 6 April 2014 to 5 August 2014. The accommodation cost Bernie's employer £99,000 in February 2012 and was previously occupied by another employee. The accommodation had a market value of £123,000 in April 2014 and an annual value of £3,600.

What is Bernie's total taxable benefit in respect of the accommodation for the tax year 2014/15?

A £1,200
B £260
C £1,460
D £1,720 **(2 marks)**

10.3 Julia is employed by C plc at a salary of £20,000 each tax year. For the tax year 2014/15 C plc paid Julia's corporate gym membership at a cost of £1,200. Julia receives no other benefits from C plc.

Which form, if any, does C plc use to report this benefit to HM Revenue and Customs (HMRC) and by what date must it be submitted to HMRC?

A P11D – 6 July 2015
B P11D – 31 May 2015
C P9D – 6 July 2015
D Tax free benefit – no form required **(2 marks)**

(Total = 6 marks)

11 Azure plc   18 mins

The following items have been provided by a UK company, Azure plc, to employees earning more than £8,500 a year.

(a)   A loan of £16,000 at 1% a year to Mr Andrews on 6 October 2014. The loan was not for a qualifying interest purpose.

(b)   A £7,000 interest free loan to Mrs Preece on 6 April 2014 which was used to finance her daughter's wedding.

(c)   The loan of a TV to Mr Charles from 6 June 2014, the asset having cost the company £800 in 2012 and having had a market value of £500 in June 2014.

(d)   A long service award in December 2014 to Mrs Davies, the company secretary, comprising a gold wrist watch costing £1,000. Mrs Davies has been employed by the company since December 1989.

(e)   Removal expenses of £9,500 to Miss Jackson in September 2014 who moved from Plymouth to Liverpool to take up a new position in the Liverpool office in July 2014.

(f)   The provision of two mobile phones to Mr Long on 6 April 2014 both of which were available for private use as well as business use. Azure plc paid £120 for the hire of each of the mobile phones for the tax year. The market value of each of the phones was £500. The cost of the calls made during the year was £300 for one of the phones and £400 for the other phone. 70% of these expenses related to business use.

Required

State in detail how each of the above items would be treated for 2014/15, computing the amount of any taxable benefit.   **(10 marks)**

12 Verdi   9 mins

Verdi is setting up a business and will be employing twelve individuals. He understands that he will need to operate the Pay As You Earn (PAYE) system for income tax and national insurance contributions.

Required

(a)   State the methods that Verdi can use to submit information electronically under the Real Time Information (RTI) system.   **(1 mark)**

(b)   State when a Full Payment Submission (FPS) must be made and outline the information that will be contained in it.   **(2 marks)**

(c)   (i)   Define a 'tax month' in relation to PAYE.   **(1 mark)**

      (ii) State the period within which Verdi must pay over income tax and national insurance contributions to HMRC for each tax month, assuming that the payment will be made electronically.   **(1 mark)**

                                                                              (Total = 5 marks)

13 Pensions   11 mins

13.1   In the tax year 2014/15, Treena earned £3,500 from part time work, trading income of £2,000 and gross bank interest of £500.

       What is the maximum gross pension contribution that Treena could have made during the tax year 2014/15 on which there would have been tax relief?

       A   £3,500
       B   £5,500
       C   £3,600
       D   £6,000   **(2 marks)**

13.2 In the tax year 2014/15, Jemima earned a salary of £90,000 and she paid a contribution of £15,000 to her employer's occupational pension scheme. Jemima has no other sources of income.

What is Jemima's taxable income for the tax year 2014/15?

A £90,000
B £75,000
C £65,000
D £61,250 **(2 marks)**

13.3 Rio started in business as a sole trader on 6 April 2012 and had the following results:

2012/13 £20,000
2013/14 £30,000
2014/15 £85,000

Rio had not made any pension provision prior to 2013/14 but on 6 April 2013 he joined a personal pension scheme and made a contribution of £27,000 (gross) on that date.

What is the maximum gross pension contribution that Rio could have made during the tax year 2014/15 on which there would have been tax relief without incurring an annual allowance charge?

A £63,000
B £113,000
C £85,000
D £73,000 **(2 marks)**

(Total = 6 marks)

14 Gary, George and Geraldine   11 mins

(a) Gary was born in 1967. He had employment income of £55,000 for 2014/15. He paid £4,000 (net) into his personal pension scheme in 2014/15. This was the first year in which he had been a member of a registered pension scheme.

Required

Calculate Gary's income tax payable. **(2 marks)**

(b) George was born in 1956. He had employment income of £45,000 for 2014/15. He paid £39,200 (net) into his personal pension scheme in 2014/15. This was the first year in which he had been a member of a registered pension scheme.

Required

Calculate George's income tax payable. **(2 marks)**

(c) Geraldine was born in 1975. She had trading income of £60,000 in 2013/14. She paid £25,000 (net) into her personal pension scheme in 2013/14. This was the first year in which she had been a member of a registered pension scheme. She has trading income of £130,000 in 2014/15.

Required

Explain the maximum net personal pension contribution that Geraldine will be able to make in 2014/15, obtaining tax relief and without resulting in a tax charge. **(2 marks)**

(Total = 6 marks)

15 Property income

15.1 Paul rents out a flat which is fully furnished. The house does not qualify as a furnished holiday letting. For the tax year 2014/15 Paul's property business income and expenses are:

	£
Rent receivable	12,000
Expenses accrued:	
Water rates	200
Agent's fee	1,200
Insurance	400

What is the wear and tear allowance that Paul can claim in the tax year 2014/15?

A   £1,020
B   £1,140
C   £1,180
D   £1,200   (2 marks)

15.2 Laura granted an 11 year lease on a property to a tenant for a premium of £30,000.

What is the amount of the premium on which will Laura be chargeable to income tax?

A   £23,400
B   £6,000
C   £30,000
D   £24,000   (2 marks)

15.3 Which of the following statements about furnished holiday lettings are TRUE?

(1)   The accommodation must be available for commercial let as holiday accommodation to the public generally for at least 105 days during the tax year.

(2)   The accommodation must not have more than 155 days in the tax year in longer term occupation.

(3)   The wear and tear allowance applies on furniture provided in the furnished holiday letting.

(4)   The income from furnished holiday lettings qualifies as relevant earnings for pension contributions.

(5)   If an individual has a furnished holiday letting and another letting, two income statements must be prepared in order to identify separate profits and losses.

A   1, 2 and 4
B   2, 4 and 5
C   1, 4 and 5
D   3, 4 and 5   (2 marks)

                                                                    (Total = 6 marks)

16 Rafe   18 mins

On 1 May 2014, Rafe started to invest in rented properties. He bought two houses in the first three months, as follows.

House 1

Rafe bought house 1 for £62,000 on 1 May 2014. It needed a new roof before it was fit to be let out. Rafe paid £5,000 for the work to be done in May. He then let it unfurnished for £600 a month from 1 June to 30 November 2014. The first tenant then left, and the house was empty throughout December 2014. On 1 January 2015, a new tenant moved in. The house was again let unfurnished. The rent was £6,000 a year, payable annually in advance.

Rafe paid water rates of £320 for the period from 1 May 2014 to 5 April 2015 and a buildings insurance premium of £480 for the period from 1 June 2014 to 31 May 2015.

House 2

Rafe bought house 2 for £45,000 on 1 July 2014. He spent £1,200 on routine redecoration and £2,300 on furniture in July, and let the house fully furnished from 1 August 2014 for £7,800 a year, payable annually in advance. Rafe paid water rates of £360 for the period from 1 July 2014 to 5 April 2015, a buildings insurance premium of £440 for the period from 1 July 2014 to 30 June 2015 and a contents insurance premium in respect of his own furniture of £180 for the period from 1 August 2014 to 31 July 2015. He claimed the wear and tear allowance for furniture.

During 2014/15 Rafe also rented out one furnished room of his main residence. He received £4,600 and incurred allowable expenses of £875.

Required

Compute Rafe's property business income for 2014/15.   **(10 marks)**

17 Computing trading income   11 mins

17.1   Which of the following items of expenditure will Walter NOT be allowed to deduct in calculating his tax-adjusted trading profit before capital allowances?

    (1)   Installing air conditioning in his workshop

    (2)   Repairing the central heating in his offices

    (3)   Redecorating his showroom

    (4)   Building a wall around his showroom car park

    (5)   Making initial repairs to a recently acquired second-hand office building which was not usable until the repairs were carried out

    A   1, 2 and 4
    B   2, 4 and 5
    C   1, 4 and 5
    D   3, 4 and 5   **(2 marks)**

17.2 Allie is a sole trader and has a profit of £160,000 on her statement of profit or loss for the year ended 31 December 2014. Included within this figure are these expenses:

(1) £3,000 legal fees in connection with renewing a 15-year lease of Allie's business premises
(2) £180 car parking fines incurred by Allie whilst visiting clients
(3) £40 hamper of food for customer

What is Allie's tax adjusted profit for the year ended 31 December 2014?

A £160,040
B £163,180
C £163,220
D £160,220

(2 marks)

17.3 Terry started in business on 6 April 2014 and prepared his first set of accounts to 5 April 2015. He elected to use the cash basis. During the year to 5 April 2015 Terry invoiced his customers for £50,200 of which £4,000 was owed as receivables at 5 April 2015. Terry incurred expenses during the year to 5 April 2015 of £20,000 of which £1,500 was owed as payables on 5 April 2015.

What is Terry's tax adjusted profit for the year ended 5 April 2014?

A £24,700
B £27,700
C £32,700
D £30,200

(2 marks)

(Total = 6 marks)

18 A Trader

27 mins

A Trader's statement of profit or loss for the year to 31 March 2015 was as follows.

	£	£
Gross profit		246,250
Other income		
Impairment trade losses recovered (previously written off)	373	
Profit on sale of office	5,265	
Building society interest	1,900	
		7,538
Expenses		
General expenses	73,611	
Repairs and renewals	15,000	
Legal and accountancy charges	1,200	
Subscriptions and donations	7,000	
Impairment losses (trade)	500	
Salaries and wages	30,000	
Travel	8,000	
Depreciation	15,000	
Rent and rates	1,500	
		(151,811)
Net profit		101,977

Notes

(1)   *General expenses include the following.*

	£
Entertaining staff	1,000
Entertaining suppliers	600

(2)   *Repairs and renewals include the following.*

	£
Redecorating existing premises	300
Renovations to new premises to remedy wear and tear of previous owner (the premises were usable before these renovations)	500

(3)   *Legal and accountancy charges are made up as follows.*

	£
Debt collection service	200
Staff service agreements	50
Tax consultant's fees for special advice	30
45 year lease on new premises	100
Audit and accountancy	820
	1,200

(4)   *Subscriptions and donations include the following.*

	£
Donations under the gift aid scheme	5,200
Donation to a political party	500
Sports facilities for staff	600
Subscription to trade association	100

(5)   Travel expenses included A Trader's motoring expenses of £2,000. 25% of his use of his car was for private purposes.

(6)   Capital allowances amounted to £2,200.

Required

Compute A Trader's taxable trading profit for the accounting period to 31 March 2015. You should start with net profit figure of £101,977 and you should indicate by the use of zero (0) any items which do not require adjustment.   **(15 marks)**

19 Margaret Webster   11 mins

On 6 April 2014, Margaret Webster acquired a country house called The Cedars and immediately started a sole trader guest house business in it. Two-thirds of The Cedars was used by guests and one-third by Margaret. The following information is relevant for the year to 5 April 2015.

(i)   Revenue was £36,000 of which £500 was owed as receivables at 5 April 2015.

(ii)   Furniture for guest use was acquired for £2,500.

(iii)   Mortgage interest paid relating to the whole of The Cedars was £7,500.

(iv)   Gas and electricity bills relating to the whole of The Cedars amounted to £7,400. Cleaning and gardening costs, again relating to the whole of The Cedars, amounted to £1,800. Margaret also spent £2,000 on providing food eaten by her and the guests. There were no amounts outstanding at 5 April 2015. The fixed rate adjustment for private use of business premises for one occupant is £350 per month.

(v)   Margaret purchased a motor car on 6 April 2014. She drove 8,000 miles in the car during the year of which 2,000 miles were for journeys relating to the guest house business. The fixed rate mileage expense for motoring is 45p per mile for the first 10,000 miles, then 25p per mile after that.

(vi)   Other allowable expenses were £2,000 of which £900 was owed as payables at 5 April 2015.

Margaret will elect to use the cash basis for accounting for the tax year 2014/15 and will use fixed rate expenses where available.

Required

Calculate Margaret's taxable trading profit for the period of account ending 5 April 2015.   **(6 marks)**

20 Capital allowances   **11 mins**

20.1   Which of the following items COULD be plant which is eligible for capital allowances?

(1)   Refrigerator for coffee shop
(2)   Extension to office building
(3)   Decorative mirror in restaurant
(4)   Sound insulation in a recording studio
(5)   A bridge

A   1, 2 and 3
B   2, 3 and 4
C   1, 4 and 5
D   1, 3 and 4   **(2 marks)**

20.2   Julian is a sole trader who prepares accounts to 5 April each year. He acquired a car for both business and private purposes on 1 October 2014. The car has a CO_2 emission rate of 165 grams per kilometre and cost £21,000. The private mileage for Julian's period of account to 5 April 2015 was 25% of the total mileage for that year.

What is the maximum amount of capital allowances that Julian can claim in respect of the car for the year ended 5 April 2015?

A   £1,260
B   £3,780
C   £2,835
D   £1,680   **(2 marks)**

20.3   Olive started trading on 1 October 2014 and prepared her first set of accounts to 31 December 2014. On 10 October 2014 she acquired machinery at a cost of £135,000.

What is the maximum amount of capital allowances that Olive can claim for the period ended 31 December 2014?

A   £135,000
B   £126,800
C   £125,450
D   £125,000   **(2 marks)**

(Total = 6 marks)

21 Tom Hardy   **27 mins**

Tom Hardy prepares accounts to 30 June. Despite substantial investment in new equipment, business has been indifferent and he will cease trading on 31 December 2018. His last accounts will be prepared for the six months to 31 December 2018.

The tax written down values at 1 July 2014 were as follows.

	£
Main pool	33,500
Short life asset (acquired 1.5.13)	4,400

Additions and disposals have been as follows.

		£
20.9.14	Plant cost	27,000
15.7.15	Car for own use cost	13,400
14.7.17	Plant sold for	340
10.5.18	Short life asset sold for	2,900

Private use of the car was 20% for all years. The car emits CO_2 of 105g/km.

At the end of 2018, the plant will be worth £24,000 and the car £10,600.

Required

Calculate the capital allowances for the periods from 1 July 2014 to 31 December 2018, assuming the capital allowances rates for 2014/15 apply throughout. **(15 marks)**

22 Saruman

14 mins

Saruman is the sole proprietor of a small engineering business. He prepares accounts annually to 5 April and has been in business since 6 April 2007.

Main pool brought forward on 6 April 2014	£52,000
Tax written down value of motor car for Saruman's use on 6 April 2014	£6,000

Private use of this car is 25%.

The following events occurred during the year ended 5 April 2015.

Disposals: 20 April 2014 – Plant £12,000 (original cost £10,000)

21 May 2014 – Motor car for Saruman's own use £7,200 (less than original cost £8,923)

20 June 2014 – Plant £800 (original cost £3,000)

Additions: 21 May 2014 – New car for Saruman's own use £19,000 CO_2 emissions 150 g/km. Private use of this car is 25%.

1 October 2014 – Car for use by sales representative £4,800 CO_2 emissions 100g/km

Required

Calculate Saruman's capital allowances for the year ended 5 April 2015. **(8 marks)**

23 Assessable trading income

11 mins

23.1 Frank started trading on 1 January 2014. He prepared his first set of accounts for the 13-month period to 31 January 2015. His tax adjusted trading profit for this period was £19,500.

What are Frank's overlap profits?

A £1,500
B £3,250
C £4,500
D £3,000 **(2 marks)**

23.2 Fredericka stopped trading on 31 March 2015. Her tax adjusted profits for the last two periods of account were:

y/e 31.1.15   £10,000
p/e 31.3.15   £2,500

Fredericka had £1,000 of overlap profit when she started trading.

What is Fredericka's taxable trading income for the tax year 2014/15?

A   £12,500
B   £11,500
C   £9,833
D   £1,500   (2 marks)

23.3 Renee commenced trading on 1 January 2014. She prepared her first set of accounts for the 18 month period to 30 June 2015.

What is Renee's basis period for the tax year 2014/15?

A   1 July 2014 to 30 June 2015
B   6 April 2014 to 5 April 2015
C   1 January 2014 to 31 December 2014
D   1 January 2014 to 5 April 2014   (2 marks)

(Total = 6 marks)

24 Mr Cobbler   27 mins

Mr Cobbler starts a business as a sole trader on 1 January 2015.

His business plan shows that his monthly profits are likely to be as follows.

January 2015 to June 2015 (inclusive)   £800   a month
July 2015 to December 2015 (inclusive)   £1,200   a month
Thereafter   £2,000   a month

Mr Cobbler is considering two alternative accounting dates, 31 March and 30 April, in each case commencing with a period ending in 2015.

Required

Show the taxable trading profits which will arise for each of the first four tax years under each of the two alternative accounting dates, and recommend an accounting date.   (15 marks)

25 Miss Farrington   27 mins

Miss Farrington started to trade as a baker on 1 January 2015 and prepared her first accounts to 30 April 2016. Adjusted profits before capital allowances are as follows.

	£
Period to 30 April 2016	47,030
Year to 30 April 2017	24,787

Miss Farrington incurred the following expenditure on plant and machinery.

Date	Item	£
1.1.15	Desk and other office furniture	2,625
4.1.15	General plant	8,070
1.3.15	Second-hand oven	5,300
25.3.15	Delivery van	5,450
15.4.15	General plant	8,555
15.5.15	Car for Miss Farrington	6,600
30.1.17	General plant	10,000
30.4.17	Mixer	1,200

The private use of the car is 35%. The car has CO_2 emissions of 103g/km.

Required

Calculate the taxable profits for the first four tax years and the overlap profits carried forward. Assume that the capital allowances rates applicable in 2014/15 apply throughout. **(15 marks)**

26 Trading losses   11 mins

26.1   Which of the following statements about trading loss relief for an individual are FALSE?

(1)   A claim to set a trading loss against general income can be restricted so that the individual has enough net income to use the personal allowance.

(2)   A trading loss carried forward must be set against the first available profits of the same trade.

(3)   A trading loss carried forward can only be used in the following six tax years.

(4)   A trading loss claim for relief against general income must be made by 31 January 22 months after the end of the tax year of the loss.

A   3 and 4
B   2 and 4
C   1 and 2
D   1 and 3   **(2 marks)**

26.2   Shelly has been a sole trader for many years, preparing accounts to 31 January each year. In the year to 31 January 2014 she made a profit of £12,000 and in the year to 31 January 2015 she made a loss of £24,000. In 2013/14 she had property business income of £1,000. She has no other income in 2014/15.

How much of the loss of the tax year 2014/15 remains to carry forward to the tax year 2015/16 if Shelley makes a loss relief claim against general income for the tax year 2013/14?

A   £10,000
B   £11,000
C   £21,000
D   £12,000   **(2 marks)**

26.3 William has been a sole trader for many years, preparing accounts to 31 March each year. In the year to 31 March 2014, William made a profit of £15,000 and in the year to 31 March 2015 he made a loss of £180,000. William has property business income of £260,000 in the tax year 2013/14. He has no other income in 2014/15.

What is the amount of the loss that William can set against his general income for the tax year 2013/14?

A   £65,000
B   £50,000
C   £83,750
D   £68,750   **(2 marks)**

(Total = 6 marks)

27 Morgan   **18 mins**

Morgan started to trade on 6 April 2010. His business has the following results.

Year ending 5 April		£
2011	Profit	12,000
2012	Profit	16,000
2013	Profit	24,000
2014	Profit	15,000
2015	Loss	(38,000)

It is expected that the business will show healthy profits thereafter. In addition to his trading income, Morgan has gross investment income of £11,000 a year.

Required

(a)   Outline the ways in which Morgan could obtain relief for his loss.   **(5 marks)**

(b)   Prepare a statement showing how the loss would be relieved assuming that relief were to be claimed as soon as possible. Comment on whether this is likely to be the best relief.

(5 marks)

(Total = 10 marks)

28 Jacques   **9 mins**

Jacques has been carrying on a sole trade for a number of years, preparing accounts to 31 July each year. His recent results have been as follows.

Year ending 31 July		£
2013	Profit	5,000
2014	Loss	(120,000)

Jacques also has property business income of £84,000 in 2013/14 and £210,000 in 2014/15.

Jacques wishes to claim loss relief against general income first for the tax year 2014/15 and then for the tax year 2013/14.

Required

Compute Jacques' net income for the tax years 2013/14 and 2014/15 after loss relief.   **(5 marks)**

29 Partnerships and limited liability partnerships

11 mins

29.1 Jess and Kate have been in partnership for many years preparing accounts to 31 December each year. Laura joined the partnership on 1 January 2015. From this date, the profits were shared equally between the three partners. The partnership had a trading profit of £60,000 for the year ended 31 December 2015.

What is Laura's taxable trading income from the partnership for the tax year 2014/15?

A £15,000
B £5,000
C £20,000
D £10,000 **(2 marks)**

29.2 Quayle and Partridge have been in partnership for many years sharing profits equally and preparing accounts to 31 March each year. From 1 May 2014 the profits were divided 1 part to Quayle and 2 parts to Partridge. The partnership had a trading profit of £96,000 for the year ended 31 March 2015.

What is Quayle's taxable trading income from the partnership for the tax year 2014/15?

A £29,333
B £4,000
C £33,333
D £32,000 **(2 marks)**

29.3 Victor is a 50% partner in a partnership which prepares accounts to 5 April each year. In the year to 5 April 2015, the partnership makes a loss of £(180,000) and Victor has other income of £60,000 in 2014/15.

What is the amount of loss relief that Victor can claim against general income in 2014/15?

A £15,000
B £50,000
C £60,000
D £90,000 **(2 marks)**

(Total = 6 marks)

30 Anne, Betty and Chloe

16 mins

(a) *Required*

Briefly explain the basis by which partners are assessed in respect of their share of a partnership's taxable trading profit. **(3 marks)**

(b) Anne and Betty have been in partnership since 1 January 2008 sharing profits equally. On 30 June 2014 Betty resigned as a partner, and was replaced on 1 July 2014 by Chloe. Profit continued to be shared equally. The partnership's taxable trading profits are as follows:

	£
Year ended 31 December 2014	60,000
Year ended 31 December 2015	72,000

As at 6 April 2014 Anne and Betty each have unrelieved overlap profits of £3,000.

Required

Calculate the taxable trading profits of Anne, Betty and Chloe for 2014/15. **(6 marks)**

(Total = 9 marks)

31 Daniel, Edward and Frank

11 mins

Daniel and Edward have been in partnership since 6 April 2006, making up accounts to 5 April. On 31 December 2014 Edward resigned as a partner, and was replaced on 1 January 2015 by Frank. For the year ended 5 April 2015 the partnership made a trading loss of £40,000. This was allocated between the partners as follows.

	£
Daniel	20,000
Edward	15,000
Frank	5,000

Each of the partners has investment income. None of them have any capital gains.

Required

State the possible ways in which Daniel, Edward and Frank can relieve their trading losses for 2014/15.

(6 marks)

32 National insurance contributions

11 mins

32.1 Natalie is a sole trader and has taxable trading profits of £41,000 for her period of account ended 31 August 2014.

What is the TOTAL amount of national insurance contributions (NIC) that Natalie has to pay for the tax year 2014/15?

- A £2,974
- B £3,195
- C £3,117
- D £3,833

(2 marks)

32.2 Nigel is an employee earning £36,000 a year, payable in equal monthly amounts. In February 2015 he received a bonus of £8,000.

What are Nigel's class 1 (primary) national insurance contributions (NIC) in respect of February 2015?

- A £1,240
- B £489
- C £343
- D £339

(2 marks)

32.3 Gina was paid an annual salary of £45,000 during 2014/15. In addition, her employer provided her with a computer for private use for which the taxable benefit is £300.

What are the national insurance contributions (NIC) liabilities?

- A Class 1 primary and secondary contributions on £45,000

- B Class 1 primary contributions on £45,000, Class 1 secondary contributions on £45,300

- C Class 1 primary contributions on £45,300, Class 1 secondary contributions on £45,000, Class 1A contributions on £300

- D Class 1 primary contributions on £45,000, Class 1 secondary contributions on £45,000, Class 1A contributions on £300

(2 marks)

(Total = 6 marks)

33 Derek and Denise
16 mins

(a) Derek is the sole employee of Rose Ltd. In 2014/15, Derek was paid a salary of £55,000 and had taxable benefits amounting to £3,000.

Required

    (i) Compute the primary Class 1 national insurance contributions payable by Derek for 2014/15. **(2 marks)**

    (ii) Compute the secondary Class 1 national insurance contributions payable by Rose Ltd for 2014/15. **(2 marks)**

    (iii) Compute the Class 1A national insurance contributions payable by Rose Ltd for 2014/15. **(2 marks)**

(b) Denise started business on 6 April 2014 as a designer dressmaker. Her trading profits in her first year of trading were £45,000.

Required

Show the Class 2 and Class 4 contributions payable by Denise in 2014/15. **(3 marks)**

(Total = 9 marks)

34 Sasha Shah
27 mins

Sasha Shah is a computer programmer. Until 5 April 2014 she was employed by Net Computers plc, but since then has worked independently from home. Sasha's income for the year ended 5 April 2015 is £60,000. All of this relates to work done for Net Computers plc. Her expenditure for the year ended 5 April 2015 is as follows:

(1) The business proportion of light, heat and telephone for Sasha's home is £880.

(2) Computer equipment was purchased on 6 April 2014 for £4,000.

(3) A motor car was purchased on 6 April 2014 for £10,000 with CO_2 of 115g/km. Motor expenses for the year ended 5 April 2015 amount to £3,500, of which 40% relate to journeys between home and the premises of Net Computers plc. The other 60% relate to private mileage.

Required

(a) List eight factors that will indicate that a worker should be treated as an employee rather than as self-employed. **(4 marks)**

(b) (i) Calculate the amount of taxable trading profits if Sasha is treated as self-employed during 2014/15.

    (ii) Calculate the amount of Sasha's taxable earnings if she is treated as an employee during 2014/15. **(7 marks)**

(c) (i) Calculate Sasha's liability to Class 2 and Class 4 NIC if she is treated as self-employed during 2014/15.

    (ii) Calculate Sasha's liability to Class 1 NIC if she is treated as an employee during 2014/15. **(4 marks)**

(Total = 15 marks)

35 Computing chargeable gains

11 mins

35.1 Which of the following assets will ALWAYS be exempt from capital gains tax?

(1) A qualifying corporate bond (QCB)
(2) Investments held in new individual savings accounts (NISAs)
(3) A plot of land
(4) A decoration for bravery

A   1 and 2
B   2 and 3
C   2 and 4
D   1 and 4

(2 marks)

35.2 Joe has chargeable gains of £16,400 and allowable capital losses of £3,000 in the tax year 2014/15. He also has allowable capital losses of £4,000 brought forward from the tax year 2013/14.

What is the correct use of these amounts for the tax year 2014/15?

A   £16,400 – £3,000 (current year loss) – £4,000 (brought forward loss) = £9,400
B   £16,400 – £3,000 (current year loss) – £2,400 (brought forward loss) = £11,000
C   £16,400 – £4,000 (brought forward loss) – £1,400 (current year loss) = £11,000
D   £16,400 – £3,000 (current year loss) = £13,400

(2 marks)

35.3 Melanie purchased a ten-acre plot of land for £80,000. In January 2015, she sold three of the acres for £36,000 with expenses of sale amounting to £1,000. The market value of the remaining seven acres of land in January 2015 was £90,000.

What is Melanie's chargeable gain on the disposal of the three acres of land in the tax year 2014/15?

A   £12,600
B   £13,600
C   £13,143
D   £12,143

(2 marks)

(Total = 6 marks)

36 Peter Robinson

18 mins

Peter Robinson made the following disposals of assets during the tax year 2014/15.

30 June 2014

Investment property for £150,000 less costs of disposal £1,280. Acquired for £79,000.

27 July 2014

Part of a plot of land. The proceeds of sale were £35,000. The costs of disposal were £700. The original cost of the land was £54,000. The remainder of the land is worth £70,000.

1 September 2014

A vase which was destroyed. It cost £12,000. Compensation of £20,000 was received on 30 September 2014. Peter bought a new vase as a replacement for £17,000 on 21 December 2014.

Peter had taxable income of £27,465 in 2014/15.

Required

Calculate Peter's capital gains tax payable for the year 2014/15.

(10 marks)

37 Chattels and the principal private residence exemption

11 mins

37.1 Edward purchased a 20th century painting for £1,500, incurring purchase costs of £75. In October 2014 he sold the painting for £7,000, incurring disposal costs of £350.

What is Edward's chargeable gain in the tax year 2014/15?

- A £1,667
- B £5,500
- C £5,075
- D £1,083

(2 marks)

37.2 Belinda purchased a ruby necklace for £7,500, incurring purchase costs of £400. In January 2015 she sold the necklace for £4,000, incurring disposal costs of £200.

What is Belinda's allowable loss in the tax year 2014/15?

- A £1,500
- B £1,900
- C £2,100
- D £4,100

(2 marks)

37.3 Roger purchased a house on 1 January 1991 and lived in it until 31 December 2002. On 1 January 2003 Roger went to live with his parents and the house was unoccupied for six years. Roger then lived in the house from 1 January 2009 until it was sold on 31 December 2014.

How many years of Roger's period of ownership of the house will be chargeable to capital gains tax?

- A Three years
- B Six years
- C 21 years
- D 10.5 years

(2 marks)

(Total = 6 marks)

38 John and Elsie

18 mins

(a) John purchased a property in England on 1 August 1992 for £40,000 and lived in it until 30 November 1994 when he moved overseas to take up an offer of employment. He returned to the UK on 1 February 1999 and took employment in Scotland until 30 April 2005. During these periods he lived in rented accommodation. On 1 May 2005 he moved back into his own house until he moved out permanently on 31 December 2011. The house was then put up for sale and was finally sold on 30 November 2014 for £120,000. At all times when John was not in the house it remained empty.

Required

Prepare a schedule of periods of exemption and non-exemption, together with the reasons where applicable.

(6 marks)

(b)   Elsie made the following disposals of assets during the tax year 2014/15.

July 2014

An oil painting for £5,000 (net of £400 commission). She had purchased this at a cost of £11,500.

February 2015

A crystal chandelier for £7,500. She had purchased this for £4,000.

Required

Calculate Elsie's chargeable gains or allowable losses on these two transactions.   **(4 marks)**

(Total = 10 marks)

39 Business reliefs   11 mins

39.1   Jane has two chargeable gains in the tax year 2014/15:

£10,000 – claim made for entrepreneurs' relief
£12,900 – no claim made for entrepreneurs' relief

She has taxable income of £13,000 in the tax year 2014/15.

What is Jane's capital gains tax liability for the tax year 2014/15?

A   £3,322
B   £1,532
C   £1,342
D   £2,142   **(2 marks)**

39.2   Norman is a sole trader. He sold Shop A in July 2014 for £80,000, realising a chargeable gain of £25,000. Norman used the proceeds to buy a Shop B for £70,000 and used the remainder as working capital.

What is the cost of Shop B for capital gains tax purposes if Norman makes a claim for replacement of business assets (rollover) relief?

A   £60,000
B   £65,000
C   £45,000
D   £55,000   **(2 marks)**

39.3   On which of the following gifts can a claim be made for gift relief?

(1)   10% shareholding in an unlisted investment company
(2)   Factory owned by an individual and used in the trade of that individual's personal company
(3)   Premises owned by a sole trader of which two thirds are used for trade purposes and one third is used for private purposes
(4)   2% shareholding in a trading company listed on the London Stock Exchange

A   1 and 2
B   2 and 3
C   2 and 4
D   1 and 4   **(2 marks)**

(Total = 6 marks)

40 Roy and Gary
14 mins

Roy was a sole trader for many years. He had bought a factory for use in his trade on 10 July 2008 for £150,000.

On 1 December 2014, Roy gave his sole trader business as a going concern to his son, Gary. The market value of the factory at that time was £260,000.

Due to restructuring of the business, Gary let out the factory to an unconnected company from 1 December 2014. He sold the factory to a developer on 1 March 2015 for £320,000.

The factory is the only chargeable asset owned by either Roy or Gary. Both Roy and Gary are higher rate taxpayers.

Required

(a) Calculate the capital gains tax payable by Roy and by Gary for 2014/15 if a claim is made for gift relief on the factory. **(3 marks)**

(b) Calculate the capital gains tax payable by Roy and by Gary for 2014/15 if no claim is made for gift relief on the factory. **(3 marks)**

In parts (a) and (b), you should assume that any other available reliefs are claimed.

(c) From your calculations in parts (a) and (b), explain why Roy and Gary should not make a claim for gift relief on the factory. **(2 marks)**

(Total = 8 marks)

41 Sharon
13 mins

Sharon is a sole trader. She acquired a freehold shop for use in the business in May 2006 for £40,000 and sold it in August 2014 for £80,000.

Sharon is considering buying a new shop. She has located two possible shops. One is a small freehold shop which would cost £72,000. The other is a larger leasehold shop with a lease of 55 years. The cost of the lease would be £90,000.

Required

Explain the tax consequences of acquiring each of the shops. **(7 marks)**

42 Kai
18 mins

Kai started in business as a sole trader in August 2008. He acquired a freehold shop for £80,000 and a warehouse for £150,000.

Kai sold his business as a going concern to Jibran in December 2014 and received £50,000 for goodwill, £90,000 for the shop and £180,000 for the warehouse. Kai also sold a plot of land to Jibran which he had not used in his business. The land cost £10,000 and Jibran paid £25,800 for it.

Other than those listed above, Kai had never undertaken any transactions which were relevant for capital gains tax purposes.

Kai's taxable income in 2014/15 was £20,000.

Required

Compute the capital gains tax payable by Kai for 2014/15, assuming that he makes any beneficial claims. State the date by which any claim must be made. **(10 marks)**

43 Shares and securities

43.1 On 14 March 2015, Caroline gave her daughter 10,000 shares in A plc. On that date the shares were quoted at £2.20 – £2.22 and there were marked bargains of £2.12, £2.18, £2.20 and £2.22.

What is the value of gift for capital gains tax purposes?

A £21,700
B £21,800
C £22,050
D £22,000   **(2 marks)**

43.2 Billy bought 1,000 shares in B plc on 10 March 2010. He purchased a further 500 B plc shares on 31 July 2014 and 250 B plc shares on 10 August 2014. Bill sold 800 B plc shares on 31 July 2014.

How are the 800 B plc shares sold on 31 July 2014 matched?

A Against 250 of the shares acquired on 10 August 2014 and then against 550 of the shares acquired on 10 March 2010
B Against 500 of the shares acquired on 31 July 2014 and then against 300 of the shares acquired on 10 March 2010
C Against 500 of the shares acquired on 31 July 2014, then against 250 of the shares acquired on 10 August 2014 and then against 50 of the shares acquired on 10 March 2010
D Against 800 of the shares acquired on 10 March 2010   **(2 marks)**

43.3 Which of the following statements about shares and securities owned by an individual are FALSE?

(1) A disposal of government securities ('gilts') by an individual is chargeable to capital gains tax.

(2) If a company makes a 2 for 1 bonus issue, each shareholder will receive 1 extra share for each 2 shares held without payment.

(3) In a rights issue the rights issue shares are paid for by the shareholder resulting in an adjustment to the cost of the shareholding.

(4) A chargeable gain does not usually arise on a takeover where new shares are exchanged for old shares.

A 2 and 4
B 1 and 2
C 1 and 3
D 3 and 4   **(2 marks)**

(Total = 6 marks)

44 Melissa

Melissa bought shares in Fisher plc as follows:

12 July 2002	3,000 shares for £21,000
17 January 2005	Bonus issue 1 share for each 1 share held
14 December 2007	Rights issue 1 share for each 3 shares held at £3.25 per share
11 July 2014	4,000 shares for £16,000

She sold 10,000 shares for £42,000 on 2 July 2014.

Required

Compute Melissa's gain on sale.   **(10 marks)**

45 Self assessment and payment of tax for individuals

11 mins

45.1 Steven and Rita wish to file their personal tax returns for 2014/15 electronically. The notice to file by HM Revenue and Customs (HMRC) to Steven was issued on 31 May 2015. The notice to file by HMRC to Rita was issued on 30 November 2015.

What is the latest filing date for each of Steven and Rita?

	Steven	Rita
A	31 October 2015	28 February 2016
B	31 August 2015	31 January 2016
C	31 January 2016	28 February 2016
D	31 January 2016	31 January 2016

(2 marks)

45.2 Tony is self-employed and his trading income is his only source of income, His income tax liabilities and Class 4 national insurance contributions (NIC) for 2013/14 and 2014/15 are as follows:

	2013/14	2014/15
	£	£
Income tax	10,000	12,500
Class 4 NIC	2,000	2,500
	12,000	15,000

How will Tony pay his income tax and Class 4 NIC for the tax year 2014/15?

A £15,000 on 31 January 2016
B £7,500 on 31 January and 31 July 2015
C £5,000 on 31 January 2015, 31 July 2015 and 31 January 2016
D £6,000 on 31 January and 31 July 2015, £3,000 on 31 January 2016

(2 marks)

45.3 Pepe has a trading loss of £80,000 for the tax year 2014/15. Due to carelessness he enters £88,000 on his tax return and makes a loss relief claim for £88,000 against his property business income for the tax year 2014/15. The property business income would otherwise have been taxed at 40%.

What is the MAXIMUM penalty that could be charged by HM Revenue and Customs (HMRC) in respect of the error?

A £3,200
B £960
C £2,240
D £640

(2 marks)

(Total = 6 marks)

46 Ash   18 mins

Ash is employed and also has a bank deposit account and owns some shares. On 5 May 2015, HM Revenue and Customs issued a notice to Ash to file his tax return for 2014/15.

Ash's total tax liability for 2013/14 was £16,800. Of this £7,200 was paid under the PAYE system, £800 was withheld at source from bank interest and £200 was suffered on dividends received during the year.

Ash's total tax liability for 2014/15 was £22,000. £7,100 of this was paid under PAYE system, £900 was withheld at source from bank interest and there was a £250 tax credit on dividends.

Ash did not make any claim in respect of his payments on account for 2014/15.

On 31 March 2016, Ash filed his tax return for 2014/15. The late filing was due to Ash's carelessness and was not deliberate.

On 30 April 2016, Ash paid the balancing payment for 2014/15.

Required

(a)   State:

    (i)   The payments Ash was required to make in respect of his 2014/15 tax liability.   **(6 marks)**
    (ii)   The due dates for the payment of the amounts in part (i).   **(2 marks)**

(b)   Compute:

    (i)   The penalty for late filing of Ash's tax return for 2014/15.   **(1 mark)**
    (ii)   The penalty for late payment of the balancing payment for 2014/15.   **(1 mark)**

(Total = 10 marks)

47 Inheritance tax: scope and transfers of value

11 mins

47.1   Bernard made a gross chargeable lifetime transfer of £260,000 in August 2010. In November 2014, he gave £420,000 to a trust for the benefit of his son and daughter. Bernard agreed to pay any lifetime IHT due.

How much inheritance tax will be payable by Bernard on transfer of value in November 2014?

    A   £87,250
    B   £69,800
    C   £88,750
    D   £22,500   **(2 marks)**

47.2   Andy and Hilda had been married for many years when Andy died in June 2007. 60% of Andy's nil rate band was unused on his death. The nil rate band at Andy's death was £300,000. Hilda died in December 2014. Her only lifetime transfers of value were cash gifts of £6,000 to her nephew in January 2014 and £10,000 to her niece in March 2014.

What is the maximum nil rate band available for use against Hilda's death estate?

    A   £504,000
    B   £520,000
    C   £510,000
    D   £495,000   **(2 marks)**

47.3 On 15 July 2014 Yvette gave £500,000 to a trust for the benefit of her grandchildren. Yvette died on 27 December 2014.

What are the due dates for inheritance tax to be paid on this transfer of value?

	Lifetime tax	Death tax
A	31 January 2015	30 April 2015
B	30 April 2015	30 June 2015
C	14 January 2015	26 June 2015
D	31 January 2015	30 June 2015

(2 marks)

(Total = 6 marks)

48 Colin   18 mins

Colin died on 20 December 2014. During his lifetime, he used his annual exemption in April each year and also made the following gifts.

Date	Gift	Recipient
21.1.08	Cash of £315,000	Trustees (Colin paid the IHT)
20.8.09	Shares worth £15,000 (value at 20.12.14 £75,000)	Daughter
19.6.10	Shares worth £88,000 (value at 20.12.14 £120,000)	Trustees (Trustees paid the IHT)

Required

(a) Explain the inheritance tax implications of these gifts during Colin's lifetime, computing any inheritance tax due. State the due dates for payment of the tax. **(6 marks)**

Nil rate bands for previous years

2007/08	£300,000
2009/10	£325,000
2010/11	£325,000

(b) Explain the inheritance tax position on these gifts as a result of Colin's death, computing any inheritance tax due. State the due dates for payment of the tax. **(4 marks)**

(Total = 10 marks)

49 Simona   18 mins

Simona died on 19 January 2015, leaving the following assets:

	£
Shares in MS plc	320,000
Life assurance policy	see note
House	175,000
Household furniture	20,000
Cash in bank	97,750
Car	5,000

Simona also had the following debts at her death:

	£
Bank loan secured on house	10,000
Credit card bills	7,000
Income tax	3,000
Gas bill	250

Note

The value of the insurance policy immediately before Simona's death was £60,000. The proceeds payable as a result of Simona's death were £250,000.

The personal representative of Simona's estate paid funeral expenses of £2,500.

Simona had not made any lifetime gifts.

Simona was widowed in September 2007. Her husband left £20,000 to his sister and the rest of his estate to Simona. He had not made any lifetime gifts. The nil rate band for 2007/08 was £300,000. Simona remarried in April 2010.

In her will, Simona left her house to her second husband and the remainder of her estate to her children.

Required

(a) Compute Simona's chargeable death estate. **(6 marks)**

(b) Explain and compute the amount of the nil rate band available to be set against Simona's death estate, assuming any elections available are made. **(3 marks)**

(c) Using your answer to part (b), compute the inheritance tax payable on Simona's death estate. **(1 mark)**

(Total = 10 marks)

50 Computing taxable total profits   11 mins

50.1   H Ltd started trading on 1 December 2013 and prepared its first set of accounts to 31 March 2015.

What are H Ltd's accounting period(s) for the period of account to 31 March 2015?

A   1 December 2013 to 31 March 2014 and 1 April 2014 to 31 March 2015
B   1 December 2013 to 5 April 2014 and 6 April 2014 to 31 March 2015
C   1 December 2013 to 30 November 2014 and 1 December 2014 to 31 March 2015
D   1 December 2013 to 31 March 2015 **(2 marks)**

50.2   L Ltd is a trading company which prepares accounts to 31 March each year. In its statement of profit or loss for the year to 31 March 2015, it has included a deduction of £3,200 in respect of the annual leasing cost for a car. The car has a recommended list price of £16,000 and CO_2 emissions of 140g/km.

What is the allowable expense in respect of the leasing cost for the accounting period ended 31 March 2015?

A   £2,720
B   £480
C   £3,360
D   £3,200 **(2 marks)**

50.3   Z Ltd is a trading company which prepared accounts to 30 June 2014. In addition to its trading activities, Z Ltd lets out an unfurnished house for an annual rent of £14,400 payable in monthly instalments. The tenant is due to pay each instalment in arrears on the last day of each month but did not pay the June 2014 instalment until 14 July 2014. There was interest of £7,500 accrued during the year to 30 June 2014 on a mortgage taken out by Z Ltd to acquire the house.

How much must Z Ltd include in its taxable total profits as its property business income for the accounting period ended 30 June 2014?

A   £13,200
B   £6,900
C   £12,960
D   £14,400 **(2 marks)**

(Total = 6 marks)

51 Elderflower Ltd

27 mins

Elderflower Ltd is a company which trades as a manufacturer of specialist soft drinks. The company's statement of profit or loss for the year ended 31 March 2015 is as follows:

	£	£
Gross profit		510,000
Other income		
Profit on disposal of office building (note 1)		54,000
Bank interest (note 2)		7,000
Expenses		
Depreciation	54,690	
Professional fees (note 3)	22,000	
Repairs and renewals (note 4)	29,700	
Other expenses (note 5)	24,400	
		(130,790)
Finance costs		
Interest payable (note 6)		(23,000)
Profit before taxation		417,210

Notes

(1)   *Disposal of office building*

The profit of £54,000 is in respect of a freehold office building that was sold on 30 June 2014 for £380,000. The chargeable gain on sale has been computed to be £45,580.

(2)   *Bank interest received*

The bank interest was received on 31 March 2015 and is the amount accrued to that date. The bank deposit is held for non-trading purposes.

(3)   *Professional fees*

Professional fees are as follows:

	£
Accountancy and audit fee	4,600
Legal fees in connection with the issue of share capital	8,800
Legal fees in connection with the issue of loan notes (see note 6)	6,400
Legal fees in connection with breach of contract by supplier	1,300
Legal fees in connection with fine for breach of health and safety legislation	900
	22,000

(4)   *Repairs and renewals*

The figure of £29,700 for repairs includes £9,700 for constructing an extension to the company's manufacturing premises and £5,400 for repainting the interior of the company's offices.

(5)   *Other expenses*

Other expenses include £2,310 for entertaining customers, £1,600 for entertaining employees and a qualifying charitable donation of £500.

(6)   *Interest payable*

Elderflower Ltd issued loan notes on 1 October 2014. The capital raised was used for trading purposes. Interest of £23,000 in respect of the first six months of the loan was paid on 31 March 2015.

(7)   *Plant and machinery*

On 1 April 2014 the tax written down values of plant and machinery were as follows:

	£
Main pool	27,500
Special rate pool (consisting of car with CO_2 emissions of 176g/km)	14,700

The following transactions took place during the year ended 31 March 2015:

		Cost/(Proceeds) £
10 May 2014	Purchased plant	20,200
5 January 2015	Sold the special rate pool motor car	(9,700)
20 March 2015	Sold a delivery van	(11,600)
31 March 2015	Purchased a motor car CO_2 emissions 107g/km	9,600

The van sold on 20 March 2015 for £11,600 originally cost £18,500. The motor car purchased on 31 March 2015 is used by the sales manager: 25% of the mileage is for private journeys.

Required

(a)   Calculate Elderflower Ltd's trading profit for the year ended 31 March 2015. Your answer should commence with the profit before taxation figure of £417,210 and should list all of the items in the statement of profit or loss indicating by the use of a zero (0) any items that do not require adjustment. You should assume that the company claims the maximum available capital allowances.

(13 marks)

(b)   Calculate Elderflower Ltd's taxable total profits for the year ended 31 March 2015.   **(2 marks)**

(Total = 15 marks)

52 Computing the corporation tax liability   11 mins

52.1   A Ltd has one 100% owned subsidiary, B Ltd. In addition A Ltd holds 40% of the shares in another company, C Ltd. Dividends of £9,000 are received from B Ltd and £4,500 from C Ltd.

How much is included as franked investment income (FII) in A Ltd's augmented profits?

A   £15,000
B   £9,000
C   £5,000
D   £4,500   **(2 marks)**

52.2   In the year ended 31 March 2015 P Ltd had taxable total profits of £280,000. The company had five companies associated with it.

What is P Ltd's corporation tax liability for the year ended 31 March 2015?

A   £56,000
B   £59,500
C   £58,750
D   £58,800   **(2 marks)**

52.3   G Ltd had taxable total profits for the year to 31 March 2015 of £590,000. It has no associated companies.

What is the amount of corporation tax payable by G Ltd for the year ended 31 March 2015?

A   £118,000
B   £121,625
C   £123,900
D   £125,375   **(2 marks)**

(Total = 6 marks)

53 Tree Ltd and Branch Ltd

18 mins

(a) Tree Ltd, a company with no associated companies, had the following results for the twelve months to 31 March 2015:

	£
Trading profits	180,000
Chargeable gain	105,000
Qualifying charitable donation paid	27,000
Bank interest received	36,000
Dividend received	29,700

The bank interest accrued evenly over the period.

Required

Compute the corporation tax liability for the year ended 31 March 2015. **(7 marks)**

(b) Branch Ltd, a company with no associated companies, had taxable total profits of £420,000 for its six month accounting period ended 31 March 2015. No dividends were received by the company during the year.

Required

Compute Branch Ltd's corporation tax liability for the period. **(3 marks)**

(Total = 10 marks)

54 Righteous plc

18 mins

Righteous plc used to make its accounts up to 31 December. A decision has been made to change its year end to 31 May. The following information relates to the period of account from 1 January 2013 to 31 May 2014.

	£
Trading profits	500,000
Bank interest accrued and received	
30.6.13	15,000
31.12.13	6,000
31.5.14	2,500
Capital gain on property sold on	
1.5.14	5,000
Qualifying charitable donations paid	
28.2.13	15,000
31.8.13	15,000
28.2.14	40,000

No capital allowances are claimed.

Required

Calculate the corporation tax liability. **(10 marks)**

55 Chargeable gains for companies

11 mins

55.1 U Ltd acquires an asset in April 2010 for £12,000, incurring costs of acquisition of £800. It spends £5,000 enhancing the asset in May 2011. U Ltd sells the asset in August 2014, incurring costs of disposal of £1,000.

How is the indexation allowance calculated on the disposal?

A   From April 2010 to August 2014 on £12,000 and from May 2011 to August 2014 on £5,000
B   From April 2010 to August 2014 on £17,800
C   From April 2010 to August 2014 on £12,800 and from May 2011 to August 2014 on £5,000
D   From April 2010 to August 2014 on £13,800 and from May 2011 to August 2014 on £5,000

(2 marks)

55.2 D Ltd sold a factory for £640,000 on 15 March 2015. It had paid £120,000 for the factory on 12 January 2010. D Ltd incurred expenses of £8,000 in buying the factory and £6,000 in selling the factory. The assumed indexation factor for the period January 2010 to March 2015 is 0.204.

What is D Ltd's chargeable gain on the disposal?

A   £478,664
B   £479,888
C   £481,520
D   £506,000

(2 marks)

55.3 F Ltd sells a factory for £200,000. The factory cost £110,000 and the indexation allowance available is £20,000. The company acquires another factory 15 months later for £187,500.

What is the amount of rollover relief which F Ltd can claim?

A   £12,500
B   £70,000
C   £77,500
D   £57,500

(2 marks)

(Total = 6 marks)

56 Long Ltd

18 mins

On 28 October 2014, Long Ltd sold its entire holding of £1 ordinary shares in Wide plc for £110,000.

Long Ltd purchased 5,000 shares in Deep plc on 10 June 2002 for £14,000. On 15 May 2008, Deep plc made a 1 for 1 rights issue at £4 per share. Long Ltd took up its full entitlement to rights issue shares.

On 7 March 2014 Deep plc was taken over by Wide plc. Long Ltd received two £1 ordinary shares and one £1 preference share in Wide plc for each £1 ordinary share held in Deep plc. Immediately after the takeover each £1 ordinary share in Wide plc was quoted at £5 and each £1 preference share was quoted at £2.50.

Required

Calculate the chargeable gain arising from Long Ltd's disposal of its shares in Wide plc.

(10 marks)

RPIs (actual and assumed)

June 2002 = 176.2   March 2014 = 255.4
May 2008 = 215.1   October 2014 = 258.7

57 Xeon Ltd

18 mins

Xeon Ltd made the following disposals in the year ended 31 March 2015.

(a)   On 31 May 2014, Xeon Ltd sold a warehouse used in its trade for £120,000. The company had bought the warehouse for £65,000 on 1 July 2003. Xeon Ltd had bought another warehouse for use in its trade for £100,000 on 1 July 2013.

(b)   On 18 June 2014, Xeon Ltd sold two acres of land for £30,000. These two acres were part of a five acre plot of land which was purchased for £21,000 on 1 April 2000. The remaining three acres were valued at £40,000 in June 2014. Xeon Ltd spent £1,000 in December 2012 on improving the two acres of land sold in June 2014.

Xeon Ltd made any beneficial claims in respect of these gains.

Required

Compute Xeon Ltd's chargeable gains for the year ended 31 March 2015 and show the cost for chargeable gains purposes of the warehouse bought on 1 July 2013. **(10 marks)**

RPIs (actual and assumed)

April 2000 = 170.1   May 2014 = 256.8
July 2003 = 181.3   June 2014 = 256.4
December 2012 = 246.8

58 Losses

11 mins

58.1   Which of the following statements about loss reliefs for a company are TRUE?

(1)   Property business losses of a company cannot be set against total profits of the same accounting period

(2)   Trade losses of a company carried forward can only be used against profits of the same trade

(3)   Trade loss relief may be given by deduction from current period total profits and those in the previous 12 months

(4)   Capital losses made by a company can be used against chargeable gains of the previous accounting period

A   1 and 2
B   2 and 3
C   1 and 4
D   2 and 4   **(2 marks)**

58.2   E plc prepares accounts to 31 December each year. In the year ended 31 December 2013 E plc had total profits of £36,000 and it made a qualifying charitable donation of £1,000. In the year ended 31 December 2014 E plc made an adjusted trading loss of £40,000, had other taxable income of £10,000 and made a qualifying charitable donation of £3,000.

What is the loss that E plc can claim to carry back to the year ended 31 December 2013?

A   £30,000
B   £33,000
C   £36,000
D   £35,000   **(2 marks)**

58.3   The following information relates to T plc for the year ended 31 March 2015:

	£
Trading income	165,000
Income from non-trading loan relationships	27,000
Chargeable gain	14,000
Trading loss b/f at 1 April 2014	(170,000)
Capital loss b/f at 1 April 2014	(3,000)

What are T plc's taxable total profits for the year ended 31 March 2015?

A   £33,000
B   £27,000
C   £41,000
D   £38,000

(2 marks)

(Total = 6 marks)

59 Ferraro Ltd   18 mins

Ferraro Ltd has the following results.

	y/e 31.3.13 £	9m to 31.12.13 £	y/e 31.12.14 £
Trading profit (loss)	6,200	4,320	(100,000)
Bank deposit interest accrued	80	240	260
Rents receivable	1,420	1,440	1,600
Chargeable gain	0	7,680	0
Qualifying charitable donations	0	1,000	1,500

Required

Compute all taxable total profits, claiming loss reliefs as early as possible. State the amounts of any losses carried forward as at 31 December 2014.   (10 marks)

60 Groups   11 mins

60.1   C Ltd had the following results for the year ended 31 March 2015:

	£
Trading income	(16,000)
Income from non-trading loan relationships	1,000
Capital loss	(5,000)

C Ltd paid a qualifying charitable donation of £4,000 on 2 February 2015.

What is the maximum amount that C Ltd can surrender for group relief?

A   £16,000
B   £20,000
C   £19,000
D   £21,000

(2 marks)

60.2 O Ltd owns 100% of P Ltd. In the year to 31 December 2014 O Ltd made a trading loss of £60,000. P Ltd had taxable total profits of £54,000 for the year to 31 March 2015.

What group relief can P Ltd claim from O Ltd which can be set against its taxable total profits for the year to 31 March 2015?

A   £40,500
B   £54,000
C   £45,000
D   £60,000   (2 marks)

60.3 A Ltd group has the following structure:

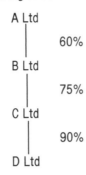

A Ltd

60%

B Ltd

75%

C Ltd

90%

D Ltd

Which ONE of the following is a chargeable gains group?

A   A Ltd, B Ltd and C Ltd

B   B Ltd and C Ltd

C   B Ltd, C Ltd and D Ltd

D   C Ltd and D Ltd   (2 marks)

(Total = 6 marks)

61 P Ltd   18 mins

P Ltd owns the following holdings in ordinary shares in other companies.

Q Ltd   83%
R Ltd   77%
S Ltd   67%
M Ltd   80%
T Ltd   70%

In each case, the conditions for claiming group relief, where appropriate, are satisfied.

The following are the results of the above companies for the year ended 31 March 2015.

	M Ltd	P Ltd	Q Ltd	R Ltd	S Ltd	T Ltd
	£	£	£	£	£	£
Trading profit	20,000	0	64,000	260,000	0	70,000
Trading loss	0	226,000	0	0	8,000	0
Property business income	0	6,000	4,000	0	0	0
Qualifying charitable donation paid	4,000	4,500	2,000	5,000	0	0

P Ltd and S Ltd are not expected to become profitable for several years.

Required

Compute the corporation tax payable for the above accounting period by each of the above companies. Assume that group relief is claimed where appropriate and in the most tax efficient manner.

(10 marks)

62 Apple Ltd

27 mins

Apple Ltd owns 100% of the ordinary share capital of Banana Ltd and Cherry Ltd. The results of each company for the year ended 31 March 2015 are as follows:

	Apple Ltd £	Banana Ltd £	Cherry Ltd £
Tax adjusted trading profit/(loss)	(125,000)	650,000	130,000
Capital gain/(loss)	188,000	(8,000)	0

Apple Ltd's capital gain arose from the sale of a freehold warehouse on 15 April 2014 for £418,000. Cherry Ltd purchased a freehold office building for £290,000 on 10 January 2015.

Required

(a) Explain the group relationship that must exist in order that group relief can be claimed. **(3 marks)**

(b) Explain how losses should be relieved (including by group relief) in order to maximise the potential benefit obtained. **(4 marks)**

(c) Assuming that reliefs are claimed in the most favourable manner, calculate the corporation tax liabilities of Apple Ltd, Banana Ltd and Cherry Ltd for the year ended 31 March 2015. **(8 marks)**

(Total = 15 marks)

63 Self assessment and payment of tax by companies

11 mins

63.1 N Ltd pays tax at the small profits rate and prepares accounts to 31 December every year.

What are the dates by which N Ltd must file its tax return and pay its corporation tax for the accounting period ended 31 December 2014 to avoid penalties and interest?

	Return date	Tax payable date
A	31 January 2016	31 January 2016
B	31 December 2015	1 October 2015
C	31 January 2016	30 September 2015
D	31 December 2015	31 January 2016

(2 marks)

63.2 Q plc has a 15-month period of account ending 31 March 2015.

What is the date by which Q plc must file its corporation tax return for the first accounting period in this period of account to avoid penalties and interest?

A 31 March 2016
B 30 June 2015
C 31 December 2015
D 1 October 2015

(2 marks)

63.3 M Ltd prepared accounts for the year ended 31 March 2015.

What is the earliest date until which M Ltd must retain its business records related to this year, assuming that no compliance check is made, and what is the maximum penalty for non-compliance?

(1) Retention date: 31 March 2017
(2) Retention date: 31 March 2021
(3) Maximum penalty: £2,000
(4) Maximum penalty: £3,000

A 1 and 3
B 2 and 3
C 1 and 4
D 2 and 4

(2 marks)

(Total = 6 marks)

64 Cyan plc

9 mins

Cyan plc prepared its accounts to 31 March for many years. In May 2014, Cyan plc decided to change its accounting date to 31 December and so prepared accounts to 31 December 2014. Its taxable total profits for this nine-month period were £1,428,571. Cyan plc did not receive any dividends during the period and it has no associated companies. In the year to 31 March 2014, Cyan plc had taxable total profits of £1,632,000.

Required

(a) Calculate the corporation tax payable by Cyan plc for the accounting period ended 31 December 2014. **(2 marks)**

(b) Show how the corporation tax liability in part (a) will be paid. **(3 marks)**

(Total = 5 marks)

65 Skyblue Ltd and Turquoise plc

18 mins

(a) Skyblue Ltd prepares accounts to 30 September each year. HM Revenue and Customs sent Skyblue Ltd a notice on 15 December 2014 requiring it to file a corporation tax return for the accounting period ended 30 September 2014. Skyblue Ltd is not a member of a group of companies.

Required

(i) Explain how Skyblue Ltd must file its return and a copy of its accounts for accounting period ended 30 September 2014. **(2 marks)**

(ii) State the filing date for the corporation tax return for the accounting period ended 30 September 2014. **(1 mark)**

(iii) State the latest date by which HM Revenue and Customs can give written notice to Skyblue Ltd that it intends to make a compliance check on the return if it is filed on 10 February 2016. **(2 marks)**

(b) Turquoise plc prepares accounts to 31 March each year. In its return for the accounting period ending 31 March 2015, loss relief for £100,000 was claimed, resulting in a reduction of £21,000 in the company's corporation tax. In fact, the loss relief available was only £10,000. The error was deliberate but no attempt was made to conceal it.

Required

(i) Compute the maximum penalty that may be imposed on Turquoise plc for this error. **(2 marks)**

(ii) Explain what is meant by an 'unprompted disclosure' in relation to an error on a tax return. **(2 marks)**

(iii) Compute the minimum penalty that may be imposed on Turquoise plc for the error if it makes an unprompted disclosure of the error. **(1 mark)**

(Total = 10 marks)

66 An introduction to VAT

11 mins

66.1 Alec has been in business since 1 June 2014 making water bottles. He will prepare his first set of accounts for the 12 months ending 31 May 2015. Alec's total taxable turnover for the seven months ended 31 December 2014 amounted to £45,000. On 1 January 2015 he received an order for water bottles amounting to £81,500 to be delivered later that month. Alec registered for VAT only when he was required to do so.

On what date will HM Revenue and Customs (HMRC) register Alec for value added tax (VAT) purposes?

A   1 January 2015
B   1 February 2015
C   1 June 2015
D   1 March 2015   **(2 marks)**

66.2 B plc is registered for value added tax (VAT). In the quarter ended 31 October 2014 it made taxable supplies (before taking account of any discounts) of £60,000, exclusive of VAT. All supplies are standard rated. B plc offers a discount of 4% to all of its customers who settle their invoices within 30 days. Only 25% of all customers (representing a quarter of the £60,000 above) pay within this time.

How much output VAT should B plc show on its VAT return for the quarter ended 31 October 2014 in respect of the above supplies?

A   £11,880
B   £11,640
C   £11,520
D   £12,000   **(2 marks)**

66.3 K Ltd received an order for machine parts on 14 December 2014. K Ltd dispatched these to the customer on 18 December 2014. An invoice was issued on 31 December 2014 and full payment was received on 15 January 2015.

What is the tax point for the sale of the machine parts?

A   18 December 2014
B   31 December 2014
C   15 January 2015
D   14 December 2014   **(2 marks)**

(Total = 6 marks)

67 Newcomer Ltd and Au Revoir Ltd

18 mins

(a)   Newcomer Ltd commenced trading on 1 October 2014. Its forecast sales are as follows.

		£
2014	October	18,500
	November	18,900
	December	23,400
2015	January	21,300
	February	22,700
	March	19,200

The company's sales are all standard-rated, and the above figures are exclusive of VAT.

Required

Explain when Newcomer Ltd will be required to compulsorily register for VAT.   **(6 marks)**

(b) Au Revoir Ltd has been registered for VAT since 1998, and its sales are all standard-rated. The company has recently seen a downturn in its business activities, and sales for the years ended 31 October 2014 and 2015 are forecast to be £75,000 and £73,500 respectively. Both of these figures are exclusive of VAT.

Required

Explain why Au Revoir Ltd will be permitted to voluntarily deregister for VAT, and from what date deregistration will be effective. **(4 marks)**

(Total = 10 marks)

68 Justin   18 mins

Justin has the following transactions in the quarter ended 31 December 2014. All amounts exclude any VAT unless otherwise stated.

	£
Purchases (all standard-rated)	
Furniture for resale	275,000
Computer for use in the business	2,400
Restaurant bills: entertaining UK customers	1,900
Petrol for cars owned by Justin and used only by his employees	2,800
Sales	
Furniture (standard-rated)	490,000
Books on interior design (zero-rated)	2,400

Only one employee's car has petrol for private motoring provided by Justin who has opted to use the fuel scale. The appropriate fuel scale charge for the quarter is £391 inclusive of VAT.

Required

Calculate the amount of VAT which Justin must pay to HM Revenue and Customs for the quarter.

(10 marks)

69 Ongoing Ltd   18 mins

Ongoing Ltd is registered for VAT, and its sales and purchases are all standard-rated. The following information relates to the company's VAT return for the quarter ended 30 April 2014:

(1) Standard-rated sales amounted to £120,000. Ongoing Ltd offers its customers a 5% discount for prompt payment, and this discount is taken by half of the customers.

(2) Standard-rated purchases and expenses amounted to £35,640. This figure includes £480 for entertaining UK customers.

(3) On 15 April 2014 the company wrote off impairment losses (bad debts) of £2,100 and £840 in respect of invoices due for payment on 10 August 2013 and 5 December 2013 respectively.

(4) On 30 April 2014 the company purchased a motor car at a cost of £16,450 for the use of a salesperson, and machinery at a cost of £21,150. Both these figures are inclusive of VAT. The motor car is used for both business and private mileage.

(5) On 30 April 2014 the company sold a motor car for £12,000 which had been used for both business and private mileage.

Unless stated otherwise, all of the above figures are exclusive of VAT. Ongoing Ltd does not operate the cash accounting scheme.

Required

Calculate the amount of VAT payable by Ongoing Ltd for the quarter ended 30 April 2014.

(10 marks)

70 Further aspects of VAT

70.1 Which of the following statement about the value added tax (VAT) cash accounting scheme are TRUE?

  (1) All VAT returns must be up to date before a trader can join the scheme.
  (2) Trader must pay 90% of the previous year's net VAT liability during the year by means of nine monthly payments.
  (3) Trader's taxable turnover (exclusive of VAT) in 12 months before application must not exceed £1,350,000.
  (4) Scheme gives automatic impairment loss relief (bad debt relief).

  A   1 and 2
  B   2 and 3
  C   1 and 4
  D   2 and 4   (2 marks)

70.2 Iris is a UK value added tax (VAT) registered trader. She sold goods with a VAT exclusive price of £30,000 to Heinrich in February 2015. Heinrich runs a business in Germany and is VAT registered in that country. Iris quoted the Heinrich's VAT number on the invoice and has proof of delivery to him in Germany. The rate of VAT in Germany on the goods would be 19%.

  What is the VAT that Iris must charge on this supply?

  A   £5,000
  B   £6,000
  C   £5,700
  D   £0   (2 marks)

70.3 X plc is registered for value added tax (VAT) and uses the flat rate scheme. In its VAT quarter ended 30 June 2014 it had a tax inclusive turnover of £110,000. This comprises of standard rated sales of £80,000, zero-rated sales of £20,000 and exempt sales of £10,000. The flat rate scheme percentage for the company's trading sector is 9%.

  What is the VAT payable to HMRC by X plc for the quarter ended 30 June 2014?

  A   £9,900
  B   £7,200
  C   £9,000
  D   £8,100   (2 marks)

                                                                        (Total = 6 marks)

71 Jason

Jason is a sole trader who has recently registered for value added tax (VAT). He buys and sells goods from and to other businesses situated elsewhere in the European Union (EU) and outside the EU. He also supplies services to business customers outside the EU.

Required

(a)   State how supplies of goods made by Jason to a VAT registered trader in another EU state will be treated for VAT.   **(1 mark)**

(b)   Explain how Jason will deal with the VAT implications of buying goods from a VAT registered trader in another EU state. State the tax point for acquisitions of goods in the UK from other VAT registered businesses in the EU.   **(5 marks)**

(c)   Explain how Jason will deal with the VAT implications of importing goods from outside the EU. You may assume that Jason is not a regular importer of goods from outside the EU.   **(3 marks)**

(d)   State how the supply of services by Jason to business customers outside the EU will be dealt with for UK VAT.   **(1 mark)**

(Total = 10 marks)

72 K Ltd and L Ltd

(a)   K Ltd is registered for value added tax (VAT). The directors of K Ltd have recently heard about the annual accounting scheme and asked you for advice on this matter.

Required

Prepare draft notes, for a meeting with the directors of K Ltd, outlining:

    (i)   The rules and qualifying conditions that the company must satisfy in order to join and continue to use the VAT annual accounting scheme   **(4 marks)**

    (ii)   The advantages and disadvantages of using the scheme   **(3 marks)**

(b)   L Ltd carries on a business as a wholesale adult clothing outlet and is registered for VAT. In recent months, L Ltd has had difficulty in obtaining payment of its invoices from its customers which has led to cash flow problems.

The directors of L Ltd have heard that there is a VAT scheme which may be advantageous for L Ltd to use. It wishes to continue to submit quarterly VAT returns.

Required

State the VAT scheme which would be advantageous for L Ltd to use and advise the directors of the conditions to join the scheme.   **(3 marks)**

(Total = 10 marks)

73 M Ltd

9 mins

M Ltd is registered for value added tax (VAT). M Ltd's main business is repairing computers. These are standard rated supplies for VAT. M Ltd also sells a small number of computing magazines which are zero rated supplies for VAT.

In the year ended 31 March 2015, M Ltd made supplies of computer repairs amounting to £82,000 (inclusive of VAT) and supplies of magazines amounting to £8,000. During this year, the company purchased standard rated supplies amounting to £10,000 (inclusive of VAT) and zero rated supplies amounting to £4,000.

The directors of M Ltd are considering using the VAT flat rate scheme.

Required

(a)   Advise the directors of M Ltd of the conditions that the company must satisfy in order to join and continue to use the VAT flat rate scheme.   **(2 marks)**

(b)   Calculate the tax saving if M Ltd had used the flat rate scheme to calculate the amount of VAT payable throughout the year ended 31 March 2015. The relevant flat rate scheme percentage for the company's main business of computing repairs is 10.5%.   **(3 marks)**

(Total = 5 marks)

BPP
LEARNING MEDIA

1 Introduction to the UK tax system

1.1   D   2 and 4

HM Revenue and Customs (HMRC) produces a wide range of explanatory notes and has the administrative function for collection of tax.

HM Treasury formally imposes taxation. Advice on minimising tax liability is provided by professional advisors such as accountants.

1.2   B   2 and 4

Inheritance tax and capital gains tax are capital taxes.

Income tax and national insurance are revenue taxes. Corporation tax is both a revenue tax (in respect of its income) and a capital tax (in respect of its chargeable gains).

1.3   C   1, 2 and 4

Inform Serena in writing that it is not possible for your firm to act for her, inform HMRC that your firm is no longer acting for Serena, and report Serena's refusal to disclose the omission and the facts surrounding it to your firm's Money Laundering Reporting Officer.

You are not required to inform HMRC about the details of Serena's omission.

2 Computing taxable income

2.1   D   £13,500

	£
Dividends £10,800 × 100/90	12,000
Building society interest £400 × 100/80	500
Interest on government security (received gross)	1,000
Total income	13,500

2.2   C   2, 3 and 4

Interest received from a New Individual Savings Account, Premium Bond prizes, and interest on NS&I Savings Certificates are exempt from income tax.

Dividends from a company and interest on government securities are chargeable to income tax.

2.3   C   £7,500

	£
Net income	105,000
Less income limit	(100,000)
Excess	5,000
Personal allowance	10,000
Less half excess £5,000 × ½	(2,500)
Available personal allowance	7,500

Although Robert was born before 6 April 1948, the higher personal allowance is reduced to the standard personal allowance due to Robert's net income (which is the same as his adjusted net income) obviously being in excess of £27,000. The standard personal allowance is then restricted by half of the excess of Robert's (adjusted) net income over £100,000.

3 Julia, Sandeep, Harriet and Romelu

> **Tutorial note.** When answering a question on residence status, start by considering whether the individual is automatically non-UK resident. If this test is not satisfied, then consider whether the individual is automatically UK resident. Again, if this test is not satisfied, then consider whether the combination of days in the UK and sufficient UK ties makes the individual UK resident.

(a) Julia was previously UK resident but is automatically non-UK resident for the tax year 2014/15 because she spends less than 16 days in the UK during that tax year.

(b) Sandeep is not automatically non-UK resident for the tax year 2014/15 because he spends 46 days or more in the UK during that tax year and does not work full-time overseas (and, in any case, has spent more than 90 days in the UK for the tax year).

He is automatically UK resident for the tax year 2014/15 because he spends 183 days or more in the UK during that tax year.

(c) Harriet was previously resident in the UK. She does not satisfy any of the automatic overseas tests since she spends 16 days or more in the UK and does not work full-time overseas.

Harriet does not satisfy any of the automatic UK tests since she spends less than 183 days in the UK, during the tax year 2014/15, has an overseas home and does not work full-time in the UK.

The 'sufficient ties' test is therefore relevant. Harriet has two UK ties:

(i) Substantive work in the UK
(ii) Available accommodation in the UK in which she spends at least one night in the tax year

Harriet spends between 91 and 120 days in the UK in 2014/15. These two ties are therefore sufficient to make her UK resident for the tax year 2014/15.

(d) Romelu was not previously resident in the UK. He does not satisfy any of the automatic overseas tests since he spends 46 days or more in the UK during the tax year 2014/15 and does not work full-time overseas.

Romelu does not satisfy any of the automatic UK tests as he spent less than 183 days in the UK, has an overseas home and does not work in the UK.

The 'sufficient ties' test is therefore relevant. Romelu has two UK ties:

(i) UK resident close family (spouse)
(ii) Available accommodation in the UK in which he spends at least one night in the tax year

Romelu spends between 91 and 120 days in the UK in 2014/15 and so he would need three UK ties to be UK resident for that tax year. Since Romelu has only two ties with the UK, he is therefore non-UK resident for the tax year 2014/15.

4 Luke

> **Tutorial note.** The personal allowance is set against non-savings income in priority to savings income.

Luke 2014/15

	Non-savings income £	Savings income £	Total £
Pension income	22,900		
Bank interest × 100/80		5,000	
Net income	22,900	5,000	27,900
Less: higher personal allowance (W)	(10,210)		
Taxable income	12,690	5,000	17,690

Working

	£
Net income	27,900
Less income limit	(27,000)
Excess	900

	£
Higher personal allowance (born before 6 April 1938)	10,660
Less half excess £900 × ½	(450)
Revised higher personal allowance (higher than standard personal allowance of £10,000)	10,210

5 Computing the income tax liability

5.1   A   £970

	£
£2,000 × 20%	400
£880 × 10%	88
£(3,290 − 880) = £2,410 × 20%	482
Tax liability	970

Non-savings income is taxed at 20%. Savings income is taxed at 10% where such income falls within the first £2,880 of taxable income. The remainder is then taxed at 20%.

5.2   C   £24,877

	£
£31,865 × 20%	6,373
£(150,000 − 31,865) = 118,135 × 40%	47,254
£(175,000 − 150,000) = £25,000 × 45%	11,250
Tax liability	64,877
Less: PAYE deducted	(40,000)
Tax payable	24,877

5.3   B   £549

	£
Net income	53,400
Less: personal pension contributions (gross)	(300)
Adjusted net income	53,100
Less: threshold	(50,000)
Excess	3,100
÷ £100	31
Child benefit income tax charge: 1% × £1,771 × 31	549

6 John and Helen

Tutorial note. In part (a), John's dividend income is between the basic rate limit and the higher rate limit, so it is taxed at 32.5%. Helen's dividends, however, fall below the basic rate limit and are consequently taxed at 10%. In part (b), John's adjusted net income is the same as his net income, since he has not made any personal pension contributions or gift aid donations in 2014/15.

(a)   *John and Helen 2014/15*

	Non-savings income £	Savings income £	Dividend income £	Total £
John				
Employment income	64,955			
Dividends × 100/90			1,211	
Bank deposit interest × 100/80		750		
Building society interest × 100/80		740		
Net income	64,955	1,490	1,211	67,656
Less personal allowance	(10,000)			
Taxable income	54,955	1,490	1,211	57,656

		£	£
Non savings income			
£31,865 × 20%			6,373
£23,090 × 40%			9,236
£54,955			
Savings income			
£1,490 × 40%			596
Dividend income			
£1,211 × 32.5%			394
Tax liability			16,599
Less: tax credit on dividend		121	
tax suffered on savings income		298	
PAYE		15,200	
			(15,619)
Tax payable			980

	Non-savings income £	Savings income £	Dividend income £	Total £
Helen				
Employment income	22,190			
Dividends × 100/90			2,820	
Bank deposit interest × 100/80		95		
Building society interest × 100/80		525		
Net income	22,190	620	2,820	25,630
Less personal allowance	(10,000)			
Taxable income	12,190	620	2,820	15,630

	£	£
Non-savings income		
£12,190 × 20%		2,438
Savings income		
£620 × 20%		124
Dividend income		
£2,820 × 10%		282
Tax liability		2,844
Less: tax credit on dividends	282	
tax suffered on savings income	124	
PAYE	2,200	
		(2,606)
Tax payable		238

(b)   John will be liable to the child benefit income tax charge for the tax year 2014/15 because his spouse has received child benefit during this tax year and he has adjusted net income in excess of £50,000 that is higher than that of Helen. Since John's adjusted net income exceeds £60,000, the child benefit income tax charge is the full amount of child benefit (£1,066) received by Helen in 2014/15. This charge will be collected under the self assessment system.

7 Michael and Josie

	Non-savings income £	Savings income £	Dividend income £	Total £
Michael				
Employment income	163,540			
Dividends × 100/90			12,111	
Bank deposit interest × 100/80		7,500		
Building society interest × 100/80		7,400		
Net income/Taxable income	163,540	14,900	12,111	190,551

	£	£
Non savings income		
£31,865 × 20%		6,373
£118,135 (150,000 − 31,865) × 40%		47,254
£13,540 × 45%		6,093
£163,540		
Savings income		
£14,900 × 45%		6,705
Dividend income		
£12,111 × 37.5%		4,542
		70,967
Less: tax credit on dividend	1,211	
tax suffered on savings income	2,980	
PAYE	59,650	
		(63,841)
Tax payable		7,126

	Non-savings income £	Savings income £	Dividend income £	Total £
Josie				
Employment income	100,000			
Dividends × 100/90			2,820	
Bank deposit interest × 100/80		950		
Building society interest × 100/80		5,250		
Net income	100,000	6,200	2,820	109,020
Less personal allowance (W1)	(6,490)			
Taxable income	93,510	6,200	2,820	102,530

BPP
LEARNING MEDIA

	£	£
Non-savings income		
£33,865 (W2) × 20%		6,773
£59,645 × 40%		23,858
£93,510		
Savings income		
£6,200 × 40%		2,480
Dividend income		
£2,820 × 32.5%		916
Tax liability		34,027
Less: tax credit on dividends	282	
tax suffered on savings income	1,240	
PAYE	33,000	
		(34,522)
Tax repayable		(495)

Workings

1 Personal allowance

	£
Net income	109,020
Less gross gift aid donation £1,600 × 100/80	(2,000)
Adjusted net income	107,020
Less income limit	(100,000)
Excess	7,020
Personal allowance	10,000
Less half excess £7,020 × ½	(3,510)
Revised personal allowance	6,490

2 Basic rate limit

£31,865 + (£1,600 × 100/80)	£33,865

8 Employment income

8.1 B £9,800

	£
Salary	8,000
Bonus received 30 November 2014 (receipts basis)	1,800
Employment income 2014/15	9,800

8.2 C 3 and 4

Diane is employed in a temporary workplace for less than 24 months, so travel from home to her temporary workplace is allowable. Erica's journey from home to Bristol is travel in the performance of duties so travel from home to the client is allowable.

Ben has a permanent workplace in Bristol and is not entitled to deduct travelling expenses from home to his workplace. Colin has two permanent workplaces so he is not entitled to deduct travelling expenses to either of them.

8.3   B   £(500) allowable expense

	£
Amount reimbursed 15,000 × 35p	5,250
Less: statutory allowance	
10,000 miles × 45p	(4,500)
5,000 miles × 25p	(1,250)
Allowable expense	(500)

9 Danni

> **Tutorial note.** Tax relief is not available for an employee's normal commuting costs but relief is available where the employee has a temporary workplace where the secondment is expected to last up to 24 months.

Danni – employment income 2014/15

	£	£
Salary		
1.7.14 – 31.12.14		
£6,000 × 6	36,000	
1.1.15 – 31.3.15		
£(6,000 × 102.5%) × 3	18,450	
Bonus		
Received 31 March 2015	10,000	
		64,450
Travel		
Home to work: not deductible	(0)	
Temporary workplace expected to last less than 24 months:		
£543 × 3	(1,629)	
Mileage allowance: 24 miles × 2 (return journey) × 5 = 240 miles		
Excess over statutory mileage allowance 240 × (0.45 – 0.30)	(36)	
Membership fees		
MCIP: professional subscription relevant to employment	(159)	
Tennis club: not wholly, exclusively and necessarily for employment	(0)	
Payroll giving		
£50 × 4	(200)	
		(2,024)
Employment income 2014/15		62,426

10 Taxable and exempt benefits. The PAYE system

10.1   B   £4,400

CO_2 emissions are 133 g/km, round down to 130 g/km

Appropriate percentage: (130 – 95) = 35 g/km in excess of threshold

35/5 = 7%

12% + 7% + 3% = 22%

List price £20,000 × 22% = £4,400

10.2   C   £1,460

		£
Annual value		3,600
Additional amount £(99,000 − 75,000) × 3.25%		780
		4,380
× 4/12		1,460

Accommodation provided for private use by an employer is taxed on the annual value plus an additional amount if the accommodation cost the company more than £75,000. The market value is only used if the accommodation was acquired more than six years prior to being provided. Both benefits are pro-rated for occupation for part of the tax year.

10.3   A   P11D – 6 July 2015

Form P11D is used to report benefits for directors and employees paid £8,500+ per tax year.

31 May following the end of the tax year is the date for providing an employee with Form P60. Form P9D is used to report benefits for other employees. The payment of gym membership is a taxable benefit.

11 Azure plc

> **Tutorial note**. The calculation of benefits is particularly important for exam purposes. Ensure that you pro-rate the benefits if they are not available for the entire year.

(a)   A taxable benefit must be computed for Mr Andrews. The benefit will equal the difference between the interest which would have arisen at the official rate and the actual interest paid. The benefit for 2014/15 is therefore £16,000 × (3.25 − 1)% × 6/12 months = £180.

(b)   The loan to Mrs Preece is less than £10,000, so the taxable benefit is nil.

(c)   Mr Charles will have a taxable benefit of the annual value of the TV, which will be computed as 20% of the value of the asset when first provided as a benefit to any employee. If the TV had been lent to an employee when it was bought, the benefit for 2014/15 would be £800 × 20% = £160 × 10/12 = £133. If the TV was first provided as a benefit in June 2014, the benefit would be £500 × 20% = £100 × 10/12 = £83.

(d)   Long service awards of tangible property to employees with at least 20 years service are not taxed provided the cost to the employer does not exceed £50 for each year of service and no similar award has been made to the same person within the previous ten years. In Mrs Davies's case the limit on value would be £50 × 25 = £1,250, so there will be no taxable benefit.

(e)   The first £8,000 of removal expenses payable to Miss Jackson will be an exempt benefit because:
   (i)   She does not already live within a reasonable daily travelling distance of her new place of employment, but will do so after moving, and
   (ii)   The expenses are incurred or the benefits provided by the end of the tax year following the tax year of the start of employment at the new location.

   Miss Jackson will be taxable on the excess removal expenses £(9,500 − 8,000) = £1,500.

(f)   The private use of one mobile phone is an exempt benefit. The private use of the second phone is a taxable benefit Mr Long can choose which phone is exempt and should therefore choose the one which has the higher phone charges.

The taxable benefit on the second phone is calculated as follows.

£

Greater of:
    20% of market value (20% × £500 = £100)
    Hire charge £120
    ie   120
Cost of calls   300
                                    420

Private use taxable benefit £420 × 30%   126

12 Verdi

> **Tutorial note.** Verdi cannot use the HMRC's Basic PAYE Tools software to report PAYE information electronically because he will have more than nine employees.

(a) Verdi can submit information electronically either using commercial payroll software or a payroll provider.

(b) A Full Payment Submission (FPS) must be made on or before any day when Verdi pays employees. The FPS includes details of:

    (i) The amounts paid to employees

    (ii) Deductions made under PAYE such as income tax and national insurance contributions

    (iii) Details of employees who have started employment for the first FPS and, for subsequent submissions, those who have started employment or left employment since the last FPS

(c) (i) A tax month runs from 6th of one calendar month to the 5th of the following calendar month.

    (ii) Verdi must pay over income tax and national insurance contributions to HMRC within 17 days after the end of each tax month if the payment is made electronically.

13 Pensions

13.1 B   £5,500

    The maximum amount of contributions attracting tax relief which could be made by Treena in 2014/15 is the higher of:

    (a) Relevant earnings which is the total of her employment income of £3,500 and her trading income of £2,000, and

    (b) Basic amount of £3,600.

    Bank interest is not relevant earnings.

13.2   C   £65,000

	£
Earnings	90,000
Less: occupational pension contribution	(15,000)
Net income	75,000
Less: personal allowance	(10,000)
Taxable income	65,000

Under net pay arrangements (most occupational pension schemes) the gross contribution is deducted from earnings so that tax relief is given at all rates of tax. Under tax relief at source (most personal pension schemes), the payment is made net of basic rate tax and higher rate relief and additional rate relief are given by increasing the basic rate and higher rate limits in the tax computation.

13.3   A   £63,000

	£
Annual allowance 2014/15	40,000
Annual allowance unused in 2013/14 £(50,000 − 27,000)	23,000
Maximum gross pension contribution in 2014/15	63,000

The annual allowance for 2012/13 is not available as Rio was not a member of a pension scheme in that year.

14 Gary, George and Geraldine

Tutorial note. Tax relief is available on pension contributions up to the higher of relevant earnings and the basic amount (£3,600). However, tax relief on contributions in excess of the annual allowance are clawed back by the excess contributions charge.

(a)   *Gary 2014/15*

	Non-savings income £
Employment income	55,000
Less personal allowance	(10,000)
Taxable income	45,000

Tax

	£
£36,865 (W) × 20%	7,373
£8,135 × 40%	3,254
45,000	10,627

Working

Basic rate limit £31,865 + (£4,000 × 100/80) = £36,865

(b)   George 2014/15

	Non-savings income £
Employment income	45,000
Less personal allowance	(10,000)
Taxable income	35,000
His income tax liability will be:	
£35,000 × 20%	7,000

Tutorial note

As George's earnings are only £45,000 for 2014/15 the maximum net contribution entitled to tax relief would be £45,000 × 80% = £36,000. Therefore the remaining £3,200 (£39,200 – £36,000) would not qualify for tax relief. Note the basic rate limit is increased by £45,000, but the taxable income falls below this limit.

(c)   In 2013/14, Geraldine has made a gross contribution of £(25,000 × 100/80) = £31,250. She therefore has an unused annual allowance of (50,000 – 31,250) = £18,750. This will be carried forward and added to her annual allowance of £40,000 for 2014/15, giving a total of £(18,750 + 40,000) = £58,750. The net equivalent (ie the amount she would actually pay) is £58,750 × 80% = £47,000.

Tutorial note

Geraldine's relevant earnings of £130,000 exceed the gross pension contributions of £58,750, so she can obtain tax relief on this contribution.

15 Property income

15.1   C   £1,180

Rent – water rates × 10%

£(12,000 – 200) × 10% = £1,180

15.2   D   £24,000

	£
Premium received	30,000
Less: £30,000 × 2% × (11 – 1)	(6,000)
Amount chargeable to income tax	24,000

15.3   B   2, 4 and 5

The accommodation must not have more than 155 days in the tax year in longer term occupation, the income from furnished holiday lettings qualifies as relevant earnings for pension contributions, and if an individual has a furnished holiday letting and another letting, two income statements must be prepared in order to identify separate profits and losses.

The accommodation must be available for commercial let as holiday accommodation to the public generally for at least 210 days during the tax year. Capital allowances are available on furniture instead of the 10% wear and tear allowance.

16 Rafe

	£	£
Rent		
House 1: first letting £600 × 6		3,600
House 1: second letting £6,000 × 3/12		1,500
House 2: £7,800 × 8/12		5,200
		10,300
Expenses		
House 1: new roof, disallowable because capital	0	
House 1: water rates	320	
House 1: buildings insurance £480 × 10/12	400	
House 2: redecoration	1,200	
House 2: water rates	360	
House 2: buildings insurance £440 × 9/12	330	
House 2: contents insurance £180 × 8/12	120	
House 2: wear and tear £(5,200 − 360) × 10%	484	
		(3,214)
Income from houses 1 and 2		7,086
Rent a room (W)		350
Total property business income		7,436

Working

Rafe should claim rent a room relief in respect of the letting of the furnished room in his main residence, since this is more beneficial than the normal basis of assessment (£4,600 − £875 = £3,725). This means that Rafe will be taxed on an additional £350 (£4,600 − £4,250) of property business income.

17 Computing trading income

17.1   C   1, 4 and 5

Installing air conditioning in his workshop, building a wall around his showroom car park and making initial repairs to a recently acquired second-hand office building which was not usable until the repairs were carried out (see *Law Shipping Co Ltd v CIR 1923*) are capital expenditure. They are not allowable as expense in calculating trading profits.

Repairing the central heating in his offices and redecorating the showroom are allowable expenses in calculating trading profits.

17.2   D   £160,220

	£
Profit per accounts	160,000
Add: parking fines	180
hamper	40
Tax-adjusted profit	160,220

The legal fees in relation to the short lease are allowable as this involves a renewal of a short lease rather than the grant of a new lease. Parking fines for the owner of a business are never allowable. Gifts of food are not allowable.

17.3   B   £27,700

	£
Revenue: cash received £(50,200 – 4,000)	46,200
Less: allowable expenses: cash paid £(20,000 – 1,500)	(18,500)
Tax-adjusted profit	27,700

18 A Trader

> **Tutorial note**. You are extremely likely to be required to adjust accounts profit in your exam to arrive at taxable trading profits. The best way to familiarise yourself with the adjustments required is to practise plenty of questions like this.

	£	£
Net profit		101,977
Add: general expenses: entertaining staff	0	
general expenses: entertaining suppliers	600	
repairs and renewals: redecoration	0	
repairs and renewals: renovation	0	
legal and accountancy: debt collection	0	
legal and accountancy: staff service agreements	0	
legal and accountancy: tax consultancy	30	
legal and accountancy: grant of short lease on new premises	100	
legal and accountancy: audit and accountancy	0	
subscription and donations: gift aid donation	5,200	
subscription and donations: political donation	500	
subscription and donations: sports facilities for staff	0	
subscription and donations: trade association	0	
impairment losses (trade)	0	
salaries and wages	0	
travel: private travel expenses 25% × £2,000	500	
depreciation	15,000	
rent and rates	0	
		21,930
Less: profit on sale of office	5,265	
impairment losses recovered	0	
capital allowances	2,200	
building society interest	1,900	
		(9,365)
Taxable trading profit		114,542

19 Margaret Webster

> **Tutorial note.** The fixed private use adjustment for private use of business premises does not apply to mortgage interest or rent on those premises. Instead, the usual proportional private use adjustment must be made.

	£	£
Revenue (cash received £36,000 – £500)		35,500
Less: furniture	2,500	
mortgage interest £7,500 × 2/3 (business use proportion)	5,000	
household expenses (W)	7,000	
fixed rate expense for motor car 2,000 × 45p	900	
other allowable expenses (cash paid £2,000 – £900)	1,100	
		(16,500)
Taxable trading profit 2014/15		19,000

Working

Household expenses

	£
Gas and electricity	7,400
Cleaning and gardening	1,800
Food	2,000
	11,200
Less: fixed rate private use proportion £350 × 12	(4,200)
Allowance household expenses	7,000

20 Capital allowances

20.1 D 1, 3 and 4

Refrigeration equipment, decorative assets provided for the enjoyment of the public in a restaurant, and sound insulation (provided mainly to meet the particular requirements of the trade) are items which could be plant for the purposes of capital allowances.

Expenditure on a building such as an office extension could not qualify as plant. A bridge is a structure and are therefore also not plant.

20.2 A £1,260

	Car	Allowances 75%
	£	£
y/e 5 April 2015		
Addition	21,000	
WDA @ 8%	(1,680)	1,260
TWDV c/f	19,320	
Maximum capital allowances		1,260

20.3   C   £125,450

	AIA £	Main pool £	Allowances £
p/e 31 December 2014			
Addition qualifying for AIA			
Machinery	135,000		
AIA £500,000 × 3/12	(125,000)		125,000
	10,000		
Transfer balance to main pool	(10,000)	10,000	
WDA @ 18% × 3/12		(450)	450
TWDV c/f		9,550	
Maximum capital allowances			125,450

21 Tom Hardy

> **Tutorial note**. The key to being able to deal with a capital allowances computation correctly is to get the layout right. Once you have done this, the figures should fall into place.

	AIA £	Main pool £	Private use car (80%) £	Short life asset £	Allowances £
1.7.14 – 30.6.15					
Brought forward		33,500		4,400	
Addition qualifying for AIA					
Plant	27,000				
AIA	(27,000)				27,000
	0				
WDA @ 18%		(6,030)		(792)	6,822
Carried forward		27,470		3,608	
Allowances					33,822
1.7.15 – 30.6.16					
Addition (not AIA)			13,400		
WDA @ 18%		(4,945)	(2,412) × 80%	(649)	7,524
Carried forward		22,525	10,988	2,959	
Allowances					7,524
1.7.16 – 30.6.17					
WDA @ 18%		(4,055)	(1,978) × 80%	(533)	6,170
Carried forward		18,470	9,010	2,426	
Allowances					6,170
1.7.17 – 30.6.18					
Disposals		(340)		(2,900)	
		18,130		(474)	
Balancing charge				474	(474)
WDA @ 18%		(3,263)	(1,622) × 80%		4,561
Carried forward		14,867	7,388		
Allowances					4,087
1.7.18 – 31.12.18					
Disposals		(24,000)	(10,600)		
		(9,133)	(3,212)		
Balancing charges		9,133	3,212 × 80%		(11,703)

> **Tutorial note**. The capital allowances are restricted as a result of the private use of an asset by the owner of the business.

22 Saruman

> **Tutorial note.** Balancing adjustments where there has been private use of the asset are restricted to the business use element.

Capital allowances computation for year ended 5 April 2015

	Main pool £	Saruman's car (75%) £	Allowances/ (charges) £
TWDV b/f	52,000	6,000	
Addition (no AIA on car)	4,800		
Disposals (10,000 + 800)	(10,800)	(7,200)	
	46,000		
Balancing charge		(1,200) × 75%	(900)
Private use car		19,000	
WDA 18%	(8,280)		8,280
WDA 8%		(1,520) × 75%	1,140
TWDV c/f	37,720	17,480	
Allowances			8,520

23 Assessable trading income

23.1 D   £3,000

First tax year (2013/14)
Actual basis
Basis period 1.1.14 to 5.4.14

Second tax year (2014/15)
Period of account in 2nd year at least 12 months so basis period is 12 months to that accounting date
Basis period 1.2.14 to 31.1.15

Overlap profits
Period of overlap 1.2.14 to 5.4.14 (two months)

2/13 × £19,500   £3,000

23.2 B £11,500

Last tax year (2014/15)
Basis period 1.2.14 to 31.3.15

	£
y/e 31.1.15	10,000
p/e 31.3.15	2,500
	12,500
Less: overlap profits	(1,000)
	11,500

23.3 B 6 April 2014 to 5 April 2015

2014/15 is the second year of trading. There is no period of account ending in 2014/15, so the basis period is the tax year.

24 Mr Cobbler

> **Tutorial note**. Significant cash flow advantages can be gained with a careful choice of accounting date.

Taxable profits for the four years 2014/15 to 2017/18

The accounts profits will be as follows.

Period ending in	Working	Accounting date 31 March £	30 April £
2015	3 × £800	2,400	
	4 × £800		3,200
2016	3 × £800 + 6 × £1,200 + 3 × £2,000	15,600	
	2 × £800 + 6 × £1,200 + 4 × £2,000		16,800
2017	12 × £2,000	24,000	24,000
2018	12 × £2,000	24,000	24,000

The taxable profits will be as follows.

		Accounting date 31 March £	30 April £
2014/15	Actual basis (1 January 2015 to 5 April 2015)	2,400	
	£3,200 × 3/4 (work to nearest month)		2,400
2015/16	Year to 31.3.16	15,600	
	First 12 months (1 January 2015 to 31 December 2015)		
	£3,200 + £16,800 × 8/12		14,400
2016/17	Year to 31.3.17	24,000	
	Year to 30.4.16		16,800
2017/18	Year to 31.3.18	24,000	
	Year to 30.4.17		24,000
		66,000	57,600

30 April is the better choice of accounting date as it will give a considerable cash flow advantage.

25 Miss Farrington

> **Tutorial note.** In a question like this, work out the capital allowances for each period of account before you think about allocating profits to tax years.
>
> Writing down allowances and the annual investment allowance are time apportioned in a long period of account.

We must first work out the capital allowances.

	AIA £	Main pool £	Private use car (65%) £	Allowances £
1.1.15 – 30.4.16				
Additions qualifying for AIA				
Desk and office furniture (1.1.15)	2,625			
General plant (4.1.15)	8,070			
Secondhand oven (1.3.15)	5,300			
Delivery van (25.3.15)	5,450			
General plant (15.4.15)	8,555			
	30,000			
AIA £500,000 × 16/12 = £666,667	(30,000)			30,000
Addition not qualifying for AIA				
Car (15.5.15)			6,600	
WDA @ 18% × 16/12			(1,584) × 65%	1,030
Carried forward		0	5,016	
Allowances				31,030
1.5.16 – 30.4.17				
Additions qualifying for AIA				
General plant (30.1.17)	10,000			
Mixer (30.4.17)	1,200			
	11,200			
AIA	(11,200)			11,200
WDA @ 18%			(903) × 65%	587
Carried forward			4,113	
Allowances				11,787

Profits are as follows.

Period	Profit £	Capital allowances £	Adjusted profit £
1.1.15 – 30.4.16	47,030	31,030	16,000
1.5.16 – 30.4.17	24,787	11,787	13,000

The taxable profits are as follows.

Year	Basis period	Working	Taxable profit £
2014/15	1.1.15 – 5.4.15	£16,000 × 3/16	3,000
2015/16	6.4.15 – 5.4.16	£16,000 × 12/16	12,000
2016/17	1.5.15 – 30.4.16	£16,000 × 12/16	12,000
2017/18	1.5.16 – 30.4.17		13,000

The overlap profits are the profits from 1 May 2015 to 5 April 2016: £16,000 × 11/16 = £11,000.

26 Trading losses

26.1   D   1 and 3

A claim to set a trading loss against general income cannot be restricted so that the individual has enough net income to use the personal allowance. A trading loss can be carried forward indefinitely.

A trading loss carried forward must be set against the first available profits of the same trade. A trading loss claim for relief against general income must be made by 31 January 22 months after the end of the tax year of the loss.

26.2   B   £11,000

	2013/14 £
Trading income	12,000
Less: trading loss 2012/13 b/f	(3,000)
	9,000
Property business income	1,000
	13,000
Less: loss relief against general income c/b from 2014/15	(13,000)
Net income	0

The trading loss available to carry forward to 2015/16 is £(24,000 – 13,000) = £11,000.

26.3   C   £83,750

	2013/14 £
Trading income	15,000
Property business income	260,000
Total income	275,000
Less: loss relief against general income	(83,750)
Net income	191,250

In 2013/14, the loss relief cap does not apply to loss relief against the trading income of £15,000. However, the cap does apply to the loss relief against non-trading income. The cap is £275,000 × 25% = £68,750. The total loss relief claim for 2013/14 is therefore £(15,000 + 68,750) = £83,750.

27 Morgan

(a)   Loss relief could be claimed:

   (i)   Against general income of the year of loss (2014/15), the investment income of £11,000

   (ii)   Against general income of the preceding year (2013/14). This would be trading profits of £15,000 plus investment income of £11,000.

   (iii)   Against the first available future profits of the same trade

(b)   **The quickest claim**

The quickest way to obtain relief would be for Morgan to use loss relief against general income in both years. The tax computations would then be as follows.

	2013/14 £	2014/15 £
Trading profits	15,000	0
Investment income	11,000	11,000
Total income	26,000	11,000
Less loss relief against general income	(26,000)	(11,000)
Net income	0	0

The balance of the loss, £1,000, would be carried forward and relieved against future trading income.

Although this proposal produces loss relief quickly, it has the disadvantage of wasting Morgan's personal allowance in both years. Morgan could, if he chose, delay his relief by carrying the loss forward. The loss would then be set off only against trading income, with the investment income using his personal allowance.

28 Jacques

Jacques – Net income

	2013/14 £	2014/15 £
Trading income	5,000	–
Property business income	84,000	210,000
Total income	89,000	210,000
Less: loss relief (W)	(55,000)	(52,500)
Net income	34,000	157,500

Working

			2013/14 £	2014/15 £
Cap is higher of:	(i)		50,000	50,000
	(ii)	25% × £89,000/£210,000	22,250	52,500
Loss capped against non-trading income			50,000	52,500
Loss against trading income			5,000	0
Loss relief			55,000	52,500

29 Partnerships and limited liability partnerships

29.1 B £5,000

y/e 31 December 2015

Profit share £60,000 × 1/3 £20,000

2014/15 basis period is 1 January 2015 to 5 April 2015 so 3/12 of this amount is taxable in 2014/15 ie £5,000.

29.2 C £33,333

y/e 31 March 2015

	£
1.4.14 – 30.4.14	
Profit share £96,000 × 1/12 × 1/2	4,000
1.5.14 – 31.3.15	
Profit share £96,000 × 11/12 × 1/3	29,333
	33,333

Current year basis applies as there is no commencement or cessation, simply a change in profit sharing ratios.

29.3 B £50,000

Victor's share of the loss is 50% ie £90,000. However, the amount of loss relief that Victor can claim against general income of £60,000 is restricted to the greater of £50,000 and 25% of Victor's adjusted total income (ie 25% × £60,000 = £15,000) ie £50,000.

30 Anne, Betty and Chloe

> **Tutorial note**. You may be asked to explain the taxation implications of a partnership as well as compute taxable income for each of the partners.

(a) Each partner is taxed like a sole trader who runs a business which starts when that partner joins the partnership, finishes when the partner leaves the partnership, has the same periods of account as the partnership, and makes profits or losses equal to the partner's share of the partnership profits or losses.

(b)

	Total £	Anne £	Betty £	Chloe £
1.1.14 – 31.12.14				
January to June	30,000	15,000	15,000	
July to December	30,000	15,000	–	15,000
Totals	60,000	30,000	15,000	15,000
1.1.15 – 31.12.15	72,000	36,000	–	36,000

Trading profit assessments 2014/15

	Anne £	Betty £	Chloe £
Profits y/e 31.12.14	30,000		
Profits 1.1.14 – 30.6.14		15,000	
Profits 1.7.14 – 31.12.14			15,000
Profits 1.1.15 – 5.4.15			
3/12 × £36,000			9,000
	30,000	15,000	24,000
Less overlap relief for Betty on cessation		(3,000)	
Profits assessable 2014/15	30,000	12,000	24,000

31 Daniel, Edward and Frank

> **Tutorial note**. Each partner can make a separate loss relief claim for his share of the partnership loss.

Daniel

Daniel can use his £20,000 loss:

(a)   Against general income of 2014/15 and/or of 2013/14
(b)   Against future trading profits

Edward

Edward can use his £15,000 loss:

(a)   Against general income of 2014/15 and/or of 2013/14

(b)   If there is a terminal loss in the last 12 months of trading, against trading profits of the tax year of cessation (2014/15) and the three preceding years, later years first (2013/14 then 2012/13, then 2011/12)

Frank

Frank can use his loss of £5,000:

(a)   Against general income of 2014/15 and/or 2013/14
(b)   Against general income of 2011/12, 2012/13 and 2013/14 (early years loss relief)
(c)   Against future trading profits

32 National insurance contributions

32.1   C   £3,117

	£
Class 2	143
£2.75 × 52	
Class 4	
£(41,000 – 7,956) = 33,044 × 9%	2,974
Total NIC 2014/15	3,117

32.2   B   £489

Total earnings received in February 2015 are £11,000 (£3,000 + £8,000)

The NIC primary limits for each month are £7,956/12 = £663 and £41,865/12 = £3,489.

NIC payable is therefore:

	£
£(3,489 – 663) = 2,826 × 12%	339
£(11,000 – 3,489) = 7,511 × 2%	150
NIC February 2015	489

32.3   D   Class 1 primary contributions on £45,000, Class 1 secondary contributions on £45,000, Class 1A contributions on £300

Class 1 primary and secondary contributions are generally payable on cash earnings. Class 1A contributions are payable on non-cash benefits by the employer only.

33 Derek and Denise

> **Tutorial note**. It is important that you can calculate and distinguish NICs for the self-employed and employed individuals. Remember that NICs in respect of benefits are only payable by employers, not employees. For self-employed taxpayers, there is a flat rate contribution and a contribution based on profits.

(a)   (i)   **Derek – Primary Class 1 NICs 2014/15**

	£
£(41,865 – 7,956) = 33,909 × 12%	4,069
£(55,000 – 41,865) = 13,135 × 2%	263
	4,332

(ii)   **Rose Ltd – Secondary Class 1 NICs 2014/15**

	£
£(55,000 – 7,956) = 47,044 × 13.8%	6,492
Less: Employment Allowance (sole employee)	(2,000)
	4,492

(iii) **Rose Ltd – Class 1A NICs 2014/15**

	£
£3,000 × 13.8%	414

(b)   **Denise – Classes 2 and 4 NICs 2014/15**

	£
Class 2 NICs	
£2.75 × 52	143
Class 4 NICs	
£(41,865 – 7,956) = 33,909 × 9%	3,052
£(45,000 – 41,865) = 3,135 × 2%	63
	3,115

34 Sasha Shah

(a)   Factors that will indicate that a worker should be treated as an employee rather than as self-employed are:

  (i)   Control by employer over employee's work

  (ii)   Employee must accept further work if offered (and employer must offer work)

  (iii)   Employee does not provide own equipment

  (iv)   Employee does not hire own helpers

  (v)   Employee does not take substantial financial risk

  (vi)   Employee does not have responsibility for investment and management of business and cannot benefit from sound management

  (vii)   Employee cannot work when he chooses but when an employer tells him to work

  (viii) Described as an employee in any agreement between parties

(b)   (i)   *Income assessable as trading profits*

	£	£
Gross income		60,000
Less: business expenses on heating etc	880	
computer – AIA	4,000	
business expenses re car (£3,500 × 40%)	1,400	
WDA @ 18% on business car (CO_2 up to 130g/km)		
£10,000 × 18% × 40% (business proportion)	720	(7,000)
Assessable as trading profits		53,000

   (ii)   *Net taxable earnings*

	£	£
Gross income		60,000
Less: business expenses on heating etc	880	
computer – AIA	4,000	(4,880)
Net taxable earnings		55,120

(c)   (i)   *Class 2 and Class 4 NIC*

		£
Class 2	£2.75 × 52	143
Class 4	£(41,865 − 7,956) = 33,909 × 9%	3,052
	£(53,000 − 41,865) = 11,135 × 2%	223
Total		3,418

(ii)   *Class 1 NIC (Primary)*

		£
£(41,865 – 7,956) = 33,909 × 12%		4,069
£(60,000 – 41,865) = 18,135 × 2%		363
Total		4,432

35 Computing chargeable gains

35.1 A   1 and 2

Qualifying corporate bonds (QCBs) are exempt assets. Investments held in new individual savings accounts (NISAs) are exempt assets.

A plot of land is a chargeable asset. Decorations for bravery are exempt assets only if awarded, not purchased.

35.2 B   £16,400 – £3,000 (current year loss) – £2,400 (brought forward loss) = £11,000

Current year losses must always be used in full against the current year gains.

If losses are brought forward then they must be used against the first available gains after the current year losses and then only enough to reduce the current year's net gains to the annual exempt amount limit of £11,000.

Therefore in this case the £3,000 must be used first and only £2,400 of the brought forward figure needs to be used.

35.3 D   £12,143

The amount of the cost attributable to the part sold is:

$$\frac{£36,000}{£36,000 \ + \ £90,000} \times £80,000 = £22,857$$

	£
Proceeds £(36,000 – 1,000)	35,000
Less cost (see above)	(22,857)
Gain	12,143

36 Peter Robinson

> **Tutorial note**. The first disposal is a basic computation. The second disposal tests the A/(A+B) formula and the third part tests compensation for the destruction of an asset.

Peter Robinson CGT payable 2014/15

Summary

	£
Investment property (W1)	69,720
Land (W2)	16,300
Destroyed asset (W3)	3,000
	89,020
Less: annual exempt amount	(11,000)
Taxable gains	78,020
CGT	
£(31,865 – 27,465) = £4,400 @ 18%	792
£(78,020 – 4,400) = £73,620 @ 28%	20,614
CGT 2014/15	21,406

Workings

1   *Investment property*

	£
Proceeds	150,000
Less cost of disposal	(1,280)
Net proceeds	148,720
Less cost	(79,000)
Gain	69,720

2   *Land*

	£
Proceeds	35,000
Less cost of disposal	(700)
Net proceeds	34,300
Less cost	
$£54,000 \times \dfrac{35,000}{35,000+70,000}$	(18,000)
Gain	16,300

3   *Vase*

	£
Proceeds	20,000
Less cost	(12,000)
Gain	8,000
Gain immediately chargeable £(20,000 – 17,000)	3,000

Remainder £(8,000 – 3,000) = £5,000 rolled into base cost of new vase.

37 Chattels and the principal private residence exemption

37.1 A £1,667

		£
Proceeds less disposal costs £(7,000 – 350)		6,650
Less: cost and purchase costs £(1,500 + 75)		(1,575)
Gain		5,075

The maximum gain is 5/3 × £(7,000 – 6,000) = £1,667

The chargeable gain is the lower of £5,075 and £1,667 ie £1,667

37.2 C £2,100

		£
Proceeds (assumed)		6,000
Less: disposal costs		(200)
		5,800
Less: cost and purchase costs £(7,500 + 400)		(7,900)
Allowable loss		(2,100)

37.3 A Three years

		Exempt	Chargeable
1.1.91 – 31.12.02	Actual occupation	12	
1.1.03 – 31.12.05	Up to 3 years any reason	3	
1.1.06 – 31.12.08	Unoccupied		3
1.1.09 – 31.12.14	Actual occupation	6	
Total		21	3

Any periods up to three years are exempt if the house is then reoccupied, so only the remaining three years of the period when Roger was staying with his parents are chargeable as Roger then went back to occupy his house.

38 John and Elsie

Tutorial note. Part (a) is a typical question examining principal private residence relief. You are asked to present your answer as a schedule (ie table) showing periods of exemption and non-exemption with reasons (ie explanation of your application of the rules). To obtain good marks you must comply with these instructions. Part (b) tests your knowledge of the chattels rules.

(a) **John – Gain on house**

	Chargeable months	Exempt months
1.8.92 – 30.11.94 – actual residence		28
1.12.94 – 31.1.99 – employed abroad any period		50
1.2.99 – 31.1.03 – up to four years work elsewhere		48
1.2.03 – 30.4.05 – up to three years any reason		27
1.5.05 – 31.12.11 – actual residence		80
1.1.12 – 31.5.13 – absent	17	
1.6.13 – 30.11.14 – last 18 months ownership		18
Totals	17	251

(b) **Elsie**

(i)   Painting

	£
Proceeds (deemed)	6,000
Less costs of disposal	(400)
Gain	5,600
Less: cost	(11,500)
Loss	(5,900)

(ii)   Chandelier

	£
Proceeds	7,500
Less: cost	(4,000)
Gain	3,500
Cannot exceed £(7,500 − 6,000) × 5/3	2,500

39 Business reliefs

39.1   C   £1,342

	£
Entrepreneurs' relief claimed	1,000
£10,000 × 10%	
No entrepreneurs' relief claimed	
£(12,900 − 11,000) = £1,900 × 18%	342
Total CGT	1,342

Gain on which entrepreneurs' relief is claimed is taxed at 10%. The other gain will be reduced by the annual exempt amount and then taxed in this case, at 18%, because Jane has total gains and income less than the basic rate limit of £31,865.

39.2   D   £55,000

	£
Chargeable gain on Shop A	25,000
Less: amount not reinvested £(80,000 − 70,000)	(10,000)
Amount available for rollover relief	15,000
Original cost of Shop B	70,000
Less: rollover relief	(15,000)
Cost of Shop B for CGT	55,000

39.3   B   2 and 3

Gift relief can be claimed for the factory owned by an individual and used in the trade of that individual's personal company. It can also be claimed for premises owned by a sole trader of which two thirds are used for trade purposes and one third is used for private purposes (although the relief will be restricted to the business part of the premises).

Gift relief is not available on investment company shares. It is only available on listed trading company shares if the company is the individual's personal company: a 2% shareholding is too small to meet this test.

40 Roy and Gary

> **Tutorial note.** When dealing with a sole trader, you should bear in mind that entrepreneurs' relief may apply to reduce the rate of tax on the gain.

(a) *Roy – CGT payable 2014/15 if gift relief claimed*

Full gift relief is available as no payment is made by Gary ie it is an outright gift.

	£
Market value at gift	260,000
Less cost	(150,000)
Gain before gift relief	110,000
Less gift relief	(110,000)
Gain after gift relief	0
CGT payable 2014/15	0

Gary – CGT payable 2014/15 if gift relief claimed

	£
Proceeds	320,000
Less cost £(260,000 – 110,000)	(150,000)
Gain	170,000
Less annual exempt amount	(11,000)
Taxable gain	159,000
CGT payable @ 28%	44,520

> **Tutorial note.** Entrepreneurs' relief is not available for Gary's disposal because he has not used the factory in his own business.

(b) *Roy – CGT payable 2014/15*

	£
Gain (as in part (a))	110,000
Less annual exempt amount	(11,000)
Taxable gain	99,000
CGT payable @ 10% (entrepreneurs' relief claimed)	9,900

Gary – CGT payable 2014/15

	£
Proceeds	320,000
Less cost	(260,000)
Gain	60,000
Less annual exempt amount	(11,000)
Taxable gain	49,000
CGT payable @ 28%	13,720

(c) If Roy and Gary make a claim for gift relief, the total tax payable is £44,520. If they do not make a claim for gift relief, the total tax payable is £(9,900 + 13,720) = £23,620, which is £20,900 less than if a gift relief claim is made. This is due to the availability of entrepreneurs' relief for Roy and the use of his annual exempt amount.

41 Sharon

> **Tutorial note.** When dealing with rollover relief look out for depreciating assets.

Sharon has made a gain of £40,000 (£80,000 – 40,000) on the sale of the shop. If she acquires a replacement shop within 3 years of the sale, she can claim rollover relief.

Freehold Shop

Less than the full proceeds have been reinvested. A gain equal to the amount not reinvested (£80,000 – £72,000 = £8,000) will remain in charge.

The remainder of the gain of £32,000 can be rolled over into the base cost of the freehold shop. The base cost will therefore be £72,000 – £32,000 = £40,000 for the purposes of computing a gain on its disposal.

Leasehold Shop

Full deferral of the gain is available as the whole of the proceeds of sale are reinvested.

The leasehold shop is a depreciating asset as the lease has less than 60 years to run. The gain is not deducted from the base cost of the leasehold shop, but is deferred until the earliest of the disposal of the leasehold shop, ceasing to use it in the business or ten years from its acquisition. The gain which will come into charge at that date will be £40,000.

If a non depreciating asset is acquired before the gain crystallises it can be rolled over into that new asset.

42 Kai

> **Tutorial note.** Gains qualifying for entrepreneurs' relief use up the basic rate band in priority to gains not qualifying for the relief.

	£	Gains £	CGT £
Gains qualifying for entrepreneurs' relief			
Goodwill		50,000	
Shop	90,000		
Less cost	(80,000)		
Gain		10,000	
Warehouse	180,000		
Less cost	(150,000)		
Warehouse		30,000	
Taxable gains		90,000	
CGT @ 10% on £90,000			9,000
Gains not qualifying for entrepreneurs' relief			
Land	25,800		
Less cost	(10,000)		
Gain		15,800	
Less: annual exempt amount (best use)		(11,000)	
Taxable gain		4,800	
CGT @ 28% on £4,800 (N)			1,344
Total CGT due			10,344

The claim for entrepreneurs' relief must be made by 31 January 2017.

Note

The basic rate band is used first by income (£20,000), then by gains qualifying for entrepreneurs' relief (£90,000). The remaining gain is therefore above the basic rate limit and so taxable at 28%.

43 Shares and securities

43.1 A £21,700

A plc

Lower of (i) $\dfrac{2.22 - 2.20}{4} + 2.20 = 2.205$ and (ii) $\dfrac{2.12 + 2.22}{2} = 2.17$

ie $2.17 \times 10,000$ £21,700

43.2 C Against 500 of the shares acquired on 31 July 2014, then against 250 of the shares acquired on 10 August 2014 and then against 50 of the shares acquired on 10 March 2010

The matching rules are first against same day acquisitions, then shares in the following 30 days and then the share pool.

43.3 B 1 and 2

A disposal of gilts by an individual is exempt from capital gains tax. If a company makes a 2 for 1 bonus issue, each shareholder will receive 2 extra shares for each 1 share held without payment.

In a rights issue the rights issue shares are paid for by the shareholder resulting in an adjustment to the cost of the shareholding. A chargeable gain does not usually arise on a takeover where new shares are exchanged for old shares ('paper for paper' takeover).

44 Melissa

Tutorial note. The matching rules are very important and must be learnt.

First match the disposal with the acquisition in the next 30 days:

	£	£
Proceeds $\dfrac{4,000}{10,000} \times £42,000$	16,800	
Less: cost	(16,000)	800

Next match the remaining shares with the share pool:

	£	£
Proceeds $\dfrac{6,000}{10,000} \times £42,000$	25,200	
Less: cost (W)	(20,625)	4,575
Total gains		5,375

Working

	No. of shares	Cost £
12 July 2002 acquisition	3,000	21,000
17 January 2005 bonus issue 1 for 1	3,000	0
	6,000	21,000
14 December 2007 rights issue 1 for 3 @ £3.25 per share	2,000	6,500
	8,000	27,500
2 July 2014 disposal	(6,000)	(20,625)
c/f	2,000	6,875

45 Self assessment and payment of tax for individuals

45.1 C Steven 31 January 2016, Rita 28 February 2016

The latest filing date for a personal tax return is usually 31 January following the end of the tax year. However, if the notice to file the tax return is issued to the taxpayer after 31 October following the end of the tax year, the latest filing date is the end of 3 months following the notice.

45.2 D £6,000 on 31 January and 31 July 2015, £3,000 on 31 January 2016

Payments on account will be made on 31 January and 31 July 2015, with the balance of being paid on 31 January 2016.

Payments on account for 2014/15 are payable based on 50% of the relevant amount (income tax plus Class 4 NIC) for 2013/14.

45.3 B £960

The maximum penalty for a careless error is 30% of the potentially lost revenue (PLR). The PLR in this instance is 40% × £8,000 = £3,200. The penalty is therefore 30% × £3,200 = £960.

46 Ash

Tutorial note. In part (a), three payments of income tax may need to be made in respect of a tax year. Two payments on account are normally made on 31 January in the tax year and on the following 31 July. A final balancing payment of the income tax due for a year is normally made on the 31 January following the year. In part (b) it is important to identify the penalty date from which the penalty will be calculated. In relation to the late payment penalty, the penalty date is 30 days after the due date for the payment of tax. For the late filing penalty, the penalty date is the date on which the return is overdue.

(a) (i) Ash's payments on account for 2014/15 are based on the excess of the 2013/14 tax liability over amounts deducted under the PAYE system, amounts deducted at source and tax credits on dividends:

	£
2013/14 tax liability	16,800
Less: PAYE	(7,200)
tax deducted at source	(800)
tax credit on dividends	(200)
'Relevant amount'	8,600

The two payments on account for 2014/15 were therefore £4,300 (£8,600/2) each.

The balancing payment in respect of Ash's 2014/15 tax liability was calculated as follows:

	£
2014/15 tax liability	22,000
Less: PAYE	(7,100)
tax deducted at source	(900)
tax credit on dividends	(250)
	13,750
Less: payments on account (part (i))	(8,600)
Balancing payment	5,150

(ii) The due dates for the payments on account for 2014/15 were 31 January 2015 and 31 July 2015.

The due date for the balancing payment for 2014/15 was 31 January 2016.

(b) (i) The penalty date for late filing of the tax return is the date on which the return will be overdue (ie 1 February 2016 which is the day after the filing date). The date of filing is not more than three months after the penalty date. The late payment penalty is therefore £100.

(ii) The penalty date for late payment of tax is 30 days after the due date. The date of payment is therefore not more than five months after the penalty date. The late payment penalty is therefore:

£5,150 × 5%   £257

47 Inheritance tax: scope and transfers of value

47.1 A   £87,250

	£
Gift	420,000
Less: AEs 2014/15, 2013/14 b/f	(6,000)
Net chargeable transfer	414,000
Less: nil band remaining £(325,000 – 260,000)	(65,000)
	349,000
IHT @ $^{20}/_{80}$	87,250

The gross chargeable transfer in August 2010 is after any exemptions but the gift in November 2014 must have the annual exemptions deducted to find the net chargeable transfer.

47.2 C   £510,000

	£
Andy's unused nil band	
60% × £325,000	195,000
Hilda's unused nil band	
£(325,000 – 10,000)	315,000
	510,000

The transfer by Hilda to her nephew is covered by her annual exemptions for 2013/14 and 2012/13 b/f.

47.3 B   Lifetime tax 30 April 2015, death tax 30 June 2015

For chargeable lifetime transfers the due date is the later of 30 April just after the end of the tax year of the transfer and six months after the end of the month of the transfer. The due date for the tax arising on death is six months from the end of the month of death.

48 Colin

> **Tutorial note.** This answer follows the 'steps' set out within the text but in a streamlined format which is equally acceptable in the exam.

(a) **IHT implications during Colin's lifetime**

21.1.08

No chargeable transfers were made in the seven years prior to 21.1.08 so all of the nil band of £300,000 remained available for use.

	£
Net transfer of value	315,000

IHT			£
	£300,000	× 0% =	Nil
	£ 15,000	× 20/80 =	3,750
	£315,000		3,750

The gross chargeable was: £315,000 + £3,750 = £318,750.

Check: tax £(318,750 − 300,000) = £18,750 × 20% = £3,750.

The IHT was due on 31 July 2008.

20.8.09

	£
Potentially exempt transfer	15,000

This was a PET so no lifetime tax was due. The transfer is treated as exempt during Colin's lifetime so no lifetime tax was due and the transfer does not enter into cumulation whilst Colin is alive.

19.6.10

Gross chargeable transfers of £318,750 had been made in the seven years prior to 19.6.10. The nil rate band remaining for use was £(325,000 − 318,750) = £6,250. The trustees pay the IHT due so no grossing up is required.

	£
Gross transfer of value	88,000

IHT			£
	£6,250	× 0% =	Nil
	£ 81,750	× 20% =	16,350
	£88,000		16,350

The IHT was due on 30 April 2011.

(b) **IHT position as a result of Colin's death**

21.1.08

Gross transfer of value	£318,750

No gross chargeable transfers were made in the seven years prior to 21.1.08 so all of the nil band at death of £325,000 remains available for use.

No death IHT payable because the transfer is within the available nil rate band (but there is no refund of lifetime tax).

20.8.09

Gross chargeable transfers of £318,750 have been made in the seven years prior to 20.8.09. The nil rate band remaining for use is £(325,000 − 318,750) = £6,250.

The value of the PET is the value at the date of the gift, not the value at the death of the donor.

Gross transfer of value		£15,000

			£
IHT	£6,250	× 0% =	Nil
	£8,750	× 40% =	3,500
	£15,000		3,500
Less taper relief @ 60% (5-6 years)			(2,100)
IHT payable			1,400

The IHT is due on 30 June 2015.

19.6.10

Gross chargeable transfers of £(318,750 + 15,000) = £333,750 have been made in the seven years prior to 19.6.10 so there is no nil band available to set against this transfer. There is no effect on the value of the transfer as a result of the increase in value of the asset between the lifetime transfer and the death of the donor.

Gross chargeable transfer	£88,000

	£
£88,000 × 40% =	35,200
Less taper relief @ 40% (4-5 years)	(14,080)
Less lifetime tax	(16,350)
Tax due on death	4,770

The IHT is due on 30 June 2015.

49 Simona

Tutorial note. Where a deceased spouse's unused nil rate band is transferred on the death of the surviving spouse and the nil rate band has increased between the deaths of the spouses, the unused nil rate band is increased pro-rata.

(a) **Simona's death estate**

	£	£
Shares in MS plc		320,000
Life assurance policy (amount of proceeds payable as result of death)		250,000
House	175,000	
Less: loan secured on house	(10,000)	
		165,000
Household furniture		20,000
Cash in bank		97,750
Car		5,000
Less: credit card bills	7,000	
income tax	3,000	
gas bill	250	
funeral expenses	2,500	(12,750)
Net death estate		845,000
Less: spouse exemption (net value of house)		(165,000)
Chargeable death estate		680,000

(b)   Simona's full nil rate band at death is available as she made no lifetime transfers.

Simona's first husband had an unused nil rate band of £(300,000 – 20,000) = £280,000. In terms of the nil rate band at Simona's death, the unused proportion is:

$$\frac{280,000}{300,000} \times £325,000 = £303,333$$

Simona's personal representatives can elect to transfer this unused nil rate band to Simona. The total nil rate band available to calculate death tax on Simona's death estate is therefore £(325,000 + 303,333) = £628,333.

(c)   The IHT on Simona's death estate is:

£(680,000 – 628,333) = £51,667 @ 40%   £20,667

50 Computing taxable total profits

50.1   C   1 December 2013 to 30 November 2014 and 1 December 2014 to 31 March 2015

If a company has a long period of account it is divided into one accounting period of 12 months and one accounting period of the remainder.

50.2   A   £2,720

	£
Leasing cost	3,200
Less: £3,200 × 15% disallowable	(480)
Allowable deduction	2,720

50.3   D   £14,400

Rent (accruals)	£14,400

The mortgage is a non-trading loan relationship and so the interest is a debit which must be set against credits from other non-trading loan relationships. There is no wear and tear allowance on an unfurnished property.

51 Elderflower Ltd

> **Tutorial notes.** You must use the layout shown when adjusting profits for taxation. The notes have been added for tutorial purposes.

(a) **Trading profit for y/e 31 March 2015**

	£	£
Profit before taxation		417,210
Add:		
Depreciation	54,690	
Accountancy and audit	0	
Legal fees – share capital (N1)	8,800	
Legal fees – loan notes (N1)	0	
Legal fees – breach of contract	0	
Legal fees – health and safety (N1)	900	
Repairs and renewals: extension (N2)	9,700	
Repairs and renewals: repainting (N2)	0	
Other expenses: entertaining customers	2,310	
Other expenses: entertaining employees	0	
Other expenses: qualifying charitable donation	500	
Interest payable (N3)	0	
		76,900
Deduct:		
Office building profit	54,000	
Bank interest	7,000	
Capital allowances (W)	25,190	
		(86,190)
Profit adjusted for tax purposes		407,920

Notes

1   Costs relating to share capital need to be added back as they relate to a capital expense. However, the fees relating to the loan notes are a loan relationship expense and thus deductible as a trading expense because the debenture is for trade purposes. Legal fees in relation to the fine are not deductible as the fine is a payment contrary to public policy.

2   The cost of the extension has been added back as a capital expense but the cost of repainting is allowable as it is a repair and therefore a revenue expense.

3   No adjustment is needed for the interest because it relates to a trade purpose loan.

Working

Capital allowances on plant and machinery

	AIA £	Main pool £	Special rate pool £	Allowances £
TWDV b/f		27,500	14,700	
Additions qualifying for AIA				
10.5.14 Equipment	20,200			
AIA	(20,200)			20,200
Additions not qualifying for AIA				
5.2.15 Car				
31.3.15 Car (N1)		9,600		
Disposals				
5.1.15 Car			(9,700)	
			5,000	
20.3.15 Van		(11,600)		
		25,500		
WDA @ 18%		(4,590)		4,590
WDA @ 8% (N2)			(400)	400
TWDVs c/f		20,910	4,600	
Allowances				25,190

Notes.

1. The private use of the car by the employee is not relevant for capital allowance purposes. No adjustment is ever made to a company's capital allowances to reflect the private use of an asset.

2. Although the only asset in the special pool has been sold, the pool of expenditure continues to be written down. A balancing allowance on the special pool can only when the trade ceases.

(b) **Total taxable profits y/e 31 March 2015**

	£
Trading profit (part (a))	407,920
Chargeable gain	45,580
Investment income	7,000
Total profits	460,500
Less: qualifying charitable donation	(500)
Taxable total profits	460,000

52 Computing the corporation tax liability

52.1 C £5,000

Dividends from associated companies are ignored for tax purposes and only dividends from non-associated companies are included in franked investment income. The figure of £4,500 must be grossed up by 100/90.

52.2 D £58,800

There are five companies associated with P Ltd so the upper limit is £1,500,000/6 = £250,000 and the lower limit is £300,000/6 = £50,000. Therefore P Ltd is a main rate company.

£280,000 × 21%	£58,800

52.3 B £121,625

Marginal relief applies

	£
£590,000 × 21%	123,900
Less: £(1,500,000 – 590,000) × 1/400	(2,275)
Corporation tax payable	121,625

53 Tree Ltd and Branch Ltd

Tutorial note. You need to calculate both taxable total profits and augmented profits. Augmented profits determine which tax rate applies, but the tax rate is applied to taxable total profits.

(a) **Tree Ltd**

	Year to 31.3.15 £
Trading profit	180,000
Chargeable gain	105,000
Investment income	36,000
Total profits	321,000
Less: qualifying charitable donation	(27,000)
Taxable total profits	294,000
FII: £29,700 × 100/90	33,000
Augmented profits	327,000

Marginal relief applies

Year to 31.3.15	£
Corporation tax (FY 14)	
£294,000 × 21%	61,740
Less 1/400 × (1,500,000 – 327,000) × $\dfrac{294,000}{327,000}$	(2,637)
	59,103

(b) **Branch Ltd**

	6 months to 31.3.15 £
Taxable total profits	420,000
Augmented profits	420,000
Upper limit £1,500,000 × 6/12	750,000
Lower limit £300,000 × 6/12	150,000

	£
Corporation tax (FY 14)	
£420,000 × 21%	88,200
Less marginal relief	
£(750,000 – 420,000) × 1/400	(825)
	87,375

54 Righteous plc

> **Tutorial note.** Where a company has a long period of account, it has two accounting periods: first 12 months and then the remainder.

	1.1.13 - 31.12.13 (12m) £	1.1.14 - 31.5.14 (5m) £
Trading income (12:5)	352,941	147,059
Investment income (15,000 + 6,000)	21,000	2,500
Chargeable gain	–	5,000
Total profits	373,941	154,559
Less: qualifying charitable donations (15,000 + 15,000)	(30,000)	(40,000)
Taxable total profits	343,941	114,559

Lower limit: £300,000 × 5/12 = 125,000

Upper limit: £1,500,000 × 5/12 = 625,000

Therefore marginal relief applies for the first 12 month accounting period and small profits rate applies for the five month accounting period.

12 m/e 31.12.13

	£
FY12	
£343,941 × 24% × 3/12	20,636
Less: £(1,500,000 – 343,941) × 1/100 × 3/12	(2,890)
FY13	
£343,941 × 23% × 9/12	59,330
Less: £(1,500,000 – 343,941) × 3/400 × 9/12	(6,503)
Tax due for y/e 31.12.13	70,573

5 m/e 31.5.14

	£
Taxable total profits/augmented profits	£114,559

Small profits rate applies for both FY13 (1.1.14 to 31.3.14 – three months) and FY14 (1.4.14 to 31.5.14 – two months). Since the same rate applies for both FYs, the computation can be combined.

	£
FY13 and FY14	
£114,559 × 20%	22,912

55 Chargeable gains for companies

55.1   C   From April 2010 to August 2014 on £12,800 and from May 2011 to August 2014 on £5,000

There is no indexation allowance on costs of disposal.

55.2   B   £479,888

	£
Net proceeds £(640,000 – 6,000)	634,000
Less: cost £(120,000 + 8,000)	(128,000)
	506,000
Less: indexation allowance 0.204 × £128,000	(26,112)
Chargeable gain	479,888

55.3   D   £57,500

	£
Proceeds	200,000
Less: cost	(110,000)
Unindexed gain	90,000
Less: indexation allowance	(20,000)
Indexed gain	70,000
Less: rollover relief (balancing figure)	(57,500)
Chargeable gain: amount not reinvested £(200,000 – 187,500)	12,500

56 Long Ltd

> **Tutorial note**. The key to success in share computation questions is to set up the three column pro-forma for the FA 1985 pool. Remember to **add** the indexed rise to the indexed cost pool!

Shares in Wide plc

FA 1985 pool – Deep plc

	No. of shares	Cost £	Indexed cost £
June 2002 Acquisition	5,000	14,000	14,000
May 2008 Indexed rise $\dfrac{215.1-176.2}{176.2} \times £14,000$			3,091
Rights 1:1 @ £4 per share	5,000	20,000	20,000
Pool at 15 May 2008	10,000	34,000	37,091

Takeover 7 March 2014

	No. of shares	MV £	Cost £	Indexed cost £
Ord shares in Wide plc	20,000	100,000	27,200	29,673
Pref shares in Wide plc	10,000	25,000	6,800	7,418
	30,000	125,000	34,000	37,091

FA 1985 pool – Wide plc ordinary shares

	No. of shares	Cost £	Indexed cost £
May 2008 Deemed acquisition	20,000	27,200	29,673
October 2014 Indexed rise $\dfrac{258.7-215.1}{215.1} \times £29,673$			6,015
Sale	(20,000)	(27,200)	(35,688)
c/f	0	0	0

Gain

	£
Proceeds	110,000
Less cost	(27,200)
	82,800
Less indexation allowance £(35,688 – 27,200)	(8,488)
Gain	74,312

57 Xeon Ltd

> **Tutorial note.** When using the part disposal formula, remember that it only applies to cost which relates to the whole of the original asset, not to expenditure incurred just on the part being sold (which is deductible in full).

Warehouse

	£
Proceeds	120,000
Less cost	(65,000)
	55,000
Less indexation allowance $\dfrac{256.8 - 181.3}{181.3}$ (0.416) × £65,000	(27,040)
Gain	27,960
Less rollover relief (balancing figure)	(7,960)
Gain left in charge £(120,000 − 100,000)	20,000

Cost of warehouse bought in July 2013

	£
Cost	100,000
Less rollover relief	(7,960)
Revised cost	92,040

Plot of land

	£
Proceeds	30,000
Less cost	(9,000)
$\dfrac{30,000}{30,000 + 40,000}$ × £21,000	
expenditure in December 2012	(1,000)
	20,000
Less indexation allowance	
$\dfrac{256.4 - 170.1}{170.1}$ (0.507) × £9,000	(4,563)
$\dfrac{256.4 - 246.8}{246.8}$ (0.039) × £1,000	(39)
	15,398

58 Losses

58.1   B   2 and 3

Trade losses of a company carried forward can only be used against profits of the same trade. Trade loss relief may be given by deduction from current period total profits and those in the previous 12 months.

Property business losses of a company are set against total profits of the same accounting period. Capital losses can only be set against chargeable gains in the same or future accounting periods.

58.2 A £30,000

E plc must make a current year loss claim against total profits if it wishes to make a claim to carry a loss back so the loss available for carry back is £(40,000 – 10,000) = £30,000.

E plc cannot keep sufficient income to cover the qualifying charitable donation. The carry back is against total profits (ie before qualifying charitable donations).

58.3 D £38,000

	£
Trading income	165,000
Less: trading loss b/f	(165,000)
	0
Non-trading loan relationship income	27,000
Chargeable gain £(14,000 – 3,000)	11,000
Taxable total profits	38,000

59 Ferraro Ltd

> **Tutorial note.** The pro forma for loss relief is important. If you learn the pro forma you should find that the figures slot into place. Note that the result of a losses claim may be that, as here, qualifying charitable donations become unrelieved.

	Accounting periods		
	12m to 31.3.13	9m to 31.12.13	12m to 31.12.14
	£	£	£
Trading profits	6,200	4,320	0
Investment income	80	240	260
Property business income	1,420	1,440	1,600
Chargeable gain	0	7,680	0
Total profits	7,700	13,680	1,860
Less current period loss relief	0	0	(1,860)
	7,700	13,680	0
Less carry back loss relief	(1,925)	(13,680)	(0)
Less qualifying charitable donations	(0)	(0)	(0)
Taxable total profits	5,775	0	0
Unrelieved qualifying charitable donations		1,000	1,500

Loss memo	£
Loss of y/e 31.12.14	100,000
Less used y/e 31.12.14	(1,860)
	98,140
Less used 9m/e 31.12.13	(13,680)
	84,460
Less used y/e 31.3.13 3/12 × £7,700	(1,925)
c/f against first available profits of the same trade	82,535

> **Tutorial note.** The loss is carried back to set against profits arising in the previous 12 months. This means that the set off in the y/e 31.3.13 is restricted to 3/12 × £7,700 = £1,925.

60 Groups   11 mins

60.1   C   £19,000

	£
Trading loss	16,000
Excess qualifying charitable donation £(4,000 – 1,000)	3,000
Amount available for group relief	19,000

60.2   A   £40,500

The lower of:

P Ltd profits 1.4.14 – 31.12.14 £54,000 × 9/12	£40,500
O Ltd loss 1.4.14 – 31.12.14 £(60,000) × 9/12	£45,000

60.3   C   B Ltd, C Ltd and D Ltd

B Ltd owns 75% of C Ltd and so is in a chargeable gains group with it. B Ltd also has an effective interest in D Ltd of 75% × 90% = 67.5%. As this is 50% or more, D Ltd is also in this gains group.

A Ltd does not own 75% or more of B Ltd and so cannot be in a chargeable gains group with B Ltd or its subsidiaries.

61 P Ltd

> **Tutorial note**. You are asked to use group relief in the most tax efficient manner. This means giving it first to companies in the marginal relief band, then to companies paying tax at the main rate.

There are six associated companies, so the lower and upper limits are £50,000 and £250,000 respectively.

S Ltd and T Ltd are outside the P Ltd group for group relief purposes. P Ltd's loss should be surrendered to Q Ltd, to bring its taxable total profits down to £50,000, and to R Ltd to bring its taxable total profits down to £50,000. The balance of £5,000 should be surrendered to either M Ltd, Q Ltd or R Ltd. In this case M Ltd has been selected. A claim by P Ltd against its own profits would have wasted qualifying charitable donations and carrying the loss forward would not obtain relief for several years.

	M Ltd £	P Ltd £	Q Ltd £	R Ltd £	S Ltd £	T Ltd £
Trading profits	20,000	0	64,000	260,000	0	70,000
Property business income	0	6,000	4,000	0	0	0
Total profits	20,000	6,000	68,000	260,000	0	70,000
Less qualifying charitable donation	(4,000)	(4,500)	(2,000)	(5,000)	0	0
	16,000	1,500	66,000	255,000	0	70,000
Less group relief	(5,000)	0	(16,000)	(205,000)	0	0
Taxable total profits	11,000	1,500	50,000	50,000	0	70,000
Corporation tax (FY14):						
at 20%	2,200	300	10,000	10,000	0	
at 21%						14,700
Less marginal relief 1/400 (£250,000 – 70,000)						(450)
Corporation tax payable	2,200	300	10,000	10,000	0	14,250

62 Apple Ltd

> **Tutorial note**. The marginal rate of tax of 21.25% is an effective tax rate only. It is never actually used in working out corporation tax.

(a) Group relief is available within a 75% group. This is one where one company is a 75% subsidiary of another company or both are 75% subsidiaries of a third company. The holding company must have at least 75% of the ordinary share capital of the subsidiary, a right to at least 75% of the distributable income of the subsidiary, and the right to at least 75% of the net assets of the subsidiary were it to be wound up.

Two companies are in a group only if there is a 75% effective interest eg if Company A holds 90% of Company B which holds 90% of Company C, all three companies are in a group because 90% × 90% = 81%.

(b) Losses should be allocated to the company with the highest marginal rate of tax. This is Cherry Ltd and Apple Ltd to the extent that taxable total profits exceed £100,000 since the small profits rate lower limit is £300,000 ÷ 3 = £100,000. Such profits are taxed at the marginal rate of 21.25%. The remainder of the loss should be set against the taxable total profits of Banana Ltd which bears tax at 21%.

As a current year loss relief claim against the total profits of Apple Ltd has to use as much loss as is available, the group relief claims surrendering losses to Banana Ltd and Cherry Ltd are made first, specifying amounts that will leave Apple Ltd with sufficient losses to reduce its taxable total profits to £100,000.

Tutorial note

The amounts of the income loss relief claims are determined after chargeable gains and losses are considered.

(c) Rollover relief for part of Apple Ltd's gain can be claimed in respect of the investment by Cherry Ltd. The excess of amount of proceeds over the amount invested remains in charge ie £(418,000 – 290,000) = £128,000.

An election should be made so that the capital loss by Banana Ltd is transferred to Apple Ltd. Apple Ltd will then be able to offset the loss of £8,000 against the gain of £128,000, leaving £120,000 chargeable.

Apple Ltd then needs £20,000 loss remaining after group relief to make a current year loss relief claim to bring its profits down to £100,000. Therefore, £30,000 losses should be group relieved to Cherry Ltd (to save tax at the marginal rate), with £75,000 (£125,000 – £30,000 – £20,000) relieved to Banana Ltd to leave the £20,000 losses in Apple Ltd.

	Apple Ltd £	Banana Ltd £	Cherry Ltd £
Trading profits	–	650,000	130,000
Net capital gain	120,000	–	–
Total profits	120,000	650,000	130,000
Less: loss relief against total profits	(20,000)		
group relief		(75,000)	(30,000)
Taxable total profits	100,000	575,000	100,000
Tax @ 20%	20,000		20,000
Tax @ 21%		120,750	

Note that the upper limit is £1,500,000 ÷ 3 = £500,000 and the lower limit is £300,000 ÷ 3 = £100,000.

63 Self assessment and payment of tax by companies

63.1 B   Return date 31 December 2015, tax payable date 1 October 2015

The return must be submitted within 12 months of the end of the accounting period and the tax paid nine months and one day after the end of the accounting period.

63.2 A   31 March 2016

The tax return must be filed within 12 months of the end of the period of account because it is not more than 18 months long. Therefore the return for the first accounting period which ends on 31 December 2014 must be submitted by 31 March 2016.

63.3 D   Retention date: 31 March 2021, maximum penalty: £3,000

A company must keep its records for six years from the end of the accounting period, if no compliance check is made.

Failure to keep records can lead to a maximum penalty of £3,000 for each accounting period affected.

64 Cyan plc

> **Tutorial note.** Companies paying corporation tax at the main rate must pay their CT liabilities in quarterly instalments.

(a)   **Cyan plc – corporation tax payable p/e 31.12.14**

	£
Upper limit £1,500,000 × 9/12	1,125,000
Cyan plc is therefore a main rate company for the period	
Corporation tax £1,428,571 × 21%	300,000

(b)   Cyan plc is required to pay its corporation tax liability in instalments because it is a main rate company (a 'large' company) and this is not the first year that it is 'large'.

The amount of each instalment and the due dates are as follows:

$$3 \times \frac{£300,000}{9} = £100,000 \text{ payable on 14 October 2014, 14 January 2015, 14 April 2015.}$$

65 Skyblue Ltd and Turquoise plc

> **Tutorial note.** For part (a), if a corporation tax return is filed after the due date, the date for written notice of a compliance check is one year after the next quarter date after the actual delivery of the return. In part (b), it is important to calculate the potential lost revenue (PLR) as a result of the error as the penalty will be a percentage of this amount.

(a)   **Skyblue Ltd – corporation tax return**

(i)   Skyblue Ltd must file its corporation tax electronically and must include a self assessment of any tax payable. Skyblue Ltd must also file, electronically, a copy of its accounts in iXBRL (inline eXtensible Business Reporting Language).

(ii)   The filing date is 12 months after the end of the period to which the return relates which in this case is 30 September 2015.

(iii)   The latest date, by which HM Revenue and Customs can give written notice to Skyblue Ltd that they intend to make a compliance check on the return if it is filed on 10 February 2016, is 30 April 2017.

(b)   **Turquoise plc – penalty for error**

(i)   Potential lost revenue as a result of the error is:

	£
£(100,000 − 10,000) = £90,000 × 21%	18,900
The maximum penalty for a deliberate, but not concealed, error is:	
£18,900 × 70%	13,230

(ii)   An unprompted disclosure is one made at a time when the taxpayer has no reason to believe HM Revenue and Customs has discovered, or is about is discover, the error.

(iii)   The minimum penalty for a deliberate, but not concealed, error with unprompted disclosure is:
£18,900 × 20%   £3,780

66 An introduction to VAT

66.1   A   1 January 2015

Alec is liable to register for value added tax (VAT) when he is aware that his taxable turnover during the next 30 days will exceed the VAT registration limit of £81,000 (the future test). HM Revenue and Customs (HMRC) will then register him from the first day of that 30-day period, in this case 1 January 2015.

66.2   C   £11,520

All discounts, whether taken or not, must be taken into account before VAT is calculated. Therefore the VAT due is £60,000 × 96% × 20% = £11,520.

66.3   B   31 December 2014

The tax point is generally the earliest of: the date of delivery, the invoice date and the cash receipt date. However, if as in this case, the invoice is issued within 14 days of delivery, then the invoice date becomes the tax point.

67 Newcomer Ltd and Au Revoir Ltd

Tutorial note. This question is a typical question on registration and deregistration. Note the importance of the dates.

(a)   The registration threshold is £81,000 during any consecutive 12 month period.

This is exceeded in January 2015:

		£
2014	October	18,500
	November	18,900
	December	23,400
2015	January	21,300
		82,100

Therefore, Newcomer Ltd must notify HM Revenue and Customs within 30 days of the end of the month the threshold was exceeded, ie by 2 March 2015.

Newcomer Ltd will be registered from 1 March 2015, or an earlier date agreed between the company and HM Revenue and Customs.

(b)   A person is eligible for voluntary deregistration if HM Revenue and Customs are satisfied that the amount of his taxable supplies (net of VAT) in the following one year period will not exceed £79,000. However, voluntary deregistration will not be allowed if the reasons for the expected fall in value of taxable supplies is the cessation of taxable supplies or the suspension of taxable supplies for a period of 30 days or more in that following year. HM Revenue and Customs will cancel a person's registration from the date the request is made or an agreed later date.

68 Justin

> **Tutorial note**. This question is a basic VAT computation. Note how the input and output VAT is accounted for in respect of petrol and that the VAT incurred on the entertaining for UK customers is blocked from recovery.

	£	£
Output VAT		
Furniture: £490,000 × 20%	98,000	
Books: £2,400 × 0%	0	
Petrol (VAT scale charge): £391 × 1/6	65	
		98,065
Input VAT		
Furniture: £275,000 × 20%	55,000	
Computer: £2,400 × 20%	480	
Entertaining: irrecoverable in relation to UK customers	0	
Petrol: £2,800 × 20%	560	
		(56,040)
VAT to account for quarter ending 31 December 2014		42,025

69 Ongoing Ltd

> **Tutorial notes**.
>
> 1   Where a discount is offered for prompt payment, VAT is chargeable on the net amount, regardless of whether the discount is taken up.
>
> 2   VAT on business entertaining is generally not recoverable. However the cost of entertaining overseas customers is recoverable.
>
> 3   Impairment loss (bad debt) relief is only available for debts over six months old (measured from when the payment is due).
>
> 4   VAT incurred on the purchase of a car not used wholly for business purposes is not recoverable. However, the subsequent sale of the car is exempt from VAT.

	£	£
Output tax		
£120,000 × 95% = 114,000 × 20% (note 1, note 4)		22,800
Input tax		
£(35,640 − 480) = 35,160 × 20% (note 2)	7,032	
£(2,100 × 95%) = £1,995 × 20% (note 3)	399	
£21,150 × 1/6 (note 4)	3,525	(10,956)
VAT payable for quarter ending 30 April 2014		11,844

Notes

1   VAT is calculated after the deduction of the prompt payment discount.

2   UK entertaining is not an expense on which input tax can be recovered.

3   The debt must be six months old to claim bad debt relief. The output tax accounted for on the supply was net of the 5% discount for prompt payment even though the discount was obviously not taken up. The same amount of input tax can therefore be recovered under bad debt relief.

4   Input tax on motor cars not used wholly for business purposes is irrecoverable. However, the sale of the car, on which input tax is irrecoverable, is exempt from VAT.

70 Further aspects of VAT

70.1   C   1 and 4

All VAT returns must be up to date before a trader can join the scheme and it gives automatic impairment loss relief (bad debt relief) because VAT is not due on a supply until payment has been received.

The turnover condition is that a trader can join the scheme if their taxable turnover (exclusive of VAT) for the 12 months starting on their application to join the scheme is not expected to exceed £1,350,000. The payment of VAT by monthly payments applies to the annual accounting scheme.

70.2   D   £0

Where goods are sold to another EU member state, the supply is zero-rated if the supply is made to a registered trader.

70.3   A   £9,900

The flat rate percentage is applied to the full tax inclusive turnover including all standard, zero and exempt supplies so the VAT liability is £110,000 × 9% = £9,900.

71 Jason

Tutorial note. Make sure that you are clear about the different procedures for dealing with VAT on goods acquired from outside and inside the EU. The overall effect will usually be the same, but there is an actual payment of VAT required for imports from outside the EU at the time of importation.

(a)   As Jason is a UK VAT registered trader, when he supplies goods to another VAT registered business within the European Union, the supply is zero-rated.

(b)   When Jason acquires goods from a VAT registered trader in another EU member state, he is liable to VAT in the UK.

He will enter the transaction on his VAT return as an output and an input so the effect is neutral.

This means that Jason is in the same position as he would have been if he had acquired the goods from a UK VAT registered trader.

The 'tax point' is the earlier of:

(i)   The fifteenth day of the month following the month of acquisition
(ii)   The date of issue of an invoice

(c)   Jason must account for VAT on the goods imported from outside the EU at the point of entry into the UK.

Jason can then deduct the VAT payable as input tax on his next VAT return.

This means that Jason is in the same overall position as he would have been if he had acquired the goods from a UK VAT registered trader.

BPP
LEARNING MEDIA

(d)   Supplies of services by a UK VAT registered trader to business customers outside the EU are outside the scope of UK VAT as the place of supply is not in the UK.

72 K Ltd and L Ltd

> **Tutorial note.** In part (a), it is a good idea to present your answer as bullet points where you are asked to prepare notes for a meeting. The main advantage of the cash accounting scheme is automatic impairment loss relief so you should have spotted that this was the relevant scheme in part (b).

(a)   **K Ltd – notes for meeting on annual accounting scheme**

(i)   *Rules and qualifying conditions*

- Must regularly pay VAT (rather than receive repayments) to HM Revenue & Customs (HMRC)

- Taxable turnover (excluding VAT) must not be expected to exceed £1,350,000 in next 12 months

- All VAT returns must be up-to-date

- Nine payments on account required, commencing at the end of the fourth month of the year

- Payments are made by direct debt

- Each payment is 10% of the net VAT payable for the previous year

- Option to pay three larger interim instalments

- Annual return must be submitted within two months of the VAT year-end and any balance paid

- If the expected value of taxable supplies by the end of a year exceeds £1,600,000, notice must be given to HMRC within 30 days and may then be required to leave the scheme

- If by the end of that year the £1,600,000 limit is in fact exceeded, must leave the scheme

(ii)   *Advantages*

- Only one VAT return each year so fewer occasions to trigger a default surcharge
- Ability to manage cash flow more accurately
- Avoids need for quarterly calculations for input tax recovery

Disadvantages

- Need to monitor future taxable supplies to ensure turnover limit not exceeded

- Timing of payments are less related to turnover (and therefore cash flow received) by business

- Payments based on previous year's turnover may not reflect current year turnover which may be a problem if the scale of activities has reduced

(b)   **L Ltd – cash accounting scheme**

The cash accounting scheme will provide automatic impairment loss relief. This is because L Ltd will account for VAT on the basis of cash paid and received and so the date of payment or receipt determines the return in which the transaction is dealt with. Therefore, VAT will not be due on a supply until payment has been received.

L Ltd can use the cash accounting scheme if its expected taxable turnover for the next 12 months does not exceed £1,350,000. L Ltd must also be up-to-date with its VAT returns and VAT payments.

73 M Ltd

> **Tutorial note.** When applying the flat rate percentage, you must include standard rated, zero rated and exempt supplies.

M Ltd – flat rate scheme

(a)   M Ltd can join the flat rate scheme if its expected taxable turnover (excluding VAT) for the next 12 months does not exceed £150,000.

   M Ltd can continue to use the scheme until its total turnover (including VAT) for the previous year exceeds £230,000.

(b)   The net output VAT for M Ltd for the year ended 31 March 2015 was £(82,000 – 10,000) × 1/6 = £12,000.

   If M Ltd had used the flat rate scheme throughout the year ended 31 March 2015, then it would have paid VAT of £(82,000 + 8,000) @ 10.5% = £9,450.

   This is a tax saving of £(12,000 – 9,450) = £2,550 for the year.

Tax tables

SUPPLEMENTARY INFORMATION

1. Calculations and workings need only be made to the nearest £.
2. All apportionments may be made to the nearest month.
3. All workings should be shown.

TAX RATES AND ALLOWANCES

The following tax rates and allowances are to be used in answering the questions.

Income tax

		Normal rates	Dividend rates
		%	%
Basic rate	£1 – £31,865	20	10
Higher rate	£31,866 to £150,000	40	32.5
Additional rate	£150,001 and over	45	37.5

A starting rate of 10% applies to savings income where it falls within the first £2,880 of taxable income.

Personal allowance

	£
Personal allowance	
Born on or after 6 April 1948	10,000
Born between 6 April 1938 and 5 April 1948	10,500
Born before 6 April 1938	10,660
Income limit	
Personal allowance	100,000
Personal allowance (born before 6 April 1948)	27,000

Residence status

Days in UK	Previously resident	Not previously resident
Less than 16	Automatically not resident	Automatically not resident
16 to 45	Resident if 4 UK ties (or more)	Automatically not resident
46 to 90	Resident if 3 UK ties (or more)	Resident if 4 UK ties
91 to 120	Resident if 2 UK ties (or more)	Resident if 3 UK ties (or more)
121 to 182	Resident if 1 UK tie (or more)	Resident if 2 UK ties (or more)
183 or more	Automatically resident	Automatically resident

Child benefit income tax charge

Where income is between £50,000 and £60,000, the charge is 1% of the amount of child benefit received for every £100 of income over £50,000.

Car benefit percentage

The base level of CO_2 emissions is 95 grams per kilometre.

The percentage rates applying to petrol cars with CO_2 emissions up to this level are:

	%
75 grams per kilometre or less	5
76 grams to 94 grams per kilometre	11
95 grams per kilometre	12

Car fuel benefit

The base figure for calculating the car fuel benefit is £21,700.

New individual savings accounts (NISAs)

The overall investment limit is £15,000.

Pension scheme limits

Annual allowance	– 2014/15	£40,000
	– 2011/12 to 2013/14	£50,000

The maximum contribution that can qualify for tax relief without any earnings is £3,600.

Authorised mileage allowances: cars

Up to 10,000 miles	45p
Over 10,000 miles	25p

Capital allowances: rates of allowance

Plant and machinery

Main pool	18%
Special rate pool	8%

Motor cars

New cars with CO_2 emissions up to 95 grams per kilometre	100%
CO_2 emissions between 96 and 130 grams per kilometre	18%
CO_2 emissions over 130 grams per kilometre	8%

Annual investment allowance

Rate of allowance	100%
Expenditure limit	£500,000

Cap on income tax reliefs

Unless otherwise restricted, reliefs are capped at the higher of £50,000 or 25% of income.

Corporation tax

Financial year	2012	2013	2014
Small profits rate	20%	20%	20%
Main rate	24%	23%	21%
Lower limit	300,000	300,000	300,000
Upper limit	1,500,000	1,500,000	1,500,000
Standard fraction	1/100	3/400	1/400

Marginal relief

Standard fraction $\times$ (U – A) $\times$ N/A

Value Added Tax (VAT)

Standard rate	20.0%
Registration limit	£81,000
Deregistration limit	£79,000

Inheritance tax: tax rates

£1 – £325,000		Nil
Excess	– Death rate	40%
	– Lifetime rate	20%

Inheritance tax: taper relief

Years before death	% reduction
Over 3 but less than 4 years	20
Over 4 but less than 5 years	40
Over 5 but less than 6 years	60
Over 6 but less than 7 years	80

Capital gains tax

Rates of tax	– Lower rate	18%
	– Higher rate	28%
Annual exempt amount		£11,000
Entrepreneurs' relief	– Lifetime limit	£10,000,000
	– Rate of tax	10%

National insurance contributions
(Not contracted-out rates)

Class 1 Employee	£1 – £7,956 per year	Nil
	£7,957 – £41,865 per year	12.0%
	£41,866 and above per year	2.0%
Class 1 Employer	£1 – £7,956 per year	Nil
	£7,957 and above per year	13.8%
	Employment allowance	£2,000
Class 1A		13.8%
Class 2	£2.75 per week	
	Small earnings exception	£5,885
Class 4	£1 – £7,956 per year	Nil
	£7,957 – £41,865 per year	9.0%
	£41,866 and above per year	2.0%

Rates of Interest (assumed)

Official rate of interest	3.25%
Rate of interest on underpaid tax	3.0%
Rate of interest on overpaid tax	0.5%

BPP
LEARNING MEDIA

Index

BPP
LEARNING MEDIA

Review Form – Paper F6 (Taxation) Finance Act 2014 (10/14)

Please help us to ensure that the ACCA learning materials we produce remain as accurate and user-friendly as possible. We cannot promise to answer every submission we receive, but we do promise that it will be read and taken into account when we update this Study Text.

Name: _____   Address: _____

_____

_____

How have you used this Study Text?
(Tick one box only)

☐ On its own (book only)

☐ On a BPP in-centre course _____

☐ On a BPP online course

☐ On a course with another college

☐ Other _____

Why did you decide to purchase this Study Text? *(Tick one box only)*

☐ Have used BPP Texts in the past

☐ Recommendation by friend/colleague

☐ Recommendation by a lecturer at college

☐ Saw information on BPP website

☐ Saw advertising

☐ Other _____

During the past six months do you recall seeing/receiving any of the following?
(Tick as many boxes as are relevant)

☐ Our advertisement in *ACCA Student Accountant*

☐ Our advertisement in *Pass*

☐ Our advertisement in *PQ*

☐ Our brochure with a letter through the post

☐ Our website www.bpp.com

Which (if any) aspects of our advertising do you find useful?
(Tick as many boxes as are relevant)

☐ Prices and publication dates of new editions

☐ Information on Text content

☐ Facility to order books

☐ None of the above

Which BPP products have you used?

Text	☑	Passcards	☐	Other	☐
Kit	☐	i-Pass	☐		

Your ratings, comments and suggestions would be appreciated on the following areas.

	Very useful	Useful	Not useful
Introductory section	☐	☐	☐
Chapter introductions	☐	☐	☐
Key terms	☐	☐	☐
Quality of explanations	☐	☐	☐
Examples	☐	☐	☐
Exam focus points	☐	☐	☐
Questions and answers in each chapter	☐	☐	☐
Fast forwards and chapter roundups	☐	☐	☐
Quick quizzes	☐	☐	☐
Question Bank	☐	☐	☐
Answer Bank	☐	☐	☐
Index	☐	☐	☐

Overall opinion of this Study Text.	Excellent ☐	Good ☐	Adequate ☐	Poor ☐

Do you intend to continue using BPP products?   Yes ☐   No ☐

On the reverse of this page is space for you to write your comments about our Study Text. We welcome your feedback.

The BPP Learning Media author of this edition can be emailed at: AlisonPriest@bpp.com

Please return this form to: Davinia McGann, ACCA Publishing Manager, BPP Learning Media Ltd, FREEPOST, London, W12 8AA

TELL US WHAT YOU THINK

Please note any further comments and suggestions/errors below. For example, was the text accurate, readable, concise, user-friendly and comprehensive?

NATALIA OSIPOVA

BECOMING A SWAN

Natalia Osipova

BECOMING A SWAN

PHOTOGRAPHS BY ANDREJ USPENSKI

First published in 2013 by Oberon Books Ltd
521 Caledonian Road, London N7 9RH
Tel +44 (0)20 7607 3637
info@oberonbooks.com
www.oberonbooks.com

Cover and book design: James Illman

A catalogue record for this book is available from the British Library.

PB ISBN 978-1-78319-022-5
E ISBN 978-1-78319-521-3

Printed and bound in India by Replika Press Pvt. Ltd.

Visit www.oberonbooks.com to read more about all our books and to buy them. You will also find features, author interviews and news of any author events, and you can sign up for e-newsletters so that you're always first to hear about our new releases.

Acknowledgements

Thank you to Oberon Books

FOREWORD

Natalia Osipova is a phenomenon, one of the most extraordinary ballerinas of the twenty-first century.

Working with her on Sir Anthony Dowell's production of *Swan Lake*, and seeing her meticulous work on the dual role of Odette/Odile, gave me great personal pleasure and satisfaction. By thoroughly learning and scrupulously polishing every movement we achieved great results together. Without doubt Natalia Osipova possesses the skilful technique of a great ballerina, which enables her to create two contrasting roles in this ballet. But she was determined to do yet more work to deepen the intense spiritual feeling in Odette's character and interpret that side of the dual role in The Royal Ballet production.

Andrej Uspenski is a dancer with The Royal Ballet. As a photographer he captures wonderful moments of our creative working atmosphere with acute sensitivity. Very precisely, with great tenderness and love for his profession, he is able to perfectly preserve fragments of progress from studying the choreographic material to perfecting it during Osipova's performance on stage. His images penetrate the inner spiritual world of the ballerina in these two completely contrasting roles of good and evil. With such a reliable partner – Carlos Acosta (Siegfried) – Osipova becomes an irresistible heroine, delicate, fragile and vulnerable. She convinces us that she is deeply in love and trusting in the second act, and later in total despair when she is betrayed by Siegfried. But by the end of the performance we share her passion as she sacrifices her earthly life for their eternal love.

I look forward to seeing Natalia Osipova in new roles, adding new ballets in her repertoire, and new artistic achievements!

Alexander Agadzhanov, *Senior Teacher and Répétiteur to the Principal Artists*

ПРЕДИСЛОВИЕ

Наталья Осипова – экстраординарная, феноменальная балерина 21-го века.

Работая с ней над "Лебединым озером", в редакции сэра Антони Доуэлла я получил огромное удовольствие и неимоверное удовлетворение от ее кропотливой работы над ролями Одетты- Одилии. Тщательное изучение и скрупулезно отшлифовывая каждое ее движение в этих ролях, мы добились с ней великолепных успехов. Безусловно, безукоризненная техника балерины, которой владеет Наталья Осипова, очень помогает ей в создании того или иного образа. Но, ей необходимо было поработать над интерпретацией этой роли в нашей постановке и внутренним духовным состоянием образа Одетты

Андрей Успенский, танцовщик Королевского балета, как фотограф, с проницательной чуткостью уловил моменты творческой рабочей атмосферы. Очень точно, с особой нежностью и любовью к своей профессии, он смог в своих фотографиях превосходно запечатлеть фрагменты развития прогресса с самого начала изучения хореографического материала до полного совершенства во время выступления на сцене.Ему удалось проникнуть во внутренний духовный мир балерины в этих двух, совершенно противоположных по характеру, ролей. Вполне естественно,что в надежных руках Карлоса Акосты(Зигфрида) наша героиня могла себе позволить быть совершенно неотразимой, нежной и хрупкой и легко ранимой, а также глубоко и доверчиво влюбленной во 2-м акте и в полном отчаяние от предательства Зигфрида в их вечной любви, готовой страстно на самопожертвование.

Мне хотелось бы пожелать Наталье Осиповой новых ролей, новых балетов в ее репертуаре и новых творческих удач!

С уважением , всегда - Александр Л. Агаджанов

Alexander Agadzhanov, *Senior Teacher and Répétiteur to the Principal Artists*

with **Alexander Agadzhanov**, *Senior Teacher and Répétiteur to the Principal Artists*

with **Boris Gruzin**, *Conductor*

with **Carlos Acosta**, *Principal Guest Artist*

NEATH AND PORT TALBOT

Those were the days

NEATH AND PORT TALBOT

Those were the days

by David Roberts

Courier

breedon **books**
PUBLISHING

First published in Great Britain in 2003 by The
Breedon Books Publishing Company Limited,
Breedon House, 3 The Parker Centre,
Derby, DE21 4SZ.

ISBN 1 85983 380 2

Printed and bound by Butler & Tanner,
Frome, Somerset, England.

Cover printing by Lawrence-Allen Colour Printers,
Weston-super-Mare, Somerset, England.

CONTENTS

An Appreciation

This book would not have been possible without the assistance of the many residents of Neath and Port Talbot who submitted their own telling images of times past, particularly readers of the *Neath and Port Talbot Courier* newspapers.

Special thanks are given to:

Cheryl Roberts
John Vivian Hughes and John Southard
Michael & Valerie Davies
Michael & Barbara Hopkins
Keith & Ann Davies
Mervyn & Betty Roberts
Brenda Thomas & Elaine Davies
Henri Griffiths, Steve Miles
Peter Stevens,
Grace & Robert Thomas,
Vernon Joseph, Colin Radford
Janet & Alan Jones,
Linda Feltham, Anne George
Mary Gregory, Tony Crocker,
Wynford Vaughan Thomas
West Glamorgan Archivist Susan Beckley and her team
and also the staff of Neath Port Talbot
Libraries and Museum Service

FOREWORD

THOSE who are already familiar with the books of images of Neath and Port Talbot produced by *South Wales Evening Post* journalist David Roberts will open this latest offering with a keen sense of anticipation, which will not be disappointed.

Others discovering the delights compiled by him for the first time are in for a treat, courtesy of the enthusiasm and dedication with which David tackles what can only be a labour of love.

Once again the photographs on view will remind us of how things were, and how much things have changed over the passing decades.

We are now well established in the 21st century, and the two proud towns featured in this volume are embarked upon the latest stage of their individual and joint journey through time. How appropriate, then, to pause and reflect on how each town has reached its current place in the ever shifting social picture of this part of South Wales.

The *South Wales Evening Post*, and its associated *Courier* titles in Neath and Port Talbot, are delighted to offer David congratulations on another job well done.

Spencer Feeney
Editor
South Wales Evening Post

MEETING THE

CHALLENGE

NEATH and Port Talbot are towns which, indelibly and undeniably, have left their mark on the world at large and continue to do so as the 21st century unfolds. Their industries, down the years, have often been at the forefront of the very toughest challenges – no mean feat when Wales itself is acknowledged as the first true industrial nation. Coal, iron, steel and tinplate have all played their part in shaping the destiny of the two towns. And in turn the people of the proud communities who now campaign under the one, proud county borough banner have played their part in the fortunes of those, and other perhaps lesser, industries.

Global change has meant the demise of many of these traditional, heavy industries and in their place the rise of lighter, high-tech production facilities in keeping with the computer age. Once again Neath and Port Talbot and their people have risen to the fresh challenge and continually strive to meet their demands. But it is not simply on an industrial front that the new has displaced the old. Perhaps the biggest, most recent evidence of this is the new, state-of-the art hospital opened on Baglan Moors. In replacing the former Neath General Hospital it accepted the challenge to continue a proud tradition and a highly respected reputation.

The many new housing developments around the County Borough further demonstrate its metamorphosis to meet changing lifestyles and hopefully demonstrate faith in the future. But there are other milestones of change, perhaps less significant, everywhere we look. And although many often fail to realise it, everyone in Neath and Port Talbot, their districts, and communities have played a part in shaping the way things are. They may have grown up, gone to school, worked or simply immersed themselves in daily life, but each has played an individual part in the heritage of what makes up Neath and Port Talbot. The pictures in this book are a reflection of that and a well-earned tribute to those people.

David Roberts

2003

AROUND TOWN

The view down New Street, Neath, from The Square, about 1900.

Looking up Station Road, Port Talbot, 1926, from outside the Grand Hotel.

The bowling green at Memorial Park, Taibach, Port Talbot, 1928.

The Forge Road, Port Talbot store of plumber and gas fitter Henry Griffiths, late 1920s.

If you wanted to buy any china or glassware in Neath in 1903 then this is probably where you would have gone. It was the stall opened on the site of the old cattle market – where The Parade was later developed – by W Mort before the opening of the town's general market. His son Godfrey and wife Tydvil are seen in front of its amazing array of goods.

Oliver's boot and shoe warehouse Queen Street, Neath, 1910.

Ena Avenue, Neath, looking towards Cimla Road, early 1920s.

Davey Richards – with a
young helper – at the
general store he ran from a
garage at Hillside, Neath,
1926.

Forge Road, Port Talbot, was thronged with people for this parade in the mid-1930s. Many of the properties on the right hand side looking up towards Velindre still had front gardens then.

The newsagents run by John Griffiths at Port Talbot, late 1940s.

A view across the rooftops of Neath town centre towards the river, 1929.

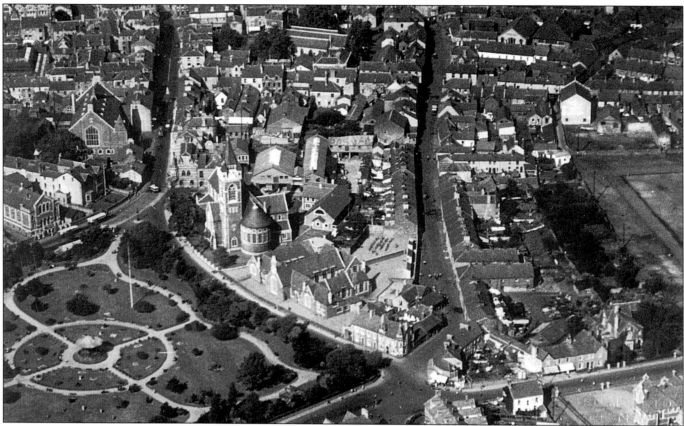

An intriguing 1929 view across a section of Neath town centre that has changed greatly due to modernisation and commercial redevelopment. The field on the right hand side is now the site of the Civic Centre.

Station Road, Port Talbot was once a busy traffic trunk route and the scene of frequent congestion as this early 1950s scene shows. In later years the street was pedestrianised.

The Square, Neath, early 1950s. Pedestrianisation was a long way off then.

Probably the biggest traffic bottleneck in Port Talbot was the junction at the top of Water Street where it met the A48 trunk road. Queues like this were frequent in the early 1950s.

A mid-1950s view of Victoria Gardens, Neath.

High Street, Aberavon, early 1950s.

Cottages at Water Street, Neath, near its junction with St David's Road, mid-1950s.

Alderman Davies Primary School, Neath, in the background, 1950. The young baby girl in the pram has grown up now and so too have the trees which today obscure this scene.

High Street, Aberavon, with Pentyla in the distance, mid-1950s.

Heavy traffic in High Street, Aberavon, made life hazardous for pedestrians in the mid-1950s.

The Gorsedd Circle at Victoria Gardens, Neath, 1960, with St David's Church in the background.

A wet mid-1950s winter's day at the railway level crossing that marked the junction of High Street Aberavon, and into the distance Station Road, Port Talbot. Traffic chaos regularly ensued when the crossing gates closed to allow trains to pass.

Bush Sports, Water Street, Neath, in 1973. It was a popular rendezvous for sportsmen and women, for decades.

Traffic and pedestrians are forced to await the passage of a train across the busy main route through Port Talbot, mid-1950s.

These buildings in Water Street, Neath, Bush Sports and Allin's the grocers were scheduled for demolition for redevelopment when this 1973 picture was taken.

Vivian Square, Aberavon, viewed from the hillside above and with the town's gasworks in the centre distance, late 1950s.

It was the route to traffic salvation for Port Talbot – work on the long-awaited M4 motorway across the town well under way above Aberavon's old Mountain Primary School, 1963.

The Bird In Hand pub, Wind Street, Neath, 1974, before its demolition to make way for the development of a Tesco store and multi-storey car park. Wilkinsons store occupies the site today.

Parts of old Aberavon had already disappeared under the demolition hammer when this picture showing early progress on the construction of the M4 through the town was taken in 1963.

The Shakespeare Inn, on the junction of Water Street and Wind Street, Neath, 1974.

The George & Dragon Inn, Water Street, Neath, where many a schoolboy could claim to have had his first drink! It had already closed when this picture was taken in 1974.

The quadrangular housing of Vivian Square once occupied this part of Aberavon, demolished to pave the way for redevelopment and the march of the M4. This was the scene in mid-1960.

Workmen
demolish Bethel
Methodist Chapel,
High Street,
Aberavon, to make
way for the M4
motorway, 1963.
Below them is the
Welcome to Town
pub also set to
suffer the same
fate.

For the sweet-
toothed, the Gem
confectionery and
tobacconists, Gnoll
Park Road, Neath –
pictured in 1975 –
was a haven.

Looking across old Aberavon, Baglan Moors and Sandfields estate, from Springfield Terrace, Aberavon, 1961.

The Ancient Briton pub, Wind Street, Neath, 1975.

The M4 motorway spans the River Afan in this view from High Street Bridge, 1968. The buildings on the left were demolished to make way for the town's redevelopment.

Many of Port Talbot's buildings had vanished by 1972 when this view across Talbot Square towards the town's distant Municipal Buildings, also under demolition, was taken.

Water Street, Neath, 1975. These properties were later demolished for the building of a Tesco supermarket and multi-storey car park.

Ready for demolition. These buildings, opposite Neath Workingmen's Club in Wind Street were demolished for redevelopment shortly after this 1975 picture was taken.

The march of progress has had a telling impact on this 1972 Port Talbot scene. The gas works has long gone and much of the site redeveloped for housing. The River Afan is on the right hand side with Newbridge Road running across the bottom of the view.

The Port Talbot Hotel, Water Street, Aberavon, mid-1970s.

Construction of a railway bridge for the main Swansea to Paddington railway line at Neath over route of the new A465 dual carriageway through the Neath Valley 1979.

Looking over the town's rooftops towards Port Talbot steelworks, April 1979.

Road and rail side by side at Neath in October 1982. The former Neath & Brecon railway junction signal box is prominent in the background while the overhead bridge carries the main Swansea to Paddington railway line. The buses were running Saturday shoppers from Banwen and Glynneath in the Dulais and Neath valleys to Swansea.

The National Schools, Aberavon, November mid-1970s. The buildings were demolished in 1976.

A 1985 addition to the Creamline Services bus fleet at Neath heads a line-up of vehicles at Victoria Gardens bus station on March 23 of that year before setting off on a then new Neath to Moortown and Skewen service. The bus station was closed for upgrading during August 2003.

A sure sign that the temperature was well-below freezing – the River Afan almost frozen over near Cwmavon, January 1983.

The view along part of Heilbronn Way, Port Talbot towards Forge Road, November 1982 before the later construction of the town's civic centre and Tesco store and car park on the right of the view.

Looking up and looking down. The clock of St David's Church, Neath stands at 10 past three on a summer's day in 1987, as a statue of one of the town's benefactors – Howell Gwynne – looks down on passers-by in the town's Victoria Gardens. The statue originally stood in the nearby forecourt at the Gwyn Hall, where his finger pointed to his birthplace, where Argos now stands.

Ysguthan Road, Aberavon, January, 1989, with the Mears and Jones grocery store in the background at its junction with Pembroke Terrace.

The Queen's Hotel, Orchard Street, Neath, mid-1980s. The hostelry later changed its name to The Canterbury.

The roundabout at Stockham's Corner, Neath, mid-1980s. Now it is a much busier meeting point for traffic.

The old Aberavon fire station at Water Street, January 1989.

Looking up Queen Street, Neath towards Victoria Gardens and the town's library, late 1980s after it had been pedestrianised.

PEOPLE POWER

Old Mam Newton, of New Henry Street, Neath, middle front, surrounded by some of the womenfolk in her family, early 1900s.

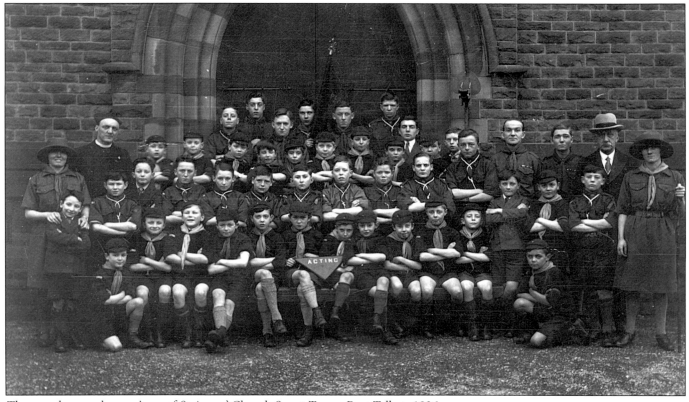

The members and organisers of St Agnes' Church Scout Troop, Port Talbot, 1926.

Members of Port Talbot's St John Ambulance Brigade Division who were winners in a competition at Clydach, on July 18, 1925.

Neath china and glassware entrepreneurs William and Tydvil Mort, with their children, early 1900s.

Members of the congregation of St Clement's Church, Briton Ferry in fancy dress, 1920s.

Second World War serviceman Joe Gubb, of Wood Street, Margam is given a send off by friends and neighbours, 1940.

A group of the younger members of Gnoll Road Congregational Church, Neath, outside the building with Sunday school teachers, possibly at Whitsuntide 1934.

A visit by The Princess Royal in the late 1940s was good enough reason to dress in traditional Welsh costume for these members of Cwmavon Urdd youth group pictured on the mountainside near Monks pool.

A detachment of the Home Guard at the Drill Hall, Cimla Road, Neath, November 4, 1944.

Some of the members of Cwmavon Urdd group who took part in the organisation's Machynlleth Eisteddfod in 1952.

The old age pensioners group at Cadoxton, Neath, celebrates its first birthday in 1952. Members are seen with officials of the group outside the village school.

Fun in the sun for these three children at Hawthorn Avenue, Baglan, Port Talbot, late 1950s.

Staff of the County Furnishers, Aberavon at the annual dance of the company's southern division, 1952. On the right are Mr Leonard Goodreid and his wife who later became mine hosts at the King Edward VII pub, London Road, Neath for many years.

Cwmavon's industrious looking sewing class, 1950s.

Friends and neighbours of surrounding streets gather in Victoria Street, Briton Ferry, early 1950s.

Youngsters at play near Victoria Terrace, Cwmavon, early 1950s.

Members of St Clements Church Mothers Union, Briton Ferry, mid-1950s.

Down the years the Salvation Army has been responsible for much good work in and around Port Talbot. Among those who made it possible were Salvationists Leonard and Dorothy Roberts seen in the early 1950s with the Port Talbot Corps flag in a lane just off High Street Aberavon.

Nothing wrong with holding your chum's hand on a winter walk – except for the fact that these two youngsters were walking on a deep frozen Neath Canal at Melyncrythan, in the late 1950s.

Some of the young people and officers of Port Talbot Salvation Army Corps, 1960.

Cub Scouts from Cimla, Neath, during a camping trip to the Ivy Tower, Tonna, late 1950s.

The Young Wives group of St Catharine's Church, Baglan, early 1960s.

The officers and committee of Neath Busmens Club, Brynhyfryd, late 1950s.

An evening out 1960s style for these members of the Young Wives group of St Catharine's Church, Baglan.

Weddings like this one at St David's Church, Neath town centre always drew crowds of onlookers in 1960 just like today.

Baglan Girl Guides, Port Talbot, on a camping trip, 1964.

Staff of Woolworths store, Port Talbot at their Christmas dinner, December 12, 1967.

Guests leave the Castle
Hotel, Neath, after a
1960 wedding reception.

A farewell party thrown for the owners of The Elms Country Club, Shelone Road, Briton Ferry , 1973.

The committee of Cwmavon Gardening Club and their wives at a civic reception given by the mayor of the former Borough of Afan, Councillor Ray Morgan, 1982.

Members of the congregation of Rehoboth Chapel, Briton Ferry during their Whitsun procession on May 30, 1982.

Miners wives from Dyffryn Cellwen in the Dulais Valley, drive home their message while collecting for the cause at Neath's Safeway store during the miners, strike, 1984.

Cubs of the 5th Port Talbot St Theodore's pack pictured with the Mayor and Mayoress of the Borough of Afan Councillor Ray and Mrs Morgan, after winning a hotly-contested Road Safety competition, 1982.

Brownies gather at Cefn Saeson Comprehensive School, Cimla, Neath, for a Thinking Day celebration, 1988.

Port Talbot Lions Club made sure everyone had a good time at this mid-1980s concert for disabled youngsters at the Afan Lido.

One of the prize-winning leeks displayed at Cwmavon horticultural show, Port Talbot 1986.

Musical director Christopher Waring-Davies and choreographer Julie Dawn with youngsters of the chorus of Briton Ferry Amateur Operatic Society's successful production of the hit musical *Oliver!* during a break in rehearsals, 1990.

Members of the congregation of Margam Abbey, Port Talbot, at a barn dance they organised on a nearby farm, late 1980s.

DISTRICT DAYS

Smoke and steam rises from some of the numerous collieries and pits that once peppered the landscape near Bryncoch, Neath, early 1900s.

Tyr Owen Row, Cwmavon, Port Talbot, early 1900s.

Garthmor Lodge, Briton Ferry, on a snowy winter's day, early 1900s.

The now demolished Jersey Beach Hotel, Aberavon, 1903. The building was gutted by fire on December 14, 1908.

The view down Villiers Street, Briton Ferry, early 1900s when it was a thriving street in a prosperous small town.

A little developed Aberavon Beach, 1903. The Jersey Beach Hotel is in the background and towering sand dunes where housing development followed.

Cwrt Sart, Briton Ferry, looking towards Neath, 1907.

Tommy Oakes outside his butcher's shop at 29 Briton Ferry Road, Neath, 1927, probably with his wife.

Wil Y Post, outside his home in Fullers Row, Cwmavon, 1910. Wil was for many years the village postman.

Margam Cottage hospital on the mountainside above Port Talbot, 1914.

This picture appeared on a Christmas card sent in 1921 to all the best customers of S E Davies butchers shop at 129 Neath Road, Briton Ferry. It shows Mr Davies with some of his family and a butcher's boy outside a shop well-stocked for the forthcoming festivities.

The Post Office on The Square at Cwmavon, 1907.

Looking out over Cwmavon from Ynysygwas, late 1930s.

Thompsons confectioners and tobacconist next door to Briton Ferry Public Hall, Neath Road, mid-1920s.

A view over Cwmavon mid-1930s.

A telling view from the air in 1934. Nearly all the fields in the picture have been swallowed up by housing development at Baglan, while the heavy industry evident has vanished too. The waterway is Briton Ferry Dock and its basin.

Residents of one of the now demolished stone-built terraces that clung to the hillside at Abercregan in the Afan Valley pose for a photograph on a sunny, late 1940s afternoon.

A young mum with her children outside one of the many prefab bungalows built at Farm Drive, Sandfields, Port Talbot, during the late 1940s to help ease the town's housing shortage.

A young lad plays on waste ground opposite his Dalton Road, Sandfields, Port Talbot home, early 1950s.

Aberpergwm House, Near Glynneath, mid-1930s.

A view of the Gnoll House with its grand conservatory, late 1930s.

A jazz band sets off to parade through the streets of Taibach, Port Talbot, early 1950s.

No parking problems for these youngsters with their trolley in 1951, on the site of Velindre Crescent, Port Talbot.

Gas lamps were still in evidence in this Briton Ferry scene near the point where the main railway line passes under Briton Ferry viaduct, September 1, 1959.

Briton Ferry Public Hall, late 1950s. Today a car sales showroom occupies the site. It was demolished in the early 1970s. The hall was used in one of the scenes of the Peter Sellers, Mai Zetterling film *Only Two Can Play* which was shot on location in Swansea.

Inkerman Row, Taibach, 1955. The building on the left was known as the Barracks. It was converted into a bungalow in 1960. The row itself was demolished in 1965.

A view from the mountainside across Baglan towards Port Talbot, mid-1965.

Newly-built private housing at Bryncoch, 1967.

The Afan Lido swimming pool and sports centre, Aberavon Beach, June 1966.

A coach travels through Caewern council estate, Neath, 1965.

The Ferry Boat Inn, Earlswood, with the Monkstone Cruising and Sailing Club's moorings on the River Neath, in the background, early 1970s. The inn became a private residence in the 1990s and has the only private mooring on the river.

Seafront housing at Aberavon Beach, June 1966. The blocks of flats were all local authority owned.

The Ivy Tower, on the hillside above Tonna, early 1970s. A landmark that can be seen from far and wide, it was originally built as a folly by the Mackworth family when they occupied Gnoll House.

Miami Beach funfair and amusement park on the Little Warren or eastern end of Aberavon Beach, 1966. It was a popular haunt for summer tourists but the site is now occupied by private housing.

Glyncorrwg in the upper Afan Valley, 1968. The railway lines, which served the village's South Pit have long since disappeared.

Cefn Saeson Comprehensive School, Cimla, Neath, 1980.

The village of Groes, Margam, shortly before it was demolished to make way for the advance of the M4 motorway. Early dismantling work was already under way on the historic Beulah or Round Chapel on a wet January 14, 1975.

Briton Ferry viaduct and Neath River bridge join to snake their way over the eastern edge of the township mid-1970s. The view shows what was the Wern aluminium works alongside the river and to the upper left the Monkstone Cruising and Sailing Club's marina under construction.

The Crown Inn on Neath Road, Briton Ferry, in the 1980s.

A huge pall of smoke billows from Mynydd Dinas at Baglan, visible from miles around, during this extensive forestry blaze in the early 1980s.

A clear demonstration of the way in which railways always seem to have cut Briton Ferry into two. This mainline view towards Neath was taken on March 5, 1983.

Looking across Cymmer towards Glyncorrwg, Afan Valley, Port Talbot, March 30, 1981.

A South Wales Transport bus tackles the twisting roadway under the viaduct at Pontrhydyfen, during November 1982 on a service from Swansea to Blaengwynfi in the Afan Valley.

TIME FOR CELEBRATION

A Whitsun procession moves along one of Neath's main streets, early 1900s.

Raising money for the First World War effort at Port Talbot, 1914.

Holding the banner high, worshippers from St Thomas Church Sunday School, Neath, are seen heading along Windsor Road as they take part in a Whitsun march, early 1900s.

This couple, Bryn Jones and his bride Marion Gubb, were the first to be married at Wesley Chapel, Taibach, Port Talbot, during August Bank Holiday, 1930.

One of the participants in Port Talbot Hospital's popular carnival parades pedals her way along Ysguthan Road, Aberavon on a heavily bedecked bicycle, 1934.

This topical float was produced by Stanford's bakery at Aberdulais, Neath, in 1920 for a harvest festival procession to a local church.

A young Port Talbot lad helps his grandmother celebrate a special birthday, 1940s style.

Harold Llewellyn and his bride Nan Richards with chief guests at their Neath wedding in 1928.

Members of the congregation of Rock Chapel, Cwmavon, Port Talbot, during their Whitsun treat, 1948.

The Dominoes was the title of this entertaining entry in Cwmavon's 1949 carnival parade.

Nurses, doctors and the matron of Neath General Hospital, Penrhiwtyn, 1934.

Staff of Neath hospital with local dignitaries pictured during a ground-breaking ceremony for a new building, 1935.

Members of Rock Chapel, Cwmavon, Port Talbot, and their families celebrate the Festival of Britain, 1951.

Residents of Evans Road, Melincrythan, Neath in happy mood at the street party they held to celebrate the Silver Jubilee of King George V, 1935.

Gwyn Nichols and Hilda Peard with bridesmaids and groomsmen after their wedding at St John's Church, Skewen, 1949.

Hat's the way! These senior citizens of West End, Taibach, Port Talbot are seen during celebrations to mark the Coronation of Queen Elizabeth II, June 1953.

Children of employees of Richard Thomas & Baldwins Wern Works, Briton Ferry at their annual Christmas party, 1946.

Time for a picture to mark the occasion for this group of mainly youngsters of the congregation of Rehoboth Baptist Chapel, Briton Ferry, after their Whitsun tea, 1950.

Some of the younger residents of Dalton Road, Sandfields, Port Talbot, tuck in at the street party organised by their mums to celebrate the Coronation of Queen Elizabeth II, June 1953.

Residents of King Street and Maria Street, Neath, united for a Festival of Britain parade, 1951.

Everyone wore a crown when residents of Farm Drive, Sandfields, Port Talbot celebrated the Coronation of Queen Elizabeth II, June 1953 – well almost!

Dudley Street, Neath, may be small, but its residents together with those of nearby Rectory Road made a big effort to salute the Coronation of Queen Elizabeth II, June 1953. Even the Rector of Neath at the time, Rev Roberts, turned up. He was the father of former Cardiff MP Michael Roberts who is pictured second right at the front.

Residents of Farm Drive, Sandfields, Port Talbot, sit down to a celebratory street tea to celebrate the Coronation of Queen Elizabeth II, June 1953.

Bunting straddled the street when residents of Greenway Road, Neath, held a party to celebrate the Coronation of Queen Elizabeth II, 1953.

Army Cadets who took part in a parade through Port Talbot when they were given the freedom of the Borough, April 1966.

This was the crowd that gathered at Bethel Chapel, School Road, Crynant in June 1953 to celebrate the Coronation of Queen Elizabeth II with a tea party.

Nearly every resident of Lewis Road, Neath, joined in the festivities to mark the Coronation of Queen Elizabeth II, June 1953.

Youngsters at Knights Road, Margam, Port Talbot, take a break from celebrating the Investiture of the Prince of Wales, 1969.

A table stretches into the distance when families in Hawthorn Avenue, Baglan, Port Talbot, staged a street party to mark the Investiture of the Prince of Wales, July 1969.

Pleased with their efforts in the piano smashing competition at Baglan carnival, 1975, are these members of Briton Ferry Steel Rugby Club.

Residents of Tonna, Neath, dressed up to celebrate the Coronation of Queen Elizabeth II, June, 1953.

Children of Middleton Street, Briton Ferry, during its Coronation celebrations, 1953.

Contestants in a charity pram race organised by Port Talbot Lions Club, 1981.

A group of employees of BP Chemicals, Baglan Bay, Port Talbot, plant, who retired in July 1982.

These were some of the participants in a party held at Briton Ferry Public Hall on the occasion of the Coronation of Queen Elizabeth II, June 1953.

A Port Talbot Guardsman with his proud family after the Welsh Guards were afforded the Freedom of Bridgend following the Falklands War, 1982.

Taking a break from the fun during their party to celebrate the Coronation of Queen Elizabeth II are these youngsters of Dudley Street and Rectory Road, Neath, June 1953.

A tree planting ceremony at Memorial Park, Taibach, Port Talbot in 1986, to honour Lord Heycock, of Taibach who is seen standing to the right of the tree accompanied by Lady Heycock.

Guests at a special evening at the Castle Hotel, Neath to mark the completion of 61 years service at Victoria Laundry, Cadoxton by Miss Gwynne Monkton, early 1960s.

Briton Ferry Cub Pack at an investiture ceremony to mark its restart, May 1978.

West Glamorgan Guide Commissioner Miss Freda Gibbins hands out Queen's Guide Awards to two Neath Guides while a fellow Guider looks on, 1978. Miss Gibbins died in 2003, aged 94.

Briton Ferry Brownies form a guard of honour after the wedding of their Brown Owl, 1982.

CHURCHES AND CHAPELS

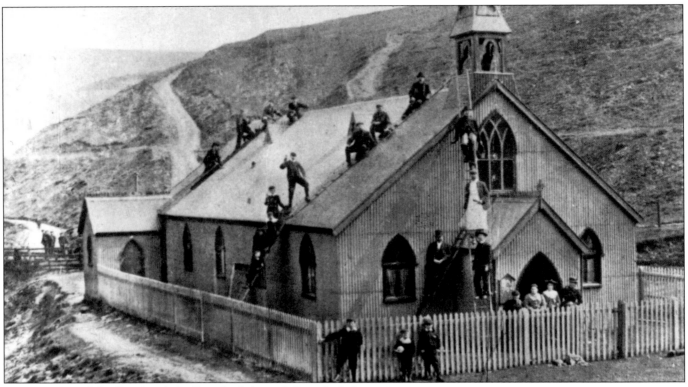

Construction of the first St John's Church, Oakwood, Pontrhydyfen, 1882.

The interior of Hope Chapel, Neath, at Harvest time, 1884, believed to be one of the oldest pictorial records of such an occasion in the town. The building is now occupied by Neath Boys Club.

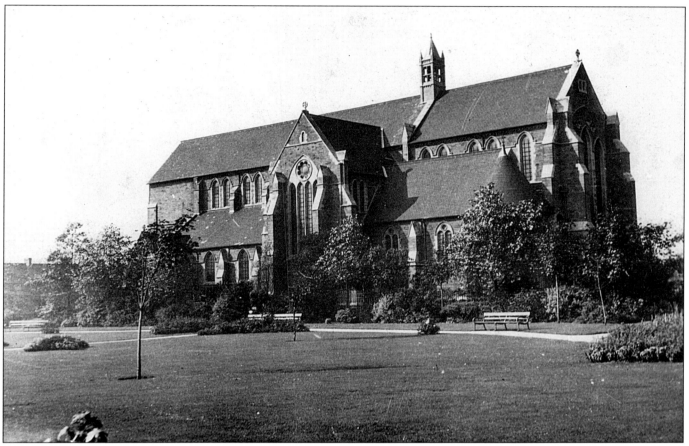

St Theodore's Church, Port Talbot, mid-1930s.

Orchard Place English Baptist Chapel, Neath 1920.

Construction work nears
completion on Neath
Methodist Church at
Stockham's Corner, 1913.

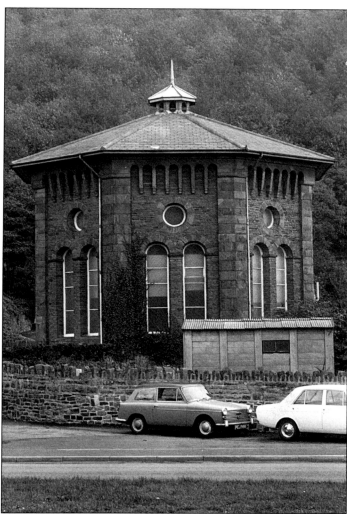

Beulah – the Round Chapel – at Groes, Margam, in 1971, before being resited in Tollgate Park nearby to make way for the M4 motorway. It is said to have been shaped like this so that the devil couldn't hide in the corners.

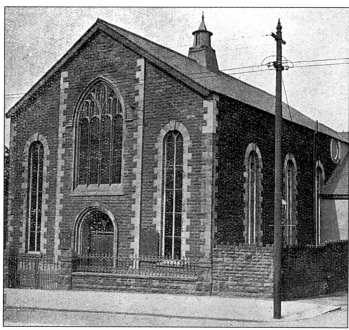

Jerusalem Chapel, Neath Road, Briton Ferry, 1921.

Holy Cross Church, Port Talbot, know as Chapel of Ease, 1980.

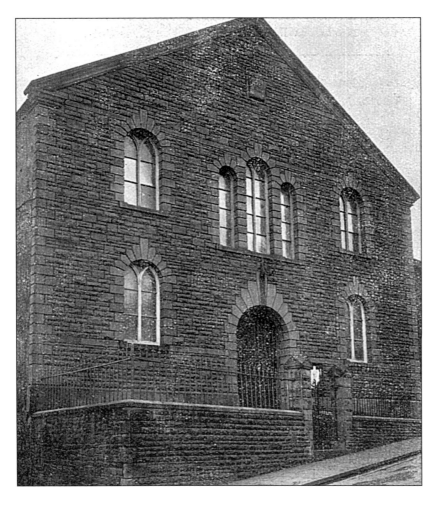

Melincrythan English Baptist Church, Herbert Road, Neath, 1921.

Penuel Baptist Church, Cwmavon, Port Talbot, November, 1982.

Sardis Chapel, Resolven, Neath, 1922.

Elim Church, Velindre, Port Talbot, 1984.

Mount Pleasant English Baptist Church, Skewen, 1922.

Wesley Methodist Church, Incline Row, Taibach, Port Talbot, 1985.

St Peter's Church, Goytre, Port Talbot, mid-1980s.

The ruins of Neath Abbey, 1960s.

St Mary's Church, Aberavon, Port Talbot, 1980s.

St David's Church, Neath, 1960s.

St Joseph's Roman Catholic Church, Port Talbot, January 1989. It was built in 1931 on the site of a former church constructed in 1862.

Wesley Chapel, London Road,
Neath, 1970.

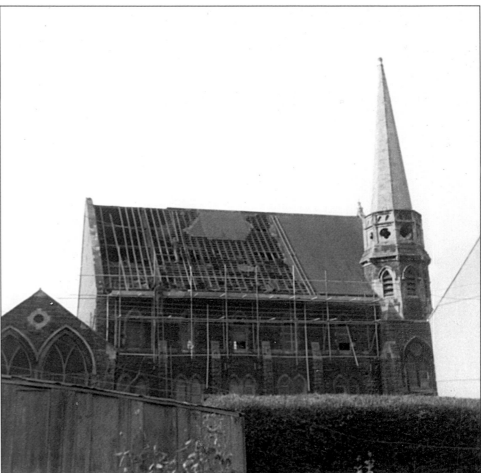

A sad end to devoted service. The
demolition men do their worst on
Ritson Street Congregational
Church, Briton Ferry, 1980.

BREAK TIME

A crowd gather on Crynant station in the Dulais Valley for a day out at Neath's September Fair, 1910.

Deacons of Gnoll Road Congregational Church, Library Road, Neath, all dressed up for a day trip, 1920s.

A day out in Briton Ferry Woods with his family in 1914 is something this First World War soldier may have looked forward to for some time.

This was the sight that would have greeted summertime visitors to Aberavon Beach in the early 1900s.

Members of the choir of St Theodore's Church, Port Talbot, with their choirmaster on a day trip to Weston Super Mare, 1930.

This group is all set for a day out to remember aboard Neath's Windsor Bus Company's first charabanc, 1920.

A crowd gathers to listen to the musicians playing in the bandstand at Memorial Park, Taibach, Port Talbot, 1930s.

Members of Bethesda Chapel, Briton Ferry on a Whitsun outing, 1939.

Members of Neath Busmens Club before setting off on an outing in the early 1950s. How did they travel? By bus of course!

A group of Port Talbot friends on a charabanc trip, 1930s.

This group of children and their mums seen outside Cimla Welfare Hall, travelled in style when they headed off for the day in 1951. They climbed aboard an N&C luxury coach.

Sun, sand and a comfortable deck chair was bliss for these Port Talbot people in July 1950.

Crynant, Neath residents on a trip to Brighton organised by villager Reg Brown, 1951.

A group of Port Talbot friends enjoys an impromptu picnic on the beach, mid-1950s.

The playground at Gnoll Park, Neath was a popular destination with these Neath children, swinging high in 1952.

Well even babies need a break in the fresh air at some time. This youngster enjoys her play in the back yard of an Aberavon home, 1951.

Families and friends from Crynant, Neath on a 1955 excursion to the Isle of Wight.

Youngsters enjoy the excitement of a ride in the swing boats at Aberavon Beach, 1952.

Employees of the Inland Revenue office at Neath on their annual outing, 1956.

Anyone else for a ride on the sands? This patient pony must have hauled thousands of passengers in his 1958 stint at Aberavon Beach.

These Port Talbot rugby fans were off to watch Wales play Scotland, 1958.

Youngsters prepare to set off for an exchange visit to Neath's twin town of Udine, Italy, August 1964.

Cheers lads! A group of Port Talbot mates during a summer holiday at Butlins Pwllheli, 1958.

Opposite: A donkey ride was one of the must-haves at Margam Fete, 1973… along with a delicious ice cream like this (below).

Penscynor Wildlife Park, Cilfrew, Neath, with its birds and animals was a mecca for people from far and wide in its heyday. The park was eventually closed and the site now occupied by housing. This picture of the late owner Idris Hale outside his home during November 1968 before opening the venture to the public will revive memories for many though.

Neath Circuit Methodist Church trip to Jersey, 1968. The picture includes Rev Colin Richards with some of the circuit youth club members.

Senior citizens from Mansel Street, Briton Ferry on a day trip, 1970.

High spirits from these pitmen from Dyffryn Cellwen in the Dulais Valley. They were dressed for a soccer match against a team of Skegness miners while on holiday during the mid-1970s.

RAILWAYS REMEMBERED

The stationmaster at Seven Sisters on the platform with some passengers, 1910.

Aberavon station, looking up towards Velindre, 1909.

A GWR pannier tank locomotive crosses Pontwalby viaduct north of Glynneath with the 7.40am Neath to Pontypool Road train on April 16, 1964.

Port Talbot Central station, 1932. It was situated behind the former Plaza cinema.

The *Doll* locomotive which for many years was a familiar sight on the the Briton Ferry industrial scene, July 30, 1959.

The 11.55am Paddington to Swansea train, with through coaches to Pembroke Dock, arriving at Port Talbot General station on July 27, 1958.

Briton Ferry station looking towards Port Talbot, early 1960s.

Two railwaymen take a break from their labours at Briton Ferry, early 1960s.

A train arrives at Neath Riverside station from Glynneath, early 1960s.

Locomotive 4134 arrives at Cymmer Afan station in the Afan Valley on June 18, 1960.

The signal box at the Neath & Brecon junction, Neath, 1960.

Aberavon Town station, June 1960.

A passenger train runs by Neath General West signal box as it enters the station, early 1960s.

The main building at Aberavon Town station, June 1960.

An empty passenger train heads through Neath Riverside station for Seven Sisters to pick up a miners, excursion to Porthcawl, 1962.

The platform and canopy at Cymmer Afan station mid-1960.

A train arrives at Cymmer Afan station early 1960s.

A freight train heads through Neath Abbey from Swansea Docks, June 2, 1962.

Railway workers at Margam up side marshalling yard, 1961.

The goods shed at Neath general station in April 1963 – it is now a car park.

Trains often needed the assistance of a banker engine to negotiate the climb up from Margam towards Pyle as this 1963 picture shows.

A locomotive awaits its next duty at Glynneath, February 1964.

The end of the line for these long-serving locomotives, at the Briton Ferry breakers yard, mid-1960s.

Two trains wait patiently for a signal to proceed on their journey from Porthcawl railway station, March 8, 1963.

The last day of passenger rail services from Cymmer Afan station to Bridgend, June 20, 1970.

A locomotive sets its train of empty wagons under the coal hopper at Blaenant Colliery, in the Dulais Valley before setting off for Aberthaw power station on December 16, 1989.

Briton Ferry rail yard was the marshalling point for this daily train of household coal bound for east Wales, April 4, 1991.

EARLY LEARNING

Some of the pupils at Sandfields Girls School, Port Talbot, with their teacher, early 1920s.

A mixed class of pupils at Jersey Marine Junior School, 1923.

Form 4, Cwrt Sart Central School, Briton Ferry, 1930.

Class 3, Sandfields Infants School, Port Talbot, 1923.

Form 3A Cadoxton Senior School, Neath, 1931 with their teacher and headteacher.

Pupils at Sandfields Girls School, Port Talbot, mid-1920s.

Pupils of Neath County School for girls with head teacher Miss Decima Jones, 1940.

A class at Port Talbot Secondary School with headmaster Mr C Reynolds, 1940.

Studying hard – pupils of Form 5A, Neath County School for Boys, 1939.

These pupils of Neath Technical School had been fruit picking while staying at Rammoth Road Camp, Wisbech, Cambridgeshire, 1951.

These pupils of Cwrt Sart School pictured with a teacher in 1954 were both prefects and members of the school tennis team.

Pupils of Cwrt Sart School, Briton Ferry with American exchange teacher Miss McGinn, February 1953.

It must have been raining heavily shortly before this class of girls at Sandfields School, Port Talbot, dutifully displayed themselves for the photographer, 1949.

A class at Central Girls Junior School, Port Talbot, St David's Day, 1950.

Pupils of Crynallt Junior School Cimla, Neath, 1956.

These pupils of the Commercial School, Pentyla, Port Talbot, were joined by teacher Mrs O'Shea and some of their friends for this youth dance at the town's Masonic Hall, early 1950s.

Pupils of Baglan Infants School, Port Talbot, early 1950s.

Children from Ynysymaerdy Primary School, Briton Ferry, take a rest during a summer nature walk, 1958.

Dinner time at Alderman Davies, Primary School, Neath, 1958.

Books at the ready for another lesson, these girls were pupils of Glanymor Primary School, Sandfields, Port Talbot, 1953.

Children who attended Trefelin Primary School, Velindre, Port Talbot, 1954.

Girls of Baglan Infants School, Port Talbot dressed in traditional Welsh costume to celebrate St David's Day, 1956.

Boys of Creunant Junior School out in the yard on a snowy March 1, 1955.

Making music with teacher Audrey Davies at the piano are these children of the percussion band at Creunant Junior School, Crynant in the Dulais Valley, 1957.

Mr Trick, headmaster of Brynhyfryd Junior School, Briton Ferry with some of his pupils, 1959.

Celebrating St David's Day 1969, a class at Crynallt Infants School, Cimla, Neath.

It was definitely summertime when this picture of a class at Cwmafan Junior School, Port Talbot was taken, early 1960s.

Boys of Alderman Davies, Primary School, Neath, with their teacher and headteacher, 1959.

Ynysmaerdy Primary School pupils, Briton Ferry, with their teacher and headteacher, 1976.

With the school buildings behind them these are pupils of Tywyn Primary School, Sandfields, Port Talbot, early 1960s.

The reception class at Crynallt Infants School, Cimla, Neath, 1979.

These children of Llansawel Nursery School, Briton Ferry were all dressed up to salute their patron saint on March 1, 1981.

A class at Trefelin Primary School, Velindre, Port Talbot, June 1961.

Nursery pupils of Neath Welsh School with their teacher at the piano and her assistant alongside, St David's Day, 1981.

Form 3A Dyffryn Comprehensive School, Margam, Port Talbot, 1965.

The lucky dip proved one of the most popular attractions at the summer fair of Neath Welsh School, Woodland Road in 1982 as this picture shows.

Pupils of Dyffryn Comprehensive School, Margam, Port Talbot, 1966.

It was the last day in primary school for this group of pupils at Crynallt Junior School, Cimla, Neath, 1984.

Pupils of Baglan Primary School, during a 1975 concert.

Form 2T Cefn Saeson Comprehensive School, Cimla, Neath, 1984.

Pupils of Tywyn Junior School, Port Talbot, 1978.

Form 5K, Cefn Saeson Comprehensive School, Cimla, Neath, 1984.

Class 1S, Cwmavon Junior School, Port Talbot, 1979.

The class of 1978 at Tywyn Primary School, Sandfields, Port Talbot.

A class of pupils at Central School, Port Talbot, with their teacher and headteacher, 1983.

Children of the nursery class at St Joseph's Primary School, Neath, on St David's Day, 1989.

WORKING AT IT

Some of the workmen who helped sink Seven Sisters pit, Dulais Valley, Neath, 1872.

Morfa Colliery, near Port Talbot, around 1910.

The Mines Rescue Company at Crynant Colliery, Dulais Valley, 1916.

Some of the nursing staff, including a ward sister at Neath General Hospital, 1927.

Cwmavon Tinplate works, Port Talbot, early 1900s.

Quarrymen at Maesmelyn Quarry, Skewen, 1920s.

Nursing staff at Neath General Hospital take a break from their duties, 1936.

Surface workers at Ynyscorrwg Colliery, Glyncorrwg, Afan Valley, early 1900s.

Staff of the Windsor Bus Company, Neath, 1936.

A pit pony and colliers at Blaen Pelenna Colliery, Tonmawr, 1900.

Special police constables at Briton Ferry, 1940.

Wil the postman at Cwmavon,
1910.

Members of Tonna Fire Brigade, Neath, early 1940s.

Wartime ambulance driver Mary Griffiths with nurse Peg Bonner and their vehicle at Port Talbot, 1940s.

Second World War munitions workers at the Metal Box factory, Neath, mid-1940s.

Waitresses at the Walnut Tree Hotel, High Street, Aberavon, 1949.

Apprentices in Port Talbot Borough Council's Burrows Yard, Aberavon, 1954.

Three of the male members of the teaching staff at Cwrt Sart Secondary School, Briton Ferry, 1953.

Retained firemen at
Briton Ferry with their
appliance, late 1950s.

These three lads were among the new intake of apprentices at the Albion steelworks, Briton Ferry, 1954.

One of the shift gangs at the Very Low Nitrogen (VLN) plant at Port Talbot steelworks, 1961.

Workman Will Dai Morris of Copper Row, Cwmavon, a well known village character, pictured in 1960.

Engineers and administrative staff of the Baglan Foundry & Engineering Company at the opening of their new premises at Melincrythan, Neath, on August 23, 1954, after relocating from Baglan.

Teaching staff at Coedffranc Girls School, Skewen, mid-1950s.

Construction work under way on Neath River Bridge, mid-1950s.

The J R Freeman & Son cigar factory at Sandfields, Port Talbot, 1972. It has since closed and been demolished.

A delivery boy with his bike, its basket laden with greengroceries from Albert Gould's store at Crynant, Dulais Valley, 1954.

A tobacco leaf is placed on a cigar-making machine at the Port Talbot factory of J R Freeman and Son, 1972, shortly after it opened.

Harry Harris, one of the last ferryboatmen on the River Neath at Briton Ferry, 1955. The giant piers of the road bridge that made the task redundant can be seen towering behind him.

Averil Williams, who at 19 became the first woman on the gardening staff of Neath Borough Council in 1956 is pictured some years later attending to one of the spectacular floral clocks she helped maintain in the town's Victoria Gardens. The theme on this occasion was road safety.

Albion steelworks, Briton Ferry, locomotive driver Ernie Harries, 1960s.

An aerial view of BP's Llandarcy oil refinery, Neath, 1969. Most of the works has now been demolished in readiness for extensive future redevelopment including shops, offices and housing.

Radiography department staff at Neath General Hospital, 1981.

Kitchen staff at Cefn Saeson Comprehensive School, Cimla, Neath, 1981.

Staff of Cefn Saeson Comprehensive School, Neath, 1981.

Miners wives from Dyffryn Cellwen in the Dulais Valley collecting for the strike fund, 1985.

Some of the miles of pipework that had to be dismantled at BP Llandarcy works after its closure, mid-1980s.

One of the gangs responsible for the demolition work at BP LLandarcy refinery, mid-1980s.

This picture shows how quickly progress was made, mid-1980s.

Breweries and bottling seem to have thrived in Neath and Port Talbot as these recently discovered stoneware jars show.

TRANSPORT AND TRADE

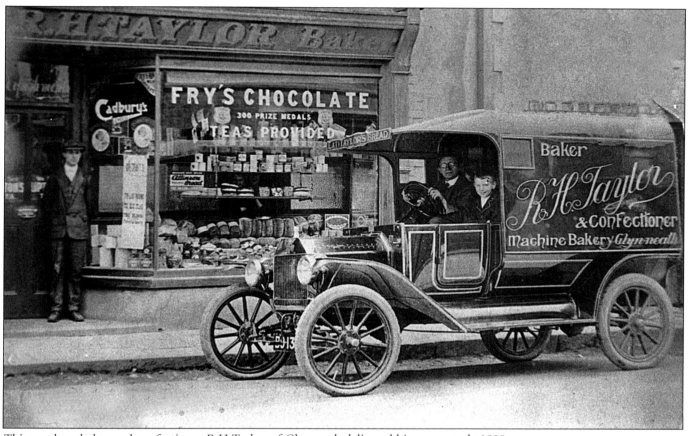

This was how baker and confectioner R H Taylor, of Glynneath delivered his wares, early 1900s.

The docks at Port Talbot, 1912.

As business expanded William Mort decided his Neath-based china and glassware business would benefit from the services of a pony and trap – and this was it, 1900.

A 1930s view of the docks at Port Talbot.

When the people of Port Talbot needed their old dry cell batteries recharged Ryans Charging Depot, of 17 Margam Terrace was one of the businesses they turned to. This motorcycle combination may be overloaded with family members in this 1934 snapshot, but normally its cargo was recharged batteries. With the demise of dry cell batteries the Ryan family turned to taxi hire to earn their living.

An early Neath charabanc, owned by David Williams, who later started the Windsor Bus Company, about 1920.

This was the cart used to transport the tools and wares of Port Talbot plumber Henry Griffiths, late 1940s. His wife Elizabeth and son Henri are at the helm on this occasion.

Briton Ferry was a busy and industrious centre of commerce in 1921 as this early aerial photograph showing the steelworks and dock confirm.

Pedal power tricycle style was one way of getting about for these Mayberry Road, Baglan, Port Talbot, youngsters 1957.

When you saw this van approaching you knew it was delivering bread for well-known Neath bakers W J Stockham. This picture was taken at Hillside, mid-1930s.

Two young Port
Talbot girls try their
hand at scooter riding,
early 1960s.

A group of motorcyclists at
Crynant, near Neath, May 1965.

Work under way on the World's biggest tidal harbour, at Port Talbot, December 1968. When complete some years later the harbour would provide a safe haven for the giant ore carriers whose cargo was so necessary for the nearby steelworks. The harbour was completed in 1969 and was opened by Queen Elizabeth II in 1970.

The parcels office in the entrance hall at Neath's newly-built station, 1972.

Margam Abbey Motors was a familiar car sales and filling station landmark on the A48 road at Margam – until it was demolished, along with the nearby village of Groes, to make way for the M4 motorway, not long after this early 1970s picture was taken.

A Creamline bus waits for passengers at Longford, Neath Abbey, mid-1960s.

A South Wales Transport single-decker makes its way through Sandfields estate on a service to Margam, December 1979.

Another ocean-going vessel awaits the indignity of the scrap cutters blowtorch at the Giant's Grave shipbreaking yard of Thos Ward, Briton Ferry, late 1960s.

Two buses pass each other on a sharp bend at Cymmer in the Afan Valley while serving passengers on routes that connected town with country, March 1981.

A congested scene at Victoria Gardens bus station, Neath in the late 1960s.

A Llynfi Motor services bus at Port Talbot bus station, January 1983. The Maesteg-based company was later absorbed into the South Wales Transport Company.

An early 1970s view of Neath River Bridge looking towards Briton Ferry from Earlswood. The pub beneath the bridge on the right is the Vernon Arms.

Traffic heads from Baglan towards Sandfields Estate over the main Swansea to Paddington railway line, along seaway Parade, 1983.

A South Wales Transport double-decker heads through Neath Abbey for Swansea, 1970.

Shipping movements at Norbrit Wharf, Briton Ferry, May 1985. At the time the wharf handled about 20 vessels a month and cargoes totalling around 20-30,000 tonnes.

A toboggan was the best way to travel for these Briton Ferry children in the snow-covered sloping grounds of Neath General Hospital, 1978.

The paddle steamer *Waverley* takes on passengers at the Norbrit Wharf, Briton Ferry before setting off on a Bristol Channel cruise, May 1989.

Fully laden with passengers, the *Waverley* paddles her way down the River Neath towards the sea, 1989, passing the towers of BP Chemicals Baglan Bay complex as she goes.

The iron ore carrier *Atlantic Superior* discharges her cargo of more than 100,000 tonnes of ore on to a conveyor at Port Talbot tidal harbour, 1989.

PLAYING ALONG

When it came to making music the Port Talbot Salvation Army band certainly had some fine musicians in its ranks when this picture was taken, just off Oakwood Lane, in the early 1920s.

A group of Briton Ferry entertainers who toured the area during the 1920s.

The Unique Concert Party who entertained scores of people with their own brand of music and comedy, at Cwmavon, 1923.

Neath Male Voice Choir, 1933, the year it performed at the London Palladium.

St Agnes Church Choir, Port Talbot, late 1940s.

Afan Ladies Choir, Port Talbot, with conductor Madam Olive Davies, late 1940s.

Port Talbot's
Western
Revellers
Concert Party,
1947. The
party was
managed by
Evan John,
second left
and included
radio
personality
Ossie Morris,
next to him.

St Catherine's Church Hall, Melincrythan, Neath was filled to capacity when these children performed the Gipsy Queen in 1934. The children were drawn from a number of local churches.

Some of the members of the Cwmavon Stewards Jazz Band, Port Talbot, early 1950s.

Briton Ferry Town Silver Prize Band, 1936 pictured in front of Briton Ferry Conservative Club.

Pilgrim's Progress as performed by Cwmavon's active YWCA drama group, September 18, 1950.

Younger members of Gnoll Road Congregational Church, Neath, during their Nativity performance, 1936.

Port Talbot's Jersey Mexican Jazz Band, early 1950s.

Some of the members of Neath Amateur Operatic Society who took part in the 1953 production of *Annie Get Your Gun* at the Gnoll Hall, now Kwik-Fit tyre depot.

The drum corps of the Afan Paraders jazz Band, Port Talbot, 1952.

The Afan Paraders jazz band, Port Talbot, on the march in 1952.

The cast of *Calamity Jane*, the successful 1959 production staged at the town's Gwyn Hall by Neath Amateur Operatic Society.

Briton Ferry Amateur Operatic Society rehearse for their production of *Wedding in Paris* at the town's public hall, 1959.

Crowds gather at Port Talbot to watch the Queen Mary Stewards jazz band in action, 1953.

Neath Amateur Operatic Society perform *The King and I*, at the town's Gwyn Hall, October 1960.

Youngsters of the Youth Club at Eastern School, Taibach during one of the many shows they staged under the direction of Leo Lloyd, 1954.

Youngsters of Ynysymaerdy School during a pantomime they performed at Jerusalem Chapel, Briton Ferry, 1973.

A 1986 concert performance by youngsters from St Mary's Church, Briton Ferry.

Cwmavon, Port Talbot, YWCA drama group take a break from rehearsals for their January 1955 production.

Briton Ferry Amateur Operatic Society members in full flight during their version of *Calamity Jane* at the Gwyn Hall, Neath, 1977.

Members of Port Talbot Charity Choir perform at Trefelin Workingmen's Club, Velindre, mid-1960s.

Two very serious cast members of a 1956 play staged by pupils of Sandfields School, Port Talbot.

GOOD SPORTS

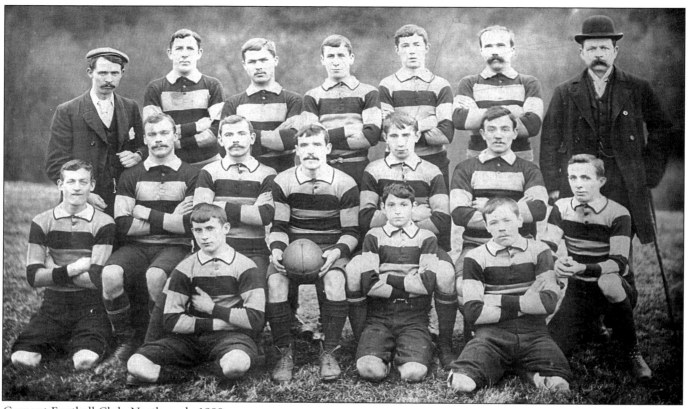

Crynant Football Club, Neath, early 1900s.

Mansel Juniors rugby XV, Port Talbot, season 1907-08.

Briton Ferry Hockey Club, 1913-14.

Mansel Juniors Rugby Club, Port Talbot, 1909-10.

The combined Neath and Aberavon rugby side, with officials, that was fielded against a touring New South Wales, Australia, team, September 1927.

Seven Sisters Rugby Club, Neath, 1928-29.

Members of The Mount Bowls Club, Hillside, Neath, 1920s.

The winners of the Port Talbot YMCA billiards trophy, 1912.

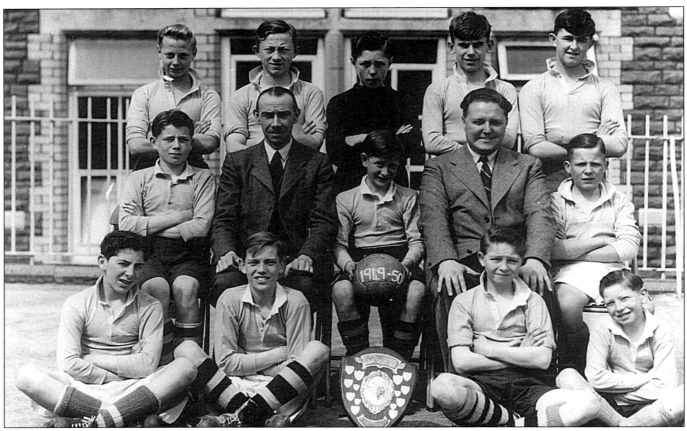

Coedffranc School, Skewen's shield-winning football team, 1949-50.

Metal Box factory tug-of-war team, Neath, late 1940s.

St Clement's Church football team, Briton Ferry, 1949-50 season.

Pontrhydyfen Juniors rugby team, 1923-24.

Metal Box factory football team, mid-1950s.

Port Talbot Ladies Bowls Club, 1941.

Supporters of Crynant Rugby Club had plenty to cheer about on this day in 1955 when their team beat rivals Seven Sisters in a thrilling local derby. There was just one point in it though – the score was Crynant 14pts, Seven Sisters 13pts.

Briton Ferry Steel Cricket Club players, late 1950s.

Cwrt Sart Secondary School, Briton Ferry, senior football team, 1954-55.

Cwmavon RFC West Wales Rugby Union Champions 1948-49.

A Metal Box Angling Club, Neath, presentation evening, mid-1960s.

Velindre Juniors rugby team, Port Talbot, 1949-50.

Park United Football Club, Melincrythan, Neath, 1960-61.

The hockey team of Dyffryn Grammar School, Port Talbot, 1960.

The Midland Metal Spinning factory cricket XI, Neath, 1966-67.

The girls athletics team at Dyffryn Grammar School, Port Talbot, 1961.

Briton Ferry Steel RFC, 1968. In only their third full season of competition rugby they won all the major tournaments organised by Neath & District Rugby Union.

The 1961 girls hockey team of Dyffryn Grammar School, Port Talbot.

Midland Metal Spinning football team which won the Neath League Open Cup quarter-finals by beating Ynysmeudwy by five goals to one, 1968-69.

Port Talbot Pigeon Club presentation evening, at the Steel Company of Wales Sports and Social Club, Margam, 1965.

Briton Ferry Athletic AFC, 1972.

Some of the participants in a special disabled games competition held at Aberavon Quins ground, Sandfields Port Talbot pose with members of the town's Lions Club which organised the 1981 event, and civic dignitaries who attended.

Briton Ferry Steel junior cricket XI, 1981.

Baglan Under-10s very successful rugby squad, 1982.